THIRD EDITION

BUSINESS MARKETING

Edward G. Brierty

Professor of Marketing
Southern Oregon University

Robert W. Eckles

Professor Emeritus
University of Houston–Downtown

Robert R. Reeder

Professor of Management
Southwestern Oklahoma State University

Prentice Hall, Upper Saddle River, New Jersey 07458

Acquisition Editor: Whitney Blake
Associate Editor: John Larkin
Editorial Assistant: Rachel Falk
Vice President/Editorial Director: James Boyd
Marketing Manager: John Chillingworth
Editing and Production: Accu-color, Inc.
Associate Managing Editor: Linda DeLorenzo
Managing Editor: Dee Josephson
Manufacturing Buyer: Diane Peirano
Manufacturing Supervisor: Arnold Vila
Manufacturing Manager: Vincent Scelta
Design Manager: Patricia Smythe
Cover Design: Robert Freese
Cover Photo: Trevor Mein/© Tony Stone Images

Copyright © 1998, 1991, 1987 by Prentice Hall, Inc.
A Simon & Schuster Company
Upper Saddle River, New Jersey 07458

Library of Congress Cataloging-in-Publication Data

Brierty, Edward G.
    Business marketing / Edward G. Brierty, Robert W. Eckles, Robert
R. Reeder. — 3rd ed.
       p. cm.
    Rev. ed. of: Industrial marketing : analysis, planning, and
control / Robert R. Reeder, Edward G. Brierty, Betty H. Reeder. 2nd
ed. c1991
    Includes bibliographical references and index.
    ISBN 0–13–757378–2
    1. Industrial marketing.   I. Eckles, Robert W.
II. Reeder, Robert R.   III. Reeder, Robert R.
Industrial marketing.   IV. Title.
HF5415. 1263.875   1998
658.8—dc21   97–23946
                                       CIP

Prentice-Hall International (UK) Limited, London
Prentice-Hall of Australia Pty. Limited, Sydney
Prentice-Hall Canada, Inc., Toronto
Prentice-Hall Hispanoamericana, S.A., Mexico
Prentice-Hall of India Private Limited, New Delhi
Prentice-Hall of Japan, Inc., Tokyo
Simon & Schuster Asia Pte. Ltd., Singapore
Editora Prentice-Hall do Brasil, Rio de Janeiro

Printed in the United States of America

10 9 8 7 6 5 4 3 2 1

To Mary and Dolores,
Our Partners and Inspiration

Contents in Brief

Contents

PART VI   COMMUNICATION STRATEGIES

xiv

PART IX   CASES

See Case Index, p. 580, for cross-reference to relevant chapters

Preface

New Edition—New Writing Team

Sports teams are not the only ones that reorganize and come back stronger than ever. As every textbook author knows, the return on personal investment sometimes seems negative. When advised that it was time to prepare a third edition, Bob and Betty Reeder decided that they would rather invest their efforts in other pursuits. This left Ed Brierty on the horns of a dilemma. He had no desire to let the text die for want of continued effort. The first two editions had provided an exciting challenge and the opportunity to remain current in his teaching field. Moreover, comments from an increasing number of adopters verified that the original goals of the team had been realized, namely, to stimulate the interest of students in the business market by providing them with a clear and applicable comprehension of this arena.

On the other hand, the prospect of taking on what had been the combined efforts of three people was, to say the least, daunting. Faculty in institutions that prioritize teaching know that terms such as *teaching assistant* and *release time* may only be theoretical concepts. But just when frustration approached the danger level, Brierty made a fortunate phone call. Bob Eckles thought he had "semiretired" from academia and writing, but enthused by the prospect of adding another successful text to his previous publications, he agreed to join the project. Bob Reeder remains on the list of authors to reflect our sincere appreciation of his invaluable past contributions and continued moral support.

Principal Objectives of the Third Edition

One overarching objective continues to be dominant: students must not only gain knowledge of but also develop a sense of curiosity and excitement about this multifaceted market. They should become eager to understand the factors that shape the decision-making of successful business marketing managers. Thus, while we humbly appreciate that faculty have allowed us to enter their classrooms and share the teaching responsibility, students remain the primary audience for this text. To that end, clarity has been favored over profundity, proven tactics over arcane or faddish theories. One should not infer from this statement, however, that everything new has been ignored; surmise instead that the old has not been condemned as unfashionable.

To accomplish the primary objective, several subsidiary objectives must be achieved:

1. Understand commonalities in the consumer and business markets that foster similar marketing strategies, while distinguishing significant differences that demand an altered approach
2. In a similar vein, differentiate strategies successfully employed across industries from those that appear industry-specific and identify the underlying reasons
3. Recognize fundamental trends occurring in domestic and/or global markets that necessitate a change in strategy or tactics
4. Appreciate the significant impact of global competition on a domestic market and the intensified challenge of transforming a domestic strategy into an effective international approach

Organization of the Text

The third edition comprises twenty-two chapters grouped into eight parts. Part I outlines the dimensions of the business market—customers, products/services, and global aspects. Part II addresses the buying process in this market and the important buyer-seller relationships. Part III considers strategy formation including market research, demand analysis and forecasting, market segmentation, product positioning, and strategic planning. Parts IV through VII explore strategies for product and services, channel, communication, and pricing. Part VIII covers competitive strategies, strategic control, and a summary chapter on international marketing. It should be emphasized that in addition to Chapter 22, major international aspects relevant to each chapter's topic are covered within that chapter.

Changes, Additions, and Improvements

The terms *industrial marketing* and *learning curve* do not fully portray their respective concepts. The industrial market is only one segment of the business market, and learning alone does not provide a firm with the full range of cost-saving opportunities. Thus, this edition refers to *business marketing* and *experience curve*.

Four new chapters have been added. Chapter 12 provides expanded coverage of business services marketing. Chapters 20 covers the broad range of competitive strategies. Chapter 21 provides in-depth analysis of the mechanisms available to monitor and control marketing efficiency and profitability. Part III, which deals with the important area of strategy formation, has been expanded from three to four chapters.

We have monitored emerging marketing concepts and those that have assumed greater importance as a result of a changing market environment. These concepts and their impact on marketing strategy are covered in the appropriate context and include:

- Artificial intelligence and expert systems
- Concurrent engineering and platform teams
- Cost-driven versus customer-driven versus competition-driven pricing
- Material requirements planning (MRP I and MRP II)
- Relationship marketing
- Sales force automation (SFA)

- Strategic alliances
- Supplier partnering (also channel member partnering)
- Twin-stream product development

Supplements

The following supplements are available to instructors:

INSTRUCTOR'S RESOURCE MANUAL

Written by John R. Brooks, Jr., of Houston Baptist University, the *Instructor's Resource Manual* provides professors with coverage of Chapter Objectives, Overviews, and Outlines as well as answers to the Discussion Questions, and Student Projects. Also included are detailed synopses of all the cases, offering analysis issues that can be used to stimulate student discussion.

TEST ITEM FILE

Contains approximately 1,500 multiple-choice, true/false, and essay questions. Each question is rated by level of difficulty and includes a text-page reference. It is available in both printed and electronic formats.

PRENTICE HALL CUSTOM TEST

Windows version   Based on the number 1 best-selling, state-of-the-art, test-generation software program developed by Engineering Software Associates (ESA), *Prentice Hall Custom Test* is not only suitable for your course, but is customizable to your personal needs. With *Prentice Hall Custom Test*'s user-friendly test creation and powerful algorithmic generation, you can originate tailor-made tests quickly, easily, and error free. You can create an exam, administer it traditionally or online, evaluate and track students' results, and analyze the success of the exam—all with a simple click of the mouse.

VIDEO LIBRARY

A special video library containing business-to-business marketing clips is available to professors.

About the Authors

Ed Brierty's career has taken several unique, self-generated turns. After 6 years of study in preparatory and theological seminaries, he decided to beget his own congregation rather than minister to one. Following brief stints with Motorola and Westinghouse in purchasing and sales positions, he joined the semiconductor division of Texas Instruments only months after the firm shipped its first mass-produced transistors. Thus began a 26-year contribution to the dramatic growth of this company and industry through a series of sales, marketing, and general management positions.

After earning a University of Chicago MBA degree, he decided it was time to start a second career "preaching what he had practiced." In 1981 he joined the faculty of California State University at Chico. Three years later, he migrated to Southern

Oregon University in the beautiful Rogue River Valley, where he teaches strategic marketing, new product development, market channels, and market research. He is currently laying plans for a still-undefined third career.

Bob Eckles also merged academic and industrial careers. His background includes 34 years as a professor of marketing, plus 8 years as a marketing practitioner in the office equipment and computer industries. He also served as a marketing research director in the cosmetics industry. During his teaching years, he acted as a marketing and management consultant.

Dr. Eckles holds an MBA degree from Miami University (Ohio) and a DBA degree from Washington University. He has authored four texts in marketing and management, numerous monographs, and more than two dozen research and trade articles.

Acknowledgments

Many colleagues and adopters have offered helpful suggestions to make this third edition even more effective than the earlier editions. We particularly want to thank Thomas Hitzelberger and Jerry Cooper of Southern Oregon University; C. Anthony DiBenedetto, Temple University; Dwight Scherban, Central Connecticut State College; Dean Siewers, Rochester Institute of Technology; Alvin J. Williams, University of Southern Mississippi, and William C. Rodgers, St. Cloud State University.

As usual, members of the Prentice Hall editorial department helped us to stay on schedule during some trying times and provided much-appreciated encouragement and counsel. Whitney Blake, John Larkin, Linda DeLorenzo, and Theresa Festa have earned particular praise.

The final task of reviewing page proof is typically a tedious and boring one for authors. In this instance, however, the experience, diligence, and delightful Celtic humor of Suzanne Wakefield of Accu-color, Inc. made it "almost enjoyable." We deeply appreciate her memorable effort.

We owe a special word of thanks to John "Rusty" Brooks for creating an Instructor's Manual that clearly enhances this text and provides students with a series of interesting and challenging projects, including the exploration of Internet sources.

Finally, for the students who are truly our customers, we hope your journey through our text will prove provocative, enlightening, and fruitful. You are the potential marketers who must carry the profession into the next century, with all of its opportunities and challenges. We wish you good luck and much success.

Ed Brierty
Bob Eckles

P A R T

Dimensions of Business Marketing

The Cat Fights Back

Caterpillar Inc., long number one [in its markets], is driving especially hard to beat off its Japanese competitors. In just 4 years, it has doubled its product offerings by producing new varieties of Cats it never would have considered in bygone times.

In those glorious olden days, a 15-foot, 73-ton Cat tractor could push, crush, and roll over the best that competition could offer. And Cat users were happily willing to pay premiums for that excellence. But in the 1980s things began to head for a sudden downturn. Construction markets collapsed, a long-term recession insidiously set in, and the U.S. dollar took flight; suddenly the number one feline found both her flanks exposed to attack by Japanese competitors. Profits fell. She saw a 1981 $579 million profit figure sink into the depths of a $953 million loss in just 3 quick years. A mandate for change was dramatically painted across her balance sheet.

She began cutting her marginally productive facilities, pruning excessive payrolls, and reorganizing her 60,000 Cat-people. She cut prices in world markets, introduced new, smaller Cats, which ranged from backhoes to farm tractors, and built a 6-year modernization program for the updating of 36 million square feet of factory space, with an estimated cost of $1.2 billion.

By late 1988, Cat sales had jumped up 22 percent, and losses had turned to profits. By the end of the year, profits totaled $616 million, exceeding all previous years.

Caterpillar, like many other firms, has felt the pressure of fierce domestic and international competition. As the following data depict, the company has also withstood this pressure quite well.

Caterpillar Performance, 1988-1995 (in Millions of Dollars)			
	Sales ($)	Profit	Profit (%)
1988	10,435	616	5.9
1989	11,126	497	4.5
1990	11,436	210	1.8
1991	10,182	−404	−4.0
1992	10,194	−2,435	−23.9
1993	11,615	652	5.6
1994	14,328	955	6.7
1995	16,072	1,136	7.1
1996	16,522	1,361	8.2

Caterpillar's primary markets—agriculture, road building, and timber—remained relatively depressed during the early 1990s. Consequently, all sales negotiations suffered from severe competitive price pressures. Caterpillar managed to maintain a fairly level sales rate, but only by meeting competitive prices. The sales and profit results from 1994 on clearly indicate Caterpillar's combined efforts to increase market share while improving manufacturing productivity.

World markets remain very volatile, and firms that choose to compete internationally can reap attractive rewards. They also face daunting downside risks. Customer demands and competitive pressures continually force firms to develop strategies that are more complex yet more flexible, goal-oriented but more responsive to fast-changing environments. An old French proverb states, "plus ça change, plus c'est la meme chose." This translates to "the more things change, the more they stay the same." Indeed, the one constant in the business market is change.

We write this third edition of *Business Marketing* with such thoughts in mind, hoping that we can convince future business marketers to treat both customers and competitors as critical elements of any strategic plan. The former represent opportunities, but only if their needs are well satisfied. The latter represent potential barriers to success, unless their capabilities are recognized and counteracted. And the market "windows of opportunity" remain open for only a short period of time. Chapters 1 through 3 attempt to provide an understanding of this market's basic elements—its environment, its participants, and its unique characteristics.

Endnote

Case example excerpted from Ronald Henkoff. "This cat is acting like a tiger," *Fortune*, 1988, pp. 71-76. Copyright © 1988 Time Inc. Reprinted with permission; all rights reserved.

CHAPTER 1

Global and Domestic Perspectives of the Business Market

Most college marketing courses concentrate on the consumer market, with perhaps one token chapter on the business market. Consequently, most students (and many fledgling practitioners) have only a vague idea of what constitutes and takes place in this largest market area. Therefore, before we can have a meaningful discourse on strategies and planning, we need to survey this market from both a global and domestic viewpoint to understand its size and importance. This chapter will introduce you to the following:

1. The size and scope of the U.S. business market
2. The impact of foreign trade and trade deficits
3. Trading partners and products that represent the most troubling deficits
4. The effect of negative consumer attitudes
5. The relative success of industrial products in world trade
6. Opportunities and fallacies regarding trade deficits
7. An analysis of the primary sectors in the domestic business market

Magnitude of the U.S. Business Market

To compare the relative sizes of the business and consumer markets in the United States, you could buy a copy of the *World Almanac* and look for a breakdown of **gross domestic product** (GDP), or you could go directly to the source, the *Survey of Current*

Business, published by the Bureau of Economic Analysis, a branch of the Department of Commerce. You would find that in 1995, GDP totaled approximately $6.7 trillion, including $4.6 trillion in **personal consumption expenditures.** Since this leaves only $2.1 trillion for all other elements, how can the business market possibly be the largest? The answer lies in how the numbers are formulated.

As we learned in macroeconomics, **gross national product** (GNP) is the market value of all goods and services produced within a time period, usually 1 year. GNP includes a portion of what is produced offshore by U.S.-based companies. Today, GDP is used more frequently and includes only domestic production. In both tabulations, only the value of end-products is counted. In other words, the value of the tires, upholstery, air conditioner, and so on is included in the retail value of the automobile. This process rightly prevents the error of double counting, but it gives a false impression of where marketing takes place and in what magnitude.

The composite of all U.S. manufacturing firms sold their output in 1994 for $3.3 trillion. Part of this total was sold directly to other manufacturers either as capital equipment (e.g., a computer system) or as components to be assembled into an end-product (integrated circuits going into a stereo system). Another portion was sold to various government agencies and institutions. Still more went to merchant wholesalers to be resold to other manufacturers, to the government, or to retailers. The total value of these resales was $2.1 trillion. Very little of the manufacturers' total output went directly to consumers.

Finally, there is the broad spectrum of services sold. This segment accounted for $2.5 trillion of the personal consumption expenditures. However, more than 30 percent of these services were purchased by businesses and government agencies. Thus, another $750 billion was added to the business or nonconsumer market.

All of these sales transactions totaled $6.2 trillion. Since the design, production, and sale of these goods and services require people, and people equate to jobs, we can now better appreciate the importance of the business market to the nation's economy.

In 1994, 116 million workers generated the $6.7 trillion GDP, for an average productivity or output of $58,000. By comparison, the 18.3 million workers in the manufacturing sector produced an average output of $182,000, and 6.1 million wholesale workers each produced $221,000 output, or 3.8 times the national average.[1,2] We will consider this factor of productivity again later in the chapter.

World Trade: Exports and Imports

Every country buys goods and services from other countries. In some instances, money is used to pay for the purchases. More regularly, an exchange or barter system is used. For example, when the United States buys rubber, textiles, and precision ball bearings from other countries to produce automobiles, we prefer to ship some of these automobiles back in payment for the raw materials and component parts. Millions of such transactions each year constitute the U.S. **merchandise trade.** A broader definition of foreign trade includes services as well as products. Table 1-1 shows the trend in the trade of goods between 1970 and 1994. Table 1-2 shows a similar trend in the trade of services.

TRADE SURPLUSES AND DEFICITS

When a country ships more abroad than it imports, it enjoys a surplus in the balance of trade; when imports exceed exports, there is a deficit. The United States has generated a substantial trade deficit in goods each year since 1980, despite the fact that we

TABLE 1-1 United States Trade in Goods: 1970-1994, Based on Census (in billions of dollars)

	Total Goods				Manufactured Goods			Agriculture			Mineral Fuels			Other Goods		
	Exp	Imp	Total	Bal	Exp	Imp	Bal	Exp	Imp	Bal	Exp	Imp	Bal	Exp	Imp	Bal
1970	43.8	40.4	84.2	3.4	31.7	27.3	4.4	7.3	5.8	1.8	1.6	3.1	-1.5	3.1	4.2	-1.1
1975	109.3	98.5	207.8	10.8	76.9	54.0	22.9	22.1	9.5	12.6	4.5	26.5	-22.0	5.9	8.6	-2.7
1980	225.7	245.3	471.0	-19.5	160.7	133.0	27.7	41.8	17.4	24.3	8.2	78.9	-70.7	15.1	15.9	-0.8
1985	218.8	336.5	555.3	-117.7	168.0	257.5	-89.5	29.3	19.5	9.8	10.3	53.7	-43.4	11.2	5.9	5.3
1990	393.6	495.3	888.9	-101.7	315.4	388.8	-73.5	39.6	22.3	17.2	12.4	64.7	-52.3	26.3	19.5	6.8
1991	421.7	488.5	910.2	-66.7	345.1	392.4	-47.3	39.4	22.1	17.2	12.3	54.1	-41.8	24.9	19.8	5.1
1992	448.2	532.7	980.9	-84.5	368.5	434.3	-65.9	43.1	23.4	19.8	11.3	55.3	-43.9	25.2	19.7	5.5
1993	465.1	580.7	1045.8	-115.6	388.7	479.9	-91.2	42.8	23.6	19.2	9.9	55.9	-46.0	23.7	21.2	2.5
1994	512.6	663.3	1175.9	-150.6	431.1	557.3	-126.3	45.9	26.0	20.0	9.0	56.4	-47.4	26.7	23.6	3.1

Bal = balance; Exp = exports; Imp = imports.

Source: Department of Commerce, International Trade Administration. 1995. *United States Foreign Trade Highlights – 1994*. Washington, D.C.: U.S. GPO.

produce a greater quantity and broader assortment of products than any other country in the world. While the reasons given for these deficits are both numerous and debatable, the magnitude is a certainty. Table 1-1 shows the broad outline of this situation. Several points should be noted. First, total goods exports have increased more than tenfold since 1970 with manufactured goods generating 70 to 80 percent of the total. Second, the United States continues to be a significant supplier of agricultural goods to the rest of the world. Third, oil imports from OPEC nations have been a major contributor to the trade deficit since the 1973 oil embargo. Finally, despite the net deficit, the United States replaced Germany in 1992 as the world's leading exporter of products and has since retained that position.

Table 1-2 indicates a much healthier trade balance in services. Tourism has grown steadily as a major industry in this country and provides substantial revenues for airlines, motels/hotels, restaurants, tour guides, and travel agencies. The increase in royalties and license fees stems from continued leadership in technology and marketing. As one indication of the importance of technological leadership and patents, Texas Instruments collected more than $2.5 billion in royalties from 1986 through 1994, primarily on semiconductor patents. During this same time period, TI's operating profit from component production totaled $2.3 billion.[3]

Impact of the Trade Deficit   If we consider the trade deficit as a major problem, we cannot devise and implement a solution without identifying the problem's source. Do specific countries contribute regularly to this deficit? Do most countries strive for a trade surplus? Are manufactured goods and imported oil the prime roots of the problem? Can the United States rectify the situation?

We start by analyzing the impact of a deficit. During the first five years of this decade, 1990 through 1994, the cumulative U.S. trade deficit exceeded $500 billion, or a yearly average of $100 billion.[4] Given the average productivity of $58,000 mentioned earlier, it would take more than 1,725,000 additional workers to generate an output equal to the annual $100 billion deficit.

Between 1990 and 1994, an average of 7.5 million Americans were unemployed. Assuming people with the right skills were in the right place at the right time (an obviously theoretical assumption), elimination of the deficit would have reduced unemployment by 23 percent. Of course, given their lower productivity figures, more than 1,725,000 workers in other countries would have lost their jobs and been unable to buy any American exports.

Regardless of the importance one places on trade deficits, they played a major role in converting the United States from the largest world creditor in 1976 to the world's largest debtor.

U.S. TRADE BY REGION

We must also analyze the balance of trade in terms of our trading partners to determine where the greatest imbalances exist. Table 1-3 provides an overview of foreign trade across geographic areas. Several points must be recognized.

First, Canada consistently ranks as the largest trading partner. Of equal importance, they have remained the largest customer, buying more than 20 percent of total U.S. exports. Canada's purchases exceed those of Japan despite an economy only one tenth the size of Japan's. However, Canada's sales continue to outstrip purchases, resulting in a 5-year deficit of $46.5 billion.

Trade with Mexico, our other North American Free Trade Agreement (NAFTA) trading partner, doubled between 1989 and 1994 in both purchases and sales, with a deficit of $2.2 billion in 1989 becoming a surplus of $1.5 billion in 1994. Those who pre-

TABLE 1-2 United States Trade in Services by Major Category, Based on Balance of Payments (in billions of dollars)

	Total Services				Travel, Fares, and Transport			Royalties and License Fees			Other Private Services			Military Defense and Miscellaneous Government Services		
	Exp	Imp	Total	Bal	Exp	Imp	Bal	Exp	Imp	Bal	Exp	Imp	Bal	Exp	Imp	Bal
1970	14.2	14.5	28.7	-0.3	5.9	8.0	-2.1	2.3	0.2	2.1	1.3	0.8	0.5	4.5	5.5	-1.0
1975	25.5	22.0	47.5	3.5	11.5	14.4	-2.9	4.3	0.5	3.8	2.9	1.6	1.3	6.7	5.6	1.1
1980	47.6	41.5	89.1	6.1	24.8	25.8	-1.0	7.1	0.7	6.4	6.3	2.9	3.4	9.4	12.1	-2.7
1985	72.9	72.8	145.7	0.1	36.9	46.6	-9.7	6.6	1.2	5.4	19.9	10.2	9.7	9.6	14.8	-5.2
1990	148.3	117.7	266.0	30.6	80.3	71.2	9.1	17.1	3.2	13.9	40.6	23.8	16.9	10.4	19.4	-9.0
1991	164.3	118.4	282.7	45.9	86.6	68.6	18.0	18.5	4.2	14.3	48.0	27.0	21.0	11.2	18.5	-7.3
1992	178.6	122.0	300.6	56.6	94.6	74.7	19.9	20.0	5.1	14.9	51.0	26.2	24.8	12.6	16.1	-3.5
1993	187.8	130.0	317.8	57.8	98.5	78.6	19.9	20.6	4.9	15.8	55.1	32.0	23.1	13.6	14.5	-0.9
1994	196.7	138.8	335.5	57.9	104.0	84.7	19.3	22.4	5.7	16.8	59.0	35.6	23.4	13.3	13.0	0.3

Bal = balance; Exp = exports; Imp = imports.

Source: Department of Commerce, International Trade Administration. 1995. *United States Foreign Trade Highlights – 1994.* Washington, D.C.: U.S. GPO.

TABLE 1-3   U.S. Foreign Trade by Geographic Area: 1990-1994 (in billions of dollars)

	U.S. Exports	U.S. Imports	Total Trade	Balance
WORLD	2,241.2	2,760.5	5,001.7	–519.3
WESTERN HEMISPHERE	838.5	878.2	1,716.7	–39.7
Canada	474.2	520.7	994.9	–46.5
Mexico	194.6	185.9	380.5	8.7
South America	108.0	123.4	231.4	–15.4
Caribbean	32.7	28.2	60.9	4.5
Central America	26.1	19.6	45.7	6.5
Other W. Hemisphere	2.9	0.4	3.3	2.5
ASIA	696.9	1,198.3	1,895.2	–501.4
Japan	245.9	505.0	750.9	–259.1
China	36.6	137.4	174.0	–100.8
East Asian NICs[1]	247.0	318.3	565.3	–71.3
Other Asian countries	91.2	156.2	247.4	–65.0
Middle East	76.2	81.4	157.6	–5.2
AUSTRALIA AND OCEANIA	52.1	25.8	77.9	26.3
AFRICA	45.3	73.0	118.3	–27.7
EUROPE	606.7	583.6	1,190.3	23.1
European Union (15)[2]	529.0	518.6	1,047.6	10.4
Eastern Europe	25.1	15.3	40.4	9.8
Non–Eu. western. Europe	52.6	49.7	102.3	2.9
SUBTOTAL	2,239.5	2,758.9	4,998.4	–519.4
REST OF WORLD	1.7	1.6	3.3	0.1
DEVELOPED COUNTRIES[3]	1,361.6	1,627.9	2,989.5	–266.3
DEVELOPING COUNTRIES	877.6	1,131.1	2,008.7	–253.5
OPEC	89.5	163.3	252.8	–73.8

[1] Includes Hong Kong, Singapore, South Korea, and Taiwan.
[2] Includes original EC-12 plus additional members: Austria, Finland, and Sweden.
[3] Includes Canada, Japan, all of Western Europe, Australia, New Zealand, and South Africa.

Source: Adapted from U.S. Department of Commerce, International Trade Administration. 1995. *U.S. Foreign Trade Highlights–1994.* Washington, D.C.: U.S. GPO.

dict a dismal failure for the NAFTA trade agreement must recognize that the current deficit lies with Canada, where wage rates are similar to ours. The trade imbalance does not stem from low Mexican wage rates.

Japan continues to be our second largest supplier. Although total trade increased approximately 20 percent over the 5-year period, exports to Japan remain stubbornly at half the level of their exports to the United States. Consequently, this trade imbalance constituted 50 percent of the 5-year deficit. Some argue that the 2:1 export-to-import ratio is fairly realistic, since Japan's 1994 GDP of $2,527 billion was only 38 percent of our $6,738 billion GDP. However, there are two other important considerations.

First, no other industrialized nation enjoys a trade surplus with every one of their trading partners as does Japan. Second, with specific reference to the U.S. deficit, this country consistently represents a greater percentage of Japan's exports than of their imports. For example, in 1994 Japan's total trade consisted of $396 billion in exports and $274 billion in imports. The United States bought $119 billion, or 31.8 percent of the exports. However, Japan bought only $53 billion of American goods, or 19.3 of their total imports.[5]

Although equality of volume appears unrealistic, equality of percentage does not. If the United States can represent 31.8 percent of Japan's exports, nothing prevents Japan from purchasing that same percentage of their imports. In 1994, Japan would have purchased $87 billion from the United States, reducing the trade imbalance from $66 to $32 billion. The 1994 data are not unique. This situation has existed since the 1970s and will be discussed from other aspects elsewhere in the text.

China and the **newly industrialized countries** (NICs) in Asia also present a consistent and growing deficit as well as unequal import/export percentages. In fact, as Table 1-4 indicates, the Pacific Rim clearly constitutes the heart of the U.S. trade deficit. Japan, China, and the NICs make up 83 percent of the 1990-1994 trade imbalance.[4] Again, trade equality would substantially reduce this problem.

A DEFICIT REDUCTION STRATEGY

Table 1-4 lists the top twenty trading partners with the largest deficits in 1994. The table also shows each country's total imports and exports along with the U.S. share. The last two columns adjust the import percentage to equal the export percentage and show the resultant increase in U.S. exports. The total 1994 trade deficit of $151 billion would be reduced by $120 billion, or 79 percent, and $71 billion of this reduction would come from the Pacific Rim countries.

TABLE 1-4   U.S. Foreign Trade Deficits by Country, and a Partial Solution (1994 data in billions of dollars)

	Total Exports	Exports to U.S.	U.S. % of Total	Total Imports	Imports from U.S.	U.S. % of Total	U.S. Deficit	Adjusted Import %	Trade Increase
Japan	$ 395.5	119.2	30.1	$ 274.3	$ 53.5	19.5	$ −65.7	30.1	$ 29.1
China	121.0	38.8	32.1	115.7	9.3	8.1	−29.5	32.1	27.8
Canada	164.3	128.4	78.1	151.5	114.4	75.5	−14.0	78.1	3.9
Germany	437.0	31.7	7.3	362.0	19.2	5.3	−12.5	7.3	7.2
Taiwan	93.0	26.7	28.7	85.1	17.1	20.1	−9.6	28.7	7.3
Italy	190.8	14.8	7.8	168.7	7.2	4.3	−7.6	7.8	6.0
Malaysia	56.6	14.0	24.7	55.2	7.0	12.7	−7.0	24.7	6.6
Thailand	46.0	10.3	22.4	52.6	4.9	9.3	−5.4	22.4	6.9
Venezuela	15.2	8.4	55.3	7.6	4.0	52.6	−4.4	55.3	0.2
Nigeria	11.9	4.4	37.0	8.3	0.5	6.0	−3.9	37.0	2.6
Indonesia	41.3	6.5	15.7	31.4	2.8	8.9	−3.7	15.7	2.1
France	249.2	16.7	6.7	238.1	13.6	5.7	−3.1	6.7	2.4
India	24.4	5.3	21.7	25.5	2.3	9.0	−3.0	21.7	3.2
Sweden	59.9	5.0	8.3	49.6	2.5	5.0	−2.5	8.3	1.6
Singapore	96.4	15.4	16.0	102.4	13.0	12.7	−2.4	16.0	3.9
Angola	3.0	2.1	70.0	1.6	0.2	12.5	−1.9	70.0	0.9
Philippines	13.4	5.7	42.5	21.3	3.9	18.3	−1.8	42.5	5.2
Saudi Arabia	39.4	7.7	19.5	28.9	6.0	20.8	−1.7	20.8	0.0
Korea, South	96.2	19.6	20.4	102.3	18.0	17.6	−1.6	20.4	2.9
Norway	36.6	2.4	6.6	29.3	1.3	4.4	−1.1	6.6	0.6
TOP 20— PERCENT OF U.S. TOTAL	2,191.1	483.1	22.0 72.8%	1,911.4	300.7	15.7 58.7%	−182.4	22.0 121.0%	119.9

Source: 1995 CIA World Factbook. 1995. Other countries' total exports and imports: U.S. Imports and Exports by Nation: U.S. Foreign Trade Highlights. International Trade Administration.

The data just cited should not be interpreted as a suggestion that Asian trade be limited. On the contrary, these countries represent tremendous trading opportunities for the next decade and beyond. Japan and the four NICs—China, Korea, Singapore, and Taiwan—continue to raise their GDP per capita, thus increasing the buying power of their consumers. The people of China have far less buying power at present, but this nation will spend countless billions to develop an industrial infrastructure. The Chinese business market has one of the brightest potentials in the world. In fairness, we must also note that United States exports to these five countries exceeded those of any other non-Asian country. In Korea, Singapore, and Taiwan, we were second only to Japan. Thus, we have the opportunity to penetrate one of the fastest growing economic blocs in the world.[6]

Trade with the European Union and in the Western Hemisphere has progressed favorably. The OPEC data reflect the danger of our dependence on imported oil. In summary, the U.S. trade balance has improved in all geographic areas except Japan, the Asian NICs, and OPEC.

As a final note, the equal division of deficits between developed and developing countries clearly indicates that this problem does not stem solely from significant wage differences. In fact, Germany, representing the largest deficit in Europe, has higher average wages than the United States.

U.S. TRADE BY PRODUCT CATEGORY

We can also analyze foreign trade by product. Table 1-5 depicts the top ten product groups in exports, imports, surpluses and deficits. As with countries, certain factors stand out.

Exports and Imports   Based on the economic theory of comparative advantage, one might conclude that a country would export certain groups of products and import others. However, the data in Table 1-5 seem to contradict this theory. Eight of the leading export product groups are also among the leading imports. Only SITC 79 (other transport equipment) and SITC 87 (scientific instruments) are not among the leading imports. Civilian aircraft, a category wherein the United States does enjoy market leadership, constitutes the bulk of SITC 79. Despite this leadership, we also imported $40 billion in this category. Likewise, exports of scientific instruments reached more than $74 billion, but imports also topped $39 billion.

While automotive vehicles (SITC 78) represent our leading import, the United States also exported more product in this category than any country except Japan. However, petroleum imports far exceed our exports, valued at $31 billion. Likewise, apparel exports of $21 billion fall far short of imports.

Deficit Products   Petroleum and its by-products created the largest deficit. Since so many applications, both industrial and consumer, require these products, usage will probably increase. Resins derived from petroleum are the base material for a broad range of plastics. They are also necessary to the manufacture of synthetic fabrics such as nylon and rayon. In short, the plastics and textile industries depend heavily on petroleum by-products.

In 1992, the United States accounted for 2.7 billion of the 22 billion barrels of oil produced worldwide, or 12 percent. However, our production plus net imports equaled 5.3 billion barrels, or 24 percent of the world's production.[7] Thus, the only alternatives to this trade deficit are greater domestic production of petroleum or discovery of viable substitutes. For example, commercial and personal motor vehicles consumed

TABLE 1-5   U.S. Trade Goods by Product Groups: 1990-1994 (in billions of dollars)

SITC*	Top Ten Exports		SITC	Top Ten Imports	
77	Elect. machinery/apparatus	199.4	78	Road vehicles	398.0
78	Road vehicles	189.3	33	Petroleum and by-products	259.5
79	Other transport equipment	173.7	77	Elect. machinery/apparatus	212.8
75	Office machines, ADP eqpt	154.9	75	Office machines, ADP eqpt	191.7
89	Misc. manufactures	116.1	84	Apparel and accessories	153.4
74	General industrial equipment	95.1	89	Misc. manufactures	143.8
71	Power generating equipment	92.3	76	Telecomm. and recording eqpt	131.4
72	Industry-specific machinery	89.0	74	General industrial eqpt	82.8
87	Scientific instruments	74.6	71	Power generating eqpt	81.5
76	Telecomm and recording eqpt	64.4	72	Industry-specific machinery	65.9
	TOP TEN TOTAL	1,248.8		TOP TEN TOTAL	1,720.8
	TOTAL PRODUCT EXPORTS	2,239.7		TOTAL PRODUCT IMPORTS	2,761.2
	TOP 10—PERCENT OF TOTAL	55.8		TOP 10—PERCENT OF TOTAL	62.3

	Top Ten Surpluses			Top Ten Deficits	
79	Other transport equipment	133.2	33	Petroleum and by-products	−228.5
87	Scientific instruments	35.6	78	Road vehicles	−208.8
57	Plastics, primary form	25.0	84	Apparel and accessories	−132.8
72	Industry-specific machinery	23.1	76	Telecomm. and recording eqpt	−66.9
59	Chemical material/products	20.0	85	Footwear	−48.9
51	Organic chemicals	12.0	75	Office machines, ADP eqpt	−33.7
54	Pharmaceuticals	8.1	67	Iron and steel	−33.6
56	Fertilizers	7.2	66	Nonmetallic minerals	−29.2
58	Plastics, nonprimary forms	5.7	89	Misc. manufactures	−27.7
55	Essential oils	5.6	68	Nonferrous metals	−20.9
	TOP TEN TOTAL	275.5		TOP TEN TOTAL	−831.0

*SITC = Standard International Trade Code.

Source: Adapted from *U.S. Foreign Trade Highlights–1994,* U.S. Department of Commerce, International Trade Administration (September 1995).

129 billion gallons of fuel (gasoline and diesel oil) in 1991.[8] Electric automobiles and mass transit could make a serious dent in this consumption, if the former become more feasible (greater distance per battery charge), and the commuting public in western metropolitan areas will make greater use of the latter. Advertisements praising cotton as the "fabric of our lives" can also reduce the deficit while creating a stronger market for cotton growers.

Consumer Preferences   Referring again to Table 1-5, the consumer market is wholly or primarily responsible for the five largest deficit categories. Automobiles, clothing, footwear, and electronic entertainment products (CD players, televisions, stereos, portable game players, and so on) accounted for $90 billion net imports in 1988, and this deficit increased to $106 billion in 1994.

While we bewail the loss of jobs to other countries, we happily buy the products that these countries produce. Every billion dollars in imports represents 5,000 to 10,000 jobs, depending on the level of productivity that one uses in the equation.

When the thought of lost jobs presents a mental dilemma, the rationalization switches to quality. "Everyone" knows that American workers simply do not produce the same quality of product that one can import from Japan, Germany, Taiwan, or Lower Slobbovia. Yet a recent, vague TV "factoid" said that 79 percent of the women and 71 percent of the men in a survey sample considered their work performance above average. Except for 1 percent of each sex, the respondents said their performance was at least average. Either these people used a low standard in defining average and above-average performance, or the other 21 and 29 percent caused all the problems.

We will discuss the impact of quality further in a subsequent chapter. For now, suffice it to say that the most difficult perceptions to change are negative ones. When a manufacturer, wholesaler, or retailer disappoints customers and forces them to seek out alternative satisfiers, it takes a monumental and time-consuming effort to regain their confidence—if it is ever regained. Quality, in the sense of product performance, affects both customer satisfaction and company reputation. When the former diminishes, the latter erodes, and customer loyalty is lost.[9]

Perhaps the trend in the automotive industry can provide some optimism and serve as a model for the recovery of lost customers. After a decade-long loss in market share, the Big Three automakers not only arrested this trend in 1991 but reversed it in succeeding years.[10] In 1995, the Big Three produced eight of the top ten selling vehicles, and Ford alone could claim five of these.[11] Part of this success stemmed from a weak dollar in relation to the Japanese yen, forcing Japanese automakers to increase their prices despite a fiercely competitive U.S. market. Another part was the result of innovative styling. But many feel that continuing efforts by the Big Three to upgrade quality and overcome a negative image finally won over a segment of the buying public.

Surplus Products   The products shown in Table 1-5 as major surpluses provide another reason to believe that American-made products can readily compete in the international market, whether the buying criteria are economic or qualitative. American aircraft manufacturers, notably Boeing and McDonnell-Douglas, maintained a major market share despite a strong competitive and political effort by the Airbus consortium, a firm backed by France, Germany, Spain, and the United Kingdom. Airbus stressed to the national airlines of every European country the importance of the European Union's developing a respectable share in this multibillion-dollar industry. They also reminded major airlines throughout the world of the danger inherent in one or two aircraft companies dominating the supply side. This battle still rages and will continue to demand superior performance by all competitors.

Manufacturing Infrastructures   American manufacturers of **capital equipment** and components have consistently maintained a trade surplus. Capital equipment includes a broad spectrum of industrial machinery used in oil drilling, mining, construction, electricity generation, and the manufacture of virtually all other end products. This category also includes the sophisticated information technologies of the computer, telecommunications, and semiconductor industries.

Every industrialized nation recognizes capital equipment as a major element of its manufacturing infrastructure, because it provides the essential support for workers in all other industries. Having to depend on another nation to supply such equipment means lagging behind them in manufacturing technology. However, the alternative of using inferior domestic equipment creates an even greater problem. The output quality invariably declines, while costs increase as a result of higher reject rates and lower worker efficiency. A trade surplus in capital equipment indicates not only a country's ability to compete in the world market but also its leadership in manufacturing technology.

Developing nations in Asia and Africa have no choice but to depend on equipment produced in the United States, Germany, Japan, or other industrialized countries.

The nations of eastern Europe must replace their obsolete manufacturing infrastructures with systems that will allow them to become productive members of the free market system.

China represents a very interesting market opportunity. On one hand, an unofficial alliance continues to develop between China, Taiwan, and Hong Kong. China possesses vast land and people resources and has a burning desire to become a world economic power. Taiwan can contribute advanced technologies and financial power, while Hong Kong provides both finances and international marketing skills.[12] The reunification of Hong Kong and China will undoubtedly accelerate this alliance and may have a negative impact on trade with the United States. However, despite logical reasons to increase mutual interdependence and to minimize trade with outsiders, a survey of Chinese procurement officials indicated their willingness to buy American industrial products based on a perception of high quality and competitive pricing.[13]

A PROMISING FUTURE FOR THE U.S. TRADE BALANCE

Economists define "market equilibrium" as that condition in which customer demand and producer output are equal. Under this condition, one can forecast future markets with relative ease. Economic skeptics, though agreeing with the definition, emphasize that we pass through this theoretical point quickly each time we journey from boom to bust or vice versa. Thus, another term, "all other things being equal," is frequently used.

To predict any future circumstance, we try to assume a set of conditions that are both reasonable and probable. The reasonable part is not too difficult, but probability grows increasingly nebulous as the world undergoes the type of changes we have witnessed during the 1980s and thus far in the 1990s. Suppose we assume that the trends discussed in this chapter continue:

1. The world economy will grow at least modestly.
2. Developing nations will seek to strengthen their infrastructures and will require both goods and services from other nations.
3. Industrialized nations will acknowledge the mutual need for a more balanced trade.
4. More American manufacturers will recognize that customer satisfaction is a prerequisite to financial success.
5. American consumers will reward those manufacturers who have earned their patronage.

If the above conditions prevail, the United States will have an excellent environment in which to strengthen its international business and economic position. We already know that American buyers, both consumers and businesses, respond more favorably to greater value and satisfaction than to point of origin. (Note that greater value and lower price are not automatically synonymous.) Studies as well as actual results show that buyers in other countries respond similarly. As long as manufacturers and service providers continue to recognize that customer satisfaction must exist before profits can be generated, a favorable trade balance should result.

The Low-Wage Problem   Some feel that the United States simply cannot compete against the output of low-wage countries. On the surface, this argument appears compelling. But consider the world textile market as a prime example to the contrary. In the United States, imported textiles rose from only a 2 percent market share in 1963 to more than 50 percent in 1990. American producers moved from New England to lower-wage states in the Southeast and eventually to foreign countries in a futile attempt to stem the tide of imports and maintain a viable position in the world market. Meanwhile, despite wage rates $4 an hour above those in the United States, Germany remained the world's leading exporter of textiles. Their primary competitor, the Italian textile industry, also had higher wage rates than American producers. What caused this apparent contradiction of common wisdom?

German textile producers followed several time-honored principles. First, they purchased the most sophisticated textile machinery (not available from American manufacturers) and installed it in modernized facilities. Then they hired skilled employees who had completed a rigorous apprenticeship program and were capable of operating the equipment. Finally, they produced the high-quality, fashionable goods sought after by a sufficiently large segment of the market. The result: satisfied customers who valued the goods made possible by well-paid, well-equipped, efficient workers whose productivity compensated for the higher wage.[14]

The Fallacy of Tariffs and Quotas   High tariffs and restrictive product quotas also fail as solutions to trade deficits. Consider the results of American (or Japanese or German) mechanisms aimed at reducing imports. If buyers still consider the products indispensable, they will continue buying but must now pay a higher price. The law of supply and demand still holds sway. Instead of hurting the supplier, the higher profits resulting from higher prices simply strengthen this firm. If the restricted nation feels unjustly penalized, it will retaliate with its own mechanisms, thereby restricting American exports.

When nations engage in an import restriction war, neither one wins. All buyers spend more, put less into savings, and further reduce the money available to upgrade production facilities. Total trade is reduced, and jobs are lost. A far better solution emanates from increased quality, increased productivity, better products at a given price, or the same products at a lower price.

The Domestic Business Market

The **manufacturing ability** of a country defines its economic growth potential. Manufacturing ability applies not only to end products but also to the raw materials and component parts that make up the end products and the production equipment required to fabricate them. As we discussed with reference to developing countries, lack of productive resources in any of these areas results in lagging behind those countries that are self-sufficient. This manufacturing capability is the industrial base of a nation's economy and the fountainhead of its business market.[15] Millions of consumers wait at the opposite end of a circuitous path to purchase many of the diverse goods and services that flow from the industrial sector.

For the sake of discussion, think of the business market as a closed-loop system. This requires the elimination of exports and imports as well as all consumer purchases. Government can remain in the picture, since it purchases about a third of the total GDP. Including government, we now have a **four-sector system** that includes natural product providers, goods-producing firms, service-producing firms, and the government. Box 1-1 depicts these sectors. Each sector requires the output of the others in order to exist. Farmers and fishers need equipment to operate their businesses, and they pay for it by selling their crops and catches to other people in the system. Manufacturers need raw materials from mining companies and component parts from other manufacturers to build end products. These products are fabricated in factories and stored in warehouses built by construction firms. Many of these products will pass through wholesalers and retailers

---

BOX 1-1

Industry Classifications
Used by the Department of Commerce

NONMANUFACTURED (NATURAL) PRODUCT INDUSTRIES

Agriculture

Fishing

Forestry

GOODS-PRODUCING INDUSTRIES

Mining

Construction

Manufacturing

   Durable goods

   Nondurable goods

SERVICE-PRODUCING INDUSTRIES

Transportation

Public utilities

Trade

   Wholesale

   Retail

Finance, insurance, and real estate

Business services

Personal services

Hospital services

Legal services

Educational services

GOVERNMENT

Federal

State

Local

Source: Department of Commerce, Bureau of Economic Analysis.

---

on their way to end users. Meanwhile, a broad spectrum of services will be provided by firms that specialize in accounting systems, market research, business loans, legal services, and day care for the children of the workers. Each firm pays for its inputs through the sale of its outputs.

We will briefly examine the four sectors of the business market, viewing them primarily as producers.

PRODUCTION INDUSTRIES

In the broadest sense, the industrial sector includes all industries that produce goods and services consumed anywhere in the economy or exported to other countries. The listings in Box 1-1 represent industrial classifications used by the Department of Commerce in their various reports. In a narrower sense, the term *industrial* applies only to producers of natural and fabricated products. For further clarity, the term *resellers* differentiates firms engaged in wholesale and retail trade from all other service providers. Government is not only the largest purchaser in the business market but also a major provider of social services.

As we discussed at the beginning of this chapter, industrial output is bought, sold, rebought, and resold at various points in the marketing continuum. This would create a serious counting problem without **value-added** accounting. Consider the following example. An independent contractor bids on the right to cut Douglas fir trees on 10 acres controlled by the Bureau of Land Management (BLM). The contractor pays the BLM, hauls the logs to a local mill, and sells them. The mill owner cuts these logs into a variety of popular lumber sizes and sells them to lumberyards and do-it-yourself outlets such as Home Depot. Building contractors buy lumber at a local lumberyard so they can build the homes they have sold to happy new homeowners. Some of these homeowners want to add a patio deck off the family room and decide to do the work themselves. They buy the necessary lumber at Home Depot. Later, they may also hire a carpenter to get rid of the mysterious tilt in the deck floor.

If the Department of Commerce added the value of all these sales together, they would overstate the total. To correct this problem, they count only the value added by each firm and contractor: The logger generates costs in cutting the trees and hauling the logs to the mill; the mill owner adds the cost of cutting the logs into lumber and marketing the lumber; the lumberyard wholesaler and Home Depot generate operating costs, as does the building contractor. The underlying price paid for the original trees is not considered until the final sales transaction—either the sale of the home or the homeowner's lumber purchase. Only the homeowner's carpentry efforts go uncounted.

Six different industries make up this example. The Bureau of Land Management represents government. The logger represents forestry, one of the natural-product industries along with fishing and agriculture. The mill manufactures durable goods (lumber products). The building contractor belongs to the construction industry. Both the lumberyard and Home Depot are resellers. If the lumberyard deals exclusively with contractors, it is a wholesaler. Home Depot might be both a wholesaler and a retailer. The difference lies in whether a firm sells to other firms or to consumers. The carpenter who had to patch up the homeowner's noble but amateurish efforts is a personal-service provider. Besides serving consumers, this carpenter might also provide business services (remodeling the offices of a local physician or CPA). In addition to exemplifying the value-added process, this scenario indicates the difficulty in properly categorizing various industrial activities.

Natural-Product Industries   Agriculture and fishing provide most of our food and beverages, including meat, poultry, seafood, fruits, vegetables, and a variety of drinks ranging from milk to fruit juice to fashionable wines. In addition, agriculture provides textile fibers, animal feeds, and convertible basics such as soybeans. Forestry obviously deals with trees and shrubbery, logs and lumber, but also provides other unassociated materials, such as maple syrup and antitoxins.

Mining and Construction   These industries either extract minerals from beneath the earth or change its surface. Mining ranges from precious metals (gold, silver, platinum) to jewels (rubies, emeralds, diamonds) to a variety of more common materials (coal, salt, gravel, sand). This industry typically accounts for less than 2 percent of the GDP, but materials derived from its output constitute 9 percent.[16]

The construction industry produces an equally diverse output. For example, there are more than 100 million dwellings in the United States. These range from single-unit houses to mobile homes to housing complexes such as townhouses and apartment buildings. The total value of these dwellings exceeds $6.7 trillion dollars. Total new construction averages $400 billion per year in constant 1987 dollars. This total includes manufacturing plants, offices, hotels and motels, hospitals, schools, churches, farm structures, petroleum pipelines, highways, sewer systems, and water supplies. Despite its overall size, small firms dominate this industry. The typical U.S. construction firm has only nine employees and revenues of $688,000[16]

Manufacturing Industries   These industries drive the rest of the economy. Unfortunately, many numbers suggest that we have taken a detour off the main road. As discussed earlier in this chapter, we import more manufactured goods than we export. This

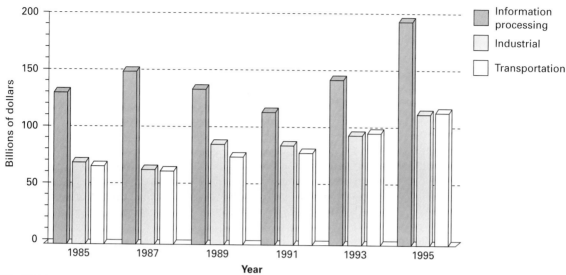

DATA: U.S. Department of Commerce, Census Bureau, *Survey of Current Business* (multiple issues) July 1988-January 1997.

Source: Adapted from Thomas A.Stewart, 1994. The information age in charts. *Fortune* (April 4, 1994):75-9.

FIGURE 1-1   Purchase of producers' durable equipment (PDE) 1985-1995. Subdivided into information processing, industrial, and transportation equipment (in constant 1992 dollars).

problem would be noteworthy even if American firms were unable to produce the imported goods. This is not the case. The numbers in Tables 1-1 and 1-5 clearly indicate that many American consumers and business customers still feel that imported goods provide better quality and better performance at an equal or lower price. Such perceptions do not change quickly.

As a consequence, 2.5 million fewer people worked in manufacturing in the United States in 1994 than did so in 1980, and the output of these industries fell steadily from 21.2 percent of GNP in 1970 to 19.5 percent in 1980 and 17.4 percent in 1994. Simultaneously, services rose from 10.8 to 12.5 to 20.2 percent of GNP over the same time period. Perhaps this is the reason some pessimists predict that the major American products of the twenty-first century will be hamburgers, soft drinks, and lawsuits.

The future, however, holds more promise than the past. Having received a "wake-up call" regarding their lagging rate of improvement, many American industries have responded with significant productivity improvements in the 1990s. The absolute level of output per worker remains the highest in the world. The United States also maintains leadership in its ability to apply high technology to the design and manufacture of products. However, note the phrase "ability to apply"; not all firms have made use of available technology. However, as Figure 1-1 indicates, American firms as a whole continue to spend more money on information processing equipment (including computers, telecommunications, and computer-aided production equipment) than on industrial or transportation equipment. It is logical to assume that this dollar distribution indicates an overt effort to increase product quality, worker productivity, and the accurate exchange of critical information.

Companies such as Motorola and Intel consistently introduce new products about the time their competitors offer a version of the obsolete product. This point will be discussed further in subsequent chapters. Finally, although the downsizing of corporations has caused pain to many displaced workers, firms that have slashed their

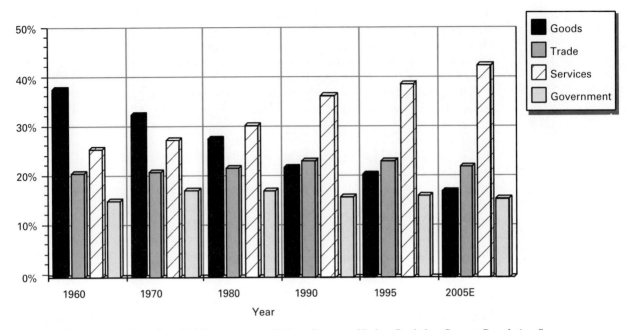

Source: Labor force statistics from U.S. Department of Labor, Bureau of Labor Statistics. *Current Population Survey* (periodic issues). Estimate is based on BLS midrange projection as of May 1996.

FIGURE 1-2 Distribution of United States employment by major sectors: 1960-1995, actual numbers; 2005, estimate.

bureaucracies, closed obsolete plants, retrained workers, and equipped them with modern technology can now compete effectively in world markets.

SERVICE INDUSTRIES

When productive capacity in the United States was growing continuously in the 1960s, no one foresaw the day when fewer than 25 percent of all American workers would be employed in the production of raw materials, homes, and factories, plus the entire spectrum of manufactured products. Yet this is precisely the situation in the 1990s. As Figure 1-2 indicates, the percentage of workers engaged in the mining, construction, and manufacturing industries has declined steadily. The Bureau of Labor Statistics (BLS) predicts a continuation of this trend through the year 2005.[17] Where will the remaining 80 percent work?

Between 1980 and 1995, 7 million workers entered wholesale and retail trade, raising the percentage of this sector from 22.5 to 23.3 percent. Despite the addition of 3 million workers at the federal, state, and municipal levels, the government sector shrank from 18.0 to 16.5 percent. The services sector was by far the largest growth area, adding 18 million of the 26 million new workers in the economy and increasing in percentage from 31.2 to almost 40 percent. The BLS predicts that almost 17 million more workers will enter the nonfarm economy between 1995 and 2005, with 14 million becoming service providers.[17]

Any discussion of manufacturing sector problems gives rise to the twin topics of worker productivity and quality of output. Indeed, the United States was rapidly losing its position as the most productive nation in terms of GDP produced per worker. However, leaving quality aside, the services sector has a more severe productivity problem than the manufacturing sector. In 1990, service-producing industries (as defined in

Box 1-1) possessed more than 80 percent of the installed computer base in the United States, employed 61 percent of all workers, but generated only 47 percent of total GDP. Thus, nonservice industries generated 53 percent of GDP, with 39 percent of the workers and 15 percent of the computer base. On the plus side, however, services continue to provide a trade surplus, as discussed earlier.

Regarding productivity, why should this important factor be lower in the services sector? The very breadth of services offered makes this question difficult to tackle. Service providers include truck drivers as well as the police who arrest those who speed, pastry chefs as well as physicians who tell us to avoid fattening foods, and college instructors as well as the bank manager who arranges student loans. Some analysts suggest the problem stems from our inability to assess properly the value of intangibles. Others feel that part of the problem lies with those service providers who do not receive fair market value for their efforts—for example, professionals who do pro bono work, hospitals that serve the indigent, not-for-profit organizations, and so on.

We do not possess all the reasons, nor the only accurate one. However, if you employ a constant factor of revenue generated per employee, the data clearly indicate a lower ratio in the service sector.

Resellers   Merchant wholesalers and retailers share in a phenomenon known as the **20/80 syndrome,** which implies that 20 percent of firms do 80 percent of the business. Although both trade segments are populated by thousands of small firms, the few largest firms enjoy the majority of all sales. For example, according to the 1992 Census of Wholesale Trade, 301,000 merchant wholesalers sold $1,822 billion in products, an average of $6.1 million each. However, only 3,746 firms, about 1 percent of all, had sales in excess of $50 million, but they accounted for $972 billion, or 53 of total sales.[18] We will discuss wholesalers and other business channel intermediaries more fully in Chapter 13.

Retailers, who will not be covered in depth in this test, provide almost a perfect example of the 20/80 syndrome. Twenty percent of all retailers had 1994 sales of $1 million or more, but they enjoyed 77 percent of all sales.[19] The retail segment is also unique because of its constant restructuring; consumers can make their purchases through an endless variety of outlets—from vending machines and door-to-door sellers to television shopping networks and through home computers. Finding ways to attract the elusive consumer provides a continuing challenge for retail marketers.

Institutions   Institutions, including hospitals and clinics, high schools and colleges, churches and synagogues, prisons, and museums, form another interesting segment of service-producing industries. Some provide public services on a not-for-profit basis and resemble the government in that respect. County hospitals and state universities meet this description. Others act with a clear profit motivation. Most HMOs and all private schools fall into this category.

Government as a Service Provider   We normally view the composite of federal, state, and municipal government as the biggest consumer in the country or as the prolific spender of our tax dollars. Government expenditures exceed 2 trillion dollars. However, the government also provides a wide range of services, some in competition with the private sector. For example, the postal service competes with United Parcel and Federal Express. Security organizations and private investigators compete on a limited basis with municipal and state police forces. Public schools compete with their private counterparts. Other government services, such as the justice system, legislative bodies, military forces, and management of public lands have no commercial equivalents.

Looking Back

To the average consumer, the business market is like an iceberg with only its tip visible. This tip is the segment of the business market in which the consumer is employed, as almost 50 percent of all American workers are. And yet, virtually all the goods and services that consumers buy must pass through this market.

All countries in the world, whether industrialized or primarily agricultural, have a need for the output of the business market; but in many instances, the limits of their own productive capabilities force them to buy products from other countries. Sometimes they can exchange products for products—in other words, export in an amount that offsets imports. Otherwise, imports must be paid for with currency, which results in a trade deficit. This is the situation in which the United States has found itself for almost 20 years. Our most nagging deficits exist with Japan, other Pacific Rim countries, and the OPEC cartel. Aside from petroleum, consumer durables and nondurables remain the largest product deficits.

We examined the domestic business market, differentiating production industries from service industries. Within the service sector, we noted the particular attributes of resellers, institutions, and the government as a service provider.

Questions for Discussion

1. Do trade deficits really present a serious problem, or does the problem exist mainly in the minds of inefficient manufacturers who want protection against more capable competitors?

2. Who is primarily to blame for continued deficits in consumer products: American manufacturers who made dissatisfying products originally or consumers who refuse to believe that current products are competitive?

3. How would you bring these manufacturers and consumers together for the betterment of both? Remember that importing products is the same as exporting jobs—20,000 jobs for every $1 billion in imports. Or is this a satisfactory situation?

4. Think of the major political and economic changes that have taken place worldwide over the past 10 to 15 years. What business opportunities have these changes created for American firms? What threats do they pose?

5. "You can't get around the fact that low-wage countries will win the battle to produce low-tech products." Support or debate this statement.

6. Do tariffs and quotas solve or create trade problems? Explain.

7. Should the federal government be involved in the provision of any services that private enterprise can supply? Why or why not?

Endnotes

1. U.S. Department of Commerce. 1995. 1994 Annual Survey of Manufactures, Report M94(AS). Statistics for industry groups and industries, Washington, D.C., U.S. GPO.

2. U.S. Department of Commerce. 1996. Annual Survey of Wholesale Trade, Report W94(AS). Washington, D.C.: U.S. GPO.

3. Standard & Poor's Industry Surveys. 1995. Electronics section. August 3, p. E28.

4. U.S. Department of Commerce, International Trade Administration. 1995. *U.S. Foreign Trade Highlights:1994.* Washington, D.C.: U.S. GPO.

5. U.S. Central Intelligence Agency. 1995. *The 1995 World Factbook.* Washington, D.C.: U.S. GPO.

6. Hal Hill and Prue Phillips, "Trade is a two-way exchange: Rising import penetration in east Asia's export economies," *World Economy* 16 (1993):687-97.

7. U.S. Department of Energy, Energy Information Administration. 1993 *Monthly Energy Review*. Washington, D.C.: U.S. GPO.

8. Department of Transportation, Federal Highway Administration, 1992 Census of Transportation. Washington, D.C.: U.S. GPO.

9. Fred Seines, "An examination of the effect of product performance on brand reputation, satisfaction, and loyalty," *European Journal of Marketing* 27 (1993):19-35.

10. "Trying to rev up," *Business Week* (January 24,1994), pp. 32-3.

11. "Trucks set pace in a so-so year," *Automotive News* (January 8, 1996):1.

12. Louis Kraar, "A new China without borders," *Fortune* (October 5, 1992), pp. 124-8.

13. Erdener Kaynak and Orsay Kucukemiroglu, "Sourcing of industrial products: Regiocentric orientation of Chinese organizational buyers," *European Journal of Marketing* 26 (1992):36-55.

14. Lester Thurow, *Head to Head* (New York, William Morrow & Co., 1992), pp. 190-93.

15. Frederick E. Webster, Jr. 1978. "Management science in industrial marketing," *Journal of Marketing* (January 1978), pp. 21-7.

16. Louis Rukeyser, *Louis Rukeyser's Business Almanac,* 2nd ed. (New York: Simon & Schuster, 1991), pp. 465-9.

17. Bureau of Labor Statistics. 1995. Report #USDL 95-485, Washington, D.C.: U.S. GPO.

18. U.S. Department of Commerce, Census Bureau 1995. *1992 Census of Wholesale Trade.* Washington, D.C.: U.S. GPO.

19. U.S. Department of Commerce, Census Bureau 1995. *1994 Annual Survey of Retail Trade* (Washington, D.C.: U.S. GPO).

Bibliography

Hill, Hal, and Prue Phillips, "Trade is a two-way exchange: Rising import penetration in east Asia's export economies," *World Economy* 16 (1993):687-97.

Kraar, Louis, "A new China without borders," *Fortune* (October 5, 1992), pp. 124-8.

Rukeyser, Louis, *Louis Rukeyser's Business Almanac,* 2nd ed. (New York: Simon & Schuster, 1991).

Seines, Fred, "An examination of the effect of product performance on brand reputation, satisfaction, and loyalty," *European Journal of Marketing* 27: 19-35.

Thurow, Lester, *Head to Head.* (New York: William Morrow & Co., 1992).

U.S. Government Publishing Office (U.S. GPO), various relevant documents:
    U.S. Department of Commerce, Census Bureau, *Census of Manufactures, Census of Wholesale Trade,* and *Census of Retail Trade* (published every 5 years; *Annual Surveys* in intervening years).
    U.S. Department of Commerce, Bureau of Economic Analysis. *Survey of Current Business.*
    U.S. Department of Commerce, International Trade Administration. Various reports on exports, imports, and productivity, by country.
    U.S. Department of Labor, Bureau of Labor Statistics, Various domestic wage, employment, and productivity reports.

CHAPTER

2

The Nature of Business Marketing

Although the basic tenets of marketing apply equally to the consumer and business markets, significant differences exist in a number of important dimensions and elements. In Chapter 1 we analyzed the business market sectors as different types of providers or sellers. We will now view these same sectors as potential customers. Recall that the business market can be viewed as a closed-loop system, with all sectors selling to and buying from each other. Depending on the sector involved, the size and number of potential customers and their buying motives vary considerably. The same is true of the relative importance of price and the choice of personal selling or advertising as the primary promotional element. Business marketers normally deal with other business professionals rather than consumers acting on their own behalf. This level of professionalism, along with different motivation, has a notable impact on the method and extent of negotiations. In this chapter, we will address the following:

1. The difference between consumer and business marketing management
2. The defining characteristics of the business market
3. Differences in the business marketing mix
4. The economic factors that influence the demand for business goods and services

Why Study Business Marketing?

With so many other employment opportunities available to college graduates, why study business marketing? That question gives rise to a paradox. Many perceptive business executives in the early 1980s foresaw the need for greater customer satisfaction and thus greater marketing competence. However, they also recognized that "the historical weakness in their firms" had been the lack of a marketing orientation, which resulted in the following[1]:

- A failure to provide proper guidance and stimulation for the development of new products
- A failure to exploit and develop markets for these new products
- An inability to define new methods for promoting products to customers in the face of major increases in the cost of media advertising and personal selling

- A failure to innovate in distribution and other areas to keep up with changing requirements of customers doing business on a multinational basis
- An attempt to meet significant new competition through traditional ways of doing business
- An inability to refine and modify product positioning
- A tendency for product managers and higher levels of management to approach problems in the same old way

Despite the recognition of these major shortcomings more than a decade ago, the problem persists in the 1990s. The marketing competence needed to correct such shortcomings often comes only through painful experience. The 1980s should have provided both the experience and the desire for correction. The best place to lay the foundation for competence is in the classroom, where situation analyses affect only grades—not jobs or profits.

In the early 1980s, one researcher surveyed business marketers to discern the areas of expertise they considered most important for success in business marketing. The top twenty rankings are listed in Table 2-1. Since these persons dictate hiring practices, their opinions provide valuable insights. As indicated, the strategic areas (marketing research, planning, forecasting, and product development) carry the greatest importance.[2] As helpful as this list and others that emphasize areas of knowledge or experience are, they do not provide insight into the personal skills and attributes that typify successful marketers: effective written and oral communication, ability to persuade and motivate, skillful problem-solving and analysis, plus a broad range of interpersonal people skills. This bears out the emphasis that all instructors put on the development of critical thinking skills and the ability to articulate one's conclusions.

Business Versus Consumer Marketing Management

While marketing managers face the same basic tasks in both markets, unique forces combine to pose special challenges for the business marketing manager. For example, in most goods-producing industries, a few firms dominate the buying power. Most suppliers are aware of these firms and focus their selling efforts on them. The seller must either penetrate these firms or settle for a modest market share. Even in the con-

TABLE 2-1   Practitioners' Ranking of Marketing Expertise

Topic	Ranking	Topic	Ranking
Market planning	1	Field sales management	11
Market analysis	2	Advertising	12
Sales forecasting	3	Sales promotion	13
Market research	4	Buyer behavior	14
Product planning	5	Buyer-seller relations	15
New product development	6	Financial interface	16
Product management	7	Price and the law	17
Pricing strategies	8	Marketing control	18
Price theory	9	Technical sales	19
Sales management	10	Proposal writing	20

Source: Adapted from Plank, Richard E., 1982. Industrial marketing education: Practitioners' views. *Industrial Marketing Management* 11:311-15

struction market, where small firms dominate, there is "reverse size pressure." Construction firms tend to buy their tools and supplies from producers who have demonstrated their ability to satisfy. Supplier size equates to market share, which indicates customer satisfaction.

Channels of distribution in the business market are shorter and crowded. The same concentrated buying (and selling) power exists among wholesalers, so that all manufacturers would like to franchise the same ones to distribute their product lines. Business buyers are well informed, highly organized professionals who are not likely to be influenced by "bells and whistles." Major purchases are made by multiple influencers who bring diverse needs and attitudes to purchasing decisions.

As in the consumer market, business marketers must define their target segments, determine the needs of those segments, design products and services to fill the needs, and develop programs to reach and satisfy each target. However, general management becomes more involved in the functions of business marketing. In fact, many business executives have difficulty in separating marketing from corporate strategy and policy.[1]

Many consumer marketing departments act independently to devise strategic changes at the retail level through alterations in advertising, promotion, and packaging. Changes in business marketing strategy, particularly in the manufacturing sector, tend to have such corporate implications as a departure from traditional engineering design and manufacturing techniques or a major shift in developmental emphasis. As was the case with Caterpillar, this may require capital commitments for new plants and equipment. (Caterpillar took 5 years and spent $200 million to revamp one 40-year-old facility.)[3] Although marketing may identify the need for such changes, top management usually makes the final decisions, with implementation and follow-through required in all functional areas.

Business Marketing Defined

Business marketing consists of *all activities required to provide goods and services to customers.* As discussed in Chapter 1, these customers include producers of both natural and fabricated products, government agencies, and service-producing organizations including institutions, wholesalers, and retailers. These diverse customers can use products and services to fabricate their own end products or to facilitate the operation of their business.

Contrasting Business and Consumer Marketing

A comparison of market characteristics will probably best illustrate these differences. As Table 2-2 indicates, notable differences exist in (1) market structure, (2) product usage, (3) buyer behavior, (4) distribution channels, (5) promotional variables, and (6) pricing strategies. Because of these basic differences plus a longer list of subtleties, we cannot agree with those individuals who insist the two markets are essentially the same and should not be considered separately.

MARKET CHARACTERISTICS

Business and consumer markets differ in their size, their geographic concentration, and their competitive natures.

TABLE 2-2	Areas of Difference Between the Business and Consumer Markets	
	BUSINESS	CONSUMER
Market structure	Geographically concentrated	Geographically dispersed
	Relatively few buyers	Mass markets
	Oligopolistic competition	Pure competition
Buyer behavior	Functional involvement	Family involvement
	Rational/task motives prevail	Social/emotional motives prevail
	Stable relationships	Less buyer-seller loyalty
	Professionalism, expertise	Less trained, often inexperienced
Decision-making	Distinct, observable stages	Vague, mental stages
	Often group decisions	Usually individual decisions
Products	Many tailored for customer	Most standardized
	Service, delivery, dependability very important	These items somewhat important
Channels	Shorter, more direct, fewer links	Longer, indirect, multiple links
Promotion	Emphasis on personal selling	Emphasis on advertising
Price	Competitive bidding	List prices with some discounts
	Complex, lengthy negotiations	Only a few factors negotiable
	End-use cost most important	Published price most important

 Size of the Market   The consumer market in the United States consists of approximately 100 million households, each of which buys a very small percentage of all consumer goods and services. By comparison, some business markets contain fewer than 100 firms. Even in those markets that contain hundreds or thousands of firms, a small number of them will dominate. This situation defines an **oligopoly,** and the majority of product markets (as opposed to services) are oligopolies. Table 2-3 provides examples of oligopolistic industries.

Though fewer in number, business customers buy larger quantities than consumers because of their size and repeat these purchases on a regular basis. Some of the volume purchases are surprising. For example, General Motors' biggest supplier does not provide tires, batteries, or any other tangible product; it is Blue Cross Blue Shield.[4] This surprising fact bears out another significant point: Many services would not survive if they had to depend on the consumer market alone.

Geographic Concentration   Figure 2-1 illustrates the geographic distribution of manufacturing plants. They tend to concentrate in the Middle Atlantic states of Pennsylvania, New York, Delaware, West Virginia, Maryland, and New Jersey; the East North Central states of Wisconsin, Illinois, Indiana, Michigan, and Ohio; the Pacific states of California, Washington, and Oregon; and the South Atlantic states of North Carolina, South Carolina, Georgia, and Florida. Most of these markets cluster in the large urban areas where manufacturing, distribution, transportation, financial, health and educational organizations exist.

Although the other regions in the U.S. are not as well populated with business organizations, some exceptions do exist. Texas, Oklahoma, Arkansas, and Louisiana in the West South Central region have only 8.3 percent of the nation's plants, but these states are strong in oil, oil related industries, and agriculture (i.e., rice, cotton, and maze). The West North Central states of North and South Dakota, Nebraska, Kansas, Minnesota, Iowa and Missouri are also rich in agricultural products, such as corn and wheat. The Mountain states have the lowest percentage of manufacturing plants in the country, but provide beef and other agricultural products. The East South Central states have the second lowest percentage and contain mostly agricultural commodities.

				Market Share		
SIC Code	Product Category	Number of Firms	Value of Shipments (in millions of dollars)	Top Four	Top Twenty	Top Fifty
3721	Aircraft	151	62,937.7	79	99	>99
3011	Tires and inner tubes	104	11,810.0	70	98	>99
3711	Motor vehicles/bodies	398	151,711.9	84	99	99
2911	Petroleum refining	131	136,579.3	30	78	97
3861	Photographic eqpt/supplies	832	22,120.5	78	89	93
3571	Electronic computers	803	38,205.9	45	82	92
2834	Pharmaceuticals	583	50,412.5	26	72	90
3661*	Telephone/telegraph eqpt	479	12,464.8	51	77	89
2011*	Meatpacking plants	1,296	6,958.7	50	79	88
3674	Semiconductors	823	32,143.9	41	72	85
3663	Radio/TV equipment	861	19,462.8	41	68	80
3714	Automotive parts/accessories	2,714	75,033.7	48	69	79
3531	Construction equipment	867	13,485.1	42	65	79
2051	Bakeries	2,180	18,142.5	34	66	78
2086	Soft drink bottlers/canners	637	25,422.5	37	61	75
3523	Farm equipment	1,578	9,616.4	47	62	71
2711	Newspapers	6,761	33,879.5	25	54	70
2721	Periodicals	4,390	22,075.0	20	46	62

TABLE 2-3 Manufacturing Oligopolies, Selected Industries: 1992 (ranked by top fifty market share)

* The dollars and market share data shown for this industry are based on Value Added rather than Value of Shipments because the latter contains a substantial and unmeasurable amount of duplication.

Source: 1992 Census of Manufactures report MC92-S-2, "Concentration Ratios in Manufacturing," U.S. Department of Commerce, Census Bureau (March 1995).

Manufacturers of computers and other sophisticated electronic products present an interesting case of plant location. They tend to concentrate in areas that have advanced teaching and research facilities and desirable living locales such as the Silicon Valley near San Francisco and Route 128 surrounding Boston. Such locations are chosen to facilitate the attraction of intelligent, educated employees, who seek both intellectual challenges and physical pleasures.

The top ten metropolitan areas in the United States have extensive business markets: New York, Los Angeles, Chicago, Washington-Baltimore, San Francisco–Oakland, Philadelphia, Boston, Detroit, Dallas–Ft. Worth, and Houston. Sizable business markets also exist in smaller but dynamic metropolitan areas such as Miami, Atlanta, Seattle, San Diego, Phoenix, Denver, Portland, and San Antonio.

Business marketers identify their customers and prospects by analyzing the location of plants, corporate offices, mills, government offices, industrial distributors, service organizations (accounting, financial, transportation, and legal), and health and educational institutions. The selection of concentration areas as target markets can result in significant savings of time, effort, and personnel.

Nature of Business Competition   The dominance of large firms affects both the selling and buying sides. When Boeing, Exxon, or General Motors generates the largest sales in their respective markets, they must also buy proportionate amounts of goods and services to produce that volume of output. This situation, wherein a few buyers

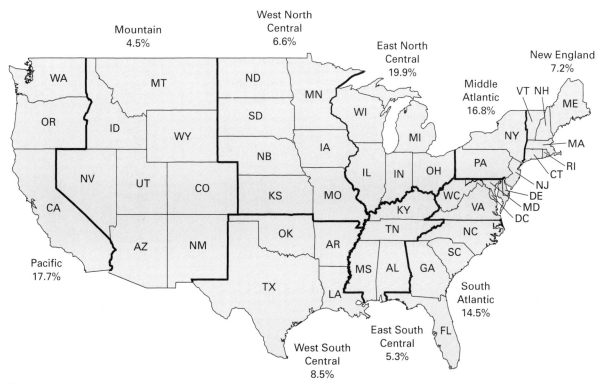

Source: U.S. Bureau of the Census, *Statistical Abstract of the United States 1993,* 113th ed. (Washington, D.C., 1993).

FIGURE 2-1 Geographical distribution of U.S. manufacturing plants.

exert a disproportionate influence on the market, is termed an **oligopsony.** Market observers wryly comment, "When GM catches cold, their suppliers get pneumonia." They refer to the fact that many smaller suppliers depend on GM to buy the major portion, if not all, of their output. When GM cuts back on production, these suppliers are put in desperate straits.

Because technological or economic advantages override geographic and political considerations, goods producers are more likely to engage in international transactions. Thus, the major finished goods exports of industrialized nations tend to be business rather than consumer goods, despite the United States consumer-goods deficit discussed in Chapter 1. Table 2-4 shows that 21 of the top 25 United States exporters in 1992 were producers of business goods. Only Philip Morris and the Big Three automakers are exceptions. Even then, *Fortune* magazine explains that much of the automotive exports are component parts shipped for assembly in Canadian and Mexican plants, with most of the completed cars returned to the United States. Table 2-4 shows that 21 of the top 25 U.S. exporters in 1994 were primarily involved in the production of business goods.

 Cooperative Competition   A dramatic shift is occurring in the relationship between high-tech industry competitors. The shift began in Japan.

Researchers and observers have long noted that the Japanese culture encourages an open cooperation between functional departments within a company. Unlike many American firms, Japanese companies have enjoyed the advantage of individual departments putting aside their provincial priorities in favor of focused corporate goals. That

		TABLE 2-4 U.S. Industrial Exporters: 1994		
Rank	*Company*	*Export sales (in millions of dollars)*	*Percent of change from 1993*	*Percent of total revenue*
1	General Motors	$16,127.1	8.1	10.4
2	Ford Motor	11,892.0	25.4	9.3
3	Boeing	11,844.0	−19.0	54.0
4	Chrysler	9,400.0	11.9	18.0
5	General Electric	8,110.0	−4.6	12.5
6	Motorola	7,370.0	47.7	33.1
7	IBM	6,336.0	−13.2	9.9
8	Philip Morris	4,942.0	20.4	9.2
9	Archer Daniels Midland	4,675.0	61.2	41.1
10	Hewlett-Packard	4,653.0	−1.8	18.6
11	Intel	4,561.0	33.9	39.6
12	Caterpillar	4,510.0	20.5	31.5
13	McDonnell Douglas	4,235.0	24.4	32.1
14	DuPont	3,625.0	3.6	10.4
15	United Technologies	3,108.0	−11.3	14.7
16	Eastman Kodak	2,600.0	16.0	15.4
17	Lockheed	2,079.0	19.3	15.8
18	Compaq Computer	2,018.0	5.0	18.6
19	Raytheon	1,867.0	−9.5	18.6
20	Digital Equipment	1,830.7	1.7	13.6
21	Allied Signal	1,818.0	7.0	14.2
22	3M	1,755.0	17.7	11.6
23	Westinghouse	1,613.0	20.6	17.5
24	Dow Chemical	1,575.0	9.2	7.9
25	Merck	1,572.5	56.7	10.5
	TOTAL	124,116.3*	13.9	15.0

* Equals 28.8% of all U.S. merchandise exports in 1994.

Source: James Aley, Lenore Schiff, and Tricia Welsh, "New lift for the U.S. export boom," *Fortune* (November 13, 1995), p. 129.

cooperative effort has also extended beyond corporate walls to competitors and suppliers. Although many have predicted that this phenomenon would never occur in the United States because of significant cultural differences, external cooperative efforts are indeed occurring with increasing regularity.

We should examine first why competitors decided to cooperate in Japan. In part, they were prompted by the powerful Ministry of International Trade and Industry (MITI). MITI has the responsibility for macroeconomic research in Japan; that is, it decides which industries should receive major governmental support in order to achieve a significant worldwide market share. Computers and semiconductors, along with automobiles and industrial machinery, have held priority status since the 1960s.[5]

However, firms such as NEC Corp., Fujitsu, Hitachi, and Toshiba—although profitable and successful—had two major concerns. First, the *cost* of developing world-class products and building the sophisticated equipment and factories necessary to produce them had reached astronomical levels. For example, the cost of building a semiconductor fabrication facility (fab) in 1994 exceeded $1 billion. Second, with product life cycles shortening and foreign competition strengthening, the _risk_ associated with such an expenditure went beyond the actual cost. Firms in Taiwan, Korea, Malaysia, Singapore, and other developing Asian countries were threatening Japan's high-tech industries, just as Japanese firms were doing in North America and Europe.

When American executives analyzed this cooperative competition more closely, they recognized some basic business tenets that had nothing to do with culture. The Japanese technology leaders simply wanted to spread the risk and beat their competition to market. A working alliance costs each firm less, might create synergistic strengths, and frequently shortens the time to market. U.S. firms could enjoy the same benefits. They did and went one step further by extending their alliances beyond national borders.

In 1992, semiconductor companies worldwide formed more than 130 **strategic alliances,** and more than half of these involved U.S. firms. Alliances between two U.S. firms were the most plentiful, followed by U.S.-Japanese partnerships, U.S.-European, and U.S.-Asia/Pacific, in that order. These alliances included licensing and second-source agreements; sales agencies; fabrication, assembly, and testing agreements; technology exchanges; joint ventures; joint development agreements; and investment, standards coordination, and procurement agreements.[6]

PRODUCT CHARACTERISTICS

Most business products are not purchased for personal use, although we might view corporate automobiles or cellular phones in that light. Manufacturing firms buy a broad variety of goods as component parts of the end products they produce. In many instances, the buying firm specifies the performance capability of these components to control the desired performance of the end product. A product used in both the business and consumer markets might have the same performance capability, but _intangibles_ such as presale consultation and postsale service assume greater importance when selling to business customers. For instance, **just-in-time** (JIT) delivery can mean the difference between a smooth-running production line and costly shutdowns.

BUYER CHARACTERISTICS

Buyers in the business market are professionally trained and technically qualified, whether they work for manufacturing firms, resellers, or institutions. These professionals generally base their buying decisions on adherence to specifications, cost-effectiveness, and dependability of supply, rather than social or psychological factors. Since many of these decisions entail technical complexity, large financial commitments, as well as considerable risk and uncertainty, the final decision will be based on the inputs of multiple individuals. _Reciprocity_ also impacts business decisions; that is, when the situation warrants, buyers will buy from their own customers.

 Stable Relationships   Many consumers change their purchasing habits and preferences frequently; not so with business buyers. Empirical studies indicate that business relationships develop over time and usually remain stable. Changes occur slowly and infrequently. Determining a potential supplier's technical, productive, and financial capability requires much time and effort, which buyers would prefer to expend on more pressing tasks.[7]

Buyer-Seller Interfaces   Agreements, orders, and contracts require offers and counteroffers; thus, considerable negotiating and information exchange takes place between various _functional specialists._ Individuals from both firms bring special knowledge and interests to the relationship. A *network* of interorganizational contacts emerges, and personal relationships develop. With the advent of JIT systems, production schedules and partnering between customers and suppliers aimed at achieving lower costs and higher quality levels, these working relationships have become even closer and more durable. New firms trying to break into the buying pattern where such relationships exist find the task difficult if not impossible.[8] This point will be covered further in Part II.

CHANNEL CHARACTERISTICS AND IMPORTANCE

Because of the need to minimize the costs of inventory and to speed up the flow from production line to the end user, business market channels tend to be *short and direct.* Most component parts moving from one producer to another go direct or through only one channel intermediary (**merchant wholesalers**). Merchant wholesalers serve as critical elements of a producer's marketing strategy. They provide local inventories, perform selling and customer service functions, take on credit risks, and essentially broaden the producer's reach into the target market.

Manufacturers' representatives (reps) form the other significant arm of the business channel. Some producers, who prefer not to take on the cost and maintenance of their own sales force, hire these sales professionals. We will elaborate on both wholesalers and reps in Part V. However, one additional aspect of international business channels should be noted here.

A producer trying to penetrate a foreign market will, in great part, succeed or fail depending on the support provided by channel intermediaries. For example, many American firms feel cut off from lucrative Japanese markets by unfair, protective government regulations. United States negotiators have spent endless time and effort in rather futile attempts to penetrate these barriers. Meanwhile, major corporate conglomerates (called *keiretsus* in Japan), such as Mitsubishi and Sumitomo, quietly make sure that products that would compete with their own output do not enter the necessary channels. They can accomplish this task because as a conglomerate, which typically includes a central bank, a worldwide trading company, and multiple goods-producers, they also control critical wholesale and retail outlets. If a maverick channel member wanted to take on Kodak cameras and film, for example, they might find it difficult to obtain Nikon and Pentax cameras. Mitsubishi holds a 27 percent interest in Nikon Corporation and a 28 percent share of Asahi Glass, Nikon's primary supplier of photographic lenses and the parent company of Pentax.[9] To be even-handed, we must note that American semiconductor producers used similar tactics during the early 1970s in a futile attempt to thwart the penetration of Japanese semiconductors into U.S. electronic equipment markets.

PROMOTION CHARACTERISTICS

Business marketers generally put the greatest emphasis on **personal selling.** Advertising lays a foundation for the sales call rather than serving as the primary communication tool. Salespeople act as consultants and technical problem-solvers, using extensive product knowledge plus an understanding of the buyer's needs. Trade shows, **catalogs,** and sales incentives consume additional promotion dollars. Most business advertising aims at corporate image-building and "door-opening" for the sales force.

Intel Corporation's innovative television and print advertising campaign entitled "Intel Inside" has been a notable exception to the general rule. Intel apparently saw the need to apply a classic strategy of **push** and **pull promotion.** While their sales force sold microprocessors quite successfully to computer manufacturers, the "Intel Inside" advertisements prompted consumers to buy only those computers that contained Intel products.[10]

PRICE CHARACTERISTICS

Business buyers and consumers do not attribute the same level of importance to price. This fact has been substantiated by repeated market studies. By definition, consumers purchase convenience and homogeneous shopping goods based primarily on price. In the same vein, if business buyers can see no difference between the offerings of two suppliers, they will also buy on price. But that "if" is very important. The two offerings will first be compared based on three criteria: product *quality, dependability* of supply, and associated *services.* If any of these criteria fall below a minimum level of acceptance, the faulty supplier has no chance of winning an order. In one study, purchasers were willing to pay a "premium price for equipment from a supplier who could provide superior technical and after-sales service"[11] (see Box 2-1).

Competitive bidding and negotiated prices are very common, and financing arrangements often serve as a deciding factor. In the case of capital goods, leasing often replaces an outright purchase as the method of procurement. Using this approach, the buyer circumvents the risk of equipment obsolescence and pays with pretax dollars. Quantity price discounts, prevalent in the business market, are seen less frequently in the consumer market, where the majority of customers buy in very limited quantities.

From the preceding discussion, one can see fundamental differences between the consumer and business markets. Some consumer marketing managers find it difficult to adjust when they transfer to the business market.

To understand more fully the differences between the markets, we must first analyze some underlying economic peculiarities of the business market.

The Economics of Business Market Demand

Consumers control business markets, because the **derived demand** for business products stems from the demand for consumer products. There would be no need for steel mills if consumers did not purchase cars, appliances, and similar end products. Conversely, consumer products would not exist unless business markets performed their

---

BOX 2-1

Never Talk Price

Inexperienced salespeople invariably start by thinking and talking price when money is the last thing they should discuss. They probably reason, "If a buyer bases decisions on quality, service, and price, how can I prove good quality and service when I'm not shipping anything? The only thing left is price."

Never talk price with anyone before you've sold him on your company and yourself. The purchaser will generally guide the salesperson he or she wants to do business with to the lower price. This leads to my first rule of selling: People buy from who they want to and make price and all other decision factors fit.

Source: Excerpted from Clifton J. Reichard, "Industrial selling: Beyond price and persistence," *Harvard Business Review* (March-April 1985). Copyright ©1985 by the President and Fellows of Harvard College. Reprinted by permission; all rights reserved.

functions. These interdependencies can result in a highly volatile demand in the business market. At the same time, the demand for business goods tends to be relatively price-inelastic, since derived demand prompts their sale, regardless of variations in producer and raw material price indices.

THE IMPACT OF DERIVED DEMAND

Derived demand means that the demand for consumer products affects not only the supply of those products but also the raw materials, component parts, equipment, and services associated with their fabrication. A small shift in demand at the consumer level can have disastrous effects at the opposite end of the derived demand chain.[12] The longer the chain, the more serious the "whip action" effect becomes in periods of boom or bust. This phenomenon is caused by the *economic accelerator principle.*

Accelerator Principle   This principle deals with changes in a product's derived demand. It underlines the fact that utter chaos or a sales bonanza may exist in a given industry when shifts in demand occur. The demand for oil products declined and crude oil glutted the markets in the 1980s, driving down the price of a barrel of crude, which was later reflected in the retail price of gasoline. The oil companies had to take immediate action by laying off personnel, restricting long-range expansion plans, and conserving their financial resources. Slight reductions in consumer demand led to more drastic cuts at the production level.

A similar correlation can be observed by watching a person's arm movement relative to the ground. The shoulder rotates only a few degrees, while the fingertips move through a wide arc. The shoulder movement represents the small change in consumer demand, and the fingertips represent the impact experienced by resellers and industrial firms.

Volatility of Demand   This "boom or bust" syndrome keeps business marketers on their toes (see Box 2-2). They must monitor not only the demand of their immediate customers but also the demand for finished consumer goods that impact their output indirectly. The accelerator effect also impacts the sale of production tools and equipment. If the demand for bicycles increases, the additional production lines will require more welding machines and pneumatic wrenches. A bicycle producer may even purchase upgraded equipment to improve both quality and productivity.

These reactions will certainly affect the equipment suppliers as they rush to meet the bicycle producer's needs. However, when bicycle sales fall, equipment manufacturers may face steep declines, forcing them to forego expansion or even to experience profit losses.

Price Variability in Business Markets   The greater the marketing (not geographic) distance between consumers and the point of production, price volatility increases, but so does *price inelasticity.* This apparent contradiction is another result of the derived demand function. Price volatility stems from the relation of demand to supply. When a shortage of copper coincides with a home construction boom, building contractors will compete for the existing copper supply and drive prices upward. They cannot build houses without copper tubing, and the increased cost is simply factored into the house price. Thus, we have *price volatility.* However, the increase in copper pricing does not result in decreased demand. As long as the demand for houses, even at somewhat inflated prices, remains high, copper demand will stay proportional. Thus, we see price inelasticity, that is, demand for copper stays

---

BOX 2-2

A Static Accelerator

Before Burroughs Corporation became an intrinsic part of Unisys, it had launched its B1000 series of small business computers in 1972. At that time, Burroughs executives saw this type of machine as a market insert that would last approximately 5 years, at which time the company could "churn" the installed customer base—sell it something newer, faster, and more profitable for the company. By 1986, 14 years later, Burroughs had introduced two generations of more advanced machines, but customers still clamored for the B1000, so every year the company shipped several hundred updated versions of the $70,000 to $200,000 computers. A company official noted, "It's a real workhorse."

Obviously, most computer marketers wanted their customers to buy the very latest and fanciest product offering. A common boast was that a new box would offer 50 percent more power at only 25 percent more cost to the customer. Many data processing managers wanted to stick with older models, especially since their managers were putting lids on capital spending. Many people were comfortable with staying "on the trailing edge of the leading edge," as suggested by one of the users. Most apt to have stayed with yesterday's hardware were manufacturers of such computer-driven equipment as factory automation hardware and medical imaging devices, who were still able to sell products built around older computers. "If you get more orders, you buy more boxes," explained a satisfied customer. The power of the marketplace was tested here. The customer prevailed.

Source: "The computers that refused to die," *Business Week* (July 21, 1986), p. 123.

---

relatively constant despite an upward swing in price. Unless business marketers stay abreast of demand and price trends, they run the risk of losing market share, profits, or both.[13]

JOINT DEMAND

The concept of joint demand applies to both the consumer and business markets, but the implications differ. A consumer who puts hamburger meat on a shopping list will often think to add rolls and mustard. If the thought does not occur, a hamburger cooked just right over charcoal still tastes delicious on bread.

Most end products fabricated in the manufacturing sector require multiple components and associated materials. In some instances of shortage, temporary substitutes can be used (bread for rolls); but frequently, the manufacturer must shut down the production line until the specified parts become available.

Business buyers also prefer to buy multiple products or complete product lines from one supplier rather than split the requirements among different suppliers. This preference has increased as partnering between customer and supplier has become more prevalent.

Resellers are similarly affected. Most business buyers prefer "one-stop shopping" for a variety of goods. This minimizes procurement costs. A wholesaler who can fill only a portion of the requirement may lose the entire order to a competitor with a more complete inventory.

CROSS-ELASTICITY OF DEMAND

The concept of **cross-elasticity of demand** involves the degree to which the price change of one product affects the demand of another. The demand for many business goods is correlated to the price of other goods. For example, the quantity of steel demanded is related to the price of a close substitute, aluminum. This *direct* relationship between the price of one good and the demand for a second holds true for all *substitute* products. The larger the number of substitutes available, the greater the cross-elasticity of demand. If the housing contractor referenced earlier finds that a type of plastic tubing will satisfactorily solve the copper shortage, his demand for plastic will increase sharply.

Other goods, such as printers and personal computers, illustrate a completely different relationship. As the price of computers falls, the demand for printers increases. Goods that exhibit an *inverse* relationship are *complementary* goods—they are used together rather than in place of one another. This is joint demand revisited.

Cross-elasticity for substitutes is always *positive;* that is, the price of one good and the demand for the other always move in the same direction. The more positive this ratio, the higher the cross-elasticity and the more obvious that the products compete in the same market. Cross-elasticity for complements is *negative;* price and quantity move in opposite directions. The more negative this relationship, the more likely that the products will be used jointly.

Looking Back

Business marketing managers face many of the problems that confront their counterparts in the consumer market plus some that are unique. For example, most industries are oligopolies. A few firms hold the major portion of the buying power; all suppliers know who these companies are and concentrate their selling efforts there. Channels of distribution are shorter and more crowded. The same oligopolistic conditions exist among wholesalers, so that all manufacturers try to franchise the same ones to distribute their product lines. Business buyers are well informed, highly organized professionals who are not likely to be influenced by psychological inducements. Business markets differ notably in six characteristics:

1. There are fewer but larger customers, often concentrated in specific geographic areas.
2. Products are chosen primarily for their functional value, to earn profits for the firm.
3. Groups commonly make buying decisions and base them on task-oriented criteria.
4. Distribution channels perform vital marketing tasks for the manufacturer in addition to simply warehousing products.
5. The primary promotional element is personal selling rather than advertising.
6. Price does not have the overwhelming importance that it has in the consumer market.

The consumer market drives the business market. A business firm's demand for goods and services depends, directly or indirectly, on consumer demand for its own output, hence the term derived demand. Unless consumers want to buy television sets, for instance, there is no need for the components that make up this end product nor the production equipment necessary to fabricate either the components or the TVs.

Another aspect of derived demand involves price elasticity. The further a product is from an ultimate consumer decision, the less a change in price will affect demand. Obviously, there are practical limits to this statement. For example, a 30 percent price increase in rubber grommets used to isolate a stereo speaker from vibrations will have little effect on the demand for stereo systems, assuming grommets sell for $10 per thousand. If the price of $200 speakers increased by 30 percent, the effect on consumer demand would be more apparent.

When products are used jointly for a common purpose, the demand for one impacts the demand for the other. Semiconductors, for example, cannot be used in an electronic circuit without a circuit board or copper wire connecting them to other circuit components.

Questions for Discussion

1. Would a marketing manager transferring from the consumer market to the business market face any philosophical or operational problems? If so, describe them.

2. In your opinion, what are the most significant differences between the consumer and business markets? Why did you choose these?

3. What problems does a marketing manager face in a business market with less than 200 customers?

4. In which strategic areas would you be willing to collaborate with competing firms? Are there any areas in which you would definitely not collaborate?

5. What are the advantages and disadvantages of having long-term agreements with only one or a few suppliers?

6. If you were the marketing manager for a start-up firm, how would you convince a dominant regional distributor to carry your product line?

7. How does a marketing strategy change when personal selling is the major promotional element as opposed to advertising?

8. Would you prefer to market the products of a firm that sold primarily on price or nonprice factors? Explain your choice.

9. How would you include derived demand into your sales forecast?

10. Does joint demand provide any additional opportunities to a business marketing manager? Explain your response.

Endnotes

1. Frederick E. Webster, Jr., "Top management's concerns about marketing: Issues for the 1980's," Journal of Marketing 45 (Summer 1981):9-16.

2. Richard E. Plank, "Industrial marketing education: Practitioner's views," *Industrial Marketing Management* 11 (1982):311-15.

3. Ronald Henkoff, "This cat is acting like a tiger," *Fortune* (December 1988), pp. 71-6.

4. Louis Rukeyser, *Louis Rukeyser's Business Almanac,* 2nd ed. (New York: Simon & Schuster, 1991), p. 190.

5. Philip Kotler, Liam Fahey, and Somkid Jatusripitak. *The New Competition* (Englewood Cliffs, N.J.: Prentice-Hall, Inc., 1985), p. 69.

6. U.S. Department of Commerce, International Trade Administration. February 1994. *1994 U.S. Industrial Outlook,* Chapter 15.

7. B.G. Yovovich, "Dos and don'ts of partnering," *Business Marketing* 77 (1992):38-9.

8. James Carbone, "Chrysler tries the partnering route," *Electronic Business Buyer* 19 (November 1993):97-9.

9. "Mighty Mitsubishi is on the move," *Business Week* (September 24, 1990), pp. 98-107.

10. Donald G. Norris, "Intel inside: Branding a component in the business market," *Journal of Business and Industrial Marketing* 8 (1993):14-24.

11. Russell Abratt, "Industrial buying in high-tech markets," *Industrial Marketing Management* 15 (1986):293-8.

12. B.G. Yovovich, "Revolutionary marketing," *Business Marketing* 78 (1993):34-8.
13. Previous section adapted from Eckles, Robert W., *Business Marketing Management* (Englewood Cliffs, N.J.: Prentice Hall, Inc., 1990), pp. 20-1.

Bibliography

Kotler, Philip, Lahey Fahey, and Somkid Jatusripitak, *The New Competition* (Englewood Cliffs, N.J.: Prentice-Hall, Inc., 1985).

Yovovich, B.G., "Dos and don'ts of partnering," *Business Marketing* 77 (1992):38-9.

"Mighty Mitsubishi is on the move," *Business Week* (September 24, 1991), pp. 98-107.

Norris, Donald G., "Intel inside: Branding a component in the business market," *Journal of Business and Industrial Marketing* 8 (1993):14-24.

CHAPTER 3 Understanding Business Markets

We analyzed the business market in Chapter 1 as a diverse group of goods-producing and service-providing industries, that is, the supply side of the market. Chapter 2 dealt with the differences that exist between the consumer and business markets in size and dispersion of market segments and application of the marketing mix. In this chapter we will focus on the business market environment, including those groups (*publics*) and environmental forces that influence market conduct and outcomes. Government, of course, represents one of the most influential of these forces. We will also look at the several industry sectors as customers, or the demand side of the market. An effective marketing strategy requires a clear understanding of customer needs, habits, and motives, plus a recognition of the environmental factors that will either enhance or constrain that strategy. The objective of this chapter, then, is to understand the following:

1. How business market participants collaborate to make the system function
2. Interested publics who influence and affect business outcomes
3. Critical environmental forces that must be recognized and monitored
4. The impact of government on the actions of business
5. The broad range of business customers and the types of products and services they purchase

Chapter 1 provided a broad overview of the various industries that comprise the business market. The log and lumber scenario (p. 15) gave a relatively simple example of these industries interacting to provide an eventual product to consumers. We also saw that much of the output produced by the business market—natural products, raw material, manufactured goods, and services—stays within the market to be consumed or used by other participants. The process by which these various outputs get to their destination, the participants in the process, and the overarching environment form the elements of the next analysis.

How well buyers and sellers understand the environment within which they operate—as well as how well they communicate and cooperate with one another—foretells their ability to withstand the environment's many surprises and shocks. The effectiveness of both organizations depends on early recognition of environmental changes and development of strategies that minimize risks and maximize opportunities.

The traditional view of marketing has been one of achieving organizational goals through satisfying the needs of identified markets by adapting the organization to deliver the desired satisfaction "more effectively and efficiently than competitors."[1] Thus, marketing strategies have been "viewed as a set of adaptive responses"; that is, marketing seems to begin with a system of environmental constraints.[2] Marketers gather and analyze information on forces in the environment, such as competitors, politics, and economics, and implement strategies to adapt to environmental demands.

Today's turbulent environment, however, demands more than adaptation. Marketers must plan proactively so that their strategies not only adapt to the environment but also affect it, whenever possible, for the benefit of the organization.[2]

The Business Market Environment

Figure 3-1 shows the interactive environment within which business firms operate. The inner circle depicts the multiple points where business firms interact, buying in some transactions and selling in others. The next circle represents various groups who can and do affect operations within the business market. The third circle indicates that a number of macroenvironmental forces affect business organizations and are not directly controllable. Government, the outer circle, has the power to exert an impact on all others within.

FIGURE 3-1 The business market environment.

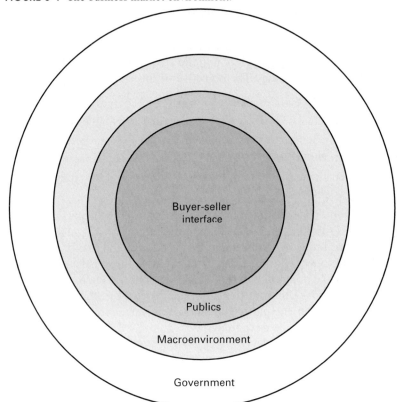

THE INTERFACE LEVEL

The interface level includes firms that sell their outputs as required inputs to other firms. In turn, the latter organizations sell their own output to those who need it. For example, mining companies sell their bauxite ore to smelters, who produce aluminum for fabricators, who convert the aluminum into sheeting for companies that sell home siding. This level contains not only *producers* and *users* of goods but also firms that serve as *facilitators* in the production, distribution, marketing, or transportation of these goods. In turn, their output might be other production factors or a necessary service. For example, an employment agency locates workers with required skills; a bank loans necessary capital; a trucking company transports finished goods across the country to a wholesaler who acts as a local warehouse and sales organization. An advertising agency creates an ad campaign that will help to move products off the wholesaler's shelf.

As Figure 3-2 shows, the complex nature of the business market allows a firm to view itself from several perspectives. It may perceive a product marketer, a material converter, an input supplier, a service provider, or even a competitor. (In this illustration, government agencies act as end users.)

Input Suppliers   As described above, business firms provide input goods and services—raw materials, component parts, labor, and capital—so that other firms can conduct their operations. We should again emphasize that current practices, such as JIT purchasing and partnering, have created buyer-seller relationships that are closer and longer lasting today than in the past.[3] When an input supplier acts essentially as an inventory depot or extension of the customer's production process, the two firms are virtually one.

FIGURE 3-2 Participants in the interface level.

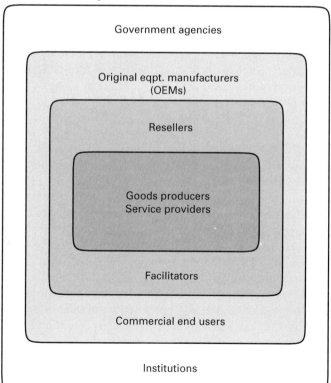

Government agencies

Original eqpt. manufacturers (OEMs)

Resellers

Goods producers
Service providers

Facilitators

Commercial end users

Institutions

The success or failure of each firm depends on the performance of the other. This is one reason that Japanese industrial giants form a *keiretsu,* or interlocked conglomerate.

Diamond-Star Motors, a joint venture between Mitsubishi and Chrysler in Bloomington, Illinois provides a vivid example of interlocked suppliers and a customer. As shown in Figure 3-3, 13 different Mitsubishi divisions and interlocked corporations act as primary suppliers of their respective products to Diamond-Star. Inputs ranging from engines to air conditioners to brakes and springs essentially come from the same company. Two other factors quell the concerns of those who would claim constraint of trade or import-mania: (1) Each of the supplier organizations is a major producer that sells to many other customers, including competitors Mazda and Honda, and (2) only two suppliers, Mitsubishi Motors and Mitsubishi Steel, provide imported goods.[4] Meanwhile, other firms trying to break into the supply loop face a formidable challenge, to say the least.

Distributors and Dealers   These channel specialists provide services that benefit both sellers and buyers. Most manufacturers prefer to concentrate their resources and efforts on the design and production processes. Even the basic marketing functions of communicating with, selling to, and serving customers far removed from the point of manufacture assume secondary importance in many production oriented firms. Thus, outside organizations that can not only perform these functions, but that do so more efficiently than the manufacturer, become valued partners.[5]

From the buyer's viewpoint, a distributor or dealer represents a local source for information, inventory, and personal service. Moreover, these product specialists carry the output of numerous manufacturers who produce associated or joint products (refer to the discussion of joint demand in Chapter 2). Thus, they provide "one-stop shopping" for the buyer, saving both time and expense.[5]

Distributors and dealers provide another valuable service because of their unique position. They interact on a regular basis with the manufacturer of a product, the users, and the manufacturer's competitors. Like the Roman god Janus, they can view an industry in both directions simultaneously, and thus make significant contributions to market intelligence. Buyers can get an overview of the technologies available to them, while producers get feedback regarding customers' plans and reactions as well as competitors' programs.

Distributors, dealers, and other channel intermediaries will be discussed further in Part V.

Facilitators   Advertising agencies and public relations firms provide the necessary *communication flow* between sellers and buyers by providing meaningful information and formulating effective media strategies. Advertising plays a vital role in reaching potential buyers and buying influencers. Rarely can sales people personally contact all buying influencers. Public relations firms are particularly useful when environmental forces necessitate the dissemination of commercially significant news to maintain or enhance the corporate image. Trade journal advertising and publicity releases aid buyers in locating and selecting potential suppliers.

Transportation and warehouse companies facilitate the *physical flow* of goods that must be delivered in usable condition and on time to customers and distributors. Goods delivered late or damaged result in production shutdowns and financial losses. Insurance companies protect against major loss, and banks provide loans in times of profit shortage.

Competitors   The actions of competitors, either domestic or foreign, can influence a company's choice of target markets, distributors, product mix, or its entire marketing strategy. Particularly in times of economic decline, technological changes, market

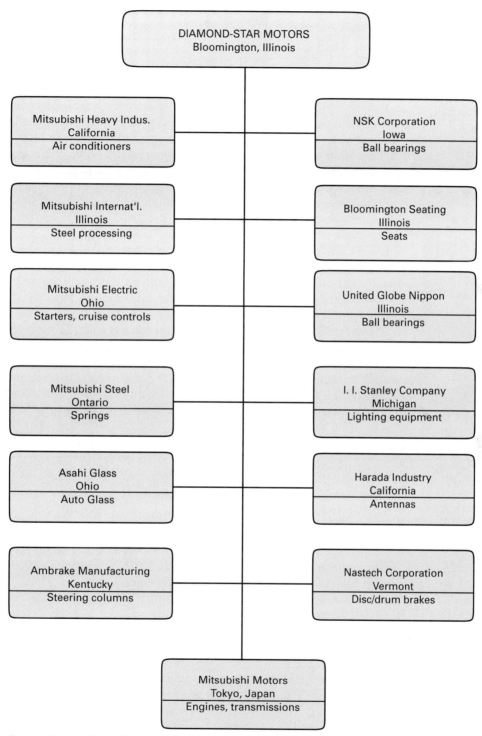

DIAMOND-STAR MOTORS
Bloomington, Illinois

Mitsubishi Heavy Indus. California	NSK Corporation Iowa
Air conditioners	Ball bearings

Mitsubishi Internat'l. Illinois	Bloomington Seating Illinois
Steel processing	Seats

Mitsubishi Electric Ohio	United Globe Nippon Illinois
Starters, cruise controls	Ball bearings

Mitsubishi Steel Ontario	I. I. Stanley Company Michigan
Springs	Lighting equipment

Asahi Glass Ohio	Harada Industry California
Auto Glass	Antennas

Ambrake Manufacturing Kentucky	Nastech Corporation Vermont
Steering columns	Disc/drum brakes

Mitsubishi Motors Tokyo, Japan
Engines, transmissions

Source: Adapted from "Mighty Mitsubishi is on the move," *Business Week*, September 24, 1990, pp. 98-107. Reprinted by permission of *Business Week*, © 1990.

FIGURE 3-3 Partnering within Mitsubishi U.S.A.

maturity or turmoil, **competitive intelligence** is vital to survival, let alone marketing success.[6] Firms usually charge all employees with outside contacts, particularly those engaged in sales and purchasing, to serve as intelligence gatherers (see Box 3-1).

Implications   Business firms are part of a chain of organizations. Each firm is both buyer and seller. As buyers, they constitute less populated markets than consumers do. Buying decisions require more technical knowledge and operational expertise. What they buy and how they decide affects the cost and efficiency of the manufacturing process as well as the quality and performance of the output products moving through the chain.

To deal with such interdependencies, business firms form long-term buyer-seller partnerships.[3] Departmental specialists in research, engineering, production, and marketing meet with their counterparts to exchange information on technological developments, process innovations, and market trends. Buyers expect more assistance from their suppliers in terms of technical innovation, quality improvement, and cost-cutting suggestions; in turn, suppliers want more specific direction regarding the needs that buyers anticipate in the future.[7]

Business marketers can no longer think domestically; they must have a global perspective. Even if they have no immediate plans to market internationally, they must still monitor the international scene for competitive threats or economic trends that will affect the domestic market. For example, the U.S. economy began to show signs of quickening recovery in the latter part of 1993. Normally, component suppliers could expect an increase in demand from equipment producers who sold globally. However, both the Japanese and German economies were in a tailspin. Producers in Japan and Germany stepped up their efforts to sell in the United States, exacerbating an already competitive market. Meanwhile, industrialists and government officials in both countries guarded their national markets more jealously than ever. Thus, American suppliers faced greater challenges rather than enhanced opportunities.[8]

BOX 3-1

Competitive Intelligence: A Valuable Strategic Tool

As corporate America enters the twenty-first century, it faces highly competitive markets. Economic growth has slowed down, competition from overseas has heightened, and many end-use industries have matured. The result is that few opportunities exist for improving performance through market growth. According to Dominick Attanasio, vice president of Planning and Business Development for Pfizer, Inc., expansion will occur mainly through market share gains. Such an environment, however, significantly intensifies competition. Thus, competitive intelligence becomes a more valuable tool for strategic planning.

The objectives of competitive intelligence are (1) to identify competitors' weaknesses, thereby providing the firm with possible new market share opportunities; (2) to anticipate competitors' market thrusts; and (3) to allow the firm to react more quickly and effectively to changes in the market.

Competitive intelligence, as practiced today, however, functions as a formal information system that monitors the external world of the organization—the industry, the markets, the industry suppliers of technology and materials, the competition, and the global economy. In the same manner that management information systems formalized information for internal operations, competitive intelligence formalizes information for tactical and strategic management.

Source: Dominick B. Attanasio, "The Multiple Benefits of Competitor Intelligence," *The Journal of Business Strategy* (May/June 1988), pp. 16-19.

PUBLICS

Multiple publics, shown in Figure 3-4, exert a significant influence over the activities of participants in the interface level. **Publics** are distinct groups that have an actual or potential interest in or an impact on a firm's ability to achieve its respective goals.[9] Publics can help or hinder a firm's effort to serve its markets. Financial institutions influence the ability to obtain funds, favorable or unfavorable press affects customer perceptions, interest groups place special emphasis on specific aspects of the firm's strategy, and the attitudes of employees and the general public directly affect the firm's efficiency and image.

Financial Publics   Financial groups, such as investment banks, brokerage firms, and individual stockholders, invest in an organization for monetary gain. This type of investment differs from that of financial organizations that serve as facilitators in the interface environment by providing operating funds as a service. Such service-providers tend to exert less pressure on organizational policies and profit generation. Institutional investors, such as public employee pension funds, tend to concern themselves with the total operation of a firm. As stockholders, they often become involved in the election of corporate management; and when dissatisfied with either management or the firm's social policies, they sell their shares.

Some institutional investors, angered by what they consider self-serving actions by some corporate managers, have begun aggressive campaigns to make management more sensitive to shareholder needs. For example, the California Public Employees' Retirement System (CALPERS), the largest U.S. publicly pension fund with assets of $80 billion and 979,000 members who happen to be consumers, forced corporate giants like Time Warner, Polaroid, Westinghouse, and Sears in 1994 to reform policies governing the choice of board members, executive compensation, and resource investment. At Westinghouse, CALPERS used 2 million shares of stock to back up their demands.[10]

When organizations deceive or mislead shareholder publics, they also face *sanctions* by the Securities and Exchange Commission, which regulates the stock market. General Dynamics, for instance, found itself under investigation by the SEC when it

FIGURE 3-4 Business market publics.

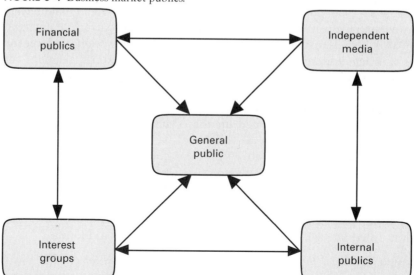

was revealed that top management had not been totally forthright with its shareholders regarding cost overruns and other problems.[11] To obtain support of the financial community, a firm must evaluate its actions in light of that public's interpretations and work to cultivate its goodwill.

Independent Media   Business firms must recognize the role that the mass media (also trade media) play and the impact they can have on corporate image and success. The media can publish news capable of either enhancing or destroying the reputation of a firm as well as its market position. Unfavorable publicity, such as General Dynamics received, can also severely hamper a company's attempt to float stock or issue bonds.

Negative publicity regarding a firm's operations can be easily triggered, particularly when sales decline, profits erode, layoffs occur, and dismissed executives leave with a multimillion dollar handshake. Bad news has always sold more newspapers and attracted more television viewers than "happy talk," as underscored by the story of the Alaskan oil spill of Exxon Corporation's tanker *Valdez* in 1989 (see Box 3-2).

Public Interest Groups   Groups representing specific interests have a conspicuous impact on business decisions. Hundreds of these groups have developed and expanded over the last two decades. Organizations like the Sierra Club and Greenpeace seek to protect the environment. Other organizations such as National Organization for Women (NOW), the National Association for the Advancement of Colored People (NAACP), and the Gray Panthers seek to protect and expand the rights of women, blacks, and senior citizens.

BOX 3-2

Can Exxon Assuage the Public?

When Joseph Hazelwood's ship ran aground, spilling 11 million gallons of crude oil on the Alaskan shores of Prince William Sound, Exxon found itself locked in a public relations offensive that many say was poorly handled. While Exxon recited statistics on what it had accomplished—60,000 barrels of oil recovered and 1,087 miles of beach rendered "environmentally stable"—the State of Alaska filed a multibillion-dollar lawsuit, claiming that the company had "cut and run with the work unfinished." T-shirts sold in Valdez, Alaska, summed up the problems that pervaded Exxon's $1 billion effort: "Cleanup '89. It's not just a job, it's a ---- waste of time."

While many say that Prince William Sound is no longer an ecological disaster, Exxon's failure to respond openly and immediately to the spill, which it called an "act of God," has cast a shadow over the oil industry. Instead of showing its concern and commitment to the public by flying to Valdez immediately after the spill, Exxon's Chairman Lawrence Rawl remained in New York, silent and unavailable to the press. To avoid the barrage of unanswered questions, other executives went underground. And Otto Harrison, Exxon's cleanup engineer, waiting for heavy cleanup equipment, set hundreds of people to wiping off the oil-laden rocks by hand, "a spectacle that fixed in the public's mind images of a bumbling and ludicrous Exxon effort."

Since the accident, environmentalists have continued to battle the oil industry and its allies, preaching energy conservation. Congress also postponed new offshore drilling in Alaska's Bristol Bay, along the California coast, and on several sections of the East Coast from Massachusetts to Florida.

Source: "A disaster that wasn't," *U.S. News & World Report* (September 18, 1989), pp. 60-69.

Public interest groups clearly limit the freedom of business firms. While some companies respond aggressively, others accept these groups as another variable to be considered in developing strategic plans and utilize their public affairs departments to establish the best possible working relationships. All participants in the interface level, however, feel the impact of these groups.

General Public   Although the general public does not normally engage in organized interaction with business, as other interest groups do, when a sizable portion of 250 million people develops a negative attitude toward a firm or industry, the impact is significant. In an attempt to win the hearts and minds of the public, environmentalists, and Congress, Exxon mobilized an army of workers in 1989 to repair the damage and launched a multimillion-dollar public relations campaign.[12] Nevertheless, the company still felt aftershocks of public indignation over the Alaskan oil spill 5 years later. Exxon was found guilty of gross negligence and directed to pay $5 billion in punitive damages to the victims of the oil spill in addition to the costs incurred in the cleanup attempt. Perhaps of equal note is that a 1994 survey of 9,100 American college students found that the space shuttle Challenger explosion was the psychological landmark of their generation, closely followed by the Persian Gulf War, the fall of the Berlin Wall, and the Exxon *Valdez* oil spill.[13]

Internal Publics   From executives and managers to factory and office workers, all employees serve as emissaries of the organization when interacting with other publics. Corporate policy must give due consideration to those on whose efforts organizational success depends. Business decisions affect employee morale; low morale detracts from organizational effort. A firm's employees spend more than two thirds of their time off the job, interacting with their families and the community. Their attitudes, good or bad, form a public perception of the company. After years of reports about adversarial relations between the Big Three automotive firms and their unions, articles began to appear in the 1980s announcing the cooperative efforts between management and workers at the Honda plant in Marysville, Ohio, Nissan's plant in Smyrna, Tennessee, and other transplanted Japanese operations.[14] Readers had to remind themselves that these were independent American workers, not the more docile citizens of Japan. Then, other articles told of union-management discussions at the Big Three that eventually led to cooperative agreements regarding work rules, increased productivity, and job protection. Although downsizing continued into the 1990s, productivity and quality improved notably, the loss of U.S. market share to imports was arrested, and profits returned to acceptable levels.[15]

Implications   Since the ultimate function of business is to satisfy the various needs of society, publics can serve (1) to announce that society is in fact being served, (2) to indicate the level of satisfaction provided, and (3) to act as a societal sounding board on which business can make its case heard.

When one of the major U.S. railroads was serving its industrial customers poorly, financial institutions were reluctant to underwrite further operations. Its own employees became demoralized, their negative perceptions further impaired the company's reputation and operations, and the value of its stocks and bonds plummeted. Stories of the railroad's problems appeared in newspapers across the nation. Government agencies and legislators began to respond, stimulated by public interest groups that wanted to avert the demise of a vital transportation company, one of the nation's primary railroads. The company mounted its own appeal through the print media and television, in the courts, and before government agencies. Today, Penn Central is a subsidiary of American Premier Underwriters and again serving America's eastern seaboard.

Business managers must always remember their primary mission—service to society—and remain sensitive to the publics who monitor and evaluate their performance. At the same time, they should not hesitate to pronounce the firm's accomplishments through corporate advertising and public relations campaigns.

THE MACROENVIRONMENT

The dynamic forces of the macroenvironment, shown in Figure 3-5, have a major impact on both the publics and interface level of the business environment. Shifts in U.S. and world economics, consumer demographics, ecology and culture, technology, and the geographic locations of suppliers and buyers alter the level and conduct of business. Market participants can adjust their marketing or operating strategy in an attempt to pacify an unhappy public, but macroenvironmental forces tend to resist the counteractions of individual firms.

The primary challenge presented by the macroenvironment is its continuous change and the accelerating rate at which change takes place. Over the last decade, dramatic changes have occurred in technologies, economics, politics, demographics, and cultural ideologies. Consider the impact of major events such as the reunification of Germany, the dissolution of the Soviet Union, the renunciation of Communism throughout eastern Europe, and the dramatic collapse of a seemingly invincible Japanese economy. As remarkable as these events were, all simply laid the groundwork for further change. Thus, business organizations must constantly stay balanced amidst unbalancing forces that, ironically, often stem from business activities.

Technology, whether emerging from an industrial, institutional, or government research lab, can cause social, economic, and even cultural changes. For example, gene splicing began in Monterey, California, where the world's scientists gathered in 1975 to decide its fate. The potential benefits of recombinant DNA are now being pursued in the research of genetic diseases, mental disorders, and certain forms of cancer. A patent was issued in 1988 for an "oil-eating bacterium," which has already been used to constrain the effects of oil spills similar to the Exxon disaster.[16]

FIGURE 3-5 Macroenviromental influences.

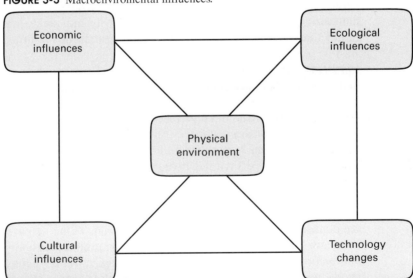

Biotechnology has not only brought about a fundamental shift in drug research and development, it also promises to increase milk production significantly and give civilization the capability of producing drought-resistant crops as well as crops that can thrive in high-salinity soil. Improved food production can eventually reduce world hunger (bringing about a change in world *demographics*), enable many of the Third World nations to become self-supporting (leading to changes in world *economics*), allow these nations to move from subsistence economies to industrial economies (ultimately changing cultural *ideologies*), and, through the production of stronger, hardier food varieties, permit a lower use of herbicides (improving world *ecology*).

Economic Influences   Both domestic and worldwide economic conditions affect an organization's ability and eagerness to buy and sell. Thus, emerging economic changes must be closely monitored.

Because of the derived nature of business demand, changes that affect consumers' discretionary purchasing power also affect goods producers, service providers, and market facilitators. When consumers tighten their belts and wait for better economic times, demand for raw materials, component parts, and associated services also declines.

When U.S. interest rates are high, the dollar tends to appreciate in comparison to major foreign currencies, increasing the price competitiveness of foreign imports and limiting U.S. exports, which further reduces the demand for American goods. For instance, during the early 1980s, the U.S. dollar was persistently overvalued with respect to foreign currencies, and many U.S. firms were forced to change their manufacturing and marketing strategies as well as their relations with key suppliers and labor unions. Beckman Instruments, for instance, had to transfer overseas the production of two product lines sold in Europe. Foreign suppliers were providing component parts at 33 percent less than U.S. firms.[17]

A decade later, the situation reversed. With a weak dollar in relation to the Japanese yen, U.S. automakers not only halted their loss of market share but regained a portion starting in 1991. Improved quality and greater productivity provided part of the stimulus; higher prices for Japanese imports provided the remainder.[15]

Shifts in economic conditions, however, do not affect all sectors of the market equally. While the demand for aluminum, transmissions, and rubber tires to produce autos may fall significantly when interest rates rise and credit tightens, the effect on the textile and chemical industries may be minimal. Therefore, firms that market to more than one industry must monitor the dissimilar impact on their various customers. We should also note that bureaucratic institutions do not always follow the same purchasing criteria employed by business firms. Commercial organizations may reduce capital goods spending during periods of high interest, while institutions will expend their capital budget lest it be reduced in the next fiscal period.[18]

Ecological Influences   Business organizations throughout the world face public reaction and government intervention when their activities pose potential danger to the earth's resources. Government officials, like those who promoted California's Proposition 65 (Box 3-3), are becoming increasingly concerned with environmental damage to the earth's water, land, air, and people. Industrial organizations involved in the manufacture of such products as chemicals and pesticides constantly pose severe threats to the environment. The disposal of waste materials from these products has already created dangerously high levels of mercury in our oceans, the now-banned pesticide DDT in our soil and food supplies, and numerous toxic-waste dump sites.

Major industrial disasters continue to occur: a poison gas leak at Union Carbide's Bhopal, India pesticide plant in December 1984 that killed 3,400 people and injured

---

BOX 3-3

Getting Tough on Toxics in California

Proposition 65, passed by California voters in November 1986, has changed the way products are packaged, labeled, and sold. Once called the Safe Drinking Water and Toxic Enforcement Act, Prop 65 (as it is popularly called) goes far beyond existing state or federal toxic control laws by forcing the hand of government and industry.

Not only does Prop 65 order the governor to create a list of chemicals "known to the state to cause cancer or reproductive toxicity," it puts the burden on business to provide "clear and reasonable" warnings to those who may be exposed to designated chemicals—whether in the workplace, in consumer products, or in the environment at large. It also set in motion an inflexible timetable for implementation and provisions for enforcement by civil suits from those who are dissatisfied.

According to David Roe, a lawyer for the Environmental Defense Fund who was a principal draftsman of the new law, this is a powerful approach that has potential repercussions in virtually every area of risk; the assessment, regulation, and management of toxic substances.

Source: Russell, Christine. 1989. "California gets tough on toxics," *Business and Society Review,* August, 47-53.

200,000 more; the Chernobyl nuclear power plant meltdown in April 1986 that sent a cloud of radioactive contaminants around the world; and the Exxon *Valdez* oil spill in March 1989 that spread 270,000 barrels of crude oil over 900 square miles of pristine waters and thousands of miles of shoreline.

And despite worldwide attention and pledges to prevent a recurrence of the *Valdez* disaster, in February 1996, a stricken oil tanker leaked 19 million gallons near one of Britain's most important wildlife conservation areas at St Ann's Head Wales. This spill far exceeded that of the *Valdez*.[19]

In a dramatic attempt to address all natural disasters plus forest destruction and overpopulation, the United Nations sponsored an Earth Summit in June 1992. More than 30,000 people and 100 world leaders gathered in Rio de Janeiro, Brazil. With so many attendees and an equally broad set of agendas, the resulting output did not contain many specific plans nor worldwide treaties. However, the participants felt that attention had at least been focused on the sad state of world ecology.[20]

Physical Environment Influences   The ability to do business at a profit demands a favorable combination of required inputs. Certain advantages stem from the natural riches of an environment, such as raw materials, water, and power, or the availability of skilled workers, experienced management personnel, and transportation facilities. Businesses that can package low-cost combinations of these factors of production often enjoy a differential advantage over competition.

Nations with histories of political stability also offer greater assurances to both buyers and sellers than those that are constantly undergoing upheaval. Tariff barriers and trade restrictions have traditionally been used by governments to close off outside competition and enhance the production advantage of domestic producers.

Location and transportation considerations, particularly when procurement requirements necessitate a close buyer-seller relationship, are often of paramount consideration in the supplier-sourcing decision. As transportation costs increase, buyers are beginning to prefer suppliers whose mining, manufacturing, or storage facilities are nearby.[21]

BOX 3-4

Coming to America

More and more managers from Japanese companies are coming to America. They are joining existing staffs of subsidiaries and branches to work with teams of their American counterparts. Integrating these newcomers into the American culture and value system is a big job, according to Sy Corenson of Hewlett-Packard's International Operations. But when U.S. managers understand the cultural differences, they can help these newcomers "get up to speed."

The first step is to recognize that differences in cultural attitudes toward work exist. For example, Americans generally are more interested in the rewards that are earned through working, such as money, status, or promotion. Japanese people, on the other hand, see work as a "consecrated" task. Work enables the Japanese manager to build a legacy that can be passed on to his sons and grandsons. In contrast to the American manager, then, the Japanese manager is more willing to take work home, to study each assignment carefully, and to work long hours.

Americans also tend to be individualistic, looking to individual performance and appraisals as the major determinants of their salaries and bonuses. The Japanese, however, emphasize group cohesiveness and consensus. Thus, while American managers expect to be held individually accountable and receive the lion's share of the bonus, Japanese managers expect to share recognition and responsibility—and any bonuses—with the group.

To avoid a collision of cultural values and work styles, Hewlett-Packard provides intensive training and orientation for Japanese managers to assist them in adjusting to the differences they find in working in the American culture.

Source: Louis A. Allen, "Working better with Japanese managers," *Management Review* (November 1988). Copyright © 1988 by American Management Association, New York. Reprinted by permission; all rights reserved.

Cultural Influences   Cultural mores, customs, habits, norms, and traditions influence the structure and function of an organization as well as the interpersonal relationships of its members. Louis Allen's article (Box 3-4) stresses the special efforts expended by Hewlett-Packard to make it easier for transplanted Japanese managers to acclimate themselves to American attitudes and characteristics. While cultural differences have little effect on the specifications of manufactured products, there is a growing trend in the United States toward entering into **joint ventures** with foreign partners to take advantage of production techniques that are the products of other cultures. For example, as we noted in Chapter 2, U.S. semiconductor firms have been more active in the formation of international alliances than their counterparts in Asia or Europe.

While these growing links between U.S. and foreign companies have taken place to improve competitive positions in the United States and abroad, they all run the risk of *cultural incompatibility*. For example, the Japanese preference for consensual decision-making and the use of quality control circles have been more difficult to establish in the United States. Despite the risks, and even though some ventures have already failed when corporate objectives diverged, more and more U.S. companies are looking for ways to team up in joint ventures with foreign partners.[22]

Technological Influences   Technological developments in the business market affect both buyers and sellers. Buyers look for enhanced profitability and market acceptance when suppliers change product designs or manufacturing process. Suppliers, in turn, hope that their target customers will maintain market share in the downstream markets that constitute derived demand. Rapidly changing technology can also restructure entire industries. The push toward a so-called "information superhighway" has already affected the computer, telecommunication, software, semiconductor, and entertainment industries.[23] While bureaucratic committees continue to discuss the future potential and pitfalls of this phenomenon, businesses have already structured a commercial prototype in Silicon Valley.[24]

The significant productivity and quality increases already achieved in U.S. manufacturing plants stem in great part from the use of computers and robotics. Computer-assisted design (CAD) coupled with a philosophy called *designing for manufacturability* (DFM) results in products that can be constructed faster, better, and more consistently. Robots now perform many of the boring, repetitive tasks that workers used to dread, and these computer-controlled machines never develop a negative attitude nor try to cut corners.[25] **Concurrent engineering** (CE) brings design engineers, manufacturing people, buyers, and marketers together at the outset of a design project, so that both DFM and market factors receive equal consideration.[26] Research and development dollars can now be directed more precisely toward consumer satisfaction.[27] Concurrent engineering will be discussed further in subsequent chapters.

Demographic Influences   The demographic environment impacts business through derived demand. World population explosion and the aging of populations in Japan, Germany, and the United States pose both opportunities and threats. In June 1996, the world's population exceeded 5.7 billion, and every hour 15,180 babies are born but only 6,131 people die for a net increase of 9,049.[28] As world population increases, it becomes more and more difficult to ration the earth's resources. The aging populations in the major industrialized countries will put further pressure on the cost of social programs. Population is also growing unevenly; nations that can least afford it have the greatest growth rates.

Sweden's population will reportedly double in 1,386 years and England's in 1,155, but India's will double in only 36 years and Mexico's in just 25.[29] Such imbalance augurs continuing economic challenges for the entire world and immediate problems for many Third World countries. At the same time, some of the problems that accompany such increases can be mitigated by use of advanced technology. For example, natural product producers have been evaluating the possibilities of farming the oceans to lessen world hunger problems.

Government's Influence on the Business Environment

Governments, charged with administering and controlling nations and their subdivisions, transcend the business environment. As global competition increases, business executives pay greater attention to the actions of domestic as well as foreign governments. In performing its multifaceted functions, government enables and facilitates but also hampers and disallows business actions.

Governmental laws, regulations, and controls affect all participants in the interface environment. Government's diversified actions, as shown in Box 3-5, include the funding of various start-up programs, effecting changes in interest rates and taxes, specifying product safety standards, sponsoring research and development, issuing regulations that protect the environment, and perhaps most important, facilitating those activities believed to be in the best interests of society.

One can easily see that government transcends the business environment. For example, government might respond to negative public opinion, stimulated by the media and involving an ecological problem that can only be resolved by banning a particular pesticide. The current producer faces a ravaged market, but the successful developer of a replacement has an exciting market opportunity.

ANTICIPATING GOVERNMENTAL ACTIONS

Business managers realize that their best approach often entails beating government to the punch. Government often yields to fervent advocacy in the face of logic, to public opinion despite major financial investment, and to the media regardless of a firm's best intentions. Government regulations often favor whichever environmental entity has the most influence in Washington D.C., the state capital, or city hall.

A business firm can thus further its best interests by changing a process or policy before being mandated to do so. At the same time, one must remember that governmental agencies can also enable and facilitate.

Perceptive business firms have reaped benefits by anticipating and assisting government with a new research project or product development. For example, new metal alloys and fabrics developed for NASA space projects have spawned entire product lines aimed at industrial and consumer applications with similar temperature, weight, or volume requirements. As discussed next, the influence of government on the business environment filters through political and legal systems as well as its many agencies and legislators.

INFLUENCING GOVERNMENTAL ACTION

Government can influence and be influenced by all levels of the business environment. Each factor of the public and macroenvironment levels influences government, whether directly or indirectly. Public interest groups fight purposely to save a wilderness area; the growing number of senior citizens, even without an overt effort, influences governmental actions regarding social security benefits.

As international competition heightens, business lobbies should try to exert even more influence. The Japanese government, through the powerful Ministry of International Trade and Industry (MITI), provides considerable aid to industries through direct financial assistance, market research data regarding technology, products, and promising world markets, and particularly, the establishment of import barriers.[30]

The United States government's last major attempt to bring financial, governmental, and industrial entities together by enabling the establishment of export trading

---

BOX 3-5

Government Activities Affecting Business

Primary government functions relating to businesses include the following:
Protecting companies from each other
Protecting consumers from unfair business practices
Protecting the larger interests of society against unrestrained business behavior
Lessening income inequality in society
Stabilizing the economy by controlling unemployment and inflation

These functions involve:
- Regulatory agencies
- Import/export regulation
- Laws and politics
- Tax levying
- Program funding
- Social programs
- Research funding
- Controlling interest rates

companies accomplished little because of adverse economic conditions during the 1980s.[31] However, government trade representatives in the early 1990s assumed a much tougher stance with trading partners, particularly Japan, who gave evidence of erecting restrictive trade barriers while simultaneously pursuing the U.S. market with increased aggressiveness. As discussed in Chapter 1 and earlier in this chapter, however, the deficit with Japan hinges on more than governmental efforts and attitude.

GOVERNMENT AGENCIES AND LEGISLATORS

A variety of government agencies regulate business activities, agencies that are charged with the responsibility of protecting businesses from each other, protecting consumers from businesses, and protecting the larger interests of society from unrestrained business behavior. The dictates of agencies such as the Food and Drug Administration, the Federal Trade Commission, the Environmental Protection Agency, and the Federal Communications Commission can affect the development of new products, their pricing and promotion, and overall marketing strategies.

With greater emphasis being put on protection of the environment and human safety, government regulation and intervention in these areas have increased. Final approval of any marketing plan must include analysis of **regulatory adherence**. Business firms employ internal or external legal staffs experienced in such analyses. They also work with key legislators at local, state, and national levels when unfavorable situations develop. Companies can act individually or jointly with other firms in an industry by forming an **industry or trade lobby**.

Implications   The importance of environmental elements will vary with the decision being made and the eventual impact on operational strategies. Construction firms specializing in highrise office buildings require support from the financial community, for instance, but are affected more by the overall strength of the economy and the current phase of the business cycle.

As global competition amplifies, the cultures and demographics of different nations impact the international marketer trying to devise the most effective promotion and distribution strategies. As the pace of technological change accelerates, firms must learn to monitor the technological environment and to develop products that leapfrog competition rather than mimic a short-lived technology.

Finally, business managers must recognize government as the single entity that transcends all environmental levels, exerts influence on all other environmental factors, and can be influenced to support the valid needs of business. If governments of other industrial nations act more effectively to shape the environment for the benefit of their own industries, U.S. industries will continue to lose worldwide market share with a concurrent worsening of the trade deficit.

Business Market Customers

Business customers can be assembled into three groups: commercial enterprises, governmental agencies, and institutions. In turn, commercial enterprises subdivide into original equipment manufacturers (OEMs), end users, and resellers.

COMMERCIAL ENTERPRISES

Commercial enterprises include all businesses that exist to **produce** or **distribute** goods or to **provide services** with the intention of gaining a profit from these activities. Manufacturing firms can range from an IBM or General Motors to a small machine shop with three employees. Yet all purchase various input resources to produce their end products and also require both physical goods and services to operate their businesses. Although corporate giants and small shops vary considerably in the size of their purchases and the number of people involved in purchasing decisions, there are some commonalities which, when recognized, make it easier to understand how the buying and selling functions interact in the business market. These commonalities will be analyzed after a brief description of each customer classification.

Original Equipment Manufacturers   This nomenclature (normally shortened to **OEMs**) refers to businesses that purchase materials and components to *fabricate* an infinite variety of end products or equipment. For example, Ford is an OEM of automotive products, IBM of computers, and Giddings & Lewis of computer-controlled machine tools. The firms that supply these OEMs with materials or components realize that derived demand for the end products will drive the OEM's purchase requirements. If the sale of Ford Tauruses and Probes accelerates, Motorola will sell more electronic engine controls, and Firestone can anticipate increased orders for tires.

End Users   When a commercial enterprise purchases products or services to *support* its manufacturing process or to *facilitate* any other aspect of its business, this firm becomes an end user. Giddings & Lewis would look on Ford, IBM, or the local machine shop as an end user, as would suppliers of grinding wheels, calculators, hand tools, paper towels, machine lubricants, or paper clips. Even though these goods are not incorporated into the user's end product, their demand still depends on derived demand. The OEM will buy only enough production equipment to fabricate the expected demand for their output, enough paper towels to serve the required number of workers, or enough file cabinets to handle the paperwork generated by that level of business.

Service providers might see customers as either OEMs or end users. A small plating shop that refinished component parts used by an OEM would see the firm in that light. But if the plater was hired to refurbish conference room furniture or cafeteria tables, the OEM would become an end user.

Resellers   Even though many of the goods that OEMs purchase are "resold" as part of their end products, this is not the type of resale that defines resellers. Distributors, dealers, and retailers purchase raw materials, component parts, or equipment that they usually resell with little or no alteration. They do *enhance* these goods, however, by providing *services* (local inventory, technical advice, credit extension, etc.) in addition to the physical output. By definition, these organizations normally do not produce restructured physical output that would classify them as OEMs. Those who do are frequently referred to as **value-added resellers**. For example, some resellers of computer and peripheral equipment will configure a complete system along with associated software for the specific requirements of a customer. They combine the products of several OEMs in this process.

Overlap of Categories   The foregoing descriptions should clarify the point that business customer classifications center on how they *utilize* the products and services purchased. Manufacturers can be either OEMs or end users. Distributors can be either resellers or end users.

It must also be noted that OEMs are very concerned about the impact that components will have on the quality and reliability of their end products. End users also worry about quality, but more in the form of consistent and trouble-free operation.

When problems do occur, they need prompt maintenance service. To resellers, quality means products that will satisfy customer needs and backup inventories that preclude non-delivery of critical orders. All of these commercial customers agree on one point: their purchases are expected to enhance the *profit-making* capability of the firm.

GOVERNMENT AGENCIES

As mentioned in an earlier chapter, the largest purchaser of business goods in the United States is a composite of the various federal, state, and local agencies that spent $1,261 billion dollars in 1995 for products and services. No one expects this figure to diminish substantially in the foreseeable future; but with the end of the cold war era, a lively debate continues on how many dollars should be taken from the defense budget and reallocated to numerous social services.

Since government purchases involve tax dollars, countless laws and regulations dictate how the purchasing process must be conducted. The result is a sizable procurement administration and practices that are highly specialized and very often confusing. When a particular product or service is needed, government buyers either negotiate directly with approved suppliers or develop detailed specifications and invite prospective suppliers (through the media) to submit a price bid in writing. The order usually goes to the lowest qualified bidder. This purchasing process will be discussed further in Part II.

INSTITUTIONS

Public and private institutions form another important classification of business customers. Private, or for-profit, institutions tend to follow processes and criteria that emulate commercial organizations. After all, they continue to exist only if they can generate sufficient profits. Public, or not-for-profit, institutions act more like government agencies; indeed, many of them are (for example, prisons, state universities and colleges, county hospitals). Some institutions follow rigid purchasing rules, while others employ more casual procedures. Effective marketing programs for institutional customers, as with any other customer group, depend on a clear understanding of their needs, priorities, and practices.

Classifying Industrial Products

In this section we return to a consideration of the manufacturing sector and the broad range of products and services that are required by OEMs and industrial end users. Although many of the concepts will be covered in greater detail in subsequent chapters, this section should provide a better understanding of how the buyer-seller interaction changes with product classifications and the impact of these changes on marketing strategies.

Table 3-1 brings several aspects of the industrial buying and selling process together. It shows that the individuals who influence or make the final purchase decision vary with product categories, and the criteria used to decide also change. On the marketing side, product categories also affect channel and pricing strategies.

RAW OR PROCESSED MATERIALS

Raw materials are used with little or no alteration. This category includes such items as chemicals, natural gas, or compressed air. They might become part of the end product or be used in some other aspect of the firm's operations (production line, engi-

TABLE 3-1 Categories of Business Goods: Decision-Makers, Criteria, Channel and Pricing Strategies

Category Descriptions	Decision-Makers	Criteria/Role Played	Channel Strategy	Pricing Strategy
Raw and Processed Materials Materials used in production or elsewhere with little/no alteration (e.g., natural gas, compressed air) or after conversion (e.g., copper, aluminum, or plastic fabricated into piece parts).	1. Purchasing 2. Manufacturing 3. Engineering 4. Mid-top management	1. Dependability, value 2. Support, flexibility 3. Quality, reliability 4. Compatibility, ability to grow with demand	Volume buyers and custom items are channeled direct; distributors usually handle lower volume of standard items.	For standard items, utilize penetration pricing or meet competition; with customized items, it is often possible to skim.
Component Parts Fabricated products that are assembled into an end product (e.g., tires, spark plugs, windows, plus other parts that become an automobile when assembled).	1. Engineering 2. Purchasing 3. Manufacturing 4. Quality control	1. Performance specs 2. Delivery, price 3. Support, flexibility 4. Quality, reliability	Components are handled like materials. Sold directly and through distributors based on type and quantity.	Treat like consumer shopping goods: if homogeneous, use penetration or compete; if heterogeneous, skim.
MRO Supplies Supplies for maintenance, repairs, and day-to-day operations (e.g., lubricants, spare parts, soap, hand towels, paper clips, and floppy disks).	1. Purchasing 2. User groups	1. Price, service 2. Quality, support	Largest portion is sold through distributors, but direct contact is maintained with major users.	Most supplies homogeneous; look for nonprice differences or face severe price wars.
Capital Goods Facilities and equipment used in the production process or in other administrative functions (e.g., lathes, drill presses, mainframe computers, elevators, plus offices, factories and warehouses).	1. Top management 2. User group 3. Engineering 4. Purchasing	1. ROI, to make or buy 2. Required performance 3. Consultants to 1 and 2 4. Primary negotiators	Most sold direct due to technical aspects, except for equipment like that made by Caterpillar, Hyster.	Stress nonprice factors: technology, fabrication, presale help, postsale service. Be unique!
Tools/Accessories Light equipment and tools costing less than capital goods and bought in greater quantity. A firm with only one main-frame computer might have many terminals. Every office has chairs and file cabinets.	1. Purchasing 2. User groups	1. Price, overall service 2. Quality, support	Like materials and components, broad distribution of catalog items for sale to small users. Major buys sold direct.	Chance for producer to provide technical edge and distributor to give superb service; if not, anticipate a price war.

TABLE 3-1—cont'd Categories of Business Goods: Decision-Makers, Criteria, Channel and Pricing Strategies

Category Descriptions	Decision-Makers	Criteria/Role Played	Channel Strategy	Pricing Strategy
Systems These may be product systems (a computer and associated software, maintenance, training, etc.) or service systems (a time-share data processing service or a periodic business audit). Both types usually involve hardware plus intensive, customized services.	1. Mid-top management 2. User group(s) 3. Engineering 4. Purchasing	1. ROI, to make or buy 2. Required performance 3. Consultants to 1 & 2 4. Primary negotiators	Most systems are sold direct, because they are specifically designed for a customer's application.	Customized systems offer a classic opportunity to stress nonprice factors and use price skimming.
Services These vary from grounds-keeping and plant maintenance to legal counsel and marketing research. There is some blurring between service systems and services.	1. User group(s) 2. Purchasing	1. Capability, buy or perform service 2. Primary negotiators	The seller also provides the service. Make the service unique or plan on heavy advertising.	Services can also be sold on nonprice differences to protect against price wars.

neering lab, maintenance department, etc.). Processed materials are raw materials that have undergone some form of conversion. Metals and plastics that have been shaped into various piece parts are common examples of processed materials (Figure 3-6).

Decision-making   Let us assume the firm requires piece parts. When specifications and quantity requirements have been determined, the purchasing department carries out the details of placing and scheduling orders, but a variety of decisions precede the purchasing process. Engineering, in conjunction with manufacturing, must write the specifications. Marketing provides a forecast of sales for the end product involved. Production planners (part of the manufacturing department) decide how much and when material is required to coincide with customer orders and the sales forecast. Company

FIGURE 3-6 An example of how raw material is processed into component parts.

Source: Courtesy PALM•DEBONIS•RUSSO•INC, advertising and Public Relations, Bloomfield, Conn.

managers might be involved in deciding whether potential suppliers are compatible in terms of commitment to quality, ability to grow, and overall business philosophy.

While the various influencers have the same goal—finding a dependable source of quality goods at an affordable price—their emphasis varies. Purchasing looks for dependable performance and quality at a price (value for the money). Engineering seeks quality goods that will perform consistently over time (reliability). Manufacturing also wants a dependable source, but one that provides supportive help and has the ability to adjust to changing circumstances (revised specs, altered delivery schedules).

Channel and Pricing Strategies   Channel strategy hinges on the volume that the buying firm will require and the nature of customer specifications. Large volume buyers are often handled directly by the selling firm (their sales force or manufacturers' reps). The same holds true for custom-made goods that are not sold to other customers. On the other hand, distributors (wholesale resellers) franchised by the supplier usually handle the requirements of smaller customers who buy standard catalog items.

Price also follows volume and specifications. Manufacturers of virtually every industrial product offer quantity discounts. The degree of competition determines how aggressively prices are set. Some firms choose to act as price leaders; others prefer to follow the lead of their primary competitors. When the buying firm sets the product specifications, price often becomes a tradeoff against these specs. In other words, the tighter the specification, the higher the price.

COMPONENT PARTS

There is little difference between this category and processed materials in principle. When difference exists, it tends to involve the degree of product complexity, although processed metal and plastic parts can be quite intricate in design and specified in very tight tolerances (Figure 3-7). The term component implies that this product, combined with a number of others, will become part of some end product. Think of the many components that make up an automobile or a computer or a jet airplane. And then imagine what might happen if only one of those components quit working.

Decision-making   Since the nature and usage of components closely parallels that of processed materials, the decision process follows a similar path. Engineering is listed ahead of purchasing to indicate that the technical description of a component tends to be more complex, particularly when interrelated moving parts are involved, or the component must operate within an electrical or electronic circuit. To further emphasize the importance of consistent, reliable operation, the *quality control* (frequently called *quality assurance*) department is shown as a major decision-influencer.

When purchasing recommends a new source that is quoting a very attractive price, proof will be required that the low price is not coincident with reduced performance. Neither engineering nor manufacturing will react to price in the same way many consumers do. Unless quality, dependability, and service meet corporate criteria, price is irrelevant.

Channel and Pricing Strategies   Components flow through the same channels as processed materials. The only difference will be the type of distributors involved. Distributors tend to specialize by the type of products they handle and the markets they serve. For example, mill supply houses might carry nothing but various forms of steel and aluminum, while the products carried by electronic parts distributors are self-evident.

1. **CONSISTENT QUALITY** Our advanced molding facility meets your most exacting requirements. Strict tolerances are maintained throughout production.

2. **ON-TIME DELIVERY** Promises don't keep production lines running. Parts do. Winzeler has been supplying the parts you need, on time, for over 45 years.

3. **CRAFTSMANSHIP** Highly skilled tool makers, working closely with our planning and gear engineering people, develop the finest tooling available. And quality tooling insures quality gears.

4. **QUALITY CONTROL** We have the latest gear checking equipment, to insure your parts meet exact specifications.

5. **EXPERIENCE** Our many years of gear making has given us the experience you need to solve your molded gear problems. Call us and get the finest molded gears at a cost-effective price.
   For more reasons why you should choose Winzeler, send for your free facilities and capabilities brochure.

Call Toll Free 1-800/621-2397
In Illinois, Call 312/867-7971

Winzeler

7355 W. Wilson Ave. • Chicago, IL 60656

Precision Made Molded and Stamped Gears

FIGURE 3-7 An example of customized component parts.

Source: Courtesy Winzeler, Chicago, Ill.

We stated in the previous section that price is usually not a stand-alone criterion. This statement does not imply that price is unimportant, but rather, that quality and service have become increasingly important in the business market. Even consumers are adopting the philosophy that "you get what you pay for." The best way to build a floor under price is to create a **competitive advantage**. Successful practitioners of this pricing philosophy prove to customers that their complete product offering, the *augmented* product, provides valuable benefits not available from competition. Without this differential, the product is just one more choice among many, and price becomes the deciding factor.

MRO SUPPLIES

MRO is a commonly used acronym for **maintenance, repair, and operations.** This category contains a broad spectrum of products that includes cleaning compounds for the maintenance crew, spare parts for various production and office equipment, and day-to-day needs ranging from computer disks to hand soap. With the exception of spare parts, which normally come from the equipment manufacturer, most other MRO items are basic products that a consumer could buy at the supermarket, hardware store, or office supply house.

Decision-making   Given the simple nature of the products, most decision-making is confined to the purchasing department with inputs from **user groups**. Users comment on the desirability of particular brands, the service afforded by current suppliers, or their personal preferences.

Channel and Pricing Strategies   The largest portion of MRO goods come *through* local distributors and dealers, who can provide local inventory, sales contact, and special services. For example, some creative resellers install computer terminals and dedicated phone lines in the purchasing department of their special customers. Buyers can check inventory and place immediate orders over the terminal. Other resellers put consigned inventories of volume products in the buyer's stockroom. A count is taken periodically (for instance, once a month) and the customer is billed only for the products used. In both examples, price becomes a minor issue. This is the kind of *differentiation* that keeps resellers out of price wars.

CAPITAL GOODS

This category includes facilities to conduct the firm's business (factories, offices, warehouses) and major equipment used in the production process or for other administrative purposes. The equipment segment might involve lathes and drill presses; a mainframe computer plus terminals or a network of PCs and servers; or elevators and escalators. All of these goods involve major financial decisions and require extended discussions and negotiations between the buying and selling firms.

Decision-making   The impact of these purchases on the buyer's scale of operations requires that sellers work closely with prospective customers. Negotiations often take many months and involve top executives in both the buying and selling firms. This is particularly true for buildings or custom-made equipment.

Executives in the buying firm concern themselves with the potential return on a major investment. During prolonged negotiating on equipment specifications, the question of *make or buy* often arises; that is, the buyer wonders whether a purchase will provide as much flexibility and performance as would be obtained by making the equipment in-house. User groups will provide significant inputs regarding performance expectations, and the engineering department will act as technical consultants to both users and executives. When specifications have finally been tied down, the purchasing manager will normally serve as the primary negotiator on terms and conditions of the sale including price.

Channel and Pricing Strategies   Because of the dollars involved and the technical complexities, most capital goods are sold through direct negotiations between the buying and selling firms. A notable exception to this statement is the **construction and mining**

equipment market. Almost 70 percent of sales in this market ($26 billion in 1992) go through industrial distributors.[32] (This market includes the type of equipment produced by Caterpillar and its competitors.) The reason for this strong variance seems to center on the need for local inventories and service. A road building contractor cannot afford to have a $500,000 piece of equipment out of operation for need of a tire or a replacement part. Trade-ins and resale of used equipment is also prevalent in this industry.

Capital goods are not sold primarily on price, but neither buyer nor seller ignores price when the negotiation involves thousands or millions of dollars. **Nonprice factors** such as special services or accelerated delivery can also be used in this category to offset price pressures.

This category also involves leasing. Many firms lease capital equipment rather than buy it. This approach allows them to deduct the lease cost as an operating expense rather than committing capital dollars and recovering the cost through depreciation. Tax implications influence the financing choice. Leasing can also be beneficial when the supplier guarantees to provide upgraded equipment in the event of a product revision or obsolescence.

TOOLS AND ACCESSORIES

This category includes products similar to capital goods in that they can facilitate either the production process or other administrative functions. They differ primarily in cost and quantity. For example, a firm may have only one mainframe computer, within and controlled by the data processing department, but hundreds of computer terminals bought specifically for accounting, engineering, production, personnel, and marketing. A production line may include a sophisticated conveyor system, but every worker will have a set of hand tools. This category also includes office equipment such as desks, chairs, file cabinets, etc.

Decision-making   The same people who make MRO supply decisions, purchasing and user groups, control tool and accessory purchases. Their choice criteria also remain consistent. Product quality related to price, brand preferences, supplier dependability, and service level influence the final choice.

Channel and Pricing Strategies   Tools and accessories also require a broad network of **resellers** to handle sales of standard items to small firms. As with materials and components, manufacturers handle larger users and the sale of custom-made products direct.

This product category offers an excellent opportunity for the producer and distributor to collaborate. The producer supplies a top-grade product backed by an impressive warranty. The distributor provides local inventory plus superb service. This combination is another effective hedge against price-cutting and profit losses.

SYSTEMS

Systems are subdivided into product systems and service systems but with a great deal of overlap. A **product system**, for instance, could include a computer network with all necessary software packages, backed by a maintenance contract, free training for new employees, and a warranty of performance. A **service system** might be provided by an accounting firm that collects data from the customer and handles all invoicing, payroll, and accounts receivable. Both examples involve hardware coupled with continuous, customized service.

Decision-making   This category gives rise to another "make or buy" decision, particularly in the case of service systems. In effect, service systems delegate part of a firm's operations to an outside contractor. Management's decision centers on the best utilization of people and resources. Outside service providers might be used in times of overload instead of hiring additional employees. The same type of decision results in hiring temporary workers instead of permanent ones.

System decision-making involves the same people and the same criteria used in capital goods decision. Capital goods decisions can also have a limited time horizon when equipment is leased instead of purchased.

Channel and Pricing Strategies   Service systems invariably bring provider and user together directly. An intermediary would serve no useful purpose. Product system purchases might have an intermediary in the form of a **value-added reseller**, whom we described earlier in the chapter. An increasingly common variety of value-added reseller deals in computer systems, supplying both hardware and software configured to a particular customer's needs. They do provide backup service and a warranty that stems from the equipment manufacturer. Worker training would simply require one additional skill within the reseller's capability.

The very nature of systems denotes customizing, specialization, and unique performance. Price tends to flex with each system. The seller has an excellent opportunity to adjust system specifications to satisfy each customer's values and price emphasis.

SERVICES

Here again, some blurring exists between service systems and services. Both connote a greater degree of intangibility than the idea of products. Business services cover an amazing spectrum, ranging from simple maintenance services to legal counsel, employee health services, and marketing research. This category will continue to broaden as long as business firms, like consumers, prefer to have others perform certain tasks or lack the ability to do for themselves.[33]

Decision-making   Those who utilize the service are in the best position to describe, monitor, and evaluate performance. In a broad but accurate sense, anyone in a business organization with appropriate authority can decide to contract for services. Thus, we could list top management who will probably hire legal counsel, members of the engineering department who will pick a laboratory to perform special environmental tests, or the persons in the marketing department who will choose an ad agency or research firm. In most but not all firms, the purchasing department serves as the primary negotiator of terms and conditions.

Channel and Pricing Strategies   As with service systems, service providers are also the sellers. They deal with buyers directly. Pricing also follows a similar format. The more a service provider can create an image of professionalism, expertise, and customer orientation, the greater the likelihood that price will play a secondary role.

Looking Back

Business firms interact with each other in a variety of ways. Thus, a manufacturer can be a material converter, a product marketer, an input supplier, a service provider, or even a competitor. The interface level includes all goods producers, resellers, and a broad range of other facilitators who perform the tasks necessary for goods to flow downstream toward business end users or the consumer market.

Publics are segments of the population who can aid or restrict business organizations. Financial institutions, workers, and unions have a direct impact. The media and public interest groups can harm a company if they develop a negative attitude toward the firm's strategy or policies. In turn, the general public or the government may pick up on this negativism and boycott or regulate its activities. Witness the impact on Exxon after the *Valdez* fiasco.

Business firms also face a variety of macroenvironments—economic, ecological, physical, cultural, technological, and demographic—over which they have little control. This lack of control necessitates continual monitoring of the environments, so that major threats and opportunities can be spotted while the firm can still act to minimize threats or capitalize on the opportunities.

Government has the greatest ability to affect the operation, plans, and policies of business organizations. This influence stems from its ability to enact laws and regulations, to limit or expand international trade, to develop supportive industrial policy or social programs, and to provide an overall environment that favors or restricts business growth.

Business firms also serve as each other's customers. Manufacturers buy goods to assemble into end products (as OEMs) or to facilitate the operation of the company (as end users). Resellers act as intermediaries, buying outputs from some businesses and selling it as input to others.

The composite of all government—federal, state, and municipal—is also a trillion dollar customer. Institutions, both private and public, also require business goods and services to operate effectively.

Finally, we analyzed the seven categories of goods and services to understand how each affects the buying practices of firms when they act as customers and the marketing strategies used when they act as suppliers.

Questions for Discussion

1. How (if at all) would your marketing approach change if your firm was a raw material producer, or a component manufacturer, or an equipment manufacturer?

2. What tradeoffs must a manufacturer consider when choosing between the use of distributors or its own regional warehouses and sales force?

3. How can a firm plan long-range (for example, planning a gradual buildup of sales) when stockholders are primarily interested in short-term returns?

4. Which public interest groups, in your opinion, are most supportive of business activities? Which are most opposed?

5. Given the current social and economic environment, do you see the mass media as allies or adversaries of business? Should the media be anything more than unbiased observers and reporters?

6. Which skill is more important to an international marketer: language proficiency or cultural understanding? Why?

7. Is it wise for U.S. semiconductor or automobile manufacturers to enter collaborative arrangements with Japanese or other foreign companies?

8. Should the United States have an industrial policy similar to that of Japan, that is, deciding which industries and technologies are most important for future economic growth and actively supporting them?

Endnotes

1. Philip Kotler, *Marketing Management: Analysis, Planning, Implementation, and Control*, 8th ed. (Englewood Cliffs, N.J.: Prentice Hall, 1994), p. 18.

2. Carl P. Zeithaml and Valarie A. Zeithaml, "Environmental management: Revising the marketing perspective," *Journal of Marketing* 48 (1984):46-53.

3. F. Ian Stuart, "Supplier relationships: Influencing factors and strategic benefits," *International Journal of Purchasing and Materials Management* 29 (1993):22-8.

4. "Mighty Mitsubishi is on the move," *Business Week* (September 24, 1990), pp. 98-107.

5. See Donald M. Jackson, Robert F. Krampf, and Leonard J. Konopa, "Factors that influence the length of industrial channels," *Industrial Marketing Management* 11 (1982):263-68; and Donald M.Jackson and Michael F. d'Amico, "Products and markets served by distributors and agents," *Industrial Marketing Management* 18 (1989):27-33.

6. Dominick B. Attanasio, "The multiple benefits of competitor intelligence," *Journal of Business Strategy* 9 (May/June 1988):16-9.

7. Jeffrey H. Dyer and William G. Ouchi, "Japanese-style partnerships: Giving companies a competitive edge," *Sloan Management Review* 35 (1993):51-63.

8. Lester Thurow, *Head to Head*. (New York: William Morrow & Co., 1992), pp. 59-66.

9. Philip Kotler, *Marketing Essentials*. (Englewood Cliffs, N.J.: Prentice-Hall, Inc., 1984), pp. 82-3.

10. Up front. *Business Week* (May 2,1994) p. 4; and Our heroes. *New Choices* (May 1994), pp. 20-3.

11. "A move to make institutions start using their stockholder clout," *Business Week* (August 6, 1984), pp. 70-1.

12. "A disaster that wasn't," *U.S. News & World Report* (September 18, 1989), pp. 60-69.

13. "Generation WHY?" *Psychology Today* 28(1995):18.

14. "The Americanization of Honda," *Business Week* (April 25, 1988), pp. 90-96; and "Shaking up Detroit," *Business Week* (August 14, 1989), pp. 75-80.

15. "The new golden age of autos," *Fortune* (April 4, [YEAR?]), pp. 51-66.

16. "Biotech comes of age: More than 100 gene-splicing companies launch a barrage of products," *Business Week* (January 23, 1984), pp. 84-94; and J.H. Barton, "Patenting life," *Scientific American* 264 (March 1991):40-6.

17. "For multinationals, it will never be the same," *Business Week* (December 24, 1984), p. 57.

18. Thomas V. Bonoma and Gerald Zaltman, 1978. Introduction. In T.V. Bonoma and G. Zaltman, eds. *Organizational Buyer Behavior*. (Chicago: American Marketing Association, 1978), p. 23.

19. "Oil ship leaks record amount in Welsh Bay," *San Francisco Chronicle* (February 22, 1996), p. A6.

20. "Rio's legacy," *Time* (June 22, 1992) p. 44.

21. Niren Vyas and Arch G. Woodside, "An inductive model of industrial supplier choice processes," *Journal of Marketing* 48(1984):30-45.

22. "Are foreign partners good for U.S. companies?" *Business Week* (May 28,1984), pp. 58-9; and Akio Morita, "Partnering for competitiveness," *Harvard Business Review* 70 (1992): 76-83.

23. "Yield signs on the info interstate," *Business Week* (January 26, [YEAR?], pp. 88-90.

24. "Truck lanes for the info highway," *Business Week* (April 18, [YEAR?]), pp. 112-14.

25. "This is what the U.S. must do to stay competitive," *Business Week* (December 16, 1991), pp. 92-6.

26. "A smarter way to manufacture," 1990. *Business Week* (April 20, 1990), pp. 110-17.

27. "Sharpening our high-tech edge," *U.S. News & World Report* (December 16, 1991), pp. 71-7.

28. Bureau of the Census, "World population clock," Washington, D.C. http://www.doc.gov/census/clock/world, June 29, 1996.

29. American Association for the Advancement of Science, *Science* 80 (November 1980), p. 11.

30. See Naoto Sasaki, *Management and Industrial Structure in Japan,* (New York: Pergamon Press Ltd., 1981), p. 95; also Philip Kotler, Liam Fahey, and Somkid Jatusripitak, *The New Competition,* (Englewood Cliffs, N.J.: Prentice-Hall, Inc., 1985), pp. 27-29.

31. Jennifer Stoffel, "Why the Export Trading Act failed," *Business Marketing* (January 1985), pp. 54-58.

32. 1992 Census of Wholesale Trade: Summary Statistics for the United States, U.S. Department of Commerce, (January 1995), pp. US10, US13.

33. Geoffrey L. Gordon, Roger J. Calantone, and C. Anthony di Benedetto, "Business-to-business service marketing: How does it differ from business-to-business product marketing?" *Journal of Business and Industrial Marketing* 8 (1993):45-57.

Bibliography

Dyer, Jeffrey H., and William G. Ouchi, "Japanese-style partnerships: Giving companies a competitive edge," *Sloan Management Review* 35 (1993):51-63.

Gordon, Geoffrey L., Roger J. Calantone, and C. Anthony Di Benedetto. "Business-to-business service marketing: How does it differ from business-to-business product marketing?" *Journal of Business and Industrial Marketing* 8 (1993):45-57.

Stuart, F. Ian. "Supplier relationships: Influencing factors and strategic benefits," *International Journal of Purchasing and Materials Management* 29 (Fall 1993):22-8.

Zeithaml, Carl P., and Valarie A. Zeithaml. "Environmental management: Revising the marketing perspective," *Journal of Marketing* 48 (Spring 1984):46-53.

PART

II

Business Buying and Buyer Behavior

Today's business products must rely on so many different critical technologies that it becomes impossible for any one company to maintain a lead in all of them. IBM's personal computers were an instant hit because of business application software developed by Lotus Development Corporation, an operating system developed by Microsoft, and a microprocessor from Intel.

No one company can keep all of its technologies in-house as General Motors tried in the 1930s and 1940s. Just as IBM needs to rely on an army of external vendors, so each vendor needs to sell to as broad a market as possible to remain profitable. Even original equipment manufacturers (OEMs) with captive technologies are not immune to this dispersion. NEC may develop a state-of-the-art memory chip for its own mainframe computers, but it can sell many times more memory chips to its competitors for use in their machines. Thus, the buying process in the business market and the interpersonal dynamics of business buyer's behavior become most critical to a seller's future success. The next two chapters will explore these dynamics.

4

The Buying Process in the Business Market

NCR Corporation defines a customer-supplier relationship as "a business rapport, bound by obligation, investment, and commonality of interest, the purpose of which is to create value." This type of pronouncement of a partnership relationship where the supplier has a dominant role is counter to the traditional arm's length, almost adversarial, interrelationship that existed in the past. This concept is being accepted by both suppliers and customers as the better way to manage business buyer-seller relationships. Ironically, as competition increases, particularly from international suppliers, American firms demand increased cooperation.[1]

This chapter covers the following concerns:

1. How the newer concepts of marketing relationships, partnering, just-in-time delivery systems, concurrent engineering, total quality management, and the horizontal organization can affect the buying process
2. What is included in organizational buying activities
3. How the buygrid model models the buying process
4. How buying centers and multiple buying influences affect the buying process
5. How a model can be used for determining the composition of the organizational buying center
6. A discussion of the objectives in organizational buying which includes both task-oriented and non-task-oriented objectives
7. How product analysis can be used to identify informational needs of key influencers

Another dimension in the buyer-seller relationship is the emphasis manufacturing firms place on the amount of time it takes to move a product from the design stage to the market, called in the trade **time to market.** The new competitive firms realize the best time-to-market accelerators are those that focus on speed in engineering, sales response, and customer service. One business futurist and venture capitalist says the corporation of the future will be highly responsive and tightly linked with its core suppliers and customers.[2] However, before such an event can occur, an organization must provide the appropriate infrastructure and must undergo cultural change. Integrated systems, sometimes called *groupware systems,* are powerful systems that will facilitate design of virtual products. They facilitate concurrent engineering and draw customer service and marketing people into the project from the very beginning.

Many exciting changes have occurred in the buyer-seller relationship in the past two decades. Once this relationship was profoundly identifiable. Lately, this relationship has become very complex. Competitive international market conditions have fostered new relationships. Greater partnering patterns have emerged where vendors no longer are merely suppliers of products and services, but have become a subunit of the manufacturer in some cases. The effects of **just-in-time** (JIT) delivery systems, the revolutionary concept of **concurrent engineering** (CE), the development of **total quality management** systems (TQM), and **team management,** sometimes called horizontal or process management, have been largely responsible for these drastic innovations. How far these innovations will take business marketing and how many firms will embrace these concepts remains to be settled. Whether or not these changes will be important and what effects they will have on business marketing, specifically on buyer-seller relationships, is unquestionable. Figure 4-1 shows this extremely delicate relationship. Coverage of these new concepts first will show how they have profoundly affected the buying process.

FIGURE 4-1 The complex process of business buying and concurrent engineering (CE), total quality management (TQM), just-in-time (JIT) deliveries, and horizontal management.

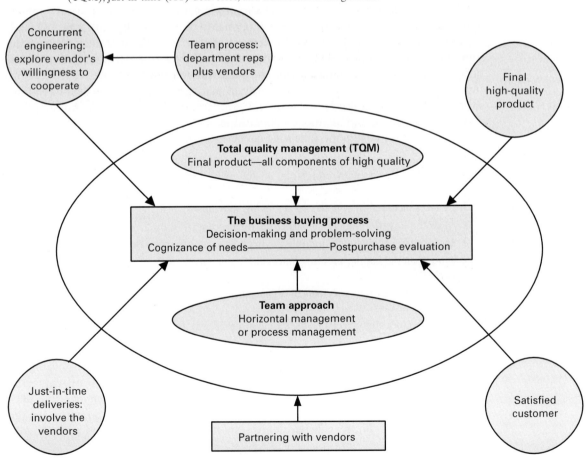

Partnering

The concept of **partnering,** that is, forming a partnership with suppliers and/or customers, has become an important part of the American business community. Popularized by the Japanese, strings of companies from many different business specialties have banded together to combat competition by lowering costs and becoming more efficient.

Suppliers in long-term relationships are able to achieve the same level of growth as firms that employ a transactional approach to servicing their customers.[3] The supplier firms can achieve higher profitability by reducing their discretionary expenses, i.e., selling, general, and administrative overhead costs, to a greater extent than their counterparts who use a transactional approach. Although outsourcing was frowned on, today outsourcing means bringing in the special talents of suppliers to design a component rather than using your own engineering department which may not have the same expertise or favorable cost structure, to design the desired component.

The Intelligent Automation (I/A) plant of the Foxboro Company is an operation that exemplifies the partnering concept. The company has received acclaim from manufacturing experts around the world. The firm believes teamwork that characterizes the plant also permeates I/A's supplier relationships. The alliances and partnerships with key suppliers have played a crucial role in making I/A one of the most studied manufacturing facilities in the United States, a prototype of the plant of the twenty-first century. Its cost breakdowns attest to its success: materials, 70 percent; overhead, 27 percent; and direct labor, 3 percent.[4] Ford Motor Company and Asea Brown Boveri, Ltd., in building a $300 million Oakville paint-finishing facility together, struck a partnership that created a genuine, mutually beneficial, win-win relationship incorporating innovations that are beyond the current practices of the Japanese automobile industry. Instead of forming a relationship around an initial and often dramatic price negotiation, Ford and ABB structured a series of repeat relationships over an extended period of time.[5]

The Japanese conducted an age-old partnering system called *keiretsu* in which strong family ties existed between manufacturer and suppliers, a structure that was given credit for bringing a product to market sooner and at less cost. The keiretsu system worked well, except when it was employed in a slightly altered form in the Japanese auto industry when Japan suffered a deep recession in the early 1990s. The manufacturer dictated behavior to the other partners. The problems were most acute among the small Japanese manufacturers, who secretly wanted more pressure from the U.S. government, which might lead to reform of the system. This pressure would enable the manufacturers to abandon their existing keiretsu suppliers while using the argument that they were responding to external pressure.[6]

Just-in-Time Delivery Systems

JIT delivery systems have forced the buying organization to include the suppliers in their production plans. Instead of ordering a large supply of goods, the buyer establishes plans via computer networking with the supplier to deliver a smaller quantity of goods more often. This strategy can greatly reduce the buyer's holding costs and free what would otherwise be storage space for use by extended production lines, improved quality control stations, and more. The seller must adjust his production plans to meet the customer's needs or else face the possibility of losing the account.

When General Motors built a $1.9 billion plant for its Saturn cars, it decided to rethink everything from the way cars are made to its relationship with workers and suppliers. The 4.1-million-square-foot plant in Spring Hill, Tennessee sits in the middle of a cornfield and is easily accessible from the interstate, making JIT deliveries possible. The number of power trains on the floor between the engine plant and vehicle assembly at any time is less than 140, which is barely enough to cover 2 hours of production. Following Japanese tradition, all material arrives at the Saturn plant directly from the supplier's dock, without passing through a consolidation point, where at one time such materials were sorted for future delivery to various sections of the plant. Suppliers are paid as the parts are consumed in production. Saturn also strives to cultivate genuine partnerships with its suppliers; that means replacing bids with long-term assignments. Saturn's suppliers can expect to have the business forever—as long as they continue to meet world-class standards for quality, delivery, and cost.[7]

Concurrent Engineering

Concurrent engineering (CE) is the concept that allows all the participants—the engineering, production, marketing, and finance departments as well as vendors—to be in on the beginning steps of a product venture to ensure cost efficiencies, proper designs that work, parts that fit, and to see that correct market needs be fulfilled. The exciting thing about concurrent engineering is that vendors are included as an integral part of their customer's organization. Such a relationship is vital to the success of the project because companies know their customer's requirements from the outset of product development.

Concurrent engineering strategy is based on time—spending more time initially to save more time downstream by designing products properly and doing what is right the first time. This foresight reduces the time it takes between product conceptualization and market availability. This shortened time span can enhance a seller's competitive position by giving the firm the absolute state-of-the-art technology with which to compete. The time-to-market bottleneck in manufacturing firms is in the combined design-engineering-manufacturing activity.[8] That is why companies such as Ford Motor Company, Cincinnati Milacron, and Ingersol Milling Machine have made it a product strategy for the 1990s.

Concurrent engineering is not without its possible disadvantages, particularly for the functionally oriented firm. The concept has five risks: (1) the ineffective-team pitfall, (2) the unobtainable-schedule pitfall, (3) the changing-product-requirements pitfall, (4) the business-as-usual parts-vendoring pitfall, and (5) the automated-everything pitfall. Xerox Corporation made CE pay by changing its culture dramatically. In functional organizations in which work teams are not part of the culture, training is essential to prepare technical staff for effective work in a team atmosphere.[9]

Total Quality Management (Continuous Improvement Process)

Marketing organizations have advocated the notion that quality products and quality service are cost effective, since wasted activities and corrective actions for errors made are eliminated when the product is made right the first time and the product is delivered to the customer with the highest-quality service. An additional thought that serving the customer's needs at a profit to the firm has permeated the concept of *total quality management* (TQM).

TQM and CE have been successful strategies, as reflected in the gradually increasing acceptance of U.S. products in the world market segments that previously considered American-made products to be inferior. However, the quality revolution is far from over; it has yet to change the heart of the manufacturing process—the material flow and the logistics system. The new factory paradigm is founded on small inventories, short cycle times, small, decentralized storerooms with real-time inventory control systems, and a simplified material flow. Factories operating under the new system can produce the same volume as traditional plants using a fourth to a half the investment in work-in-progress inventory.[10]

The Horizontal Organization

Also called team, reengineering, or process management, the **horizontal organizational** concept is organized around a process, not a task. It has a shallow or flattened organizational hierarchy in which teams are used to manage everything. Most important of all, the horizontal organization is driven by customer satisfaction, not stock appreciation or profitability. Profit will come when a firm satisfies its customer's needs. Team performance is rewarded. Maximum contact (partnering), in which employees have direct contact with customers and suppliers, is encouraged. Supplier or customer representatives are added as full working members of in-house teams when they can be of service. Finally, the concept suggests that managers trust staffers with raw data but train them how to use it to perform their own analysis and make their own decisions.[11]

These new concepts and perspectives have changed not only business buyer behavior but also the characteristics that people must have when they work with these concepts inside the buying organization. A new breed of engineers is needed with a different set of skills, namely, how they work with others, particularly in manufacturing departments, both within and outside their companies. The trend toward teamwork ties in with the move to CE, in which engineering, manufacturing, and marketing personnel cooperate from a product's inception. IBM, GE, and Parker Hannifin all want engineers who are grounded first in science, physics, and engineering and second in good communication skills, leadership, and interpersonal skills.[12]

Regardless of the new concepts that have improved the buying environment, the bottom line is still, as it has always been, that buying decisions are a function of the different individuals personalities involved and the criteria they apply in making the purchase decisions.[13]

Organizational Buying Activities

Organizational buying activities center on the level of experience and information that firms have in purchasing certain products and services. Routine purchases do not require the buyer to possess much information since he can rely on past experience. If a purchase decision is new, however, the buyer must obtain extensive information because of the firm's lack of experience with the product, service and the suppliers. When buying a new computer, for example, the buyer would have to know his needs to match the computer's characteristics, its programming capabilities, the need for any peripheral equipment, maintenance services availability, and the supplier's reputation and its capability to provide those services. With the intense interdependence that exists among firms today, the importance of long-term relationships becomes of paramount concern.

Buying activities also consist of various phases of decision-making. Depending on the type of buying situation, whether it is routine or new, these phases will vary in their degree of importance. Effective business marketing strategy, then, requires that marketers focus their attention on the buying situation, the phase of its decision-making process, and what criteria various influencers will emphasize in the final purchase decision.

The Buygrid Model

The concept of business buying behavior can be simplified by dividing the process into its various phases, which can then be analyzed in different buying situations. This process aids the seller in identifying the specific decision phases, the information needs of the purchasing organization, and the criteria that buyers may be considering when making the purchase.[14] A conceptual model called the **buygrid model** is useful for visualizing the different combinations of buying phases and buying situations.

As shown in Table 4-1, the buygrid model incorporates three types of buying situations: (1) the *new task,* (2) the *straight rebuy,* and (3) the *modified rebuy,* in addition to eight phases in the buying decision process. The model provides an easy reference for dividing the complex business decision buying process into distinct segments that are useful in recognizing critical decisions and specific informational needs.

BUYING SITUATIONS

Since business buyers have different levels of experience and needs for information, the same purchase in two different organizations could evoke markedly different purchasing strategies. One firm may see the purchase of a new computer as a new task because of the firm's lack of experience in this area, whereas another firm may see the same situation as a modified rebuy. Therefore, marketing strategy must begin with identifying the type of buying situation the buying firm is facing.[13]

New Tasks In the new task buying situation the buyer must obtain the greatest variety of information to explore alternative solutions to his purchasing problem because of his lack of experience. These problems may have developed because the buyer's customers may have changed, or a product line has been expanded, or costs must be cut and efficiency must be increased as a result of new or changed competition. Frequently, this type of buying situation is handled by a buying center comprising representatives of various departments working as a team. They must quickly expand their knowledge to cope with these new purchasing uncertainties. Products perceived to be complex by the buyers will most likely be subjected to a group decision-making process rather than left to the sole discretion of the purchasing agent.[15]

Modified Rebuy Decision-makers enter into a modified rebuy situation when they believe that significant benefits such as quality improvements or cost reductions may be derived from reevaluating workable alternatives. Often well-defined criteria may be used in this situation, but some uncertainty may exist concerning the switch to a new supplier because of unhappiness with a current supplier. Usually this purchase situation is handled by an individual purchasing agent, except where large expenditures are involved and approval of a buying center or a top executive is required.

			Buyclasses	
		New Task	*Modified Rebuy*	*Straight Rebuy*
B u y P h a s e s	1. Anticipation or recognition of problem (need) and a general solution			
	2. Determination of characteristics and quantity of needed item			
	3. Description of characteristics and quantity of needed item			
	4. Search for and qualification of potential sources			
	5. Acquisition and analysis of proposals			
	6. Evaluation of proposals and selection of suppliers			
	7. Selection of an order routine			
	8. Performance feedback and evaluation			

TABLE 4-1 A Buygrid Analysis Framework for Business Buying Situations

NOTES

1. The most complex buying situations occur in the upper left portion of the bugrid matrix, when the largest number of decision makers and buying influences are involved. Thus, a new task in its initial phase of problem recognition generally represents the greatest difficutly for managements.

2. Clearly, a new task may entail policy questions and special studies, whereas a modified rebuy may be more routine and a straight rebuy essentially automatic.

3. As buyphases are completed, moving from phase 1 through phase B, the process of "creeping commitment" occurs, and there is diminishing likelihood of new vendors gaining access to the buying situation.

Source: Marketing Science Institute Series, *Industrial Buying and Creative Marketing* by Patrick J. Robinson, Charles W. Faris, and Yoram Wind. Copyright © 1967 by Allyn & Bacon, Inc. Reprinted by permission.

Straight Rebuy   Straight rebuys are the most common situations generally performed by a purchasing agent. The buyer-seller relationships will exist as long as delivery is prompt, quality is consistent, and price is reasonably competitive.[16] This scenario characterizes the predominant view among many purchasing agents; hence alternative solutions are seldom evaluated. The seller attempts to reach this level of partnership with his customers by providing the needed service and more. However, change is a constant that the seller must face as new individuals are involved, new and different problems appear, and competitors attempt to unseat established business relationships with better service, lower prices, and superior products.

PHASES IN THE PURCHASING DECISION PROCESS

As shown in Figure 4-2, by tracing the activities that occur in the business buying process, it is not difficult to uncover the critical decision phases and evolving information requirements of buying situations.[17] Unlike the mental consumer decision processes of problem recognition, information search, information evaluation, purchase decision, and postpurchase behavior involving one or a few people, the business decision-making process is largely a set of observable stages that can involve a number of people in every step along the way. As seen in Figure 4-2, phase 3, for example, is the description of the characteristics and quantity of the needed item. The original

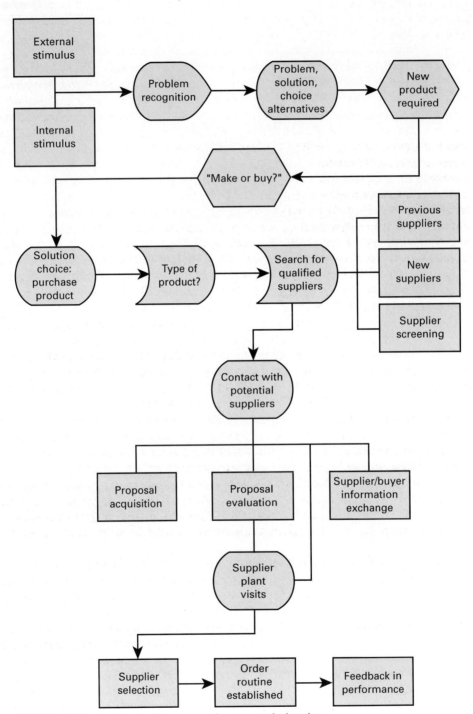

FIGURE 4-2 Purchasing decision process in a new task situation.

developers of the buygrid model wrote, "Since this description becomes the basis for action by people inside and outside of the buying organization, it must be detailed and precise to facilitate later phases in the buying process."[18]

Phase 1: Anticipation or Recognition of a Problem (Need)   The purchasing decision process is triggered by the buying organization's recognition of a problem, need, or potential opportunity to improve the company's efficiency and bottom line. This recognition may originate within the company, i.e., outmoded, equipment, break downs, unsatisfactory in quality or availability, new managers insist on change, or present suppliers do not perform to desired quality levels. The need recognition may originate outside the buying organization with a marketer who recognizes a company need and convinces the buying organization that the seller can improve the company's operating performance by buying a given product or installing a given service.

Research has shown that new product ideas frequently originate with customers, therefore, early involvement in the new task/problem recognition phase offers the marketer a differential advantage over competitive suppliers.[19] Given the movement to concurrent engineering in many firms, this phase is an absolute *must* for sellers to penetrate early or be left behind when companies are invited into a discussion about a new product development with a potential customer. All the information which follows is based upon this first phase since it is the most critical of all eight phases in the buying process.

Phase 2: Determination of the Characteristics and Quality of Needed Items
Problem recognition provokes the buying organization into resolving the problem with precise, analyzed alternative actions that will seek answers to such questions as: "What performance specifications need to be met?" "What are the application requirements?" "What types of goods and services should be considered?" and "What quantities will be needed?"

Technical product specifications such as punch presses, drop forges and conveyer belt systems are prepared by either the engineering department or the user department. When nontechnical products such as lubrication for a section of the production line are involved, the user department (production/operations) might determine that products currently on the market could solve the problem. While influencers from outside the department may be used, or insist on being used, as in the case of the purchasing department providing price information, critical decisions and information needs at this phase lie chiefly within the user department.

Phase 3: Description of the Characteristics and Quality of the Needed Item
Many suppliers do not become aware that a buying situation is in progress until the firm begins its outside search for information about products, sub components, and prices. Here a definite advantage accrues to the marketer who helped to trigger the need in the first phase of the buying process. A partnering position at this stage is even better, because here the vendor would be consulted as the expert to provide the characteristics and quantity of the needed item without the hassle of competing with other vendors. During this phase, the company prepares the product specifications that will determine who will eventually receive the order. If concurrent engineering has been followed, the lucky supplier would have already been involved in this determination.

Phase 4: Search for and Qualification of Potential Sources   Once the specifications and workable solutions have been determined and precisely described, the buying organization searches for alternative sources of supply. Here the purchasing department can exercise much influence as it provides most of the data for possible vendor sources. Other departments may provide information, and hence influence, about costs, vendor reliability, and the feasibility of JIT operations with a vendor. Obviously, the decision makers have determined which suppliers will be considered as potential vendors. If a strong partnership relationship existed between the buyer and seller, this phase would not be necessary since the vendor would have helped to establish the specifications in the first place and would become the anointed supplier.

Phase 5: Acquisition and Analysis of Proposals   Requests for specific proposals are made to qualified vendors in this phase. In a straight rebuy situation, the buyer may simply contact the chosen vendor to obtain up-to-date information about prices, delivery times, and mode of shipment, so phases 4 and 5 may appear as the same step. For modified rebuys, more time would be spent on the analysis of the proposals submitted. New task buys probably would take the most time and months may expire before a final decision is made. Quality of both product and service, and the vendor's past efforts, could be the hallmark identification for the winning vendor.

Phase 6: Evaluation of Proposals and Selection of Suppliers   The various proposals are weighed and analyzed to determine which vendor or vendors can match the product or service specifications and the desired price and delivery requirements. Subsequent negotiations may be needed to produce the desired finite results relative to prices, delivery and long-term commitment or other aspect of the vendor's proposal.

Personal tastes and personalities cannot be ruled out, but the company that is well liked and can give the customer the best overall product and service will generally win the order, plus the strong possibility of a long-term partnering relationship.

Phase 7: Selection of an Order Routine   Orders are forwarded to the vendor, and status reports are sent to the user department. The inventory levels will be established, and the JIT routines will be determined, if such a possibility exists. The user department views this phase as just the beginning. Delivery, setup, and training, if necessary, will transpire next.

Phase 8: Performance Feedback and Evaluation   Similar to the first phase, this last phase in the buying process is also critical. The customer has had his aspirations raised as the result of the need analysis, product specifications, and proposal submitted; now the vendor must deliver on his promises. This phase involves a determination by the user department as to whether the purchased item has solved the original problem. Because this time can be a difficult phase for the vendor (since some of the variables are not completely controlled by him), it behooves the buying organization to analyze the performance and provide feedback to all the interested parties for further evaluation. Feedback that is critical of the chosen vendor can cause the various members of the decision-making unit to reexamine their positions. When this reexamination occurs, views regarding previously rejected alternatives become more favorable.[16]

MARKETING IMPLICATIONS

The direction of marketing strategy is greatly affected by both the purchasing situation and the decision phase of the customer. Progressively greater amounts of data will be needed by organizational buyers as the purchase situation changes from a straight rebuy to a modified rebuy, and to a new task situation. Information needs, as well as individual involvement in the purchase decision, will also be affected by the phase of the purchasing process. Anderson, Chu, and Weitz[20] found that when organizational buyers are facing a new task, they will be (1) uncertain about their needs and the appropriateness of the possible solutions; (2) more concerned about finding a good solution than getting a low price or assured supply; (3) more willing to entertain proposals from "out" suppliers and less willing to favor "in" suppliers; (4) more influenced by technical personnel; and (5) less influenced by purchasing agents. Hence, the marketing strategy depends on both the purchasing situation and the decision-making process.

The most important phases affecting marketing strategy, particularly for a new task or modified rebuy situation, are phases 1 through 5. While Table 4-2 summarizes how the following discussion of marketing strategy differs over these phases and buying situations, the astute marketer should be aware that not all organizational members may view the buying situation from the same perspective; for instance, a purchasing agent might view a given buying situation as a new buy, and an engineer might view it as a straight rebuy. Such a situation could occur when an engineer, for instance, was routinely involved with a product or supplier, much to the chagrin of the purchasing department, while he was employed with a different company within the same industry.[19]

Phase 1: Problem Recognition   In the new task situation, marketing opportunities depend on anticipating, recognizing, and understanding customer problems to provide the right information and assistance at the right time. This task is difficult, since problem recognition is largely internal to the buying firm. A seller's firm would stand a better chance of being selected as a potential vendor if it had been well recognized because of past experience under a concurrent engineering system.

A straight rebuy situation is rather routine and the "in" supplier should maintain a close relationship with the user and purchasing personnel. To prevent the buying situation from moving to a modified rebuy situation, a close monitoring of the product

TABLE 4-2   Appropriate Marketing Strategies Over Various Buying Situations and Phases

Phase	New Task	Modified Rebuy	Straight Rebuy
1. Problem recognition	Anticipate problem; use advertising and creative salespeople to convince buyers of problem-solving capabilities.	In supplier: maintain quality/service standards; out supplier: watch for developing trends.	In supplier: maintain close relationship with users and buyers; out supplier: convince firm to reexamine alternatives.
2. Solution determination	Provide technical assistance and information.	In supplier and out supplier: stress capability, reliability, and problem-solving capabilities.	Same as phase 1.
3. Determining needed item	Provide detailed product/service information to decision-makers.	Same as phase 2.	Same as phase 1.
4. Searching for and qualifying supplier	In supplier: maintain dependability; out supplier: demonstrate ability to perform task.	In supplier: watch for problems; out supplier: demonstrate ability to perform task.	Same as phase 1.
5. Analyzing proposals	Understand details of customer problem/needs; make timely proposals.	Understand details of customer problem/needs; make timely proposals.	Make timely proposal.

Source: Marketing Science Institute Series, *Industrial Buying and Creative Marketing* by Patrick J. Robinson, Charles W. Faris, and Yoram Wind. Copyright © 1967 by Allyn & Bacon, Inc. Reprinted by permission.

and service quality is mandatory. Research has shown that customers dissatisfied with present suppliers often react by changing suppliers without first attempting to correct the problems with the present supplier.

Suppliers not currently considered as a vendor to a firm have to develop systematic sources of information to detect and respond to any developing trends that might lead to a modified rebuy situation. For example, the salesperson may overhear a conversation or be told of competitive actions within the firm by a friendly insider who voices dissatisfaction with the company's current supplier. However, if the customer is happy with the present supplier, the "out" supplier must offer extraordinary advantages to the customer in the form of a new cost savings, state-of-the-art product that the customer can't turn down.

Phase 2: Determining Solutions Characteristics   The marketing opportunities in this phase consists of providing information, technical assistance, and suggested direction while the customer is in the process of narrowing solutions. In the new task and the modified rebuy situations, for both the "in" and the "out" supplier, the task is one of gaining acceptance for participation in the firm's problem-solving process. The marketer's past history with the customer, including his corporate and personal reputation is very significant to establish in the customer's mind that they can provide capable technical assistance to the purchasing firm. "In" suppliers should have previously established their capability record by producing quality service. "Out" suppliers need to stress their general capability, reliability, and problem-solving skills and address any special information requirements made by the customer to differentiate their skills relative to their competitors.

The marketing task in the straight rebuy situation requires the vendor to maintain a flow of information through mailings, new product development, and calls on a periodic basis to make sure that all things are running smoothly. Frequent calls also can detect any problems which might arise that can be taken care of before any customer dissatisfaction might sets in.

Phase 3: Characteristics/Quality of Needed Item   In the new task and modified rebuy situations, the buying firm's decision-makers are primarily interested in the total offers that competing suppliers can provide, particularly those related to products and support services. The marketing opportunities in this phase depend on detailed product, production, and service information provided by the sellers. In this phase, the seller has the best chance to influence the preparation of specifications which could favor their organization's products and services. For straight rebuy situations, essentially the seller would follow the same strategy as in phase 2.

During the first three phases, it becomes imperative that the decision-maker be found, but often the seller is the last to know this person's identity. Obviously the decision-maker does not make blatant statements and tends to melt into the background to hide his identity so the marketer doesn't concentrate his efforts on him. The normal buyer-seller pattern for straight rebuy situations is the purchasing department. For modified rebuys, either the purchasing department or a buying center, an ad hoc group of executives formed to accomplish a given task, are involved. The difference between whether the buying center and/or purchasing would be involved is a function of the product class and its costs. Frequently, a new task situation would require a buying center to contain the decision-maker if the cost of the product class is high. A low-cost new task item could be handled and decided by the purchasing department.[21] However, in all straight rebuy and modified rebuy situations, the purchasing agent plays an important role in influencing the final decision, regardless of the costs. The decision-maker and significant influencers in problem recognition and solution choice phases are often executives found in middle or top management, engineering in high-tech firms, manufacturing, and research and development.[13]

Phase 4: Searching for and Qualifying Suppliers   In the new task and modified rebuy situations, out suppliers must demonstrate an ability to perform the job. As in the case of Ford Motor Company, technical experts may visit plant facilities, examine equipment, and talk with technical personnel. The out supplier's marketing task in a modified rebuy situation is to convince the potential customer that superior value, such as better quality control, faster deliveries, or significant cost savings are possible. For the in supplier in a straight rebuy situation, the task is to maintain performance and communication flow so that the customer will not consider alternative suppliers.

Phase 5: Acquiring and Analyzing Proposal   Marketing strategy in the new task or modified rebuy situation should be directed at understanding the specific details of the customer's problems and providing technical assistance. This may include cooperative involvement in cost studies, product testing, and evaluation. During this phase it is also critical for the supplier, particularly in the new task situations, to determine the relative importance of the various specification details to the customer. These details will fall into three basic categories:

1. What is essential to solve the problem (e.g., electric motor with 1-horsepower output)
2. What is desirable, but not essential (e.g., weight less than 25 pounds)
3. What is added for clarification only (e.g., painted black with white letters)

With this understanding, the supplier is in a much better position to emphasize those factors of greatest importance to the customer and avoid designing product characteristics that increase cost without increasing the customer's value perception. This understanding also allows the supplier to know which specifications are open to value-enhancing revisions (for example, our standard 30-pound, 1-horsepower motor will cost 15 percent less than a 25-pound version requiring special metal alloys).

In the straight rebuy, in suppliers should make timely proposals and quotations upon request. The goal, as in the previous phases, is to maintain quality service to prevent or forestall a shift to a modified rebuy.

Phase 6: Postpurchase Relationships   A satisfied customer becomes a potential new order. Before the sale, a seller can supply information, influence the buyer, and listen and respond to the buyer's needs. After the sale, the most critical events transpire, relative to any future business. Does the buyer receive help from the seller to avoid nasty logistical surprises, get help to find the proper personnel, and receive help from the seller to avoid the inevitable conflict that often exists over the purchase within the buyer's organization.[22]

Buying Centers and Multiple Buying Influencers

A successful marketing communication strategy must address the significant variation in information needs of those individuals involved in the purchasing decision as it progresses through its many phases. A major task, then, facing the business marketer is identifying the individuals who are in any way involved in the purchasing decision process, that is, the **decision-making unit.** However, the relative importance of buying center members, as perceived by the purchasing agents, can shift based on the type of product and the decision situation.[23]

A decision-making unit may consist of only one person, but it is normally a group of individuals "who share a common goal or goals which the decision will hopefully help them to achieve, and who share the risks arising from the decision."[24]

It is not uncommon to encounter groups consisting of fifteen to twenty individuals, and some have been known to involve more than fifty people.[25] Another study demonstrated that buying center size was a function of both the phase in the purchasing process and the buying situation with the buying center size being more highly correlated with buying phase than buying situation.[26] The buying center size, according to this study, varied from 2.67 to 5.10, with a grand mean of 3.95 or 4 individuals. In business marketing these decision-makers are referred to as the *buying center.*[27]

IDENTIFYING BUYING CENTER MEMBERS

The **buying center** is an "informal, cross-departmental decision unit in which the primary objective is the acquisition, impartation, and processing of relevant purchasing-related information."[28] Generally, people become involved in the buying center for one of two reasons: (1) they have formal responsibility, such as the user, the decider, and so on, although this is not always discernible, or (2) they have importance as a source of information.[29] The emphasis of this discussion is on the influence functional areas exert on the purchase decision system. Table 4-3 indicates how these various functional areas are involved in the purchasing decision process over different buying situations.

Marketing   When a purchasing decision has an effect on the marketability of a firm's product such as altering the product's materials, packaging, or price, marketing

TABLE 4-3   Buying Center Influence Matrix

Phase	*New Buy*	*Modified Rebuy*	*Straight Rebuy*
Need identification	Engineering Purchasing Research and development Production	Purchasing Production Engineering	Production Purchasing
Establishment of specification	Engineering Purchasing Production Research and development	Engineering Purchasing Production Research and development Quality control	Purchasing Engineering Production
Modification and evaluation of buying alternatives	Engineering Purchasing Research and development	Purchasing Engineering Production	Purchasing Engineering Production
Supplier selection	Purchasing Engineering Research and development Quality control	Purchasing Engineering Production	Purchasing Engineering Production

Source: Earl Nauman, Douglas J. Lincoln, and Robert D. McWilliams, "The purchase of components: Functional areas of influence," *Industrial Marketing Management,* 13 (1984):113–122. Copyright © 1984 by Elsevier Science Publishing Co., Inc.

people become active influencers in the purchase/decision process. The perspective of marketing in the purchasing process is "Will it enhance salability?" since the purchase of parts and materials tends to influence the salability of final products. This relationship exists in many companies, but firms who embrace CE or TQM systems involve the marketing department at the onset to be sure that customer satisfaction and the product's ultimate salability are ensured.

Manufacturing   Manufacturing plays a very significant role when new products or new models are being developed. Manufacturing is responsible for determining the feasibility and economic cost considerations of producing end products. Manufacturing works with marketing to complete the price determinations. Engineering decisions have to be made on specifications, parts, and materials. In addition, equipment needs, costs, and impact on current production are given careful consideration by the manufacturing department. Manufacturing, which is often the user of products purchased, maintains a strong influential position in the purchasing process by giving purchasing a continuous supplier performance update. With these actions, manufacturing has a key position in the selection and retention of suppliers and the allocation of quantities among suppliers.

It might be noted that manufacturing will not willingly accept technical changes, even obvious improvements, with complete enthusiasm. This situation is one of the cultural changes that must be made when a firm embraces concurrent engineering. Top management holds production/operations primarily responsible for product cost reductions, and product or manufacturing changes have a tendency to increase costs, at least temporarily, because the learning curve is interrupted (see Chapter 18).

Research and Development   Research and development departments are involved in the initial development of product prototypes and processes and set broad specifications for component and material criteria, minimum end product performance standards, and, occasionally, manufacturing techniques. Since the department has many products in different stages of development, it's important that the marketing department become involved very early, for two reasons. First, the earlier the marketing department becomes involved in the development process, the greater the chance of incorporating a product favorable to the customer into the final design. Second, by understanding the direction in which customers or prospective customers are moving, the marketing department is better able to plan the direction of their own promotional efforts. In progressive companies, engineers and manufacturing people already believe the marketing department should be involved early in the product development process, because they want to see their efforts become successful marketing ventures as much as anyone else.

General Management   Top management becomes involved in the purchasing process when the firm is faced with an unfamiliar situation not related to day-to-day activities, or when purchasing decisions are likely to have major consequences on the firm's operations and bottom line, or when the purchase is a harbinger of the company's taking a new direction. For example, the purchase of a executive airplane or the purchase of a new drop forge for an improved manufacturing system is most likely to be strongly influenced by top management. Such major acquisitions are also likely to be decided at the top, with little information requested from the lower levels. When top management is directly involved in a purchase, it is likely to be actively involved in establishing guidelines and criteria for future purchases of similar products.

Purchasing   As you can see in Table 4-4, contrary to popular belief, purchasing is not the most central activity in the buying process.[30] Research consistently indicates that the purchasing department's dominant sphere of influence falls within phases 4, 5, and 6 of the purchasing decision process—when specifications of products to be purchased have been established and suppliers have been qualified.[25] The buying center size is also reduced in the supplier selection phase, phase 4, from its largest size in phases 1 and 2—recognition of need and determination of characteristics of quality of the needed item. Establishment of buying alternatives and evaluation of buying alternatives are relatively complex decisions which result in the need for more participants in the buying center. Seller selection decisions are less complex and information is more concentrated among fewer participants; thus, the buying center is smaller.[25]

TABLE 4-4 The Most Central Individual(s) in Each Buying Center for the Purchase of Capital Equipment

Type of Company	Equipment Purchase	Central Figure(s)
Chemical manufacturer	Heat exchanger	Purchasing manager
Industrial safety products manufacturer	Automatic drilling machine	Engineer and vice president of manufacturing
Steel mill furnace manufacturer	Standby oil heating system	Purchasing manager
Steel manufacturer	Coke oven	Purchasing manager
	River tow barge, galvanized steel processor	Vice president of production
Water transportation and construction companies	Locomotive crane	Purchasing manager
Heating equipment manufacturer	Large industrial press	Engineer
Specialty steel manufacturer	Hot piercer mill	Purchasing manager
	Steel plate leveler	Manufacturing engineer
Industrial products distributor	Plasma cutting equipment	Vice president of operations
	Storage shelving	Director of materials
Metal and wire manufacturer	Wrapping machine	Division manager
Aerospace and automotive products manufacturer	Metal working Machine tool	Divisional purchasing Manager
Paper products manufacturer	Banding system	General manager Project manager
Steel mill builder	Processing pump	Project manager
Refractory	Forklift trucks	Plant purchasing manager
Pipe fabricator	Presses	Safety engineer, maintenance Supervisor
Petroleum products manufacturer	Gasoline storage tank	Buyer
Power plant builder	Nuclear load cell	Job-shop order department manager
Mining equipment manufacturer	Executive office desk	Purchasing agent
Chemicals and scientific instrument distributor	Medical instruments	District vice president of sales
Electrical parts distributor	Recessed lighting	Company vice president
Electrical parts manufacturer	Resistor	General manager and Purchasing manager
Building materials manufacturer	Pump	Engineer
Cement manufacturer	Forklift truck	General manager and vice president

Source: Adapted from Wesley J. Johnston and Thomas Bonoma, "The buying center: Structure and interaction patterns," *Journal of Marketing* 48 (Summer 1981):143–56. Reprinted by permission of the American Marketing Association.

Because purchasing agents are specialists who have negotiation experience, knowledge of buying products, and close working relationships with suppliers, they are the dominant decision-makers and influencers in repetitive, straight, or modified rebuy situations. They also exercise a high level of influence over selected types of purchases when uncertain environmental conditions are present, as when the probability of interrupted supply or shortage is high.[27]

INFLUENCE PATTERNS VARY

It is important to note that functional responsibility and job titles often are not true indicators of the relative influence of buying center members in a purchase decision task. Any one person can assume several or all the roles shown in Box 4-1. Since buyers have differing levels of experience and use different problem-solving approaches in various situations, role influence will vary over the different phases of the purchasing process, depending on the purchasing situation, the number of individuals involved, the complexity of the purchase, and the functional lines involved.[31]

Identifying the various roles of buying center members across functional lines is important to both marketing managers and salespeople in developing the most

---

BOX 4-1

Buying Center Roles

PRIMARY ROLES

Deciders. Those organizational members who have formal or informal authority who actually make the buying decision. Identifying deciders, or decision makers, is often the most difficult task. In routine purchases of standard items, the buyer is usually the decider. However, in complex purchasing decisions, the officers of the company are often the deciders. An engineer who designs specifications such that only one vendor can meet them becomes, in effect, an informal decision maker.

Influencers. Those individuals inside or outside the organization who influence the decision process (directly or indirectly) by providing information on criteria for evaluating buying alternatives or by establishing product specifications. Technical people, such as design engineers and quality control inspectors, typically have significant influence in the purchase decision. Individuals outside the buying firm, such as architects who draw up building specifications, may also assume this role.

SECONDARY ROLES

Users. Those organizational members who use the products and services. Users may exert from a minor to a very significant degree of influence on the purchasing decision. They may even initiate the purchasing process and play an important role in defining purchase specifications.

Buyers. Buyers are organizational members who have formal authority in the selection of suppliers and in the implementation of procedures involved with purchasing. In complex purchasing, buyers might include high-level officers of the company who may well be the decision makers. Buyers may be involved in developing specifications, but their major role is in selecting suppliers and negotiating purchases within buying constraints.

Gatekeepers. Those organizational members who control the flow of information into the buying center. This can be done by controlling printed information and advertisements, as well as by controlling which salespersons are allowed to speak to individuals within the buying center.

Source: Adapted from Frederick E. Webster, Jr., and Yoram Wind, *Organizational Buyer Behavior* (Englewood Cliffs, N.J.: Prentice Hall, Inc., 1972), pp 77–80.

effective marketing communication strategy. This situation is exacerbated by CE concepts when team members from many functions work together from the start-up of a product project. The salesperson must determine the major deciders and initiators of new product projects and must keep these individuals informed of the seller's new product or subcomponent developments. Obviously, this activity is not an easy task, since most firms do not want a sales rep to know the intimate secrets of the firm. Therefore, the sales rep should be cognizant of the customer's activities and in some cases actually initiate some of the product ideas through good creative selling: identifying a customer's needs and then matching an appropriate product to fulfill this need.

GATEKEEPERS' INFLUENCE

Understanding the role of the gatekeeper is crucial in the development of business marketing strategy. Information can be filtered by the individual or individuals who play the gatekeeper role, since they can stand between the information source and its destination. Gatekeepers can exercise some control over the buying process by withholding from the decision-makers any information that does not coincide with their own opinions. Purchasing managers may be involved primarily in such a role, since they are often close to the purchasing action and could have the most vested interests if a favorite supplier of theirs appeared to be losing the order. [32]

The basic functions of the purchasing department are to negotiate prices, place orders on the best terms in accordance with requisitions, nurture supplier relationships, and expand orders to ensure a smooth flow of supplies. Purchasing agents often wish to expand beyond these functions and feel that they have more important contributions to make by keeping management informed of developments in materials, sources, and price trends. Therefore, they want to be consulted before requisitions are drawn up, and this tends to enhance and protect their position as gatekeepers.[33] Business salespeople often take on expanded roles to bypass purchasing agents to ensure that the information gets to those who are in authority and should receive it.[34] Such expanded roles take the form of dinner, theater, golf, shared hobbies, and personal friendships. A salesperson cannot afford to stand on the sidelines, but instead, becomes involved with influencers right down to the product user and product decider levels which often by-pass the purchasing department.

IDENTIFYING KEY BUYING INFLUENCERS

Because members of buying centers change with every different type of product, the task of identifying key buying influencers for a particular purchasing process becomes quite complex. Furthermore, research indicates that key influencers are most often located outside the purchasing department. For example, in buying centers for highly technical products, purchasing agents, engineers, scientists, production/operations and quality control personnel are usually included in the buying center; the engineers and scientists, however, have the greatest level of influence.[35]

Key buying influencers are those who are capable of swaying other influencers, either knowingly or unknowingly.[36] For example, a buying center involved in the purchase of capital equipment may consist of ten or fifteen buying influencers, yet three or four of these influencers are able to influence the others because of their authority, knowledge, information, or gatekeeper status. The ability to identify influencers and sell them on product attributes (customer benefits) is vital to good marketing strategy.

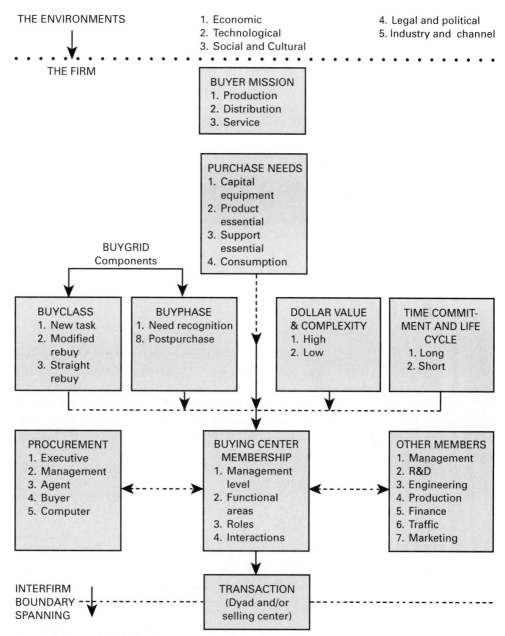

Source: Mattson, Melvin R, "How to determine the composition and influence of a buying center," *Industrial Marketing Management* 17 (1988):200-14. Reprinted by permission.

FIGURE 4-3 A model for determining the composition of the organizational buying center.

A Model for Determining the Composition of the Organizational Buying Center

The composition and varying influences within the buying center will change, depending on the buying situation and the phase in the purchasing decision process.[37] Mattson has developed a model, shown in Figure 4-3, which assists marketers in analyzing and predicting buying center membership and influence. The variables shown in

Figure 4-3 relate to the buying firm's environments, mission, purchase needs, and organizational structure.

ENVIRONMENT AND MISSION

Environment and mission may place constraints on how organizational authority is delegated, or change the level of managerial interest in a particular purchase decision. In industries with strong channel leaders, for instance, a firm may not be allowed flexibility in its choice of transportation carriers. Where no channel leaders exist, transportation decisions may be totally perfunctory or be made by habit rather than by choice of the firm.

Different organizations have different missions that affect the importance of the purchasing decision. For example, automobiles will have a different function in the ability of Hertz to serve its mission than they would to serve the mission of Bethlehem Steel. The determination of a firm's mission, according to Mattson, is the first step in determining who in the buying organization will be interested in the purchasing decision. A firm that employs a CE system, with its attendant team project concept, makes this step extremely important, since the salesperson must be involved very early for the buying process to be successful.

PURCHASE NEEDS

Identifying influencers and buying center composition depends on the marketer's understanding of the product's potential uses and priorities within the firm. For example, when products are developed to a department's specifications, that department may also specify the supplier. This priority is particularly true when the department has experienced a favorable relationship with a given supplier who they trust and respect. The importance of building trust between buyer and seller appears to be the glue in this dyadic relationship. Salespeople in all trade relationships should operate from positions of honesty and reliability, because these directly aid the buyer's developing trust in the seller.[38]

BUYCLASS/BUYPHASE

As previously discussed, in the new task buying situation buyer center membership tends to be larger at the first four phases than in the modified or straight rebuy situation. Departmental influence also tends to vary with the type of product and the buy phase and, while each buy phase may have different buying center members, purchasing is generally represented in each phase with varying degrees of influence per phase. More influence is exerted by purchasing in the later phases of the buying decision process after the critical initial phases have been settled. The marketer who calls only on the purchasing department may miss all the action and have not become aware of a potential sale until after the fact. In addition, the purchasing department's influence becomes more important as the products and the method of purchase becomes more routine.

DOLLAR VALUE AND COMPLEXITY

Purchasing agents use dollar value as an indication of management involvement in the purchasing decision process and level of criteria to be employed. In very small firms, when the dollar amount is relatively large, purchasing managers generally have little influence. In medium-sized firms, purchasing agents have more authority as the relative size of each purchase gets smaller. In large firms, the authority of purchasing managers decreases as purchasing decisions become more compartmentalized and purchasing managers become specialists.

TIME COMMITMENT AND LIFE CYCLE

Purchasing activities tend to vary with the buying firm's product life cycle. While the buy class suggests that the amount of management involvement decreases as the firm moves from a new task to a straight rebuy, Fox and Rink have found that purchasing's involvement is high during the product decision introduction stage and maturity stages of the buying firm's product life cycle.[39] This finding suggests that the seller wants to ensure a successful product introduction by keeping purchasing involved to monitor material prices and potential suppliers. In the maturity stage of the product's life cycle, purchasing is actively searching for new suppliers as the company attempts to either change the product or substantially improve its promotion. As time horizons increase, buyers and sellers tend to develop mutually beneficial relationships and purchasing decisions can become routine; thus, decisions are delegated to managers lower in the hierarchy.

BUYING CENTER MEMBERSHIP, PROCUREMENT, AND OTHER MEMBERS

As discussed, buying center involvement can be determined by examining functional areas of influence. The higher the level of managerial interest, however, the lower the influence of the purchasing department. This does not mean that business marketers should overlook the importance of the purchasing department; because of purchasing's special knowledge, their involvement in asset management teams, and their negotiating skills, purchasing department members are highly influential during the interorganizational steps of the purchasing process.

Business buying must be viewed as a multidimensional, complex process that is affected by organizational, individual, social, and environmental variables. Therefore, purchasing decisions are frequently team decisions that often overlap among several departments and top management. More firms develop products using teams than ever before, further complicating the business marketer's job.

Objectives in Organizational Buying

Before vendors can respond effectively to customer information needs, they must understand the various criteria that customers use in evaluating potential suppliers. Different groups of individuals will view the supplier's offering from their unique perspectives. While business buying tends to reflect organizational goals, organization members are influenced by both task and nontask objectives.

Task-oriented objectives involve pragmatic considerations such as price, quality, reciprocity, meeting production specifications, delivery times, service, and return on investment. Nontask objectives center on such personal factors as the desire for job security, recognition, promotion, and salary increases. When suppliers' offerings are similar in product attributes, price, and delivery, buyers have little basis for task-oriented choices. Since they can effectively satisfy organizational goals through several suppliers, buyers often tend to be more influenced by personal factors, or nontask objectives. However, when significant differences exist in product/service factors, business buyers are more accountable for their choices and tend to place more emphasis on economic factors.[40]

The problem facing the business marketer is to define the buying goals of organizational buyers. This task is difficult at best. Generalizations of organizational buying objectives across business buying decisions cannot be made with any degree of accuracy. In fact, research indicates that buying center members often employ different criteria in evaluating suppliers.[41] Purchasing agents, for example, may value price and delivery factors; engineers may value product quality, validity, and reliability; controllers and finance managers may value return on investment; and production/operations people may value JIT obligations of zero inventory, on-time deliveries, and high-quality component parts. Furthermore, the importance of each criterion is increased by the type of purchase under consideration. The challenge is to examine the purchasing decision from the buying firm's point of view, determine the roles of buying center members, and ascertain the task and nontask objectives that motivate key buying influencers very early in the buying process. Box 4-2 shows how buying influencers rank the factors that affect their supplier choice decision.

TASK-ORIENTED OBJECTIVES

Organizations that are in business to make a profit are predominantly oriented to purchasing at the lowest possible price while avoiding compromises on technical service, price quality, and certainty of delivery. Nonprofit organizations, however, are concerned with budgetary constraints, and buying at the lowest possible price may be necessary to operate within predetermined budgets. Therefore, economic task objectives that achieve the organizational goals are a significant consideration to the marketer.[42]

Price   Buyers are concerned with the *evaluated price* of a product, that is, the level of satisfaction or value a buyer derives from the purchase of a given product compared with the price paid. In evaluating the price, a number of factors are considered, namely, "What is the cost of the material processing?" "How much scrap or waste will result from the use of the material?" "How much power will the machine consume?" "What is the return on investment on the capital equipment purchased?" The purchase of a piece of capital equipment provokes the notion that an increase in productivity and/or reduced labor costs can materialize.

Price, however, cannot be considered in isolation. A supplier who has a reputation for high-quality products and dependable delivery and service may be awarded a contract even though his prices are higher than those of a competitor. To the buyer, the costs of shutting down manufacturing because of faulty equipment, missed deliveries, or dealing with an unreliable supplier may far outweigh the greater product price. Business marketers, then, should not overestimate the importance of price; they should also know that low bidders often fail to meet other important criteria of the buyers.[40]

Services   Product services are required by business buyers to achieve organizational goals. Such services include technical training, availability of spare parts, repair capability, on-time deliveries (especially in the case of JIT contracts), and, the most difficult of all, delivery of the promised product quality. Long-term contracts, common in JIT and CE systems, require the seller to meet the expectations of the buyer or else lose the contract. This requirement is even more important than the specific price involved.

Technical contributions of suppliers are highly valued wherever equipment, materials, or parts are in use. Many buyers tend to favor suppliers with reputations for being technical leaders in their field. Replacement parts should be available for organizations who do their own repairs. Complex office machines, computers, and

---

BOX 4-2

Ranking of Factors Motivating Buying Influences in Various Departments in Selecting Suppliers of a Standard Business Product

Accounting Department

1. Offers volume discounts
2. Regularly meets quality specifications
3. Is honest in dealings
3. Answers all communications promptly
5. Has competitive prices
5. Handles product rejections fairly
5. Provides needed information when requested (such as bids)

Production Control Department

1. Can deliver quickly in an emergency
2. Ships products when wanted (for example, when move-up and/or push-back deliveries are necessary)
3. Regularly meets quality specifications
4. Is willing to cooperate in the face of unforeseen difficulties
4. Is helpful in emergency situations

Purchasing Department

1. Regularly meets quality specifications
2. Advises of potential trouble
2. Is honest in dealings
2. Provides products during times of shortages
5. Is willing to cooperate in the face of unforeseen difficulties
5. Delivers when promised
5. Provides needed information when requested (such as bids)
5. Is helpful in emergency situations

Manufacturing Engineering Department

1. Delivers when promised
2. Is honest in dealings
2. Provides products during times of shortages
4. Regularly meets quality specifications
5. Can deliver quickly in an emergency

Quality Control Department

1. Regularly meets quality specifications
2. Is honest in dealings
3. Allows credit for scrap or rework
3. Provides products during times of shortages
5. Has a low percentage of rejects

Special Machinery Engineering Department

1. Provides products during times of shortages
2. Regularly meets quality specifications
3. Has a low percentage of rejects
4. Delivers when promised
5. Is honest in dealings

Tool Design Department

1. Is honest in dealings
2. Has technical ability and knowledge
2. Handles product refections fairly
2. Allows credit for scrap or rework
2. Invoices correctly
2. Provides products during times of shortages
2. Answers all communications promptly

---

*Duplicate numbers indicate ties in rankings. A standard product was defined as having three or more of the following characteristics: (1) low unit cost, (2) little additional information required, (3) few people involved in the purchase, (4) short commitment (one year or less) to the product, and (5) little or no supplier modification of the product needed before use.

Source: Sibley, Stanley D., "How interfacing departments rate vendors," *National Purchasing Review* 5 (1980): 11, Reprinted by permission.

manufacturing equipment may require installation and intensive training. The marketer who can offer sound advice, training, spare parts, and quality products and services very often has a differential advantage over his less capable competitors.

Quality   Organizational buyers search for quality levels that are consistent with specifications and the intended use of the product. The buyers are reluctant to pay for extra quality yet are unwilling to compromise specifications for a reduced price. The critical factor is uniformity or consistency in product quality that will guarantee uniformity in end products, reduce costly inspections and testing of incoming shipments, and ensure a smooth blending with the production process. JIT systems seldom inspect incoming goods, but if the proper tolerances and quality "specs" are violated, the JIT agreement could be in jeopardy. Close communication and cooperation with the customer are required to maintain the optimum working customer relationships under JIT and CE systems.

Assurance of Supply   An assurance of a steady supply of parts and materials is of paramount importance to prevent the possibility of plant shutdown caused by an interruption in the flow of supplies, which would result in costly delays and lost sales. Physical distribution services rank second to product quality in influencing the purchasing decision.[43]

Delays caused by a supplier's labor problems, strikes, accidents, fires, or natural disasters motivate purchasing agents to seek out at least two suppliers for greater assurance of supply. When a buyer chooses to spread a given order over two suppliers, one becomes the favored supplier and receives the bulk of the order, whereas the second supplier receives what is left. The marketer should realize the policies that customers follow in seeking continuity of supply and develop a marketing strategy around them. JIT systems are built on zero inventory systems, in which an assured supply of parts and materials is delivered to the customer at specific times to keep the customer's production system flowing.

Reciprocity   Giving consideration to selecting suppliers because of their value as customers is known as *reciprocity*. The objective of reciprocity is for the buyer and seller to reach an agreement on an exchange of business that is mutually beneficial and has become an important part of the trade relations responsibility of purchasing and materials management.[44] Reciprocity is legal if it is not enforced through coercive power, or if a reciprocal agreement does not substantially lessen competition. Purchasing managers may initiate reciprocal agreements to "meet their firm's basic purchasing needs."[45]

NONTASK OBJECTIVES

People join organizations to accomplish personal objectives such as greater status, promotions, salary increases, increased job security,[46] and social interaction.[47] In the sphere of business marketing, it has been found that major factors that influence the purchasing decision are social considerations such as friendship, reputation, and mutually beneficial interactions.[50]

Organizations work best when people accomplish personal and organizational goals simultaneously. A buyer can take pride in achieving a personal objective by making a correct buying decision that also satisfactorily serves an organizational objective. In this instance, a single action accomplishes two different objectives. To avoid an incomplete picture of organizational buying, vendors need to keep both sets of objectives in mind. A department head in the buying organization will think about the purchase of a new product that will increase efficiency, reduce costs, and generally make his or her department more productive, as well as how this productivity will reflect on his or her managerial abilities as seen by superiors. However, the seller should never suggest such a situation, but let the buyer infer the consequences. Marketers can open doors to future business by simply remembering to send a letter of thanks. Marketers should show their appreciation and give praise to a buyer for giving them the order, or even show appreciation to the buyer's supervisor. At the same time, caution must be exercised to avoid overemphasizing the buyer's personal goals at the expense of the organization's objectives.

Product Analysis for Identifying Information Needs of Key Influencers

A product is a bundle of utilities with promises to be kept. Any one promise may be highly significant to certain individuals, and only incidental to others. Product characteristics are viewed by influencers in accordance with how well those characteristics assist in meeting task objectives and the impact they have on different functional areas, including how important the buyer and/or user appear to superiors for making the buy decision. However, if the promises are not kept, the impact can be disastrous. Equally important is the translation of product characteristics into need satisfactions, or customer benefits. As stated in the classic example, "Customers don't want 1/4-inch drill bits; they want 1/4-inch holes." Therefore, marketers must understand which need satisfactions are important to those who buy or influence buying. When information needs vary, no single sales presentation can be targeted simultaneously to the purchasing agent, the engineer, and the vice president of manufacturing.

Product analysis consists of developing a list of criteria considered relevant to the needs of the target market, assigning weights to each of those criteria, and developing a rating scale to determine whether the product under consideration has a high or low probability of success in the marketplace. Lists of product criteria that specifically relate to functional areas of customer firms can also be developed. By questioning purchasing agents and other influencers within the customer firms, and by exercising judgment based on past experience, weights can be assigned to the importance of criteria for various functional areas. It is invaluable for the business marketer to be able to "read" and understand each member in the customer firm; to do otherwise is courting failure.

Where weights are comparatively high, effective communication strategy must be developed to reach key influencers involved with those functional areas. For instance, in Table 4-5 the product analysis matrix for a new computer installation pinpoints the relevant information needs of key functional influencers. Information most important to management involves knowledge of the supplier's technical competency (.4) and personal training ability (.5). Purchasing, on the other hand, is more concerned with expansion capabilities (.4) and maintenance service (.4), than with installation (.1) and training (.1). Comptrollers are vitally interested in the investment payback period (.7). Marketing communication strategy must be developed to address these concerns of the various functional people, and emphasis should correlate with the levels of importance these different people assign to their information needs.

Looking Back

Insights into how business organizations purchase goods and services enable the business marketer to reach the right influencers with information that satisfies their various needs. Business purchasing is a problem-solving process that evolves in sequential

TABLE 4-5 Product Analysis for a New Computer Installation

Product Information Needs	Functional Influencers				
	Marketing	Engineering	Management	Comptroller	Purchasing
Technical competency	.2	.2	.4		
Expansion capability	.1	.2	.1	.1	.4
Installation		.1			.1
Credit terms				.2	
Personnel training	.3	.3	.5		.1
Programs	.4	.2			
Investment payback period				.7	
Maintenance service					.4
	1.0	1.0	1.0	1.0	1.0

steps. The level of a firm's experience with purchasing problems is the key to how the marketer should define the buying situation—new task, modified, or straight rebuy. Each situation requires a different type of response from the business marketer. This delicate set of circumstances is further enlarged by some of the newer practices such as TQM, CE, JIT deliveries, and the development of teams for product innovation. All these practices necessitate that the business marketer have a most cordial relationship with the customer so that he or she can be invited to participate in the very early phases of the buying process (when all the most critical decisions are made, including which seller will receive the order).

Influencers involved in these earlier phases tend to have more power affecting the final choice. Marketing efforts must, therefore, be concentrated at these critical phases, and marketers must be continually on the search for who is making *what decisions,* based on *which criteria.*

Marketing strategy is influenced by the number and background of influencers in the buying center who may cut across functional lines, particularly in concurrent engineering situations, and assume several different roles during the purchasing decision process. Task as well as nontask objectives of buying influencers should be considered. As buying influencers move through the purchasing decision process they have information needs that must be met if they are to evaluate alternatives and make the best supplier selection. Such information needs are product and service related and should be viewed with regard to the firm's task objectives and the product's impact on functional areas. Since various influencers will evaluate product characteristics from their individual perspectives, product analysis can and should be used to identify the major interests of key influencers and their respective information needs.

Questions for Discussion

1. In which phases of the purchasing process will upper management most likely be involved? At what stage should the marketer attempt to become involved? What types of action should be taken? If the firm practices concurrent engineering, when should the marketer become involved?

2. As an "out" supplier, would it be possible to penetrate a firm by offering (a) very attractive prices or (b) substantial improvements in production efficiencies?

3. Business marketers seldom call on their counterparts in the buying firm. What advantages might accrue to the seller if a relationship were to be established in this area? Would concurrent engineering affect this relationship in any way?

4. Consider this scenario: A young, insecure buyer is clearly acting as an information gatekeeper. The order cannot be won unless important information reaches the decision-makers, but unfortunately, the buyer will not pass along the information and cannot be bypassed without his knowledge and subsequent wrath. How can a creative salesperson turn this potentially disastrous situation into a clear-cut advantage?

5. Functional areas are generally perceived to have varying amounts of influence across both the purchase situation and purchase phases. In a new task purchasing situation, some authorities believe that the engineering department will have the most influence, whereas in modified or straight rebuy situations, the purchasing department will have the most. Discuss how this could be so.

6. Analyze the Balfour Corp., a medium-sized (several hundred employees) manufacturing firm in the process of purchasing, for the first time, an expensive, multipurpose computer system to be used by various functional departments. List the individuals and name the one or more roles they will play in this buying situation. What would the situation be like under a concurrent engineering system?

7. What would your reaction be if advised that social and psychological persuasion played no part in the business buying process? How would you prefer to differentiate consumer and business buying motives?

8. One authority has concluded that the type of buying situation a firm is facing is not as important in the buying decision process as are other factors such as the product under consideration, whether concurrent engineering is practiced, and the market/economic environment. Do you agree?

Endnotes

1. Sang-Lin Han, David T. Wilson, and Shirish P. Dant. "Buyer-supplier relationships today," *Industrial Marketing Management* 22 (1993):331-8.

2. Richard Pastore, "A virtual visionary," *CIO* 6 (1993):46-9.

3. Manohar U. Kalwani and Narakesari Narayandas, "Long-term manufacturer-supplier relationships: Do they pay off for supplier firms?" *Journal of Marketing* 59 (1995):1-16.

4. James Morgan, "Building a world class supply base from scratch," *Purchasing* 5 (1993):56-61.

5. Sherwood C. Frey, Jr. and Michel M. Schlosser, "ABB and Ford: Creating value through cooperation," *Sloan Management Review* 35 (1993):65-72.

6. Maryann Keller, "The keiretsu unravels," *Automotive News* 174 (1994):11.

7. Ernest Raia, "Saturn: Rising star," *Purchasing* 115 (1993):44-7.

8. Joseph Vesey, "The new competitors: They think in terms of 'speed to market'," *Production and Inventory Management Journal* 33 (1992):71-7.

9. Jean V. Owen, "Concurrent engineering," *Manufacturing Engineering,* 109 (1992):69-73.

10. James K. Allred, "Changing the manufacturing paradigm: A blueprint for U.S. industrial competitiveness," *Industrial Engineering* 25 (1993):16-17.

11. John A. Byrne, "The horizontal corporation," *Business Week* (December 20, 1993), pp. 76-81.

12. James Braham, "Employers demand new skills," *Machine Design* 64 (1992):42-7.

13. Earl Naumann, Douglas J. Lincoln, and Robert D. McWilliams, "The purchase of components: Functional areas of influence," *Industrial Marketing Management* 13 (1984):113-22.

14. Joseph A. Bellizzi and Philip McVey, "How valid is the buy-grid model?" *Industrial Marketing Management,* 12 (1983):57-62.

15. Richard G. Jennings and Richard E. Plank, "When the purchasing agent is a committee," *Industrial Marketing Management* 24 (1995):411-19.

16. Peter Doyle, Arch G. Woodside, and Paul Mitchell, "Organizations buying in new task and rebuy situations," *Industrial Marketing Management* 8 (1979):7-11.

17. Discussion based on Chapter 9 of Gordon T. Brand, *The Industrial Buying Decision.* (New York: John Wiley & Sons, 1972); J.M. Stevens, and J.P. Grand, *The Purchasing/Marketing Interface* (New York: John Wiley & Sons, 1975); and Patrick J. Robinson, Charles W. Faris, and Yoram Wind, *Industrial Buying and Creative Marketing* (Boston: Allyn & Bacon, Inc., 1967), pp. 11-18+.

18. Patrick J. Robinson, Charles W. Faris, and Yoram Wind, *Industrial Buying and Creative Marketing.* (Boston: Allyn & Bacon, Inc., 1967), p. 3.

19. Eric Von Hippel, "Successful industrial products from customer ideas," *Journal of Industrial Marketing* 42 (1978):39-49.

20. Eric Anderson, Wujin Chu, and Barton Weitz, "Industrial purchasing: An empirical exploration of the buyclass framework," *Journal of Marketing* 51 (July 1987):71-85.

21. Robert W. Eckles and Timothy J. Novotny, "Product class as the major determinant of the industrial buying center's decision maker." In David M. Klein and Allen E. Smith, eds., *Marketing Comes of Age* (New Orleans: Southern Marketing Association, 1984), p. 94; and Joseph A. Bellizzi, and C.K. Walter, "Purchasing agent's influence in the buying process," *Industrial Marketing Management* 9 (1980):137-41.

22. Philip C. Burger and Cynthia W. Cann, "Post-purchase strategy, a key to successful industrial marketing and customer satisfaction," *Industrial Marketing Management* 24 (1995):91-8.

23. Judith M. Schmitz, "Understanding the persuasion process between industrial buyers and sellers," *Industrial Marketing Management* 24 (1995):83-90.

24. R.D. Buzzell and others. *Marketing: A Contemporary Analysis,* 2nd ed. (New York: McGraw-Hill Book Co., 1972), p. 62.

25. G. Van Der Most, "Purchasing process: Researching influences is basic to marketing planning," *Industrial Marketing* 61 (1976):120.

26. Robert D. McWilliams, Earl Naumann, and Stan Scott, "Determining buying center size," *Industrial Marketing Management* 21 (1992):43-49.

27. Frederick E. Webster, Jr. and Yorum Wind, *Organizational Buying Behavior.* (Englewood Cliffs, N.J.: Prentice Hall, Inc., 1972), p. 6.

28. Robert W. Speckman and Louis W. Stern, "Environmental uncertainty and buying group structure: An empirical investigation," *Journal of Marketing* 43 (1979):56.

29. Gordon T. Brand, *The Industrial Buying Decision.* (New York: John Wiley & Sons, 1972), p. 30.

30. Joseph A. Bellizzi and C.K. Walter, "Purchasing agent's influence in the buying process," *Industrial Marketing Management* 9 (1980):143-56.

31. Murray Harding, "Who really makes the purchasing decision?" *Industrial Marketing Management* 51 (1966):76.

32. Thomas V. Bonoma and Gerald Zaltman, Introduction. In T.V. Bonoma and G. Zaltman, eds., *Organizational Buying Behavior* (Chicago: American Marketing Association, 1978), p. 14.

33. Mary Ellen Mogee and Alden S. Bean, "The role of the purchasing agent in industrial innovation." In T.V. Bonoma and G. Zaltman, eds., *Organizational Buying Behavior* (Chicago: American Marketing Association, 1978), p. 126.

34. George Strauss, "Work flow frictions, interfunctional rivalry, and professionalism: A case study of purchasing agents." In A.H. Rubenstein and C. Haberstroh, eds., *Some Theories of Organizations.* (Homewood, Ill.: Richard D. Irwin, Inc., 1966).

35. James R. McMillan, "Role differentiation in industrial buying decisions: Proceedings of the American Marketing Association," (Chicago: American Marketing Association, 1973), pp. 207-11.

36. E. Raymond Corey, *Industrial Marketing: Cases and Concepts.* (Englewood Cliffs, N.J.: Prentice Hall, Inc., 1983), p. 97.

37. Melvin R. Mattson, "How to determine the composition and influence of a buying center," *Industrial Marketing Management* 17 (1988):205-14.

38. Paul Dion, Debbie Easterling, and Shirley Jo Miller, " What is really necessary in successful buyer/seller relationship?" *Industrial Marketing Management* 24 (1995):1-9.

39. Harold W. Fox and David R. Rink, "Purchasing's role across life cycle," *Industrial Marketing Management* 7 (1987):186-92.

40. Philip Kotler, *Marketing Management:Analysis, Planning, Implementation, and Control,* 8th ed. (Englewood Cliffs, N.J.: Prentice Hall, Inc., 1994), p. 210.

41. J. Patrick Kelly and James W. Coaker, "Can we generalize about choice criteria for industrial purchasing decisions?" In Kenneth L. Bernhardt, ed. *Marketing: 1976 and Beyond.* (Chicago: American Marketing Association, 1976), pp. 33-43.

42. Discussion based on Richard M. Hill, Ralph S. Alexander, and James S. Cross, *Industrial Marketing.* (Homewood, Ill.: Richard D. Irwin, Inc., pp. 54-8, 1975); and E. Raymond Corey, 1983. Industrial Marketing: Cases and Concepts. (Englewood Cliffs, N.J.: Prentice Hall, Inc., 1983), pp. 36-7.

43. William D. Perreault, Jr. and Frederick A. Russ, "Physical distribution services in industrial purchasing decisions," *Journal of Marketing* 40 (1976):3-10.

44. Lamar Lee, Jr. and Donald W. Dobler, *Purchasing and Materials Management.* (New York: McGraw-Hill Book Co., 1971), pp. 90-91.

45. Gregory D. Upah and Monroe M. Bird, "Changes in industrial buying: Implications for industrial marketers," *Industrial Marketing Management* 9 (1980):117-21.

46. Delbert J. Duncan, "Purchasing agents: Seekers of status, personal and professional," *Journal of Purchasing* 2 (1966):17-26; and George Strauss, "Tactics of lateral relationships: The purchasing agent," *Administrative Science Quarterly* 7 (1962):161-86.

47. Thomas V. Bonoma and Wesley J. Johnson, 1978. "The social psychology of industrial buying and selling," *Industrial Marketing Management* 17:213-34.

Bibliography

Banting, Peter, Jozsef Beracs, and Andrew Gross, "The industrial buying process in capitalist and socialist countries," *Industrial Marketing Management* 20 (1991): 5-13.

Bellizzi, Joseph A., and C.K. Walter, "Purchasing agent's influence in the buying process," *Industrial Marketing Management* 9 (1980):143-56.

Drumwright, Minetle E. "Socially responsible organizational buying: Environmental concern as a noneconomic buying criterion," *Journal of Marketing* 58 (1994):1-19.

Han, Sang-Lin, David T. Wilson, and Shirish P. Dant, "Buyer-supplier relationships today," *Industrial Marketing Management* 22 (1993):331-8.

Henthorne, Tony L., Michael S. LaTour, and Alvin J. Williams, "How organizational buyers reduce risk," *Industrial Marketing Management* 22 (1993):41-8.

McWilliams, Robert D., Earl Naumann, and Stan Scott, "Determining buying center size," *Industrial Marketing Management* 21 (1992):43-9.

Venkatesh, R., Aljay K. Kohli, and Gerald Zaltman, "Influence strategies in buying centers," *Journal of Marketing* 59 (1995):71-82.

Interpersonal Dynamics of Business Buyer Behavior

Organizational buying behavior is ultimately influenced by forces within the organization as well as by the business environment. The status and operating procedures of purchasing, the degree of involvement and interaction of various groups, and the differing perceptions among group members all have a significant impact on purchasing decisions. Knowledge of these forces is an essential ingredient in the development of an effective business marketing strategy.

The purpose of this chapter, then, is to discuss the following:

1. How purchasing activities within the organizational structure influence buying behavior
2. The joint decision-making process and its interface with the firm and the firm's buying centers
3. How some psychological factors relating to groups and individuals result in differences in their approaches to buying
4. The conflicts and resolutions in joint decision-making
5. How organizational buyers choose and evaluate suppliers

Effective and responsive business marketing strategy rests on the marketer's knowledge of how organizational buying behavior is affected by forces within the organization. Seldom does an organizational buyer make a decision in isolation. Purchasing decisions are influenced by organizational, group, and individual forces, as well as forces within the external environment.[1]

The position of the purchasing department and its status within the organization has a significant influence on business buying behavior. Purchases are also affected by a complex set of decisions made by the several individuals in buying centers—individuals with different levels of information and expertise and different backgrounds, who interact at different stages of the purchasing decision process. For marketing strategy to be successful, the business marketer must have a clear understanding of how organizational groups interact, the amount of influence the various group members may possess, and how this influence varies throughout the purchasing decision process.[2]

The Purchasing Department's Influence on Interpersonal Buyer Behavior

Contributing to the recognition and the growing status of purchasing is the realization that efficient and effective purchasing, through the use of *material requirements planning* (MRP), *partnering, concurrent engineering* (CE), and *just-in-time* (JIT) *inventory control systems,* is a key factor in maintaining profits and alleviating cash flow problems. JIT and partnering bring suppliers into the decision-making loop. CE shows the importance of having accurate marketing information. All these newer concepts (discussed in Chapter 4) underscore the importance of the purchasing department and thus increase purchasing's influence.

PURCHASING MANAGEMENT'S EXPANDING ROLE

Purchasing managers are dominate in repetitive straight rebuy and modified rebuy purchase situations because their knowledge of suppliers, pricing, and their close relations with vendors.[3] Two of their primary functions are to (1) to secure vendor information and (2) maintain up-to-date pricing information. Once the buying center acquires the technical specifications of the proposed product to be purchased, and when vendors have been qualified as legitimate sources, the purchasing department assumes a position of power. This position of power is ensured by purchasing's status as an authority in the procurement area, its technical competence and credibility, its position as a repository of data, and its top management support.[3] Purchasing managers perceive themselves as the most important individual purchaser and to be one of the most influential members of the buying center, particularly in the area of supplier selection decisions.[4]

The corporate manager of procurement programs for Raytheon, Arnold Lovering, believes many purchasing people have a mentality that "they get no respect."[5] He responds, "Have you earned it?" A well-rounded purchasing professional needs to have knowledge and understanding in seven areas of purchasing and materials management:

1. Negotiating skills—the most important area, concerning tactics, strategies, planning, risk analysis, and ethical considerations
2. Cost and price analysis—direct and indirect costs, fixed and variable costs, learning curves, cost models, and cost breakdowns
3. Material control—MRP, organizations, forecasting, and JIT inventory management
4. Purchasing law—uniform commercial code, law of agency, sale of goods, Occupational Safety and Health Administration (OSHA) rules, antitrust laws, contract terms, buyer remedies, and warranties
5. Traffic and transportation—shipping modes, shipping memos, bills of lading, freight classification, rates and tariffs, and good receiving practices
6. Subcontract administration—federal acquisition, types of contracts, production cost visibility, competition, sourcing, and contract management
7. Purchasing standards of conduct—supplier relations (gifts, favors, services, discounts) conflicts of interest, and confidential information

THE PURCHASING DEPARTMENT'S ORGANIZATION

The typical purchasing department, as seen in Figure 5-1, is headed by the purchasing manager or director of purchasing, to whom one or more purchasing agents report. Within each of the purchasing agents sections are a number of buyers, each of whom specializes in the purchase of specific types of materials. In a large department, assistant buyers are often assigned when the load warrants the need. Once orders are placed with a vendor, another major function of the department—expediting—comes onstream. Expediters promptly execute the shipment of an order if the delivery date has been extended by the seller, or if the buyer's needs require a sooner-than-promised delivery. Expediters also check frequently with the supplier on the progress of the order throughout the vendor's manufacturing process.

PURCHASING'S IMPRESSIONS OF MARKETERS AND IMPLICATIONS

In business marketing, particularly in industrial marketing, sales reps spend much of their time maintaining relationships with their customers. However, one study suggests that buyers believe that some sellers know little about the industrial buying environment and are not very adept at receiving and interpreting cues about purchasing people to indicate the level of trust they had for each of several pertinent members of the buying committee.[6] The shocking fact was that the least trusted members of the *role set* were members of the buyer's own marketing department and the sales representatives who called on them, in that order. It isn't enough for a sale rep to be motivated to get the order; to achieve success, the sales rep must be aware of all the interpersonal variables that make up the buyer's personality and the nature of the buyer's environment.

FIGURE 5-1 A purchasing department's organization.

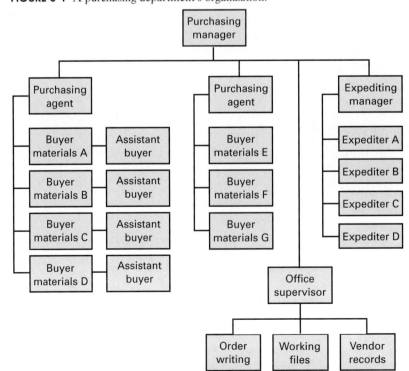

The average business firm spends approximately 60 percent of its sales dollars on materials, services, and capital equipment.[7] Purchasing is now being viewed as *asset management through asset utilization and inventory control.*[8] Today purchasing managers regularly attend meetings with other major functional departments of the firm. A typical **asset management** team includes procurement specialists, cost/price analysts, and engineers.[2]

MATERIAL REQUIREMENTS PLANNING (MRP)

One major change in the purchasing function is the use of **material requirements planning** (MRP), as shown in Figure 5-2. In an MRP system, a firm estimates its future sales, schedules production accordingly, and then orders parts and materials to coordinate with production schedules so that inventories will not become too large or too small. MRP is conceptually simple, but in practice it can require diverse considerations. An input part, for example, may be used at more than one stage in a production process that takes place over a period of time. Thus, multiple deliveries may be necessary to minimize inventory costs and existing inventories must be continuously monitored to accommodate any inaccuracies in sales forecasts and subsequent production. JIT contracts are often related to MRP plans.

To use MRP, a growing number of firms are combining the functions of purchasing, transportation, inventory control, receiving, and, in some instances, production control under one functional area called materials management. For example, to improve its accuracy of inventory records and achieve its objective of a 15 percent annual growth, Tennant Company reorganized the functions of purchasing, production planning, and material planning into one 33-member unit. One of the advantages of

FIGURE 5-2 An integrated material requirements plan and purchasing.

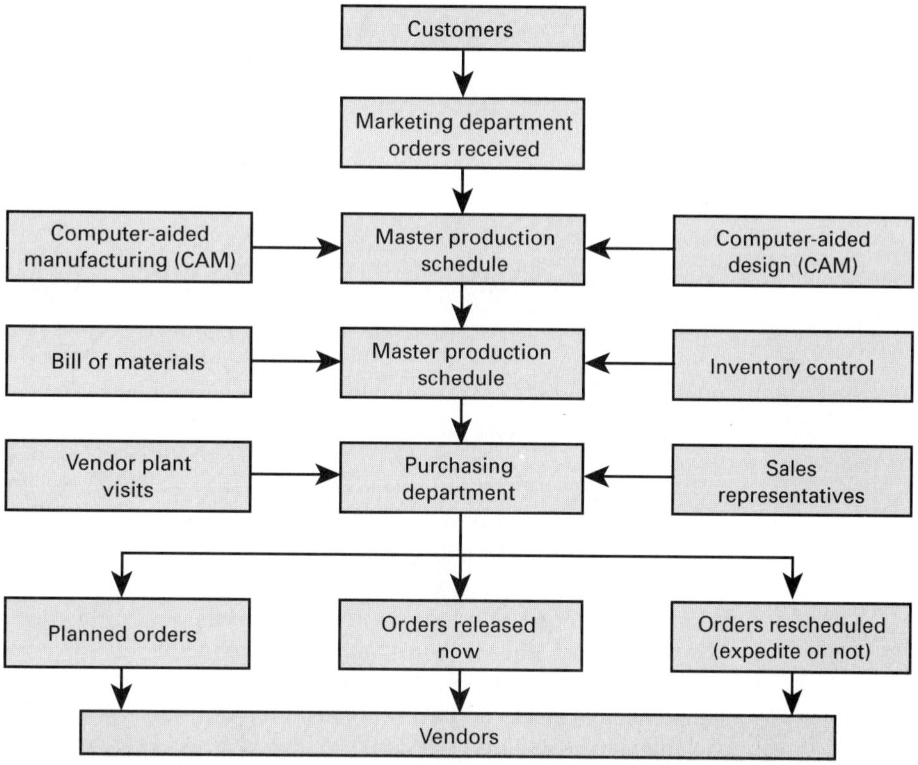

Tennant's reorganization, shown in Figure 5-3, is that procurement specialists have more time to negotiate with vendors, to work on cost reduction plans, and to consult with engineers on prototype products.[9]

To keep track of orders and the various supply sources available, many organizations have also begun using computers, some of which are directly linked to suppliers. Since irregular deliveries and defective parts furnished by suppliers can require numerous adjustments in a producer's MRP scheduling, these computerized systems are used to find and eliminate weak suppliers.[10]

In general, the effectiveness of MRP depends on the buyer notifying the supplier of material needs in advance of production schedules. Since irregular deliveries and defective parts furnished by suppliers can require numerous adjustments in a producer's MRP scheduling, suppliers who sell to organizations using MRP must work closely with customer firms to ensure that MRP systems are effective. The resultant benefits of MRP to both the supplier and customer, however, are controlled inventory levels, better management of production costs, timely deliveries, and an overall increase in efficiency and effectiveness of operations.[11]

MEETING THE MRP CHALLENGE WITH MRP II

With the advent of new software tools, marketers' detachment and their occasional hostility to manufacturing is changing fast. That's because the new technologies—once marketers learn the ropes—can be used to make companies become marketing driven rather than manufacturing oriented.

In recent years, with the increasing computerization of production scheduling and inventory control, the information networks of manufacturing databases have begun to extend into marketing offices. These systems are described as *integrated manufacturing systems* and include formerly independent departmental databases. It is no easy task, but the ultimate goal of the integrated database is to get the entire business enterprise operating as a team.

This concept is being embraced thanks to a relatively new yet controversial system that is catching on fast in companies across the country: *manufacturing resource planning* (MRP II).[12]

CENTRALIZED PURCHASING

In addition to MRP, there is a growing tendency toward *centralized purchasing.* Important differences in buying behavior occur between centralized and decentralized purchasing functions.[3] When purchasing is centralized, purchasing specialists concentrate their attention on selected items, developing extensive knowledge of supply and demand conditions. Thus, the specialists are more familiar with cost factors that affect the supplying industry, and they understand well how vendors within the industry operate. This specialized knowledge, when combined with the volume buying that centralized purchasing controls, increases the firm's buying strength and its supplier options.

Centralized purchasers also tend to place different priorities on selected buying criteria. In contrast to local units, where the emphasis is more on short-term cost efficiency and profit considerations, centralized units place more emphasis on long-term supply availability and supplier relationships. Further, influencers outside the purchasing unit appear to have more influence on purchasing decisions at the local level. Engineers and other technical personnel are inclined to be overly specific in their preferences regarding materials, component parts, and sources of supply. Less specialized, nontechnical local purchasing agents often lack the expertise and self-perceived status to challenge these preferences.[3]

FIGURE 5-3 Tennant Company's reorganization plan for materials management.

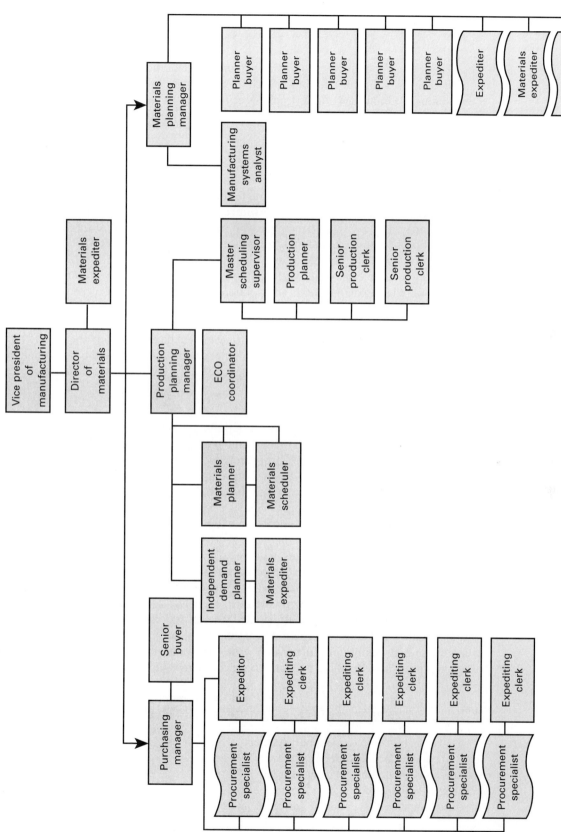

Source: Margaret Nelson, "MRP war-gaming via market simulation." *Business Marketing* 69 (September 1984):20-2. Reprinted by permission of *Business Marketing*. © Crain Communications, Inc.

BUYER TECHNOLOGY

The advent of computers has significantly improved the function of purchasing. Typical computer applications in purchasing include calculating economical order quantities, determining optimal lead times, tracking critical delivery schedules, and monitoring supplier performance indices. In fact, computers have been the primary factor in the implementation of MRP, JIT, and CE[13] (see Table 5-1).

While many significant advancements in computer applications of purchasing decisions remain for the future, computer systems are already employed in highly repetitive buying because of their ability to handle such tasks faster, cheaper, and more accurately than individual buyers. Although totally computerized handling of new task buying situations is unlikely in the near future, computerized data analysis allows purchasing managers more time to evaluate and negotiate with potential suppliers.[14] With the advent of the newest techniques, computers serve an even bigger role in the buyer-seller relationship than they did a few years ago.

Highly focused companies with sourcing operations that bear little resemblance to today's purchasing departments will dominate business in the next century.[15] Almost every aspect of the process of acquiring materials and services will have changed from what were and are considered the best practices of the 1990s. A new level of professionalism will involve experienced individuals who will be experts in planning and analyzing long-term product and organizational needs and in choosing the best available internal or external source for an item or service.

MARKETING IMPLICATIONS

MRP and centralized purchasing have a definite impact on business marketing programs. To remain compatible with the growing professionalism of purchasing managers who are more technical and financially oriented in their approach to buying, marketers must keep up to date with the business purchasing practices. Buyers are not only becoming more professional, but in many cases, the scope of their responsibility has broadened considerably. Sales people must possess the tools necessary to respond properly to the needs of business and be able to provide information on a broad range of functions and buying criteria.

Marketing to business firms will be even more difficult for "out" suppliers because of the close buyer-seller relationships that develop through MRP, JIT, CE, and partnering. To serve their customers better, "in" suppliers will eventually find it necessary to computer-link directly with the customer. The use of computer systems for MRP, JIT, CE, and partnering will also necessitate that suppliers constantly monitor product quality and delivery capability. Suppliers will not have the luxury of delivering a less- than-high-quality product if they wish to remain a long-term supplier. And as relevant as JIT systems have become, some companies violate the system in times of

TABLE 5-1 How Purchasing Uses Its Computers (percent of computerized departments)	
We have an on-line decision support system.	37.2
We do on-line purchase order processing.	56.5
We do batch processing of purchase orders.	56.5
We use computers for preparing status reports.	65.6
We use computers for special off-line problem-solving applications.	31.5

Source: "Computers begin to take off in purchasing departments," *Purchasing* (1985). Copyright © 1985, Cahners Publishing Company.

rising demand. "JIT does not allow for those inevitable problems, like a rail strike," according to an executive in a sports and fitness equipment manufacturer, thus giving the "out" suppliers a chance to be included.[16]

Individual Buying Motives

Both rational and emotional buying motives exist in business marketing. The organization's buying center personnel, individual buyers, or a buying committee want to satisfy the organization's needs, but they also want to satisfy their own needs in the process.

RATIONAL NEEDS

The overt, rational needs for the organization include all the "on the table" variables, such as the product's price, quality, service, that it meets production specifications, that delivery times are acceptable, and considerations of reciprocity.

Price   Price affects a firm's bottom line. It is a measure of value that can be registered in a *return on investment* (ROI) statement. Price is not as important as purchasing people would like to have the marketers believe. When a product is sold on price only, the subsequent quality and service could be suspect. Selling a product by emphasizing the product's quality and service and mitigating the product's price helps to develop trust, respect, and eventually a solid partnership.

Quality   Quality to the buyer means the right materials, design, fit with other parts, appearance, and consistency of quality. The highest quality can also be the cheapest means of manufacture: producing a first-time high-quality product reduces makeovers, returns, delays, needless inspections, customer dissatisfaction, and lost future orders. In a highly competitive global market, only high-quality products will survive in the long run. Buyers understand this competitive struggle and demand the highest quality, given the price. To be successful, JIT systems require that the highest quality product be supplied the first time if the seller is to have any chance of contract renewal.

Focusing on improved quality is valuable only if improvements are linked to enhanced customer satisfaction. Customer satisfaction is an overall evaluation of the supplier based on the purchase and the consumption experience over time. The customer's perception of quality makes the customer the ultimate judge of quality.[18] One study indicated that the following factors greatly affect a customer's perception of quality: (1) technological leadership—products are performance leaders; (2) the product or service provides competitive advantage—that is, it helps to improve the customer's time to market and is the seller is willing to work with us to meet schedules; (3) the seller is responsive to day-to-day issues—provides quick answers to design problems, listens to the customer's problems, and visits the customer's locations with teams to better understand their business; (4) offers distribution services—gives the customer a choice of buying direct or through distributors; (5) offers technical resources and expertise—provides competitive lead times and demonstrates systems solutions and comprehensive process controls; and (6) the seller is sensitive to operational concerns—notifies the customer of any design, material, or process changes and gives advance notice of new products.[17]

Product Service   Service includes training, repair, replacement if damaged in shipment, spare parts, information, installation of a new system, and cost reduction or value analysis, which is a study of how to maximize the cost-benefits in the purchase of machines, materials, and subassemblies. Some companies thrive on sales to the after-market, which involves goods and services sold after the major product has been sold. Partnering requires a lasting relationship to be successful and a set of good products (replacement products) and services provided after the initial sale of a product.

Customer Service   Engaging in improved customer service can greatly enhance a seller's competitive advantage. This type of service refers to customer-driven responses to meeting the customer's needs above and beyond the servicing of the product. This includes seller's systems be designed to be customer friendly; employees trained to be customer oriented; employees view business from the customer perspective; and employee service performance be used as a promotion criterion. In addition, customer research and feedback become an integral part of the seller's organization by including working closely with existing customers; encourage feedback from customers; seek long-term contacts with customers; and offer better service for important customers.[18]

Meeting Product Specifications   Meeting tolerances for individual product standards may vary by customer. For one customer a specific tolerance means a part that fits the customer's assembly operation. For another customer, tolerance may mean absolute perfection in manufacture and in appearance. Japanese companies specify the latter tolerance limits and many American companies have followed suit. No longer can "getting by" suffice; now perfection is demanded by most global customers.

Delivery Times   This presents the first or second most popular buyer's complaint. Missed promised product or service delivery times can mean lost time for the start of a new project, or a missed delivery time can represent a buyer's huge investment is idled and no returns are forthcoming. Both situations are serious and a seller's reputation may be injured to the extent that a new supplier may be sought by the buyer.

Reciprocity   A common practice today are marketers who quiz their purchasing departments to find vendors who will buy their products, will use mild pressure to these vendors to buy from them. The premise used is that if we buy from you, you must buy from us with a hidden motivator that if not, why should we buy from you. Although very subtle, a violation of this gentlemen's agreement could prove to be costly for the vendor.

EMOTIONAL NEEDS

Many buyers, purchasing agents, users, and decision-makers find it expedient to unload their heavy psychological burdens or achieve gratification of a variety of psychological needs in the purchase of a given product. These needs include basic psychological needs, perceived risks, status, rewards, and friendships.

Psychological Needs   Some people in the buying firm feel it necessary to unload the kinds of psychological burdens most often created by oppressive bosses, lower-than-desired pay, lack of prestige, and sometimes low self-esteem or self-concept. These depressed members of the buying center, or any other unit concerned with the purchase of a product, may seek recognition of their importance, power, prestige, and attention from a more receptive outside audience. The seller must sometimes be willing to listen to such tales of woe if he or she wants to form a lasting relationship such as partnering.

Perceived Risks   Nervous and uncertain buyers, deciders, influencers, users, and gatekeepers often falter when a sale is nearing completion. Questions such as "How much will the product cost in total terms?" "Can the company afford this much?" "Will I be reprimanded for making this decision?" Obviously, the last question is not verbalized by the buyer, but in many companies, justifying the purchase weighs heavily on the buyer who made the decision. This thought process could manifest itself in any comments such as: "Who made the decision to buy this ----?" A seller must build a strong case that encompasses any possible retorts the decider may face after the sale and delivery of the product.

Status and Reward   Although a product and/or services are purchased, to meet organizational, the needs of the buying committee, individuals and others needs also must be met. In this way, the buyers perceive what the purchase will mean to their future with the organization, their peer recognition, and how the purchase will make them look in the eyes of their superiors. The astute seller realizes the dual nature of the buying problem and can cater to any relevant buyers' needs.

Friendship   Many business relationships between buyers and sellers are built on a sincere sense of trust and respect. This relationship is fundamental for partnering and concurrent engineering that fosters friendships that may last for many years. Trust is an integral part of any marketing relationship, and much of the success enjoyed by sellers and buyers is based on this mutual trust and respect they have for each other.[19]

Joint Decision-Making

While methods of reaching buying decisions differ widely, even within the same firm, there appear to be underlying patterns of organizational structure and behavior that may establish similarities for analyzing organizational decision-making. Whereas recent evidence indicates that when supplier loyalty is high, modified or straight rebuy purchasing decisions are frequently made by individuals within the firm. Studies have shown that the number of organizational members involved in a buying decision depends on (1) the characteristics of the firm (e.g., organization orientation and size); (2) the type of purchasing situation (e.g., routine versus new task); (3) the perceived importance of the product (e.g., risk involved); and (4) the available resources for handling the purchase (e.g., degree of centralization).[20] Sheth[21] refers to these areas in his model (Figure 5-4) as company-specific factors (1, 4) and product-specific factors (2, 3).

Many models have been developed in attempting to explain **organizational buying behavior.**[22] The use of business buyer-behavior models gives those who wish to understand and affect business buying behavior a common and useful starting point. One of the most intuitively appealing of these models is the Sheth model of business buyer behavior. Although not all of its many considerations have yet been empirically substantiated, it offers insight into the factors that appear to influence organizational buying behavior within the organization.

The Sheth model focuses on the complex relationships involved in joint decision-making. While the model appears complicated, it is quite useful for examining organizational buying behavior from the perspective of (1) the conditions that precipitate joint decision-making; (2) the psychological world of the individuals involved; and (3) the inevitable conflict among those involved in the decision process, and resolution of this conflict.[26]

The decision-making process in foreign markets takes on a whole new world of a buying group, as governmental units play an important hand. Although few data are available, one study investigated the procurement process in Czechoslovakia for pol-

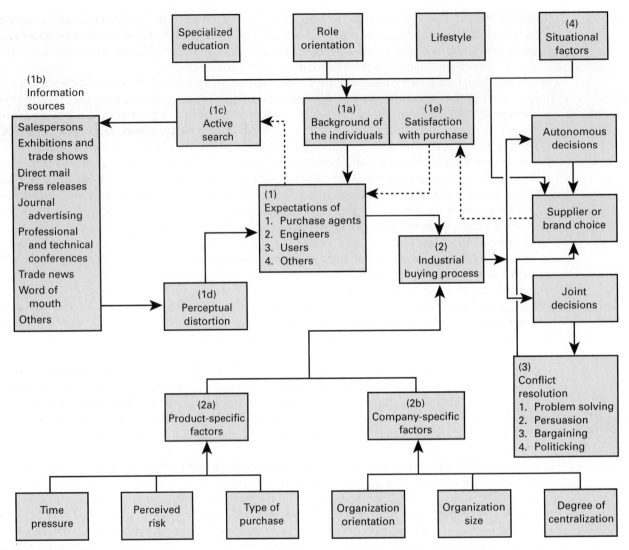

Source: Jadish N. Sheth, "A model of industrial buyer behavior," *Journal of Marketing* 37 (1973):50. Reprinted by permission of the American Marketing Association.

FIGURE 5-4 A model of industrial buyer behavior.

lution control equipment, before the country separated and became the Czech Republic and Slovakia. Governmental offices, particularly the Ministry of Finance, along with the Federal Committee for the Environment, were responsible for any legislation and coordination with business firms. However, the firms making the purchase made the investment subject to the ministries' advisement regarding technical solutions to environmental problems and the commercial aspects of foreign trade.[22] Some firms have tried to operate without governmental help and have had bad experiences, so it is likely that Czech firms will keep at least some ties to contacts with various governmental agencies, and a specific foreign trade organization that has a monopoly in the subindustry can activate the actual procurement process.

Regardless of the model involved, a more mundane approach can be taken. The engineers at Case Corporation asked a long-term customer to fly to Burlington, Iowa to assess the company's new loader-backhoe. The customer was initially skeptical, but after three grueling 11-hour days of pushing dirt around and comparing the new Case machine against that of its competitors, Caterpillar, Inc., and Deere & Co., the customer was overwhelmed. The customer's feedback was incorporated in the new design, and Case reaped big profits for the first time in years.[23]

CHARACTERISTICS OF THE FIRM

Findings from a recent study indicate that two characteristics of the firm appear to have a strong influence on the number of influencers involved in the purchasing decision: (1) the size of the firm as determined by the number of employees and (2) the firm's orientation (profit versus nonprofit).[24]

Table 5-2 indicates that as the size of the firm increases, the number of influencers involved in the purchase decision increases. This table also indicates that more influencers are involved when the organization is a nonprofit institution or governmental agency. Two variables may account for these findings: (1) functional areas tend to be more specialized in larger firms, and (2) nonprofit, governmental, and educational organizations, because of their high visibility, are more accountable to the public sector, and thus, more individuals may be involved as a safeguard and cross-check. Table 5-2 also indicates that as the purchasing situation moves from a modified rebuy to a new task, more influencers are involved.

Purchase Situation Influence   As Table 5-3 shows, the greater the importance and complexity of the purchase situation, the greater the vertical involvement, lateral involvement, and extensity. Thus, greater numbers of people will be involved in the buying center, and they will come from other divisions and departments as well as from other levels in the hierarchy.

TABLE 5-2 Average Number of Persons Influencing the Decision in a Modified Rebuy and New Task Purchasing Decision With the Firm's Characteristics as Parameters		
	Average Number of Persons Influencing Decisions	
Characteristics	*Modified Rebuy*	*New Task*
Number of Employees		
Less than 100	1.82	1.96
100–250	1.97	2.10
251–500	1.58	2.00
501–1000	1.85	2.63
1001–1500	3.16	2.75
Over 1500	2.60	2.81
Significance level	.0001	.165
Function of the Firm		
Manufacturing	1.90	2.20
Service for profit	1.86	2.40
Nonprofit, government, education	2.58	2.70
Significance level	.005	.165

Source: Adapted from Lowell E. Crow and Jay D. Lindquist, "Impact of organizational and buyer characteristics in the buyer center," *Industrial Marketing Management* 14 (1985):49-58. Reprinted by permission.

TABLE 5-3 Positive Relationships Between Situational/Organizational and Buying Center/Interaction Variables

	Organizational Structural Variables			*Purchase Situation Attributes*		
	Formalization (increased written communication)	*Centralization (control of purchasing)*	*Importance*	*Complexity (long time frame)*	*Novelty (from rebuy to modify rebuy)*	*Capital Good versus Service*
Vertical involvement				+		+
Lateral involvement	+		+	+	+	
Extensivity	+		+	+		+
Connectedness		+				

Source: Wesley J. Johnston and Thomas V. Bonoma, "The buying center: Structure and interaction patterns," *Journal of Marketing* 45 (1981):143-56. Reprinted by permission of the American Marketing Association.

Organizational Influence　　The more complex an organization is, as indicated by more written communications, the greater the lateral involvement and extensivity will be and the less the connectedness will be within the organization. As more written communications are required by a buying organization, more people are called on to help in the buying decision. However, since many of the communications are in written form (such as purchase orders), there is less face-to-face communication. On the other hand, when sign-off power for purchasing decisions is concentrated at corporate headquarters (as is often the case in formal organizational structures), the degree of connectedness between buying center members tends to be high. This connection is a result of the amount of interaction that must take place to see that everything is in order before the decision can be moved upward.

MARKETING IMPLICATIONS

The Czech and Case studies give the marketer important insights to assist in determining the size and interaction of buying center members. Two variables that have an impact on buying center size are the firm's characteristics and the type of purchasing situation the firm is in, neither of which is difficult to determine. Secondary data are available for determining organizational size and orientation, and salespeople are quite adept at discovering the type of purchasing task customer firms are facing.

Insight into the degree of vertical and lateral involvement, extensity, and connectedness (and how these patterns are affected by both the purchasing situation and organizational structure) is quite useful for developing a proactive communication strategy. Marketers who anticipate that various hierarchical levels will be involved in complex purchasing decisions can structure a sales force that embodies individuals who can relate to various hierarchical levels.

The greater the degree of lateral involvement, the greater the potential for diversity of viewpoints in the buying organization. Thus, the potential to influence the buying organization lies in communicating with different functional areas within the firm. As lateral involvement increases, the more important it is to have a broadly trained sales force with access to the expertise of the different functional specialists within the firm.

Extensity and connectedness affect the buyer's ability to process information. When the various people involved in a purchasing decision communicate directly, information is processed quickly and relatively accurately. However, in those purchasing situations, which are important and complex, it should be recognized that the buying center will be larger and less connected.

When there are several divisions in the buying firm and the purchasing department is centralized, it should be recognized that face-to-face communications in the buying center will tend to decrease. When a high degree of centralization exists, it may only be necessary to persuade the purchasing manager of the vendor's capabilities. When the purchasing manager's control is low, marketers will find it necessary to influence other members of the buying center, each with a unique perspective of the purchasing problem.

Psychological Factors Influencing Individual Decision-Making

Knowledge of the similarities and differences in the psychological worlds of individuals involved in the buying center, and how their behavior can affect the purchase decision, is critical in directing the firm's communication strategy. It is not unusual to find purchasing, engineering, manufacturing, and marketing personnel involved both individually and jointly at various phases in the purchasing decision process, particularly in a modified or new task purchasing situation. Because of the differences in their psychological makeups, expectations regarding the potential of alternative suppliers to satisfy a number of different purchasing criteria will substantially differ in any given purchasing task. Two significant factors, as indicated in Sheth's model,[25] appear to account for these differences: (1) role orientation and (2) information exposure.

DIFFERENCES IN ROLE ORIENTATION

Because of different areas of functional responsibility, each individual has a different perception of his or her role in the decision process. Thus, he or she tends to view the importance of the various buying criteria differently. Purchasing agents, for instance, look for price advantage and economy in shipping; engineers look for quality and pretesting.

Because of the fact that organizations typically reward individuals for achieving their respective departmental goals, they will also have experienced different levels of satisfaction with past suppliers. Purchasing agents, for example, are rewarded for economic achievement, meaning lowest price or greatest value; engineers for product performance, meaning product validity and reliability. The result is that the respective objectives and reward criteria of individuals may conflict when applied to selection of a supplier.

DIFFERENCES IN INFORMATION EXPOSURE

Expectations, and thus objectives, are further influenced by the type and source of information exposure. Purchasing agents, because of their position within the organization, are not only exposed to greater amounts of commercial sources of information but also are normally assigned the task of actively searching for information. Personnel in the engineering and production departments, however, typically have a disproportionately smaller amount of information. What information is obtained is often gathered primarily through trade reports, professional meetings, and word of mouth.

Perhaps because of individual educational pursuits and lifestyles, information is also subject to the individual's cognitive process of selective distortion and retention:

the tendency to systematically select, change, and retain information so that it conforms to prior knowledge, expectations, or needs. Therefore, given the different goals and values of individuals, the same information will be interpreted differently, leading to further differences in expectations and objectives.

PERCEIVED RISK IN THE VENDOR SELECTION PROCESS

Business purchasing decisions often involve an element of functional risk, such as uncertainty with respect to product or supplier performance, or psychological risk, such as negative reactions from other organizational members. The greater the uncertainty in a buying situation and the greater the adverse consequences associated with making the wrong choice, the greater the **perceived risk** in the purchasing decision.[26] The different types of perceived personal risk associated with making buying decisions and how purchasing agents rank them are shown in Table 5-4.[27]

When uncertainty exists in any given purchasing decision, research indicates that decision-makers tend to reduce the level of risk by remaining loyal to existing suppliers who represent a known entity. Decision-makers also tend to adopt one or more of the following strategies in an attempt to minimize or avoid the perceived risk[29]:

1. Reduce uncertainty—uncertainty may be reduced by gathering additional information, such as consulting with other influencers or visiting potential suppliers' plants.

2. Play the odds—through sophisticated, quantitative methods of vendor analysis and selection, often involving expected value analysis, which considers both the probability of and magnitude of the consequence, the business buyer can "play the odds" by selecting the supplier with the most favorable expected value.

3. Spread the risk—the consequences of choosing the wrong supplier can also be reduced through multiple sourcing, thus enabling buyers to choose the proportion of risk to be assumed by allocating it among different suppliers.

TABLE 5-4   Magnitude of Various Components of Perceived Personal Risk

Component	Average Risk*	Rank
You will feel personal dissatisfaction	6.32	1
Your relations with the users of the purchased product will be strained	5.13	2
The status of the purchasing department will decrease	3.59	3
Your next performance review will be less favorable	3.41	4
You will have less chance for promotion	2.92	5
Your next raise will be smaller	2.71	6
You will lose status among your peers	2.68	7
You will lose your job	2.25	8
Your personal popularity will diminish	1.78	9

*Where risk is computed as the product of seriousness (1 = annoying but not serious; 2 = somewhat serious; 3 = very serious) and probability (1 = not probable; 2 = somewhat probable; 3 = very probable).

Source: Jon M. Hawes and Scott H. Barnhouse, "How purchasing agents handle personal risk," *Industrial Marketing Management* 16 (1987):287-92. Copyright © 1987 by Elsevier Science Publishing Co., Inc. Reprinted by permission.

A recent study, however, indicates that strategies for handling risk may be related to the way in which decision-makers approach the situation.[29] In attempting to reduce uncertainty, buyers may adopt decision-making strategies such as (1) using performance measures (such as examining past historical data of current suppliers, looking for guaranteed performance levels, or using break-even criteria), (2) using expected value analysis, and (3) choosing between certainty and risk.

According to the findings, when historical data alone are utilized, or buyers prefer certainty to risk, buyers tend to split their orders between suppliers, thus avoiding or minimizing the uncertainties involved in the purchasing decision. However, when suppliers are willing to guarantee performance, reducing the element of risk considerably, buyers resort to this "split decision" less often.

When **break-even analysis** or expected **value analysis** is employed, buyers are more willing to accept the elements of uncertainty. The assumption for this phenomenon, under the use of break-even criteria is that decision-makers may be expected value maximizers. However, in the case of expected value analysis, buyers appear to be willing to accept the best course of action given the possible consequences—choosing those suppliers that have the most favorable expected value.

Another time-worn way of reducing buying risks is to have more than one supplier per item. A study was conducted to determine whether the reduction of uncertainty in the purchase decision provides the motivation for choosing multiple and/or single sourcing strategies. A random sampling of 80 purchasing managers from electronics firms reviewed the buying situations, that is, need uncertainty, market uncertainty, and transaction uncertainty. The results indicated that there is no relationship between any type of uncertainty and a preferred sourcing strategy. Thus, knowledge about a purchaser's preferences for single or multiple sources would benefit marketers in their segmentation and target selection process.[30]

MARKETING IMPLICATIONS

The significance of these findings relate more to "out" suppliers than to "in" suppliers. In view of the fact that supplier loyalty represents a formidable obstacle for "out" suppliers, the most effective strategic approach for "out" suppliers is to offer performance guarantees as part of their proposals. Out suppliers might also want to consider encouraging split procurement, offering their services as a backup or secondary supplier, and, whenever an opportunity exists to service a portion of a new account, be willing to accept it when submitting a proposal.

In developing marketing strategy, however, both in and out suppliers should be aware of buyers' decision strategies in reducing uncertainty and how these strategies affect supplier choice. Business salespeople should, for instance, emphasize guarantees when applicable or the expected value considerations of their offer.

Conflict and Resolution in Joint Decision-Making

Whenever two or more individuals have to reach an agreement concerning issues such as product specifications, information credibility, vendor capabilities, multiple sourcing, contract terms, or order routines, the potential for conflict exists.[31] The potential for conflict emanates from differences in expectations regarding suppliers, differences in the evaluative criteria employed, differences in buying objectives, and differences in the decision-making styles of the individuals involved.[25] Whether conflict is good or bad depends on the type of conflict that emerges and how it is resolved. Conflict that supports the goals of the organization and improves the firm's performance rather than hinders it is good. What is important from the marketer's perspective is how conflict is resolved.

When conflict is resolved through cooperation and the search for a mutually beneficial solution, joint decision-making tends to be rational. However, when conflict is resolved through bargaining or politicking, joint decision-making tends to be based on irrational criteria.

CONFLICT-RESOLUTION STRATEGIES

As shown in Figure 5-5, when conflict arises, individuals may resort to several different types of conflict-resolving strategies[32]:

1. Competing—"Let's do it my way!": The desire to win one's own concerns at the other party's expense—the desire to dominate, to yield no quarter, to envision the interaction as a win-lose power struggle; assertive, uncooperative behaviors.

2. Accommodating—"I see your point of view.": The desire to satisfy the other's concerns without attending to one's own concerns—peaceful coexistence, perhaps entertaining long-term motives; unassertive, cooperative behaviors.

3. Collaborating—"Maybe we can work this one out.": The desire to fully satisfy the concerns of both parties—sharing responsibility, problem-solving, in-depth exploration of issues, reaching a mutually beneficial agreement; assertive, cooperative behaviors.

4. Avoiding—"Better let the situation cool down before we act.": Exerting an attitude of indifference to the concerns of either party, not immediately addressing the conflict—diplomatically sidestepping an issue, postponing an issue until a more opportune time, or withdrawal from a threatening situation; unassertive, uncooperative behaviors.

5. Compromising—"Let's split the difference!": The desire to reach an expedient, mutually acceptable agreement that is somewhere short of total satisfaction for either party—exchanging concessions or seeking a middle-ground solution; intermediate in both assertive and cooperative behaviors.

Perhaps the most prevalent, yet ignored, form of conflict resolution found among buying center members is **coalition formation.**[31, 33] When coalition is used to resolve conflict,

FIGURE 5-5 Resolution strategies.

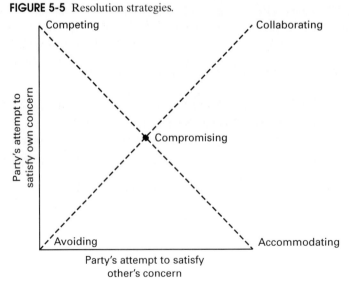

Source: Ralph L. Day, Ronald E. Michaels, and Barbara C. Purdue, "How buyers handle conflicts," *Industrial Marketing Management* 17 (1988):153-69. Copyright © 1988 by Elsevier Science Publishing Co., Inc. Reprinted by permission.

individuals within the formation attempt to cooperate with specific other group members to enhance their competitive position with respect to the entire group. Since a coalition tends to enhance the individuals' influence and represents a positive channel for airing and resolving conflict, it may be the most rational approach to conflict resolution.

The type of **conflict-resolution strategy** that individuals use, however, depends on several mediating variables, such as the characteristics of the purchase situation, the size of the buying center, the network of communication links and the individuals base of power in the organizational buying decision.[31]

For example, two important reasons for utilizing **coalition** behavior are (1) the rewards available through various coalitional alternatives and (2) the resource/power positions of group members.[40] It is not unusual for individual objectives and reward criteria to be in conflict when applied to group decision-making because of the differences in expectations of the individuals involved. *Coalition formation* is one way of neutralizing conflict (that is, joining with other individuals who have the same objectives and reward systems to strengthen one's position in the conflict situation). Coalition formation is also a means of compensating for power inequalities among the participants and enhancing each individual's influence on the decision. When alliances form between weaker group members, more strength results to bargain for control of the group decision.

POWER IN CONFLICT RESOLUTION

It is becoming increasingly important for marketers to understand and identify the source of power held or sought by key decision-makers in customer firms.[34] The use of power in resolving conflict is common in business buying.[35] Unfortunately, power does not always correlate with organizational rank or the functional area of an individual. Buying centers do, however, tend to display one dominant power base. It may be a combined power base (for instance, purchasing and marketing, or engineering and production)[31] or an individual with little formal power who is able to stop or hinder a purchase by virtue of his or her attributed power.[34] As Table 5-5 indicates, common bases of power include **reward, coercive, legitimate, personality,** and **expertise power.**[34, 36]

Reward Versus Coercive Power   The ability to influence a purchasing decision by granting monetary, social, political, or psychological benefits refers to reward power. The opposite of reward power is coercive power. Coercive power depends on fear of the ramifications which could result from noncompliance and the coercer's ability and discretion to impose the penalty. Threats are not the same as having the power to impose them.

Legitimate Power   The power to reward or coerce is closely related to an individual's formal position within the organizational structure. Legitimate power grants

TABLE 5-5   Sources of Power in Conflict Resolution

Reward power	The ability to influence a decision by granting monetary, social, political, or psychological benefits
Coercive power	The ability to impose monetary or psychological punishment
Legitimate power	Formal authority or position within the organizational structure
Personality power	The ability to inspire and convince others because of one's own physical appearance or attitude, wit, charm, or status
Expertise power	The possession, access to, or even the withholding of information

Source: French, J.R., and Raven, B.H. 1959. The bases of social power. In Cartwright, D., ed. *Studies of Social Power.* Ann Arbor: University of Michigan Press, pp. 150-67.

one the right to reward or punish (coerce) to carry out organizational tasks or functions. When authority is granted to prescribe behavior, both reward and punishment are used to bring about the desired behavior. Such power is exercised in the superior/subordinate relationship and in the control of resources laterally between departments and divisions: for example, the computer department manager may elect to make additional computer time available to the marketing department if certain concessions are agreed on.

Expert Power   In the area of organizational buying behavior, expert power has been found to be a more important source of influence over other buying center members than legitimate power.[33] Purchasing behavior, particularly in a new task situation, has a relatively high element of risk. Uncertainty may exist in the need itself, the technical aspects of the product, in market availability, whether funds are available, or with respect to delivery dates or terms of the sale.[37] An important source of credible information for reducing the uncertainty is the expertise of another buying center member. Furthermore, when the purchasing decision cuts across functional areas, as in the case of a computer purchase, hierarchical lines of authority over the purchase tend to become diffused.

IDENTIFYING POWER BASES

In a small firm, it is not unusual to find a combination of several power bases, such as organizational authority and personality power, being enjoyed by a single member of a buying center. On the other hand, in a large diverse firm, purchasing decisions may be subject to influence by a number of individuals relying on various sources of power. Effective marketing strategy rests on the ability to determine which individuals hold and use power to influence various decisions, or if coalitions of power exist.[31]

The power obtained through one's organizational position and through the ability to reward and punish is frequently discernible in a simple organization chart. There are of course other rewards and punishments that are given by peers and subordinates that are not so easily discernible, such as a secretary who bars a salesperson's visit to a purchasing manager or another member of the buying center because of a real or imagined discourteous treatment.

A marketing person contacting a new organization might begin with the assumption that the organizational hierarchy appropriately depicts power bases, but that person should be aware of other buying center members who seem to have unexplained influence. Those buying center members with expertise are often easily discernible because of their questions, apparent comprehension, or job function.

MARKETING IMPLICATIONS

The more detailed the salesperson's understanding of how power is distributed within the buying center and the resulting interactions (how conflict is resolved), the better his or her ability to communicate effectively with buying center members. For example, when individuals within the buying center are politicking, it is possible for a salesperson to find herself in the middle of opposing interests. An awareness of the situation may enable the salesperson to decide which political camp will best serve the company's interest and thus develop a strategy that may bridge the gap between the opposing parties.

It is wise to acknowledge those who hold power bases and give them the attention and respect consistent with their power. In this regard, the amount of time spent with various buying center members should be related to their ability to influence decisions. Spending an undue amount of time and effort to persuade an ineffective buying center member, who is consistently overruled, can work to the disadvantage of a vendor.

The Buying Committee

So far, much of our discussion has focused on the **buying center.** A more formalized buying center, the buying committee, is used extensively in the resellers' market and by many business organizations, particularly when purchasing is centralized. In the resellers' market, organizations such as food chain retailers form buying committees that meet on a regular basis to decide on new product purchases. In the institutional side of the business market, institutions such as universities and hospitals often appoint temporary buying committees to make joint decisions regarding which products can best satisfy organizational needs. And, in the commercial side of the business market, representatives from engineering, production, and accounting often establish formal buying committees to review and approve major purchases. Committee buying is also prevalent in the government side of the business market.

In the typical **buying committee,** one or two individuals set the direction while "rubber stamp" decision-makers go along. Determining who these direction setters are and understanding their motives is the key in selling to buying committees.[38]

✔ Committee buying generally involves a lengthy selling process during which the vendor meets much more frequently with individuals on the buying committee than with the entire committee. While the salesperson must provide product-related information to all accessible committee members, the real selling effort needs to be targeted to those one or two individuals who are most influential on the committee. Identifying those individuals and determining the structure of the decision-making unit depends on an analysis of the seller's past experience with the buying firm with respect to product purchases, technical expertise of committee members, individual personalities and objectives, and organizational structure.[38]

Buyer-seller interpersonal relationships are strongly affected by the newer technology; techniques and practices in modern companies such as concurrent engineering; horizontal information flows; corporate networking; organizational intelligence; and technology fusion. These newer phenomena simply make the buying center and the supplier relationships more complex and necessitate a greater integration between buyer and seller where innovations must be shared on a long-term basis. This integration is particularly true in Japanese firms, which have the made the transition from imitator status to world-class innovator status in the 1990s.[39]

Supplier Choice and Evaluation

Regardless of the diversity of expectations and objectives, buyers seek to find the best possible source of supply for their respective needs. In repetitive purchasing situations, such as a straight or modified rebuy where buyers are familiar with current suppliers and the purchase involves a standardized product, it may be a simple matter of choosing a supplier from the list of sources already identified and evaluated.[40] A supplier may even be recommended for selection on the basis of reciprocity considerations. For example, in one study it was noted that buyers sometimes want to favor a specific vendor in return for a favor.[41]

In a new task situation, or when the purchase involves a substantial expenditure or the quality of the needed product is critical, the selection may involve an extensive search to find the one qualified supplier. When no current source of supply exists, it may even require that the firm work with many suppliers to develop the needed product.

The development of a new source can take months, even years. In some cases, the buying organization may have to help a supplier develop the necessary level of needed performance by providing financing for equipment, by assisting in developing job scheduling and quality control techniques, or by participating in the development of bid preparations and cost accounting procedures.[42] Such a situation is prevalent under partnering relationships.

SUPPLIER CHOICE AND QUALIFYING PROCESS

How buyers choose and qualify suppliers depends on the type of buying situation and the importance of the purchase in terms of complexity and dollar value. Purchasing may even evaluate the supplying firm's position in the industry, its progressiveness, its interest in the firm's order, and its cooperative attitude.[40] Factors important to buyers in the supplier selection process are shown in Table 5-6.

Qualifying factors, however, may limit buyers' choice of suppliers. For instance, with the increasing cost of transportation, buyers may limit their choice to local suppliers, or in the case of dependency on uninterrupted shipments, the suppliers' capacity and capability may become a deciding factor in supplier choice.[41]

EVALUATING SUPPLIER PERFORMANCE

Qualification of suppliers does not end with the purchase. The real test of a supplier is the ability to perform effectively and consistently over time. This performance record is the deciding factor as to whether the supplier will continue as the "in" supplier or be replaced. Buyers use both objective and subjective evaluations to rate suppliers' performance. Supplier evaluation, however, generally involves four basic considerations: quality, service, delivery, and price. The most common methods used to evaluate suppliers are (1) the categorical method, (2) the weighted-point method, and (3) the cost-ratio method.

The Categorical Method   The least precise of the three methods is the categorical method, because supplier evaluation is based on the experience and opinions of the user departments. Thus, the evaluation is subjective rather than objective. A list of significant performance factors is drawn up by purchasing, and users merely assign a grade

---

TABLE 5-6   Ten Criteria Viewed as Most Appropriate in Measuring a Buyer's Performance

1. Making purchases that arrive on time
2. Making purchases that pass incoming Quality Assurance inspection
3. Meeting target costs
4. Knowledge of commodities in the buyer's area of responsibility
5. Ability to control purchase order cycle time
6. Ability to cultivate qualified suppliers
7. Ability to perform work with a minimum of errors
8. Ability to determine the bottom price a supplier will take
9. Amount of complexity of commodities in buyer's responsibility
10. Providing timely responses to inquiries from suppliers and internal customers

Source: Thomas E. Hendrick and William Ruch, "Determining performance appraisal criteria for buyers," *Journal of Purchasing and Materials Management* 24 (1988) 18-24.

of plus, minus, or neutral to each factor. At regularly scheduled meetings (usually monthly), the ratings are discussed, and those suppliers with overall high, low, or neutral ratings are notified.

While the categorical method is nonquantitative, it is an inexpensive way for the buyer to keep records of supplier performance. The main disadvantage to the vendor, however, is that it relies heavily on the memory and opinion of the different evaluators and is subject to their perceptual biases.

The Weighted-Point Method   Under the weighted-point method, the organization assigns weights to the different evaluation criteria. While any number of evaluative factors may be included, the assigning of weights to each factor enables the buyer to develop a composite performance index that can be quantitatively used to compare suppliers.

For example, if quality and delivery are the first and second most important performance factors, with frequency of cost-reducing suggestions and price being third and fourth in importance, then quality might be given a weight of 40, delivery 30, cost-reducing suggestions 20, and price 10. A performance score can then be developed for each factor, and the factor scores of each supplier can be totaled for comparative analysis of supplier performance. Buyers can also assign acceptable and unacceptable ranges to apply to the composite ratings of competing suppliers (such as excellent = 85 or above, acceptable = 84 to 75, unacceptable = 74 and below). An example of a composite rating for one supplier is shown in Table 5-7.

The advantage of the weighted-point method of supplier evaluation to the buyer is that a number of evaluative criteria can be proportioned to correspond with the values of the firm. It also forces the buyer to define the key attributes of a supplier and objectively evaluate them, thus minimizing much of the subjective evaluation that occurs under the categorical method.

The regular notification of suppliers concerning their respective performance assists in isolating supplier problems, stimulates improved supplier performance, and, most important, strengthens the buyer-seller relationship.

The Cost-Ratio Method   The cost-ratio method, based on the use of cost analysis in evaluating suppliers, has become increasingly important in the way purchasing managers evaluate suppliers.[43] Under this method, all identifiable purchasing costs are related to the value of products received. When the ratio of costs to products is high, the supplier's rating is low; when the ratio is low, the supplier's rating is high. While the choice of costs depends on the products involved, quality, delivery, service, and price are the most commonly used categories.

TABLE 5-7   **Weighted-Point Method of Supplier Evaluation**

Factor	Weight	Actual Performance	Performance Score
Quality	40	90% acceptable	$40 \times .9 = 36$
Delivery	30	90% on schedule	$30 \times .9 = 27$
Cost-reducing suggestions	20	% of total received = 60	$20 \times .6 = 12$
Price	10	125% of lowest price $100/125 = .8$	$10 \times .8 = 8$
		Total composite performance score = 83	

Source: Adapted from Gary J. Zenz, *Purchasing and the Management of Materials.* (New York: John Wiley & Sons, Inc., 1981) p. 140. Copyright © 1981. Reprinted by permission.

	TABLE 5-8 Summary of Suppliers' Cost Comparisons					
Supplier	Quality/ Cost Ratio (%)	Delivery/ Cost Ratio (%)	Service/ Cost Ratio (%)	Total Cost Penalty (%)	Quoted Price per Unit ($)	Net Adjusted Price per Unit ($)
A	2	1	−4	−1	95.50	94.55
B	2	3	+2	+7	95.00	101.65
C	2	1	+1	+4	94.75	98.54
D	1	1	−1	+1	95.25	96.20

Source: Adapted from Gary J. Zenz, *Purchasing and the Management of Materials* (New York: John Wiley & Sons, Inc., 1981), p. 140. Copyright © 1981. Reprinted with permission.

From the buyer's perspective, costs associated with quality include such factors as visits to the vendor's plant, evaluation of samples, inspection of incoming shipments, and the costs associated with defective products (for example, unusual inspection procedures, rejected parts, and manufacturing time lost due to defective parts). Thus, when cost-ratio methods of supplier evaluation are used, not only can purchasing managers rationalize lowest total cost suppliers, they can also measure nonperformance costs.[57]

To arrive at a cost/quality ratio, the vendor's quality cost is totaled and equated to the value of goods received. For instance, if the buyer's quality costs were $8,000, and the value of the purchase $800,000, the cost/quality ratio would be 0.01 or 1 percent.

Cost ratios are also computed for costs associated with delivery, such as the cost of paperwork involved in expediting the order, telephone follow-ups, factory downtime and rescheduling because of delayed shipments, and emergency transportation. However, the intangible costs of supplier service capability such as financial stability, geographical location, innovativeness, and flexibility in providing short lead time, are difficult to measure and evaluate but often considered necessary to the evaluation. Intangible costs are measured by assigning relative weights to each factor considered important by the firm. Once costs have been computed, they are combined with the supplier's quoted prices to determine the "net adjusted price."

A summary of cost comparisons for four suppliers is shown in Table 5-8. As you can see, under this method of supplier evaluation, the buying organization assigns a minus (−) weight for favorable service and a plus (+) for unfavorable service. In this example, supplier B had a bid price of $95.00, but a total cost penalty of +7 percent (2 + 3 + 2 = 7). Thus, the adjusted net cost to the buyer was $101.65. The firm will select the supplier with the most economical total offer that fulfills other salient criteria considered important to the firm such as company image and supplier reputation and attitude, rather than the supplier with the lowest bid—supplier A in this example.

MARKETERS CAN ALSO DEVELOP SUPPLIER RATING SYSTEMS

Business marketers must be aware of the criteria that buyers employ in evaluating their offerings. Since buying organizations have varying objectives, requirements, and structures, the evaluation criteria used will differ from firm to firm. Each buying organization will have product and service needs that are unique to its operation. The systematic evaluation of suppliers by buyers, however, offers the marketer unique opportunities. By developing a rating system based on customer criteria, a similar system can be used by the selling firm to[44]:

1. Promote and enhance the *value* of the company's product and services
2. Provide *special control* over items that customers consider critical to their operation
3. Substantiate *performance* in response to customer requests
4. Improve *efficiency* of internal planning and control
5. Supply *hard data* in support of contract negotiations

Benefits to the marketer include more effective buyer-seller communications, better customer services, and thus enhanced buyer-supplier relationships. As buyers increase their use of the computer, and purchasing becomes more expert and centralized, the performance of suppliers will be subject to greater quantitative and qualitative scrutiny. Therefore, business marketers must view their product offering from the perspective of the buying organization. The use of a self-evaluation based on customer needs, is one way of ensuring this view.

Looking Back

Business marketers must thoroughly understand the influence of business purchasing practices on organizational buying behavior. The power and status of purchasing has been enhanced by such factors as material requirements planning, JIT purchasing, CE, partnering, centralized buying, and advanced quantitative techniques brought about by increased computer technology. Where the purchasing function is centralized, buyers tend to become specialists in repetitive buying situations, are long-term rather than short-term oriented, and have more influence on the purchasing decision than those at decentralized locations.

Business purchase decisions are often the outcome of interactions that take place between various members of the buying center. Thus, it is important for marketers to understand the interaction, the leadership patterns, and the formal and informal network of communication among buying center members. The number of organizational members involved in the buying center depends on the characteristics of the firm, the type of purchasing situation, the perceived importance of the product, and the resources available for handling the purchase.

Group decision-making is affected by the different personalities, experiences, organizational functions, and perceptions of the individuals involved. In joint decision-making, the potential for conflict is always present because of the differences in goals and expectations among organizational members. When conflict occurs, individuals resort to one of several means of resolving it, depending on their respective sources of power.

After applying a wide range of criteria, both subjective and objective, to the choice of a supplier, firms usually evaluate and monitor supplier performance through the use of formal rating systems. These systems center on supplier attributes that are important to the firm such as quality, service, delivery, and price. Vendor rating systems can range from the easily administered categorical plan to the more complex cost-ratio method.

Questions for Discussion

1. Is the combination of purchasing, material flow, and production control into one functional department a logical, evolutionary change or simply "empire building" by or for the purchasing manager? Justify your opinion.
2. The advantages of a JIT purchasing system to a large-scale, continuous-flow manufacturing operation are fairly obvious. However, would this system have any advantages for a smaller-scale, discontinuous job-order type of operation?

3. From a marketer's perspective, what are the advantages and disadvantages of dealing with a modern, centralized purchasing function compared with a decentralized department of the 1960s? From the same perspective, what are the advantages and disadvantages of working with the concurrent engineering concept? Would partnering make it any easier for the marketer?

4. Suppose that you were asked to compare the impact of social classes and reference groups on consumer buying with vertical and lateral involvement in the business buying process. Is there any logical comparison? If so, describe it.

5. The buying committee of the Logan Corporation is made up of a chief engineer who wants technical innovation regardless of price, a purchasing agent committed to driving component costs down, and a manufacturing manager who insists on maintaining the status quo so manufacturing costs can be stabilized. How can a seller develop a strategy to handle these contradictory objectives when no type of partnering system is used, but where many suppliers are called in to bid on a proposal?

6. "In selling to a committee, it is definitely more effective to make an initial presentation to the group as a whole and then handle objections and problems in separate, individual sessions." Agree or disagree with this statement and explain why.

7. Consider a situation in which three different members of Sunheath Chemicals are involved in a purchasing decision for a computer. The scientist wants a service that generates a particular output form; the manager wants a service emphasizing low cost and speed of information recovery; and the librarian wants a service in which his department plays a role. Discuss how sources and bases of power might have an impact on the situation. Considering the risk involved in such a purchase, what types of strategies might these decision-makers employ?

8. If a selling firm wants to encourage an evaluation visit by a potential customer, what steps can it take beforehand to increase the probability that the visit will be made, and what actions during the visit will increase the likelihood of a fair and objective evaluation?

9. Given a choice, which evaluation method would you prefer that your customers employ—categorical, weighted-point, or cost-ratio? Why?

Endnotes

1. Frederick E. Webster, Jr., and Yoram Wind, 1972. *Organizational Buying Behavior.* (Englewood Cliffs, N.J.: Prentice-Hall, Inc., 1972), pp. 26-37.

2. Earl Naumann, Douglas J. Lincoln, and Robert D. McWilliams, "The purchase of components: Functional areas of influence," *Industrial Marketing Management* 13 (1984):113-22.

3. E. Raymond Corey, *The Organizational Context of Industrial Buying Behavior.* (Cambridge, Mass.: Marketing Science Institute, 1978), p. 34.

4. Donald W. Jackson, Jr., Janet E. Keith, and Richard K. Burdick, "Purchasing agent's perceptions of industrial buying center influence: A situational approach," *Journal of Marketing* 48 (1984):75-83.

5. Robert D. Franceschini, "Becoming a top purchasing pro starts with commitment," *Purchasing* 15 (1986):39.

6. Ronald E. Michaels, Ralph L. Day, and Erich A. Joachimsthaler, "Role stress among industrial buyers: An integrated model," *Journal of Marketing* 51 (1987):28-45.

7. Robert R. Reck and Brian G. Long, "Purchasing: A competitive weapon," *Journal of Purchasing and Materials Management* Fall 24 (1988):2-8.

8. See Upah, Gregory D., and Bird, Monroe M. 1980. Changes in industrial buying: Implications for industrial marketers. *Industrial Marketing Management* 9:117-21; Gary J. Zenz, *Purchasing and the Management of Materials,* 5th ed. (New York: John Wiley & Sons, Inc., 1981), pp. 6-7; and Mayer, Wolfgang U., "Situational variables and industrial buying," *Journal of Purchasing and Materials Management* 19 (Winter 1983) 21-26.

9. Margaret Nelson, "MRP war-gaming via market simulation," *Business Marketing* 69 (September 1984):20-2.

10. See John C. Fisk, "MRP: A tool for product and sales management," *Industrial Marketing Management* 7 (1978):32-6; and Joseph R. Biggs, Donald C. Bopp, Jr., and William M. Champion, "Material requirements planning and purchasing: A case study," *Journal of Purchasing and Materials Management* 20 (Spring 1984):15-22.

11. See Gary J. Zenz, *Purchasing and the Management of Materials*, 5th ed. (New York: John Wiley & Sons, Inc.1981); and Gregory D. Upah and Monroe M. Bird, "Changes in industrial buying: Implications for industrial marketers," *Industrial Marketing Management* 9 (1980):117-21.

12. John Couretas, "The challenge to marketing of integrated manufacturing databases," *Business Marketing* (March 1985), pp. 10, 51.

13. Gary J. Zenz, *Purchasing and the Management of Materials*, 5th ed. (New York: John Wiley & Sons, Inc., 1981), p. 372.

14. David T. Wilson and H. Lee Mathews, Impact of management information systems upon purchasing. *Journal Of Purchasing* 7 (1971):48-56.

15. James B. Morgan, "Purchasing 2000: Spell the function with an S for supply," *Purchasing* 110 (1991):48-9+.

16. "Just-in-time inventories fade in appeal as the recovery leads to rising demand," *The Wall Street Journal* (October 25, 1994), p. A2+.

17. William J.Qualls and José Antonio Rosa, "Assessing industrial buyer's perceptions of quality and their effects on satisfaction," *Industrial Marketing Management* 24 (1995):359-68.

18. William G. Donaldson, "Manufacturers need to show greater commitment to customer service," *Industrial Marketing Management* 24 (1995):421-30.

19. Robert M. Morgan and Shelby D. Hunt, "The commitment-trust theory of relationship marketing," *Journal of Marketing* 58 (1994):20-38.

20. W. E. Patton III, Christopher P. Pluto, and Ronald H. King, "Which buying decisions are made by individuals and not by groups?" *Industrial Marketing Management* 15 (1986):129-38.

21. Jagdish N. Sheth, "Research in industrial buying behavior—today's needs, tomorrow's seeds," Marketing News 13 (1980):14; and Robert W. Hass, *Industrial Marketing Management*, 2nd ed. (Boston: Kent Publishing Co., 1982), pp. 77-84.

22. Johan Roos, Ellen Veie, and Lawrence S. Welch, "A case study of equipment purchasing in Czechoslovakia," *Industrial Marketing Management* 21 (1992):257-63.

23. "Case digs out from way under," *Business Week* (August 14, 1995), pp. 62-63.

24. Lowell F. Crow, and Jay D. Lindquist, "Impact of organizational and buyer characteristics on the buying center," *Industrial Marketing Management* 14 (1985):49-58.

25. Jagdish N. Sheth, "A model of industrial buyer behavior," *Journal of Marketing* 37 (October 1973):50-56.

26. Raymond A. Bauer, "Consumer behavior as risk taking." In R.L. Hancock, ed. *Dynamic Marketing for a Changing World.* (Chicago: American Marketing Association, 1960), pp. 389-400.

27. Jon M. Hawes and Scott H. Barnhouse, "How purchasing agents handle personal risk," *Industrial Marketing Management* 16 (1987):287-93.

28. T.W. Sweeney, H.L. Mathews, and D.T. Wilson, "An analysis of industrial buyers' risk reducing behavior: Some personality correlates," Proceedings of the American Marketing Association. (Chicago: American Marketing Association, 1973); and D.T. Wilson, "Industrial buyers' decision making styles," *Journal of Marketing Research* 8 (1971):433-36.

29. Christopher P. Puto, Wesley E. Patton III, and Ronald H. King, "Risk handling strategies in industrial vendor selection decisions," *Journal of Marketing* 50 (1985):89-98.

30. Raydel Tullous and Richard Lee Utecht, "Multiple or single sourcing?" *Journal of Business and Industrial Marketing* 7 (1993):5-18.

31. Michael H. Morris and Stanley M. Freedman, "Coalition in organizational buying," *Industrial Marketing Management* 13 (1984):123-32.

32. Ralph L. Day, Ronald E. Michaels, and Barbara C. Perdue, "How buyers handle conflicts," *Industrial Marketing Management* 17 (1988):153-169.

33. Robert J. Thomas, "Bases of power in organizational buying decisions," *Industrial Marketing Management* 13 (1984):209-17

34. Thomas V. Bonoma, "Major sales: Who really does the buying?" *Harvard Business Review* 60 (1982):111-19.

35. George Strauss, "Tactics of lateral relationships: The purchasing agent," *Administrative Science Quarterly* 7 (1962):161-186.

36. J.R.P. French and B.H. Raven, "The bases of social power," In D. Cartright, ed. *Studies of Social Power.* (Ann Arbor: University of Michigan Press, 1959); and Samuel B. Bachrach and Edward J. Lawler, *Power and Politics in Organizations.* (San Francisco: Jossey-Bass, Inc., Publishers, 1980).

37. Richard N. Cardoza, "Situational segmentation of industrial markets," *European Journal of Marketing* 14 (1980):264-76.

38. John W. Wingate and Joseph S. Friedlander, *The Management of Retail Buying.* (Englewood Cliffs, N.J.: Prentice-Hall, Inc., 1978), pp. 235-37.

39. B. Bowonder and I. Miyake, "Japanese innovations in advanced technologies: An analysis of functional integration," *International Journal of Technology Management* 8 (1993):135-156.

40. Stuart F. Heinritz and Paul V. Farrell, *Purchasing Principles and Applications,* 5th ed. (Englewood Cliffs, N.J.: Prentice-Hall, Inc., 1971), p. 222.

41. Niren Vyas and Arch G. Woodside, "An inductive model of industrial supplier choice processes," *Journal of Marketing* 48 (1984):30-45.

42. B. Charles Ames and James D. Hlavacek, *Managerial Marketing for Industrial Firms.* (New York: Random House, 1984), p. 57.

43. Robert M. Manzka and Steven J. Trevcha, "Cost-based supplier performance evaluation," *Journal of Purchasing and Materials Management* 24 (1988):2-7.

44. David Wieters and Lonnie L. Ostrom, "Supplier evaluation as a new marketing tool," *Industrial Marketing Management* 8 (1979):161-166.

Bibliography

Barclay, Donald W., 1991. Interdepartmental conflict in organizational buying: The impact of the organizational context. *Journal of Marketing Research* 28:145-59.

Bonoma, Thomas V., "Major sales: Who really does the buying?" *Harvard Business Review* 60 (1982):111-19.

Day, Ralph L., Ronald E. Michaels, and Barbara C. Perdue, "How buyers handle conflicts," *Industrial Marketing Management* 17 (1988):153-69.

Ganesan, Shankar, "Determinants of long-term orientation in buyer-seller relationships," *Journal of Marketing* 58 (1994):1-19.

Gilbert, Faye W., Joyce A. Young, and Charles R. O'Neal, "Buyer-seller relationships in just-in-time purchasing environments," *Journal of Business Research* 29 (1994):111-20.

Helper, Susan, "How much has really changed between U.S. automakers and their suppliers?" *Sloan Management Review* 32 (1991):15-28.

Henthorne, Tony, Michael S. Latour, and Alvin J. Williams, "How organizational buyers reduce risks," *Industrial Marketing Management* 22 (1993):41-48.

Holmlund, Maria, and Soren Kock, "Buyer-perceived service quality in industrial networks," *Industrial Marketing Management* 24 (1995):109-21.

Lancione, Dick. "The reporting relationship of customer service," *Industrial Marketing Management* 24 (1995):19-26.

Manzka, Robert M., and Steven J. Trevcha, "Cost-based supplier performance evaluation," *Journal of Purchasing and Materials Management* (Spring 1988), pp. 2-7.

O'Neal, Charles, and William C. LaFief, "Marketing's lead role in total quality," *Industrial Marketing Management* 21 (1992):133-43.

Perdue, Barbara C., "Ten aggressive bargaining tactics of industrial buyers," *Journal of Business and Industrial Marketing* 7 (1992): 45-52.

Sharma, Arun, and Douglas M. Lambert, "How accurate are salespersons' perceptions of their customers?" *Industrial Marketing Management* 23 (1994):357-65.

Thomas, Robert J., "Bases of power in organizational buying decisions," *Industrial Marketing Management* 13 (1984):202-17.

Wilson, Elizabeth J., Gary L. Lilien, and David T. Wilson, "Developing and testing a contingency paradigm of group choice in organizational buying." *Journal of Marketing Research* 28 (1991):452-66.

Strategy Formation in the Business Market

Business marketing is an extremely competitive environment as each business firm attempts to satisfy its customers' needs. Sometimes these customer bases overlap and become intertwined among various business suppliers; this necessitates the development of sophisticated intelligence systems to determine what competitors are currently doing and, more important, what they are thinking about doing.

To combat these competitive actions, many extensive market research studies may have to be developed to determine the proper products, channels, prices, and promotions to use to be competitive. The firm must analyze both present and potential market demand and then make the most appropriate sales forecast based on properly segmenting markets, choosing target markets and then positioning the right products via promotion. Finally, the firm must plan and develop detailed market strategies to win in the competitive marketplace and to achieve the company's planned objectives and stated mission.

In Part III we will consider all of these aspects of business marketing and some of the most critical decisions business marketers must face daily.

6

CHAPTER

Marketing Intelligence Systems and Market Research

Assessing market opportunities is basic to strategic planning (which will be covered in Chapter 9). In our increasingly competitive and changing world, effective market performance depends on the continuous gathering and analysis of information on customers, competitors, and internal and external forces to support strategic decision-making. This chapter discusses the various methods that business-to-business organizations use to gather and analyze relevant marketing information to identify marketing opportunities and mitigate problems. When you have completed this chapter, you should be able to do the following:

1. Understand the importance of business marketing intelligence systems
2. Understand the role of marketing research in strategic decision-making
3. Understand how secondary and primary data are collected and used
4. Become aware of the vast changes taking place in the area of secondary research
5. Appreciate the business applications of decision support systems and the software for them

Strategic Decision-Making

Strategic decision-making must be based on knowledge gained from **marketing intelligence systems** (MkIS), which are concerned with data about market potential, customer segments, and other forces in the firm's internal and external environment. Thus, to analyze, plan, implement, and control marketing strategy effectively, information must be gathered, organized, and analyzed. The assessment of environmental opportunities and threats, and the company's capacity to respond, however, must be performed with systematic care. According to a study of more than 400 business firms, 70 percent of today's business organizations use **marketing research** in the strategic decision-making process to analyze **market potential, market share,** sales, business trends, and competition. They also use market research to establish sales forecasts (covered in the next chapter) and quotas for customers and territories, to study new product acceptance and potential, and to determine market characteristics.[1] This chapter is concerned with how organizations systematically assess the marketing environment through marketing intelligence and marketing research.

COMPUTERIZED SYSTEMS

As the nation moves into the era of *computer-designed support systems,* the perspective and use of MkIS systems and research in strategic decision-making is changing considerably. Computerized systems store, calculate, and retrieve data and enable managerial interaction to facilitate decision-making at conveniently located terminals. Thus, today's decision-makers use both primary and secondary research via a dynamic manager/machine interface in which a synergistic effect is achieved in analyzing the marketing environment and mitigating problems.[2]

New product development has been one of great risk-taking ventures in business marketing. An example of the lack of good competitive intelligence and good market research can be illustrated in some new products that bombed. Steven Jobs, the co-inventor of the original Apple personal computer and developer of the subsequent NeXT computer, used a revolutionary concept called an optical drive in the NeXT computer. He realized that an early product introduction was absolutely necessary, but customers did not want it after they saw it. Customers wanted the conventional floppy drive; the new feature made it tough to switch work from a PC to the NeXT computer. Although Jobs insisted that NeXT was the right product, he overlooked one thing: it is important to get to the market swiftly, but it's even more important to get quality and pricing right the first time, even if it means delay.[3] If he had believed the last statement to be true, he would have succeeded.

When executives at Hewlett-Packard's Medical Products Group studied ten of their new-product failures along with ten of their successes, they were surprised to identify a total of fourteen essential tasks that determined which products worked and which did not. The steps covered a wide range of corporate skills. Among the tasks were (1) figuring out which new products play to a company's core strengths, (2) understanding how a new product should be marketed, and (3) getting an early fix on a project's costs. The company found that if just two of the fourteen tasks were missed, the product failed.[3]

LOW-COST AMERICAN FIRMS

Many American companies have reversed their downturn of the 1980s by using the latest management techniques and practices. The U.S. economy has shifted gears and has become one of the low-cost manufacturers in the world as the nation's economy has seen a resurgence in the technology sector. Feeding this sense of economic well-being has been a stunning acceleration in American manufacturing productivity.[4] America has steadily increased its share of world merchandise exports and has reclaimed its global leadership in this crucial area. Its stellar performance in technology and trade reinforces the notion that the United States is again the world's preeminent economic power.

A McKinsey analysis shows that American manufacturing companies lead Japan in productivity by 17 percent and Germany by 21 percent.[4] The study also shows that

American workers are more efficient than Japanese workers in four of nine industries. Several factors account for driving this productivity gain. First, U.S. companies have more leeway than their global competitors do to use layoffs as a way of cutting costs. Second, because it has more open markets, the United States is far more vulnerable to foreign competition than countries such as Japan and Germany, which countries have protected many industries from exports. Open markets in the U.S. have fostered a drive for better communications and information within business firms and better information flows with suppliers to increase efficiencies and improve a firm's market competitiveness.

Need for Business Marketing Information

When the accounting and consulting firm Coopers & Lybrand investigated 250 American corporations concerning profit management for at least the next 20 years, it found that more attention to effective marketing planning and strategy will be required. The company reported that marketing strategy is the "most significant planning challenge" facing today's corporations.[5] MkIS systems are the key steps in achieving such a goal. According to Coopers & Lybrand, regardless of industry or type of business, remaining competitive requires that a firm adhere to the following:

1. Reorient planning techniques and processes with competitive marketing strategy as the driving force
2. Develop sound forecasts of the shape and dynamics of markets, including economics, public policy, and business trends
3. Realize that marketing strategy is not price-cutting or promotional faddish, but rather a productive adaptation of all corporate resources to new opportunities in the marketplace
4. Understand that marketing expenses are investments affecting all areas of a firm from inventory management to distribution, from cash flows to cost accounting

The executives' ability in a business firm to ingest and digest copious quantities of pertinent data and then translate these data into profitable actions can ensure the firm's future. New products, new technology, new markets, and growth are necessary ingredients for any future viability. This search process narrows down to having the right products in the right markets at the right time—all the time.

After studying many successful and unsuccessful firms, John Clark gives nine major reasons for a company's failure: (1) failure to adjust to changing times; (2) improper handling of the market; (3) failure to introduce new products; (4) failure to terminate products, lines of products, or whole divisions; (5) lack of a favorable image; (6) lack of use of a marketing concept; (7) overdiversification; (8) lack of a competitive strategy; and (9) improper implementation of the business functions.[6] Many of these actions were the direct result of insufficient market data or management's improper use of marketing information. The firms became isolated and began to act autonomously. Firms that failed or were forced to reorganize because of improper use of information included International Harvester, Texas Instrument's personal computer division, Monsanto's consumer product's division, and Federal Express' fax systems.

Differences in Business and Consumer Intelligence Systems

Although business marketers require research and information as much as consumer marketers, a decided difference exists between the two. *Consumer marketing* has an established base of concepts, strategic and operating principles, and information processes. *Business marketing* and particularly its subsets, *industrial marketing, commercial marketing,* and *institutional marketing,* suffer some of the pangs of deprivation, disinterest, and discontinuity in competitive intelligence. A key reason for consumer marketing advancing faster than business marketing is the low cost and ready availability of information concerning consumer markets. Irwin Gross, the former head of DuPont Company's corporate marketing research division, and subsequently the executive director of the Institute for the Study of Business Markets at Pennsylvania State University believes business-to-business marketing's knowledge is still in the primitive stage of growth compared with its needs. "Market research and intelligence can no longer be treated as a sporadic and optional activity. It must be seen as a critical part of doing business, as it already is in consumer marketing."[7]

Marketing Intelligence System Essentials

According to Daniel Marcus, director of the business marketing practice of Elrick and Lavidge, a Chicago-based marketing research and consulting firm, there are five essentials tasks or activities that serve core marketing objectives and satisfy the question about "the most bang for the marketing buck."[8] All five areas are indigenous to marketing information systems:

1. Identify the best customers and customer groups.
2. Learn precisely what they (the customers) want and need from the marketer.
3. Determine the company's and competitor's marketing strengths and weaknesses.
4. Identify the company's most and least profitable products.
5. Measure the size and growth rate of each market segment.

Marcus's analysis, pared down to the bare essentials, would give the best customer profiles, including customer identification, industry, size, location, and sales history. Once the customers were identified, the second essential would be the analysis of their needs and wants. A detailed understanding of the technological and psychological needs of the customer would be necessary. Third, determination and the analysis of what the customers think are the company's and competitor's strengths and weaknesses help to determine how and where the company should direct its actions and/or restructure its weaknesses. Fourth, if the best and worst products are known, managers would have a better idea for placement of their best efforts. By having access to monthly and annual sales data by product and product line, cost-of-sales data, overhead allocations, general and administrative expenses, calculations of gross profit, profit margins, and net profit for each product and product line would assist in this effort. Last, knowing who to sell to and which product attributes and types of products to combine into a total product or service offering, as well as knowing the segment size and growth, would indicate how much the firm is likely to sell. "Sophisticated marketing means planning and implementing strategies that achieve and maintain competitive advantage in served markets."[8]

Definition of a Marketing Intelligence System

Discussing the pros and cons of an MkIS system may appear glib, but the essential nature or need for such a system is an absolute necessity. A marketing intelligence system (MkIS) consists of people, equipment and procedures to gather, sort, analyze, evaluate, and distribute needed, timely, and accurate information to marketing decision-makers.[9]

Components of a Marketing Intelligence System

Before managers can make effective decisions, they must have reasonable amounts of useful and pertinent data to use, in conjunction with their managerial creativity. Much data are available to describe the composition of business markets, including The Standard Industrial Classification (SIC) code system and the County Business Patterns description of businesses. However, two difficulties arise using these data: (1) vast amounts of data have to be manipulated, and (2) SIC's format is quite restrictive, and data have to be mapped to fit SIC's format.[10] Thus, data collection and analysis rests with the individual firm. Many online data banks exist to ease the pressure, however.

As shown in Figure 6-1, a business marketing intelligence system is composed of four major subsystems: (1) internal accounting system, (2) external market intelligence system, (3) *analytical marketing system,* and (4) the marketing research system.[10]

INTERNAL ACCOUNTING SYSTEM

Accounting provides much useful data for marketing analysis. Accounting is the system that reports the activities of a firm including orders, sales, accounts receivables, inventory levels, out-of-stock items, back ordered items, inventory movement by item, costs of materials and labor, landed costs, and so on. Business marketing managers can analyze these data to identify problems and trends and predict potential opportunities, advantages and disadvantages they might experience in the future. Sufficient warning of these impending failures or fortunes can provide the lead time managers need to analyze and organize their resources to manage future events. For example, one of the success prerequisites is to get a handle on product costs as soon as possible, which is not an easy situation unless management is adamant in its demands. If a product's direct costs (traceable costs) are known early in the game, then a costs trail exists for marketing managers to work with to make the proper product decisions. If the deci-

FIGURE 6-1 Marketing information system (MkIS).

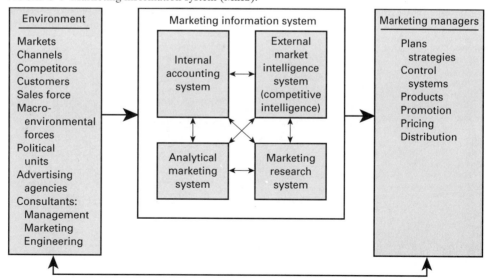

Marketing decisions and communications

Source: Adapted from Philip Kotler, *Marketing Management: Analysis, Planning, and Control,* 5th ed. (Englewood Cliffs, N.J.: Prentice Hall, 1984, p. 189). Copyright © 1984; adapted by permission of Prentice Hall.

sions turn out to be faulty, then the managers can take corrective actions to put the product back on the road to success with a good marketing information system.

Lifeblood of the Firm   The lifeblood of any business is the flow of sales orders into the firm and their shipping and billing, as shown in Figure 6-2. Field salespeople initiate the major process by closing orders in the field and transmitting the sales order to the home office. Billing creates a multipart invoice from the order that is subsequently distributed throughout the office and plant. If the order can be filled out of stock, the order is processed, packed, and shipped to its destination with a copy of the invoice used as a packing slip enclosed. If the order has to be back-ordered, a copy of the invoice is sent to production planning for processing and a notice is sent to the customer informing him of the order's disposition.

Order, Billing, and Shipping   The company usually does not receive any revenue until the order is billed and shipped, so any delay that occurs in the order-filling process can be costly to the firm. Computers can track an order's progress through the plant, warehouse, and transportation modes to expedite the order's delivery and enhance the customer's satisfaction. International Shoe closed the order-billing-shipping loop by inputting retail store audits into their computer system on a weekly basis so that production could determine which styles/colors/sizes should be produced and shipped to designated parts of the country.

EXTERNAL MARKETING (COMPETITIVE) INTELLIGENCE

The image of trench coats, binoculars, spies, and wiretaps is called to mind as some observers believe marketing or competitive intelligence is in some way similar to mil-

FIGURE 6-2 Order processing systems and cash flow.

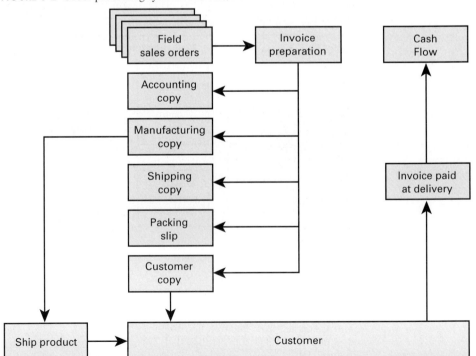

itary or governmental intelligence. However, the trademark trappings of military and government intelligence have little in common with business marketing and **competitive intelligence systems** and practices. Although some business competitive intelligence systems have used some cloak and dagger techniques, the vast majority of firms have discovered less strenuous and effective methods are more acceptable for the rapidly growing function of competitive intelligence.[11] Mr. Leonard Fuld, President of Information Data Search, a Cambridge, Massachusetts intelligence-gathering company, claims that four reasons rule out the need for clandestine operations[12]:

1. Information for decisions is needed, not trade secrets. It is more important to know what a competitor is going to do, rather than discover secret operations.
2. People will talk, anyway. People will share information as long as the gatherer is not "pushy."
3. A wealth of sources exists. Online databases and other sources are so plentiful, secret operations are not necessary.
4. Piecing the puzzle together. Creative researchers can take apparently commonplace sources and turn them into powerful intelligence tools.

Marketing intelligence data can be gathered in many ways. The great majority of real world intelligence gathering is rather unexciting. Reading technical journals, maintaining libraries of business, industrial, commercial, and institutional and other business books, periodicals, newspapers, magazines, and pamphlets provide the basis for a workable marketing intelligence system (MkIS). Listening to others talk and to pick up pertinent information that may be helpful in determining an analytical direction for managers, is most helpful. Online data sources, fax machine transmissions, computer databases, and other search programs can provide a wealth of data can be analyzed to develop useful information.

The truly creative researcher can take commonplace data from many different sources and turn them into powerful intelligence tools by piecing together bits of information and constructing a total mosaic. For example, a researcher may not be able to acquire a competitor's income statement, but might be able to construct a relatively accurate statement by using public filings about the competitor's borrowings, plant size, and number of employees. He then pieces these data together with industry statistics and data from the company's operations to create an entire operating pattern for a competitor.

ANALYTICAL MARKETING SYSTEM

General Electric, IBM, and others make extensive use of advanced techniques for analyzing marketing data. An **analytical marketing system** consists of a statistical bank and a model bank. Included in the statistical bank are the traditional statistical procedures for extracting meaningful information from data, plus the multivariate statistical techniques such as multiple regression analysis, discriminant analysis, factor analysis, and cluster analysis.

The **model bank** includes an assortment of models, developed by management scientists, which will help marketing managers make better decisions. As seen in Box 6-1, the models can range from descriptive models to more complex mathematical models. Use of these models exists among larger business-industrial firms, but many have not been put to use by smaller business firms for lack of understanding or assumed inaccuracy of their results. In a highly competitive international business market, it behooves the marketing manager to use effective analytical tools that offer him help in deriving correct marketing decisions.

Since a substantial body of evidence indicates that high *market share* directly affects a firm's profitability, gaining market share becomes an important company

---

BOX 6-1

Analytical Marketing System—Model Bank

DESCRIPTIVE MODELS

Macro model
Micro model
Micro behavioral model
Queuing model

DECISION MODELS

Optimization models
   Differential calculus
   Mathematical programming
   Statistical or Bayesian decision theory
   Game theory
Heuristic models

VERBAL MODELS

GRAPHICAL MODELS

Logical flow
Network planning
Casual analysis
Decision tree
Functional relationship
Feedback system

MATHEMATICAL MODELS

Linear or nonlinear models
Static or dynamic models
Deterministic or stochastic models

Source: Philip Kotler, *Marketing Management: Analysis, Planning and Control,* 5th ed. (Upper Saddle River, N.J.: Prentice Hall, Inc., 1984), pp. 213-22. Reprinted by permission of Prentice Hall.

---

goal. For example, a model of *price, quality, and value* (PQV) uses the survey approach and provides an overarching logic that can integrate survey insights into a framework for strategic analysis. Such a model, developed from empirical studies and consulting experience, considers factors such as quality weights, market quality score, general mean, and strata confidence intervals. Incidentally, one study suggests that an ideal market share percentage and profitability relationship is between 65 and 70 percent. To go any higher or lower, the return on investment would decrease.[13]

MARKETING RESEARCH SYSTEM

The most formal of the four subsystems of the business MkIS system is the marketing research system, which can be defined as the systematic and objective approach to the development and provision of information for the marketing management decision-making process.[14]

Marketing researchers probe problem areas in search of possible solutions or, if not attainable, they probe to obtain a better realization and identification of a problem area by hoping to establish a possible cause and effect relationship. Marketing research uses scientific methods of inquiry in search for facts and solutions. This search can cover broad vistas in marketing, (research and development) R&D, manufacturing, distribution, corporate planning, and general management, as pictured in Figure 6-3. Most business research designs use both exploratory and descriptive approaches, rather than experimental. The last design is impossible since the variables would be very difficult to manage. These

LIMITATIONS OF AN MKIS SYSTEM

The widespread use of computers and particularly PCs, facilitates a growing use of online data, which condition can be disturbing to a manager. Using massive databases and the Internet, managers can swiftly change plans and target new niches.[15] These

Source: Adapted from Donald D. Lee, *Industrial Marketing Research* (Westport, Conn.: Technomic Publishing Co., Inc., 1978), p. 9

FIGURE 6-3 The interfaces of marketing research.

massive amounts of data can create information overload. The most successful drug companies keep abreast of the changes in their field by making and maintaining close connections with the scientific community at large, allocating resources across a wide range of therapeutic areas to end up with the most advantageous mix of products and actively confronting the tension between organizing by function and organizing by product group. In addition the companies use sophisticated resource-allocation procedures and hire the best technical people available.[16]

Another disadvantage of the use of an information system is the host firm's lack of use. The benefits of an active MkIS may not be properly used by a business firm. Major U.S. companies have been spending more money than ever to gather information, but much of the money has been wasted on building ineffective computer databases that have collected the wrong information, in the wrong bundles, and with inappropriate indexing. Anyone who has researched the SIC codes can attest to the inappropriateness that these data offer for marketing research. One study revealed the companies surveyed spent an average of $450,000 a year to track their competition, but some companies in this survey folded their MkIS systems because of a lack of an interested audience.[17] Two major problems appeared to exist: (1) holding top management's interest in maintaining an appropriate budget and (2) keeping file folders or databases current.

Unlike companies that emphasize hardware systems and the use of extensive data banks, many successful firms have maintained a well-run, small, but effective MkIS system.[18] Many of the most successful intelligence departments did not build (nor did they plan to build) databases, since they relied solely on manual filing systems and an active network of internal experts and published reports such as magazines, newspaper articles, databases, and annual reports for their business intelligence. Those companies who used databases kept them small and simple. The emphasis was placed on useful intelligence data—not how big or how important specific mechanics of an MkIS system became.

Business Marketing Research

Competitiveness in both foreign and domestic markets can be enhanced if the industrial firm uses timely, appropriate information rather than only maintaining data. Although luck does play a role in being successful, more often good logic, hard work, and taking the right research direction are the best attributes to successful business marketing research management.

General Motors engineers were notorious for ignoring customer input or delaying market research until the final stages of car development—when it was too late to make product changes. By contrast, during the development of the Oldsmobile Aurora, teams were used who consulted extensively with consumer focus groups, even before the first designs were drawn. The teams held twenty so-called clinics nationwide, interviewing more than 4,200 consumers—the biggest such sampling in GM history.[18] Aurora was the first graduate of GM's Five-Phase Vehicle Development Process, so it offered an unusual window into the approach the carmaker counted on to help it churn out a steady stream of appealing new cars and trucks. The five phases were (1) determining what customers want, (2) using that knowledge to develop the vehicle concept, (3) converting concepts into vehicles, (4) developing process, and (5) manufacturing. At last, GM had begun listening to its customers. Many large companies are taking advantage of these newer information concepts, but most small companies do not use the services of marketing consultants because of the expense. A typical focus group session can cost approximately $3,000, while an inexpensive market strategy study can cost about $20,000, which can be cost prohibitive.[19]

DIFFERENCES BETWEEN BUSINESS AND CONSUMER MARKETING RESEARCH

While the basic objectives of marketing research apply in both the business-industrial and consumer market arenas, due to the business marketing environment and the nature of organizational buying and behavior, significant differences exist between business and consumer marketing research.[20]

Technical Orientation   When compared with consumer marketing researchers, business marketing researchers are considerably more technically oriented because of their interaction with engineers, production, and purchasing personnel during the collection of data and the development of technical reports.

Concentrated Access to Information   Because of the smaller concentration of business-industrial buyers, information sources tend to be concentrated. Thus, there is greater reliance on secondary data sources, exploratory studies, and expert judgment.

Survey Techniques   Because it is normally easier to identify specific respondents within a much smaller sample base, personal interviewing rather than telephone or mail is the predominant survey tool.

Respondent Cooperation   For a variety of reasons, such as time constraints and hesitancy to give information, data from industrial respondents are often more difficult to obtain than they are from consumers. Hesitancy among a firm's own salespeople to provide information is also a problem. If the research involves seeking unbiased information about customers, according to several studies, often the sales force does not possess the ability or the willingness to provide unbiased information about their customers.[21] Salespeople see their job as selling to the customer, not of providing the company with information about their customers.

DECISION-MAKING

Tremendous and constantly increasing amounts of easily accessible information have inspired much recent thought in the area of decision-making. One direction of thought holds that despite the ominous amount of information and the high-tech methods used to obtain much of it, smaller organizations should gain access to and take advantage of the information. One researcher points out that many newly created information sources are inexpensive, easy to access, easy to interpret, and relevant even to small, day-to-day business decisions.[22]

Two engineers established themselves as a consulting firm and, in an effort to obtain clients, ran trade journal ads that cost $15,000. However, the ads resulted in only one project, which yielded no more revenue than the cost of the ads. Based on this disappointment, the engineers contacted a marketing firm for help. That firm used several online databases to analyze and segment the market. It billed the engineers only $3,000 and provided names of 50 potential clients. The engineers then conducted a direct mail and phone campaign, offering half-day seminars on quality assessment and production enhancement. Thirty of the companies requested the seminar. After the seminars, the engineers obtained contracts totaling more than $300,000.[23]

Amitai Etzioni describes another direction of thought, which he calls "humble decision-making." Among other avenues of decision-making, he compares it to rationalism and incrementalism. Rationalism involves evaluating all possible courses of action, while incrementalism employs many very small decisions. Etzioni holds that rationalism is no longer feasible in view of the great amounts of information available. He says that decision-making no longer resembles evaluating an "open book" but more of "an entire library of encyclopedias under perpetual revision." Incrementalism involves "trying this or that small maneuver without any grand plan or sense of ultimate purpose."[24]

On the other hand, humble decision-making incorporates a "generalized consideration of a broad range of facts and choices followed by detailed examination of a focused subset of facts and choices."[24] As a method lying somewhere between rationalism and incrementalism, humble decision-making can be viewed as necessitating a number of facilitating concepts.

Focused trial and error, the first facilitating concept, involves searching based on logic or intuition, as well as periodic checking to assure that one is still on course, according to Etzioni. Another concept is tentativeness, which involves "a willingness to change directions" when the results are not satisfactory—thus the term *humble* decision-making. *Procrastination,* another useful concept, relates to a willingness to delay a decision so that a better decision might be made at a later date. The concept of decision staggering involves effecting the decision in increments over time, rather than all at once. This spacing enables the marketer to evaluate whether increments are having the expected results. *Fractionalizing* is a concept similar to procrastination. Etzioni says that it "treats important judgments as a series of subdecisions and may or may not also stagger them in time." For example, buying a truck may involve several subdecisions, and some of those decisions might be delayed to await the publication on consumer satisfaction surveys. Hedging bets, yet another facilitating concept, involves implementing the decision in more than one area, or in other words, not putting all the eggs in one basket. Maintaining strategic reserves, another facilitating concept, would lead to maintaining reserves in case of adversity. Etzioni's final implementing concept is that of reversible decisions. It is a way of avoiding "over commitment" and involves making decisions that can be easily reversed; for example, before buying a truck, one might lease it with an option to buy, thus allowing for a chance to better evaluate the vehicle before assuming a hefty financial obligation.[26]

Business marketing research is not a panacea in any sense of the word. Many products have been developed without extensive research. One of the great product successes, which did not entail formal research, was the Sony Walkman. The Japanese engineers, along with Sony's CEO, thought it was a good, useful product and decided to manufacture and market it. The rest is history.

Seiko, the Japanese watchmaking firm, brings out a new model they think the customers will like; if it doesn't sell, they simply discontinue its manufacture. Obviously, these are consumer products, but they do illustrate where good a priori logic can answer many questions before a full-blown formal research study is undertaken. American firms are more noted for undertaking or underwriting formal research studies, whereas the Japanese are less prone to do so, thus saving the companies many costs in the process.

Foreign marketing research takes on many other dimensions that are in contrast to American marketing research. This difference can be illustrated by the following example. The tremendous growth in the Asian markets of China, Hong Kong, South Korea, Malaysia, Singapore, and Taiwan in the 1980s and 1990s has whetted the appetites of many manufacturers through the world. One basic assumption that these economies will foster tremendous consumer product demand and hence generate a huge business-industrial product and service demand boom could prove false. If the consumer demand takes place, then the business-derived demand will certainly follow.

China is the world's fastest-growing economy (percentage-wise) and promises great potential for future growth. As one local official of the Chinese Communist Party in a village near Shanghai put it: "The role of the Communist Party today is to make everybody rich."[25] However, will these new-rich buy new products or put the extra income into savings? If the Chinese cultural ways prevail, much of the money may be saved rather than spent, meaning the expected consumer growth market could become an illusion.

The Business Marketing Research Process

Figure 6-4 illustrates the nine logical steps in the marketing research process, is the fourth component of a business firm's intelligence system. Although the business sector is double that of the consumer goods and services sectors, management is not always aware of the need for research, and even when management commissions the work, the internal or external researcher can find it challenging to develop the needed information.[26] Much of the difficulty lies in the nature of business markets. Some important characteristics of business markets include (1) the purchase decision is a complex process involving a number of individuals; (2) where there are few customers, market research often involves a detailed examination rather than a sampling; (3) in most business markets, a few companies account for most of the volume; and (4) with longer product life cycles in the business sector, product introductions are more risky.[28] These business risks are all the more reason to make more accurate and least costly business marketing decisions. Although the research steps in the business research process are similar to the consumer research process, the environment for the business research process is entirely different, in that a few complex organizations, knowledge-able individuals, and expensive, technical products usually are involved.

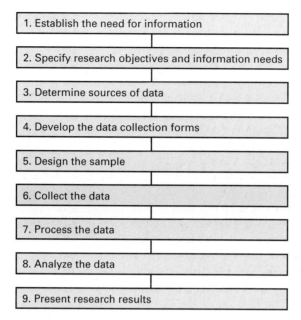

1. Establish the need for information

2. Specify research objectives and information needs

3. Determine sources of data

4. Develop the data collection forms

5. Design the sample

6. Collect the data

7. Process the data

8. Analyze the data

9. Present research results

FIGURE 6-4 Steps in the marketing research process.

Source: Thomas C. Kinnear and James R. Taylor, *Marketing Research,* 3rd ed. (New York: McGraw-Hill Book Company, 1987, p. 20). Reprinted by permission.

JUSTIFY THE NEED FOR THE DATA

Before any research can be started, the first step in the research process is to establish the need for the information. Can the problem, as defined, be satisfied with a priori reasoning without enduring all the hassle and expense of a formal research study? Does the problem justify the need for formal research? Problem definition provides the research with direction and purpose. Research is expensive and time consuming, but to collect data to simulate a solution or give the illusion that progress is being make is unpardonable. Illusion occurs when fuzzy objectives and fuzzy information needs are used. Reports that were due every 3 months may be demanded every day, for example.[27]

Companies are radically rethinking the product-development process and finding out that in regard to marketing research, they need to place more emphasis on tapping the insights and expertise of "lead users" or customers and potential customers that are on the cutting edge of the use of the company's products. The key to identifying lead users involves finding users who have needs that foreshadow general demand and then selecting those that stand to obtain the highest benefits from the solution of those needs.[28]

ESTABLISH RESEARCH OBJECTIVES

The second step is a statement of the research's objectives or problem definition and the specific information that is needed to achieve these objectives. Both tasks give direction and purpose to the research. Why is this research being conducted? What specific information is needed? The answers to both questions may not always be cut and dried. An industrial firm usually knows why the research is being conducted, but the researchers may not always know what specific information is needed. A business marketing research person cannot afford the luxury of simply collecting data because of the complexity of the research environment. Direction must be determined with a hypothesis or stated objective.

When General Motors took the gigantic step toward factory automation to achieve more production efficiency, its managers were shocked later to learn that a once mothballed California assembly plant, with outmoded equipment, had became its most efficient plant. With the help of Toyota managers, productivity in the Chevrolet Nova plant in California increased to twice the average level in General Motor.[29] The difference was the way the Toyota managers organized and operated the plant and its people. Perhaps GM did not seek the correct data by asking the right questions, or they obtained an insufficient amount of the needed data.

DETERMINE SOURCES OF DATA

The third step is to determine the secondary data sources available. Technical people might want to collect primary data first, but because of excessive costs, and also the opportunity that "inaccurate data" could intervene, secondary sources should be exhausted first. These sources include both internal and external sources to the firm. Previous research work, company records, commercial trade magazines, journal articles, industry reports, government reports, and other secondary sources are some of the best secondary sources (see Box 6-2). If sufficient data are not provided by the secondary sources, primary sources have to be tapped. Primary data may be collected by mail, telephone (telemarketing in some cases), personal interviews, observation, experimentation, *technical focus research,* customer attitude research, and market simulation.

Many secondary data sources used in business marketing research, such as Predicasts and the Census of Manufacturers, have their data arranged in accordance with codes established by the Office of Management and Budget of the federal government, as described in the *Standard Industrial Classification Manual.* These codes, commonly referred to as SIC codes, categorize business establishments in the United States according to the industries in which they are engaged.

As shown in Table 6-1, the U.S. economy is divided into eleven divisions, A through K. Within each division, major industry groups are classified by two-digit numbers.[30] For example, all manufacturing firms are in division D, with the two-digit numbers (ranging from 20 to 39) indicating major manufacturing industries within that division. Industry subgroups are further delineated by a third digit; detailed industries by a fourth digit—the longer the number, the more detailed the industry being defined. For example, SIC 2491213 includes manufacturers of lumber and wood products of more than 15 feet in length. Thus, a producer of forklifts that are capable of carrying lengthy wood poles can consult the SIC Manual and determine that code 2491213 designates industrial firms that produce wood poles, piles, and posts that are more than 15 feet long.

SIC Code Limitations   Effective use of SIC data requires an understanding of their major limitations. First, SIC codes are not completely up-to-date; for example, in recent years they have been updated on an average of about every 4 years. Second, SIC codes are based on the major product produced or operation performed by the establishment; thus, the classification assigned to an individual establishment will depend on the "principal product or operation." Where two or more products are produced, the principal product is determined by the one with the largest amount of activity associated with it—either by the amount of value added, sales, or shipments. Third, several different types of firms are often aggregated under one SIC code. Thus, for many marketers, the four-digit codes are not as "clean" as they should be. In fact, according to one industry source, as many as 100 different industries are lumped into a single four-digit code.[31]

Secondary Sources for Industrial Information Systems
(Partial List)

GOVERNMENT PUBLICATIONS

Census of United States
Census of Manufactures
Census of Business
Census of Agriculture
Census of Housing
Census of Population
Minerals Yearbook (U.S. Bureau of Mines)
Federal Reserve Bulletin (Federal Reserve
   Board)
*Monthly Catalog of United States Government
   Publications* (Superintendent of Documents,
   Washington, D.C.)
Marketing Information Guide (U.S. Department
   of Commerce)
Monthly Checklist of State Publications (The
   Library of Congress)
Survey of Current Business
Business Statistics (every two years)
County Business Patterns
Distribution Data Guide
Congressional Committee Reports
U.S. Industrial Outlook
International Trade Commission Reports

**TRADE AND PROFESSIONAL
ASSOCIATIONS AND PUBLICATIONS**

American Iron and Steel Institute
National Association of Retail Druggists
Aerospace Industries Association
American Marketing Association
American Medical Association
National Electrical Manufacturers' Association

Marketing Communications
Business Marketing

PRIVATE BUSINESS RESEARCH FIRMS

R.L. Polk and Company
A.C. Nielsen Company
Market Research Corporation of America
F.W. Dodge Corporation
Audits and Surveys Company
Herman B. Director Associates
Daniel Starch Company

PRIVATE DIRECTORIES

Thomas Register of American Manufacturers
McRae's Blue Book
Sweet's Catalog Service
Moody's Industrial Manual
Dun and Bradstreet Middle Market Directory
Standard and Poor's Register or Corporations

UNIVERSITY RESEARCH ORGANIZATIONS

Office of Industrial Development Studies
   (University of Missouri)
Survey Research Center (University of Michigan)
Institute of Business and Economic Research
   (University of California Berkeley)

FOUNDATIONS AND INSTITUTES

National Industrial Conference Board
Committee for Economic Development
Resources for the Future, Inc.
Brookings Institute

Overall, the advantages of SIC codes outweigh the disadvantages, as evidenced by the large number of secondary information sources that use them.

To overcome the fact that data are gathered by "establishments" and are assigned a SIC by the primary product produced or operation conducted, the business marketer can also turn to the Census of Manufacturers, a reference that uses two ratios to indicate the degree of error involved: (1) the primary product specialization ratio and (2) the coverage ratio. Specialization ratios are used to indicate the percentage of total shipments for a given four-digit industry that is accounted for by its primary product

TABLE 6-1	The Standard Industrial Classification System

The SIC Manual Provides Codes for 11 Industries, A through K

Division	Industry Classification	First Two-Digit SIC	Major Groups Within Industries
A	Agriculture, forestry, and fishing	01-09	20 Food and kindred products
B	Mining	10-14	21 Tobacco manufactures
C	Construction	15-17	22 Textile mill products
D	Manufacturing	20-39	23 Apparel...
			24 Lumber and wood products ...
.	.		.
.		.	.
K		.	.
		.	.

And 2 additional digits for industry series within major groups:

2441	Nailed wood boxes and shook
2448	Wood pallets and skids
2449	Wood containers ...
2491	Wood preserving
	.
	.
	.

The Census of Manufactures provides additional codes up to 7 digits:

24912	Wood poles, piles, and posts ...
2491211	15 ft or less in length
2491213	More than 15 ft in length
	.
	.
	.

Source: Adapted from Office of Management and Budget, *Standard Industrial Classification Manual* (Washington, D.C.: U.S. Bureau of the Census, 1982); and *Census of Manufactures: Wooden Containers and Miscellaneous Wood Products* (Washington, D.C.: U.S. GPO, 1985).

or operation—the higher the ratio, the higher the production activity associated with the primary product; indicating a more homogeneous industry. Thus, where ratios exceed 90 percent, the data can be considered more reliable.

Computerized Secondary Data Sources   The *Encyclopedia of Information Systems and Services* now not only speaks of the availability of so many on-line databases, but also of CD-ROM data, and data available on "disk, and magnetic tape."[32] One study indicated that not only are organizations satisfied with more accessible information but in one instance, engineers chose to use a more accessible though lower quality source.[32] These data sources not only make a great amount of information readily available, but they usually do so at relatively low cost, ranging from 50 to a few hundred dollars per hour. One study, receiving responses from 34 large firms, each with over 5,000 employees and over $100 million in sales (in random SIC codes), indicated that computerized data sources are used an average of 61.2 times per year by each firm, an average far exceeding that of any other secondary data source[33] (Table 6-2). Time and money can also be expended collecting a good deal of redundant or even irrelevant, data. A person with experience can usually bypass irrelevant data and quickly locate valuable information. Examples of some databases are included in Table 6-3. Because

TABLE 6-2 Average Yearly Usage of Forecasting Sources	
Name of Source	*Average Times Used per Year*
Census of Manufacturers	3.0
Annual Survey of Manufacturers	1.9
County Business Patterns	2.8
Input-Output Analysis	1.9
Business Conditions Digest	3.2
Survey of Industrial Purchasing Power	3.0
SIC codes	37.2
Computerized Data Sources	61.2
Trade Association Publications	36.9
State and Local Industrial Directories	21.9

TABLE 6-3 Some Online Databases		
Database	*Description*	*Producer*
PTS Annual Reports Abstracts	Provides national and international data from than 175,000 abstracts pertaining to 4,000 companies. Covers industries, companies, products, and services. Firms are classified by SIC code, name, and several other methods. Data updated monthly.	Predicasts, Inc.
Disclosure Database	Provides extracts on more than 12,000 companies based on their Securities and Exchange Commission reports. Data updated weekly. Also available on CD-ROM.	Disclosure, Inc.
The WEFA Group	Formed by a merger of the Chase and Wharton Econometric groups. Provide multiple databases and econometric models that cover all major sectors of the U.S. economy as well as much international data.	The WEFA Group
Commerce Business Daily (CBD)	Provides daily data on U.S. government purchasing and selling.	U.S. Department of Commerce
Dow Jones News/Retrieval	Makes up-to-the-minute business and financial information available. It contains 40 online databases containing both national and international information.	Dow Jones & Co., Inc.

For a thorough listing of indices, see the *Information Industry Directory* (1998) and its periodic updates, produced by Gale Research Company, Detroit, Mich.

of their training and experience with computerized data sources, librarians are well qualified to do computer searches; in fact, many of them are being lured from their jobs in public or academic institutions by higher-paying business organizations.

Noncomputerized Secondary Data Sources   Numerous sources of free data are available such as business periodicals, trade magazines, newspapers, business reference services, federal banks, and annual operating reports listed in such sources as Dunn & Bradstreet, Moody's, and Standard and Poor's industrial surveys. One marketing researcher claims that for less than $400, a firm can purchase a core of reference books that will provide the essential noncomputerized secondary data sources for market research and planning. He states that "for every significant economic activity, there is (1) an association that represents it, (2) a government agency that monitors it, and (3) a magazine that covers it."[34]

Government Sources   Government, at all levels, gathers and publishes a great deal of economic data on a national, state, and county basis (four-digit codes), and on a product-by-product basis (seven-digit codes). Since these data are classified by SIC codes, they allow for analyzing data on an industry-by-industry basis. The challenge, however, is to develop familiarity with these sources to understand how they can be used in the area of business marketing research, and to develop the credibility level of these sources.

Some of the government publications that are most useful to business marketers are presented in Table 6-4. Because of the considerable data these reports contain, only the *Business Conditions Digest* can be maintained on a current, up-to-date basis. For example, although the Census of Manufacturers is scheduled to be released every 5 years, in practice it takes a number of additional years to release it so that the data it contains on release is already dated. There is, however, a positive side to using these dated sources. The information they provide is available from few other sources; they provide excellent starting points (or *benchmarks*) for additional research; they can be quite useful in indicating what market share was; and in industries that change slowly and where SIC codes sufficiently differentiate, they can be of considerable use in researching such areas as markets that need more attention, sales force routing, designing distribution channels, and market share analysis.

The director of Faxfinder, a marketing research firm, depends on the Census of Manufacturers as a benchmark of industrial production for determining which companies dominate a given market, and is also used in designing distribution channels.[35] However, government statistics have to be considered with the understanding that not all governmental statistics are absolutely correct. The government's limited research staffs used to collect much of the macro data may actual distort the very economic situations it purports to report.[36] For example, statistics such as gross domestic product (GDP), producer price index (PPI), or capacity utilization say far more about what's happening in old-line manufacturing industries than they do about such leading-edge companies as Microsoft, Disney, MCI, Fidelity, and Intel.[37]

The survey can be used alone or in conjunction with the sources listed in Table 6-4. Since the survey does use four-digit SIC codes and does not give SIC codes for firms with less than 100 employees, using it in conjunction with government sources can be beneficial. It is also an excellent source for determining whether some of the data presented in those government sources are still current.

In addition to the sources indicated in Table 6-4, the *Thomas Register of American Manufacturers* and *MacRae's Blue Book* are also good sources of information.

DEVELOP RESEARCH INSTRUMENTS

The fourth step and subsequent steps are related to generating new data. Data collection forms, research instruments, or personal interview questionnaires have to be developed. This procedure is a most critical step, since the use of improper forms or poorly worded questions could damage the integrity of the data collected, generating inaccurate or distorted data. For example, attitude research does not take a large universe and costly equipment, but if improperly conducted, the results could be stilted with improper judgments drawn.[37]

TABLE 6-4   Reference Sources for Marketing Research and Planning

Name	Producer	Description
Census of Manufactures	U.S. Department of Commerce	Provides data for industries, states, and SMSAs. Data involve materials consumed, employment, payroll, value added, and capital goods expenditures, among others. *Problems:* Different firms lumped under same SIC code. Census lacks currency.
Annual Survey of Manufacturers	Bureau of Census	Provides same industry data (employment, payroll, value of shipments, etc.) as the *Census of Manufactures.* Also provides data on assets, rents, supplemental labor costs, fuels, etc. Intended to cover the 4 interim years between issues of the Census. *Problems:* Although the Survey is intended to be issued during each year the Census is not issued, this rarely occurs.
County Business Patterns	Bureau of the Census	Provides information on numbers of employees and payrolls be state counties for various SIC codes. *Problems:* A sampling of the reports indicates they are issued 2 years after the data are obtained.
Survey of Business (Input-Output Analysis)	Office of Business Economics (U.S. Department of Commerce)	Provides data showing value of outputs of 370 industries and what portions of the outputs various industries purchase. Also shows percentages of outputs (e.g., industry A sells 10% of its output to industry B, 30% to industry C, etc.). If, then, industry B is expected to increase production 50%, sales to B can be estimated. *Problems:* A firm in industry A wishing to forecast sales to industry B must first have a forecast of B's production/sales. A firm must then determine how similar firms are within industry B and determine how similar it is to firms within industry A. Data are for industries, not products. In reality firms within industries can differ widely in what they produce and consume.
Business Conditions Digest	Bureau of Economic Analysis (U.S. Department of Commerce)	Provides economic time series data on a monthly (and timely) basis. Includes about 150 time series classified by their relationship to fluctuations in economic activity. These include leading, roughly coincident, and lagging indicators relative to business cycle peaks and troughs. Monthly historical data are included (as far back as 1950). This publication is produced and distributed in a timely fashion. Its numerous indices offer the researcher the opportunity to find existing data which can indicate future changes in sales, business trends, etc.

SAMPLE DESIGN

Sample design is the fifth step. A clear definition of the total population of the universe to be tested must be determined and a sample that is characteristic of this universe must be drawn. Usually *probabilistic* (stochastic, or random) or *nonprobabilistic* samples are taken, depending on the data's availability. The correct size of that sample is important because it affects the accuracy of the subsequent research. Confidence intervals and standard deviations must be chosen to maintain an accurate sample size and universe representation, based on probability. A standard statistics book would provide further details not covered here.

DATA COLLECTION

The sixth step is the data collection process. Business people carry their personal feelings into the business. The human factors of perception, memory, interpersonal relationships, ethnocentricism, and basic communications may help to contribute to the distortion of some of the data collected. Proper training of data collectors and interviewers is essential for research quality control to eliminate "faulty data."

Business marketers rely heavily on secondary data sources. When research objectives cannot be met by secondary data sources, primary data must be collected. Surveys are the most common method of obtaining primary data in the business market. Surveys involve questioning subjects and collecting their responses through person-to-person interviews, telephone interviews, or mailed questionnaires. Responses can be recorded directly by the respondents themselves or by researchers who may complete the questionnaires, take notes, or record the data.[38] Although individuals may be surveyed, the use of groups is generally restricted to surveys of knowledgeable people within the business marketer's firm. Apple's handheld Newton computer could possibly have some application in personal interviews, since Apple soon realized that some market research is necessary to determine a target market. Could Newton be a case in point of technical people developing a product few customers want but that may fit the needs of the business market?

Unstructured Surveys   In general, surveys in the business market are unstructured and nondisguised. Unstructured surveys consist of asking respondents open-ended questions (questions that require more than a yes or no answer) to encourage in-depth responses so that motivations, priorities, problems, perceptions, and attitudes can be better understood and evaluated by the researcher. Nondisguised surveys use straightforward, open questions that do not attempt to hide the purpose of the survey, as is often done in the consumer area.[1]

Formal unstructured, nondisguised surveys, while flexible and effective, are more difficult to undertake and require the use of skilled interviewers and sophisticated analysts. Thus, they are relatively more costly and time consuming.[40]

Structured Surveys   Structured surveys—questionnaires that seek specific, quantifiable answers—are used in the business market, though not to the extent of unstructured surveys. For instance, the primary planning instrument of one multinational corporation is a questionnaire that is mailed to its own salespeople for completion rather than directly to customers or distributors. When salespeople can complete the questionnaire for a single customer without contacting the customer for additional information, the questionnaire may take up to 4.5 hours to complete. However, when salespeople must contact customers or other sources, this can consume up to 15 hours to complete.[39]

Although structured surveys are more easily quantified and lead to more standardized information, they are normally used only when the sample population is relatively large, the market is not concentrated, and the information of interest consists of measuring awareness and knowledge, attitudes and opinions, or prior and present buyer behavior.[20]

Surveying Individuals   Surveying individuals in the business market is not as difficult, or as costly, as in the consumer market because customers are more geographically concentrated and thus easier to contact. Further, since unstructured surveys are the preferred means of gathering information, surveys tend to be more qualitative than quantitative in nature.

Surveying Customers   The major problem with surveying individuals within current and potential customer firms is that these individuals are often hesitant to cooperate, or unwilling to share information with their suppliers because they are afraid that (1) the information may be used against them during negotiations, (2) it may cause the seller to develop unreasonable expectations or make premature commitments, and (3) the information may inadvertently or knowingly be disclosed to the buyer's competitors.[40] Not only are they hesitant about disclosing information, they may color data—particularly if data are requested by a trade association—so that competitors will be misinformed or misled. Thus, secondary data in trade magazines that have been made available by business buyers are not of the same quality as are secondary data in the consumer market.[43] Concurrent engineering, partnering and other more modern concepts may help to overcome some of these disadvantages.

Customers frequently need assistance in determining what they want or might need, especially since they are often unaware of new products that are still in the R&D laboratories. If the customers could see and use the new product, they could better decide whether they needed it. Thus, creating the experience helps to educate the customer and create the need. Toward this end, technical-market research is an innovative, technology-driven process to understand the mind of the customer so that the customer's need can be better translated into new products by designers, engineers, and marketers. The use of planning processes such as technical-market research and "antenna shops" (letting the customer experience products still in the labs) encourage innovative, collaborative ways for R&D organizations to become a higher value-added resource in the customer satisfaction process, which results in more timely actions with fewer "false starts" for the manufacturer.[41]

Surveying Experts   The more limited nature of business research budgets, the concentration of information among a limited number of people, and the limited numbers of customers all encourage obtaining data from a relatively few experts, internal or external to the firm. Within the firm, for instance, technical information can be obtained from R&D, engineering, manufacturing, and service personnel, as well as from salespeople who may be quite knowledgeable with respect to customers' needs. External experts may be from customer and prospect firms or may be industry consultants, trade journal editors or association executives, government officials, and university professors. External experts are often located by asking internal experts to identify them.[1]

Surveying Groups   Focus group interviewing is often beneficial in business marketing. It is conducted much the same way as a group discussion: the trained moderator ensures that (1) a thorough discussion of all items about which a client wants to learn is conducted; (2) everyone becomes involved; (3) monopolists are held in check; and (4) the moderator gives frequent and brief summaries, asks open-ended questions, and never expresses a personal opinion. Focus groups are faster and less expensive than most other types of research, and they are flexible in that they can include examination of unplanned areas.[42]

Business marketers made a startling discovery when it was found that a modified focus group interview, called **technical focus research,** was applicable to business marketing. Business people carry their feelings into the business, even when they buy business products.[42] Even engineers with graduate degrees might accept or reject a product for quite irrational reasons such as an irrelevant earlier experience with a vendor. "I've been giving company X a million dollars worth of business a year" said one panelist in a focus group session, "Yet when I needed another copy of a manual, the company wanted 50 bucks. Well, I paid the 50 bucks...but next time I need computer equipment...."[43]

Group discussions not involving expert moderators have also proven to be an effective means of obtaining primary data with regard to customers' needs or current satisfaction, market characteristics, and competitors' actions, particularly when sales people are involved in the discussions. Sales people, because of their day-to-day interaction with customers, tend to be knowledgeable with respect to market, industry, and customer trends. When estimates are needed from experts, data collection may be approached by the following means[44]:

1. **Group discussion**—in which experts are gathered and asked to discuss an issue collectively and produce a group estimate
2. **Pooling individual estimates**—in which experts are asked to discuss an issue collectively and produce individual estimates that can be pooled into a single estimate
3. **Delphi method**—in which a group of experts are asked separately to provide individual estimates and assumptions that are reviewed, averaged, and returned with comments. Requests for a new round of estimates are then made, and the process continues until the estimates converge

The use of simple averages of individual estimates has been shown to be considerably more accurate than the more sophisticated Delphi technique in predicting future events.[44] Though business companies continue to use the Delphi technique, one review indicated it was "unreliable and scientifically unvalidated." It appears that the feedback of results at each round of estimating causes certain estimators to yield to group opinion, which difference biases the final results.[45]

Improving Group Surveys   A number of suggestions have been made for improving formal group methods of obtaining data such as (1) using larger groups, (2) using more than one group, (3) avoiding the hasty acceptance of forecasts, (4) attempting to find disconfirming information, and (5) institutionalizing "devil's advocates."

Benefits of Group Surveys   There is a positive side to formal, future-oriented, group research. First, it has beneficial side effects such as creating improved communications and coordination, and causing people to be more motivated and future oriented in their thinking.[47] Additionally, experts sometimes know of key future events that would not be reflected through statistical techniques based upon historical data. Also, sometimes there are no extant historical data available. Group survey information can be used also to revise the data collection instrument before conducting primary research.

Competitive Intelligence Surveys   Because of dramatically increasing competition and a stagnant economy, gathering competitive intelligence has received a great deal of attention. The developments resulting from that attention, coupled with the rather clandestine nature of gathering such intelligence, make this area of research intriguing and thought-provoking. Competitive research is an area that makes use of a number of previous types of survey methods as well as additional methods. Box 6-3 lists some possible competitor information–gathering strategies suggested by one research organization.

DATA PROCESSING

Data processing is the seventh step, which includes editing and coding of the data so the data can be easily analyzed to develop meaningful results. After editing and coding, the data are ready for tabulation by computer.

ANALYZING THE DATA

Once tabulated, the data are analyzed in the eighth step to determine the results. This process is an attempt to make the analysis consistent with the objectives and informational needs discussed in step two. Caution must be taken to separate useful

---

BOX 6-3

Competitive Intelligence Strategies

TAKING A LOCAL APPROACH

Search publications from the hometown of the competitor; newspapers and city business publications, as well as regional publications. Phone calls to authors of articles will often yield much additional worthwhile information.

INTIMATE CONTACTS

Try contacting your competitor's suppliers, distributors and customers, since they may know and share "intimate details."

EDUCATED GUESSING

In the case of private companies, try researching some similar public companies—this can allow some educated guessing.

TAPPING INTO UNIVERSITIES

Companies are generally open to students and written accounts of competitors are thus often easily accessible through dissertations, company cases, and various written student projects.

CALLING IN THE REPS

As both your reps and your competitors are close to your customers, your reps' opportunities to learn about the competition are very close at hand.

COMBING THROUGH CASES

Your attorneys can often access court cases and records that will yield valuable insights regarding competitors.

FEDERAL, STATE, AND MUNICIPAL FINDINGS

Government agencies can frequently provide records regarding competitors' future actions; construction permits regarding new facilities, for example, or applications relating to new products or services.

SOMEONE HAS THE ANSWERS

Remember that if you devote enough thought to the question "Who would know about this?" there will, with few exceptions, be someone, somewhere, who knows.

data from illusions. Respondents may have given answers to questions about which they had little or no knowledge.[46] Many software packages can be used in this step such as MIDAS, an acronym for Market Image Data Analysis System.[47] Companies can build the system themselves using a combination of hardware and software, according to the developers. This type of system uses Express, Metaphor, and SPSS software.

Several uses for primary market research data have been used other than for market research. The most common uses are image and perception feedback, data pertinent to possible new product introductions, benchmarking for subsequent research, and an attempt to determine company status preparatory to business planning. There are more subtle, effective uses of good primary research, especially when the research is directed at existing customers. several relatively unexploited uses of primary research by industrial companies are employee recruiting, total responsiveness management, employee training, supplier partnering, self-promotion, and the creation of employee customer consciousness.[48]

PRESENTING THE FINDINGS

The ninth and last step in the marketing research process is the presentation of the results to management oral and written communications. Communication of results is the key to effective marketing research. Many well-researched and well-analyzed projects have been stymied because of a poor or inadequate presentation to management. Conversely, some well-presented projects, not as well researched and analyzed, may have been enthusiastically received by management.

Computer-Supported Decisions

In very recent years, computer systems have come to play a new and important role in presenting research findings. To understand that role, it should be explained that when information systems were first computerized, the role of the computer was essentially to speed up information handling. These systems, referred to as management information systems (MIS), used computers to store, perform calculations on, and provide retrieval of data. Thus, MIS systems were "backward looking" systems because they involved accumulating data for various periods of time, entering them into the computer system, and then generating periodic reports of past events.[49]

Currently available computerized systems enable managers to utilize computers to produce analyses of research findings, to provide real-time information (information stored into a computer as the information becomes available), and to be what may be termed "forward looking." For example, these systems allow managers to ask questions such as, "What will result if we increase the price of a particular product 10 percent?" called, "what-if" questions. In other words, computerized systems can now access computer decision-making programs, databases, historical and current status reports, projected reports, and even recommended courses of action (Figure 6-5). They can also forecast changes in sales, profits, market share, operating costs, and competitor reactions, as well as other environmental reactions that might occur.[50] These more advanced computerized systems are called *decision support systems* (DSS) because, as their name implies, they directly support the managers' decision-making. In doing so, DSS not only performs all these analyses, but also presents them through terminals located on the desks of decision-makers.

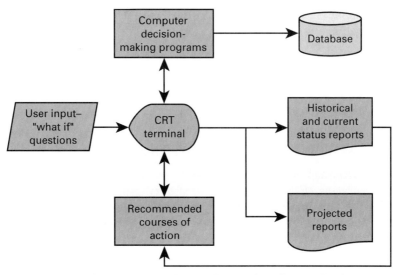

Source: Robert Thierauf, *Decision Support Systems for Effective Planning and Control.* (Upper Saddle River, N.J.: Prentice-Hall, Inc., 1982), p. 27. Reprinted by permission of Prentice Hall.

FIGURE 6-5 Interactive decision-making process of decision support systems (DSS).

Decision Support Systems

To illustrate how DSS performs, marketers can use response curves, one of the tools used by DSS (Figure 6-6). Figure 6-6 indicates that as the number of salespeople increases from 10 to 20 to 30, sales will change from some reference period by multiples of 0.5, 1.0, and 1.3. If, for example, the company's sales during reference period 19XX was $500,000, and the firm increases the size of its sales force from 20 to 30, its sales forecast would be for 1.3 X $500,000, or $650,000.

DSS response curves can also use empirical data (real data obtained through sampling and/or company records) to evaluate sales force size, territorial design, and sales effort. Since decisions regarding these three factors are interrelated, DSS (which has capabilities of examining interrelationships) is extremely useful. DSS response curves

FIGURE 6-6 Sample response curve.

Source: Adapted from Steven Alter, *Decision Support Systems: Current Practice and Continuing Challenges.* (Reading, Mass.: Addison-Wesley Publishing Co., 1980), p. 11. Reprinted by permission of Addison-Wesley Longman Inc.

are also used to examine individual customers, groups of customers, salespersons' characteristics, company products, competitive products, and competitors' reactions.

Decision support systems are intended to "be able to reflect the way managers think, be flexible and adaptive through ease of modification, support managers in a complex process of exploration and learning, and evolve to meet changing needs, knowledge and situations."[51] In effect, decision support systems offer a great advance in the performance of research and the presentation of research findings.

EXECUTIVE INFORMATION SYSTEMS

Although only a handful of software suppliers presently offer *executive information systems* (EIS), users find them very promising. EIS are intended to make great amounts of current information attractively available to top management. Rather than DSS future-oriented types of information, EIS present current information; thus, EIS answer "what is" questions rather than the "what if" questions typically answered by DSS. EIS information can be supplied from internal organization sources as well as by commercially supplied secondary information sources. To make the use of such systems attractive to top management, access to information is provided through such devices as the computer mouse and touch-screen programs that can quickly access a variety of menu possibilities. These devices pull up reports, graphs, and summaries in formats that top managers prefer, information that can be even more closely examined for more detail. These systems are not intended to replace DSS, but to enhance it by tailoring voluminous amounts of existent data in ways which top managers prefer, and then making it exceptionally easy to retrieve that data. The manager who can determine how the company is doing, compared to other firms shown through an on-line database, can better make future-oriented DSS decisions.[52]

Artificial Intelligence

Computer systems usage has given marketing information and marketing research systems a boost toward achieving the ultimate position in the future for business marketing managers. The ultimate information system would be to turn on a computer and follow the menu to solve a specific marketing problem. These facilities and technologies exit and fall under a broad range of technologies called **artificial intelligence** (AI). AI could help to revolutionize both marketing informational systems, and, in some cases, drastically change how marketing research, and even business marketing management, is practiced.

Many marketing applications of AI have been in use. DEC and Litton Industries use an expert system (XSEL) to help salespeople determine which products their customers need. Using a regular terminal, the system asks the salesperson 15 to 20 multiple-choice questions about what the customer wants and needs. With the information from the salesperson's answers and the product and technical data already loaded into the computer, a report is issued within a day that recommends the best system for the customer and explains those recommendations in detail. It designs sales proposals quickly, reduces human error, and forces salespeople and customers to specify what they want computer systems to do, making the entire process much more efficient and user friendly.

The application of expert systems in business marketing requires some basic managerial guidelines. Three areas must be analyzed before these systems can become effective: (1) it is important to identify a specific problem; (2) all available relevant data should be gathered, organized, and codified; and (3) the particular expert system approach should be identified.

Looking Back

To survive in fast-paced international competition, competitors must be aware of competitive activity, government regulations, and market needs. Executives' ability to digest large quantities of data may make the difference between the firm's success or failure.

Business marketing intelligence systems do not have well-defined variables as in the case of consumer MkISs but do require a constant stream of information, including the identity of customers, customer wants and needs, competitive strengths and weaknesses, the profitability of each product, and the potential growth rate of each market segment.

Marketing intelligence systems have four components: (1) an internal accounting system, (2) an external marketing or competitive intelligence system, (3) an analytical marketing system, and (4) a marketing research system. Each system contributes specific types of data, which have to be turned into usable or actionable information without having the reverse effect of overpowering the managers by supplying too much data.

Marketing research is the most formal and elongated system of the four components of the marketing intelligence system. Its intent is to identify problems and seek workable solutions. Because of wide swings in business sales resulting from derived demand, data analysis methods can be complex. Decision support systems that take advantage of several computer capabilities have become increasingly popular in performing business research in recent years.

Questions for Discussion

1. Discuss the various ramifications of the need for business managers to have the proper marketing information, in the right quantity and quality, to make the proper marketing decisions.

2. If and when a business firm fails, what typically are the major reasons for its demise?

3. What are the differences between the business and consumer marketing information systems? Elaborate on these differences as the systems might be used to forecast steel consumption in the automobile industry.

4. Of the four components of an MkIS, which system has the most pronounced problem solving orientation and which is oriented toward analytical or mathematical input? Why?

5. If an MkIS is the lifeblood of a business, how can it harm the firm's viability if, in addition to the proper data, it also provides superfluous data and generates data from respondents who were not qualified to answer some of the questions asked?

6. External or competitive intelligence includes many major functions, but which function in this system necessitates the use of reading and listening as major inputs?

7. What are the chief limitations of an MkIS operation? Why?

8. What are the nine steps in the business marketing research system? Which are the most critical? Why?

9. A poorly designed system that generates a poor study may sell better than a well-researched and well-analyzed study—if the first study had a better-communicated presentation. Discuss the pros and cons of this statement.

10. What is artificial intelligence and how can a business marketing information system make good use of it in a business situation?

Endnotes

1. William Cox, *Industrial Marketing Research* (New York: John Wiley & Sons, Inc., 1979).

2. Robert Thierauf, *Decision Support Systems for Effective Planning and Control* (Englewood Cliffs, N.J.: Prentice-Hall, Inc., 1982), pp. 26-27.

3. "Flops, Too Many New Products Fail, Here's Why—And How To Do Better," *Business Week* (August 16, 1993), pp. 76+.

4. "America Cranks It Up, The Resurgent U.S. Economy Shifts Gears and Really Starts to Produce," *U.S. News and World Report* (March 28, 1994), pp. 57 -60.

5. Van Mayros and Dennis J. Dolan, "Hefting the data load: How to design the MkIS that works for you," *Business Marketing* 73 (March 1988):47+.

6. John B. Clark, *Marketing Today, Success, Failures and Turnarounds* (Englewood Cliffs, N.J.: Prentice-Hall, Inc. 1987), p. 217.

7. Irwin Gross, "Why all of industry needs research ," *Business Marketing* 72 (April 1987):112+.

8. Daniel Marcus, "The strategic research you absolutely need," *Business Marketing* 71 (October, 1986):55-60.

9. Philip Kotler, *Marketing Management, Analysis, Planning, Implementation, & Control,* 8th ed. (Englewood Cliffs, N.J.: Prentice-Hall, Inc.,1994), p. 126.

10. Dennis G. Morris, "This industrial revolution lacks excitement," *Marketing News* 20 (January 3, 1986):16.

11. "Report rise in use of 'J.R.' research tactics," *Marketing News* 18 (May 25, 1984):1.

12. Leonard Fuld, "Don't confuse corporate intelligence with 'I Spy,'" *Marketing News* 12 (September 22, 1986):38.

13. Joachim Schwalbach, "Profitability and market share: A reflection on the functional relationship," *Strategic Management Journal 12* (May ,1991):299-306.

14. Thomas C. Kinnear and James R. Taylor, *Marketing Research, An Applied Approach,* 3rd. ed., (New York: McGraw-Hill Book Company, 1987), p. 18.

15. "Small fry go online" *Business Week* (November 20, 1995), pp. 158-164.

16. Rebecca Henderson, "Managing innovation in the information age," *Harvard Business Review* 72 (January/February, 1994):100-105.

17. "Study: Many firms foolish with intelligence funds," *Marketing News* 20 (January 3, 1986):44.

18. "GM's Aurora: Much is riding on the luxury sedan—and not just for Olds," *Business Week* (March 21, 1994), pp. 88+.

19. Kevin McDermott, "Who needs experts?" *D & B Reports* 39 (May/June 1991):22-5.

20. William Cox and Luis Dominguez, "The key issues and procedures of industrial marketing research," *Industrial Marketing Management* 8 (1979):81-93.

21. Arun Sharma and Douglas M. Lambert, "How accurate are salespersons' perceptions of their customers' needs," *Industrial Marketing Management* 23 (October 1994):357-65.

22. Alan R. Andreasen, "Simple, low-cost marketing research: A manager's guide," *Marketing News* 18 (May 25, 1984), Section 2, pp. 6-9.

23. Ken Landis, "Focus: Information goldmines," *Online Access* (September-October 1987), pp. 46-55.

24. Amitai Etzioni, "Humble decision-making," *Harvard Business Review* 67 (July-August 1989):122-126.

25. "Tooling up for a new era in foreign fffairs," *U.S. News & World Report* (March 28, 1994), pp. 10-11.

26. William H. Drucker, "Research also is vital for business marketers," *Marketing News* 27 (September 13, 1993), p. 17.

27. Lester C. Thurow, as quoted in "Productivity: Why it's the No. 1 underachiever," *Business Week* (April 20, 1987), p. 54.

28. B.G. Yovovich, "New product cycle playing bigger role," *Business Marketing* 79 (January, 1994):33.

29. "Making brawn work with brains," *Business Week* (April 20, 1987), p. 57.

30. John Couretas, "What's wrong with the SIC code....and why," *Business Marketing* 72 (December 1987):108-16.

31. Mary Culnan, "Environmental scanning: The effects of task complexity and source assessability on Information Gathering Behavior," *Decision Sciences* (April 1983), pp. 194-206.

32. Robert Reeder, Richard Sewell, and Betty Reeder, "A survey of empirical industrial marketing research," (Southwestern Oklahoma State University, 1988), p. 3, unpublished.

33. Stephen M. Baker, "Find marketing data fast!" *Sales and Marketing Management* (December 6, 1982), pp. 32-36.

34. John Couretas, "Counting smokestacks: Census help for marketers," *Business Marketing* 69 (January 1982):86-88.

35. "The real truth about the economy," *Business Week* (November 7, 1994), pp. 110-13+.

36. David R. Brand, "Reap the rewards of attitude research," *Business Marketing* 71 (October, 1986):62.

37. William Emory, *Business Research Methods* (Homewood, Ill.: Richard D. Irwin, Inc., 1980), p.87.

38. David Grace and Tom Pointon, "Marketing research through the salesforce," *Industrial Marketing Management* 9 (1980):53-58.

39. Frederick Webster, Jr., "Management science in industrial marketing," *Journal of Marketing* 44 (January 1978):21-7.

40. Antonio S. Lauglaug, "Technical-market research—get customers to collaborate in developing products," *Long Range Planning* 26 (April, 1993):78-82.

41. "Unveiling market segments with technical focus research," *Business Marketing* 71 (October 1986):66+.

42. Philip Kotler, "A guide to gathering expert estimates," *Business Horizons* 13 (October 1970):78-87.

43. Robert M. Hogarth, "Methods for aggregating opinions." In H. Jungermann and G. de Z Zeeuw, eds., *Decision-making and Change in Human Affairs* (Dordrech, Holland: D. Reidel Publishing Co., 1977), pp. 231-235.

44. H. Sackman, *Delphi Assessment: Expert Opinion, Forecasting, and Group Process* (Santa Monica, Calf.: Rand Corporation, April 1974).

45. Albert J. Unger, "Projectable surveys: Separating useful data from illusions," *Business Marketing* 71 (December 1986):90+.

46. "Firms that will succeed are those that search for the golden touch," *Marketing News* (May 8, 1987), p.1.

47. Dick Gorelick, "Good research has obvious—and not so obvious—benefits," *Marketing News* 27 (September 13, 1993), p. 16.

48. Robert Thierauf, *Decision Support Systems for Effective Planning and Control* (Englewood Cliffs, N.J.: Prentice-Hall, Inc., 1982), pp. 26-27.

49. Steven Alter, *Decision Support Systems: Current Practice and Continuing Challenges* (Reading, Mass.: Addison-Wesley, 1980), p. 19.

50. Keen and G. Wagner, "DDS: An executive mind-support system," *Datamation* (November 1979), p. 117.

51. Mary Lou Jordan, "Executive information systems make life easy for the lucky few," *Computerworld* (February 29, 1988), pp. 51-57.

52. Diane Lynn Kastiel, "Computerized consultant," *Business Marketing* 72 (March 1987):52+.

Bibliography

"Artificial intelligence: The goal is to store an expert's real knowledge on a disk," *Marketing News* 21 (February 27, 1987):1.

Drucker, William H., "Research also is vital for business marketers," *Marketing News* 27 (1993):17.

Donath, Bob, "For a leg up, try "satisfaction segmentation," *Marketing News* 25 (1991):14.

Feik, LuAnne, "Where in the world is research support available?" *Marketing News* 27 (March 1, 1993):R1+.

Martensen, Anne, "A model for marketing planning for new products, *Marketing & Research Today* 4 (1993):247-67.

Wingrove, Tim, "The changing face of the research market," *Marketing* 98 (1993):15.

CHAPTER 7

Demand Analysis and Sales Forecasting

In addition to information, intelligence, and research systems, as discussed in the previous chapter, business marketing managers have to understand two more managerial tools—**demand analysis** and **sales forecasting.** Managers have to understand their market and sales potentials to accurately predict the sales for each product. Sales forecast data are very important since they are used as the basis for most of the firms' subsequent planning and budgeting/accounting procedures and are used for any possible future changes made in the product/market plans developed by the company.

In this chapter the important concerns are these:

1. The new technologies and the existence of intra-firm conflicts
2. The effects of partnering, total quality management (TQM), concurrent engineering (CE), and customers
3. The difference between market potential and sales potential
4. The research facilities available for measuring market and sales potential
5. Sales forecasting techniques, including both quantitative and qualitative
6. Using market intelligence, market research, demand analysis and sales forecasts to select markets and develop marketing strategies

Business Demand and Sales Forecasting Complexities

Business marketing demand analysis and sales forecasting has become more complex as the result of the market dynamics and the rapid change in technology. The computer industry, for example, has changed the practices of business with countless technological breakthroughs. Just a few years ago, it would have been unusual for a airframe manufacturer to use computer-aided design and computer-aided manufacturing (CAD-

159

CAM) exclusively for designing a new airframe, but Boeing designed the Boeing 777 airframe to achieve closer specifications using CAD-CAM. The Boeing 777, touted as the company's market entry for the twenty-first century, was the company's first paperless plane (paperless manufacturing) where the CAD-CAM designed fuselage sections fit together so precisely that the completed plane looked as though it were carved from a smooth block of marble; it lacked the ripples common in past airliner bodies that had to be shimmed to fit.[1] Boeing developed the 777 to combat Airbus's widebody plane, which was already in production, to serve the market's needs for the twenty-first century. The 777 was forecast to fit the future needs of the market, as well as being a defensive move to combat Airbus's intrusion into Boeing's market lead.

Other new computer business markets have blossomed in groupware, online services, improved customer service, document management, servers, networks, databases, printers, voice recognition, storage protection, fax machines, scanners, pen notebooks, flash technology, advanced fiberoptics, wireless technology, video conferencing, graphics technology, data compression, object orientation, virtual reality, geographic systems, and many more.

Each new product or service in the burgeoning computer field requires extensive demand analysis and sales forecasting analysis for the company to determine which market segments to tap and the commensurate marketing strategy to follow. Demand analysis and sales forecasting was considered a relatively difficult process in the past, but with the new computer technology and the new customer relationships discussed in the previous chapters, demand analysis and sales forecasting have become a more complex problem for business marketers.

Although the inevitable need to forecast must be implemented, sales forecasts can fail or miss the target for at least seven reasons[2]:

1. Unexplained assumptions
2. Limited or misplaced expertise
3. Lack of imagination
4. Neglect of constraints
5. Excessive optimism
6. Mechanical extrapolation of trends
7. Overspecification

Forecasters must keep the potential for these errors in mind so that what they anticipate will more closely match the future realities.

NEW TECHNOLOGIES

Apple Computer, International Business Machines, and Motorola combined efforts to develop and produce a new, $1 billion high-speed microprocessor called PowerPC that used a revolutionary *RISC* design (an acronym for reduced instruction set computing). The RISC design processor had the potential to do more work for less money and less electric power than the *CISC* (or complex instruction set computing) microprocessor, most of which was made by Motorola's fierce competitor, Intel. It was hoped that Apple's and IBM's flagging fortunes, at the time, could be resuscitated. A successful PowerPC could blaze a trail for other computer manufacturers such as DEC, Sun Micro-systems, and Mips Technologies.

Apple introduced a new line of Macintosh computers using the PowerPC, and Intel responded with the Pentium chip, whose development was an updated version of CISC architecture. The backers of the PowerPC claimed that it was faster, less costly to manufacture, used less power, and was only 40 percent as big as the Pentium.[3] For Apple Computer, it meant a bet-the-company adventure. Apple forecast that a million PowerPC Macs, about a quarter of its total computer production, would be sold. Apple's major problem was that Macintosh software applications such as word processing, spreadsheets, and desktop publishing were limited, with only 50 programs ready at the time of the Power Mac's introduction. Apple banked on Microsoft to have PowerPC software written for its Word and Excel programs. A wrong forecast could have cost Apple a great deal of their future viability.

INTRA-FIRM CONFLICTS

In contending with all of the uncertainties of the future, it is reassuring to note that business production people have come to realize the importance of the customer and the importance of sales forecasting based on customer demand, rather than based only on statistical data, devoid of future customer activity input. Conflict has existed between production and marketing for some time.[4] Although these departments are dependent on each other, this conflict centers on the method of forecasting sales: production uses quantitative data, whereas sales and marketing use both quantitative and qualitative analysis of the customer's future expectations and future activities. For example, production people may forecast sales of backloader machines for the coming year by using an average of the backloaders sold in the previous 3 years. Marketing people may use the same historical statistics but modify them based on anticipated aggregate economic activity and anticipated customer sentiment in the construction business. The requirement for backloaders is driven by **derived demand**, that is, the demand for residential properties. The more houses to be built, the higher the demand for backhoes.

Marketing peoples' forecasts may change frequently based on the dynamics of the marketplace, but production people quickly become perturbed when this occurs. Changing forecasts disrupt production's planning process and their determinations of material requirements, forcing production managers to redo their plan. Fortunately, this situation may be changing. As noted in a production publication, the awareness of the customer's importance is reflected in the following quote: "Facing a bottom-line-conscious marketplace and increasing pressure from domestic and overseas competitors, manufacturers have been forced to reassess established practices. They now recognize that products need to be brought to market more quickly without compromising quality and that processes need to be honed to ensure cost-competitiveness."[5]

THE EFFECTS OF PARTNERING, TQM, CE, AND MARKET-DRIVEN DOWNSTREAM CUSTOMERS

Markets are not as free and open as they once were. Business pacts have always existed, but today elongated and lasting pacts, via partnering, and between buyers and sellers, has become a way of business to compete with overseas sellers. The fundamental transformations during the 1980s focused on reshaping the internal operations of business organizations. In contrast, developments in the 1990s and beyond tend to be different, with the focus of change shifting, broadening, and becoming more subtle and complex, and unquestionably, involving the marketing function in a central position.[6]

Many business firms realize that downstream, final consumer demand is an important factor in determining their own demand and the subsequent sales forecasts. Derived demand considerations have moved many companies toward concentrating on the realities of the consumer market and how the value-adding chains are working to meet changing needs and marketing research efforts. DuPont, for example, changed its thinking to emphasize the market-driven nature of its business.[6]

Demand Analysis

Forecasting is predicting, projecting, or estimating some future event or condition that is outside the full control of an organization.[7] Forecasting is viewed as comprising two elements: (1) market potential and (2) sales potential. **Market potential** is the totality of market wants, needs, and desires that would manifest in sales for a given product or service, in a defined business market, at a given moment in time, for all companies in that industry. Of course, the nature of business marketing includes derived demands, and the market potential calculation would have to take this situation into consideration. **Sales potential**, on the other hand, is the total market share of that market potential that one company could possibly achieve for a given product or service in a defined business market at a given moment of time. Sales forecasts are different from sales potential, since forecasts are affected by the marketing efforts (promotion, channels, price, and market choice) of an individual seller, competition, and the prevailing general economic conditions.[8] Sales forecasts are a subset of the existing sales potential. Business marketing must also consider the derived demand situation, as well. A *product sales forecast* is the expected level of a given product's sales volume, based on a chosen marketing plan and an assumed marketing environment for that product.[9] Figure 7-1 shows the intricate relationship between demand analysis and sales forecasting.

Market and Sales Potentials

Market potential represents a maximum sales opportunity from which the company's sales forecasts can be derived. Titanium is a silvery gray, light, strong, metallic element often used as an alloy in steel, or combined in refractory materials, or used in industrial coatings. Airframe manufacturers are the largest users of titanium because of its properties of strength and lightweight.

The airframe market potential for titanium would include all the possible airframe manufacturers who had acquired or anticipated commercial and/or government

FIGURE 7-1 Product demand analysis and sales forecasting process.

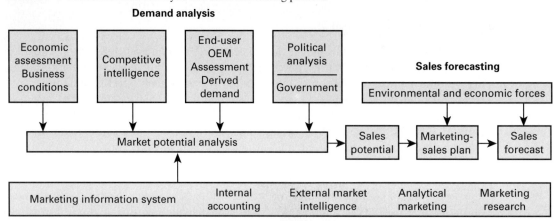

contracts to build new airframes, namely, Boeing, McDonnell-Douglas, Northrup, and others. Each firm working on a current government or private sector contract would be analyzed to determine the quantity of titanium they would use by investigating the size of their unfilled contracts, their monthly output and engineering "specs" of the types of airframes being manufactured. The total quantity of titanium demanded by present users could be extrapolated from these data to provide the marketers the basis for an eventual sales forecast.

Sales potential can be determined by investigating the marketing company's strengths and weaknesses compared with those of their competitors, within the context of the givens in the market environment. Company size, financial strength, technical capability, sales force size, previous technical experience, personalities, and, of course, the company's ability to develop a marketing strategy all would help to determine the size of the company's sales potential.

Market potentials can be very tenuous, because they are subject to many changes. Economic, environmental, competitive, and governmental forces may interplay and drastically change the market's potential demand for a specific company's titanium. Congress may not allocate the necessary funds for the development and production of future aircraft that would use titanium. A commercial firm such as Continental Airlines or United Airlines might reduce the size of the expected order or split the order between Boeing McDonnell-Douglas or Airbus. Therefore, an industrial firm supplying titanium is at the mercy of the market variables and must learn to cope with the demand situation to survive.

Measuring Market and Sales Potential

Forecasting the future always entails a degree of soothsaying, but to measurably reduce unjustified and unqualified forecasts, one general method is used to judge market potential, called the **market build-up method**.[9]

Business producers frequently use the market build-up method for estimating their potential purchases, because accuracy demands they be able to identify all or most of their potential buyers. The build-up method employs isolating one of a number of factors that relates to a firm's future sales, and then adding these factors together to arrive at the sales potential for the company. If John Deere wanted to forecast future tractor sales, they would look at the trends in three variables: (1) the number of independent farm units or family farms and agribusiness units; (2) the age of currently owned tractors of the type being forecast; and (3) the number of tractors sent to the junk yard. These factors would provide replacement demand and any *delta*, or change, in the demand for new tractors. When these factors are added together, Deere could better estimate its sales potential.

Three general measures can be employed in the market build-up method to provide reasonable data to determine market and sales potential. They include (1) statistical series methods, (2) market surveys, and (3) input/output analysis.

Statistical Series Methods

Statistical series methods provide one major approach for a forecaster's prognostications. A single series and/or a number of series are chosen to stabilize a forecast. The logic assumes one series or set of series can be found to be highly correlated with a product's past sales data. Knowing the forecast of this one series or set of series, as provided by other sources, could be used to help predict a product's future sales potential.

If a single-series approach is used, perhaps the best choice for industrial goods is "value added" by manufacturer from the *Census of Manufactures*. However, these data are not always up-to-date, nor are they ever available to most companies by market area of interest. The next best option is a statistical series for employment that is correlated with "value added" by manufacturer and is available by both industries and establishment.[8] Employment statistics are useful because they often correlate with a customer's need for machine tools, supplies, raw materials, and other industrial products. The semiconductor industry uses a leading indicator to predict its future sales.[10] The semiconductor industry's so-called book-to-bill ratio has been a reliable series. This ratio is a 3-month moving average of U.S. orders or bookings compared with a 3-month moving average of billings or shipments. If the ratio is 1.26, this figure means that for every $100 of product shipped, semiconductor manufacturers receive orders valued at $126. The higher the ratio, the better the future prospects.

GOVERNMENT'S CENSUS OF MANUFACTURES, COUNTY BUSINESS PATTERNS, AND SURVEY OF INDUSTRIAL AND COMMERCIAL BUYING POWER

A valuable secondary source is the **Census of Manufactures** published by the Commerce Department, which lists the manufacturers by industry type, among other things. This report is valuable for estimating a firm's market potential.

The **County Business Patterns** lists the number of employees, payrolls, and the number of establishments, by SIC code. A valued supplemental source was the **Survey of Industrial and Commercial Buying Power** (SICBP) conducted by *Sales and Marketing Management* magazine. This survey provided the best and most usable data for business marketers, but the magazine discontinued the service in 1989. Some of these reports can still be received by writing to the magazine. The County Business Patterns (CBP) does provide a finer breakdown by SIC codes than the SICBP. However, the CBP is published only every 4 years, creating gaps in the data. The shortage of reliable market data sources places an extra burden on the marketer's creativity and endurance when analyzing both quantitative economic data and qualitative data.

SIC LIMITATIONS

Despite the usefulness of the government's SIC data, four major limitations exist.[11] First, the total output of a multiple-product firm must be assigned to a single four-digit industry to simplify the data collection and presentation. This limitation over-states shipments and understates the establishment's secondary products or services. Second, the nondisclosure rule bars the Census Bureau from publishing any data that could disclose the operations of a specific company. A large establishment that dominates a county's statistical listing cannot by law be listed, thus excluding these shipment/receipts data from that county's total. Third, SIC data are heavily weighted toward manufacturing firms as compared with service firms, hence distorting data on services. Fourth, the classification of the data is confusing. For example, if a particular product is branded by a distributor (Bushnell), it will not show up in the same category (binoculars) as its parent company (Bausch & Lomb), makers of optical equipment. Bushnell would be dumped together with distributor data, hence distorting the data.

LEADING TIME SERIES

One important secondary source of economic data managers can use is time series. These data can be correlated with a firm's historical sales data. Managers and forecasters search constantly for a historical indicator series that either (1) leads the business cycle turning points, (2) is coincidental to these points, or (3) lags the business cycle's turning points, as seen in Table 7-2. Regardless of the series used it is important that the best match be found that can be used to predict a product's sales volume If a lag economic series matches the history of the product's sales history, then it can be used to forecast the product's sales by over laying one series on the top of the other. If the lag series gives any appropriate signal of changes by turning upward or downward *before* the company's sales turns up or down, then the lag series can be used to predict the product's future sales by observing what the lag series has already done. The lead and coincident series can be used the same way.

Many economic series exist and are available in the **Survey of Current Business** such as Gross Domestic Product, Industrial Capacity Used, Unemployment, Leading Economic Indicators (LEI), as seen in Table 7-1, and Industrial Production. A good example of a leading series is the **Business Week Index,** which contains seven groups of economic data from which one or many series can be used by many industrial firms to predict U.S. production and sales data. The index includes production indicators such as steel, automobiles, trucks, electric power, and so on; foreign exchange including the Japanese yen, German mark, British pound, and so on; prices of gold, steel scrap, foodstuffs, copper, and so on; leading indicators including stock prices, corporate bond yields, bond ratings such as Aaa, industrial material prices, business failures, real estate loans, and so on; monthly economic indicators such as money supply, M1 (currency and checking accounts), banks' business loans, free reserves, and so on; money market rates for federal funds, prime commercial paper, certificates of deposit (3 months) and Eurodollars (3 months).[12] If any one series or a combination of series in this index correlates with a given product sales history, then a predictive tool may be at hand.

BUSINESS CYCLE ANALYSIS

It is very helpful to look for the significant turning points (see Table 7-2) in aggregate economic activity so an estimate of market potential may be developed with some fine-tuning. If business fluctuations in the past have either correlated with industry sales or the business cycle has been used as an sales indicator, cycle analysis can be a valuable tool. If a new product is involved, business fluctuations could indicate waves of optimism or pessimism directly affecting the derived demand status of the industrial product.

New products and services do not have the luxury of using historical data, per se. New ventures must scratch out a sales forecast in the best way they can. When a group of about twenty big Silicon Valley companies, including Intel, Sun Microsystems, Hewlett Packard, Packard Bell and Apple Computer, planned to jump-start the most ambitious electronic marketplace yet for the information superhighway, called, CommerceNet, its success was almost a total unknown. The consortium used the Internet system and was designed to rely heavily on Internet programs called World Wide Web and Mosaic, which programs would hide from buyers and sellers the Internet mind-numbing minutiae and complexity. The group believed that after two decades of use by engineers, scientists, and adventurous PC owners, the Internet system was at a turning point. The chief quantitative data used by the group to predict the future, besides the strong movement by the market in this direction, was that an estimated 40,000 U.S. companies routinely exchanged electronic invoices and other business forms directly from one company to another, which exchange was called electronic data interchange

TABLE 7-1 Business Cycle Indicators (Composite Indexes)

Series No.	Series Title and Timing Classification	Year 1994	1994 June	July	Aug.	Sept.	Oct.
	The Leading Index						
910	Composite index of leading indicators, 1987=100 (L,L,L)	101.7	101.7	101.7	102.3	102.3	102.2
	Percent change from previous month	.2	.2	0	.6	0	–.1
	Percent change over 3-month span, AR	2.3	1.2	3.2	2.4	2.0	0
	Leading index components:						
1	Average weekly hours, mfg. (L,L,L)	42.0	42.0	42.0	42.0	42.1	42.1
5	Average weekly initial claims for unemployment insurance, thous. (L,C,L)	337	339	335	323	321	329
8	Mfrs.' new orders, consumer goods and materials, bil. 1987$ (L,L,L)	1,430.51	117.72	115.36	122.00	120.15	120.80
32	Vendor performance, slower deliveries diffusion index, percent (L,L,L)	60.1	59.7	57.2	61.4	62.1	64.7
20	Contracts and orders for plant and equipment, bil. 1987$ (L,L,L)	531.47	44.82	43.63	44.54	46.57	45.73
29	Index of new private housing units authorized by local building permits, 1987=100 (L,L,L)	86.4	85.2	85.0	87.5	90.0	88.4
92	Change in mfrs.' unfilled orders, durable goods, bil. 1987$, smoothed (L,L,L)	–.71	–.12	–.16	–.43	–.49	–.41
99	Change in sensitive materials prices, percent, smoothed (L,L,L)	1.72	1.84	2.36	2.50	2.37	2.16
19	Index of stock prices, 500 common stocks, 1941-43=10, NSA (L,L,L)	460.33	454.83	451.40	464.24	466.96	463.81
106	Money supply M2, bil. 1987$ (L,L,L)	2,764.9	2,769.0	2,769.3	2,757.4	2,750.4	2,743.1
83	Index of consumer expectations, U. of Michigan, 1966:1=100, NSA (L,L,L)	83.8	82.7	78.5	80.8	83.5	85.1
950	Diffusion index of 11 leading indicator components:						
	Percent rising over 1-month span	59.5	45.5	40.9	77.3	59.1	45.5
	Percent rising over 6-month span	70.4	72.7	81.8	77.3	90.9	72.7
	The Coincident Index						
920	Composite index of coincident indicators, 1987=100 (C,C,C)	113.9	113.6	113.7	114.4	114.7	115.3
	Percent change from previous month	.4	.4	.1	.6	.3	.5
	Percent change over 3-month span, AR	4.5	2.9	4.3	3.9	5.7	5.0
	Coincident index components:						
41	Employees on nonagricultural payrolls, thous. (C,C,C)	114,034	113,943	114,171	114,510	114,762	114,935
51	Personal income less transfer payments, bil. 1987$, AR (C,C,C)	3,664.7	3,649.3	3,654.2	3,665.0	3,683.6	3,735.7
47	Index of industrial production, 1987=100 (C,C,C)	118.1	118.0	118.2	119.1	119.0	119.5
57	Manufacturing and trade sales, mil. 1987$ (C,C,C)	6,688,534	554,024	549,987	565,578	564,681	566,945
951	Diffusion index of 4 coincident indicator components:						
	Percent rising over 1-month span	83.3	75.0	75.0	100.0	50.0	100.0
	Percent rising over 6-month span	100.0	100.0	100.0	100.0	100.0	100.0
	The Lagging Index						
930	Composite index of lagging indicators, 1987=100 (Lg, Lg,Lg)	97.5	97.4	97.6	97.8	98.4	96.8
	Percent change from previous month	.3	.6	.2	.2	.6	.4
	Percent change over 3-month span, AR	3.5	5.1	4.2	4.2	5.0	6.7
	Lagging index components:						
91	Average duration of unemployment, weeks (Lg, Lg, Lg)	18.8	18.4	19.0	18.9	18.8	19.3
77	Ratio, mfg. and trade inventories to sales in 1987$ (Lg, Lg, Lg)	1.47	1.47	1.49	1.45	1.46	1.46
62	Change in labor cost per unit of output, mfg., percent, AR, smoothed (Lg, Lg, Lg)	–2.3	–3.7	–3.5	–3.6	-2.6	.1
109	Average prime rate charged by banks, percent, NSA (Lg, Lg, Lg)	7.14	7.25	7.25	7.51	7.75	7.75
101	Commercial and industrial loans outstanding, mil. 1987$ (Lg, Lg, Lg)	384,184	378,803	382,721	385,007	391,859	398,455
95	Ratio, consumer installment credit outstanding to personal income, percent (Lg, Lg, Lg)	14.86	14.84	14.90	15.07	15.14	15.09
120	Change in Consumer Price Index for services, percent, AR, smoothed (Lg, Lg, Lg)	3.1	3.0	2.8	3.0	3.1	3.1
952	Diffusion index of 7 lagging indicator components:						
	Percent rising over 1-month span	61.3	71.4	64.3	71.4	100.0	57.1
	Percent rising over 6-month span	62.5	64.3	57.1	71.4	71.4	85.7
940	Ratio, coincident index to lagging index, 1987=100 (L, L, L)	116.7	116.6	116.5	117.0	116.6	116.7

Source: Survey of Current Business (August 1995), p. C-1.

	1994		1995						
	Nov.	*Dec.*	*Jan.*	*Feb.*	*Mar.*	*Apr.*	*May*	*June*	*July*
	102.3	102.5	102.5	102.2	101.8	101.2	101.0	101.2	101.0
	.1	.2	0	−.3	−.4	−.6	−.2	.2	−.2
	.8	1.2	−.4	−2.7	−5.0	−4.6	−2.3	−.8	—
	42.1	42.1	42.2	42.1	42.0	41.5	41.4	41.5	41.3
	327	325	329	330	330	352	380	369	367
	123.24	124.93	125.28	122.58	121.31	118.98	119.27	119.31	119.43
	65.2	65.7	62.6	62.5	56.7	56.1	52.9	51.2	50.4
	47.67	44.65	48.85	49.83	50.80	47.63	51.13	52.11	48.52
	85.7	89.6	81.6	80.9	77.9	78.4	78.4	80.5	85.5
	−.19	.21	.61	.87	.75	.19	−.22	−.67	−.92
	2.17	2.14	2.10	1.73	1.51	1.34	1.23	.99	.51
	461.01	455.19	465.25	481.92	493.15	507.91	523.81	539.35	557.37
	2,742.1	2,739.5	2,740.1	2,728.5	2,728.0	2,727.4	2,733.4	2,755.9	2,763.8
	84.8	88.8	88.4	85.9	79.8	83.8	80.1	84.1	87.4
	63.6	59.1	50.0	27.3	27.3	31.8	40.9	68.2	54.5
	63.6	36.4	27.3	18.2	27.3	27.3	—	—	—
	115.8	116.4	116.6	116.9	117.0	116.7	116.7	117.1	117.3
	.4	.5	.2	.3	.1	−.3	0	.3	.2
	6.1	4.6	3.9	2.1	.3	−.7	.3	2.1	—
	115,427	115,624	115,810	116,123	116,302	116,310	116,248	116,498	116,553
	3,727.3	3,751.4	3,763.3	3,776.8	3,789.2	3,784.1	3,766.4	3,786.0	3,806.4
	120.3	121.7	122.0	122.1	122.0	121.2	121.2	121.1	121.3
	572,659	578,177	577,427	577,835	576,415	571,204	575,322	579,894	—
	75.0	100.0	75.0	100.0	50.0	12.5	37.5	75.0	83.3
	100.0	100.0	100.0	100.0	75.0	66.7	—	—	—
	99.4	99.5	100.0	100.7	101.1	101.8	102.1	102.6	102.3
	.6	.1	.5	.7	.4	.7	.3	.5	−.3
	4.5	4.9	5.3	6.6	7.4	5.7	6.1	2.0	—
	18.2	17.8	16.7	16.9	17.5	17.7	16.9	15.6	16.5
	1.45	1.44	1.45	1.45	1.46	1.48	1.47	1.47	—
	−.5	−1.8	−2.2	.9	2.0	1.8	.7	.4	.8
	8.15	8.50	8.50	9.00	9.00	9.00	9.00	9.00	8.80
	398,638	402,981	407,523	412,295	416,565	425,224	424,948	427,934	431,089
	15.33	15.35	15.42	15.41	15.58	15.74	16.00	16.08	—
	3.1	2.9	3.1	3.4	3.6	3.9	4.0	4.0	3.9
	57.1	50.0	78.6	64.3	78.6	64.3	50.0	64.3	40.0
	92.9	92.9	100.0	100.0	100.0	100.0	—	—	—
	116.5	117.0	116.6	116.1	115.7	114.6	114.3	114.1	114.7

TABLE 7-2 Cyclical Indicators: Composite Indexes

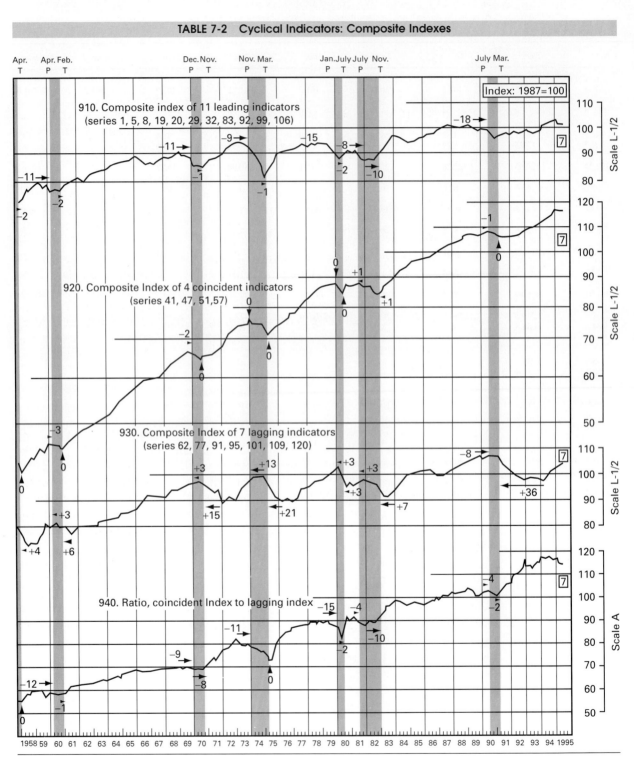

Source: Survey of Current Business (August 1995), p. C-7.

(EDI). In addition, the existence of computerized reservation systems, networks for hospital suppliers, auto parts, and insurance, were also seen as impressive trends that indicated a strong potential.[13]

Market Surveys

Long a standard means of acquiring data for market analysis, surveys are conducted among many groups to upgrade and update any statistical series data. Personal interviews, and mail or telephone surveys are conducted by the company's sales force, industry experts, distributors, dealers, the customer's purchasing people, and the customer's technical and marketing people to gain a reasonable estimate of a product's market potential. These methods are very helpful for new or untested products where no historical sales data experience exists or where no statistical series can be found useful for correlation analysis. The magazine *Industrial Distribution* surveyed the members of the American Supply and Machinery Manufacturers Association to project what actions were necessary to survive in today's hectic distribution arena. DuPont surveyed its business customers to determine whether its customers were willing to pay a premium price for some of its new products.[14] Case Corporation asked a long-time customer to assess the company's new loader-backhoe machine. Many of the customer's recommendations were included in the product's final design. Addition surveys of farmers and contractors were made by Case to forecast the new loader-backhoe's potential success.[15]

Sales Forecasting

After the preliminaries of forecasting market and sales potentials are completed, the serious task of developing a workable sales forecast for a specific product must be undertaken. This development entails forecasting both (1) the customer's organizational responses to the given strategy used and (2) the expected effectiveness of the level of the marketing effort. A sales forecast is the result of first, the sales potential; second, the marketing strategy used; and third, the level of the marketing effort. The forecast is not the result of the size of the market or sales potential only. However, any business marketing sales forecast is subject to derived demand. If USX wanted to forecast its sales for rolled sheet steel, it would have to forecast consumer demand for cars, refrigerators, freezers, washers, dryers, and any other consumer product that used a rolled-sheet steel component. Then the company would have to account for any of its customers' reduction or increase in rolled sheet steel usage. In the car business, manufactures have substituted many steel components with plastic components, which action gives great concern to the rolled sheet steel manufacturers.

If the projected sales forecast for a given marketing strategy fails to meet the organization's goals and objectives, numerous opportunities exist to change the situation. Any of the marketing mix variables can be recast into more workable strategies, or the budget can be altered to change the level of the marketing effort. Therefore, products, promotion, market segments, salespeople, marketing service, technical assistance, pricing, and physical distribution can be changed in some form to adjust to the most desired strategy and marketing effort levels. For these reasons, test marketing is very appropriate for products used in quantity. For exclusive business goods such as the Cray Super Computer, which went out of business due to lack of orders, test marketing would have been out of the question. Cray installed one of its super computers in a government agency as a test to acquire a track record of engineering performance data for promotional use with potential customers. Any new business product, if possible, should be tested on the market or installed in some potential customer's business.

SALES FORECAST OBJECTIVES

Forecasting future performance is an important requirement for costing, planning manpower planning, batch sizing for production, and delivery date projections, in addition to all the requirements of marketing.[16] Sales forecasts, as used in many areas of business marketing management, may include developing sales quotas; determining sales compensation; establishing sales incentive plans; developing finished goods inventory needs; creating advertising and promotional plans; formulating sales expense policies; establishing sales territories and sales personnel needs; developing distribution plans, transportation and storage facilities; and developing future product strategies, if needed.

FORECAST TIME FRAMES

Typical forecast time frames can cover 3, 6, 12, or 18 months in length, or, in some special cases, 5 years or more. Since sales forecasts have multiple uses, different approaches must be taken to achieve the desired results. Most managers will want the forecast results to extend into the future as far as possible, but the managers should choose the right techniques for the chosen period of time.[7] The shorter the time horizon, the higher the accuracy; conversely, the longer the time frame, the lower the accuracy of the forecast. Some organizations forecast for years into the future. Boeing's forecast of the future of the 777 extended into the twenty-first century. Power and water plants forecast as far as 30 or 40 years into the future. Microchip manufacturers, on the other hand, may forecast for only 18 to 24 months.

FORECASTING UNCERTAINTIES

Forecasting incorporates soothsaying, logic, judgment, solid mathematical relationships, understanding of the data involved, and the manager's guess as to what the results should be. A sales forecast attempts to reduce the uncertainties to a manageable size. Dealing with the future can never be eliminated or reduced to to the point at which any perfunctory marketing strategies can be used. Some business and industrial managers are bewitched by these uncertainties, since many deal only with hard data most of the time. Given these uncertainties of the future, as a hedge, forecasters use several techniques. One technique assumes a primary role in determining the forecast; other techniques used provide checks on the first technique's reliability.[17]

In all techniques used, judgment and consensus among a few or many individuals become vital ingredients in enhancing forecast accuracy. However, the greater the accuracy desired, the greater will be the costs as additional techniques are added, as seen in Figure 7-2.

Costs can grow faster than the desired accuracy; thus the cost-benefits become a "wash." The Internet has many firms in the computer, information processing, and telecommunications fields positioning themselves for a significant role in the information highway's future. It has been estimated that this industry is the growth industry of the latter part of the1990s. Microsoft has spent millions of dollars in researching its role in the information highway.[18] Among Microsoft's areas of interest are natural language, speech recognition, decision-making programs, new user interfaces, operating systems, video programming, interactive TV interfaces, pocket computers, set-top

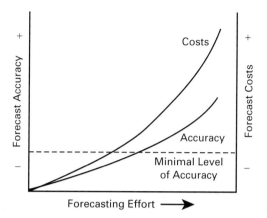

FIGURE 7-2 The sales forecast and cost trade-off.

boxes, and interactive TV services. All the firms have forecast a bright future for the Internet and are willing to invest in its future. Strange as it may seem, the same techniques used on the Internet are now successfully being used on the *Intranet* for intra-plant communications by Compaq, AT&T, and others.

Forecasting Techniques

Complementary techniques must be chosen so that the ultimate sales forecast will contain the fewest errors and provide the greatest reality. Techniques can range from qualitative (judgmental) to quantitative (mathematical). The choice of the array is a function of the time frame being forecast, the costs of the forecast techniques involved, the degree of forecast accuracy desired, availability of past data, and where and how the forecast will be used. However, the level of sophistication for the organization and the people involved must be a match for the qualitative-quantitative technique used.[7]

QUALITATIVE FORECASTING APPROACHES

Very popular among business firms because of the nature of the firm's markets, qualitative or judgmental techniques include buyer surveys, executive surveys, sales force inquiries, and the Delphi method. Some judgmental techniques have been shown to have superior accuracy compared with many more sophisticated quantitative techniques.[19] This unexpected phenomenon exists for numerous reasons. Judgmental techniques are more flexible and easier to use and do not suffer from the most typical built-in mathematical bias—what has happened in the past will continue to happen in the future.

Survey of Buyer's Intentions   Forecasting can be an art form in which the seller anticipates what present business customers or potential business customers are likely to do under given conditions. A firm's research department may question their own customer's purchase intentions toward a given product or product line, or even let the customer use a new product to gain market acceptance. Biases can enter this process if the customers are aware of the study's sponsor. A more reliable survey is conducted by the Department of Commerce, which has published an annual **Survey of Capital Equipment Buying Plans,** as reported by business executives. These surveys have been very accurate and used widely to construct sales forecasts for capital equipment manufacturers. Over one 17-year period, for example, the average error in business investment predictions was less than 5 percent.[20]

Executive Surveys   A low-cost and easy method of achieving a sales forecast makes the executive survey approach very popular. Executives from sales, marketing, product management, production/operations, finance, and top management participate in estimating a product's future sales. A composite of the opinions culminates in the sales forecast. The obvious downside is the approach's inherent propensity to provide a forum for the executive's biases and prejudices.

Sales Force Composite Inquiries   Sales force composite inquiries take the approach of a bottom build-up summation of each salesperson's forecast. The salespersons in the field are in the best position to witness any changes in their own territories since they deal with customers on a daily basis. Their judgment is substantiated by their knowledge of their respective market. Salespeople are not good market researchers, or even good forecasters, as interpreted by home-office people, because the salespeople frequently see the home office's sales forecast requests as only time-consuming intrusions. As salespeople see it, their job is to sell and foster customer relations, but salespeople are also a very fine source of forecasting information. Mead Johnson, a pharmaceutical manufacturer, tried to overcome this prevailing sales force obstacle by inviting each sales representative into the home office to play golf and get some general relaxation. In the interim, they questioned the sales force to gain sales forecasting information.

Delphi Method   Similar to the executive surveys, the Delphi method is a systematic way of converting executive opinions into an acceptable consensus. A series of estimating rounds are initiated, with each contributor's identity remaining anonymous. After the first round of written opinions about the probability of future sales, all the results are combined and issued as a consensus to each contributor's second-round analysis. Subsequent rounds are initiated as needed until a total consensus is achieved. This technique is most useful for long-term forecasting and for unique types of products because of the technique's customized approach to the forecasting problem and its ability to forge a consensus of expert opinions. Defense contractors faced the problem of technology transfer in which their production techniques had to be converted to civilian use because of the downturn in defense orders. After many brainstorming sessions using modified Delphi techniques, these contractors concluded that the future offered little solace to the millions of engineers, managers, and skilled workers whose skills, developed over a lifetime, were no longer in demand.[21]

QUANTITATIVE FORECASTING APPROACHES

Quantitative techniques are more rigorous in appearance, appear more scientific, and are frequently easier to sell to top managers. The two major quantitative types are (1) time series and (2) causal regressive.[22]

The increased use of computers and the considerable number of software programs available have led to greater usage of quantitative methods of analyzing data.[23] Software programs make available simple but highly useful techniques for analysis (Table 7-3). For example, computerized cross-tabulations can summarize data quickly and provide researchers with useful comparisons of portions of data that are arranged into easily readable matrices. Table 7-4 shows a simplified cross-tabulation matrix for analyzing customer attitudes on salesperson visits.

An analysis of Table 7-4 indicates that twice as many customers in the Illinois territory feel that salesperson visits are excessive, compared with the impressions of the

Computer Capability	Market Potentials	Market Characteristics	Market Shares	Business Trends	New Products/Line Extensions	Competitive Activities	Sales (Analysis)	Distribution Channels	Acquisitions	Imports/Exports	Marketing Planning Inputs
TABLE 7-3 Use of Computers for Measurement											
Provided by External Vendors											
Databases											
Time series	X	X	X	X	X	X	X	X	X	X	X
Secondary literature	X	X	X	X	X	X		X	X	X	X
Input/output services	X	X	X		X		X	X	X		X
Time-series software		X		X	X			X			X
Multivariate software		X	X		X	X	X	X	X		X
Computerized planning systems		X				X	X		X		X
Created Internally											
Databases											
Time series	X	X	X	X	X	X	X	X	X	X	X
Other intelligence	X	X	X	X	X	X		X	X		X
Input/output tables	X	X	X		X		X	X	X		X
Sales reporting systems		X	X		X	X	X	X		X	X
Marketing intelligence systems	X	X	X	X	X	X	X	X	X	X	X

*Source:*Applications for computers in industrial marketing research progress during the 1970s. Reprinted by permission from Craig M. Collins, "Major industrial marketing research computer system developments will be in graphics and planning in '80s," *Marketing News* 13 (April 4, 1980): 5.

TABLE 7-4 Sample Cross-tabulation Matrix

No. of Salesperson Visits	Target Markets			
	Illinois	*California*	*Texas*	*Total*
Excessive	10	0	5	15
Satisfactory	60	10	7	77
Too few	12	5	0	17
Total	82	15	12	109

customers in the Texas territory. If Table 7-4 were an actual computer printout, it would also contain percentages that would show 42 percent of the customers in Texas feel-salesperson visits are excessive, compared with 12 percent in Illinois. Such comparisons, provided by cross-tabulation software, considerably enhance the understanding and usefulness of secondary and primary data.

Some simple quantitative techniques exist that often may prove to be satisfactory without incurring the higher costs of more complex quantitative techniques. These procedures include the (1) naive method, (2) moving averages, and (3) exponential smoothing.

Naive Method   This is one of the simplest time series methods as well as being most accurate, since it uses the most recently observed values. The basic assumption is that what happened last week, or last month, or last year will continue to happen next week, next month, or next year. Often more sophisticated mathematical methods may not always provide better results, in spite of their increased costs because the naive method's lack of extemporaneous conjecture. For example, if the company's sales for its ball bearings was growing at a 3 percent pace, then a naive forecast would dictate a 3 percent pace would continue with no change.

Moving Average   In short-run analysis, a major concern is the randomness element. One of the easiest ways to minimize the impact of randomness is to average several of the past values. Whether a 3-month, 6-month or 12-month moving average is used, the results can be smoothed. For example, if a sales manager wanted to forecast monthly shipments to a specific geographical region, it might be advisable to use a 3-month moving average. As seen in Table 7-5, averaging 3 months smooths the process by removing the more erratic seasonal factors.

This approach assumes that a series' future will be an average of its past, which assumption can offer some advantages and some disadvantages. If a suddenly abrupt change occurs, the moving average can be an advantage because it would not be affected as much as would a trend line. The crucial disadvantage in using a moving average is determining the ideal number of periods to include in the average. A large number of periods make the forecast slow to react, but a small number of periods can lead to rapid response to changes in the series, which may be incorrect. Since all periods are given equal weight, starting from the oldest to the newest, moving averages fall short of being able to follow trends.

Exponential Smoothing   Instead of using a constant set of weights, as in the previous examples, an exponentially decreasing set of weights is used in this technique.

TABLE 7-5   Three-Month Moving Average

		1994	Average	1995	Average
	Jan	274	—	291	292
	Feb	463	—	397	324
	March	398	378	336	341
S	April	276	379	312	348
A	May	379	225	346	331
L	June	425	360	392	350
E	July	450	418	414	384
S	Aug	465	447	426	411
	Sept	380	432	403	414
	Oct	322	389	357	395
	Nov	301	334	320	360
	Dec	285	303	298	325

$$F_{t+1} = \frac{S_t + S_{t-1} \ldots + S_{t-n+1}}{n}$$

F_{t+1} = forecast for next period

S_t = sales in the current period

n = number of periods in the moving average

The more recent values receive more weight than older values to increase accuracy. The main decision lies in the selection of an appropriate value for smoothing the constant. This innate problem may be overcome by testing two or more smoothing constants against actual data to determine which has less error.

The simplest form of exponential smoothing can be expressed by the equation

$$F_{t+1} = F_t + a(X_t - F_t)$$

where F_{t+1} is the forecast for the present time period and a is the weight given to the difference between the actual value of the variable in the present time period (X_t) and the forecasted value.

The use of simple predictive techniques, however, can lead to incorrect predictions and costly errors, because in most situations, they do not include a sufficient number of variables for accurate forecasting, as the exponential smoothing formula reflects. This problem in predicting arises in the industrial market because derived demand is considerably affected by such factors as world political and economic conditions, the cost of money, the level of disposable income, the stage of the business cycle, seasonable considerations, the availability of resources, and many other factors that must be considered.

Many firms use more sophisticated programs, such as linear regression and time-series models, to analyze predictive data. Thirty-four large firms in random SIC code areas indicated that time series and linear regression techniques ranked one and two in business world forecasting techniques, with sales force composites a close third.[24] Comparatively, however, all other statistical techniques ranked much lower (Table 7-6).

CAUSAL OR REGRESSIVE TECHNIQUES

The two major components of causal or regressive techniques are (1) simple or linear regression and (2) multiple regression. Table 7-7 lists commonly used linear regression terms.

Simple or Linear Regression   In a simple or linear regression, the relationship between two variables, such as sales (Y) and an independent variable such as number of salespeople (X), can be represented as a straight line:

$$Y = a + b(X)$$

where a is the Y intercept and b shows the impact of the independent variable, number of salespeople. The best fit of the data can be found by deriving the values of the a and

TABLE 7-6 Average Yearly Usage of Statistical Tools

Name of Tool	Average
Delphi Technique	1.8
Exponential Smoothing	2.4
Linear Regression	8.7
Time Series	10.6
ARIMA/Box-Jenkins	1.0
Decision Support Systems	2.8
Venture Analysis	2.0
Executive Panels	3.2
Sales force Composites	6.0

TABLE 7-7 Commonly Used Linear Regression Terms	
X variable	The variable used to predict, also called the independent or predictor variable.
Y variable	The variable being predicted, also called the dependent, criterion, or predicted variable.
b coefficient	The amount of an X variable necessary to estimate a change of one unit in the Y variable.
Beta coefficient	The b coefficient determined after the X and Y date have been normalized; that is, the data for each variable are entered into the regression only after they have been changed from their raw b form into the number of standard deviations they are above or below the average.
Syx (standard error)	The standard deviation running along each side of the regression line. After computing the regression, for any particular value of X, there is a 68% chance that the predicted Y will fall between one standard error above and one standard error below the regression line.
t test	A test used to determine if a particular b coefficient is large enough to be meaningful (other than zero) or if that particular predictor variable should be omitted. Sometimes called Student's t test.
F test	A test to determine whether an entire set of different X variables (GNP, disposable income, etc.) is meaningful enough to be used as a set or if one, some, or all of them should be replaced.

b coefficients. The *least squares method* may give a more satisfactory fit, however. The least squared estimates of the coefficients are values that minimize the squared differences between the actual sales data and the values predicted by the equation, thus providing a better fit (Table 7-8). Linear regression enables the forecaster to predict the value of the dependent variable (*Y,* sales volume), but its greatest drawback is in knowing how much past data *(X)* to include in the calculation of the forecasting formula. Looking at Table 7-8, if the data were chosen for only years 1, 2, and 3, the formula would forecast a steep incline in sales. If years 4, 5, and 6 were chosen, the formula would predict a steep decline in sales. One way to overcome this disadvantage would be to plot all data first and then choose a sufficient number of periods to "wash out" the bias.

Multiple Regression   In the use of this technique, a forecaster can use a computer to build a model on past relationships that have existed among sales and several other independent X variables. A multiple-regression calculation R squared could be determined by taking the two or more independent variables' estimated values for the period to be forecast and plugging them into the formula. If sales for a derived demand product, such as roller bearings Y, were to be found, values for these independent variables would have to be calculated: X_1, sales by OEM automobile producers; X_2, sales by OEM material handling equipment manufactures; and X_3, sales to industrial distributors for resale to end users.

$$Y = b + b_1X_{t1} + b_2X_{t2} + b_3X_{t3}$$

A computer program is used for multiple regression of the dependent variable from which we derive the coefficients for X_{t1}, X_{t2}, and X_{t3}, their standard errors, the partial coefficients of determination, the coefficient of multiple determination, and perhaps one or more measures of significance, such as the t-ratio or the F-test values.[25]

TABLE 7-8 Catculating a Simple of Linear Regression

	Time X	Sales Y	XY	X^2
	1	274	274	1
	2	463	926	4
	3	398	1,194	9
	4	276	1,104	16
	5	379	1,895	25
Sum	15	1,790	5,393	55
Average	3	358.0		

$Y = a + bX$

$$b = \frac{n\Sigma XY - \Sigma X \Sigma Y}{n(\Sigma X^2) - (\Sigma X)^2} \qquad\qquad a = \bar{y} - b\bar{X}$$

$$b = \frac{5(5,393) - (15)(1,790)}{5(55) - (15)^2} \qquad\qquad a = 358.0 - (2.3)(3)$$

$b = 2.3 \qquad\qquad\qquad\qquad\qquad a = 351.1$

$Y = 351.1 + 2.3X$

Choosing X Variables   Care must be taken in choosing X variables that will accurately predict the level of Y. Some industrial companies use numerous, very broad X variables, such as gross national product, national income, or population statistics, and prepare what are called *econometric models.* Most researchers, however, try to limit the number of predictor variables to as few as possible. This reduction saves time and money in collecting and processing data and is particularly important when several linear regression models are run frequently. Also, there is increasing evidence that simpler regression and time-series models perform as well as (and often better than) those that are more complicated.[26]

Using Lag Variables   It is worthwhile for researchers to spend extra time locating X variables for which data become available before the period the company is attempting to forecast. For example, one roofing-shingle manufacturer predicts future sales using, among other variables, present building permits. The data for this building permit X variable are available before the period Y is to be predicted. This X variable is called a *lag variable.* The use of lag variables allows researchers to predict on the basis of data from events that have already occurred rather than basing predictions on data that are projected to occur at the same time as their forecasts.

To locate lag variables, researchers obtain data from several, preferably easily accessible, indices and compare plots of that data against plots of the variable to be predicted. Past data for the Y variable are plotted alongside past data for various indices of X variables, but one, two, or three time periods behind the X variable data. Researchers then visually observe the plotted data to determine whether they are related positively or negatively; that is, both the X and Y data move up and down together or both move in opposite directions. If the two variables appear to be related (move in a positive or negative relationship), as shown in Figure 7-3 (for a positive relationship), researchers can use the X indices to predict or study the relationship. Further study of the relationship can involve using the X indices to predict values of Y for different past time periods, or it can involve determining how well the variables X and Y are correlated.

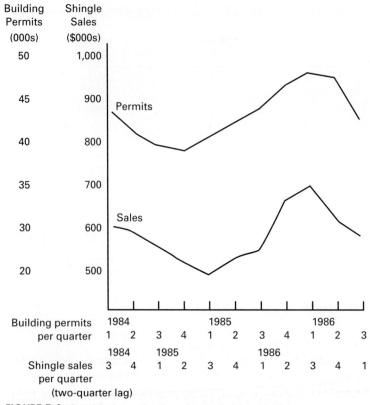

FIGURE 7-3 Graphic determination of a single lag variable.

Correlation Analysis   Linear regression computer programs usually produce two coefficients, the coefficient of correlation and the coefficient of determination, which estimate how well X and Y are correlated (whether X is related to Y). The coefficient of correlation, which ranges between the positive or negative one, indicates whether X and Y are positively or negatively related. The nearer the coefficient is to negative or positive 1.00, the greater the relationship between the two variables. The coefficient of determination (the square of the coefficient of correlation) ranges between 0 and 1.00 and indicates what percentage of the variation in Y is explained by X. The closer the coefficient of determination is to 1.00, the more likely it is that X is a good predictor of Y.

Computer Programs   There are several excellent software programs that perform linear regression. Dynacomp's Regression I, which is inexpensive and is said to be available for all computers, has several worthwhile features: it provides automatic data sorting, plots both data and curves, and produces the coefficient of correlation.[27] A frequently used program for computers is the Statistical Package for the Social Sciences (SPSS) package.

UNDERSTANDING LINEAR REGRESSION

To guide research efforts and evaluate and adjust the findings, marketing managers must understand the strong and weak points of linear regression, such as *standard error, multicollinearity, autocorrelation, heteroscedasticity,* and *nonlinearity.*

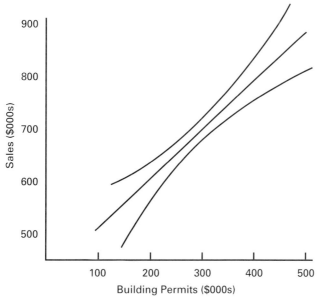

FIGURE 7-4 Sales regressed on building permits.

Standard Error   Although linear regression is normally more effective than simpler predictive models, it does have its own inherent problems. One such problem involves the standard error. As Figure 7-4 indicates, the standard error allows the forecaster to establish confidence intervals for estimates. When the researcher is forecasting Y based on an X value near the center of the X's (300 in Figure 7-4), the standard error will be smaller than when the researcher is forecasting Y based on an X value more distant from the center X value. Thus, when an unusually high or low X value occurs, indicating a forecast that would require the organization to make larger adjustments than usual, the standard error—and thus the confidence interval of the forecast,—become less accurate.

     Four other problems (although not common to all regression models) that present difficulties in preparing or interpreting linear regression models are discussed next.

Multicollinearity   **Multicollinearity** refers to using predictor variables that are very much the same (more correlated among themselves than with the variable they are predicting). Either of two such variables may alone predict well, but when both variables are used, very little additional information is added. Although this situation does not adversely affect forecasting, researchers attempt to avoid multicollinear variables, since much time and money can be spent gathering data that add little predictive ability.

Autocorrelation   **Autocorrelation** can be seen on a plot of actual data points around a regression line (Figure 7-5). Sometimes the actual data points seem to be related to one another rather than to the line, as when several adjacent points are above the line and then when several adjacent points go below the line. The points are correlated among themselves, or autocorrelated, and seem to be marching to a different drummer than to the line. When autocorrelation is present, an overestimate in one period will likely be followed by an overestimate in the next, while an underestimate will likely be followed by another underestimate.

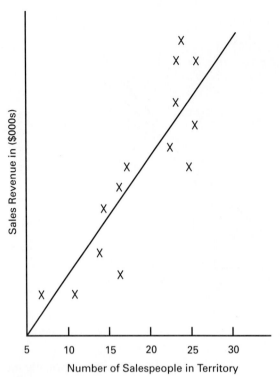

FIGURE 7-5 Graphic determination of autocorrelation.

Heteroscedasticity   **Heteroscedasticity** occurs when the variance of a Y variable is not constant for different X values. This condition reduces the accuracy of the standard error and thus the accuracy of the confidence interval of estimates. To determine whether heteroscedasticity exists, some computer programs will present a plot of the "error data"; that is, they will plot the actual input data around a line that represents the mean of Y for different X levels (Figure 7-6).

Nonlinearity   **Nonlinearity** refers to situations in which Y variables do not have straight-line relationships with X variables. This situation is true of learning curves, where X represents quantity produced and Y represents total production costs. If researchers do not recognize the nonlinearity and assume a straight-line relationship, forecast estimates and confidence intervals will be incorrect. The presence of nonlinearity can best be determined by having the computer plot a regression graph for the data entered and examining the plotted points.

TIME SERIES ANALYSIS

Time series models can be used to predict future values on the basis of the historical patterns of that variable. The basic assumption is "what has happened in the past will continue to happen in the future."[28]

    Time series is used to analyze changes in a variable on the basis of events and their periods of repetitive occurrence. Time periods of significant events that tend to repeat themselves are long-term trends, such as business cycles, seasonal differences, and even trading-day effects (the occasional occurrence on a long holiday). Figure 7-7 graphically displays the characteristic, long-term trend line, the shorter-term (usually 3- to 7-year) business cycle fluctuations, and the fluctuations occurring

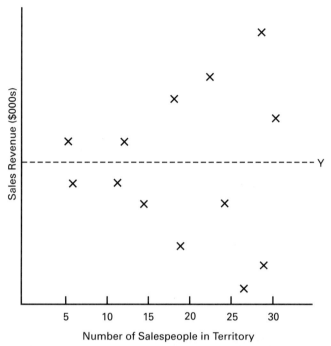

FIGURE 7-6 Graphic determination of heteroscedasticity.

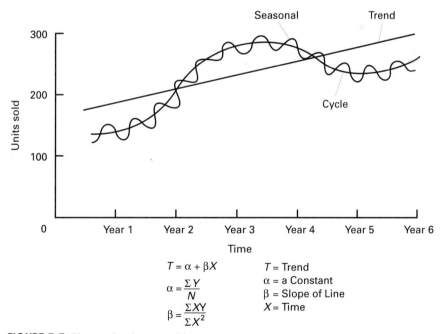

$$T = \alpha + \beta X$$

$$\alpha = \frac{\Sigma Y}{N}$$

$$\beta = \frac{\Sigma XY}{\Sigma X^2}$$

T = Trend
α = a Constant
β = Slope of Line
X = Time

FIGURE 7-7 Time series decomposition.

within each year. The model's predictions are frequently achieved by multiplying variables using the equation

$$Y = T + C + S + I$$

where *T, C,* and *S* stand for trend, cyclical, and seasonal effects and *I* stands for irregular effects (some usually unpredictable one-time special events).

Various methods are used to adjust for trading-day effects, the simplest method being to adjust the predictive data before performing any calculations. For example, assume that a major trade show occurs on either the last 2 days of June or the first 2 days of July. If one attempts to predict for an upcoming month of June during which the trade show will not take place, the data for each June in previous years are adjusted to remove the effects of the trade show before any calculations are performed.

Interestingly, like exponential smoothing, moving average, and simple trend analysis methods, time series uses only data for the variable to be predicted. However, time series' greater predictability in many situations results from partitioning the data in accordance with the recurring cyclical, seasonal, trend, and trading-day events; that is, the effects of many other variables are brought to bear on time series predictions.

The original data are decomposed in four major stages, one for each factor, as shown in Figure 7-7, until either the trend or cyclical components remain. Once these two factors are established, their extensions can be used for the forecast. Trend is used most often, since it provides the beta factor, which is the slope of the trend line. Extending the trend line provides the forecast.

ARIMA (BOX-JENKINS) MODELS

Autoregressive-integrated-moving average (ARIMA) or Box-Jenkins models evaluate trend, cyclical, seasonal, and even trading day effects but have a sounder statistical foundation than do other simpler methods of performing time-series analysis[29] (see Table 7-9). ARIMA models (1) provide better forecasts than do management experts in 30 out of 40 forecasts,[30] (2) yield better forecasts than do exponential smoothing and other models,[31] and (3) perform better—by a factor of 2 to 1—than do large econometric models.[32] Because of the long-term buyer-seller relationship, business forecasters are in a better position to obtain data for several past periods, making ARIMA

TABLE 7-9   ARIMA Software

IBM-Mainframe (S/370 and up)
Informetrica, Ltd.—AMS-FS

Time-series forecasting for high volume applications. Features census XII seasonal adjustment, Box-Jenkins for short-term forecasting and trend projections for medium and long-term applications. Sold six since 1975.

IBM PC-MS/DOS
Automatic Forecasting Systems, Inc.—Autobj, Autobox, Boxx, EZF, MTS, SimBoxJ
[SimBoxJ] "Generates from 1 to 5 discrete time series. Calculates data by multiplying random numbers and user-specified Box-Jenkins equation. Handles univariate transfer function, single intervention and Vector ARIMA models. Sold 36 since 1985. Cost $195.
Lionheart Press, Inc.—Sales and Market Forecasting
Apple Macintosh; PC-MS/DOS compatible. . . Shows how to use forecasting techniques including Box-Jenkins ARIMA models and how to relate company time-series to economic time-series. Provides selection of U.S. Department of Commerce time-series so techniques can be learned using real-life data. Sold 1,000 since 1984. Cost $145.

Source: Data Sources. (New York: Ziff-Davis Publishing Co., 1990, pp. J-277-J-278).

models more appropriate for business. Customarily, 35 or more periods of past data are needed, although at least 50 are recommended, which for recent products precludes the use of ARIMA.

The label for this group of models, *autoregressive-integrated moving average,* is derived from three factors. First, these models use linear regression to regress present Y values against lagged Y values. Regressing Y on previous Y's leads to the term *autoregressive* and the equation

$$Y_t = a + b_1 Y_{t-1} + b_2 Y_{t-2} + e_t$$

Table 7-10 shows the meanings of Y_t, Y_{t-1}, and Y_{t-2}; each term refers to an entire column of data.

FORECASTING LIMITATIONS

When foreseeing the future, a bit of insight used in conjunction with rigorous analysis becomes very useful. It would be difficult to say that luck plays a role in forecasting, but it does. Many practicing forecasters are happy if their predictions fall within five percent of actuality. The mark of a good forecaster is not one who can predict trends, but one who can predict the turning points. Accuracy in forecasting is a function of the forecaster knowing the right blend of both quantitative and qualitative tools mixed together with some good situational analysis and much good common sense. Examples of inaccurate forecasts are legends, i.e., Apples under estimation of the future success of the PowerPC and Digital's entrance into the PC market for offices in the home.

Using Intelligence, Research, Demand Analysis, and Sales Forecasts to Select Markets and Develop Strategies

Chapters 6 and 7 describe how these data-gathering techniques and analytical methods serve the business marketing organization. The following case illustrates the use of many of the techniques and procedures.

SITUATION

Timken Roller Bearing Company developed a hard steel roller bearing that promised a broad usage in steel-rolling mills throughout the world. In a steel-rolling mill an ingot of molten steel is rolled into sheet steel through a process of sequential shaping and rolling (squeezing) motions, similar to when one squeezes a tube of toothpaste, with the fingers rolling the pliable contents. As the ingot gets smaller and wider, it develops

TABLE 7-10   Autoregression Columns

Time Periods	Original Y Data	One-Time Period Lag	Two-Time Period Lags
1	45	—	—
2	43	45	—
3	40	43	45
4	36	40	43
5	35	36	40
6	31	35	36

an ever-expanding length that can shoot down the rolling mill at speeds of 60 miles per hour or more. These shoots contain roller bearings on which the extending pliable sheet steel travels.

MARKET INTELLIGENCE AND MARKETING RESEARCH

Since the potential market is largely restricted to steel-rolling mills, other applications should not be overlooked. The seller's intelligence system could investigate the "happenings" in the entire steel industry to determine whether new plant construction, plant remodeling projects, and plant abandonment projects were under consideration or were in process. Published reports and studies should be carefully scrutinized. Data gathered would indicate a strong resurgence of the steel industry in the U.S. and Brazil was occurring. South Korea, Japan, West Germany, United Kingdom, and France intended to modernize some of their steel plants.

Marketing research investigations indicate potential customer location, company size, product usage patterns, and possible other applications within the steel industry and in other industries. Research turns up the important fact that the world's overbuilt steel rolling mill capacity will not justify the development of new plants, but the situation justifies the modernization of existing plants to keep them competitive in the world market.

DEMAND ANALYSIS AND SALES FORECASTING

Demand analysis determines the potential quantity needed and on order by inspecting the data generated by the intelligence department and the marketing research department. The sales potential developed from such an analysis culminates in the worldwide need for 3,050 bearings for each of 23 plants in need of modernization construction project. Further analysis uncovers that of the twenty-three plants, the owners are willing to modernize fifteen plants in the next three years.

Sales forecasts develop the sales potential of 45,750 (3,050 × 15). The forecasters consider the company's marketing effort, possible competition, and the customer's willingness to venture into the new, drastically improved product area. Analyzing these data and perspectives, sales forecasts set a likely goal of a 10 percent market share, or 4,750 bearings.

MARKET SELECTION, PRODUCT POSITIONING, AND PRODUCT STRATEGY

Given the sales forecast, the marketing department develops plans to achieve this sales volume objective. The market with the least resistance appears to be the plants that have considered modernization but that are concerned with exorbitant financial outlays in maintenance fees for existing bearings. Since Timken's bearings are heavy duty and long lasting, their maintenance costs would be minimal.

Positioning strategy would be dictated by the above analysis. Timken's bearings would be touted as the Cadillac or Mercedes of the steel industry. As such, the initial costs might be higher, but over the long run, the company's bearings would be less expensive and more cost effective.

Marketing strategy for the bearings is determined by the market segment chosen, the locations of the potential customers, and the size of the orders, which determines revenues, costs, and residual profits. Product design is altered to meet the target market needs. The promotions department develops a Cadillac imagery campaign. Distribution plans to ship the product directly to the customer and to have it installed by the company's own engineers. Pricing is developed to reflect the Cadillac imagery and to perpetuate the company's ability to produce a high-quality bearing.

SALES FORECASTING AND INTERNATIONAL MARKETS

Sales forecasting takes on an entirely different perspective when one is working in international markets. Many reasons account for this difference and will be covered in Chapter 22. However, to get a taste of the difference, Table 7-11 shows the top 25 countries in the world, ranked by gross domestic product (GDP), as the countries may appear to American firms as a marketing opportunity or a competitive threat. This opportunity or threat rating is based on potential demand, ease of market entry, relative stability of government, literacy rates, and estimated business purchasing power as indicated by per capita purchasing power. Some countries are listed as a threat, such as Japan; however, Japan is also a strong potential market for American business goods when and if Japan and the United States ever resolve their trade differences.

TABLE 7-11   Major Economies that Represent a Threat or Opportunity to U.S. Firms Ranked by GDP (based on purchasing power parity), 1994

Country	*Population (millions)*	*GDP (billions of dollars)*	*Literacy Rate (%)*	*Opportunity or Threat*
United States	263.8	6,738	97	NA
1. China (PRC)	1,203.1	2,979	78	Both
2. Japan	125.5	2,527	99	Threat
3. Germany	81.3	1,345	99	Opportunity
4. India	937.0	1,254	52	Opportunity
5. France	58.1	1,080	99	Opportunity
6. United Kingdom	58.3	1,045	99	Opportunity
7. Italy	58.2	1,000	97	Opportunity
8. Brazil	160.7	886	81	Threat
9. Mexico	94.0	729	88	Opportunity
10. Russia	149.9	721	98	Opportunity
11. Canada	28.4	640	97	Opportunity
12. Indonesia	204.0	619	82	Opportunity
13. Spain	39.4	516	96	Opportunity
14. South Korea	45.5	508	96	Both
15. Australia	18.3	375	99	Opportunity
16. Turkey	63.4	305	79	Opportunity
17. Netherlands	15.5	276	99	Opportunity
18. Taiwan	21.5	257	86	Opportunity
19. Poland	38.8	191	99	Opportunity
20. Belgium	9.9	182	99	Opportunity
21. Saudi Arabia	18.7	173	62	Opportunity
22. Sweden	8.8	163	99	Opportunity
23. Switzerland	7.1	148	99	Threat
24. Austria	8.0	139	99	Opportunity
25. Denmark	5.2	103	99	Opportunity

Source: The U.S. Central Intelligence Agency, *1995 World Factbook.*

Looking Back

Demand analysis is the study of market potentials that exist at a given time for a specific product for all companies in a given industry. The demand is the culmination of the wants and needs of individual final consumers who create derived demand for business organizations which can satisfy these needs.

Sales potential is the slice of the total market potential demand that one company might perceive as indigenous to its abilities to best serve this market slice. Sales forecasts are the actual sales a given firm anticipates receiving, given a set marketing and sales plan, marketing effort, allocation of resources, and market environment.

Measuring market and sales potential is a prerequisite to developing a successful sales forecast. Numerous primary and secondary statistical sources are available; namely, county business patterns, SIC codes, and analysis of business cycles. Each source of data helps to shed some light into the future black box and helps to reduce the sea of uncertainty which surrounds sales forecasting.

Forecasting techniques can be classified into two groups: qualitative and quantitative. Qualitative techniques are surveys of buyer's intentions, expert opinions, and using a technique called the Delphi method. Quantitative techniques include simple mathematical routines such as naive method, moving averages, exponential smoothing, simple and multiple linear regression, correlation analysis, time series, and autoregressive-integrated-moving average commonly called Box-Jenkins.

Questions for Discussion

1. Managers manage the future by being able to predict the future. Discuss the various ramifications of this statement.

2. How may the marketing information system, discussed in the previous chapter, be used to establish market and sales potentials?

3. What is the difference between market and sales potential? How can this difference be used when forecasting the sales of machine lathes for use in woodworking plants in the European Economic Community?

4. Analyze how market and sales potential may encounter pitfalls along the way. Give examples of each.

5. Why may *county business patterns* provide more specific help to the forecaster than the GNP data contained in the Survey of Current Business?

6. How can SIC codes, lead time series, and business cycles be used to develop the market potential for the sale of airframe fittings for the Boeing 777?

7. Input/output analysis has the most contribution when managers wish to design what type of forecast?

8. Find an index in the *Business Conditions Digest* that, when lagged, enables you to predict production of synthetic rubber and rubber products (rubber and tires and tubes). Tell why you believe the index to be a good predictor.

9. Why are more simplistic quantitative tools such as exponential smoothing more accurate than a more sophisticated tool such as the Box-Jenkins model? What prerequisites are necessary to make the Box-Jenkins model more accurate?

10. Discuss the major forecasting values offered by multiple regression as used for forecasting the sales for an industrial oil field supplier of drill pipe.

Endnotes

1. "25 Breakthroughs that are changing the way we live and work: Americans are embracing the latest technology to remain on the cutting edge," *U.S. News & World Report* 119 (May 2, 1994):46-60.

2. Joseph F. Coates, "Why forecasts fail," *Research Technology Management* 36 (1993):4-5.

3. "An audacious high-wire act," March 14, 1994. *U.S. News & World Report* 119 (March 14, 1994):60-4.

4. Paul A. Konijnendijk, "Dependence and conflict between production and sales," *Industrial Marketing Management* 22 (1993):161-67.

5. John Shea, "Project management: Evolving to meet today's realities," *Manufacturing Systems* 7 (1993):24-8.

6. B.G. Yovovich, "Revolutionary marketing," *Business Marketing* 78 (1993):34-8.

7. Paul A. Herbig, John Milewicz, and James E. Golden, "The do's and don'ts of sales forecasting," *Industrial Marketing Management* 22 (1993):49-57.

8. William E. Cox and George N. Havens, "Determination of sales potentials and performance for an industrial goods manufacturer," *Journal of Marketing Research* 14 (1977):574-78.

9. Philip Kotler, *Marketing Management, Analysis, Planning, Implementation, and Control*, 8th. ed. (Englewood Cliffs, N.J.: Prentice-Hall, Inc., 1994), p. 249.

10. "Leading indicators for chip makers rose again in May," *Wall Street Journal* (June 9, 1987), p. 19.

11. *Sales and Marketing Management*, April 27, 1987. p. 36.

12. Business Week index. *Business Week* (May 9, 1994), p. 99.

13. "Truck lanes for the info highway: Commerce Net, a bazaar for Silicon Valley, may help shape a far larger business infrastructure," *Business Week* (April 18, 1994), pp. 112-14.

14. "DuPont takes new approach," *Business Marketing* 79 (June 1994):38.

15. "Case digs out from way under," *Business Week* (August 14, 1995), pp. 62-3.

16. Denis K. Towill, "Forecasting learning curves," *International Journal of Forecasting* 6 (1990):25-38.

17. Ruth M. Corbin, 1985. Managers' judgment significant. In Al Migliaro and C.L. Jain, eds. *Understanding Business Forecasting.* (Flushing, N.Y.: Graceway Publishing Co., 1985), p. 5.

18. "Microsoft hits the gas," *Business Week* (March 21, 1994), pp. 34-5.

19. J. Scott Armstrong, "Relative accuracy of judgmental and extrapolative methods in forecasting annual earnings," *Journal of Forecasting* 2 1983):437-47; and Mark M. Moriarity and Arthur J. Adams, "Management judgment forecasts: Composite forecasting models, and conditional efficiency. *Journal of Marketing Research* 21 (1984):239-50.

20. Morris Cohen, "Surveys and forecasting." In Butler, William F., and Kavesh, Robert A., eds. *How Business Economists Forecast.* (Englewood Cliffs, N.J.: Prentice-Hall Inc., 1966), pp. 60-62.

21. "Flying blind into a turbulent future," *U.S. News & World Report* 117 (December 7, 1992): 58-60.

22. Spyros Makridakis and Steven C. Wheelwright, "Forecasting: Issues and challenges for marketing management," *Journal of Marketing* 43:(1977):24-38.

23. Neil Seitz, *Business Forecasting On Your Personal Computer.* (Reston, Va.: Reston Publishing Company, Inc., 1984).

24. Robert Reeder, Richard Sewell, and Betty Reeder, "A survey of empirical industrial marketing research" [unpublished]. (Weatherford, Okla.: Southwestern Oklahoma State University, 1988), p.3.

25. See any specialized statistics book for a more detailed discussion of these statistical concepts and techniques.

26. Robin Hogarth and Spyros Makridakis, "Forecasting and planning: An explanation," *Management Science* 27 (1981):115-38.

27. Dynacomp Catalog No., 28. Rochester, N.Y.: Dynacomp, Inc., p. 54

28. Bruce L. Bowerman and Richard T. O'Connell, *Forecasting and Time Series* (Belmont, Calif.: Duxbury Press, 1979), p. 21.

29. This discussion is based on Spyros Makridakis, Steven Wheelwright, and Victor McGee, *Forecasting Methods and Applications.* (New York: John Wiley & Sons Inc., 1983), pp. 356-9.

30. Kenneth Lorek, Charles McDonald, and Dennis Patz, "A comparative examination of management forecasts and Box-Jenkins forecasts of earnings," *The Accounting Review* 51 (1976), p. 331.

31. V.A. Mabert, "Statistical versus sales force—executive opinion short-range forecasts: A time series analysis case study," *Decision Science* 7 (1976):310-18.

32. Thomas Naylor, Terry Seaks, and D.W. Wichern, "Box-Jenkins methods: An alternative to econometric models," *International Statistical Review* 40 (1972):123-37.

Bibliography

Barius, Bengt, "Simultaneous marketing: A holistic marketing approach to shorter time to market," *Industrial Marketing Management* 23 (1994):145-54.

Cox, William, and Luis Dominguez, "The key issues and procedures of industrial marketing research," *Industrial Marketing Management* 8 (1979):81-93.

Herbig, Paul A., John Milewicz, and James E. Golden, "The do's and don'ts of sales forecasting," *Industrial Marketing Management* 22 (1993):49-57.

Kendall, David L., and Michael T. French, "Forecasting the potential for new industrial products," *Industrial Marketing Management* 20 (1991):177-83.

Whitlark, David B., Michael D. Geurts, and Michael J. Swenson, "New product forecasting with a purchase intention survey," *Journal of Business Forecasting* 12 (1993):18-21.

CHAPTER 8

Market Segmentation, Target Marketing, and Positioning

The success of a business marketing strategy rests on the marketer's ability to identify, evaluate, and select attractive target segments. Effective market selection allows the firm to allocate its resources wisely and results in the achievement of organizational objectives within those markets served. In this chapter, we will discuss the following:

1. Market segmentation—its benefits, requirements, and cost
2. The importance of selecting the appropriate macro and micro segmentation variables
3. The process of evaluating potential targets and creating an effective product position
4. Factors influencing the choice of alternative target marketing strategies
5. Additional issues to consider when segmenting international markets

Few firms can afford to pursue all potential markets, nor can they ignore the negative impact of such an approach on their profitability. Thus, the task facing a firm is to identify, evaluate, and choose those markets in which it can compete most effectively. In choosing its target markets, however, the firm is not only choosing a customer base but also the competitive, technical, political, and social environments in which it will compete. This is not an easy decision to reverse. As Raymond Corey elaborates[1]:

> Having made the choice, the company develops skills and resources around the markets it has elected to serve. It builds a set of relationships with customers that are at once a major source of strength and a major commitment. The commitment carries with it the responsibility to serve customers well, to stay in the technical and product-development race, and to grow in pace with growing market demand.

Market choices should thus be based on the unique competencies and competitive advantages that the firm can bring to bear on that market.

189

Market Segmentation

Since business customers, like consumers, differ in their needs, resources, and buying attitudes, a practical approach to understanding these differences is to identify variables by which potential buyers can be segmented. Market segmentation attempts to identify groups of firms similar in their purchasing needs, product expectations, and responses to marketing programs.[2] These firms do not have to be similar in company structure, size, or end-markets, although similarity in such factors can provide a basis for more finely tuned segmentation. We will discuss this point further (see p. 194).

Business marketing managers attempt to find the best product-market match, that is, the most likely customers for each of their products. Symbolically, this match should be as close as a hand inserted into a well-fitted glove. All of the seller's capabilities and goals—product benefits, price, delivery, technology, personnel skills, and profit goals—should match with the buyer's desires and expectations—product needs, costs, delivery requirements, technical support, personnel training, and profit goals. Finding these compatible markets is the substance of market segmentation. For example, the fledgling technology of protein engineering, the next boom in biotechnology, is deciphering the structure of proteins and changing them to produce a new generation of drugs, plastics, and industrial chemicals. The new enzymes will improve many existing products and create many new uses, necessitating expanded use of more detailed market segmentation.[3]

Given the considerable difference between business customers, marketers find it difficult to determine which segmentation variables are the most or least likely to provide a desirable fit. Compounding the problem, Shapiro and Bonoma state that most business marketers use segmentation as a way to explain what has happened rather than as a means to plan and predict what will happen.[4]

The end result is that many business marketers do not use segmentation analysis as vigorously as their consumer market counterparts and thus forsake the benefits that could accrue.

On the other side of the same coin lies another potential problem. A firm must recognize that it cannot reap the benefits of segmentation if its organizational structure, channel system, or sales force stays focused on corporate goals rather than market needs.[5]

BENEFITS OF MARKET SEGMENTATION

The benefits derived more than offset the difficulties involved in identifying individual market segments.[6] These benefits fall into three main categories:

1. The seller is in a better position to spot and compare new market opportunities as well as potential threats.
2. The seller can create separate marketing programs aimed at more completely satisfying the needs of different buyers. This creates a **competitive advantage.**
3. Targeted plans and programs, based on identified needs and habits of specific markets, result in better allocation of company resources and higher profits.

When a firm seeks to expand its volume, effective market segmentation analysis will uncover the degree of customer satisfaction by comparing each segment's needs against the offerings of other suppliers. Low current satisfaction indicates a marketing opportunity, assuming the firm can do better than its competitors and produce an acceptable profit.

When a firm merely wants to maintain market share, constant surveillance of individual market segments will usually spot competitive or environmental threats before they reach a crisis stage. In short, market segmentation analysis provides both offensive and defensive intelligence.

BUSINESS MARKET SEGMENTATION CONSTRAINTS

Special organizational and environmental problems may militate against market segmentation.[9] Not every perceived opportunity becomes a profitable venture. Following are some of the specific instances in which segmentation in business markets is not useful:

1. The market is so small that marketing to a portion of it is not profitable. Therefore, a brand or product would have to appeal to all segments and level of users. A manufacturer of diesel engines may not find it profitable to produce and market jet engines at the same time.

2. Heavy users make up such a large proportion of the sales volume that they appear to be the only relevant target. Public utilities consume such large quantities of coal for generating electricity that they cast a long shadow over other users of coal.

3. A specific product or brand is so dominant in the market that it draws its appeal from all segments and levels of users, thus giving an illusion that segments do not exist. GE electric motors fall into this category.

REQUIREMENTS FOR EFFECTIVE MARKET SEGMENTATION

Regardless of the method chosen to segment the business market, the variables selected for analysis should always be[8]:

- *Measurable:* Information on the variables chosen should exist and be obtainable either through secondary or primary information sources.
- *Relevant:* The variables chosen should impact on decision making for a significant number of potential customer groupings and relate to important differences across customer groups regarding responses to different marketing programs.
- *Operational:* The variables chosen should be related to differences in customer requirements and buying behavior. They should indicate marketing approaches with respect to products, pricing, communication, or distribution.

Market Segmentation Involves Costs   Business firms segment their markets primarily to allocate their resources more effectively and to maximize return on investment. Thus, the resulting segments should be sufficiently large and profitable to warrant attention and different enough to warrant individual marketing programs.

Unfortunately, a segmentation strategy involves added costs in obtaining and analyzing data, and in developing and implementing separate marketing and manufacturing plans to serve each segment effectively. The strategy must therefore result in sufficient additional sales volume and profits to justify its costs. Before implementing a segmentation strategy, the marketer should develop an estimate of the costs versus the benefits.

MARKET SEGMENTATION AND PRODUCT POSITIONING

Market segmentation, however, is not the same as target marketing. As discussed earlier, **market segmentation** is the process of dividing a market into groups of potential customers who are similar in needs, expectations, and response to marketing stimuli. The seller selects variables that identify this market segment and develops a marketing mix that best fits the market's expectations and anticipated response.[2]

Target marketing is the process of selecting one or more of these market segments and developing products and programs tailored for each segment.[6] As Figure 8-1 illustrates, market segmentation is the first in a series of steps that ultimately enables a firm to

Source: Adapted from Philip Kotler, *Marketing Management: Analysis, Planning, Implementation, and Control,* 8th ed. (Englewood Cliffs, N.J.: 1994), p. 265. Adapted by permission.

FIGURE 8-1 A market segmentation and product positioning model.

maximize the return on its investment. Market segments must be identified and evaluated, attractive target markets selected, and decisions made as to how the firm will compete in those markets before product positioning and marketing mix strategies can be developed.

Basis for Segmenting Business Markets

There is no magic formula for segmenting the business market. The marketer should try different variables, either alone (which may be sufficient in some cases) or in combination. For segmentation variables to be meaningful, however, they must involve characteristics that are easily identified, understood, and discernible.[10] While consumer markets are typically segmented on the basis of demographic and psychographic variables, business marketers segment using a macro/micro approach (see Box 8-1). *Macrosegmentation* deals with differences between industries and business organizations. *Microsegmentation* involves differences in the criteria that are related to the purchasing decision-making process and the behavior of those individuals involved in these decisions.[11] Because of the fundamental differences between organizational and individual buyer behavior, Wind and Cardozo have recommended that market segmentation be approached in two stages: (1) identify definable macrosegments and (2) subdivide those macrosegments into appropriate microsegments.

Macro Variables

Table 8-1 lists some of the macro variables that business marketers can use during the first stage of market segmentation. Most of these variables are not difficult to identify and are easily obtained through secondary sources of information such as trade directories and publications, general business magazines and directories, government reports, market research companies, and a company's regular sources of information.

INDUSTRY CHARACTERISTICS

Many firms produce products and services that can be targeted to different, even dissimilar, industries. For example, computer manufacturers can market their products to such diverse industries as health, finance, forestry, and retailing. For these marketers, effective strategies will depend on a clear understanding of the similarities and differences between these industries. For example, while retailers, banks, and hospitals have

---
BOX 8-1

Unisys: Lining Up Business Targets

Rapidly changing technologies, shifting customer needs, and increasing competition in almost every part of the computer industry have forced Unisys Corporation, based in Blue Bell, Pennsylvania, to segment its markets, which include workstation and mainframe computer users, by what it calls a "line of business" approach.

"You have to understand what's driving change in the customer's business and ask, 'Why are they buying this stuff?'" says Richard Williams, Unisys' vice president of marketing strategy and development. So Unisys looks at the end user. The needs of a bank are different from the needs of the motor vehicle department or a plastics plant. In putting that knowledge to work, Unisys segmented the market into six commercial and governmental clusters: the industrial and commercial markets, financial services, the communications and airlines markets, the public sector, the federal government, and the defense department. Each of those clusters is further seg-

mented. For example, the public sector market comprises four groups: state and local agencies, educational institutions, health care providers, and utility companies. Each of these groups is again split. The health care group, for instance, includes hospitals, health maintenance organizations, and private practices.

In implementing its marketing segmentation strategy, Unisys reorganized its direct salespeople according to the industries they covered, launched a lead-sharing program to boost the success of its resellers in *vertical market,* advertised heavily in vertical business publications, and launched a third-party program to develop industry-specific products and services. For example, by signing a product development and marketing agreement with Jack Henry & Associates, a software developer in the financial market, a software program was adapted to handle all the operations needed to run a small bank.

Source: Kate Bertrand, "Harvesting the best," *Business Marketing* 73 (1988):44-6. Reprinted by permission.

TABLE 8-1   Examples of Macrosegmentation Variables

Categories	*Examples*
Industry	Agriculture, mining, construction, manufacturing, reselling, finance, services
Organizational Characteristics	
Demographics	Customer's level of risk-taking, desire to innovate, type of supplier relationships, number of suppliers
Size and location	Business volume, growth record, convenient to transportation, degree of operational decentralization
Economic factors	State of market economy; industry growth rate and cyclicality; customer's market share, ability and desire to expand
Competitive forces	Number and strength of competitors, ease of entry into market, ease of penetrating potential customers
Purchasing factors	Decision makers and their priorities, centralized or decentralized, major influencers on final purchase decision
End use markets	Manufacturers of end-products, commercial contractors, wholesalers and retailers, banks and other financial institutions
Product application	Component in specific end-products, consumer home or recreational usage, resale, production line or office productivity

Source: Adapted from Norman Weiner, "Customer demographics for strategic selling," *Business Marketing* (May 1983):78+. Reprinted by permission of *Business Marketing.* © Crain Communications, Inc.

some common needs with respect to computing, many of their applications are markedly different, as are their attitudes and approaches toward purchasing.

Significant differences may also be present within an industry. Consider, for instance, the use of computer hardware and software within the finance industry. While commercial banks, stock brokerage houses, savings and loan associations, and insurance companies are all part of this industry, their product and service requirements differ considerably. Thus, in some instances, further subdivision of industries is necessary to obtain a more operable segmentation strategy.[4]

ORGANIZATIONAL CHARACTERISTICS

Demographics   Business organizations, like consumers, have identifiable demographic characteristics (Table 8-2). Larger organizations, like larger families, have different purchasing requirements (e.g., volume purchasing accompanied by quantity discounts) and will respond differently to marketing programs than will firms with lower volume. Larger producers may choose to ignore small users because their volume needs cannot be provided profitably; on the other hand, smaller producers may want to avoid large companies because the volume requirements exceed production capacities and their price demands are more severe.[12]

Businesses can also be defined psychographically. For example, some firms are risk-takers in their purchasing decisions, willing to try new technologies to obtain an edge in their end markets. Other firms try, at all costs, to avoid change. In another vein, some buyers will form very close and long-lasting relationships with only a few suppliers.[13] Others will deal at arm's length with many suppliers, shifting from one to another based on temporary expedients (lower price, faster delivery, and so on).

TABLE 8-2 Applications of Customer Demographic Analysis	
Long-Range Applications	*Short-Range Applications*
Determine critical factors, and establish a profile of the potential profitable customer	Establish minimum order sizes
Evaluate new sales territories for future sales development	Establish cold-customer prequalifications criteria
Evaluate customer potential for proposed new plant sites	Evaluate sales territory potentials
Assess the company's long-term vulnerability to business economic cycles	Determine specific factors for poor sales and profit performance by individual sales reps
Determine the form of the selling organization	Determine which accounts to relinquish to competitors
Evaluate the customer base for a proposed acquisition within the same industry	Appraise monthly or quarterly performance of sales territories and sales managers
Determine target industries for future product and sales development	
Evaluate the quality of the company's current sales force	
Evaluate a competitor's customer base	

Source: Norman Wiener, "Customer demographics for strategic selling," *Business Marketing* 68 (May 1983), pp. 78+. Reprinted by permission of *Business Marketing.* © Crain Communications, Inc.

Business Marketing, a well-known trade publication, has repeatedly emphasized the importance of organizational demographics as a selling tool in the business market and the fact that too few marketers make use of these variables in developing and implementing their strategies. The analysis of customer demographics in conjunction with potential sales and profitability can provide valuable insights for the development of long-range as well as short-range strategy.

Customer location can also be important. For example, businesses value on-time delivery. Suppliers may bypass distant and widely dispersed markets because of the negative impact on inventory, transportation, and warehousing. Location also affects sales force organization and deployment. Borg-Warner, for instance, produces mechanical seals for slurry coal pipelines. They provide more coverage in West Virginia, Pennsylvania, and Illinois, where coal mines are concentrated.

Decentralized versus centralized procurement is another important variable because of its impact on the purchasing decision. As discussed in Chapter 5, when purchasing is centralized, the purchasing manager's power and specialization, the criteria emphasized, and the composition of the buying center are directly affected. Thus, *purchasing factors* provide a solid base for further segmenting firms within industries.[14] They also guide the organization of a sales force to better serve the needs and attitudes of targeted customers (e.g., national account versus local account emphasis).

↝ **End Use Markets**   Potential customers can also be segmented by the end use markets they serve. Their markets directly affect their own buying potential. Consider three hypothetical companies in Oregon. The first has been making and selling equipment to the timber and fishing industries; the second manufactures parts for the computer and semiconductor industries; the third provides marketing services to the many diversified organizations serving tourism. If a firm were selling office equipment, which of these companies would command its time and attention?

Economic and environmental factors have decimated the timber and fishing industries. Sales volumes have been dropping for a decade with little promise of a foreseeable turnaround. On the other hand, a growing number of domestic and foreign high-tech firms have sited plants in Oregon and are already building additions to handle their growing volume. One of these companies is already the largest employer in the state. The firm involved in tourism is supported by a state initiative to grow this industry and provide both revenue and jobs lost in timber and fishing. Tourism is already the second largest industry in terms of revenue.

This information would certainly influence the office equipment supplier's marketing strategy to the extent that it shows the impact of derived demand (discussed in Chapter 2). In short, business marketers cannot accurately assess the sales and profit potential of a customer without considering the attractiveness of the customer's served market or markets. ↵

↝ **Product Application**   The manner in which a product is used carries important implications. The application can influence product quality, durability, flexibility, ancillary services, and price. Equally important are the implications regarding customer expectations and priorities. Thus, product application can provide helpful information for the segmentation process. As a simple example, consider the various implications of computers used in a classroom, a research laboratory, an accounting office, and the family den.

TABLE 8-3	Examples of Microsegmentation Variables
Categories	*Examples*
Organizational Characteristics	
Purchasing situation/stage	New task, modified or straight rebuy; stage in the purchasing process
Customer experience stage	Life-cycle stage of the product coupled with customer's adoption characteristics (innovator, early adopter, laggard)
Customer interaction needs	Degree of dependence on supplier for product application assistance and choice of purchase-decision criteria
Customer innovativeness	An innovator or follower in technology
Organizational capabilities	Operational, technological, and financial resources and capabilities
Purchase Situation Variables	
Inventory requirements	Material requirement planning, just-in-time systems
Purchase importance	Degree of perceived risk, financial commitment, time pressures
Purchasing policies	Market-based prices, closed bids, or leasing preference
Purchasing criteria	Supplier reputation, low bidder, available services, product quality
Buying-center structure	Key influencers and primary decision-makers
Individual Variables	
Personal attributes	Demographics, personality, nontask motives, perceptions, attitude toward risk
Power structure	Relative strength of functional departments, ability of purchasing department to make final decisions, method of conflict resolution used most frequently (collaboration, compromise, avoidance, etc.)

Micro Variables

Macrosegmentation allows the identification of variables that are similar across industries. Microsegmentation, as Table 8-3 indicates, allows the marketer to subdivide those segments further through the analysis of specific organizational and individual criteria that are more directly related to the purchasing decision or product expectations. The specificity of these variables, however, usually rules out the use of secondary data (Box 8-2). Marketers must obtain primary information either through the company sales force or by conducting special market studies.

ORGANIZATIONAL VARIABLES

Purchasing Situation/Phase   As discussed in Chapter 4, the type of purchasing situation directly affects marketing strategy, particularly communication strategy. In the new task situation, for instance, the seller's success in market penetration depends on the ability to solve customer problems, to provide vital information to key decision makers, and to work effectively through all phases of the purchasing decision process.[15] On the other hand, in a straight rebuy situation, "out" suppliers must convince customers to reevaluate current suppliers by offering superior product advantages or sig-

---

Why Microsegmentation? Potential Customer Organizations Differ in the Composition of Their Buying Centers

Potential customer organizations differ in their need specification dimensions—that is, in the dimensions they use to define their requirements. They also differ in their specific requirements along these dimensions.

Potential customer organizations differ in the composition of their buying centers—in the numbers of individuals involved, their specific responsibilities, and in the way they interact.

Decision participants, or individual members of the buying center, differ in their sources of information as well as in the number and nature of the evaluation criteria used to assess product alternatives.

Source: Jean-Marie Choffray and Gary Lilien, "Assessing response to industrial marketing strategy," *Journal of Marketing* 42 (1978):20-31. Reprinted by permission of the American Marketing Association.

TABLE 8-4 Effects of Customer Experience in the Engineering Plastics Industry

	Customer Groups	
	Inexperienced	*Experienced*
Decision-making unit	Applications engineers	Purchasing agents
Decision-making process	New task, 2 years	Routine repurchases, four to five per year
Marketing Policy Areas		
Dominant produce benefits	Technical assistance, applications support	Performance, availability, price
Price/value considerations	Enhanced competitive position	Low cost
Sales program	Account management via industry specialists	Field sales on geographic
Key success factors	Account management and technology	Low cost of goods sold, low or parity prices

Source: F. Stewart DeBrucker and Gregory L. Summe, "Make sure your customers keep coming back," *Harvard Business Review* (Jan/Feb 1985). Copyright © 1985 by the President and Fellows of Harvard College; all rights reserved.

nificant price differences. Thus, segmentation across the Buygrid continuum is an important microstep in examining the buyer's purchasing needs, information requirements, and the structure of the buying center and interaction patterns.[16]

Customer Experience (or Product Life Cycle Considerations)   Customers unfamiliar with products (during product introduction) tend to assign purchasing responsibility to individuals within their organization who are capable of dealing with the uncertainties involved. They also tend to be attracted by a specific vendor's reputation and proven technology.[17] As familiarity increases, they tend to shift purchasing responsibility to functional specialists or purchasing agents who are more price sensitive, and supplier support programs begin to decline in value, opening the door for new suppliers. Thus, as Table 8-4 shows, the level of customer experience not only affects the composition of the decision-making unit and the decision-making process, it also affects marketing strategy for current as well as potential customer firms. In mature business markets, sellers must consider customer preferences for price versus services as an important added segmentation factor.[18]

Although customer experience can evolve with the product life cycle, the transition from inexperienced to experienced customer often occurs independent of product maturity. Since desired product benefits are identifiable and predictable as customers move from inexperience to experience, customer experience level can provide a basis for further refinement of microsegments.[17]

Marketers of higher technology products must recognize this alteration in customer expectations and priorities across the product life cycle (PLC) and adjust their marketing mix accordingly.[19] For example, technology alone may provide the primary edge over competition during the introduction stage but be supplanted by production flexibility, price, or even an advanced technology during maturity.

Customer Interaction Needs   When complex or strategically important products are involved, final purchasing decisions often hinge on the buyer's response, favorable or otherwise, to the seller's marketing stimuli during the decision-making process. Since product packages must be adapted to customer needs, the buyer-seller relationship often involves considerable interaction.

Although partnerships and relational marketing have become increasingly popular concepts, not all buyers want such relationships; some want transactional relationships that begin and end with a particular buying situation. Marketers can profit by developing a coordinated approach to foster these diverse working arrangements.[20]

Customer Benefits   Benefit segmentation—identifying customers with similar needs and desired results—can provide a very useful analysis. Moreover, this approach minimizes the danger that the marketer will be introspective rather than market oriented. In other words, product features should be a means to an end, a way of providing desired benefits to the customer. Benefit identification helps the formulation of product design, pricing, distribution, promotion, and marketing support decisions. It also prompts a study of competitive offerings, thereby providing a picture of relative strength or weakness in technology, marketing, and product-line breadth. In fact, an increasing number of marketing authorities consider segmentation by benefits as one of the most effective approaches in business markets.[21]

Organizational Capabilities   Organizations can also be segmented on the basis of their operating, technical, or financial capabilities. For example, companies that operate on tight inventories may be more attracted by supplier delivery capability. On the other hand, where financial capabilities are weak, supplier discounts may be more important than supplier delivery factors. Technical strength or weakness can also be an important segmentation variable. For instance, according to Shapiro and Bonoma, chemical industry firms that are technically weak "traditionally depend on suppliers for formulation assistance and technical support."[4]

PURCHASE SITUATION VARIABLES

Individual organizations vary in their philosophies and approaches to purchasing requirements. While the organization of the purchasing function will influence the size and operation of the buying center, other factors such as inventory requirement needs (MRP and JIT), the importance of the purchase, general purchasing policies, purchasing criteria, and the structure of the buying center may also be useful microsegmentation variables.[14]

Inventory Requirements   As discussed in Chapter 5, manufacturers who employ MRP and JIT inventory systems have a notable impact on business marketing programs. They put greater emphasis on technical and financial issues in their buying decisions and operate with a broader scope of responsibility. Marketing to these organizations not only requires a sales force that is skilled in negotiating and human relations, it also requires the ability to deliver defect-free products, on time, on a regularly scheduled basis. Segmentation on the basis of inventory requirements provides a means of differentiating those potential customers whose demands are viable and potentially profitable.

Purchase Importance   When products are applied differently across organizations, classifying them on the basis of their perceived importance can prove useful. For instance, a manufacturer of off-road equipment will perceive greater risk in the purchase of heavy-duty grease used to lubricate sealed bearings and less risk when buying the same product to keep in-plant handcarts running smoothly. The first purchase affects the performance of the end product; the latter buy has a minor impact on operations.

The degree of *perceived risk* in the purchase of some product categories can have a direct influence on the size, composition, or behavior of the decision-making unit. The greater the risk, the more individuals and departments are involved and at higher organizational levels. When multiple influencers, departments, or organizational levels are involved, the marketing effort must expand and intensify to satisfy organization needs[15] (see Box 8-3).

Purchasing Policies   Potential customers may also be segmented on the method by which they determine *target pricing* of their purchases. Automobile manufacturers and major retailers, for example, have historically negotiated on the basis of supplier costs (i.e., a capped profit margin). A majority of industrial firms negotiate based on current market prices, always seeking greater value for the

---

BOX 8-3

Segmentation on the Basis of Customer Service Levels

Traditionally, since the early 1970s, distribution service has been seen as an augmented part of the product offering; thus, customer service levels emerge over time to meet corporate objectives. But customer service represents a potent force in competitive strategy, and one way to obtain a competitive advantage is to redevelop and tailor customer service mixes to meet market needs.

The idea that customers will react in different ways to changes in service levels is nothing new. Indeed there has been a good deal of research which advocates the segmentation of a firm's customers using the service level expected by different groups of customers. Customers' perceptions with respect to service needs differ. Indeed, within a given market, different customer types may also have different priorities in relative importance of activities. It is therefore of great importance for a company planning to enter a market to investigate the service levels expected by different customer types before developing its customer service offering. . . . This is particularly important when one realizes that customer service is an integral part of the product offering and possesses demand-generating properties in the same way as other factors in the marketing mix.

Source: Norman E. Marr, "The impact of customer services in international markets," *International Journal of Physical Distribution and Materials Management* 14 (1984):33-40. Reprinted by permission of MCB University Press Ltd., Bradford, West Yorkshire, England.

dollar. Most government purchases stem from sealed bids. With growing regularity, firms are leasing their purchases, particularly for capital goods, rather than making an outright purchase.[4]

Purchasing Criteria   Purchasing criteria also differ across organizations, product categories, and situations. Lehmann and O'Shaughnessy have identified five types of criteria that will vary in their degree of importance, depending on the purchasing situation (Table 8-5). For instance, where products are standardized, economic criteria tend to dominate. Since nonstandardized, complex, or novel products appear to generate a degree of uncertainty with respect to product application, performance criteria dominate. Depending on organizational capabilities, in some instances, service factors may dominate over technical capabilities.[22]

Marketers can also segment customers on their preferences for single or multiple sources.[23] With the broadened use of JIT buying techniques and partnering, the relationship between buyers and sellers has become increasingly tighter, making it more difficult for new sources to gain a share of the business.

Structure of the Buying Center   Organizations can also be segmented on the basis of the people involved in the purchasing decision process. As discussed in Chapter 5, the buying center has often included personnel from marketing, engineering, and accounting, in addition to purchasing.

Three major business trends will accelerate multi-functional purchase decisions. These trends or concepts are concurrent engineering, partnering, and the restructuring of firms into **horizontal organizations** made up of many project teams. It is assumed that the concepts of material requirement planning (MRP) and JIT inventory control will continue.

CE brings a multifunction team together at the initial product design stage. The team continues to collaborate through the new task purchasing phase and *into full production.*[24] Project teams extend the concurrent engineering concept by keeping the

---

TABLE 8-5   Categories of Buyers' Choice Criteria

Criteria	Explanation
1. Performance criteria	These criteria evaluate the extent to which the product is likely to maximize performance in the application(s) envisaged for it.
2. Economic criteria	These criteria evaluate the anticipated cost outlays associated with buying, storing, using, and maintaining the product.
3. Integrative criteria	These criteria evaluate the willingness of suppliers to cooperate and go beyond minimal standards in providing services to integrate their efforts in accordance with the buyer's requirements.
4. Adaptive criteria	These criteria evaluate the extent to which the buying firm may have to adapt its plans to accommodate uncertainty about the capability of the supplier to meet the buyer's requirements for production and delivery.
5. Legalistic criteria	These criteria evaluate the impact on the buying decision of legalistic or quasi-legalistic constraints (e.g., government regulations, company policies and practices).

Source: Donald R. Lehmann and John O'Shaughnessy, "Decision criteria used in buying different categories of products." *Journal of Marketing* 38 (April 1074): 36-42. Reprinted by permission of the American Marketing Association.

multifunctional group together *through the life of the product* rather than reverting to separate functional departments.[25] **Partnering** adds additional members to the decision-making team—suppliers. Firms that developed successful total quality management (TQM) programs (including Motorola, Xerox, Saturn, Intel, and Hewlett-Packard) learned early on that such programs could not succeed unless the control process and dedication extended backward to the suppliers of parts, materials, and services. These suppliers did not have to analyze the buying center from a distance—they were part of it.[26]

INDIVIDUAL VARIABLES

Personal Characteristics   Purchasing decisions are ultimately made by individuals. While decisions are influenced by organizational variables and policies, one can segment the business market by the characteristics of individuals involved in the purchasing situation (e.g., demographics, personality, non-task-related motives, individual perceptions, and risk management strategies). For example, Krapfel and Brannigan-Smith[10] have found that experience (measured in years of experience in market research positions) was significantly related to buyers' price sensitivity. Also, some buyers are more willing to take risks, whereas others avoid them. Willingness to take risks, however, appears to be directly related to personality variables such as intolerance of ambiguity or self-confidence.[4] Further, some buyers are more influenced by the need for social relationships than are others and tend to maintain those relationships rather than switch suppliers.

Although data in this area are difficult to obtain, salespeople find this segmentation category very helpful, particularly when they can get prior knowledge of a potential customer's habits and preferences.

Power Structures   As discussed in Chapter 5, individuals within organizations tend to hold reward, legitimate, or expert power. Firms can be segmented on two dimensions: the functional departments and individuals who hold the power and the process by which this power is exerted.

For example, some companies are called *technocracies* because of the dominant position enjoyed by scientists and engineers. Others are driven "by the numbers" and look regularly to accountants and finance personnel for a myriad of decisions that affect other operating units. In exercising power, some firms require that upper-level managers make all major decisions. This is a strong indication that the firm has not adopted the concept of horizontal organization. If it had, decisions would more likely be delegated to those who would also carry them out.

Since interfunctional decision conflicts are often resolved by collaboration, compromise, or coalitions, marketers can sharpen their communication and negotiation strategies by determining how a potential customer is likely to make purchase decisions, who will play an influential role, what their priorities are, and which of these priorities might be subject to compromise.

A Macro/Micro Segmentation Process

Figure 8-2 shows the *five nests* advocated by Bonoma and Shapiro[4] in their macro/micro approach to business market segmentation. Working from the outside to the inside, the analyst would start with the first nest, demographics.

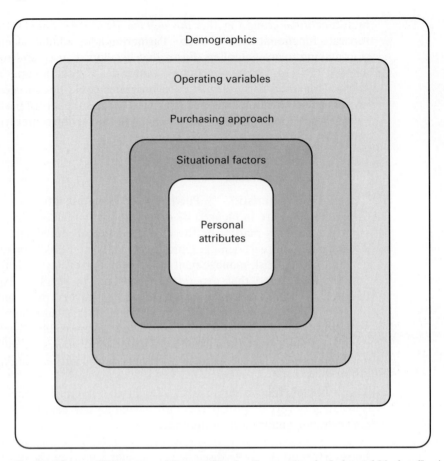

Source: Thomas V. Bonoma and Benson Shapiro, *Segmenting the Industrial Market.* (Lexington, Mass.: Lexington Books/ D.C. Heath and Co., 1983).

FIGURE 8-2 The nested segmentation approach.

DEMOGRAPHICS

The variables in the demographic nest are the industry, company size, and company location, all relating to the customer's needs and usage patterns. Industry provides a broad understanding of product and service needs. Company size affects the size of a potential order, which forces the seller's attention on their own ability to produce and manage the delivery of the product. Customer location impacts the seller's sales force organization, its territorial placement, and associated physical distribution factors.

OPERATING VARIABLES

The second nest, operating variables, contains three relatively stable components: company technology, product and brand-use status, and customer capabilities. Company technology, both product and manufacturing process, can determine buying needs. The technology used indicates the company's needs for tooling, test instruments, components, and appropriate support systems. Product and brand-use status would help to isolate common experiences with a brand or product, thus enabling the seller to categorize similar buyers. Customer capabilities includes organizational strengths and weaknesses that could help to classify a company's attractiveness and its "fit" with the seller's abilities to provide satisfaction. For example, Digital Equipment Corporation specializes in selling its minicomputers to customers who are able to develop and maintain their own software, and Prime Computer sells computers to business customers who do not need the extensive "hand-holding" services offered by IBM, Unisys, or NCR.

PURCHASING APPROACH

The third nest, purchasing approach, investigates five components: purchasing function organization, power structures, buyer-seller relations, general purchasing policies, and purchasing criteria. The organization of the purchasing function helps to determine the size, location, and levels of authority that exist in a customer's purchasing unit, which affects the size, location, and cost of the seller's sales force. Power structures that exist within specific customers impact on the type of suppliers they would choose. As discussed earlier, the seller could pursue a firm with a powerful engineering unit that dominated purchasing, or the potential customer's power base could lie in the manufacturing department and/or the general manager. Either situation would help to determine required sales force talents, product/service features to emphasize, and the broad outline for a successful selling strategy. These interrelations were discussed at length in Chapter 3. General purchasing policies, such as leasing, bidding, and doing business with only well established vendors, would dictate policy to those suppliers willing to do business within these constraints. Purchasing criteria are those product and organizational benefits deemed necessary for vendors to satisfy before a buyer-seller relationship can be established.

SITUATIONAL FACTORS

The fourth nest, situational factors, has three components: urgency of order fulfillment, product application, and size of order. Urgency of order fulfillment would be a function of the customer's inventory on hand, and the availability of suppliers to meet their needs in the allocated delivery time. The use of JIT purchasing practices would carry further implications. Product application challenges the seller's ability to satisfy both technical product needs and product servicing. Size of the order would suggest a seller concentrate on those customers whose normal orders would mesh with the seller's production economies of scale.

PERSONAL CHARACTERISTICS

The fifth and last nest analyzes the potential fit between the buying center member's personal characteristics and those of the seller. These factors include motivation, individual perceptions, acceptance of risks by the seller, personal attention to a buyer demands, the meticulousness of the buyer, and the matching of the buyer's personality traits with similar sales representative's personality traits.

The nesting approach encourages the integration of all five nests starting at the macro level and moving down to the micro level for successful industrial market segmentation analysis. However, as previously mentioned, market segmentation involves definite costs. "The more a market is segmented, the more expensive it is."[4] Thus, the degree of market segmentation depends on how detailed customer knowledge must be for effective use. As the marketer moves from macrosegmentation into microsegmentation, more intimate knowledge of potential market segments is required. While macro variables are rather easily obtained from available secondary data sources, such is not the case with micro variables.

In the business market, research studies are often required to determine which buyer attributes at the micro level best explain segment differences. Moreover, as segmentation moves from organizational variables, to purchase situation variables, to individual characteristics, more and more intimate contact with prospects becomes necessary. Finally, operational and personal attributes can change significantly from one buying situation to another, even within the same company. Therefore, as Bonoma and Shapiro argue, market segmentation *should begin with macro variables,* working inward to the more personal areas only as far as necessary. In other words, once the segmentation scheme seems "good enough," further efforts should cease.

A Market Segmentation and Product Positioning Approach

Doyle and Saunders advocate a more integrated approach to business market segmentation.[27] Historically, old-line manufacturers of basic materials such as steel, aluminum, chemicals, forest products, and mining in the United States and Western Europe have been forced to implement survival strategies. In view of their pressured profits, overcapacity, fewer orders, and fierce domestic and foreign competition, these firms have had to retrench, cutting costs in the short run, switching from basic commodities into faster growing niche markets, and concentrating on "value-added" specialty products. These changes required firms to develop new types of skills, including market segmentation analysis and the generation of product positioning strategy.

Figure 8-3 shows Doyle and Saunders' seven-step model for industrial market segmentation and product positioning. Notably, Doyle and Saunders emphasize product benefits. This approach probably runs less risk of overlooking potential markets, since the emphasis is placed on product benefits offered, rather than on customer character-

FIGURE 8-3 Seven-step model for market segmentation and product positioning.

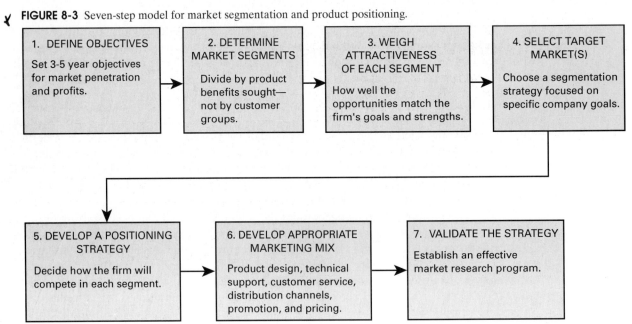

Source: Peter Doyle and John Saunders, "Market segmentation and positioning in specialized industrial markets, *Journal of Marketing* 49 (Spring 1985):24-32.

istics as in the nested approach. The process includes defining objectives, determining market segments, evaluating alternative segments, selecting target markets, developing a positioning strategy, developing the marketing mix, and validating the strategy.

DEFINE OBJECTIVES

Technologically oriented managements often overestimate their ability to overcome competitive forces when entering a new market that requires the establishment of accurate, quantitative, realistic market and financial objectives. Competitors are likely to resist any new entrant into their markets, particularly if high fixed costs, high exit barriers, and committed strategic plans are at stake. If a firm has modest market share goals and would be content to slip into a new market, then a lower risk niche strategy, perhaps aimed at a segment that other firms have either overlooked or cared not to penetrate, would be appropriate. If this same firm desires a major market share on entering the market, then attacking the most lucrative, competitive segment, would be the most appropriate strategy.

DETERMINE MARKET SEGMENTS

In business marketing, sales depend more on a product's benefits and its end use than on psychological or socioeconomic characteristics of the buyer. The buyer often buys a variety of specialty products from different suppliers to satisfy different needs and purposes. Therefore, it is often more beneficial to segment by product benefits instead of customer characteristics.[28] Apple Computer fueled their comeback in 1986-1987 by marketing Macintosh's high-quality desktop publishing capabilities to the business market rather than continuing with schools and home PC markets as their primary targets.[29] This type of analysis provides a more effective insight into the expectations of a market and the rewards for repositioning a product in that market.

EVALUATE ATTRACTIVENESS OF ALTERNATIVE SEGMENTS

Once the segments have been identified, management must evaluate the opportunities each segment offers. Segment choice triggers a firm's competitive strategy, which can produce many future ramifications for the organization. Such a choice should not be treated lightly, since the firm's future may hang in the balance.

SELECT TARGET MARKETS

Large multinationals can operate in many market segments, but most new entrants into a given market have to select one or a few segments. Limited financial and managerial capacities prevent a broader scope of activity, which might spread their resources too thin and set them up as a takeover target. The number of segments in which a company competes is determined by its shared goals, the flexibility of its manufacturing base, and the heterogeneity of the market's requirements. Satellite Industries (SI), a Minneapolis manufacturer, found a perfect heterogeneous niche when they chose to penetrate the Japanese market with their American designed and built portable toilets. The superior product won the acclaim of Japanese users for its comfort, style, and quality of construction.[30]

DEVELOP A POSITIONING STRATEGY

After the choice, management must decide how it will compete in these segments. Success requires a sustainable strategy differentiated from competitors. A higher probability of success can be achieved if the marketing mix is so uniquely arranged that it is unmatched by competitors. The success of SI stemmed from product differentiation rather than market segmentation. The latter strategy tends to create target markets that are homogenous. Product differentiation aimed at satisfying a generic need allows the firm to penetrate a heterogeneous market successfully.[31]

DEVELOP THE MARKETING MIX

Once the target market or markets and the positioning strategy have been chosen, the company must tailor a marketing mix to complement its planned positioning. This requires compatible decisions on product design, distribution channels, personal selling, advertising and sales promotion, technical support and service, and pricing.

VALIDATE THE STRATEGY

Success or failure depends on how well the market segmentation and product positioning strategies work. Follow-up research in the market should be undertaken to test the reliability of the findings.

Although a variety of statistical methods exist, many business segmentation studies use benefit models because conceptually, benefit segmentation is well suited to industrial products.[21] Rather than looking for potential customers who might purchase a product, companies profit more by matching product benefits with potential needs. The latter approach prompts the company to explore markets not previously believed to have potential.

When Unisys' original Burroughs division was started in the late 1800s, their first product was an adding machine manufactured for banks. They were so confident of the quality of this machine that they planned to go out of business when every bank in the country had purchased at least one machine. The company unknowingly segmented their market by type of customer, completely ignoring the needs of other businesses that had needs similar or identical to banks. Fortunately, someone in the company recognized that other businesses added, subtracted, multiplied, and divided data, which prompted the company to expand and tap into these "newly discovered" market segments.

A Cautionary Note About Benefit Segmentation

It can be very dangerous for business product managers to apply consumer segmentation approaches, since so many business market niches are less than a hundred customers. Stephen Livers, president of Larwin/Livers Associated, Inc., believes the best approach is to promote the product's benefits, but warns marketers appealing to niches to be aware of three traps[32]:

1. *Be wary of selling product features* instead of benefits. Users want to know what's in it for them, because new product features may thrill the development engineers, but customers want to know the benefits.

2. Havoc may reign on those who do not *match product benefits to the customer*. A 5-cent-per-unit savings might impress a manufacturer of $9.95 hair driers, but it doesn't even raise the eyebrows of a $5,000 computer manufacturer.

3. Messages that appeal to the broad market rather than to the niche are dangerous. Sales messages need to *stress the priorities and desires of specific users.*

Livers reinforces his perspectives with an example in the electronics industry.[32] During a downturn that made it too costly for manufacturers to run trade journal ads and print new catalogs, one company's marketing manager came up with a brilliant solution to spend the budget on a one-time, full-color, multipage, tear-out ad and use reprints as the new catalog. A week after the catalog was published, customers began returning "free literature" request cards. The only up-to-date information the company could provide was a reprint of its ad, which encouraged even more requests for literature. After the sales department sorted through these requests, they found most of the requests came from students, engineers working for companies not in the market, and other typical literature collectors. The only true sales leads came from prospects already contacted by the company's sales force. Sales remained flat and layoffs followed.

Target Marketing Strategies

Market segmentation and evaluation analyses help the marketer determine where opportunities exist, which segments are most attractive, and what marketing strategy seems appropriate. These analyses completed, decisions must be made as to which segments will be served, that is, *targeted*. In addition, the firm must decide whether the targeted segments are relatively similar or different. Four alternative target marketing strategies are available, influenced by the perceived segment similarities and differences: undifferentiated, differentiated, concentrated, and niche marketing.

UNDIFFERENTIATED MARKETING

When the company produces relatively standardized products or services and sells these in a horizontal market (i.e., a broad spectrum of industries), an undifferentiated marketing strategy may be the most appropriate choice. *Undifferentiated* implies that the firm ignores segment differences and develops a single marketing program that will focus on market commonalities in the hope of appealing to the broadest possible customer base. For example, manufacturers of equipment lubricants and common hardware market their products to all types of manufacturing facilities, since product usage varies little by customer type.

Although undifferentiated marketing is defended on the basis of cost economies, marketers must remember that "there is no such thing as a commodity. All goods and services are differentiable."[33] To persist and survive, a firm should strive for a unique advantage over its competitors. For example, as Levitt notes[33]:

> On the commodities exchanges, dealers in metals, grains, and pork bellies trade in totally undifferentiated generic products. But what they sell is the claimed distinction of their execution—the efficiency of their transactions in their clients' behalf, their responsiveness to inquiries, the clarity and speed of their confirmations, and the like. In short, the offered product is differentiated, though the generic product is identical.

Undifferentiated marketing strategy exposes an organization to competitive attack by firms that do differentiate. Customers do not simply buy physical products. When delivery expectations or supplier flexibility is erratic or only partially fulfilled, customers have not received the "augmented" product they expected and may turn to other sources. Thus, when highly similar products are marketed, organizations must take steps to ensure that other marketing mix factors differentiate them from competitors.

DIFFERENTIATED MARKETING

A firm may also choose to offer its output to a number of segments whose service needs, product usage, or market responses are appreciably different. Recognizing these differences, the firm uses a separate market program in each segment to achieve higher sales, a greater market share, and a more favorable image by satisfying each targeted segment more completely.

A differentiated marketing strategy, however, increases overall costs in product development, manufacturing, marketing, and administration; hence the theory that greater customer satisfaction leads to higher sales and profits must become a reality.

CONCENTRATED MARKETING

Even though diverse segments exist whose needs could be satisfied through product and market variations, a firm with limited resources or risk aversion may choose to pursue a large share in only one or a few markets. With a well-conceived marketing strategy, the firm can still achieve a strong market position within the chosen segments as well as operating economies.

As its sales and operating profits grow, the firm can expand into other segments already recognized as desirable business opportunities. By this time, their knowledge of the marketplace will have increased, their operating efficiencies improved, and their ability to compete enhanced (Box 8-4).

NICHE MARKETING

Niche marketers segment the market into finer, more homogeneous clusters than firms using differentiated marketing.[34] For instance, Coca-Cola has segmented its market into four distinct niches: regular Coke drinkers, diet Coke drinkers, caffeine-free Coke

---

BOX 8-4

Niche Marketing Is Gaining Favor

Niche marketing takes the market segmentation of the 1960s one step further. In fact, it is by definition a process of finer and finer market segmentation. . . . Moreover, it's a strategic approach to marketing which is gaining favor among business and industrial product and service marketers.

. . . Similar to the way in which some consumers prize a toothpaste more for its teeth-whitening ability than for, say, its decay preventative qualities, different groups of industrial and business product buyers have different needs for the same type of product. . . .For example, in the industrial and commercial lighting field, some buyers will be more concerned with reliability of the product while others put greater emphasis on energy efficiency (long-term cost), and a third group emphasizes low price (acquisition cost) as its primary buying interest. . . . Nor are important factors solely part of the product itself. A vendor's delivery reliability, service support and overall image, for example, can be more important than physical product characteristics or price for certain buyers.

Therefore, the task facing . . . business/industrial product marketers. . . is one of identifying the niches in which a company competes best, then creating products and a marketing presence in those niches which beats the competition.

. . . Most package goods marketers have learned the value of niche marketing. But only recently are business/industrial marketers adopting niche strategies. . . . Increasingly, they are realizing that technology, direct selling and price alone are not enough to succeed. The marketplace is teaching them that few, if any, manufacturers can be all things to all buyers.

Source: Joseph F. Barone, "Niche marketing: What industrial marketers can learn from consumer package goods," *Business Marketing* 69 (1984):56+. Reprinted by permission.

drinkers, and diet caffeine-free Coke drinkers. Thus, niche marketing enables an organization to provide products (or product versions) to buyers with specific desires and preferences. And it is "a strategic approach to marketing which is gaining favor among business and industrial product and service marketers."[4]

Creative business marketers recognize the infinite variations that customers can prefer in any element of the marketing mix. They also recognize the futility and prohibitive cost of trying to satisfy all of these variations. Thus, they monitor current and potential users in a target market to determine (1) whether a need or problem is emerging that demands a new marketing mix, or (2) whether the market can be subdivided into niches (as before—measurable, relevant, and operational) that require unique benefit packages that the firm can provide efficiently and profitably.

Both buyers and sellers drive the formation of niches. Because of the information revolution, new technical and financial data are quickly disseminated worldwide. Buyers know more about the products available to them and sellers, armed with an unprecedented amount of market information, can identify new needs and create marketing mixes to satisfy them.

For example, the growing concerns of electronic equipment manufacturers to protect their proprietary designs created a demand for customized chips—a demand that semiconductor producers answered by developing regional design centers and software to enable customers' engineers to design all or part of a chip themselves. Thus, niche marketing resembles differentiated marketing but deals with customer needs on a smaller scale, in greater detail, to provide faster and more complete satisfaction. The goal of greater market share and higher profits remains unchanged.

✓ Product Positioning

MATCH AND COMMUNICATE

Regardless of how markets are covered, the firm must develop and communicate, for every market selected, a positioning strategy that clearly differentiates its offering from that of competitors. Regardless of their competitors' strengths or weaknesses, the firm must clarify some distinct position or image in the minds of prospective customers[35]:

> Positioning starts with a product. A piece of merchandise, a service, a company, an institution, or even a person. . . . But positioning is not what you do to a product. Positioning is what you do to the mind of the prospect. That is, you position the product in the mind of the prospect.

Success in any market, whether consumer or business, depends on the firm's ability to create this unique position in the prospect's mind. Marketers accomplish this by carefully matching the prospect's needs and expectations with the firm's distinct competencies or advantages. In short, the closer the match between needs and strengths, the firmer the position.

Business positioning strategy has its limitations. Typical positioning studies provide useful information regarding a firm's relative strength in individual market segments. However, the information tends to relate this strength to competitive products rather than the qualitative value of customer response. Customer response studies in turn provide a useful and systematic method of comparing segmentation strategies.[36]

THE POWER OF LOGIC

Businesses should not let challenges or limitations dissuade them from developing a positioning strategy. An old adage suggests, "When creativity gets difficult, try simple logic." For example, research has continually reaffirmed the major criteria that companies use in choosing suppliers. Product quality, supplier dependability, relevant services, and end-use cost invariably top the list. Now the marketer's task becomes one of finding corporate strengths that notably match one or more of these criteria and communicating that fact to the target market.

When Chrysler Corporation hired Lee Iacocca in 1978 to rescue it from oblivion, he called on knowledge acquired during a 20-year automotive career. He knew that Chrysler had fallen from a 20+ percent share of the U.S. automotive market in the 1950s to less than 5 percent. He also knew that Chrysler used sound engineering designs in their cars, but consumers perceived all "Detroit iron" as vastly inferior to foreign products in overall quality. Unless that perception could be changed, the future looked very bleak.

Price and warranties often serve as surrogates for quality in the minds of customers. Raising price under existing market conditions would only have made matters worse. But what about warranty? All auto manufacturers, including Chrysler, were offering a 2-year, 24,000-mile warranty. In a bold move, Iacocca approved a change to 5 years and 50,000 miles. With a new image and product innovations like the minivan, Chrysler doubled its market share during the 1980s.

CRITICAL QUESTIONS TO ANSWER

Before embarking on a positioning strategy, marketers must address several critical questions and develop operable answers. The questions are simple to ask but difficult to answer and often require the firm to evaluate in detail its differential advantages with respect to competitors.[35] These questions are:

1. *What position do we own?* Positioning strategy begins with an assessment of what prospects already perceive because it is much easier to work with what is already there than to develop an entirely new strategy.

2. *What position do we want to own?* This question requires the firm to develop a position that will best serve it over the long term. While it is possible to compete successfully with an industry leader, going head-to-head is often more valiant than realistic. A better strategy would begin with the present position and lead the prospects toward a new mental image. Chrysler's warranty strategy provides an excellent example of this approach: determine what position is already owned by the firm in the minds of prospects and then relate them to a new position.

3. *Whom must the firm outgun?* This question ensures that the firm realizes it is not alone in the market, and prospects will compare its positioning strategy with that of competitors. An effective positioning strategy places the firm where no one else dominates.

4. *Once chosen, can the firm stick it out?* Today's markets are dynamic and volatile. Regardless, a firm must be prepared to stay with its basic position despite changing circumstances. This does not suggest a failure to adapt, but rather, a consistent image. A firm will change its pricing structure over time, for example, but should not change from a higher-price position to a cut-rate image, or vice versa. Wal-Mart and Nordstrom's have both developed successful positions in the same broad market but have remained poles apart.

5. *Does the firm match its positioning strategy?* A desired positioning must be founded in reality. Unless the firm adopts products, services, and policies that clearly support the positioning, prospects will spot the deception and turn from neutral to negative.

International Market Segmentation

All of the macro and micro variables, the potential benefits and pitfalls, and the alternative strategies that apply to domestic business markets are also applicable to international markets, but when a company attempts to market offshore, its efforts are further affected by cultural, political, economic, and special competitive issues. Moreover, conflicting schools of thought debate how each of these topical areas can best be handled. Let's consider each area briefly, with no attempt at an exhaustive coverage.

CULTURAL ISSUES

Every foreign country provides its own unique set of marketing opportunities and threats. Thus, regardless of a firm's point of origin, it will face additional challenges when it expands beyond national borders. In the opinion of many marketing professionals, cultural differences pose the greatest challenge, because they have such a broad impact and can affect all elements of the marketing mix. In our current context, culture includes traditions, beliefs, habits, and attitudes as well as product usage and business infrastructure.

Language probably represents the most apparent cultural difference and has a direct impact on promotion. A dual-language dictionary might seem an obvious solution to this challenge, but a marketer cannot simply translate American expressions or concepts into another language without understanding the associated traditions, habits, and attitudes.

Language errors are sometimes humorous. In the 1950s, General Motors decided against changing the name of its highly successful Chevrolet Nova before its introduction in Mexico. Everyone is impressed by a bright new star in the heavens, which is the English translation of a *nova,* so a popular American advertisement was translated directly into Spanish. Unfortunately, *va* is a form of the Spanish verb meaning "to go," and *no* has a similar meaning in virtually every language—thus, "no go." GM executives learned too late why their ad was met with derisive laughter.

Very few products have true international appeal. Coca-Cola is a notable exception, and IBM had established an international reputation in technology and service before losing ground in the PC market. Other products either require significant modification or confront opposing traditions. For example, automobiles must have right-hand drive in many countries, and electrical appliances must operate on 220-volt, 50-cycle power lines. Most Islamic nations will not accept any consumable product with alcoholic content. Dehydrated foods and beverages and powdered infant formulas eliminate the need for refrigeration but require a potable water supply. Prepared foods save time and energy but insult many homemakers, who consider a meal their personal creation "made from scratch."

The type of physical distribution system taken for granted in the United States did not exist even in the industrialized nations of Europe 30 years ago. Today, such systems have become commonplace in western Europe, North America, Japan, and a few other Asian countries. The rest of the world requires manufacturers to establish their own intermediate wholesale and warehousing operations.

Labor-management relations change significantly from one global region to another. While these relations have recently been more harmonious in the United States, they have been deteriorating in other industrialized nations such as France, Germany, and Japan. Cultural differences also have a major impact on the role of women in the workplace, expected benefits beyond wages, the amount of delegated decision-making, and a host of other human resource issues.

POLITICAL AND ECONOMIC ISSUES

Pricing policies may seem simple to devise, since the law of supply and demand is universal. A number of factors, however, make this process quite complex. First, three economic concepts are closely related: national economic strength, standard of living, and consumer buying power. In turn, each concept stems from three factors: the value of all goods and services produced within the country (GDP), total population, and the resultant GDP per capita. Table 8-6 provides this information for selected countries in 1994.[37]

By general consensus, countries are considered relatively affluent if their GDP per capita is above $10,000. North American and most western European countries fall in this category. Countries whose GDP per capita falls between $1,000 and $10,000 are considered "middle class." This category includes a mixture of eastern European, Middle East, and Latin American countries, plus some African and Asian nations. The majority of African and Asian countries, however, fall into the low income category below $1,000 per person. Products that represent everyday purchases in the affluent countries are unattainable luxuries in much of the world. Many American companies are developing strategies to penetrate the mass markets in Asia, particularly India and China. These two countries represented 37 percent of the world's population (consumers) in 1994. Some economists predict that China, currently enjoying unprecedented growth, will be the next great economic power. Let us analyze current data and recent trends in order to evaluate the future potential of these markets.

Gross world product (GWP) in 1994 approached $31 trillion, having grown by 3 percent during the year.[37] Average growth of 3 percent in the GDP of industrialized nations (60 percent of GWP in 1994) and 6 percent average growth among developing countries (34 percent of GWP) was partly offset by a further 11 percent drop in the former USSR/Eastern Europe area (now only 6 percent of GWP). China and India together accounted for slightly less than 14 percent of the output despite their population. Thus, the standard of living—or consumer buying power—in these two countries was only 46 percent and 25 percent, respectively, of the world average. How will these numbers change during the twenty-first century?

Table 8-7 provides some answers. The Population Reference Bureau estimated the population growth rates. The GDP growth rates represent high and low consensus estimates. To calculate real economic growth, nominal growth must be reduced by the rate of inflation. However, this adjustment alone is not enough, since true economic power is measured by the buying power of the country's consumers, or GDP per capita. Lester Thurow holds that "no country can become rich without a century of good economic performance and a century of slow population growth."[38] Although India has had some success increasing its productive output, its population growth rate remains very high. Projections indicate that it will replace China as the most populous country by the year 2100.

Despite the foregoing comments, the figures in Table 8-7 indicate that both China and India will spend billions of dollars and create millions of jobs to build their industrial and sociopolitical infrastructures. Much of the necessary technology will be imported. The jobs will increase consumer buying power and a demand for consumer products. These countries will indeed represent major business markets.

Since manufacturing wages closely parallel GDP per capita, American firms often locate production facilities in the target market countries. This strategy provides several advantages. The company is viewed as a "neighbor" who provides jobs and supports the local economy rather than as a foreign interloper. Tariffs and other import restrictions are often avoided. Strong nationalistic attitudes ("buy local products") are supported rather than challenged. In most instances, the cost of production and distribution is optimized.

TABLE 8-6 Gross Domestic Product, Population, and GDP/capita for Selected Countries, 1994 (ranked by GDP per capita)

	GDP (millions of dollars)	Population (thousands)	GDP/capita (U.S. $)
High Income Countries (GDP/cap ≥ $10,000)			
United States	$6,738,000	263,800	$25,850
Hong Kong	136,100	5,500	24,530
Canada	640,000	28,400	22,760
Switzerland	148,000	7,100	22,080
Japan	2,527,000	125,500	20,200
Singapore	57,000	2,900	19,940
France	1,080,000	58,100	18,670
Sweden	163,000	8,800	18,580
United Kingdom	1,045,000	58,300	17,980
Italy	1,000,000	58,200	17,180
Germany	1,345,000	81,300	16,580
Taiwan	257,000	21,500	12,070
Korea, South	508,000	45,500	11,270
Middle Income Countries (GDP/cap $1,000-9,999)			
Saudi Arabia	173,000	18,700	9,510
Malaysia	166,800	19,700	8,650
Argentina	270,800	34,300	7,990
Mexico	729,000	94,000	7,900
Chile	97,700	14,100	7,010
Thailand	355,200	60,300	5,970
Costa Rica	16,900	93,400	5,050
Poland	191,000	38,800	4,920
Russia	721,000	149,900	4,820
China	2,979,000	1,203,000	2,500
Philippines	161,400	73,300	2,310
Pakistan	248,500	131,500	1,930
El Salvador	9,800	5,900	1,710
India	1,253,900	936,500	1,360
Vietnam	83,500	74,400	1,140
Low Income Countries (GDP/cap < $1,000)			
Korea, North	21,300	23,500	920
Haiti	5,600	6,500	870
Laos	4,000	4,800	850
Madagascar	10,600	13,900	790
Cambodia	6,400	10,600	630
Angola	6,100	10,100	620
Burundi	3,700	6,300	600
Somalia	3,300	7,300	450
Ethiopia	20,300	56,000	310
WORLDWIDE	$30,700,000	5,733,700	$5,400

Source: U.S. Central Intelligence Agency, *The 1995 World Factbook* (Washington, D.C.).

	TABLE 8-7 Projected Economic Power of China, India, and the United States		
	Annual Growth	*1994*	*2024*
China			
Population (000)	0.9%	1,203,000	1,574,000
GDP ($ million)	5.0%	$2,979,000	$12,875,100
	3.5%	$2,979,000	$8,361,400
GDP/capita ($)	4.1%	$2,500	$8,180
	2.6%	$2,500	$5,310
India			
Population (000)	1.4%	936,500	1,421,200
GDP ($ million)	3.5%	$1,253,900	$3,519,400
	2.5%	$1,253,900	$2,630,100
GDP/capita ($)	2.1%	$1,360	$2,475
	1.1%	$1,360	$1,850
United States			
Population (000)	0.7%	263,800	325,200
GDP ($ million)	3.0%	$6,738,000	$16,354,900
	2.0%	$6,738,000	$12,205,000
GDP/capita ($)	2.3%	$25,850	$50,290
	1.3%	$25,850	$37,530

Source: Population projections from *1995 Population Date Sheet* (Washington, D.C.: Population Reference Bureau, Inc., 1995).

However, the company can also face unexpected difficulties. For instance, the host country may put restrictions on the exportation of profits. Thus, when the firm makes more profit than is required to keep this facility running smoothly, government regulations may prevent the transfer of money to a needy operation in another country. Also, as advanced technologies make the manufacturing process more complex, laborers with sufficient and appropriate skills become harder to find.

A third conflicting issue centers on the legal definitions of predatory pricing and unfair business practices. In the United States, for example, the Robinson-Patman Act clearly states that a company must charge the same price to all customers who buy "like goods and quantity." In other words, any firm that purchases 100 pieces of product X can expect to pay the same price as all other purchasers who buy the same product in the same quantity. The primary purpose of R-P is to maintain fair competition. In every other country, pricing normally results from a temporal decision as to what the market will bear. In similar fashion, pricing below cost to gain a foothold in a desired market does not carry the stigma that it does here. "Dumping" implies an environmental problem, not a marketing problem.

COMPETITIVE ISSUES

In addition to the differing attitudes toward pricing and other business practices, a company may face formidable barriers when trying to break into foreign channels of distribution. Nowhere is this situation more evident than in Japan. Japanese retailing is still dominated by the keiretsu system of interlocked companies that are tied to each other by capital investment, contractual arrangements, or both.[39] As a result, major Japanese manufacturers of consumer goods (e.g., Sony, Fujitsu, Toshiba, Hitachi) can essentially block foreign competitors from Japanese consumers, with or without government regulations or sanctions. However, the Tokyo Chamber of Commerce has suggested that products aimed at specific market niches, as compared to mass-market products, may find their way on to retail shelves more readily.[39]

One study suggests that firms entering any foreign market with a new product can learn from the history of deregulation in the United States. Successful firms that began as low-cost suppliers gravitated quickly toward specific market segments rather than remaining low-cost and undifferentiated.[40] Another study reported the opinions of American and European industrial product manufacturers regarding the aspects of marketing in the new European Community. With little variance, these industrialists felt that product quality, market segmentation, product differentiation, and more efficient distribution networks would be key elements in any successful marketing strategy.[41]

Looking Back

For a marketing strategy to succeed, the firm must identify markets that it can serve competitively with its resources and capabilities. Business customers—industrial firms, institutions, government agencies, and resellers—differ in their needs, buying attitudes, and practices. To understand those differences and to identify attractive market segments, business marketers must undertake market segmentation.

A number of variables exist for segmenting the business market on both macro and micro levels, but to be useful, these variables must be measurable, relevant, and operational. Moreover, the chosen variables should identify the market segments whose needs best match the firm's ability to satisfy. Given the additional costs involved, the benefits of segmentation should be weighed before a strategy is finalized, and the marketer should limit segmentation detail to the level that can be effectively used.

Since market segmentation only pinpoints potential business opportunities, the marketer should evaluate the profit potential of each before selecting specific targets. Competitors must also be evaluated because they represent alternative choices available to potential customers.

The choice of markets to serve depends on company resources, product-market homogeneity, the stage of the product life cycle, and competitors' marketing strategies. The company can select among an undifferentiated, differentiated, concentrated, or niche market strategy. Finally, the company must decide how to position itself within the marketplace, that is, what image to create within the minds of customers.

International markets offer similar segmenting opportunities, but they also represent additional challenges and constraints. These issues exist in the areas of culture, politics, economics, and unique competitive situations. Each national market should be studied in depth with reference to the specific product or service that the company intends to sell.

Questions for Discussion

1. To ensure its continuing success, a firm offering a product or service to several end use markets must evaluate the ability of each market to help the firm achieve its goals. Explain the steps you would take and the criteria you would use to make such an evaluation.

2. It has been proposed that complex purchasing decisions "can be segmented on the basis of the amount of conflict associated with each decision." If this is true, then conflict would depend on the role of those involved in the decision process. How would you assess the roles played by the various individuals involved in the purchasing decision?

3. There are identifiable costs involved in segmenting markets and serving targeted segments effectively. Describe the several categories of costs and explain why the level would increase with the degree of segmentation.

4. "Any product or service can be differentiated, even a commodity that seems to differ from competitors' offerings only in price." Explain why you agree or disagree.

5. With the example of any product or service you choose, describe how you would use the "nested" or macro-micro method of segmentation.

6. One business marketer recently observed, "I can't see any basis on which to segment my market. We have a 15 percent market share for our type of plastics fabrication equipment. There are eleven competitors who serve a large and diverse set of customers, but there is no unifying theme to our customer set or to anyone else's." Does this knowledge actually form a basis for segmenting this market? Justify your response.

7. Explain why a company's experience or inexperience with a product could affect its buying decisions, and how this difference would impact your market segmentation strategy.

8. Having successfully penetrated target markets in the United States, what steps would you take to identify and evaluate attractive international segments?

Endnotes

1. E. Raymond Corey, "Key options in market selection and product planning," *Harvard Business Review* 53 (1975):119-128.
2. Jay L. Laughlin, and Charles R. Taylor, "An approach to industrial market segmentation," *Industrial Marketing Management* 20 (1991):127-36.
3. "Design proteins: The next boom in biotech," *Business Week* (April 13, 1987), pp. 94+.
4. Benson P. Shapiro and Thomas V. Bonoma, "How to segment industrial markets," *Harvard Business Review* 62 (1984):104-10
5. Sally Dibb and Lyndon Simkin, "Implementation problems in industrial market segmentation," *Industrial Marketing Management* 23 (February 1994):55-63.
6. Philip Kotler, *Marketing Management: Analysis, Planning, Implementation, and Control,* 8th ed. (Englewood Cliffs, N.J.: Prentice Hall, 1984), p. 264.
7. Shirley Young, Leland Ott, and Barbara Feigin, "Some practical considerations in market segmentation," *Journal of Marketing Research* 15 (1978):404-412.
8. Frederick E. Webster, Jr., *Industrial Marketing Strategy.* (New York: John Wiley & Sons, Inc., 1979), pp. 74-5.
9. Thomas V. Bonoma and Benson P. Shapiro, "Evaluating market segmentation approaches," *Industrial Marketing Management* 13 (1984):257-68.
10. Robert E. Krapfel, Jr., and Darlene Brannigan-Smith, "An experimental approach to segmenting buyers of marketing research," *Industrial Marketing Management* 14 (1985):27-34.
11. Yoram Wind and Richard N. Cardozo, "Industrial marketing segmentation," *Industrial Marketing Management* 3 (1974):155; and Richard N. Cardozo, "Segmenting the industrial market." In Robert L. King, ed. *Marketing and the New Science of Planning.* Chicago: American Marketing Association, 1968), pp. 433-440; and Ronald E. Frank, William F. Massy, and Yoram Wind, *Market Segmentation.* Englewood Cliffs, N.J.: Prentice Hall, Inc., 1971).
12. Mark VanClieaf, "Identifying your most profitable customers," *Business Quarterly* 61 (Winter 1996):54-60.
13. Michael Barrier, "Call it supplier satisfaction," *Nation's Business* 82 (1994):56+.
14. Carl R. Frear, Mary S. Alquire, and Lynn E. Metcalf, "Country segmentation on the basis of international purchasing patterns," *Journal of Business and Industrial Marketing* 10 (1995):2-3.
15. Richard N. Cardozo, "Situational segmentation of industrial markets," *European Journal of Marketing* 14 (1980):264-276.

16. Thomas S. Robertson and Howard Barich, "A successful approach to segmenting industrial markets," *Planning Review* 20 (1992):4-11.

17. E. Steward DeBruicker and Gregory L. Summer, "Make sure your customers keep coming back," *Harvard Business Review* 63 (1985):92-8.

18. V. Kasturi Rangan, Rowland T. Moriarty, and Gordon S. Swartz. "Segmenting customers in mature industrial markets," *Journal of Marketing* 56 (October 1992):72-82.

19. Edward T. Popper and Bruce D. Buskirk, "Technology lifecycles in industrial markets," *Industrial Marketing Management* 21 (1992):23-31.

20. James C. Anderson and James A. Narus, "Partnering as a focused market strategy," *California Management Review* 33 (Spring 1991):95-113.

21. Cornelis A. DeKluyver and David B. Whitlark, "Benefit segmentation of industrial products," *Industrial Marketing Management* 15 (1986):273-86; Mark L. Bennion, Jr., "Segmentation and positioning in a basic industry," *Industrial Marketing Management* 16 (1987):9-18; and Robin T. Peterson, "Small business usage of target marketing," *Journal of Small Business Management* 29 (1991):79-85.

22. Donald R. Lehmann and John O'Shaughnessy, "Decision criteria used in buying different categories of products," *Journal of Marketing* 38 (1974):36-42.

23. Raydell Tullous and Richard Lee Utecht, "Multiple or single sourcing?" *Journal of Business and Industrial Marketing* 7 (Summer 1992):5-18.

24. Brad Morely, "Management's competitive weapon," *Industry Week* 24 (1992):44.

25. Tim Clark, "The team approach to marketing: AT&T units coordinate efforts in developing technology products," *Business Marketing* 78 (1993):27+.

26. Greg Hutchins, "Partnering: A path to total quality in purchasing," *National Productivity Review* 11 (1992):213-30; and Jeffrey H. Dyer and. William G. Ouchi, "Japanese-style partnerships: Giving companies a competitive edge," *Sloan Management Review* 35 (1993):51-63.

27. Peter Doyle and John Saunders, "Market segmentation and positioning in specialized industrial markets," *Journal of Marketing* 49 (1985):24-32.

28. James W. Peltier and John A. Schribrowsky, "The use of need-based segmentation for developing segment-specific direct marketing strategies," *Journal of Direct Marketing* 6 (Summer 1992):44-53.

29. "Apple's comeback with a more versatile Macintosh," *Business Week* (January 19, 1987), pp. 84+.

30. "Here's a U.S.-Japan trade venture that's truly flushed with success," *Wall Street Journal* (November 28, 1986), p. 13.

31. Wendell R. Smith, "Product differentiation and market segmentation as alternative marketing strategies," *Marketing Management* 4 (Winter 1995):63-5.

32. "Beware the 'beasts' of textbook techniques," 1987. *Marketing News* 21 (April 10, 1987):36.

33. Theodore Levitt, "Marketing success through differentiation of anything," *Harvard Business Review* (January-February 1982):83-91.

34. Joseph F. Barone, "Niche marketing: What industrial marketers can learn from consumer package goods," *Business Marketing* 69 (November 1984):56+.

35. Al Ries and Jack Trout, *Positioning: The Battle for Your Mind.* (New York: Warner Books, 1982).

36. Mark L. Bennion and William H. Redmond, "Modeling customer response in an industrial commodity market," *Industrial Marketing Management* 23 (December 1994):383-92.

37. U.S. Central Intelligence Agency. *The 1995 World Factbook* (Washington D.C.: 1995).

38. Lester Thurow, *Head to Head.* (New York: William Morrow, 1992), p. 207.

39. Dave Barrager, "Global trends: Japan begins to open the door to foreigners—a little," *Brandweek* 34 (1993):14-16.

40. Joel A. Bleeke, "Strategic choices for newly opened markets," *Harvard Business Review* 68 (September-October 1990):158-65.

41. Massoud M. Saghafi, Donald Sciglimpaglia, and Barbara E. Withers, "Strategic decisions for American and European industrial marketers in a unified European market," *Industrial Marketing Management* 24 (March 1995):69-81.

Bibliography

Barone, Joseph F., "Niche marketing: What industrial marketers can learn from consumer package goods," *Business Marketing* 69 (1984): 56+.

Barrier, Michael, "Call it supplier satisfaction," *Nation's Business* 82 (1994): 56+.

Bertrand, Kate, "Harvesting the best," *Business Marketing* 73 (1988):41+.

Bonoma, Thomas V., and Benson P. Shapiro, "Evaluating market segmentation approaches," *Industrial Marketing Management* 13 (1984):257-68.

Cardozo, Richard N., "Situational segmentation of industrial markets," *European Journal of Marketing* 14 (1980):264-76.

Choffray, Jean-Marie, and Gary L. Lilien, "Industrial market segmentation by the structure of the purchasing process," *Industrial Marketing Management* 9 (1980):331-42.

DeBruicker, F. Steward, and Gregory L. Summe, "Make sure your customers keep coming back," *Harvard Business Review* 63 (1985):92-98.

DeKluyver, Cornelis A., and David B. Whitlark, "Benefit segmentation for industrial products," *Industrial Marketing Management* 15 (1986):273-86.

Doyle, Peter, and John Saunders, "Market segmentation and positioning in specialized industrial markets," *Journal of Marketing* 49 (Spring 1985):24-32.

Dyer, Jeffrey H., and William G. Ouchi, "Japanese-style partnerships: Giving companies a competitive edge," *Sloan Management Review* 35 (1993):51-63.

Henderson, Bruce D., "The anatomy of competition," *Journal of Marketing* 47 (1983):7-11.

Hutchins, Greg, "Partnering: a path to total quality in purchasing," *National Productivity Review* 11 (1992):213-30.

Krapfel, Robert E., Jr., and Darlene Brannigan-Smith, 1985. "An experimental approach to segmenting buyers of marketing research," *Industrial Marketing Management,* 14 (1985):27-34.

Laughlin, Jay L., and Charles R. Taylor, "An approach to industrial market segmentation," *Industrial Marketing Management* 20 (1991):127-36.

Levitt, Theodore, "Marketing success through differentiation of anything," *Harvard Business Review* 60 (1982):110.

Peterson, Robin T., "Small business usage of target marketing," *Journal of Small Business Management* 29 (1991):79-85.

Popper, Edward T., and Bruce D. Buskirk, "Technology lifecycles in industrial markets," *Industrial Marketing Management* 21 (1992):23-31.

Robertson, Thomas S., and Howard Baris, "A successful approach to segmenting industrial markets," *Planning Review* 20 (1992):4-11.

Shapiro, Benson P., and Thomas V. Bonoma, 1984. "How to segment industrial markets," *Harvard Business Review* 62 (1984):104-110.

CHAPTER

Planning Marketing Strategies

If business marketers are to meet the challenges of today's rapidly changing markets and ever-growing global competition, marketing decisions must be based on well-conceived, clearly defined strategies. How well strategy is conceived, and the success of its implementation, however, greatly depends on careful coordination between marketing and all the other functional areas of the firm. The objectives of this chapter are to discuss:

1. Some of the problems involved in developing strategic plans in the business market and how these problems may be solved

2. Strategic planning at the corporate level, business level or strategic business unit (SBU) level, product level and the areas which must be assessed if resulting decisions are to be successful

3. The role of business marketing in the strategic planning process

Success in the business market depends on recognizing the importance of applicable strategic planning. Knowing where the organization is headed and knowing how to get there by using the company's scarce resources properly summarizes strategic planning. To deal with all the factors that can affect a firm's viability and its ability to grow profitably, management must design and follow (assuming the environment does not change) a viable strategic planning process. Such a process consists of developing a system of objectives and plans to allocate scarce company resources while striving to achieve the company's objectives. **Strategic planning,** then, involves an organization in recognizing, anticipating, and responding to changes in the marketplace to ensure that company resources are directed toward achieving those market opportunities which are consistent with the firm's capabilities.

↜ Strategies, Plans, and Tactics

Strategies consist of long-term objectives and plans to which an organization can relate its particular characteristics and capabilities to customers, competitors, and regulators.[1]

Plans consist of the various actions that must take place if resources are to be utilized effectively in implementing strategies. Thus, plans are more specific and detailed, answering such

219

questions as: "What will be done?" "Who will do it" "When will it be done?" and "How much will it cost?"

Tactics are the on-the-spot decisions made during the planning execution stage to ensure that plans are modified with events that materialize during a planning period. In this chapter, the concern is with how the business firm identifies with and can utilize the strategic planning process.

Nature of Strategic Planning

Success in the business market depends on a firm's recognition that strategic planning is a necessity. This plan should enable an organization to recognize and respond to various market changes, opportunities, and threats it might encounter.

Strategic planning takes place at three different levels for most businesses: (1) The corporate level, (2) the business level or **strategic business unit** (SBU) level, and (3) the functional or product level.[2]

An SBU is a self-contained operation within a corporation that is responsible for the manufacture and/or marketing of a service, a product, or a related product line.[3] This SBU can be a division, plant, district, or profit center operation as defined by the organization. The SBU is not part of the corporate level. Strategic marketing planning, sometimes called strategic business planning or business level planning, is the strategic planning process used at the SBU level. However, marketing opportunities and constraints are considered at all three levels.

Corporate Level   Strategic planning at the corporate level takes a broad-brush approach as it sets direction when it decides four important variables. First, what are the corporate mission and objectives? Second, in which markets should the corporation compete? Third, which present resources should be used and what are the resources that should be acquired? Fourth, how can the company's scarce resources be allocated profitably among the firm's chosen markets?

SBU Level   Strategic marketing planning at the SBU level defines all the aspects of its competitive moves in the marketplace. This includes the interrelationships among production, inventory, R&D, and investment decisions whenever business and marketplace decisions are made.

Product Level   Here the individual product's tactical plan (pricing, promotion, packaging, and distribution) is developed. This includes (1) specific product design, (2) potential buyer benefits, (3) market characteristics, (4) targeted market segment, (5) possible competition, (6) market and competitor's weaknesses and strengths, and (7) allocation of the firm's financial and organizational resources.

Business Strategic Planning Conflicts

Each business function can easily become too parochial and isolated from the broad perspectives that must be taken by top management. When tasks and objectives are in disharmony among several departments, planning processes can be jeopardized. These difficulties arise largely from three factors: (1) functional interdependence, (2) product complexity, and (3) buyer-seller interdependence.[4] Potential areas of conflict may exist between the marketing and engineering departments as well as between marketing and production/operations. A study investigated how production and sales departments of 54 small and medium-size industrial firms in the Netherlands coordinated their plans and activities in relation to their logistics structure. Interviewing data suggested there were problems in long-term capacity planning because of the high amount of market uncertainty for this time frame.[5]

Successful planning depends on cooperation between the different functional areas. Whenever tasks and objectives are different or unclear between two or more departments, a strong tendency for disharmony exists. As Table 9-1 highlights, potential areas of conflict exist between marketing and engineering. Such basic matters as new product development, product quality, and technical services may cause disharmony. Potential conflict also exists between marketing and manufacturing in such areas as sales forecasting and production planning. Marketing and R&D may have conflicts in many areas also, particularly when product features for new products are developed, if the two departments have different design criteria. Conflict may arise between marketing and R&D when new products are designed and sold to specific target markets. The mar-

TABLE 9-1   A Catalog of Potential Conflicting Areas Between Marketing/Engineering

Areas	Marketing Responses	Engineering Responses
New product design	They don't give us products we can sell. By the time we get them to design the product, it will be obsolete.	We're limited in what we can design because we have to keep it simple for marketing.
Breadth of the product line	We need more variety.	We have too much variety now.
Product appearance	Our line looks so inferior.	Our line does not need a lot of fancy window dressing.
Product problems	Why can't engineering make workable products?	Neither the customer nor our marketing department understands the product and how it is supposed to work.
Product promotion	The information we get from engineering is so dull and technical that no one would read it.	The information that marketing includes is so exaggerated. We could get sued for false advertising.
Packaging	It looks so cheap and functions so poorly that it makes our products hard to sell.	Trying to package so many products while holding costs down is extremely difficult.
Quality	Why can't we have reasonable quality at reasonable costs?	We must design so many products with numerous options that it is hard to maintain quality and keep costs down.
Technical	We need a technical expert to soothe customers even though they really do not have a problem.	We don't have enough manpower to hold the hand of some pet customers of marketing.
Warranty	Engineering always goes by the book, they don't understand that you have to bend a little.	Marketing wants us to pay the full amount of every claim, even an invalid one.

Source: J. Donald Weinrauch and Richard Anderson, "Conflicts between emgineering and marketing units," *Industrial Marketing Management* 11 (1982):291-301. Copyright © 1982 by Elsevier Science Publishing Co., Inc.

keting personnel may visualize one design, but R&D develops another. Product quality and its perception by the two different departments may cause additional conflict.[6]

MARKETING AND ENGINEERING CONFLICT

Engineering personnel focus on the product's design for attaining product validity: does the product do what it is supposed to do?; and product reliability: does the product do the same thing all the time? Marketing personnel tend to focus on how the product or service can be used to satisfy the customer's needs. Clearly, marketing people must become involved with engineers concerning new product design and new product conceptualization to bridge this significant divergence in points of view. Progressive business firms often hold joint meetings with all business functions represented, especially when conceptual activities such as concurrent engineering are practiced.

MARKETING AND MANUFACTURING CONFLICT

Conflicts also exist between marketing and manufacturing. Manufacturing forecasts sales using quantitative analysis, whereas marketing may use both quantitative and qualitative analysis. Product quality may be seen by manufacturing as durable, less expensive to make, and cost effective for the production/operations department. Marketing concentrates on the product's cost to the customer and the quality of service offered the customer. Manufacturing wants a simplified production planning process, whereas the marketing department has a tendency to change its forecasts and disrupt the production people's equilibrium. Operations people, for example, fail to see why marketing people cannot make a sales forecast for the next 6 months without constantly changing it. Every change in the forecast forces production planning people to revise their materials requirement planning (MRP) reports, which are used as the bases for planning which products are to be produced, the quantities, types, and design of parts and supplies needed; the available suppliers; and the coordinated timing to meet all the requirements for these events.

RESOLVING CONFLICTS

Alleviation of conflict begins with developing an understanding of the basic causes of interdepartmental conflict. As discussed in Chapter 5, conflict arises because each area is evaluated and rewarded on the bases of different criteria. Each area has different functions with different perceptions by the individuals involved. Conflict can also arise through differences in how departmental individuals perceive their prestige, power, and knowledge. An empire builder in one department can demand that another department bow down to the first department's demands. If customers are involved in the struggle, an enlightened company would lean toward the customer's perspectives. Budget constraints, rapid company growth, and the rapid pace of technological change can also yield potential areas of conflict between departments because costs affecting a department's "bottom line" are involved.

Marketing executives can assist in alleviating conflict by building their marketing plans around each functional area's ability to service the firm's markets and customers and by analyzing the strengths, weaknesses, and competitiveness of each respective department area, using a similar approach to analyzing the strengths and weaknesses of customers and competitors.[7]

Organizational Design for Interfunctional Cooperation   While many types of organizational structures exist, organizations are typically designed around what Galbraith and Nathanson have defined as the segmentation of work into roles. These roles include production, finance, and marketing. Further, these roles can be recombined into departments or divisions around functions, products, regions, or markets.[8] To resolve conflict and disputes between areas of specialty and to ensure that broad organizational goals will be obtained, coordination of the various functional activities is normally achieved vertically through the hierarchy of authority or through committee work and liaison roles.

Decision Support Systems   A computer software tool, **decision support systems** (DSS), contributes much toward integrating personnel in different departments, enabling a firm to use its competitive advantages better and to overcome interdepartmental conflict. Decision support systems are computer systems developed to aid managerial decisions by making state-of-the-art quantitative models that can analyze proposed actions by evaluating how these actions would affect all primary areas of an organization. For example, if a DSS were to analyze the effects of a product's price reduction, it would be able to include in its analysis all major considerations, such as the effects such actions would have on (1) the amount of product sold, (2) product inventory levels, (3) manufacturing scheduling of materials and manufacturing processes, (4) input availabilities for all affected variables, (5) the capital expenditures necessary, (6) additional revenues that may be realized, and (7) the anticipated competitor's reactions.

All firms have to realize their competitive viability is a tenuous matter and inefficiencies only create greater costs and delays, including the most tragic cost of all, the loss of valued customers. Communications among the various functions within a firm have to be improved by direct association and by formal training. The coordination by top management with all of the SBU's strategic planning people can ensure a lower level of conflicts. The creation of a marketing strategy center has been proposed where functionally integrated marketing strategy can be formulated to curtail much of the existing conflicts.[9] This center would be used as a diagnostic tool and mechanism in guiding organizational redesign and used as a vehicle for highlighting the multifunctional nature of business marketing decision making. Concurrent engineering practices, total quality management and better communications procedures are steps in the right direction. These concepts are illustrated in Figure 9-1, the planning arch. As illus-

FIGURE 9-1 The planning arch.

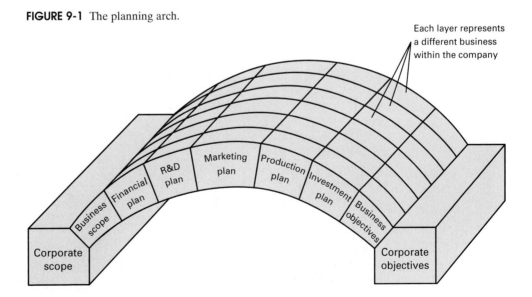

trated, the planning arch is positioned in the most critical part of the arch, but the entire structure would fall if it were not for the two stabilizing building blocks—corporate scope and corporate objectives.

Managing the Development of Strategic Planning

Strategic planning, however, is not the total answer to marketing success; the firm must be managed effectively. Many companies are coming to recognize that effective management does not lie solely in the area of strategic decision-making but also depends on other factors. According to one of the world's leading consulting firms, McKinsey & Company, strategy is only one of seven factors that the best-managed organizations exhibit.[10]

As a result of studying a large sample of excellently managed companies such as IBM, Boeing, and 3M, and discovering that their strengths included more than strategy, structure, and systems, consultants at McKinsey added four other factors. Figure 9-2 shows the seven factors that McKinsey considers necessary for a company to perform successfully over time.

The first three factors—strategy, structure, and systems—are what McKinsey sees as the hardware of success. The next four—style, staff, skills, and shared values—are seen as the software of success.

Style refers to the fact that employees share a common style in behaving and thinking, sometimes referred to as "culture." *Skill* refers to the fact that the necessary skills needed to carry out the strategies, such as marketing planning and financial analysis, have been mastered by the firm's employees. *Staffing* means that the company has hired capable people and placed them in the right positions to take full advantage of their respective talents. The last factor, *shared values,* means that employees share the same guiding values and mission, that is, an excellently managed company has a driving purpose and philosophy that is known and practiced by everyone.

FIGURE 9-2 McKinsey's seven-S framework.

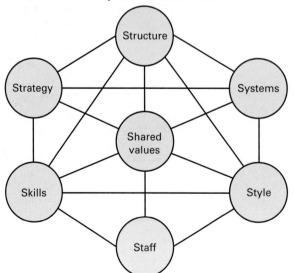

Source: Thomas J. Peters and Robert H. Waterman, Jr., *In Search of Excellence: Lessons From America's Best Run Companies.* (New York: Harper & Row, Publishers, Inc., 1982). Copyright © 1982 by Thomas J. Peters and Robert H. Waterman, Jr. Reprinted by permission of Harper & Row, Publishers, Inc.

STRATEGY: AN INTELLECTUAL AND SOCIAL PROCESS

In his study of large international companies, Horovitz[11] has discovered that management is becoming more and more concerned with three areas that are believed to be the key to quality in strategic decision making: (1) the organization structure, (2) the planning process, and (3) the activating modes used to produce strategic changes (people and style).

According to Horovitz, the concerns of management in the development of strategy, shown in Table 9-2, are best understood when viewed from two dimensions: (1) the steps necessary to formulate and implement strategy and (2) the processes that are used. Steps involve:

1. Strategy formulation—deciding in which direction to go
2. Strategy implementation—deciding how the organization is going to get there internally

The processes by which strategies are formulated and implemented involve:

1. *An intellectual process:* A decision-maker, through certain methodologies and tools, thinks through the best way to formulate a strategy and the organizational arrangements that best suit the orientation chosen, or helps managers better define their long-term orientations.

TABLE 9-2 Concerns in Strategic Management

Steps	Process	
	Intellectual	*Social*
Strategy formulation	What are the prospects in a particular industrial sector? Can we handle a changing environment with our current resources and capabilities? What should we do in our current businesses? How can profits be restored? What businesses should we be in? What portfolio should a business have, given its objectives? What firms can be bought? What units/activities should be sold?	How should the responsibilities to prepare, present, defend, and carry out plans (SBUs) be defined? How much more should be spent on planning processes and systems in the organization? How can staff be involved and a balance of viewpoints be maintained? How can innovative ideas be fostered and the right issues be addressed? How can checks be made to ensure that plans presented make sense? How can priorities be selected? How should no/yes be said? How can corporatewide spirit and concerns be instilled?
Strategy implementation	How well does the structure fit the purpose? How can our efforts be organized to generate new businesses, innovation, and new strategic alternatives? What delegation is required for fast adaptation to changes in the marketplace? How detailed should we plan the different aspects of the business? What information is needed and at what level to respond to the requirements of markets, to anticipate problem areas, and to trigger in advance strategic responses? What training and reward systems best fit our strategy?	How can we get our managers to think strategically? How can we get people committed to make it happen? How can new ideas be made standard practice? How can individual motivation be kept high? How can we ensure that broad objectives are carried out effectively through the chain of command? How can efforts be mobilized around a few values and objectives? How can withholding of information, deformation of purpose, resistance to change, and defiance toward innovation be prevented?

Source: Jacques Horovitz, "New perspectives on strategic management," *Journal of Business Strategy* 4 (Winter 1984). Copyright © 1984 by Warren, Gorham & Lamont, Inc., Boston, Mass. All rights reserved.

2. *A social process:* Through the planning process, the members of an organization participate one way or the other in the formulation of strategy. The people's profile and ability, as well as the CEO's activating mode, will determine whether and how well the strategies actually "happen." These factors also ensure that the actual behavior within the organization supports the accomplishment of the purpose.

✦ THE CORPORATE MISSION IN THE DEVELOPMENT OF STRATEGY

All successful companies exhibit a distinct and widely shared culture that directs corporate strategy.[12] A corporation's culture, like a society's culture, "is reflected in the attitudes and values, the management style, and the problem-solving behavior of its people."[13] The foundation for the development of that culture lies in a systematically and comprehensively developed mission statement.[14] It is the company mission, or purpose, that provides the basis for the culture that guides executive action and directs the formulation and implementation of strategy. When management addresses such fundamental questions as "Which business are we in?" "Who are the customers we serve?" and "Why does this organization exist?" the organization achieves a heightened sense of purpose and direction.

A well-conceived mission statement should provide a view of what an organization seeks to accomplish and the markets and customers it seeks to pursue now and in the future. It should be broadly outlined or implied, rather than specified, to enable the organization to expand or contract its business domain as it attempts to adjust to environmental change. As a business grows, or is forced by environmental pressures to alter its product/market/technology position, the need will arise to redefine the company mission.

↙ The Strategic Planning Process

As shown in Figure 9-3, the components of a strategic plan are (1) the mission statement, (2) opportunity and threat analysis, (3) monitoring the external environment, (4) differential advantage analysis, (5) internal company analysis, (6) portfolio analysis, (7) establishment of company objectives, (8) choice of market segments and competitive activities, (9) implementation of strategies and realignment of resources, and (10) evaluation of performance.

OPPORTUNITY AND THREAT ANALYSIS

The question "What business are we in?" can only be answered through the accurate evaluation of present and future marketing opportunities and threats. Opportunity and threat assessment shapes organizational efforts, determines how resources should be deployed, and guides the organization's future.

Opportunity Analysis   Opportunity analysis is undertaken to anticipate favorable situations within the scope of the firm's present or future domain capabilities. A marketing opportunity depends not only on environmental factors, but on the organization's actual and potential resources as well. Kotler defines a company marketing opportunity as an attractive arena for company marketing action in which the particular company would enjoy a competitive advantage.

Threat Analysis   Environmental threats must be identified and evaluated with respect to their seriousness and probability of occurrence to enable management to

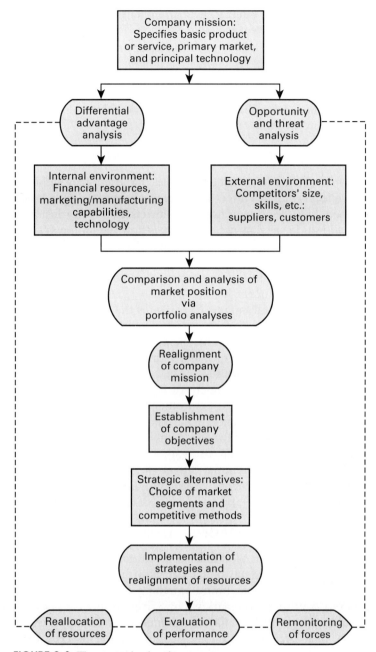

FIGURE 9-3 The strategic planning process.

adopt strategies to counteract them. An environmental threat is a threat that is likely to significantly affect the strategic planning process over the planning horizon. Kotler has identified such a threat as a challenge posed by an unfavorable trend or development in the environment that would lead in the absence of purposeful marketing action, to the erosion of the company's position.[15]

The purpose of assessing opportunities and threats is to enable an organization to capitalize on its ability to develop, maintain, and defend a specific position in the market. This assessment involves:

1. Monitoring the external environment for forces that are likely to affect markets and the demand for current and future products
2. An internal analysis of the firm to identify its strengths and weaknesses with respect to its management, its organizational structure, and its current position in the market and to identify its future capabilities
3. An external analysis to determine which market opportunities the organization should pursue and which threats should be assessed as to their implications for company planning and marketing decision making

MONITORING THE EXTERNAL ENVIRONMENT

A firm's external environment consists of those forces within the interface, public, and macro levels that can affect its strategic alternatives. Of course, forces in a firm's environment have positive or negative impacts. Zenith, for instance, whose major business domain was in the consumer market, is now the nation's largest supplier of computer terminal monitors in the institutional and government market—selling mainly to colleges and the military. Zenith's move into the business market arena was prompted by a decade of competitive price cutting that led to a loss of market share in all three of its consumer product areas.[16]

Environmental monitoring requires the analyses of past developments and current situations, as well as future projections to discover trends and identify likely opportunities and threats. One such environmental threat occurred to Intel when it tried to overlook a small problem with its Pentium chip, but once the flaw was discovered by a mathematics professor, the news spread rapidly on the Internet and the flaw was magnified to the detriment of Pentium sales.[17] It relies on quantitative analysis such as time-series analysis and other extrapolation methods that are useful in projecting economic and demographic data, as well as management judgment. To monitor political developments, foreign competition, or other issues that may affect their future, many organizations also gather information from government sources such as the Bureau of the Census, the Bureau of Economic Analysis, and the Bureau of Labor Statistics, as well as from banks and universities, or from services such as the *Yankelovich Monitor.*

COMPETITIVE ADVANTAGE ANALYSIS

At the heart of successful marketing strategy is differentiation. Effective differentiation or competitive advantage brings with it recognition and reward in such forms as customer awareness, brand switching, improved sales, better market shares, and heftier cash flows. "The survival of a firm requires that for some group of buyers, it should enjoy a differential or competitive advantage over all other suppliers."[18] Every firm occupies a unique position in the market, differentiating itself from others on the basis of product or service characteristics, management or engineering expertise, geographical location, or some other area that gives it a specific distinctive competency.[19]

A firm's competitive advantage is subject to change as elements within its external environment neutralize its existing position. The marketing environment is never static. Marketing success requires an ongoing evaluation of the firm's distinctive competencies and its position of competitive advantage within the marketplace. A threat in one market may lead to an opportunity in another, but only when a firm is able to transfer its distinctive competencies in such a manner as to develop a new competitive advantage.

INTERNAL COMPANY ANALYSIS

Three ingredients are essential for successful strategic planning: (1) it must be consistent with conditions in the external environment, (2) it must be realistic in terms of the requirements it places on the firm, and (3) it must be carefully executed.[20] The purpose of an internal company analysis, then, is to identify the specific strengths and weaknesses on which strategic planning should be based. In seeking to take advantage of opportunities, yet minimize the impact of threats, an organization must develop its strategies around its key strengths, or distinctive competencies. This task is accomplished by reviewing the company's past and present performance with respect to its products and markets and the trends and characteristics of the industry. Specifically, the organization should analyze sales trends by product lines, customer groups, geographic regions, alternative materials used in products, services provided, product design features, differences in channels of distribution, the cost and profitability of the respective areas, and its industry position.

PORTFOLIO ANALYSIS

The increased complexity of the business environment, coupled with the multiproduct, multimarket, and multinational nature of business marketing, has led many organizations to develop their strategies around portfolio analysis. Portfolio analysis enables organizations to make better decisions with respect to which market or product should be maintained, which expanded, which phased out or deleted, and which new ventures should be pursued. Several organizations have developed analytical models to assist them in selecting the appropriate marketing strategy.

Identifying Strategic Business Units   The first step, however, in portfolio analysis is to carefully identify strategic business units (SBUs) within the company. Ideally, an SBU, which is a single business, would have a distinct mission, a responsible manager, and its own competition; be independent of other business units; benefit from strategic planning; and be planned independently of other business units.[15] For instance, General Electric has identified 49 separate business areas.

Business Screening   General Electric's business screen is used to combine a number of factors into a composite value to determine each SBU's strengths and weaknesses and to assess environmental factors that represent risks and opportunities. Thus, the method uses multiple factors to assess each unit's business strengths and market attractiveness.

The business screen matrix, presented in Figure 9-4, is divided into nine cells to represent high, medium, and low market attractiveness and strong, average, and weak business strengths. Each cell is placed into zones to represent high, medium, or low overall attractiveness. The horizontal axis is traditionally labeled "Business strengths"; the vertical axis, "Market attractiveness."

Industry attractiveness is defined as a composite projection of the size and growth potential of the market, competitive structure, industry profitability, and environmental impact (e.g., economic, social and legal considerations). Organizational strength is viewed as a function of market size and growth rate, technological position, image, price competitiveness, product quality, sales force effectiveness, market location, profitability, environmental impact, and caliber of management.[21] The strategies that a business screen might suggest, depending on where an SBU is located, are shown in Table 9-3.

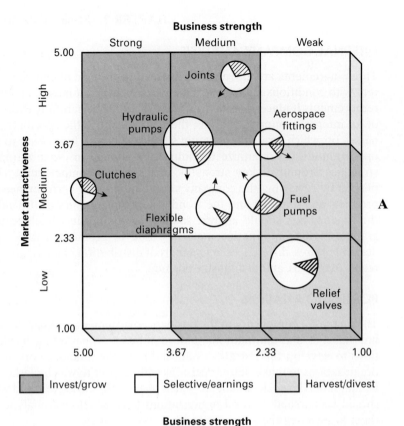

Business strength

	Strong	Medium	Weak
	5.00	3.67	2.33

Market attractiveness — High / Medium / Low

5.00 — 3.67 — 2.33 — 1.00

Joints

Hydraulic pumps

Aerospace fittings

Clutches

Flexible diaphragms

Fuel pumps

Relief valves

A

5.00   3.67   2.33   1.00

■ Invest/grow   □ Selective/earnings   ▨ Harvest/divest

Business strength

	Strong	Medium	Weak
High	PROTECT POSITION • Invest to grow at maximum digestible rate • Concentrate effort on maintaining strength	INVEST TO BUILD • Challenge for leadership • Build selectively on strengths • Reinforce vulnerable areas	BUILD SELECTIVELY • Specialize around limited strengths • Seek ways to overcome weaknesses • Withdraw if indications of sustainable growth are lacking
Medium	BUILD SELECTIVELY • Invest heavily in most attractive segments • Build up ability to counter competition • Emphasize profitability by raising productivity	SELECTIVITY/MANAGE FOR EARNINGS • Protect existing program • Concentrate investments in segments where profitability is good and risks are relatively low	LIMITED EXPANSION OR HARVEST • Look for ways to expand without high risk otherwise, minimize investment and rationalize operations
Low	PROTECT AND REFOCUS • Manage for current earnings • Concentrate on attractive segments • Defend strengths	MANAGE FOR EARNINGS • Protect position in most profitable segments • Upgrade product line • Minimize investment	DIVEST • Sell at time that will maximize cash value • Cut fixed costs and avoid investment meanwhile

Market attractiveness

B

Source: Philip Kotler, *Marketing Management, Analysis, Implementation, and Control,* 8th ed. (Upper Saddle River, N.J.: Prentice Hall, Inc., 1994), as modified by permission from George S. Day, *Analysis for Strategic Marketing Decisions* (St. Paul, Minn.: West Publishing, 1986), pp. 202, 204.

FIGURE 9-4 Market attractiveness: **A,** portfolio classification and **B,** strategies.

TABLE 9-3   Strategies Suggested for the Placement of SBUs in the Business Screen Matrix

| Organizational Strength | Industry Attractiveness | | |
	High	Medium	Low
High	Premium: Invest for growth Provide maximum investment Diversify worldwide Consolidate position Accept moderate near-term profits	Selective: Invest for growth Invest heavily in selected segments Share ceiling Seek attractive new segments to apply strength	Protect/refocus: Selectively invest for earnings Defend strengths Refocus to attractive segments Evaluate industry revitalization Monitor for harvest or divestment timing
Medium	Challenge: Invest for growth Build selectively on strengths Define implications of leadership challenge Avoid vulnerability—fill weaknesses	Prime: Selectively invest for earnings Segment market Make contingency plans for vulnerability	Restructure: harvest or divest Provide no unessential commitment Position for divestment Shift to more attractive segment
Low	Opportunistic: Selectively invest for earnings Ride market Seek niches, specialization Seek opportunity to increase strength (e.g., acquisition)	Opportunistic: Preserve for harvest Act to preserve or boost cash flow out Seek opportunistic sale Seek opportunistic rationalization to increase strengths	Harvest or divest: Exit from market or prune product line Determine timing so as to maximize present value

Source: D.D. Monieson, "An overview of marketing planning," *Executive Bulletin No. 8* (Ottawa: The Conference Board of Canada, 1978), p. 5.

The advantages of using business screening are twofold. First, it allows SBUs to be ranked intermediately between high and low and strong and weak. Second, it forces management to consider a wide range of strategically relevant variables. Once businesses have been evaluated and positioned, the appropriate marketing strategies can be determined. For example, business units falling in the "high overall attractiveness" zone should be given heavy marketing support; those in the "low overall attractiveness" should be considered for either harvesting (cultivating) or divesting (phasing out or deleting).

Profit Impact of Marketing Strategies[22]   Portfolio models, such as the business screen model, imply the need for measuring return on investment for a given business unit, under given industry and market conditions, following a given marketing strategy. Some methods of measurement have emerged from a unique research project called **Profit Impact of Marketing Strategies** (PIMS).

According to PIMS' findings, those factors having the greatest impact on ROI are market share relative to the company's three largest competitors, the value added to a product by the company, industry growth, product quality, level of innovation/differentiation, and vertical integration (ownership of other channel members). With respect to cash flow, PIMS' data suggest that growing markets and high levels of investment drain cash, while high relative market share improves cash flow. PIMS information is conveyed to participating firms through the following reports:

Par reports—showing average return on investment and cash flow on the basis of market, competition, technology, and cost structure, which enables managers to consider what would be reasonable expectations for their business and what control standards to set.

Strategy sensitivity reports—predicting effects of strategy changes on short-run and long-run ROI and cash flow.

Optimum strategy reports—suggesting combinations of strategies that will maximize results in income or cash flows.

Look-alike reports—examining tactics of similar competitors, both successful and unsuccessful.

Integrated Portfolio Models   In an empirical study of 15 SBUs, using PIMS data, Wind, Mahajan, and Swire found that where an SBU is placed in a matrix depends on the type of portfolio model being used, as well as the factors used to determine high/low industry growth and share, or industry attractiveness and organizational strengths. Specifically, the researchers have discovered that a minor change in the definition of the dimensions used, the rules used to divide those dimensions into low or high categories, how those dimensions are weighted, and the cutoff points used can result in a different classification of the SBU involved (i.e., a business may appear to be located in a high-high position in one model, but a high-low position in another model). Thus, they advise that rather than use a single portfolio model, integrated models should be used to take advantage of various methods of classification as well as to test the sensitivity of portfolio classifications of particular models. Such an integration would eliminate the risk "involved in employing a single standardized portfolio model as a basis for portfolio analysis and strategy." They further suggest that the classification of an SBU with respect to the dimensions used, cutoff rules, and weights be carefully examined.[23]

Evaluating the Portfolio Matrix   It may make little difference, however, which type or combinations of portfolio matrices are used. Their main purpose is to identify the character and market position of a firm's business portfolio. Thus, once the matrices are constructed, their classifications should be supplemented by additional analysis that adds to what the matrices indicate and that further indicates which strategies should be pursued. As Hofer and Schendel point out, those additional analyses should include the following:

1. An assessment of each SBU's industry to identify key trends and market changes, strengths and weaknesses of competitors, technological changes, and supply conditions
2. An examination of the firm's competitive position within each industry and how it ranks on factors important to successful performance in those industries
3. An identification of opportunities and threats that might arise in each area
4. An assessment of corporate resources and skills needed to improve the competitive strength of each SBU
5. A comparison of the relative short- and long-run attractiveness of each SBU
6. An evaluation of the overall portfolio to determine whether the mix of SBUs is adequately balanced; for example, whether there are sufficient cash-producing SBUs in relation to the number of those that are heavy cash consuming, so that internal control is maximized with respect to resource deployment

ESTABLISHING COMPANY OBJECTIVES

In effect, opportunity and threat analysis is the intermediate step between defining the firm's mission and the setting of corporate objectives. Analysis may reveal that to take advantage of an environmental opportunity, or avoid a threat, the organization may have to redefine its business domain, adopt a more effective strategy, or both.

While mission statements identify the underlying design, aim, or thrust of a company, objectives are the specific results desired. For example, the mission statement of Nicor, Inc., reads[24]:

> The basic purpose of Nicor, Inc., is to perpetuate an investor-owned company, engaging in various phases of the energy business, striving for balance among those phases so as to render needed satisfactory products and services and earn optimum, long-range profits.

To achieve its underlying thrust, Nicor must develop specific objectives in such areas as profitability, return on investment, and technological leadership. Thus, a specific corporate objective to optimize profits might read—double earnings per share within five years with increases in each interim year.

Objectives are important in the strategic planning process because they provide people with a specific sense of their role in the organization; lead to consistency in decision making among the various functional managers; stimulate exertion and accomplishment; and most importantly, provide the bases for specific planning, corrective actions, and control.[15] Other criteria for establishing useful objectives are outlined in Table 9-4.

✦ Marketing's Role in the Strategic Planning Process

Successful planning at both the corporate level and the business level depends on the ability of marketing to generate ideas for new product development; to spot and evaluate new market opportunities; to develop detailed marketing plans; to implement and evaluate ongoing results; to take corrective action where necessary; and to determine when a business venture is no longer viable. However, since the success of marketing planning in the business arena is greatly dependent on the activities of other functional areas, marketing's role in the strategic planning process involves analyzing and interpreting market requirements to enable corporate management to decide how best to respond.[25]

TABLE 9-4 Criteria for Establishing Useful Objectives	
Acceptable	When objectives are consistent with managers' perceptions and preferences, they are more likely to be pursued. If objectives are inappropriate, unfair, or offensive, management may ignore or even obstruct their achievement.
Flexible	In the event of unforeseen or extraordinary changes in the firm's environment, objectives must be capable of modification.
Motivating	If objectives are to stimulate exertion and accomplishment, they must be set high enough to provide a challenge and yet not so high as to cause frustration or so low as to be easily attained.
Consistent	Objectives must be consistent and suited to the overall mission of the firm as well. Objectives that are inconsistent or unsupportive of company goals can be counterproductive.
Understandable	If objectives are to be achievable, they must be stated in clear, meaningful, and unambiguous terms. Managers at all levels must have a clear understanding of what is to be achieved and the criteria by which they will be evaluated.
Achievable	To be achievable, objectives must be realistic and feasible. Thus, they should come from the company's external and internal analysis, not out of wishful thinking.

One study was conducted to determine the reasons for new product success or failure. Of the 123 technical firms involved with 203 new products reviewed, the study indicated that the five key success factors were (1) product superiority (delivering unique benefits to customers), (2) strong predevelopment research, (3) sharp and early product definition, (4) a strong market orientation with constant customer contact and input, and (5) quality of execution of key activities in the new product process.[26] The study provides further evidence that all functions must work together to obtain a viable and lasting strategic plan.

The relationship between marketing and the various business units during the strategic planning process is shown in Figure 9-5. Marketing supplies each unit with information and opinion inputs (step 1), which are analyzed and evaluated by each unit (step 2), which then establishes its mission and formulates its objectives (step 3). Once each business unit has established its mission and objectives, marketing managers can formulate marketing plans (step 4), implement them (step 5), and evaluate the results (step 6), which triggers the next cycle in the strategic planning process.[15]

✔ SITUATIONAL ANALYSIS

As Figure 9-6 shows, marketing plays a major role in the development of strategic plans, particularly at the SBU level. Each business unit within a firm relies on marketing "as the main system for monitoring opportunities and developing marketing objectives and plans for achieving that business's objectives."[30] To carry out their role in the strategic planning process, marketing managers (1) assess the current market situation and (2) determine forces that will affect the market situation during the future planning period. Situational analysis is the information gathering stage in which marketing managers assimilate and assess external or market related information and internal or company-related information to assist each business unit in identifying opportunities and threats to make the best of its competitive advantages. Current and potential market opportunities, marketing objectives, and marketing plans cannot be determined without knowing where the company presently stands in its total marketing environment.[27]

A necessary part of marketing's role in analyzing and interpreting market requirements, then, is to assess realistically the present and future market situation and identify the company's strengths and weaknesses with respect to its present and future capa-

FIGURE 9-5 The relationship between marketing and strategic planning.

Source: Philip Kotler, *Marketing Management, Analysis, Planning, and Control,* 7th ed. (Upper Saddle River, N.J.: Prentice Hall, Inc., 1984). Copyright © 1984 by Prentice Hall; reprinted by permission.

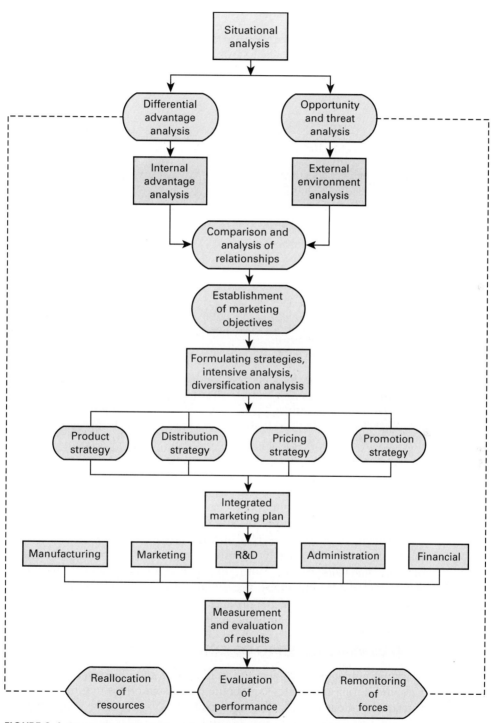

FIGURE 9-6 The business marketing planning process.

TABLE 9-5	Internal and External Information Gathering in the Situational Analysis		
Internal Information		*External Information*	
Categories	*Types of Information*	*Categories*	*Types of Information*
Organization	Company mission, objectives; company growth strategies; portfolio plans, organizational problems, power center/ struggles/weaknesses	Environmental factors	Cost and availability of needed resources: economic conditions (e.g., recession, inflation and interest rates); technological/social changes; environmental policies/ regulations; industry/business regulations
Financial resources	Profitability by product/market geographic areas; cost data by product/market geographic areas; budgets; financial ratios; credit position	Market conditions	Market size/growth; geographic concentration; market share/sales penetration
Forecasts and projections	Sales and market share forecasts and projections by products/ markets; production and manpower forecasts	Market segments	Rate of product usage, product applications and benefits; decision makers' and influencers' receptivity to sales force, advertising and promotion, prices, price changes, and channel arrangements
Operating capabilities	Manufacturing/production/purchasing capacity; quality of engineering and R&D; service facilities/expertise; inventory levels	Channels	Present channel relations; motivation of channel members; costs of alternative arrangements; inventory levels, f.o.b. points; effect of pricing strategies
Competitive strengths and weaknesses	Current status of company products, sales force, distribution advertising and promotion, compared with that of competitors	Competitors	Number, location, and market share; strengths and weaknesses with respect to products, prices, advertising and promotion, channels, R&D, engineering; possible competitive reactions

bility of competing in the marketplace. The types of information that marketing managers most often seek during the situation analysis stage are outlined in Table 9-5. A management trend that emerged in the early 1990s involves new ways to combine market research with the strategic planning process. A growing willingness on the part of many managers is to put normative data in abeyance and to question some of the standard methods of planning. These managers are using situation-specific assessments where the situation in which a product may be introduced and/or used can lead to the identification of more meaningful customer segmentation.[28]

ESTABLISHING MARKETING OBJECTIVES

Marketing objectives are derived directly from the objectives set forth by each business unit during the strategic planning process and the situational analysis. Given the assessment of current and future market situations, specific marketing objectives are normally established in terms of some desired sales volume, market share, gross margin, profits, and return on investment. Since performance is usually measured in relation to desired objectives, marketing objectives should have those attributes discussed in Table 9-4, Criteria for Establishing Useful Objectives.

FORMULATING MARKETING STRATEGIES

Once marketing objectives have been determined, alternative marketing strategies must be analyzed. Two levels of analysis are available for determining strategic marketing alternatives[15]: (1) intensive analysis, which identifies possible strategic alternatives within the company's current business areas, (2) integrated growth which suggests that a company should look backwards and forwards within its present business, and (3) diversification analysis, which identifies strategic alternatives outside the firm's current business areas.

Intensive Analysis   Intensive analysis consists of reviewing existing business units (i.e., portfolio analysis) to determine whether opportunities exist for improving their performance.[29] When the current product/market position has not been fully exploited, the potential for market share growth exists. Through more aggressive marketing efforts such as offering quantity discounts and increasing advertising and selling efforts, current customers can be encouraged to buy more, and, where competitors are weak, their customers can be attracted.

Strategic alternatives may also be generated by developing new markets through regional, national, or international expansion or by developing differentiated product versions that appeal to new market segments. Or new markets segments may be generated by the development of improved products for present markets (e.g., improving product features, creating different quality versions, or developing additional models and sizes).

Intensive analysis in planning is reinforced with the occurrence of shorter product life cycles that challenge companies to achieve market penetration quickly, with the goal of achieving steep acceleration of the sales curve before further technological change dilutes the product's potential. Rapid sales acceleration is particularly important for technology-based products, which are seeing life cycles grow ever shorter.[30]

Integrated Growth Analysis   By looking at integrating forward, backward, or horizontally, within the same business, a firm may reap some benefits such as discovering new sources of revenue and possibly lowering some costs. A company could acquire some of its suppliers, industrial distributors, or sell direct to OEMs. If such options are not available, then diversification remains as a viable alternative.

Diversification Analysis   By looking outside its present product/market area for opportunities that are both highly attractive and are related to its business strengths and distinctive competencies, the firm may also discover strategic alternatives via diversification. Three types of diversification are worth considering: (1) concentric diversification, which consists of searching for new products that have technological and/or marketing synergies with the firm's existing product lines and that will appeal to new customers; (2) horizontal diversification, which consists of adding new, technologically unrelated products that appeal to the firm's present customer base; and (3) conglomerate diversification, which consists of seeking new businesses that are totally unrelated to the company's present technology, products, or markets.

Mobility Barriers   Factors that may inhibit a firm's entry into new businesses or industry segments have been generalized as mobility barriers. Mobility barriers consist of factors that may be deterrents to a shift in the strategic position of one firm and advantages to another.[31] These barriers can be described as follows:

1. *Economies of scale*—can force an organization to enter a market on a large scale or accept the cost disadvantages inherent in low production volume. Economies of scale may exist in research, marketing, distribution, and finance as well as manufacturing

2. *Product differentiation*—can create customer loyalty, which would force a competitive organization to spend heavily to overcome this loyalty. Where products are clearly differentiated, product distinctiveness can be a strong entry barrier.

3. *Capital requirements*—can be a clear barrier to entry where substantial capital is needed for physical facilities, R&D, advertising, credit, inventories, and other areas.

4. *Cost disadvantages*—an organization may be impeded from market entry due to the considerable expenditures necessary to overcome a lack of experience in proprietary technology, existing supplier relationships, location, or existing assets.

5. *Access to distribution channels*—market entry may be difficult if channels are limited or an organization is required to develop entirely new channels.

6. *Government policy*—market entry may be difficult if license requirements and environmental and safety regulations, can serve to give entrenched firms significant advantages over potential entrants.

Developing Marketing Strategy

Once strategic alternatives have been decided on, the development of marketing strategy rests on (1) market segmentation analysis, (2) target-market selection, and (3) the development of the marketing mix strategies.

INCREASED IMPORTANCE OF SBU LEVEL PLANNING

The shift from a words-oriented to a numbers-oriented planning process gave rise to a false sense of certainty at the corporate level.[32] Corporate organizational staff planning groups laid out how each operating unit's (SBU) future was to be handled. These groups were armed with popular planning models dictated for individual corporate SBU's from on high. These corporate people were rarely close enough to the realities of the marketplace to see the actual competitive environment the SBU was facing on a daily basis. Disaster struck in many places because outmoded plans, used by the SBUs, were too specific and detailed and prevented the SBU's ability to accommodate local market conditions.

Although widely used among business firms, strategic planning was not the panacea it was once thought to be, and some scholars and firms lost some faith in the process.[33] Strategic planning took its toll in the marketing, R&D, and operations areas as financial strategy grew in importance and often dominated the other areas. Costs, profit projections, and cost ratios became the heart of many strategic plans. Marketing is not an area that can be delegated to a small group of managers using only financial goals; marketing is and always has been concerned with the whole business as seen from the customer's perspective. With this holistic emphasis, some firms have shunned the purely financial constraints and returned to the marketing concept with its customer orientation.[34]

THE THREAT OF NEW MARKET ENTRANTS

The significance of this structural element depends on the barriers to entry that exist and the reactions the newcomer can expect from the industry's members. The barriers to entry are factors such as economies of scale of production and marketing; product differentiation; capital requirements; ability to switch costs from one function to another; access to distribution channels; cost disadvantages incurred, for example, because of a favorable location; and government policy that favors one company over another.

INTENSITY OF RIVALRY AMONG EXISTING COMPETITORS

The competitive jockeying for market niches and market share fosters price competition, advertising battles, product introductions, and increased customer services. This pattern of action and reaction promotes nearly equally balanced competitors, a slow industry growth, high fixed costs, and products that lack differentiation.

PRESSURE FROM SUBSTITUTE PRODUCTS

Substitute products place a ceiling on the prices a firm can profitably charge. IBM clones battle each other for market position since they are substitutes for each other. IBM tolerated this situation for years until it introduced its PS/2 system to regain its market leadership. Then IBM began to prosecute copyright violators such as Fujitsu, Japan's largest computer manufacturer.

COMPETITIVE ADVANTAGE STRATEGY

Michael Porter considers a business firm has to practice three distinct competitive strategies to maximize its viability when coping with the three competitive forces covered in the previous section. These approaches are (1) maintain an overall cost leadership, (2) practice product or service differentiation, and (3) focus on a particular market segment rather than try to be everything to everybody. These competitive strategies should be incorporated into, and become the firm foundation for, a strategic marketing plan.

OVERALL COST LEADERSHIP

Cost leadership entails aggressive construction of efficient economy of scale facilities, vigorous pursuit of cost reductions, tight cost and overhead control, avoidance of marginal customer accounts, and cost minimization in areas like R&D, sales force, service, advertising, and so on. Having a low cost position yields the company higher returns and provides the company a defense against present and potential competitors. Emerson Electric, Texas Instruments, Black and Decker, and Du Pont have gained a reputation for their low cost control. Many other companies are attempting to downsize their organizations to control costs and produce profits such as GM, Boeing, Chrysler, Ford, IBM, Unisys, and Digital.

PRODUCT OR SERVICE DIFFERENTIATION

Crown Cork and Seal has developed a "niche" in metal cans via its outstanding customer service record. Caterpillar Tractor is widely known for its durable product, dealer network and excellent spare parts availability. IBM is known for its augmented marketing where it offers product, service, training, and software as a complete bundle. Differentiating itself from its competitors provides a defense against its competitors via brand loyalty, lower sensitivity to price, and higher margins. Customers acknowledge the firm's superiority in product design, customer service, delivery, support, and satisfaction. Market share is easier to attain when a specific product "owns" a particular market segment or niche because of the product's features, price, quality, and its producer's customer support.

FOCUS ON A SPECIFIC MARKET TARGET

Cost leadership and product differentiation are very necessary, but without focusing these efforts toward the market segment that possesses the greatest market opportunities for this superior product, the triad of competitive strategy would be defeated. Matching the right product with the right market segment to gain a market niche enhances the firm's ability to defend itself against competitors and generate its desired profit. One study that focused on 2,578 firms in Minnesota and Pennsylvania found that strategies with a narrow scope of segmentation generally prevailed in industries near the supply chain's end while strategies that adopt a broad approach tend to predominate in industries near the beginning or middle of the supply chain.[35]

Strategic Marketing Planning Objectives

The strategic marketing plan is a problem-solving sequence that according to Abell and Hammond, involves four sets of related decisions:

1. Defining the business (Where do we stand? What will the future be like? Where should we be heading?)
    a. Product and market scope (Which customers are to be served? What technologies are required?)
    b. Product and market segmentation (Does the firm recognize differences between customer segments.
2. Determining the mission or role of the business (sales growth, market share, ROI, net income, market opportunities and company's capabilities)
3. Formulating functional strategies (marketing, operations, R&D, service, distribution)
4. Budgeting (resource allocation, financial decisions, proforma income statements, balance sheets, and cash flow statements)

A strategic marketing plan is not the same as a marketing plan; it is a plan which includes all aspects of an organization's strategy which could possibly interface with the marketplace, including production, R&D, finance, human resources, sales and marketing. Abell and Hammond's perspectives characterize the basic nature of planning's objectives to be a company that must be aware of the specific business it is in or in which it wants to be. Then and only then can the organization's mission or role be set.

Planning forces a company to state its perceptions about the scope, potential and trends in a given market and forces the company to analyze the market opportunities and threats that can shape a its future. Explicitly, it requires the firm to acknowledge its strengths, weaknesses, functional strategies, market position, and who its competitors are, both primary and secondary in a given market. Planning requires that a firm's SBU's objectives and its strategies be identified and evaluated. Philosophically, the planning process builds a management team consensus behind the SBU's strategies and tactics.[33]

MARKET SEGMENTATION AND TARGET MARKETING

Market segmentation analysis is fairly well recognized by most marketing managers and can be thought of as a process of dividing a larger market into submarkets, each having different demand patterns, needs, buying styles, and responses to various suppliers' marketing strategies. Market segments must be assessed, however, in terms of market potential, competition, customer profiles, and the company's capability in serving them. How business markets are segmented was covered in Chapter 8. The important point is that marketing planning cannot be undertaken until the firm has carefully chosen those markets it is capable of serving. For example, IBM's chairman, Louis V. Gerstner, Jr., in an approach to change the giant's fortunes, changed a portion of "Big Blue's" direction by focusing on gaining ground in the fast-growing market for smaller computers linked in networks in an attempt to increase the company's business payoff from its research programs, thus forcing a drastic change in the company's strategic planning.[33] Assessment of potential target markets must be based on the following:

1. Their current size: which must be sufficient if marketing objectives in terms of sales volume, market share, profitability, or return on investment are to be achieved

2. Their potential for future growth: if the firm is to realize a sufficient return for its efforts to serve a particular market

3. Whether they are owned or over occupied by existing competition: if the firm is to assess realistically its capability of penetrating a particular market

4. Whether there exists a relatively unsatisfied need that the firm can satisfy better than its competitors

FORMULATING MARKETING MIX STRATEGY

Once a target market has been identified, marketing strategy can address the components of product, place, price, and promotion. Box 9-1 briefly outlines the decision areas covered by these four components.

Decisions with respect to how product lines, features, quality levels, services, and new product development will be used to satisfy customer needs must be clearly formulated and integrated with manufacturing, R&D, and technical services.

Since products or services must be delivered to customers when and where they are wanted, distribution strategy is primarily concerned with developing the right combination of factors (e.g., inventory levels, storage facilities, and transportation modes) to ensure consistency with the total marketing strategy.

Promotion strategy defines the manner in which the firm will communicate with its target market and provides the basis for formulating personal selling, advertising, sales promotion, and media selection plans. Not only must promotion strategy be consistent with other strategic components, it must be closely integrated with financial strategy due to cost requirements.

Pricing strategy, because of its influence on demand and supply, profitability, customer perception, and regulatory response must be carefully developed in conjunction with internal factors (e.g., cost, return on investment, and profitability). When strategies in the four areas of the marketing mix are properly developed, they should produce a synergistic marketing effect.

DEVELOPING MARKETING PLANS

Successful marketing planning, requires careful timing and implementation. Abel has suggested that in many industries there are "strategic windows"—limited periods of time during which a firm may successfully adopt and implement a completely new strategy.[37] Thus, timing is particularly critical when a firm is developing, or radically changing, its strategy. The North American Free Trade Agreement (NAFTA) is a case in point where strategic windows can change, since the agreement incorporates liberalization and market-closing measures.[38] For example, the apparel provisions of NAFTA will relieve Mexico of burdensome quotas in the North American market but will impose ultrastrict rules of product origin on the industry, hence restricting strategic planning for many companies.

Scheduling is a useful means of controlling the timing of activities, as well as the deployment of resources, in implementing plans. Scheduling can be accomplished

---
BOX 9-1

Industrial Marketing Strategy Components

PRODUCT PLANNING AND DEVELOPMENT

1. Distinguish product from that of competitors as viewed by customers.
2. Offer only one product and try to attract all buyers (i.e., use an "undifferentiated" strategy).
3. Develop separate products and marketing programs for each market segment (i.e., use a "differentiated" strategy).
4. Create new uses for existing products (through improved performances and/or exclusive features).
5. Diversify into new markets with new products, either through acquisition of companies or through internal development of new products.
6. Establish product leadership through development of quality products.
7. Develop new products for commercialization consideration each year, beating competition to marketplace and establishing a reputation for innovation.

DISTRIBUTION

1. Warehouse products at locations that enable quick delivery to each distributor and customer.
2. Provide additional outlets to reduce distribution cost per sale.
3. Use only one warehouse to minimize inventory control problems.

SALES/SERVICE

1. Expand geographic area of operations to penetrate high-potential regions not currently approached.
2. Reshape distribution channels (i.e., dealers, distributors, agents, and company sales force) to satisfy market buying preferences more closely.
3. Develop more competent sales force and/or dealer/distributor organization.
4. Require sales force to improve its knowledge of customers and their products.

5. Employ target marketing to identify and reach high-potential customers and prospects.
6. Maximize reciprocal purchases with suppliers where prudent.
7. Increase sales effort on most profitable products and customers.

ADVERTISING/PROMOTION

1. Employ "push" strategy to encourage dealers, distributors, and company sales force to move your product lines (good margins, bonuses, services, advertising, and promotional subsidies).
2. Employ "pull" strategy to stimulate customer demand through increased brand, concept, and product acceptance.
3. Maximize advertising and promotion coverage to increase volume, which will permit mass production and distribution.
4. Address advertising and promotion to key customers and "best" prospects to maximize the benefits of these expenditures in a limited market segment.

PRICING

1. Set low price for new products to discourage competitive entry into market.
2. Set low price for products to encourage high sales volume, which permits mass production and low unit cost.
3. Provide minimum "extra" services to permit lower prices.
4. Price parts, service, and repairs at cost or with slight markup to gain maximum goodwill.
5. Price products to obtain principal profit on original sale rather than on follow-up service and parts.
6. Offer quantity discounts to encourage larger unit purchases.

Source: Adapted from Cochrane Chase and Kenneth L. Barasch, *Marketing Problem Solver.* (Radnor, Penn.: Chilton Book Co., 1977), pp. 79-80. Reprinted by permission.

through the use of such techniques as the *critical path method* (CPM) and *program evaluation and review technique* (PERT). Both CPM and PERT are especially useful when major changes in purchasing or production schedules are called for in the implementation of marketing plans.

IMPLEMENTING AND CONTROLLING MARKETING PLANS

Once marketing strategies and plans have been determined, they must be implemented. To evaluate and control strategy performance, standards for control must also be established. Since marketing strategies and plans are formulated to achieve objectives, these same objectives can be used to establish standards against which performance can be measured, such as objectives regarding profit, market share, and sales penetration. The company's historical trends can also be used to establish objective targets in these areas. Industry trends, such as sales per salesperson or percentage return on sales, can also be used.

Evaluation and control methods "make it possible not only to determine better the impact of current marketing activities on costs, revenues, and profits but also to respond more quickly to opportunities and threats."[39] A number of different performance measures are available for purposes of control:

1. *Sales analysis:* Provides valuable data and serves as an early warning system for identifying declining or rapidly growing sales.
2. *Sales performance analysis:* Compares sales volume to predetermined objectives or quotas and provides a benchmark against which to evaluate sales. Sales can also be compared to last year's sales, competitors' sales, forecasted sales, or industry sales.
3. *Marketing cost analysis:* Measures marketing expenses against their magnitude and gives insight into the costs of doing business and the patterns of these costs.
4. *Contribution margin analysis:* Subtracts direct costs from sales to determine contribution to overhead and profits.
5. *Net profit analysis:* Subtracts both direct and indirect costs from sales to determine profitability.
6. *Return on investment analysis:* Compares profits to the assets involved in generating profits to measure marketing productivity.

Common performance measures and the extent of their use in the business market are shown in Table 9-6.

Schedules and Control Charts   Schedules and charts are two common and logical types of control tools. As mentioned, CPM and PERT are used to plan and monitor schedules of activities. *Gantt charts* can also be used. Control charts are used more for repetitive-type activities to detect when an activity deviates significantly enough to warrant investigation.

Reports   To assist those persons responsible for implementing, evaluating, and controlling marketing strategy, companies' information systems produce periodic reports. These reports are helpful if they are prepared so as to report on how well objectives are being accomplished. Too frequently, though, once an information system begins producing reports relative to particular objectives, it will continue to do so, long after the objectives have changed.

Budgets   Budgets are an excellent control and evaluation tool, usually established for a 1-year period and projecting costs for each budgeted category, such as sales and

TABLE 9-6 Common Performance Measures Used in the Business Market	
Measure	*Percentage of Responding Firms*
Customer Performance Measures (n = 116)	
Sales volume by customer (units or dollars)	90.5
Sales volume as compared to a predetermined objective set for the customer	48.3
Contribution of customer profit	41.1
Net profit of customer (sales less direct costs less indirect costs allocated)	24.1
Return on assets committed to the customer	9.5
Product Performance Measures (n = 142)	
Sales volume by product (units or dollars)	91.5
Sales volume as compared to a predetermined quota by product	54.2
Market share by product	59.9
Expenses incurred by product	40.0
Contributions of product to profit (sales less direct cost)	75.4
Net profit of product (sales less direct costs less indirect costs allocated)	57.0
Return on assets committed to the product	28.9
Order Size Performance Measures (n = 37)	
Sales volume by order size (units or dollars)	81.1
Sales volume as compared with a predetermined quota set for order sizes	18.9
Expenses incurred in relation to size of order	43.2
Contribution of a particular order size to profit (sales less direct costs)	45.9
Net profits of each order size (sales less direct costs less indirect costs allocated)	35.1
Geographic Area Performance Measures (n = 110)	
Sales volume by area (units or dollars)	91.8
Sales volume as compared to a predetermined quota for the area	70.0
Expenses incurred for sales to a particular area	38.2
Contribution of a particular area to profit (sales less direct costs)	25.5
Net profit of each area (sales less direct costs less indirect costs allocated)	11.8
Return on assets (committed to a particular area)	7.3

Source: Adapted from Donald W. Jackson, Jr., Lonnie L. Ostrom, and Kenneth R. Evans, "Measures used to evaluate industrial marketing activities," *Industrial Marketing Management* 11 (October 1982):269-74. Copyright © 1982 by Elsevier Science Publishing Co., Inc.

advertising. Since each budgeted item can be isolated for departments and individuals, deviations can be traced to the responsible activities or persons.

Sales and Cost Analysis   Sales and cost analyses are an effective means of discovering unexpected problems. Since sales analyses are subdivided by product, product line, customer type, and geographic area, components that need attention can be easily pinpointed. Where possible, when costs are separated and matched to specific products, product lines, customers, and geographic areas, profit measures can also be obtained.

Marketing Audits   A marketing audit consists of a systematic, periodic assessment of the entire marketing program with respect to its objectives, strategies, activities, organization structure, and individual personnel. It also includes an assessment of the firm's environment with respect to company image, customer characteristics, competitive activities, regulatory constraints, and economic trends. To ensure that an audit is carried out objectively and in an unbiased manner, however, it should be performed by persons who have no vested interests in the findings.

Looking Back

Corporate level, SBU level, and product level represent the three levels of business planning. Successful planning in the business market, as compared to the consumer market, requires a higher degree of functional coordination. Top management and marketing management must search for ways to overcome the traditional isolation of functional areas—isolation that is brought about by (1) the inherent conflict between marketing and other functional areas, (2) organizational structures that are typically internally oriented rather than externally oriented, and (3) the failure to incorporate input from other functional areas into marketing decisions.

Marketing's role in strategic planning should be one of analyzing and interpreting market requirements to assist management in deciding how to respond best. This planning involves gathering, analyzing, and interpreting external, or market-related information as well as internal, or company-related information in order to spot opportunities and assess the company's strengths and weaknesses with respect to competing in the marketplace.

The development of marketing planning, which is an intellectual and a social process, consists of determining the opportunities and threats which may exist in the firm's external environment; determining the firm's differential advantage; analysis of the firm's internal strengths and weaknesses; analysis of the firm's business and product portfolios; develop company objectives, plan competitive marketing strategies; and implement and control the specific marketing plans that evolved from the planning process.

Implementing and controlling marketing strategy involves the development of specific plans with respect to how the marketing mix will be formulated to deliver the desired satisfaction of the target markets and how the specific marketing plans will be monitored for corrective marketing actions, if necessary.

Questions for Discussion

1. A large component manufacturer was recently revising one of its leading product lines for the automotive industry. Engineers wanted a simple, cost-effective, technically consistent product line. Marketing wanted the technical aspects varied for product differentiation. After months of customer dissatisfaction and inefficient engineering designs and tests, the issue was still unresolved. What are the real issues involved and how would you solve them?

2. "Japanese companies place less reliance on the formal and conceptual aspects of formulating marketing goals and strategies and more emphasis on the implementation and human relations aspects than do American companies." Would this emphasis work in American organizations?

3. "People's behavior, judgment, and past experience and the CEO's style very much influence the quality and type of strategic decisions made." Do you agree?

4. The objective behind portfolio analysis is to "emphasize the balance of cash flows by ensuring that there are products that use cash to sustain growth and others that supply cash. The problem with concentrating on cash flow to maximize income and growth is that strategies to balance risks are not explicitly considered." If this statement is true, what other factors would you consider in developing your strategy besides organizational strengths and industry attractiveness?

5. "The success of any marketing strategy depends on the strength of the competitive analysis on which it is based." Thus, before marketing strategy can be developed, specific competitors must be identified and their strengths and weaknesses evaluated. "Yet present concepts of competitive analysis in marketing are almost useless." If these statements are true, can you improve on them?

6. "A marketing strategy is the manner in which company resources are put at risk in the search for differential advantage." Do you agree? If so, what are the firm's sources of differential advantages? How can management calculate the strength of its differential advantages?

Endnotes

1. Henry L. Tosi and Stephen J. Carroll, *Management,* 2nd. ed. (New York: John Wiley & Sons, Inc., 1982), p. 196.
2. Donald L. Bates and David L. Elderedge, *Strategy and Policy,* 2nd ed. (Dubuque, Iowa: William C. Brown Co., Publishers, 1984), p. 12.
3. Bernard A. Rausch, *Strategic Marketing Planning* (New York: American Management Association, 1982):1-2.
4. Frederick E. Webster, Jr., "Management science in industrial marketing," *Journal of Marketing* 42 (January 1978):21-27.
5. Paul A. Konijnendijk, "Dependence and conflict between production and sales," *Industrial Marketing Management* 22 (August 1993):161-7.
6. J. Donald Weinrauch and Richard Anderson, "Conflicts between engineering and marketing units," *Industrial Marketing Management* 11 (1982):291-301.
7. Benson P. Shapiro, "Can marketing and manufacturing coexist?" *Harvard Business Review* 46 (September-October 1968):100-11.
8. J.R. Galbraith and D.A. Nathanson, *Strategic Implementation: The Role of Structure and Process* (St. Paul, Minn.: West Publishing Co., 1978):12-16.
9. Michael D. Hutt and Thomas W. Speh, "The marketing strategy center: diagnosing the industrial marketer's interdisciplinary role," *Journal of Marketing* 18 (Fall 1984).
10. See Thomas J. Peters and Robert H. Waterman, Jr., *In Search of Excellence: Lessons From America's Best-Run Companies* (New York: Harper & Row, Publishers, Inc., 1982):9-12.
11. Jacques Horovitz, "New perspectives on strategic management," *Journal of Business Strategy* 4(3)(Winter 1984):19-33.
12. "Corporate culture," *Business Week* (October 27, 1980):148-60.
13. George A. Steiner, John B. Miner, and Edmund B. Gray, *Management Policy and Strategy,* 2nd. ed. (New York: Macmillan Publishing Co., 1982), p. 477.
14. John A. Pearce II, "The company mission as a strategic tool," *Sloan Management Review* (Spring 1982):15-24.
15. Philip Kotler, *Marketing Management: Analysis, Planning, Implementation, and Control,* 8th ed. (Englewood Cliffs, N.J.: Prentice Hall, Inc., 1994), p. 81.
16. "Zenith wants to give the boob tube a brain," *Business Week* (May 6, 1985):69-72.
17. James G. Kimball, "Intel Wipes Out Surfing the Net, few master online PR wave," *Business Marketing* 89 (January 12, 1995): 1+.

18. Wroe Alderson, "The analytical framework for marketing." In Ben M. Enis and Keith K. Cox , eds., *Marketing Classics: A Selection of Influential Articles,* 4th ed. (Boston: Allyn & Bacon, Inc., 1981):24-34.

19. Laurence D. Ackerman, "Identity strategies that make a difference," *Journal of Business Strategy* 8 (May-June 1988):28-32.

20. John A. Pearce II and Richard B. Robinson, Jr., *Strategic Management.* (Homewood, Ill.: Richard D. Irwin, Inc., 1982), p. 155.

21. See, for example, Charles W. Hofer and Dan Schendel, *Strategy Formulation: Analytical Concepts* (St. Paul, Minn. West Publishing Co., 1978):32-34; and William K. Hall, "SBUs: Hot, New Topics in the Management of Diversification," *Business Horizons* 21 (February 1978), p. 20.

22. See Paula Smith, "Unique Tool for Marketers: PIMS," *Dun's Review* 108 (October 1976):95-106; Sidney Schoeffer, Robert D. Buzzell, and Donald F. Heany, "Impact of Strategic Planning on Profit Performance," *Harvard Business Review* 52 (March-April 1974):137-45; and D.F. Abell and J.S. Hammond, *Strategic Marketing Planning* (Englewood Cliffs, N.J.: Prentice-Hall, Inc., 1979):272-278.

23. Yoram Wind, Vijay Mahajan, and Donald J. Swire, "An empirical comparison of standardized portfolio models," *Journal of Marketing* 47 (Spring 1983):89-99.

24. Donald L. Bates and David L. Elderedge, *Strategy and Policy,* 2nd. ed. (Dubuque, Iowa: William C. Brown Co., 1984), p. 97.

25. B. Charles Ames, "Marketing planning for industial products," *Harvard Business Review* 46 (September-October 1968):100-111.

26. Robert G. Cooper and Elko J. Kleinschmidt, "Screening New Products For Potential Winners," *Long Range Planning* 26 (December 1993):74-81.

27. Robert W. Haas and Thomas R. Wotruba, *Marketing Management: Concepts, Practice and Cases* (Plano, Tex. Business Publications, Inc., 1983):285-9.

28. Greg Wood, "Different stokes," *Journal of Business Strategy* 14 (September/October 1993), p. 28.

29. H. Igor Ansoff, "Strategies for Diversification," *Harvard Business Review* 35 (September-October 1957):113-24.

30. Thomas S. Robertson, "How to reduce market penetration cycle times," *Sloan Management Review* 35 (Fall 1993):87-96.

31. John H. Grant and William R. King, *The Logic of Strategic Planning* (Boston: Little, Brown & Co., 1982):48-9.

32. R.T. Lenz, "Managing the evaluation of the strategic planning process," *Business Horizons* 30 (January-February 1987):34-9.

33. Todd M. Helmeke, "Strategic business unit market planning," *Business Marketing* 69 (November 1984):43.

34. Frederick E. Webster, Jr., "The rediscovery of the marketing concept," *Business Horizons* 31 (May-June 1988):29-39.

35. Nancy N. Carter, Timothy M. Stearns, and Paul D. Reynolds, "New venture strategies: Theory development with an empirical base," *Strategic Management Journal* 15 (January 1994):21-41.

36. Steve Lohr, "I.B.M. Chairman Lays Out Catch-Up Plan," *New York Times* (March 25, 1994), p. D3.

37. Derek F. Abell, "Strategic Windows," *Journal of Marketing* (July 1978):21-29.

38. Alan M. Rugman and Michael Gestrin, "The Strategic Response of Multinational Enterprises to NAFTA," *The Columbia Journal of World Business* 28 (Winter, 1993):18-20+.

39. Donald W. Jackson, Jr., Lonnie L. Ostrom, and Kenneth R. Evans, "Measures Used to Evaluate Industrial Marketing Activities," *Industrial Marketing Management* 11 (October 1982):269-274.

Bibliography

Choffray, Jean Marie, and Gary L. Lilian, "A decision support system for evaluating sales prospects and launch strategies for new products,"*Industrial Marketing Management* 15 (1986):75-85.

Gupta, Anil K., amd V. Govindarajan, "Build, hold, harvest: Converting strategic intentions into reality," *Journal of Business Strategy* 4 (Winter 1984):34-47.

Helms, Marilyn M. and Peter Wright, "External considerations: Their influence on future strategic planning," *Management Decision* 30 (1992):4-11.

Kulpinski, Mary E., "The planning process—continuous improvement," *Journal of Business and Industrial Marketing* 7 (Spring 1992):71-6.

Martensen, Anne, "A model for marketing planning for new products," *Marketing and Research Today* 4 (November, 1993):247-67.

McDonald, Malcolm H. B., "Strategic marketing planning: A state-of-the-art review," *Marketing Intelligence and Planning* 10 (1992): 4-22.

McDonald, Malcolm H.B., "Ten barriers to marketing planning," *Journal of Business and Industrial Marketing* 7 (Winter 1992):5-18.

Mintzberg, Henry, "The pitfalls of strategic planning," *California Management Review* 36 (Fall 1993):32-47.

Ramaswany, Venkatran, Hubert Gatignon, and David J. Reibstein, "Competitive marketing behavior in industrial markets," *Journal of Marketing* 58(April 1994):45-55.

Scofield, Todd C., and Donald R. Shaw, "Avoiding future shock,"*Sales and Marketing Management* 145 (January 1993):16+.

"Strategic marketing: Redesigning the business to reach customers in the nineties," *Planning Review* 20 (July-August` 1992):1-48.

Product
and Service
Strategies

America Lacks Business Creativity

Last year, I was invited to speak to about 100 researchers who worked at the Bell Laboratories at AT&T. The Bell Laboratories have about seven people who have won the Nobel Prize. To me, it seemed that I would be speaking before some of the greatest men of our time. . . . As you must know, the transistor and the semiconductor, which are at the root of the current revolution in industry, were invented at the Bell Laboratories. . . .

The basic message I brought that day was that this type of research was extremely significant academically in terms of both science and culture, but to be significant from the standpoint of business and industry, two other types of creativity, in addition to the creativity required to make the original invention, were absolutely necessary.

Industry requires three types of creativity. The first, of course, is the basic creativity necessary to make technological inventions and discoveries. This alone, however, does not make for good business or good industry.

The second type of creativity that is necessary involves how to use this new technology—and how to use it in large quantities and appropriately. In English, this would be called "product planning and production creativity."

The third type of creativity is in marketing, that is, selling the things you have produced. Even if you succeed in manufacturing something, it takes marketing to put the article into actual use before you have a business.

The strength in Japanese industry is in finding many ways to turn basic technology into products and using basic technology. In basic technology, it is true that Japan has relied on a number of foreign sources. Turning technology into products is where Japan is number one in the world.

• • •

The next three chapters focus on creativity and innovation, product design and process improvement. And, as Morita wisely adds, we will examine the essential interaction between engineering, production, and marketing.

Endnote

Discussion excerpted from Akio Morita, *The Japan That Can Say "No."* Published in Japanese by Kobunsha Publishing Ltd. (1989). English translation originally appeared in the Congressional Record, v. 135 (November 14, 1989).

10

Business Products and Their Life Cycles

Successful marketing strategy centers on two essential elements—products and markets. While distribution, promotion, and pricing decisions must also focus on the customer, the product is the element that must ultimately satisfy customer needs. Product decisions also involve considerable risk, and when ill conceived, can be very costly. New product design, development, and introduction entail significant company investment. Further, with the increased pace of technological change, products may become obsolete before the firm has recouped its development costs. This chapter, then, focuses on the following:

1. The aspects of a product that influence a business customer's buying decision
2. Duties and challenges involved in the management of a business product line
3. Differences between product and market management
4. Development, modification, and deletion decisions associated with a product's life cycle
5. Systems marketing compared with product marketing

Arguably, product decisions represent the most important and complex decisions facing management. These decisions affect both the firm's internal operations and its external environment, because it is the product through which the firm aligns its resources with the market environment to achieve organizational objectives. Product decisions also shape distribution requirements, establish promotion needs, and set the limits on price—the other three elements of the marketing mix.

Within the firm, product decisions unite the diverse interests of the various functional departments. The joint and cooperative efforts of research and development, engineering, manufacturing, inventory control, technical services, and marketing are essential to create and deliver an irresistible product to potential customers.

Product strategies have two primary goals: (1) to set guidelines for the development of new products and (2) to ensure that these products support corporate and marketing objectives. Since product strategy decisions often involve the modification of current products as well as the development of new ones, these strategies affect the entire organization. For example, the introduction of a new product can reduce the sales of other products in the line, affect corporate profits, and alter production schedules.[1] Given this organizational impact, product strategies require an integrated effort to be effective.

What Is a Product?

Product decisions ultimately depend on the marketer's understanding of what will satisfy a particular market. Thus, before considering the issues involved in product strategies, we should establish a product definition. A business buyer views a product as multidimensional—a combination of basic, enhanced, and augmented properties.

BASIC PROPERTIES

Basic properties constitute the **generic product** and make it what it is. These properties define the ability to perform various functions that may benefit individual buyers in different ways.

Consider a forklift truck. A warehouse manager sees it as a tool to stack boxes higher and make better use of a high-ceilinged building. The employee-benefits supervisor sees a means of reducing absenteeism resulting from back injuries. The financial officer views it as a rational investment with high potential return. Each of these individuals evaluates the same basic product but in terms of different derived benefits.[2]

ENHANCED PROPERTIES

Enhanced properties differentiate the generic product from its competition through additions or deletions. These properties may include performance features, styling, size, weight, and quality.

For example, a computer buyer expects the product to perform basic functions such as word processing or spreadsheet formation. However, the addition of spelling and grammar checkers eases the task of communicating clearly and accurately. In like manner, spreadsheets that can insert complex functions with a simple keystroke simplify data analysis.

A deletion may involve a reduction in size or weight without compromising performance. Compact automobiles provide a good example, except in the minds of those who must ride in the back seat.

AUGMENTED PROPERTIES

Augmented properties provide the buyer with benefits beyond the capability of the physical product. These are usually intangible benefits and include training, technical assistance, availability of spare parts, maintenance and repair services, on-time delivery, generous warranties, and financing terms. Business buyers seldom base purchase decisions solely on basic and enhanced properties. As Theodore Levitt explained[3]:

Competition is not between what companies produce in their factories, but between what they add to their factory output in the form of packaging, services, advertising, customer advice, financing, delivery arrangements, warehousing, and other things that people value.

Product Strategy Involves Continual Change

Products exist to satisfy customer needs, but these needs change as customer environments and circumstances change. In turn, the product must also change to maintain customer satisfaction. For instance, firms in the semiconductor industry must build redesigned plants every 2 or 3 years to keep pace with rapidly changing technology. Each new microprocessor has a significantly greater number of individual transistors and requires more elaborate production equipment. Intel's evolutionary 286 series provides a dramatic example of this exploding technology (Figure 10-1).

When customers revise their operating procedures or redesign their end products, suppliers face potential product modification or even the obsolescence of current products. Changing laws, politics, or economics can also impact customer needs, which in turn can alter product requirements, trigger product obsolescence, create new product opportunities, or alter customer expectations regarding other aspects of the product offering.[4]

Sales and profits also change over time as a product moves through its life cycle. At product maturity (the point of market saturation), a decision must be made between modification to maintain market share or withdrawal to prevent profit loss. Because many products eventually reach the decline stage, replacements must be developed for the firm to maintain and increase its profitability.

Product strategy, then, entails a continuous process of evaluating product/market positions to determine (1) whether changes should be made in current products, and (2) whether products should be added or dropped.

FIGURE 10-1 Evolution of Intel's 286 series of microprocessors.

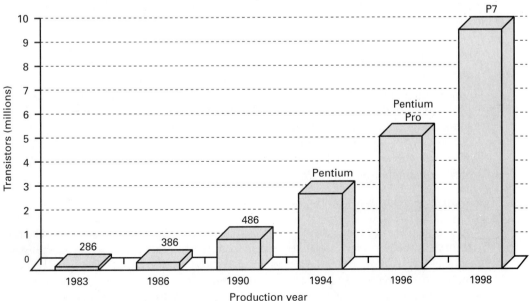

The Variety of Business Products

Business products are those goods and services used by organizations in their operations as well as the products they produce and/or resell to other firms. The term *industrial product* usually refers to components that will be used as part of a manufactured product or equipment that enables an industrial firm to carry out its operations. (Refer to Chapter 3 for a more detailed breakout of these products.) Industrial products are a subset of *business products,* which refers to all products and services not sold to the ultimate consumer but that are used by a broad variety of businesses, including insurance firms, investment banks, management consultants, advertising agencies, medical clinics, and so on.

A typical business firm's product assortment contains hundreds or thousands of individual items differentiated by design, price, size, label, or performance specifications. The complexity of managing these individual items as each moves through its respective life cycle has forced companies to create systems and organizational structures to cope with this process. The **product manager** (PM) plays a vital role in many of these organizational structures.

Business Product Management

ORIGINS OF PRODUCT MANAGEMENT

Procter & Gamble (P&G) originated the product manager concept in 1927 so that the firm could set strategy for, monitor, and control each product line within its broad assortment. P&G used the title **brand manager.** Companies that market branded consumer products continue to prefer this title. Each of these managers monitors the life cycle of one or several related products using the same brand (e.g., Tide, Bold, Crest, Ivory, and so on) and develops a strategy for maximum market penetration and product profitability. Being in a staff position, a brand manager's authority flows by delegation directly from the vice president of marketing. However, lacking line authority, the brand manager also requires persuasive powers to convince engineers that a product needed redesign, or to obtain more coverage from the advertising department, or to receive preferential treatment from manufacturing.

MATRIX MANAGEMENT

This matrix management system presents problems, both to the PM and to those required to support the PM's strategy. As seen in Figure 10-2, the PM must interact with all other business functions, not only those in marketing, but in engineering, production, finance, and legal. The need to satisfy the marketing vice president and to work effectively with all the other functions can create frustration as well as stress. Power struggles and adverse company conditions can aggravate the situation and even trigger the elimination of the PM's position.

MAKING THE CONCEPT WORK

The product management concept can actually contradict sound management practices unless the necessary steps are taken. Commensurate authority must accompany responsibility. A manager with too much delegated authority but little responsibility can become a tyrant. In contrast, a challenging level of responsibility with little authority breeds bottlenecks and delays. Since the PM position exists primarily to increase efficiency and results, the latter scenario directly contradicts this purpose.

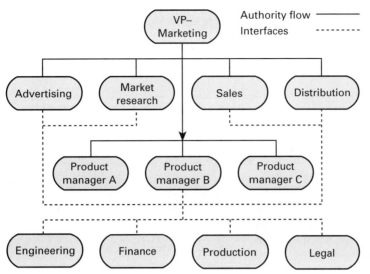

FIGURE 10-2 Product manager's matrix position.

Over time, firms have recognized that the PM approach does not solve all multi-product problems. When a firm's product line includes unrelated offerings that use separate technologies and serve different markets, the establishment of autonomous product divisions may be the best approach as long as the volume of business can support this type of organization. In other instances, separate marketing groups supported by a centralized production facility may provide satisfactory service at a greater profit margin. In short, the PM concept serves as the preferred organizational structure when the alternatives of autonomous product divisions or multiple marketing/sales groups are ineffective or impractical.[5]

Making the PM concept effective requires detailed planning, constant commitment, and clear lines of authority and responsibility. Top management must support the position and enforce it when under fire. In addition, the position requires a clear and detailed job description because of significant differences in responsibility, authority, and organizational structure from company to company.

WIDESPREAD USE OF BUSINESS PRODUCT MANAGERS

Business PMs have become very prevalent. A survey among Fortune 500 firms found that 75% of the responding companies used product managers.[6]

Duties and Responsibilities   As shown in Table 10-1, the majority of business PMs oversee a product's progress, initiate ongoing product alterations and new product specifications, determine a product's phase out and deletion, are responsible for product profitability, decide on target markets, initiate market research, and develop a product's budget and promotional strategy. Less than a majority have primary authority over product additions, promotional mix variables, channel selection, and control criteria.[6]

Unlike the original concept for brand managers, business PMs have responsibility for their product's ongoing profitability but lack total authority to determine its future success or failure. This authority rests with the chief marketing executive.

TABLE 10-1 General Duties and Responsibilities of a Business Product Manager (N = 69)	
Duties	*Percent of Responses**
Oversee product progress	91
Decide the nature of or initiate changes in ongoing products	70
Initiate product reengineering	67
Determine need and timing for product deletion	65
Determine need and timing for product phase-out	65
Determine which markets a product will enter or depart	64
Initiate and control new product conceptualization	64
Responsible for product profitability	62
Develop and present product budget request	61
Initiate price changes	58
Present promotion strategy	57
Initiate market research analysis	57
Set pricing strategy	55
Develop sales goals and objectives	55
Member of product committee	55
Develop product control criteria	45
Primary decider on which new products to add	42
Determine channel of distribution	39
Chair product committee	36
Decide nature of promotional mix (personal selling, advertising, sales promotion, publicity)	35
Control package changes	25

*NOTE: Some respondents gave more than one answer.

Source: Robert W. Eckles and Timothy J. Novotny, "Industrial product managers: Authority and responsibility," *Industrial Marketing Management* 13 (1984):73. Copyright © 1984 by Elsevier Science Publishing Co., Inc.

Authority Over Other Functions   Only a minority of business PMs have direct authority over other corporate functions, as shown in Table 10-2. The largest percentage of this minority have authority over advertising, market research, R&D, and product quality control departments. Although these PMs exercise more control over advertising than any other function, they have little involvement with day-to-day advertising operations, since these activities are subcontracted to advertising agencies.

Business Product Manager's Characteristics   Business PMs have five important responsibilities[7]:

1. Product strategy: designing a product strategy that matches the product with identified market needs

2. Product planning: the full range of activities necessary to market the product—goals, sales and profit forecasts, promotional and sales plans, post-sale service plans, and so on

3. Monitoring of product development: the difficult challenge of balancing competing company interests; BPMs must know when to cajole, when to be gently encouraging, when to threaten, and when to concede

TABLE 10-2   Business Product Manager's Authority Over Other Functions
(N = 31)

	Percent of Responses				*Number of*
Function	*None*	*Little*	*Moderate*	*Extensive*	*Respondents*
Production planning	10	10	53	27	30
Financial control	36	19	48	7	27
Financial budget changes	14	18	50	18	28
Sales management	18	4	68	11	28
Advertising	7	10	30	53	30
Market research	13	10	30	47	30
Research and development	0	22	39	39	31
Product quality control	6	16	42	36	31
Salespeople	17	17	45	21	29

Source: Robert W. Eckles and Timothy J. Novotny, "Industrial product managers: Authority and responsibility," *Industrial Marketing Management* 13 (1984):74. Copyright © 1984 by Elsevier Science Publishing Co., Inc.

4. Product marketing: the steps involved in a product's introduction, promotion, pricing, and distribution

5. Product business activities: those tactics that impact financial return on product investment—its success or failure.

In a broad sense, business product management is the ultimate managerial job because BPMs must have four kinds of relevant experiences: (1) management experience, (2) marketing experience, (3) technical experience, and (4) business experience. BPMs must understand the subtleties of having power and influence without line authority and be able to link company capabilities with customer needs. Some BPMs have "graceful technical incompetence"—which translates into knowing enough jargon and facts to surprise technical people occasionally with a brilliant insight. They need not understand how to build a product; in fact, BPMs may suffer when they let technical details obscure marketing goals. Finally, BPMs should have a solid business intelligence that includes the ability to negotiate for their day-to-day and long-range planning needs. They should also recognize if and when a product and its plans make good "business sense."

A company with a well-organized, strategically prepared product management function will be more likely to develop winning products, increase revenues, and enjoy satisfying profits than competitors who operate as reactive followers. As Randolph notes, if there is "a single function that comes closest to being a critical marketing success function for industrial and consumer products alike, it's the product management function."[7]

Another study of Fortune 500 firms found that most commercially successful product innovations occurred when an intrapreneur was involved in the venturing process.[8] Product managers are the most likely candidates for the intrapreneuring role.

Product Versus Market Management

A company that sells a variety of products into one market often uses *product* managers. Each PM concentrates on a relatively narrow product line. However, when a product line serves several diverse markets with a variety of applications, competition, and market conditions, the primary need for concentration and experience swings from product to market. In this instance, *market* managers are more appropriate, with each individual concentrating on the needs and conditions of a specific market. These two categories, product and market managers, allow the firm to concentrate on the area where the differences are the greatest—products or markets.

PRODUCT/MARKET MANAGEMENT SYSTEMS

When a variety of products is sold into multiple markets, the firm is faced with a dilemma. If product managers are used, they will tend to focus on their products rather than the varying needs of each market. On the other hand, market managers will bring greater attention to bear on market needs but may lack the breadth of knowledge necessary to make effective product decisions. To overcome this dilemma, a growing number of firms use a product/market organizational matrix. Within this matrix, market managers concentrate on the needs of a specific market and the development of strategies to serve those needs. Simultaneously, product managers concentrate on the technology, applications, and competition associated with their product lines.[9] Figure 10-3 depicts a product/market matrix employed during the 1960s by the semiconductor division of Texas Instruments.

Product/market management systems, however, frequently lead to conflict as managers strive to fulfill their respective areas of responsibility. Product managers who concentrate on selling their own products may ignore the best interests of customers. For example, when the matrix in Figure 10-3 was active at Texas Instruments, the germanium transistor manager tried to keep alive a product line that was already in decline. The silicon transistor manager strove to have his products take over markets previously dominated by germanium. Meanwhile, the integrated circuit manager generated strategies that would grow this new product category by obsoleting all discrete transistor applications.

TI customers received conflicting recommendations when they asked for application assistance. Market managers were expected to look across these "competing" product lines and make recommendations that best satisfied their customers' needs. However, some recommendations tended to be fatally biased and adversarial to corporate profits and strategic goals.

FIGURE 10-3 Product-market management matrix.

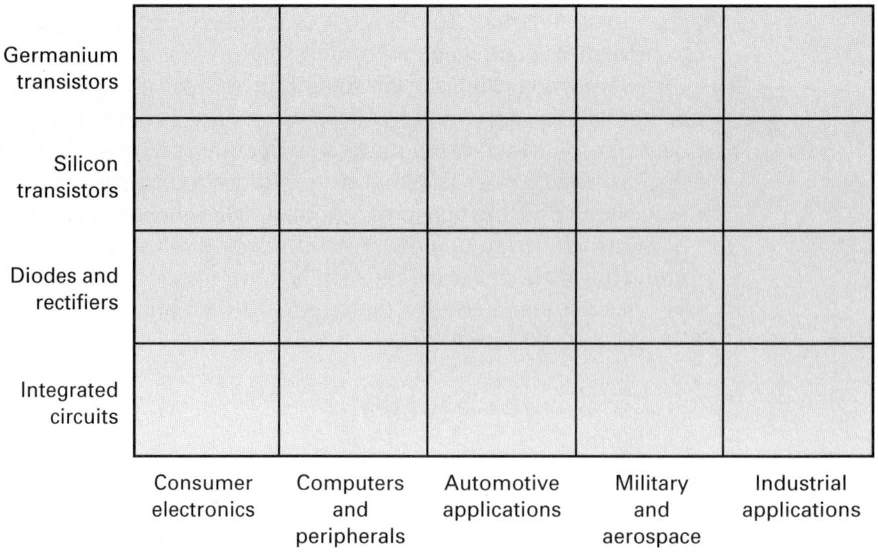

	Consumer electronics	Computers and peripherals	Automotive applications	Military and aerospace	Industrial applications
Germanium transistors					
Silicon transistors					
Diodes and rectifiers					
Integrated circuits					

BOX 10-1

Product Manager Versus Market Manager Roles

MARKET MANAGER ROLES

1. Develop an understanding of customer and end user operations and economics to determine how the existing product/service package can be improved to provide a competitive edge.

2. Identify related products and/or services that represent attractive opportunities for profitability.

3. At regular intervals, summarize for top management the most attractive opportunities in the marketplace. Recommend a strategy to capitalize on them.

4. Develop a reputation for industry expertise among key customer and end user groups. Bring know-how to bear on negotiating major orders and the training and development of salespeople.

PRODUCT MANAGER ROLES

1. Protect the pricing integrity of products. See that pricing policies and practices in one market do not jeopardize the company's position or profit structure in another.

2. Maintain product leadership by making certain that product design, cost, and performance characteristics are not only responsive to customer needs in all markets, but are also not inadvertently altered to meet the needs of one market at the expense of the company's position in another.

3. Ensure that product is responsive to the market needs while protecting the engineering and production process from becoming cluttered with a proliferation of small-lot, custom, or special orders.

4. Ensure that production scheduling and capacity are intelligently planned to meet current and anticipated aggregate demand of various markets profitably.

5. Provide the in-depth technical and/or product knowledge required to support selling efforts in major and complex applications.

Source: Excerpted from Charles Ames, "Dilemma of product market management," *Harvard Business Review* (March-April 1971), pp. 66-143. Copyright© 1971 by the President and Fellows of Harvard College; all rights reserved.

Although such conflicts tend to arise, they can provide a positive element when properly managed. If nothing else, they force the analysis of alternative strategies that would otherwise be ignored. The head of marketing or even company management might eventually have to arbitrate the final decision.

Ames[9] defined the basic roles of product and market managers within the product/market management system. These roles are shown in Box 10-1. Once roles are defined, the chief marketing executive must ensure that the managers work together in a participative manner. This executive has the responsibility of synthesizing the efforts of the product manager and market manager to capture the best of both perspectives. The system should inspire these managers to work together symbiotically for the good of the organization, choosing the action that is best for the firm as a whole, whether that decision emphasizes a product or a market point of view.

Product Management Phases

To understand its control function better, product management may be viewed as three overlapping phases. These phases are depicted in Figure 10-4. The first phase is *product development and addition*, which begins with the recognition of some market opportunity. This phase obviously precedes the introduction stage of the *product life cycle* (PLC) and continues into the growth stage. The second phase is *product modification*,

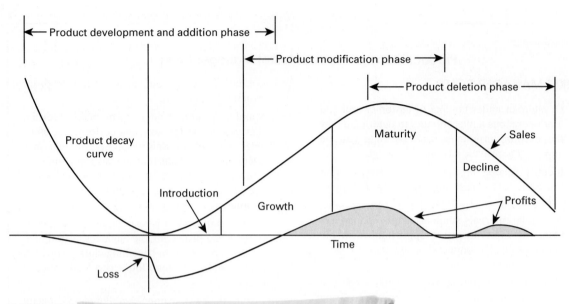

FIGURE 10-4 Phases of product management as related to a product's life cycle.

which can begin early in the growth stage and continue well into maturity. The third phase is *product deletion,* which begins during maturity and can continue into the decline stage.

These three phases overlap because mechanisms triggered in one phase impact managerial decisions in the next phase. This overlapping sequence helps to maintain a continuity of effort. With sufficient notice of an impending event, PMs can establish required plans and ensure implementation in a timely fashion. Since PMs cannot manage the past or change the present, they must plan for the future. Effective planning requires accurate and timely forecasting of future events to formulate strategy, to develop contingency plans, and to construct monitoring and control systems.

PHASE I: PRODUCT DEVELOPMENT AND ADDITION

Either suppliers or customers can originate new product ideas. The idea for a handheld calculator originated with semiconductor manufacturers looking for a high-volume use of integrated circuits. Chemical engineers at Koppers, Inc., developed the ubiquitous plastic coffee cup as a way of using the otherwise useless by-product of a common chemical process. Arm and Hammer ingeniously converted a century-old baking ingredient into an air freshener when the majority of women stopped baking at home. And people were scarcely looking for a reject adhesive when 3M introduced Post-it note pads. In these instances, solutions arose before customers expressed their desires.

On the other hand, a wide range of products have arisen from the urgent need of prospective buyers or the dissatisfaction of current users. For example, the Polaroid camera answered the universal desire of photo buffs for "instant photographic gratification." Compact automobiles provided a widely desired compromise between luxurious but costly comfort and economy of operation. In some instances, wholesalers or retailers may relay the message regarding unsatisfied customer needs to product manufacturers.

The Race to Be First   In the fast-moving electronics industry, many analysts concede the majority share of a new-product market to the innovator and another substantial portion to the first follower. Thus, only 20 percent remains for slower entrants.[9]

A McKinsey & Co. study cited in *Business Week* reported that a firm that exceeds its R&D budget by 50 percent to introduce a product on schedule subsequently loses only 4 percent of its potential profits. On the other hand, staying within budget and getting to market 6 months late can reduce profits by 33 percent.[10] These data obviously entice high-tech firms to reach the market ahead of their major competitors. One must recognize, however, that the researcher emphasized that these data referred only to high-tech products with short life cycles.[11] Other studies dealing with less complex products and/or longer life cycles have produced conflicting data.

Despite informational conflicts, many industrial firms have adopted the "first to market" strategy. Indeed, both practitioners and researchers welcome any *new product development* (NPD) process variation that produces nothing but positive results—better products, lower costs, greater market share, and enthused employees. The debate centers on whether *accelerated product development* (APD) yields such results without offsetting costs and problems.

Although studies indicate that being first to market rewards the firm with a larger market share, speed-to-market must not replace product quality as the primary goal of the development process. The ultimate market leader is usually the firm with the product that is substantially better than that of the competition in some way.[12]

Means of Accelerating the NPD Process   Firms that struggle to reach the market ahead of competition seek ways to speed up the NPD process. One study analyzed the process to determine approaches that might trigger acceleration. The researchers suggested a hierarchy of these approaches descending from most to least promising and provided their perception of potential benefits and limitations for each approach.[11] Table 10-3 summarizes these findings.

The list of potential limitations indicates that APD definitely poses offsetting problems. For example, the strategy of out-sourcing, popularly promoted as a step to reduce costs, may actually result in higher costs. In addition, the innovative firm may lose part or all of its proprietary edge. Cutting steps to save time often involves a reduction in vital information (e.g., testing to confirm technical results, assumptions regarding market needs rather than solid research, and so on). Hence more decisions are made under uncertainty with a commensurate increase in risk.[13]

Costs of Accelerating the NPD Process   In another study, Crawford also praises APD as a potentially rewarding strategy but decries its broadspread acceptance without an analysis of the downside. His concern focuses on five areas of hidden costs that stem from a speeded-up process[14]:

1. APD works best with *incremental innovation* (small-step improvements) rather than major breakthroughs. Since firms have limited resources and energy, efforts expended on minor innovations reduce the efforts spent on breakthrough projects.

2. The key steps omitted in APD often involve *critical information* that deals either with technical accomplishment or market circumstances. APD prompts the mind set that "there just isn't time to wait for answers."

3. *Small teams* are touted as the best structure for APD, because bureaucracy and inflexibility are minimized. However, when management commissions a small project team to create a new product, members connect future fame and fortune with completion of the project and market a new product, ready or not.

4. When pushed to produce results, people tend to improvise with what is available rather than working to develop necessary processes. The result is a *compromised solution* to a market problem.

TABLE 10-3 Hierarchy of NPD Acceleration Approaches With Potential Benefits and Limitations

Approach	Potential Benefits	Potential Limitations
1. Simplify: Any action that makes processes, communications, and interfaces easier to perform and manage	Increases understanding of technology/design Enhances external/internal human relationships Simplifies reports, documents, controls Greater understanding = increased trust Flatter, more effective organizations	Failure to meet customer requirements Higher costs if external sources augment process Failure to meet design criteria Lack of project status detail; inadequate control Increased trust = tendency toward "group think"
2. Eliminate steps: Shorten or eliminate unnecessary NPD operations; evaluate tasks on their contribution to customer satisfaction	Forces logical make/buy decisions Puts authorization/approval at lower levels Eliminates redundant tests and inspections Reduces "not invented here" attitude	Use of external sources may reduce proprietary advantages Senior managers reluctant to delegate Vendors may not upgrade their quality
3. Parallel processing: Use methods such as CPM and PERT to perform tasks simultaneously	Actualizes twin-stream concept Increases interdisciplinary knowledge Fosters greater teamwork	Potential for confusion Possible increase in stress levels; working with greater uncertainty Need more communication, teamwork training
4. Eliminate delays: Identify unused slack time; break bottle necks; eliminate backlogs	Clearer up-front thinking; vision Encourages early investigation of long-lead items, processes	Hurried acceptance of the NPD vision Early technology and financial analyses may trigger poor estimates Early launch may trigger inadequate marketing
5. Speed-up: Use technology (e.g., CAD, CAM) to proceed faster without losing quality	Forces use of new technologies Streamlines organization for more efficiency	Higher stress levels Danger of inadequate documentation Reduced safeguards (e.g., testing) = greater risk

Source: Murray R. Millson, S.P. Raj, and David Wilemon, "A survey of major approaches for accelerating new product development." *Journal of Product Innovation Management* 9 (January 1992):53-69.

5. Pressure to produce also puts team members under *stress.* In addition, the firm's suppliers feel the pressure, and customers can end up with unsatisfied needs.[14]

Aside from the potential problems generated by APD, being first to market has its own downside. With no precedent to use as a guide, the innovative firm must depend solely on its own market research and intuition. Research data obtained from a volatile market may be of questionable reliability. To complicate matters, the development phase of a new product may take several years between the collection of market data and the availability of production units. Market desires and priorities can change substantially during the interim. Some auto manufacturers, for example, celebrated the fact that their 1995 models took "only" 3 years to develop. By comparison, the development cycle took 5 to 6 years during the early 1980s.

Being first also means that there will be no opportunity to use *reverse engineering.* This term refers to a competitor who obtains an early sample of a new product and takes it apart to analyze its component parts and fabrication. Reverse engineering can save countless hours and dollars and occasionally result in an improved product. Thus, the competitor may actually leapfrog ahead of the innovator.

The primary factor prodding a company to innovate may be the desire to perpetuate itself. Every product has a finite life, heading toward obsolescence from its
very inception. An innovative firm must either obsolete itself with a second-generation
product or wait for competition to trigger the obsolescence.

Product Additions   Another popular tenet, supported by the former director of
GE's central R&D division, holds that the initial breadth of a new product line should
be relatively narrow, with its benefits aimed at satisfying specific customer needs.[15] A
study of the magnetic resonance imaging (MRI) equipment field found that firms who
entered the market early but broadened their product lines gradually had the best
profit performance. This would suggest that both *timing* and *product scope* are critical
elements in a firm's product portfolio strategy.[16]

These findings do not rule against additions to a new product line. To the contrary, a firm should add product variations either as a proactive move to penetrate
newly discovered market segments or as a reaction to attempted leapfrogging by competition. Product additions represent one means of accelerating growth—and potential
profits—in short-lived technology markets.[17]

New Product Acceptance   While some new products enjoy instant success, others
require considerable time and marketing effort before significant growth begins.
Electronic calculators, for instance, replaced their mechanical predecessors prac-
tically overnight, whereas electric typewriters took 14 years (1926-1940) to achieve
market acceptance.

Product acceptance in the business market depends on how the product fits into
the buyer's *total use system.* Generally, use systems involve other products, other persons, and a developed system of what Wasson[18] termed "habitual skills." These skills
involve (1) perceptions of the expected satisfaction sources, (2) perceptions of the
social role of the user in relation to the product, and (3) perceptions of the value of the
satisfaction obtained.

Habit systems, once developed, are not easily changed. The slow acceptance of
the electric typewriter stemmed from the inability of users to break old habits and
develop new ones. Typists could not rest their fingers on the electric keyboard, as they
had done on manual typewriters, but had to hold them poised above the keyboard.
Adjustment to this new typing style involved time, frustration, and much spoiled work.

On the other hand, since the calculator design changes were mainly internal and
did not affect operator performance to any degree, this innovation enjoyed ready
acceptance. Thus, products that fit into the buyer's use system or habitual skills are
adopted more rapidly than those that require habit changes. Early product acceptance
and market growth hinge on customer education and the development of a positive
mind-set toward change.

Considering the perceived risks that buyers associate with change, marketers
must conduct vigorous research before the development process begins. The primary
objectives are to identify the most important performance requirements of the eventual product and to preclude any potential problems in the use of the product.[19]

Strategic Plan for Phase I   When products have the potential for rapid acceptance
(i.e., entail a *low* level of learning), the marketer can expect to meet vigorous competition. Plans should focus on staying well ahead of potential competitors. With slowly
accepted products (i.e., those that require a *high* level of learning), marketing strategy
should focus on market development.

The introductory plan includes strategies for distribution, promotion, selling, and pricing. (The details of these strategies will be covered in Chapters 11 through 19.) After target market identification, all strategies should aim to educate potential customers as quickly as possible on the benefits of the product and the reasons why it should replace the product currently in use. The plan must also include a forecast of sales revenue, an expense budget, and a projection of profits.

Although complete and ready for implementation, the product plan cannot be considered unalterable. To do so would court disaster. Contingency plans should exist that the marketer may or may not implement, depending on the actions of competition, the reaction of customers, and the stability of economic and environmental factors.

PHASE II: PRODUCT MODIFICATION

Although a product's strategic plan includes contingency plans to cope with the future's uncertainties, the product may become stymied and lose its market acceptance. Sales may never reach forecast level, costs may remain unacceptably high, or competition may successfully play leapfrog. If the marketer still feels that the underlying product concept has merit, modification of the product or other elements of the marketing mix should be considered. This decision marks the start of the product modification phase.

The need for rejuvenation may stem from a variety of market forces: a superior competitive product, technological developments in the industry, altered market needs that essentially obsolete the product, or governmental regulations that prohibit or restrict its sale. Sometimes company actions foster the need to rejuvenate a product.[20] For example, an industrial equipment manufacturer suffered a decline in sales because of poor brand imagery and customer service, but management continued to cut corners on product quality to meet foreign competition. Needless to say, the equipment died a slow, painful, and needless death. Regardless of the cause, the decision either to rejuvenate a product or to delete it should be carefully considered and effectively implemented.[20]

Product Mix Scan As illustrated in Figure 10-5, a monthly scan of the product mix can isolate and identify those products not performing up to standards. Such a procedure helps the product manager predict which products may experience difficulties in the near future. Products deemed worthy of effort move into modification for corrective activity or rejuvenation.

Modification may involve a product's design, its target market, its promotion, pricing, or distribution system, or the manufacturing process. Modification usually aims at an increased rate of growth, improved profitability, or maintenance of market share in the maturity stage. If successful, the modification could even move a mature product into a new growth sequence, enhancing its profit contribution and extending its usefulness to the firm.

Identifying Causes of Poor Product Performance Determining the correct modification activity for a troublesome product requires three diagnostic elements: (1) an objective analysis of the situation, (2) close attention to customer inputs, and (3) translation of the inputs into effective decisions and actions.

Avlonitis, in a study of 20 business firms, found that management tends to identify poor product performance on the basis of *profitability* factors (e.g., product cost structure, production methods, and product design).[21] Thus, when products deviate from some established performance measure, accountants and engineers measure the total costs associated with the product, analyze the product's design and production method, and make judgments regarding the feasibility of reducing costs. However, a more revealing picture of the product's market position results when sales force opinions are added.[21]

These opinions provide essential inputs regarding competitive activities and customer attitudes. Quite often a product's declining market share has nothing to do with the physical product, but rather the services that enhance (or diminish) the product's image.

Even when the physical product is at fault, poor performance seldom stems from only one factor. When investigators identify and analyze product performance deviations, they frequently discover that weak performance results from multiple interrelated factors. Table 10-4 shows the range of reasons cited by respondents as the cause of unsatisfactory product performance.

Choosing Alternative Corrective Actions   According to Avlonitis's study, alternative corrective actions may involve (1) cost reductions, (2) product modifications, (3) price changes, (4) promotion changes, or (5) channel changes. The majority of respondents felt that the first step should be a search for ways to *reduce cost* through product redesign, improved parts and materials sourcing, or a modernization of plant and equipment. The most popular action used, as Table 10-5 indicates, is product modification primarily aimed at cost reduction. Some favored a price increase; others, a price decrease.

TABLE 10-4   Reasons Given for Unsatisfactory Product Performance (N = 20)

Reason	Percent of Respondents*
Uncompetitive price	35
Production problems (inferior technology, difficult assembly, etc.)	30
Low volume product, uneconomic batch size	30
Too costly to produce and market	25
High cost of manufacture	25
Overengineered	20
Market dominated by competitors	20
Unexpected customer requirements/specifications	10
Low selling price	10

Source: George J. Avlonitis,"Revitalizing weak industrial products," *Industrial Marketing Management* 14 (1985):93-105. Copyright © 1985 by Elsevier Science Publishing Co., Inc.

TABLE 10-5   Actions Taken to Correct Poor Product Performance (N = 20)

Corrective Actions	Percent of Respondents*
Product modifications (primarily for cost reduction)	75
Increase in selling price	45
Product improvement	35
Decrease in selling price	30
Development of new markets	15
Increase in promotion budget	10
Increased push by sales force	10
New distribution channel(s)	5

Source: George J. Avlonitis,"Revitalizing weak industrial products," *Industrial Marketing Management* 14 (1985):93-105. Copyright © 1985 by Elsevier Science Publishing Co., Inc.

Coping With Market Factors   The computer industry provides numerous examples of successful modification plans as well as some failures. Manufacturers have continuously redesigned their products to hold more data, compute faster, handle new applications, or improve old applications with new technology. "Innovate or face demise" has become the prevalent philosophy of the industry. Electronic giants such as General Electric and Honeywell worked on mainframe computers for years, only to drop out of the market when the combination of other mainframes plus the rapid growth of desktop computers made their positions untenable.

New firms such as Atari, Commodore, and Osborne got in on the "ground floor" of the desktop industry but concentrated on the home entertainment market, ignoring both the business and education markets that provided the primary growth for these products in the 1980s. All three have dropped by the wayside.

On the other hand, Compaq was founded by former Texas Instruments engineers who became frustrated by TI's lack of a definitive computer marketing plan. They left TI and entered the market as an alternative to IBM in the MS-DOS world and as a technological competitor to Apple. Instead of taking the low-price route traveled by most other IBM "clones," they pursued a high-quality, superior service strategy. When their higher prices began to stifle growth, Compaq changed both strategy and top management. They embarked on an aggressive pricing policy coupled with the rapid introduction of new products, each aimed at a distinct market segment. As a result, Compaq emerged as the industry leader at the end of 1994, based on total sales for the year.

Impact of Component Technology   Technological breakthroughs in component or material technology may induce users to modify their end-products. The chemical industry, for example, has developed revolutionary materials that can be used in many industrial applications as a replacement for steel or aluminum. These materials, called composites, possess the strength of steel but do not rust or suffer from environmental deterioration.[22] These composites have been used on offshore oil rigs where salt water causes severe corrosion.

The automotive industry has replaced a number of metal engine parts with ceramic substitutes that can better withstand extremely high temperatures. Such replacements provide the competitive advantage of better engine performance, reduced cost and frequency of repair, and increased customer satisfaction.

Try to visualize modern laptop or notebook computers without the existence of multimegabyte RAMs, microprocessors like the Pentium or PowerPC, long-lived batteries, and flat-screen displays.

The above examples all typify *component life cycles*. These are smaller life cycles that have a profound impact on product life cycles.[23] Component life cycles generally occur when leading-edge components, originally exclusive to one supplier, become commonplace as a result of the entry of multiple competitors. Eventually, refinements and improvements cease, the technology becomes obsolete, and the component is replaced by another with more desirable attributes.

When component life cycles end abruptly, users face potential input shortages, product obsolescence, and loss of market share. Companies that maintain a tight partnership between their designers, procurement personnel, and their suppliers, enjoy a greater likelihood of developing an effective end-of-life strategy for obsolete components.[23]

Strategic Plan for Phase II   As market demand increases, product design and other aspects of the total offering must be changed to satisfy the needs of the low-end market segment, the premium segment, or both. Product availability should remain strong, or competitors will be encouraged to enter the market. Regarding price, many firms overlook the need to lower price as costs decrease and competition increases. Experience has proven that new competition has a lesser impact on an existing firm when it links price reductions to cost decreases.

By the time market demand peaks, buyers have already found suppliers whose offerings satisfy their needs fairly well, and they are neither searching for new suppliers nor seeking alternative methods to satisfy needs. Marketing strategy, therefore, should be directed toward keeping current users satisfied and finding new market segments that might adopt the product given proper inducement and benefits.

PHASE III: PRODUCT DELETION

As shown in Figure 10-5, if a product does not warrant modification, the product manager must analyze current organizational and environmental factors to determine whether the product should be deleted immediately or phased out over time.

FIGURE 10-5 Product modification alert and deletion system.

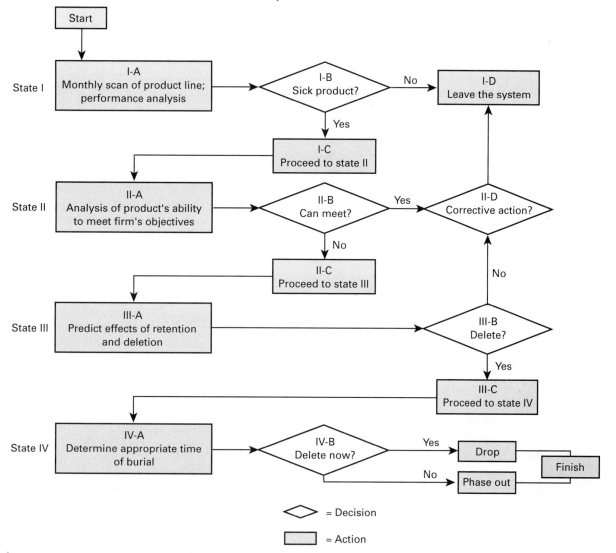

Difficulty in Deleting Business Products   Companies sometimes retain unsuccessful business products because of a high initial investment or the product manager's hopeful belief that the item might resume its growth in the future. Products that do not enjoy instant success usually receive a lengthy trial period before being deleted. A manufacturer of fans used in air conditioning systems had a policy that a new product would not be deleted without an 18-month market trial. Many firms become emotionally attached to "the product that made us what we are" and postpone the deletion decision beyond the time dictated by economic realities.

Product Deletion Decisions   In the business market, product deletion decisions center primarily on *marketing* and *financial* considerations. A study of more than 100 engineering firms concluded that a product's deletion depends on its contribution to overhead, its effect on the profitability and sales of other products, and its effect on customer relationships.[24] However, when a product's deletion lowers production output or requires the development of an appropriate substitute, the decision hinges on whether the substitute can be developed quickly, and whether the firm can tolerate the loss of interim revenue.

When a product involves 15 percent or more of a firm's resources and sales revenue, its deletion can cause serious repercussions both within and outside the firm. Therefore, product managers cannot act without considering the impact on sales, profits, employees, customer relations, and competitors' reactions. Box 10-2 outlines some of the most important considerations. The relative importance of each factor varies, however, with the industry's technology and size, the number of products manufactured by the firm, and the nature of competition.

Strategic Plan for Phase III   The deletion phase presents a classic example of *opportunity cost analysis.* The product manager must decide whether the firm will realize a greater return by maintaining a product line or by shifting resources to another alternative. Three market *Cs* will have an impact on the decision—company, customers, and competition. Short-term profits and long-term market strength often suggest contradictory decisions. Dropping a product might produce higher immediate profits but leave unhappy customers searching for an alternative source. If a competitor stands ready to oblige, this could signal the start of a serious market share decline.

BOX 10-2

Factors to Consider in Product Deletion Decisions

The effect of product's deletion on:

1. Full-line policy
2. Corporate image
3. Sales of other products
4. Customer relationships
5. Profitability of other products due to transfer of production overhead allocation
6. Profitabilty of other products due to transfer of selling overhead allocation
7. Profitability of other products due to transfer of distribution overhead allocation
8. Fixed and working capital
9. Employee relationships
10. Reassignment of managerial time and effort
11. Reallocation of resources
12. New product potential
13. Existence of substitutes
14. Potential reactions of competition

Source: George J. Avlonitis, "Product elimination decision making: Does formality matter? *Industrial Marketing Management* 14 (1985):41-52. Copyright © 1985 by Elsevier Science Publishing Co., Inc.

From another viewpoint, dropping a product simply because of market decline could be an economic mistake. As an example, Texas Instruments shifted their emphasis from germanium to silicon transistor technology in the early 1960s. But unlike competitors who dropped germanium production entirely, TI continued producing for those firms whose end-products required the unique characteristics of germanium. Volume contracts were negotiated with guaranteed quantities and fixed prices. The decision proved to be quite profitable and allowed TI to maintain leadership in both technologies.

Determining the Stage of a Product's Life Cycle

One can discuss the stages of a PLC far easier than a marketer can identify the current stage of a given product. Consider, for example, a slowdown in a product's growth. This could indicate the beginning of the maturity stage. It could also indicate a loss of share in a growing market because of the entrance of strong competition. Still again, the answer may lie in the introduction of a superior product that has begun to obsolete the original product and send it into decline. In short, a symptomatic change in the slope of a PLC curve can stem from a variety of causes. Until the precise cause has been identified, the symptom cannot be appropriately treated. Fortunately, market factors exist that can yield a relatively strong indication of the cause behind the symptom.

NUMBER AND STRENGTH OF COMPETITORS

Opportunistic firms, wishing to share in a promising new market, normally enter during the growth stage and begin to leave during maturity. Thus, the largest number of competitors will exist during the latter part of the growth stage, or what some refer to as *early maturity.* However, after some firms have pulled out of the market, those that remain normally have strong staying power. Thus, overall competitive pressure remains high throughout maturity.

INCREASED PRICE EROSION

Price erosion and aggressive or troubled competitors usually go hand in hand. The aggressive ones push for a dominant market position during the growth stage. Some will stress nonprice benefits; others will cut price. Those who remain into the maturity stage must either take business away from competitors or cease to grow. Since product differentiation tends to decline across the PLC, price becomes the weapon of choice.

This eventual pressure on price reconfirms the need to design into every new product a "bundle of benefits" that buyers will readily acknowledge and value. This approach decreases the likelihood that buyers will consider the product overpriced and increases the supplier's chances of achieving a reasonable profit, even in a competitive market.[25]

CUSTOMER FORECASTS

The forecasts of a company's sales force usually serve as the primary "outside world" input into production plans. Product types and quantities are derived from these forecasts. Unfortunately, sales force forecasts often suffer from two viruses: *provincialism* and *optimism.* Each salesperson sees only his or her territory. Market trends that start elsewhere and have not yet affected this territory go unnoticed and unreported. At the same time, when a salesperson learns of a market slowdown, pride often replaces objectivity so that the forecast reflects what "ought to be true" rather than hard realities.

A firm's customers also make forecasts for their markets and end products. They, too, use sales force inputs. But the information that reaches the production and purchasing departments has been subjected to "managerial judgment," which comprehends a broader geographic scope and adds a degree of pragmatism. Moreover, a customer's end product is closer to the ultimate consumer market than is the component or business service provided by vendors. Thus, consumer market trends become apparent sooner than they do further back in the supply chain.

PLCS OF OLDER, SIMILAR PRODUCTS

When a firm introduces a new-to-the-world product as opposed to a product extension, foreward visibility is particularly poor. However, older products that have served the same market in time past may increase the visibility to some degree. For example, in the early days of the semiconductor industry, the trends of the much older vacuum tube served as a very useful surrogate. Both products were subject to seasonal changes in the consumer electronic sector as well as funding trends in the military market.

The writer used these market factors across three decades of volatile market changes and found their usefulness continual over time. It should again be emphasized, however, that the process of locating a product's actual PLC stage (particularly the change from growth to maturity) involves considerably more effort and risk than the theoretical discussion of this phenomenon.

Systems Marketing

Theodore Levitt emphasized that buyers do not purchase a product solely for its own value.[26] Rather, they buy an *augmented* product, a package of interrelated products and services from a single supplier. Consequently, many sellers have adopted the practice of systems marketing.

In systems marketing, the supplier not only sells a group of interrelated products, but associated operating procedures, management routines, inventory control, and other service components to meet a particular buyer's needs. For example, many equipment manufacturers include maintenance, emergency repairs, and training services as part of their systems.

Systems marketing may involve (1) *product systems,* composed of capital goods and the associated operating supplies; (2) *systems contracting,* which provides a computerized order entry routine for low-value, frequently-ordered maintenance, repair, and operating (MRO) supplies; and (3) *service systems,* which involve integrated and customized services, such as information processing or management consulting, to help customers manage their businesses better. Thus, systems marketing may refer to products and supplies, products and services, or customized services that provide an integrated solution.[27]

SYSTEMS MARKETING IS SERVICE MARKETING

Systems marketing, in essence, provides a combination of products and services tailored to meet an individual customer's needs. Thus, the vendor becomes the customer's consultant, armed with a wide-ranging capability to solve a myriad of problems. For example, before designing and installing a pollution control system, the supplier would perform an analysis of the customer's operations to determine the extent to which air, water, or solid-waste pollution existed. Having defined the extent of the problem, the supplier would work with the customer to develop a system that (1) met all pertinent codes, (2) fit the operating demands of existing and planned facilities, and (3) represented the greatest reliability at an affordable cost.[28]

THE ELEMENTS OF SYSTEMS MARKETING

The essential characteristic of a good system is its ability to solve a customer problem. This requires (1) identification of the problem in financial terms (i.e., what the problem is costing the customer), (2) the use of technology to provide a profit improvement solution, and (3) overall management of the system.[28] No effective system can be developed without a thorough understanding of customer needs. This requires a clear understanding of customer operations and interaction with a wider range of influencers and decision makers than in the marketing of products.

Systems marketing stems from a fundamental premise of marketing: customers do not buy products—they buy benefits. They will readily pay for the solutions to critical problems. However, systems marketers must accept a broader range of responsibilities than product marketers; as indicated by the following list, they must[28]:

1. Develop general system designs capable of satisfying a broad set of market needs
2. Analyze the needs of the individual customer from both a technical and financial perspective
3. Recommend and develop the best solution for these needs
4. Ensure timely delivery to coincide with other operations
5. Install and debug the system
6. Assist in the conversion to a new system where an older one existed
7. Maintain the system and update it when appropriate
8. Guarantee that the system will perform as promised

BENEFITS OF SYSTEMS MARKETING

Systems marketing provides both the seller and buyer with benefits not normally realized from products. In selling an entire system, the supplier provides all the associated products and services required by the customer. Simultaneously, the supplier realizes increased revenues from this combined sale, promotion costs decrease due to consolidated advertising, and the productivity of the sales force rises. Replacement of the system by a competitive offering does not normally occur because of the cost involved and the customer's established confidence in the original seller.

Customers save the cost of development, reduce the risk of system obsolescence, and minimize the expense of spare parts inventory and maintenance personnel. At the same time, they enjoy the specialized expertise of the supplier plus the latest system technology. In reality, systems marketing does result in a win-win situation as long as both parties uphold their responsibilities.

Looking Back

Business products involve much more than the psychological or social value associated with many consumer goods. Most decisions made by professional buyers will stem from three primary factors: the quality and reliability of the product, the dependability and service of the supplier, and the combined impact of these elements on profitability.

Given the complexity of product decisions and their impact on the entire firm, product development, modification, or deletion strategies require a coordinated effort across functional departments. The three line functions of an industrial firm—engineering, manufacturing, and marketing—must work in concert to ensure timely, practical, and profitable decisions. In today's competitive markets, most firms will also involve outside agencies in this decision-making—suppliers on the input side and channel intermediaries on the output.

To a product manager, the innovation cycle begins before the product life cycle. Together they constitute a time continuum along which product strategies are continually developed and revised. A profitable product line depends on precise timing and overall scope. Being first to market offers both substantial profit opportunities and potential risks.

A large number of firms today earnestly engage in a race to reach the market first. However, when this race triggers accelerated product development (APD), a new set of potential problems can arise and with these, a set of hidden costs that may offset the advantages of being first.

Product lines should be broad enough to serve specific target markets but narrow enough to provide optimal profits. Products should be modified in recognition of changing market needs and deleted when resources can be more profitably applied to other opportunities.

Systems marketing involves a combination of physical products and associated services that provide a customer with a technical/financial solution to a specific problem. Both seller and buyer accrue benefits that are not usually realized from the sale and purchase of products alone. However, a much closer relationship is required for the effective application of systems marketing.

Questions for Discussion

1. Many business firms have adopted product management to put increased emphasis on product planning, promotion, and profitability. Most business product managers reach this position through sales or engineering.
   a. Discuss whether someone who only possesses knowledge of business marketing and product strategy could perform well in this position without prior sales or technical experience.
   b. How do the responsibilities of business product managers differ from those of their counterparts in the consumer market?

2. Chester Wasson has pointed out that business marketers "must be aware of the real differences in the rapidity of market acceptance and of the consequent differences in product life cycles" when developing product strategies. Discuss these differences and how they affect business marketing strategy.

3. There seems to be a dilemma between introducing a new product ahead of competition and risking the potential problems associated with accelerated product development. Can you solve or at least minimize the dilemma? How would you do this?

4. Avlonitis has pointed out that product revitalization decisions and product deletion decisions "represent the key alternative courses of action that a company can undertake in response to either current or projected unsatisfactory product performance." He concludes that these decisions must be considered together. Do you agree or disagree with this conclusion? Why?

5. Regarding systems marketing, decide whether the components of the system and the system itself be standardized or customized. What factors did you consider in reaching your conclusion?

6. According to Theodore Levitt, during the 1990s "... the emphasis will be on systems contracts, and buyer-seller relationships will be characterized by continuous contact and evolving relationships to affect the system." Explain your reaction to this statement.

Endnotes

1. William Lazer and James D. Culley, *Marketing Management* (Boston: Houghton Mifflin Co., 1983), p. 476.
2. Ralph G. Kauffman, "Influences on industrial buyers' choice of products: Effects of product application, product type, and buying environment," *International Journal of Purchasing and Materials Management* 30 (Spring 1994):29-38.
3. Theodore Levitt, *The Marketing Mode* (New York: McGraw-Hill Book Co., 1969), p. 2.
4. Gordon E. Greenley, "Tactical product decisions," *Industrial Marketing Management* 12 (1983):13-18.
5. B. Charles Ames and James D. Hlavacek, *Managerial Marketing for Industrial Firms* (New York: Random House, 1984), p. 341.
6. Robert W. Eckles and Timothy S. Novotny, "Industrial product managers: Authority and Responsibility," *Industrial Marketing Management* 13 (1984):71-5.
7. This section adapted from Robert H. Randolph, "The product management key to marketing success: Will it cure advanced technology marketing ills?" *Business Marketing* (September 1986), pp. 104+.
8. Byron L. David, "How internal venture teams innovate," Research Technology Management 37 (March/April 1994):38-43.
9. B. Charles Ames, "Dilemma of product/market management," *Harvard Business Review* (March-April 1971), pp. 66+.
10. "A smarter way to manufacture," *Business Week* (April 30, 1990), pp. 110+.
11. Donald G. Reinertsen, "Whodunit? The search for new-product killers," *Electronic Business* (July 1983), pp. 62-6.
12. Jack R. Harkins, "Originality sacrificed by CAD?" *Appliance Manufacturer* 42 (June 1994):11.
13. Murray R. Millson, S.P., Raj, and David Wilemon, "A survey of major approaches for accelerating new product development," *Journal of Product Innovation Management* 9 (January 1992):53-69.
14. The foregoing section is adapted from C. Merle Crawford, "The hidden costs of accelerated product development," *Journal of Product Innovation Management* 9 (2)(1992):188-99.
15. Roland W. Schmitt, "Successful corporate R&D," *Harvard Business Review* 63 (May-June 1985):32-40.
16. Jill D. Teplensky, John R. Kimberly, and Alan L. Hillman, "Scope, timing and strategic adjustment in emerging markets: Manufacturer strategies and the case of MRI," *Strategic Management Journal* 14 (October 1993):505-27.
17. Thomas S. Robertson, "How to reduce market penetration cycle times," *Sloan Management Review,* 35 (Fall 1993):87-96.
18. Chester R. Wasson, "The importance of the product life cycle to the industrial marketer," *Industrial Marketing Management* 5 (1976):229-308.
19. Michael S. Austin, "Design research complements traditional tools," *Marketing News* 28 (August 29, 1994):27.
20. Theodore Karger, "Diagnostic research can provide treatment for old, ailing brands," *Marketing News* (September 12, 1986), p. 18+.
21. George J. Avlonitis, "Revitalizing weak industrial products," *Industrial Marketing Management* 14 (1985):93-105.

22. "Chemical giants are turning to new materials," *Wall Street Journal* (June 24, 1986), p. 6.

23. Robert B. Handfield and Ronald T. Pannesi, "Managing component life cycles in dynamic technological environments," *International Journal of Purchasing and Materials Management,* 30 (Spring 1994):20-7.

24. See George J. Avlonitis, "Product elimination decision making: Does formality matter?" *Journal of Marketing,* 49 (Winter 1985):41-52; and George J. Avlonitis, "Advisors and decision-makers in product eliminations," *Industrial Marketing Management* 14 (1985):17-26.

25. Kenneth N. Thompson, Barbara J. Coe, and John R. Lewis, "Gauging the value of suppliers' products: buyer-side applications of economic value pricing models," *Journal of Business and Industrial Marketing* 9(2)(1994):29-40.

26. Theodore Levitt, "After the sale is over," *Harvard Business Review* 61 (September-October 1983):87-93.

27. Albert L. Page and Michael Siemplenski, "Product systems marketing," *Industrial Marketing Management* 12 (1983):89-99.

28. Mack Hanan, James Cribbin, and Jack Donis, *Systems Selling Strategies.* (New York: AMACOM, 1978), p. 7.

Bibliography

Bloom, Paul N., "Effective marketing for professional services," *Harvard Business Review* 62 (September-October 1984): 102-10.

Crawford, C. Merle, "The hidden costs of accelerated product development," *Journal of Product Innovation Management* 9 (2) (1992):188-99.

Dawes, P.L., and P.G. Patterson, "The performance of industrial and consumer product managers," *Industrial Marketing Management* 17 (1988):73-84.

Eckles, Robert W., and Timothy J. Novotny, "Industrial product managers: Authority and responsibility," *Industrial Marketing Management* 13 (1984):71-5.

Handfield, Robert B., and Ronald T. Pannesi, "Managing component life cycles in dynamic technological environments," *International Journal of Purchasing and Materials Management* 30 (Spring 1994):20-7.

Kauffman, Ralph G., "Influences on industrial buyers' choice of products: Effects of product application, product type, and buying environment," *International Journal of Purchasing and Materials Management* 30 (Spring 1 994):29-38.

Lambkin, Mary, and George S. Day, "Evolutionary processes in competitive markets: Beyond the product life cycle," *Journal of Marketing* (July 1989):4-20.

Millson, Murray R., S.P. Raj, and David Wilemon, "A survey of major approaches for accelerating new product development," *Journal of Product Innovation Management* 9 (January 1992):53-69.

Page, Albert L., and Michael Siemplenski, "Product systems marketing," *Industrial Marketing Management* 12 (1983):89-99.

Randolph, Robert H., "The product management key to marketing success: Will it cure advanced technology marketing ills?" *Business Marketing* (September 1986):104+.

Robertson, Thomas S., "How to reduce market penetration cycle times," *Sloan Management Review* 35 (Fall 1993):87-96.

Sonnenberg, Hardy, "Balancing speed and quality in product innovation," *The Canadian Business Review* 20 (Autumn 1993):19-22.

Teplensky, Jill D., John R. Kimberley, and Alan L. Hillman, "Scope, timing and strategic adjustment in emerging markets: Manufacturer strategies and the case of MRI," *Strategic Management Journal* 14 (October 1993):505-27.

11

Strategic Innovation and New Product Development

The new product development process has always presented a challenge, one that tests a company's market knowledge, technical competence, and financial strength as well as its willingness and ability to innovate. As markets exhibit increased global competition and faster rates of technological change, both governments and businesses will place great emphasis on R&D, new products, and technological innovation.[1] Firms that do not create new products—or at least respond effectively to the creations of competitors—will find themselves obsolete in an unsympathetic marketplace.

In this chapter, we will examine the following:

1. The multiple sources for new product ideas
2. The impact of innovation on a firm's productivity and competitiveness
3. Innovation applied to manufacturing and marketing
4. Organizational alternatives for new product development
5. Marketing's role in the development process
6. The need for total company involvement

Developing and marketing new products is a costly venture that entails commitment and risk. Research indicates that about 40 percent of all new products that reach the market fail during the introductory stage.[2] We shall examine some of the major causes of product failure.

Innovation does not stop with the creation of new products. Firms must also upgrade their production techniques and marketing methods to remain competitive. In fact, American firms are losing more business to foreign competition as a result of production and marketing shortcomings than to a lack of product creativity.[3] We will examine this phenomenon along with possible remedies.

What Is a New Business Product?

Booz, Allen, and Hamilton identified six categories of new products in terms of their newness to the company and to the market[4]:

1. *New-to-the-world* products: new products that create an entirely new market
2. *New-to-the-firm* products: products that allow a firm to compete in an established market for the first time
3. *Additions* to existing product line: products that supplement a company's established product lines
4. *Improvements/revisions* to existing products: new products that provide improved performance or greater perceived value and replace existing products
5. *Repositionings:* existing products aimed at new markets or market segments
6. *Cost reductions:* new products that provide similar performance at a lower cost

A firm generally pursues a mix of these new products. The Booz, Allen, and Hamilton study found that only 10 percent of new products are new to the world. Such products represent the greatest risk, because they are new to both the company and the market. A distribution of the six categories is shown in Figure 11-1.

Who Dreams Up New Products?

New product ideas come from a variety of sources both inside and outside the company. Within the firm, ideas can come from manufacturing, sales, engineering, and management personnel as well as from formally structured development groups. Outside

FIGURE 11-1 Types of new products.

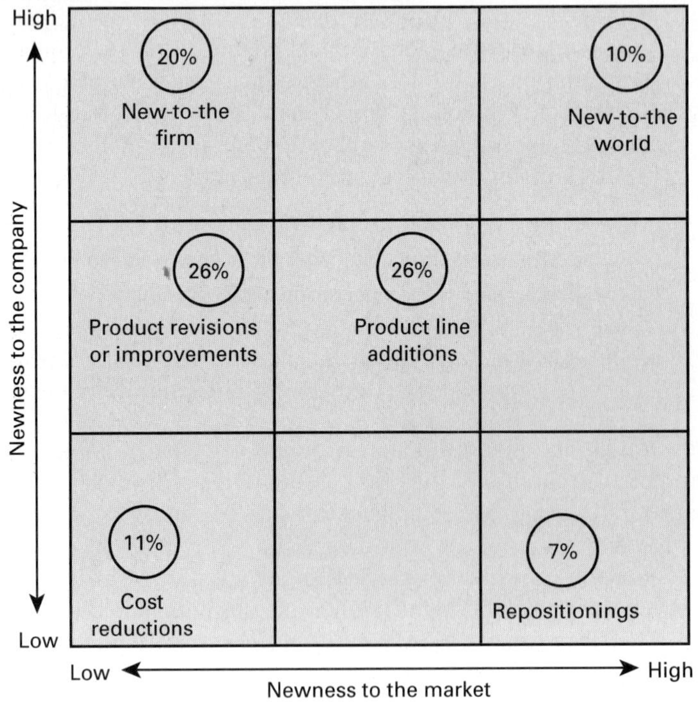

Source: Adapted from *New Products Management for the 1980s* (New York: Booz, Allen, and Hamilton, 1982). Reprinted by permission.

sources include distributors, independent researchers, competitors, government agencies, and existing or potential customers.

NEW PRODUCT IDEAS FROM WITHIN THE COMPANY

Some observers of American industry have concluded that product innovations can stem only from small entrepreneurial companies, because large firms are too bureaucratic and stultified by unimaginative policies and practices. Unfortunately, a number of large corporations justify this conclusion. Others, however, contradict it.

Intrapreneuring   The term *intrapreneur* implies the presence of entrepreneurial activities *within* business organizations, including firms the size of 3M, Bell Atlantic, Hewlett-Packard, Motorola, and Xerox. Intrapreneurship, or corporate entrepreneurship, usually requires a major restructuring of corporate strategies and thinking. The role of innovator is removed from a narrow organizational realm and invested in all employees. Firms happily discover that many employees want to grow personally by making significant contributions to the firm and will do so when provided with the necessary freedom, encouragement, and resources.[5] They take on the motivated mindset of entrepreneurs, hoping to reap the rewards of success and willing to accept the consequences of failure. This level of dedication will develop only in an environment that indicates total management commitment coupled with a patient attitude, a corporate culture capable of change, and a realistic set of measurable expectations.[6] The results at Bell Atlantic are one indication of what a proactive, planned intrapreneurial program can accomplish. Three years after its inception in 1990, 130 intrapreneurs had championed more than 100 projects, at least 15 products were on or near the market, and 15 patents had been awarded. Potential revenues for these projects were estimated at a minimum of $100 million within 5 years.[7]

One study, which focused on 139 Fortune 500 firms plus 149 smaller companies, concluded that the most successful product innovations resulted when an intrapreneur was involved in the internal venturing process. The study also concluded that the least successful ventures were those in which the product concepts began in the R&D department, even though these products exhibited the greatest degree of technical innovation.

Because of the many freedoms allowed to intrapreneurs, the process violates most bureaucratic principles and practices. Therefore, intrapreneurs have little hope for success unless this concept receives support from top management.[8]

NEW PRODUCT IDEAS FROM CUSTOMERS

Manufacturers who practice the marketing concept realize that all new product ideas should be aimed at satisfying some market. Thus, they welcome product ideas from customers seeking a solution to a specific problem. Some early research centered on the question of whether or not industrial firms used customer ideas in developing new products. Some concluded affirmatively, others negatively.[9] A possible explanation of these contradictory findings may stem from the prolonged delay between an original idea formation and its conversion into a commercial product. By the time the idea becomes a market reality, the originator has been forgotten, or the developing company contracts a sense of ownership and assumes credit for the idea.

Customer Needs and Technology Efforts   There is no longer any question about the importance of customer input into the new product development process. When the idea originates with a customer, this input is automatic and usually quite detailed. When the idea stems from a supplier's internal efforts, prompt customer evaluation is essential.

Cooper's studies repeatedly indicate the importance of *early market research* to ensure a good fit between a proposed product and market needs.[10] Crawford encourages a "dual-drive" approach to innovation, which requires the supplier to identify and analyze an important unmet customer need and match that need with the specific technology that can satisfy it. The key to this approach is a constant communication link between marketing and engineering throughout the development process.[11] Product development should not result in overemphasis on either technology or the market. The emphasis should be placed on achieving the proper balance between the two areas.[12]

A Focused Effort   An effective R&D program follows several guidelines. First, it seeks to satisfy the needs of *specific* customers or markets. Very few firms have the capability, or even the desire, to satisfy all the diverse needs in their target markets. Thus, they develop a set of criteria to screen for desirable business opportunities and assign some individual or group this screening responsibility.

Second, an R&D program should center on "generally known" needs in the target markets. For example, all customers want computers that will handle more data faster and at less cost. Such needs may also be described as *latent* or unsatisfied. Satisfying latent needs gives the firm the prestige of being first and a lead over competition in developing production volume and efficiency.[13] This head start provides an eventual cost advantage, the cause and potential uses of which will be discussed in Chapters 18 and 19.

Third, an effective R&D program should also try to expand on those technologies that represent the firm's strengths. Use of a *proven* technology is one of the factors that increases the probability of a product's success.[14] Technologies can become obsolete, however, just as products do. For example, between 1960 and 1983, the semiconductor industry obsoleted five basic fabrication technologies and countless minor variations of these.

Thus, it is necessary to evaluate which customer needs will be considered, to choose a technology capable of satisfying those needs, and to recognize when the technology and needs are no longer compatible.

Satisfying the Changing Needs of Key Customers   Business marketers must be especially sensitive to the changing needs of industry leaders, particularly if the industry is an oligopoly. When a few companies represent the bulk of an industry's buying power, a supplier cannot afford to dissatisfy, let alone ignore, their needs.

Current industry leaders do not always remain dominant, however. Geographic areas such as Silicon Valley contain many firms that have been in business less than 5 years but already possess considerable buying power. Consequently, business marketers not only face the challenge of satisfying current industry leaders, but must also identify and penetrate future leaders. This penetration is difficult because future leaders often emerge in conjunction with, or because of, new technologies. Their needs may be incompatible with a potential supplier's current capabilities. Firms willing and able to satisfy these new needs strengthen their own industry position.

Innovation and Competitiveness

In the last decade of the twentieth century, it might be beneficial to analyze where American industry stands internationally in the areas of technology, innovation, and overall competitiveness. Such an analysis can clarify the impact of technology and innovation on a firm's competitive position, but it requires the consideration of several associated factors and the establishment of certain relationships.

AN HISTORICAL PERSPECTIVE OF PRODUCTIVITY

Productivity is a good starting point, because it defines what level of output competing firms (or nations) are able to achieve with a given input level, or, more simply put, what they can do with what they have. Grayson and O'Dell, in a book obviously aimed at removing any complacency from the minds of American industrialists, provide an excellent long-range perspective on this issue.[3]

Based on gross domestic product per employee (GDP/employee), the United States remained ahead of nine other leading industrialized nations in 1985 (see Table 11-1). Two other aspects require consideration, however, before this lead can be properly evaluated.

Previous Productivity Leaders   First, the United States is the third nation since 1700 to lead the world in productivity. The Netherlands led during the eighteenth century. Nations were not then industrialized in today's sense of the word, but the Dutch surpassed other European countries in textile production, shipbuilding, insurance, banking, and international trade. Italian manufacturers in Genoa, Milan, and Venice decried the "cheap" Dutch textiles that invaded and captured their home markets.

As a result of the Industrial Revolution, the United Kingdom assumed productivity leadership by the 1780s. Throughout most of the nineteenth century, the United Kingdom was the financial and technological powerhouse of the world. The British dominated the coal, iron, and cotton cloth markets, and London became the financial center.[3]

Although its lead had already begun to decline, the United Kingdom in 1870 enjoyed about the same position that the United States had in 1985, as indicated in Table 11-2. By the 1890s, however, the United Kingdom lost its lead to the United States and became a relatively weak follower in the twentieth century. A multitude of factors, many beyond the scope of this text, caused this dramatic fall, but British creativity was not at fault. Primarily, American firms developed the ability to mass produce, at lower cost, products that the British invented.

One must also analyze the relative productivity growth rates of the ten countries between 1975 and 1985. As shown in Table 11-1, the United States ranked dead last in productivity improvement during this time interval. Table 11-2 shows the shift in the

TABLE 11-1 Real Gross Domestic Product per Employee, 1985			
Country	*1985 (U.S. dollars)*	*Relative Level**	*Annual Growth, 1975-1985(%)*
UNITED STATES	35,370	100	0.7
Canada	33,071	94	1.5
France	28,756	81	2.2
Italy	28,650	81	2.5
Belgium	28,331	80	2.3
Netherlands	27,872	79	0.7
Norway	27,447	78	2.5
Germany	26,669	75	2.0
United Kingdom	24,688	70	2.1
Japan	24,122	68	3.1

*Based on U.S. = 100.

Source: Adapted from C. Jackson Grayson, Jr., and Carla O'Dell, *American Business: A Two-Minute Warning* (New York: The Free Press, 1988), p. 39. (Time base revised.)

TABLE 11-2 Productivity Leaders, 1870, 1985, and 1994				
	1870			*1985*
UNITED KINGDOM*	100		United States	143
Netherlands	93		Canada	134
Belgium	93		France	116
United States	88		Italy	116
Canada	76		Belgium	115
Italy	55		Netherlands	113
Germany	54		Norway	111
France	53		Germany	108
Norway	50		UNITED KINGDOM*	100
Japan	21		Japan	98

	1985	*Annual Growth 1985-1994 (%)*		*1994*
UNITED STATES[†]	100	3.3	UNITED STATES[†]	100
Canada	94	1.7	Italy	85
France	81	3.1	Canada	82
Italy	81	3.8	France	80
Belgium	80	2.6	Belgium	75
Netherlands	79	2.1	United Kingdom	73
Norway	78	1.6	Netherlands	71
Germany	75	1.5	Norway	68
United Kingdom	70	3.8	Japan	67
Japan	68	3.0	Germany	64

*United Kingdom = 100.

[†] United States = 100.

Data: U.S. Department of Labor, Bureau of Labor Statistics, *International Comparison of Manufacturing Productivity* (September 8, 1995), Table 2.

Source: Adapted from C. Jackson Grayson, Jr., and Carla O'Dell, *American Business: A Two-Minute Warning* (New York: The Free Press, 1988), p. 86. (Time periods revised by author.)

rankings between 1870 and 1985 using the United Kingdom as the base. The British fell from first to ninth place because of their dismal productivity growth.

Table 11-2 also shows the 1985 rankings using the United States as the base. It lists the productivity growth rates for the period 1985 to1994 and the resultant rankings in 1994. During this period, the U.S. rate of improvement lagged behind only Italy and a resurging United Kingdom. Meanwhile, two major competitors in world markets—Germany and Japan—showed signs of decreasing gains as did our top trading partner, Canada.

Future Possibilities   Future rankings clearly depend on future productivity gains. Significant changes can occur over relatively short periods of time and for a variety of reasons. Table 11-3 shows what would happen over a 20-year span (1994 to 2014) using two different productivity growth rates. If the United States and the other nine nations maintain their 1985-1994 performance, the rankings in 2014 will show some significant changes. Italy and the United Kingdom will continue to rise in the rankings, whereas Japan, Canada, and Germany fall back.

TABLE 11-3	Future Productivity Leadership, 2014		
	Using 1985-1994 Growth Rate (%)		*2014 GDP per Employee (1985 U.S. dollars)*
UNITED STATES	3.3	UNITED STATES*	89,958	100
Canada	1.7	Italy	85,235	95
France	3.1	United Kingdom	73,175	81
Italy	3.8	France	70,283	78
Belgium	2.6	Belgium	58,949	66
Netherlands	2.1	Japan	56,696	63
Norway	1.6	Canada	54,060	60
Germany	1.5	Netherlands	50,450	56
United Kingdom	3.8	Norway	43,859	49
Japan	3.0	Germany	41,008	45
	Using 1990-1994 Growth Rate (%)		*2014 GDP per Employee (1985 U.S. dollars)*
UNITED STATES[†]	3.8	UNITED STATES*	98,826	100
Canada	3.4	Italy	88,102	89
France	2.7	Canada	74,951	76
Italy	4.0	United Kingdom	73,562	74
Belgium	2.1	France	64,213	65
Netherlands	2.5	Netherlands	55,074	56
Norway	2.2	Belgium	53,580	54
Germany	1.9	Norway	49,164	50
United Kingdom	3.8	Germany	44,175	45
Japan	0.5	Japan	35,001	35

*U.S. = 100.

Source: Concept adapted from C. Jackson Grayson, Jr., and Carla O'Dell, *American Business: A Two-Minute Warning* (New York: The Free Press, 1988), p. 86.

Data: U.S. Department of Labor, Bureau of Labor Statistics, *International Comparison of Manufacturing Productivity* (September 8, 1995).

If these ten nations duplicate their 1990-1994 performance, the United States, Italy, Canada, and the U.K. will benefit but Germany and Japan will continue to fall back.

Let us now consider factors that can affect productivity for better or worse.

Why American Productivity Declined   As mentioned earlier, the United Kingdom's fall from leadership stemmed in great part from the ability of American manufacturers to copy British products, improve on them, and produce them at a lower cost. One potential scenario for the United States bears a close resemblance. International competitors are copying American product ideas, improving on them, putting them into production rapidly at low cost and with high quality, and beating us in the marketplace. Grayson and O'Dell attribute this productivity slowdown to five underlying causes[3]:

1. The United States had very little international competition from 1946 through the 1960s. We enjoyed what Lester Thurow called an *"effortless superiority."*

2. Affluence spawned *complacency*. A desire for the good life continued to grow, but the willingness to make sacrifices for it diminished.

3. *Government programs and policies* in the 1960s and 1970s gave higher priority to equity and social justice than to productivity and efficiency.

4. Both government and business neglected the *human dimension*. Government underinvested in education; business viewed its work force as a production variable, not a partner in the planning process.

5. Both the economy and the population are *aging*. The daring, vitality, and goal orientation of youth are being replaced by a desire for security and the status quo.[3]

The productivity projections in Table 11-3 do not constitute a prediction. In fact, Japanese productivity has already improved over the dismal results of the early 1990s. Happily, American results also continue to improve. We will return to this encouraging point shortly.

THE RELATIONSHIP OF INNOVATION TO PRODUCTIVITY

If we interpret innovation narrowly to mean only *the creation of new things,* then its relationship to productivity is weak. However, innovation should also *denote new and better ways of doing what has been done before.* Besides the creation of new products, innovation also involves designing products that can be produced more efficiently, devising methods to improve the overall production process, and even increasing the effectiveness of the marketing and distribution functions. When viewed from this perspective, innovation becomes not just an element of productivity but a significant contributing cause.

THE RELATIONSHIP OF INNOVATION TO COMPETITIVENESS

A direct relationship of innovation to competitiveness seems evident, whether we view innovation as the creation of new products or as an improved method of producing and delivering current products. If a new product gives increased satisfaction to customers, the producer should enjoy a stronger competitive position. In the same vein, if two firms supply similar products, the one with a more consistent and higher quality, a lower cost, and a more dependable delivery cycle should end up with the lion's share of the market.

The electronics industry, and the semiconductor segment in particular, serves as an excellent example of both issues. We will use this industry as our analytical framework. At first glance, this example may appear too limited, but a closer view should reveal its broad application.

The Impact of Technology

THE VACUUM TUBE

The electronics industry stemmed from two American inventions—De Forest's triode vacuum tube and the Hazeltine feedback amplifier circuit. The combination of these two technologies paved the way for several major industries: radio broadcasting, wireless telegraphy, and long-distance telephone service. In turn, these industries spawned a host of other component and end product industries. Electronics dramatically improved Edison's phonograph, initial research began in video transmission, and the fledgling aircraft industry had the electronic tools necessary to make commercial flight safe and profitable. In the 1940s, vacuum tubes became the primary components of the first computers.

Vacuum tubes, however, had several major shortcomings. They generated heat, which negatively affected their reliability, and their power requirements put an excessive drain on batteries. Moreover, their size increased the bulk and weight of the end products. All three factors had a negative impact on portable and airborne applications.

THE MICROELECTRONIC REVOLUTION

In the 25-year span between 1948 and 1973, the electronics industry was changed dramatically by three more American inventions: the transistor, the integrated circuit, and large-scale integration.

The Transistor   Scientists at Bell Telephone Laboratories (BTL) announced their major invention in 1948. Because these small devices simultaneously solved the problems of limited reliability, excess size, and power drain, transistors rapidly supplanted vacuum tubes in a multitude of portable and airborne applications. Moreover, they paved the way for a broad spectrum of new products that could capitalize on their form and function.

A Redistribution of Market Power   When BTL announced the development of the transistor, three firms—RCA, GE, and Sylvania—held a combined 70 percent of the $500 million vacuum tube market. Their reaction to the transistor was mixed.

RCA was the leading producer of radio receivers and transmitting equipment as well as the owner of the National Broadcasting Company (NBC). General Electric was also a major producer of radio equipment and myriad other electrical products. Sylvania, which began as a light bulb competitor of GE, diversified into vacuum tubes and then purchased a radio manufacturer to give it a toehold in the equipment market. Thus, while the transistor represented exciting opportunities for the equipment divisions of these companies, it also posed a very serious threat to their tube business. Consequently, when BTL offered licenses in 1953 to any interested firm for $25,000, the three tube companies responded but mounted only cursory developmental efforts in this new technology.

Three other firms took a far more enthusiastic and aggressive position. Texas Instruments, only a $19 million firm in 1953, saw the opportunity for tremendous growth. Motorola, already heavily involved in consumer radios and two-way communication equipment, wanted to diversify into the component market, supported by the guaranteed volume of their sizable in-house requirements. Raytheon, a leading producer of airborne equipment and hearing aids, saw transistor technology as a means of improving its equipment performance. These three firms, plus Fairchild Camera and Instrument, were the leading semiconductor producers in 1960. It should be noted that Sony, despite strong resistance from the Japanese government, also bought a BTL license in 1953.

The Integrated Circuit   Two scientists, Jack Kilby at TI and Robert Noyce at Fairchild, working independently but concurrently, developed a means of incorporating a number of transistors, diodes, resistors, and capacitors within a single chip of silicon. In effect, an entire circuit was contained in this chip; hence the name *integrated* circuit (IC).

Kilby announced his breakthrough first, but Noyce developed an improved "planar" process and applied for a patent within 5 months of TI's 1960 application. After TI had filed a lawsuit, the courts decided that Kilby and Noyce should be considered co-inventors, and any firm desiring to produce these new devices would require licenses from both TI and Fairchild. Nippon Electric (NEC), Hitachi, and Sony were among a number of Japanese firms that applied for licenses.

ICs transformed electronic circuits into simple components. Engineers who had previously devoted their time to circuit designs could now work at the system level. This fact alone increased engineering productivity, but ICs had an even greater impact on small companies with limited R&D budgets. As ICs continued to grow in complexity (i.e., more functional circuitry on one chip) and to decline in cost, these small firms could enter a product market by simply buying the proper ICs and/or copying a competitor's electronic hardware. This also meant that remaining competitive in any market would require the constant updating of a product's electronic content.

Large-Scale Integration   Noyce and several other key executives at Fairchild left to form a new firm, Intel, with the intention of concentrating on complex ICs. They quickly developed several memory ICs with a capacity of 1K (more precisely, 1,024 bytes, or characters). While working under contract to develop a family of custom ICs for a group of Japanese calculator firms, Intel designers found that they could not meet the prescribed space limitations with individual chips. They decided to put all the functions on one chip of silicon. Their successful outcome was a *microprocessor,* sometimes called a "computer on a chip." The Japanese firms were skeptical about the device and gave Intel the right to market what eventually became the 8080—an industry standard and the heart of the first desktop computers.

With the microprocessor and some early memory chips, Intel essentially created a breakthrough in large-scale integration. During the 1970s and early 1980s, Intel and a few other manufacturers managed to quadruple the capacity of memory chips every few years (4K, 16K, 64K, 256K, and 1 Meg). By 1988, development work had started on a 4 Meg (4,000,000 byte) chip. Several Japanese producers played major roles in this sequential development process.

Further Change in Market Power   In 1970, ICs comprised only 15 percent ($300 million) of a worldwide $2 billion semiconductor market. Discrete devices (transistors, diodes, and silicon controlled rectifiers) constituted the balance. By 1980, the semiconductor market had grown to $13 billion, with ICs comprising 70 percent. Once again, the market power base had changed. Texas Instruments and Motorola were the leading producers. Intel joined the leadership ranks, but Fairchild and Raytheon slipped badly. Asian and European manufacturers held about one third of the market.

During the 1980s, even more dramatic shifts occurred. By 1990 the worldwide semiconductor market grew to $58 billion, with ICs constituting 83 percent, or $48 billion. Between 1980 and 1988, Japanese producers increased their market share from 29 to 54 percent, while American producers dropped from 60 to 33 percent. European and other Asian producers held the remaining 13 percent. Japanese firms (NEC, Toshiba, Hitachi) occupied the top three positions, the leading American firms (Motorola, TI, Intel) were in the next three slots, followed by three more Japanese firms plus a Dutch/American conglomerate (Phillips/Signetics). The development work of the Japanese in large-scale integration paid off handsomely when the desktop and portable computer market mushroomed and the demand for ever-larger memory chips seemed insatiable. Some forecasters predicted that American semiconductor manufacturers would lose the market just as radio and TV producers had lost theirs earlier.

Fortunately, some of the most impressive technological and productivity gains were made in this industry during the early 1990s. Instead of increasing, the Japanese worldwide market share fell back to 41 percent, whereas American producers regained 43 percent. Intel became the worldwide leader on the strength of its dominating position in microprocessors. Motorola and TI maintained strong positions in custom-designed circuits for multimedia computer applications and telecommunications. Japanese firms remained strong primarily in high-production memory chips.

FORESEEING SOME TRENDS, MISSING OTHERS

In a special 1980 issue entitled "The Reindustrialization of America," *Business Week* observed[15]:

> Barring some spectacular breakthrough, the most significant driving forces in high technology for the balance of this decade will be continuations of two current trends in electronics. First is the steep decline in the price of computing power. Second, and linked to the first, is the spread of the microprocessor into an ever-widening array of products . . . .
>
> Microelectronics will be the keystone technology not only because it is the world's fastest-growing industry. Even more potent than its sheer dollar volume is its pervasiveness. There will be few markets where "dumb" products can long compete against more sophisticated, computerized units . . . .
>
> [In addition, with] computer-aided design (CAD) and computer-aided manufacturing (CAM), it will be progressively less expensive for companies to . . . not only turn out new product designs much faster, but also . . . to make sure that the designs provide quality and reliability as well as the lowest possible manufacturing costs.

Business Week's predictions were quite accurate. Semiconductors, particularly microprocessors and memory chips, have indeed permeated virtually every segment of the electrical and electronic industries. In addition, a wide variety of previously mechanical ("dumb") products have been converted to electronics, everything from hand-held game machines to automated process-control systems. Table 11-4 provides a partial indication of microelectronic pervasiveness.

TABLE 11-4   Some Common Microelectronic Applications

Generic Category	*Specific Applications*
Automotive controls	Dashboard indicators, comfort controls, engine controls (fuel, ignition, exhaust), brake system, diagnostic systems
Banking	Automatic teller machines (ATMs), electronic fund transfers, credit card systems, check readers
Computers	Magnetic disk and drum controls, memories, central processors, intelligent terminals, optical and laser readers, multiplexors
Consumer entertainment	Radios, TV sets, video and audio recorders, still and movie cameras, video games, TV satellite dishes
Design and engineering	Computer-aided design (CAD), computer-aided engineering (CAE), design for manufacturing and assembly (DFMA)
Household controls	Washers, dryers, sewing machines, microwave and convection ovens, blenders, thermostats, alarm systems, light dimmers
Manufacturing	Measuring and test equipment, process monitoring and control, robotics, machine tool controls, computer-assisted manufacturing
Medical systems	Body scanners, heart pacemakers, patient diagnostic and monitoring systems, electronic aids for speech, sight, and hearing impairment
Office productivity	Data and word processing, electronic files, dictation equipment, electronic mail, copiers, printers, retrieval systems
Telecommunications	Data and voice transmission, mobile and portable phones, telephone system exchanges, facsimile equipment, paging and answering devices

The Diffusion of Innovation

Three key factors triggered this dramatic change in market composition. First, as *Business Week* correctly foresaw, microelectronic "building blocks" have simplified the production of even complex electronic systems, and a firm with limited technological expertise and/or financial resources, but armed with the right components, can become an instant competitor.

Second, by combining computer technology with creative personnel, aggressive competitors can leapfrog the design of an innovator's product or devise a more consistent and economical production process. Japanese firms have been particularly adept in this area of innovation. For example, Sharp Electronics devotes a significant portion of their R&D activities to automated design (CAD) and manufacturing (CAM) technologies. Producers worldwide recognize Sharp's R&D output as models for low-cost design and high-volume production efficiency.[16] As another example, Sony made a commercial success of the audiotape and videotape recorder technologies that Ampex invented but chose not to market. Table 11-5 lists some of the more significant products that were invented in the United States and later copied by foreign manufacturers. American producers have not only lost worldwide market share, but are losing their domestic markets as well (shades of Italian textile producers and the inroads of eighteenth century Dutch textiles). Ironically, the 1980 *Business Week* article cited earlier was entitled "Technology Gives the U.S. a Big Edge."

Third, all firms that intend to be major players in the broad-based electronics market of the twenty-first century are developing *vertically integrated* technological capabilities. In other words, they already are, or are taking steps to become, self-sufficient in the component, end product, production equipment, and control system technologies necessary to ensure world-class costs and quality. These firms, which exist in

TABLE 11-5   Penetration of Imports Into U.S. Product Markets

Products	Import Share of U.S. Market (%)			
	1975	*1980*	*1987*	*1993*
U.S.-Invented Technologies				
Audiotape recorders	90	90	100	100
Videotape recorders	90	99	99	99
Color TV	20	40	90	99
Telephones	5	12	75	72
Machine tool controls	3	21	65	60
Semiconductors	29	35	36	37
Computers	3	4	26	28
Other Basic U.S. Industries				
Footware	21	37	62	75
Apparel	8	14	32	73
Motor vehicles and parts	19	21	28	24
Farm machinery	11	15	20	23

Data: All 1993 data and other industry data for previous years from International Trade Administration, *U.S. Industrial Outlook* (annual issues).

Source: U.S.-invented technologies data for 1975, 1980, and 1987; cited in "Back to basics," *Business Week* (June 16, 1989), p. 17. Reprinted by permission of *Business Week,* © 1989.

every industrialized country, include Siemens of West Germany, Philips of the Nether-lands, Olivetti of Italy, Thomson-CSF of France, Northern Telecom of Canada, Sam-sung of Korea, Acer of Taiwan, and a host of Japanese firms—Fujitsu, Hitachi, Mat-sushita, Mitsubishi, NEC, Sharp, Sony, and Toshiba.

TECHNOLOGY CAN ALTER THE TRENDS

Elements of this same microelectronic revolution can help to alter the 1980s trends, particularly the declining market shares of American producers. Ford Motor Company provides an excellent example.

Ford's Resurgence   Ford decided in 1982 that quality improvement was only one of their challenges—their product lines also needed a major redesign to give them greater physical appeal. The Taurus and Probe were to be the symbols of corporate resurgence. When the Taurus was introduced in 1985, Ford's share of the U.S. automo-tive market was only 18.8 percent. By the first quarter of 1989, that share widened to 23.4 percent, the company's strongest showing since 1978.

To supply this greater volume, output of cars and trucks from North American plants had to be increased by more than 700,000 units. After seeing their output plunge by 49 percent between 1978 and 1982, Ford management was very reluctant to build new factories. However, one relatively small plant was built in Mexico with a 73,000-car capacity. Second shifts were added in two other plants, increasing their output by about 140,000. The remainder of the added output, more than 500,000 vehicles, resulted from *increased production efficiency* in existing plants.[17] In 1988 alone, Ford reduced manu-facturing costs by $1.2 billion, thus becoming the nation's most profitable auto producer.

By 1992, the Ford Taurus had replaced the Honda Accord as the top-selling auto-mobile in the United States and maintained that leadership through 1995. In 1995, Ford had five vehicles among the top ten automotive best-sellers (three cars and two light trucks).[18] In fact, U.S. nameplates commanded seven of the top ten slots, as shown in Table 11-6.

Other Productivity Gains   During the 1980s, IBM stopped buying printers for their personal computers from Seiko Epson Corporation. Originally, IBM felt that they could

TABLE 11-6   Automotive Sales Leaders in the United States, 1995

Model	1995 Sales
1. Ford F-Series Pickup	691,452
2. Chevrolet C/K Pickup	536,901
3. Ford Explorer	395,227
4. Ford Taurus	366,266
5. Honda Accord	341,384
6. Toyota Camry	328,602
7. Ford Ranger	309,085
8. Honda Civic	289,435
9. Saturn	285,674
10. Ford Escort	285,570

Source: "Trucks set pace in so-so year," *Automotive News* (January 8, 1996), p. 1+.

not improve on Epson's costs, which resulted from an assembly time of only 30 minutes. Yet in 1985, IBM launched its Proprinter line from an automated Kentucky factory that can produce almost 500,000 printers a year, with an assembly time of only 3 minutes.[19]

TI did equally well with an infrared gun sight supplied to the Pentagon. Assembly time was reduced 85 percent, the number of parts 75 percent, and the number of assembly steps 78 percent.[19]

NCR Corporation designed an electronic cash register that snaps together without nuts, bolts, or rivets. An NCR manufacturing engineer assembled the unit in less than 2 minutes—*blindfolded.*[19]

Design for Manufacturability and Assembly (DFMA)   All of these examples have one thing in common: manufacturers utilized relatively inexpensive computer software programs developed by Boothroyd Dewhurst Inc., a small New England firm founded by two British professors who emigrated to the United States after their ideas were ignored by British industry.

Boothroyd Dewhurst emphasizes the basic concept that design decisions can have significant economic implications. Although the design stage itself may expend only a minor portion of the total product cost, decisions made during this stage determine 70 to 95 percent of all manufacturing costs. Moreover, changing a design after it reaches the production line costs ten times as much as catching it on the drawing board—and 100 times as much if the change is made in the middle of the production cycle. The National Science Foundation began supporting Boothroyd's research in 1977. Business firms began adding their support in 1978, led by AMP, Inc., and soon joined by Digital Equipment, GE, Westinghouse, Xerox, IBM, TI, and Ford.[19]

In the mid-1980s, IBM's Rochester, Minnesota plant faced the alternatives of reducing its product development cycle time or going out of business. The average development cycle was 4 to 5 years, so that the market need often disappeared before the product was introduced. By concentrating on customer needs, designing for manufacturability, and reducing design changes, IBM cut the development time to 28 months. Since 1988, the Rochester operation has cut production costs by 66 percent and inventory by 57 percent. Customer satisfaction increased substantially as a result of notable improvements in product and service. Moreover, the Rochester division won the Malcolm Baldrige National Quality Award in 1990.[20]

NECESSARY CHANGES IN RESEARCH METHODS AND GOALS

While technology can provide significant opportunities for innovation and increased productivity, American producers must make additional changes to take full advantage of these opportunities.

A Series of Small Steps   Researchers in many American industries have traditionally concentrated on major breakthroughs. They have sought to create technologies and products that represent a quantum leap beyond that which exists. According to the research director of NEC Corporation, Japanese innovation "is the result of tiny improvements in a thousand places." A Japanese chemist adds, "Real industrial innovation spans the search for new materials, process technology, successful manufacturing schemes, and successful marketing." As a result, American homes are filled with Japanese consumer electronic products that are the result of continuous improvements in cost and performance.[21] As discussed earlier, American breakthrough inventions created many of these markets, but the Japanese style of innovation eventually captured them.

Research as a Team Effort   Virtually all surveys of new product successes and failures have found that *early interaction* of R&D, engineering, manufacturing, and marketing personnel is essential to success.[22] Innovative firms assemble *multifunctional teams* that bring these diverse disciplines together in the earliest stages of a project.[23] However, the team concept does not fit well into traditional companies organized by function. These firms still cling to the "bucket brigade" approach. Research develops an idea that is passed on to engineering for design. Manufacturing gets a list of specifications, without prior discussion, and tries to discern the best way to make the thing. Marketing eventually must find customers for something that nobody wants.[21]

To develop technologically superior products that reach the market on time, companies must establish clear product strategies and systematic processes that interconnect R&D activities with the marketing, engineering, and manufacturing functions. In addition, engineers and marketers must find a way to communicate their different perspectives and work in parallel on any development project. Multifunctional teams can facilitate this process.[24]

R&D Linked to Corporate Strategy   R&D and corporate strategy should benefit from a natural synergy: (1) both involve extended time horizons; (2) each is mutually concerned with maintaining long-term corporate strengths; and (3) both provide future business opportunities. Despite these commonalities, there often exists a wide chasm between the two functions. This problem can usually be alleviated by opening regular lines of communication. Corporate planners gain a better understanding of technology and its impact, while R&D adds a stronger and more perceptive marketing orientation to its efforts.[16]

Product Development Strategy

New product development strategy begins with an unsatisfied need. As Peter Drucker has pointed out, most successful new products are geared toward some *specific application,* some known need. Thus, "the innovation that creates new users and new markets should be directed toward a specific, clear, and carefully designed application."[25] The marketing department must provide this direction.

THE NEW PRODUCT DEVELOPMENT PROCESS

As a product evolves from an idea to a commercial reality, it passes through a series of stages, the sum of which comprises the new product development process. During this process, three questions must be considered in sequence[26]:

1. Is there a *market* for the idea?
2. Can the idea be *transformed* into a physical product?
3. Can the physical product be manufactured and marketed *profitably*?

Each of these questions gives rise to a set of criteria that must be weighed to arrive at a final decision. The first question involves market criteria, the second, product or technology criteria, and the third, financial criteria. Box 11-1, although not intended to be an all-inclusive list, indicates the type and range of these criteria.

Marketing Implications   Several important points arise from these questions and the resulting criteria. As suggested before, product development should center on customer needs. If a customer promotes the product idea, the first question has

---

BOX 11-1

New Product Evaluation Criteria

MARKET CRITERIA

1. Present size
2. Growth potential
3. Current or new customers
4. Number of competitors
5. Strength of competitors
6. Price consciousness
7. Technical service required
8. Suitability of present channels
9. Variety of identified end-uses
10. Impact on present products

TECHNOLOGICAL CRITERIA

1. Degree of innovation
2. Differential advantages
3. Lead time over competition
4. Patentable product/process
5. Estimated product life
6. Amount of know-how required
7. Past experience with technology
8. Technical feasibility
9. Strength of competing technologies
10. Other resources required

FINANCIAL CRITERIA

1. Initial investment level
2. Expected sales revenue
3. Profit-to-sales ratio
4. Expected return on investment

5. Cost-to-price
6. Expected cash flow
7. Payback period
8. Net gain/loss on other products

---

been answered. If the idea originates in-house, market research to locate an existing or potential need must take place as early as possible in the development process.[14] Various studies yield similar but varying lists of reasons for new product failures. However, as Crawford suggests, virtually all of these reasons can be grouped into three categories[27]:

1. No real need for the product exists.

2. The product fails to satisfy the need adequately or has offsetting deficiencies.

3. Some significant aspect of the marketing strategy is mishandled or flawed.

Second, the reasons for product failure clearly indicate the need for a complete and objective definition of customer needs. Business firms often equate the customer's need to the capability planned for the product; that is, "If we can't do it, they don't need it!"

Third, the dominant criteria will change during the development process. Some may quarrel with the sequence of the criteria, particularly the trailing position of financial data. However, unless marketers can identify an attractive market whose needs will be adequately satisfied, and engineers indicate that they can develop the necessary product, financial analysis becomes a fruitless exercise.

Organizing for Effective Product Development

Every firm has a choice of organizational structures. Each choice presents certain strengths and limitations, with the best format for a given firm contingent on its size, resources, and degree of innovativeness. Before selecting any option, the firm should ponder several issues that will have an impact on the R&D process.

AN ATMOSPHERE TO ENCOURAGE RISK-TAKING AND INNOVATION

Many business organizations avoid risk whenever possible. To such firms, innovation means change, and change induces unnecessary risk. Their product development programs tend to be, at best, a defensive response to the innovations of more progressive competitors. They fail to recognize, or refuse to believe, that change externally induced by competition can be more harmful than internally-generated change.

Even firms willing to accept the potential risks of innovation may unwittingly create an environment hostile to such innovation. For example, undue emphasis on short-term profits often restricts projects that do not promise fast results. Employees get the message that status-quo thinking is rewarded. Such an attitude not only limits innovation but jeopardizes long-term profits.

A 1988 study of 897 American companies in 40 industry groups sought to determine whether any correlation exists between company performance—measured by profit margins, return on assets, and productivity per employee—and the level of R&D spending per employee. To approximate the real-world lag, company performance in 1987 was measured against average R&D spending for the four year period 1983 through 1986.

The researchers found no significant correlation between R&D spending and return on assets, but the correlation between R&D spending and productivity was well beyond 99.9 percent, and the correlation with profit margins exceeded 99.5 percent.[28]

One cannot draw, however, meaningful comparisons between companies in different industries. Firms in industries with evolving technologies, for example, normally spend more on R&D than those in old-line businesses. One should also note that some researchers question whether R&D is a leading or lagging indicator of sales and profits; that is, whether firms spend more as a result of growing profits. The analyst who conducted the referenced survey feels quite certain that R&D spending, particularly in high-tech industries, is the driving force for sales and profits, not the beneficiary.[31]

EVERY PRODUCT SHOULD HAVE A CHAMPION

The term *product champion* (or its equivalent) appears with increasing frequency in business literature and conveys a concept that a growing number of practitioners support. Some see this champion as a company-oriented manager who inspires subordinates to find better ways of doing things.[3] Others describe a champion in somewhat begrudging terms as "the zealot or fanatic in the ranks ... not a typical administrative type ... apt to be a loner, egotistical and cranky. But he believes in the specific product he has in mind."[29]

Theodore Levitt sees the champion in the context of creativity and innovation, concepts that he feels are often confused: "Creativity is *thinking up* new things. Innovation is *doing* new things.... Ideas are useless unless used.... There is no shortage of creativity or creative people in American business. The shortage is of innovators.... Creative people tend to pass the responsibility for getting down to brass tacks to others.... The scarce people are the ones who have the know-how, energy, daring, and staying power to implement ideas. . . . Creativity without action-oriented follow-through is a barren form of behavior."[30]

Chakrabarti cited a study of 45 cases involving product development programs based on NASA innovations. Figure 11-2 outlines the results of this study. In 17 of the cases, the presence of a product champion could be clearly identified. In the remaining 28 cases, no such champion was perceived. Products that reached the test marketing

	Successful cases	Unsuccessful cases	Total
Product champion clearly present			17
No evidence of a product champion			28

Source: Adapted from Alok K. Chakrabarti, "The role of champion in product innovation," *California Management Review* 17 (Winter 1974):58-62.

FIGURE 11-2 Impact of a champion on product success.

stage or commercial launch were considered successful. Sixteen of 17 such products had a champion. Products that did not progress beyond technical feasiblity were deemed less successful. Only one of these 28 products had a champion.

Success Requires Consensus If others perceive a product champion as a loner or maverick, this perception will not aid the product's cause. The decision to adopt a new product idea is a collective decision made by members of several functional departments: engineering, manufacturing, finance, marketing, and perhaps corporate development. The champion, whether a maverick or not, must have the ability to bring these diverse members together in support of the product idea.[31]

Qualities of a Product Champion To be effective, a product champion must possess certain knowledge, abilities, and traits including these[31]:

1. *Technical competence:* the ability to analyze a product's capabilities, weaknesses, and potential applications plus the respect of others who must be convinced of these findings
2. *Company knowledge:* a clear understanding of corporate goals, financial resources, and marketing strategies so that only products supportive of these factors will be fostered
3. *Market knowledge:* the ability to assess a product's market potential realistically and to create a strong fit between a market's needs and the product's strengths
4. *Drive and assertiveness:* a strong desire to see a product succeed plus the perseverance to overcome obstacles and adversaries
5. *Political astuteness:* the unique ability to create consensus, communicate persuasively, and prod others to action without creating animosity; the knowledge to identify power centers and gain their support

The foregoing list strongly implies that product champions are neither in excess supply, nor can they be easily trained. However, management can structure an organization in such a way that potential champions may step forward more readily. In other words, volunteers respond more favorably to positive inducements.

CENTRALIZED VERSUS DECENTRALIZED R&D

Firms can either centralize or decentralize their R&D activity. As Figure 11-3 depicts, a functional compromise has merit. In this arrangement, the company conducts its theoretical or basic research at the corporate level, with the results communicated to all operating divisions. For example, the research scientists may hold quarterly seminars

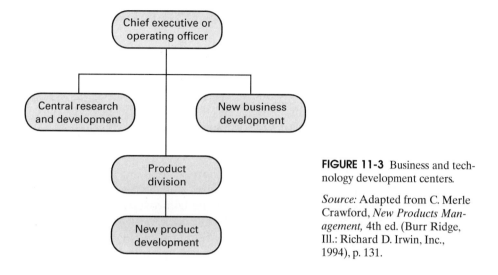

FIGURE 11-3 Business and technology development centers.

Source: Adapted from C. Merle Crawford, *New Products Management,* 4th ed. (Burr Ridge, Ill.: Richard D. Irwin, Inc., 1994), p. 131.

to update the engineering staffs of product divisions on the progress of various research projects. When a product division feels a particular technology could further its financial and marketing goals, it takes over the project and conducts applied research, which converts the basic technology into one or more commercial products. Some firms even use differential terminology, referring to centralized R&D and decentralized product development or product engineering.

The centralization of basic research has several advantages. First, it frees research scientists from the time constraints and pressures of a line operation, and provides them with an atmosphere more conducive to creative effort. Second, it consolidates all basic research into one location, making it more visible to the operating divisions while encouraging the synergistic exchange of ideas. Third, it allows an operating division to pick up any new technology that will enhance its business. Scientists are notorious for delaying the application of theoretical research on the premise that "it isn't perfected yet."

Centralization of basic research can have a major drawback. As discussed earlier, R&D should be closely aligned with the strategic direction of the firm. Unless provided with at least broad guidelines, research scientists may spend too much time and effort on technologies that do not readily support the firm's strategic thrust.[16] To avoid this possibility, top management should provide scientists with appropriate commercial guidance and review their research activities on a regular basis (either quarterly or semiannually). This review process also enhances communication by providing management with a better understanding of technology and giving R&D a stronger market orientation.[16]

New Business Development Department   As previously evidenced, innovation does not always have a technical focus. A firm might be interested in finding business opportunities with no direct relation to its current products, but that can provide desirable, synergistic effects (as when General Motors bought Hughes Electronics to gain greater expertise in computer-aided design and manufacturing). Since product divisions normally lack the interest and expertise to search for such opportunities, management establishes a staff department to perform this task (refer again to Figure 11-3). This department normally coordinates any mergers or acquisitions.

Organizational Alternatives for New Product Development

Industrial practitioners and academic researchers generally agree that new product development (NPD) projects can be staffed, organized, and managed in five different structural arrangements. Although the terminology employed may vary slightly, the underlying principles remain constant. Table 11-7 outlines these five structures.

STRENGTHS AND WEAKNESSES OF THE ALTERNATIVE STRUCTURES

A number of detailed studies have focused on NPD structures in an attempt to discern the most effective approach. These studies have generated some answers but almost as many questions along with some controversies. Several findings, however, are relatively clear. For example, referring back to the six categories of "new" products, simple line extensions or minor product improvements do not require separate organizational structures. In fact, a project matrix or project team would represent organizational overkill and actually impede progress. Thus, functional or functional matrix structures can handle such projects easily. On the other hand, new-to-the-world or new-to-the-firm projects exhibit complexities that require special focus and integration that the simpler structures cannot provide. In these instances, the project matrix or project team provides the required concentration and integration.[32] Let's examine the opposite ends of the structural continuum.

FUNCTIONAL STRUCTURE (NEW PRODUCTS COMMITTEE)

When a company does little innovating, a full-time new product operation would prove inefficient and wasteful. In this instance, an ad hoc committee examines and evaluates new product ideas that originate anywhere in the organization. Top management usu-

TABLE 11-7   Alternative NPD Project Structures

Structure	Description
Functional	The project is divided into segments and assigned to relevant functional areas (engineering, production, cost accounting, etc.) or groups within these areas. Functional and upper-level managers jointly coordinate the project.
Functional matrix	An assigned project manager with limited authority coordinates the project across the functional areas involved. Functional managers retain responsibility and authority for work done in their areas.
Balanced matrix	An assigned project manager oversees the project and shares responsibility and authority with functional managers. The project manager jointly directs activities with the appropriate functional manager, and they jointly approve many decisions.
Project matrix	An assigned project manager has primary responsibility and authority for completing the project. Functional managers provide necessary personnel and technical expertise.
Project team	An assigned project manager takes charge of a project team composed of personnel from the various functional areas and assigned to the project full-time. The functional managers have no direct involvement.

Source: Adapted from Erik W. Larson and David H. Gobeli, "Organizing for product development projects," *Journal of Product Innovation Management* 5 (September 1988):180-90.

ally staffs such a committee with managers from engineering, manufacturing, marketing, and finance. This committee meets at some interval appropriate to handle the workload (often monthly). The primary strengths of such a committee are these: (1) members view each other as experienced equals and progress fairly well toward a balanced, consensus opinion; (2) bureaucratic delay is minimized since the members usually report directly to top management; and (3) additional members can be added and then dismissed as needed, keeping the overall committee at an effective size.

On the negative side, committee members are not development specialists and tend to view this activity as secondary to their daily operating responsibilities. Given this attitude, they may indeed reach a consensus, but one of questionable strategic value. Further, with corporate managers sitting in at irregular intervals, none of the committee members assumes a strong leadership position. There is no product champion.

PROJECT TEAM (VENTURE TEAM)

The project team, also referred to as a venture team, resembles a new products committee in that its members come from the various functional departments and serve on a temporary basis (i.e., until the product has been fully developed). For that reason, the team leader must gain the full commitment of members and overcome their provincial viewpoints. The project team deals with only one development project at a time. Thus, if more than one project exists, there must be multiple teams.

Project teams more often exist in larger companies and work on major projects that are not readily assignable to any operating division. In this sense, they are similar to new business development units, although the latter entities usually concentrate on business aspects rather than the associated technology. At the completion of their projects, venture teams may be spun off into new operating departments or even separate subsidiaries.

The primary strengths of a project team are the speed and flexibility with which it can handle complex projects. These attributes stem from the singular focus of the group. This focus creates a sense of team identity and project ownership, which can generate extraordinary levels of commitment.[32] Project teams can develop technological opportunities of a magnitude unattainable through other organization forms.[33]

On the downside, the freedom and authority level of the venture team can trigger some serious interorganizational conflicts. To prevent such conflicts, top management must ensure that the resources allocated and attention given to the venture team and operating divisions are reasonably balanced.[33] In the short term, project teams tie up personnel and resources that cannot be shared with other corporate entities. In the longer term, something must be done with team members at the completion of the project. These individuals often experience career anxiety because they have lost touch with ongoing corporate activities and may not have another project waiting.[34]

PRODUCT MANAGER

Whether a company leans toward the permanence and expertise of a functional matrix or the flexibility and spirit of a project team, it must somehow interweave the needs of the market with its technological capabilities and financial resources. As discussed before, the developing product needs a champion. Although a project manager is assigned to the functional matrix, this person has too little authority to serve as a true leader. Only within a project matrix or as the leader of a project team does this person have sufficient delegated authority to lead by virtue of position.

When a NPD project represents a major investment, top management may try to "create" a champion. They look for someone with technical competence, market knowledge, strong interpersonal skills, and a goal-oriented nature. These skills and traits define a well-qualified product manager. Product managers can originate in any functional area but come most frequently from marketing.

Some companies, particularly in high-tech industries, fear that a marketing person will either lack the technical competence to make realistic product evaluations, or be too customer-oriented to make unbiased business decisions. An engineer with some market experience—such as an application engineer—is frequently chosen as a preferred alternative. R&D personnel are perceived as too far removed from the business activities to be effective in this position, while manufacturing personnel often lack both in-depth technical knowledge and marketing experience.

These trade-off considerations only serve to emphasize the range of skills and experience necessary for someone to function effectively as a product manager. Regardless of their background specialization, product managers must function with an objective, broad-based perspective. An ideal candidate often has a technical undergraduate degree, an MBA, and several years' experience selling and/or designing similar products.

Product Managers Versus NPD Managers   A lively debate continues as to whether product managers should have responsibility for ongoing products as well as new product development. One can construct compelling arguments either for or against a combined responsibility. These arguments parallel the strengths and weaknesses of functional committees and project teams. Functional committees, while keenly aware of current market conditions, suffer because members frequently give secondary attention to their NPD responsibilities. Project teams, conversely, have no distractions but can lose touch with market dynamics because of their isolation from customers and competition.

Personal experience and observation leads the writer to believe that the most effective product manager is one who can devote sufficient time to the development process, but whose decisions are based on firsthand knowledge of current market conditions. The critical issue centers on an individual—supported by a capable staff—who has the experience, drive, and creativity to cope with this combined, but synergistic, responsibility. Even these conditions prove inadequate unless the product manager has the unwavering support of corporate executives who appreciate the vital importance of an effective NPD program.[35]

AN OVERVIEW OF ORGANIZATIONAL ALTERNATIVES

All of the alternative organizations serve the same basic purposes: (1) to free general managers from direct involvement in the NPD process, (2) to bring together the multifaceted talents and inputs necessary for the success of the project, and (3) to separate the project, as much as possible and practical, from the pressures and distractions of ongoing business operations.

Given the complexity of this process and its potential impact on the growth and profitability of the firm, however, top management can neither delegate its ultimate decision making nor assume a disinterested "rubber stamp" posture regarding new product choices and strategy. This does not mean that senior officers should approve data sheets, price schedules, or advertising campaigns. It does, however, emphasize that top management retains the responsibility to ensure that each new product strategy has a positive impact on corporate goals. For example, a skimming price strategy probably will not jibe with an objective of maximized sales growth. Similarly, each new product strategy must fit with existing product strategies. This fit becomes particularly critical when the firm has autonomous product divisions, each with its own NPD program.

The New Product Development Process

The NPD process probably places greater pressure on a company to operate in a collaborative mode than any other business function. The concepts of a horizontal organization, multifunctional teams, partnering, and concurrent engineering, all play a role.

In time past, most companies treated the NPD process as a linear activity, with responsibility passed sequentially from one department to another, each operating relatively independent of the others. For example, R&D created a basic technology and passed it on to product engineering, who developed a commercial product. Manufacturing received the design specifications without the opportunity for discussion or modification. Marketing was eventually told to prepare appropriate promotion and distribution strategies prior to product launch. In many instances, the firm had not even surveyed the market to determine its needs and interests.

MARKET-CREATE-MAKE

The scenario described above followed the classic create-make-market paradigm. The NPD process began with the creation of a technology or product and continued through the marketing phase. However, when researchers studied Japanese firms in the 1980s to discover their "secrets to success," they found a significant difference in the sequence of events. Japanese firms spend a much greater percentage of their research budget studying a target market *before* the internal NPD process began.[14]

In a comprehensive study involving 203 new industrial products developed by 123 North American firms, two of the key factors separating winners from losers were (1) a strong predevelopment research effort and (2) a clear market orientation with constant customer contact and input.[36] Thus, the market-create-make paradigm seems to produce more winners for North American firms as well.

CONCURRENT ENGINEERING AND PARTNERING

The similar concepts of concurrent engineering and multifunctional teams stem from the combined goals to reach the market *sooner* and do so with a product that satisfies customers *better*. These goals lead to the associated needs for product quality, competitive pricing, and dependable service.

Instead of the linear process, concurrent engineering involves all affected departments at the outset. Engineering, manufacturing, marketing, purchasing, customer service, and technical support personnel become part of a multifunctional team to ensure that all aspects of the new product are considered and analyzed from the start. As discussed earlier in this chapter, all functional departments of the company should interact in setting the R&D strategy. Similarly, this multifunctional approach should continue into the NPD process.

Since many end products are essentially an assembly of individual components, the NPD process should involve suppliers as early as possible. Such involvement can lead to higher quality of the end product by optimizing component performance. It can also lead to lower costs by eliminating unnecessary specifications, duplicate testing, and redundant inventories.[37]

THE TWIN STREAMS OF DEVELOPMENT

Even though the process is described as new product development, the company is preparing its marketing plan simultaneously. Figure 11-4 depicts this parallel process. Based on the initial market research, the mutltifunctional team develops a product

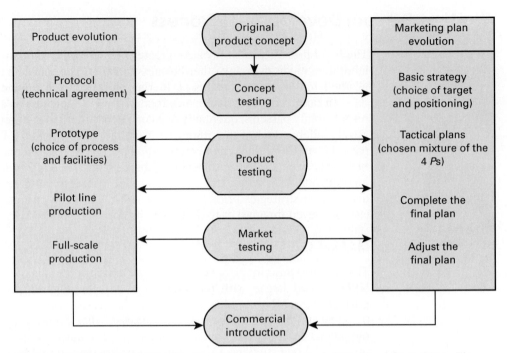

Source: Adapted from C. Merle Crawford, *New Products Management,* 4th ed. (Burr Ridge, Ill.: Richard D. Irwin, Inc., 1994). p. 131.

FIGURE 11-4 The twin streams of development.

concept (i.e., what the product should do for its user). This concept is then tested on potential users to determine whether they understand, appreciate, and would buy a product with these capabilities. Assuming a successful concept test, the technical team sets about to create a prototype that will embody the concept's attributes.

Marketing/Engineering Protocol   In this context, "protocol" means a basic agreement between engineering and marketing team members regarding customer needs and technical feasibility.[2]

Two aspects of this agreement are particularly important. First, marketing should describe their requirements in terms of customer *benefits* or *performance characteristics,* not product features. In other words, they should describe the product in terms of what it does rather than what it is. In addition, marketing subdivides these benefits into three categories: essential, desirable, and trade-offs. Essential benefits cannot be compromised; they represent the product's primary advantage. Desirable benefits remain so only if they do not detract from the essentials. For example, miniaturization may be desirable only if it does not detract from product reliability or ease of use. Trade-offs are benefits that impact each other negatively. Price and total performance level are common trade-offs and must often be negotiated before the development process is completed.

The second important aspect of the agreement concerns the limits of marketing's inputs. These inputs require specific knowledge of customer needs, competitors' capabilities, and general market conditions. In other words, marketing provides information that deals with its area of expertise. The description of the physical product should be limited to those features necessary for customer satisfaction or competitive positioning (e.g., the product must weigh less than x pounds or be smaller than y cubic inches). Engineers should have the freedom to utilize technology in whatever fashion will optimize performance and profitability. A written agreement tends to protect engineers from constant changes in performance goals; it also gives marketing greater assurance that the eventual product will meet the original goals.

A study by Gupta and Wilemon[38] confirms the need for a continuous interchange between marketing and R&D (engineering) personnel. Moreover, certain factors enhance the quality of this interchange. First, R&D managers prefer market data that helps them understand the business implications of their technical decisions. Second, they put greater faith in the information provided by marketers perceived as being technically competent. Finally, they prefer to receive information as a continuous flow throughout the development process. This latter point bears out the validity of Crawford's twin-stream concept.

Product Concept-Strategic Goal Compatibility   To ensure that the product will support a strategic thrust, business objectives and marketing strategy must precede product development; that is, the firm must first decide what business it wants to be in and what quantitative goals it seeks to achieve. These goals determine the screening criteria to be used in evaluating potential products. For example, in the 1960s, Texas Instruments established several underlying criteria for all new semiconductor products. Each had to be capable of sustaining a 15 percent compound growth rate over its life cycle, while generating a 25 percent pretax return on assets. Also, except for those products aimed at countering competition, new products had to stem from unique design or fabrication techniques that would afford a differential cost and/or performance advantage. The growth criterion forced marketers to search out the most promising business opportunities; the demand for differential advantage minimized "me-too" design efforts, while increasing the probability that products would provide a high satisfaction level in specific applications. The profitability criterion served as the cornerstone for financial analysis.

PRELIMINARY BUSINESS ANALYSIS

After prototype development and product testing but before pilot line production, (which may occur 3 to 6 months after concept testing), the firm should have enough information about customers, competitors, volume potential, tentative pricing, technology, investment level, and estimated production cost to make a first-pass financial analysis. Financial criteria (see Box 11-1, p. 290) help to determine whether or not the product should proceed toward commercial introduction.

The conversion of a concept into a physical product can represent a significant portion of the total development cost, particularly for firms that require an elaborate pilot facility to prove production feasibility. In these instances, the preliminary business analysis is of major consequence. Other firms, whose development costs are relatively modest, may choose to skip this stage entirely on the basis that most of the numbers come from conjecture, forecast, and guesswork. Research indicates that many project managers consider financial criteria the most important screening factors and will not ignore them at this point.[39]

In either case, some firms lack adequate resources, which forces them to drop otherwise promising projects. Combining the business analysis with other selection criteria provides the firm with a means of choosing the best projects for further development, while other projects are either dropped or put on indefinite hold.

The two preceding paragraphs assume that product concepts are truly innovative. If, on the other hand, the concepts are merely revisions of earlier developments, the financial data would be mostly factual and the decisions relatively simple.

PILOT LINE PRODUCTION

Several important events will occur during this stage. The product concept has been converted into a physical reality, proving technical feasibility. The manufacturing department, at least on a limited volume basis, will now confirm or negate its ability to reproduce the product within the cost estimates and performance guidelines previously established. The marketing department, when functional samples are available, will approach selected customers to verify that the product's attributes do satisfy specific application requirements. It is also important to reaffirm the market potential that was estimated earlier. During an extended development process that consumes a year or more, significant changes can occur in market and economic conditions, competitive capabilities, and customer priorities. A product concept that held great promise a year ago may be virtually obsolete today.

Designing to Cost Goals   Another aspect of the development stage is particularly important to marketers of industrial products. Given the profit-oriented nature of business buying decisions, price plays a key role. As opposed to consumer goods such as designer jeans or automobiles, business products afford little status or ego satisfaction to justify a higher price. Consequently, price should be as important a design criterion as product performance or quality. Many firms, however, allow price to be a random result rather than a specific goal. Costs drive selling price rather than a target selling price dictating a maximum acceptable cost. An example may help to clarify this point.

Suppose that the XYZ company is developing a computer-controlled, multihead drill press capable of productivity and accuracy levels unobtainable with current equipment. The firm has surveyed the market and found that customers are willing to pay approximately $5,000, a 20 percent premium over the price of conventional drill presses. XYZ can normally generate an acceptable profit by doubling its direct labor and material cost to establish an original equipment manufacturer (OEM) sales price.

The preferable approach in this instance would be to set a $2,500 labor and material cost goal along with essential performance criteria. Engineering and manufacturing would know how much latitude in cost they had to achieve the necessary performance. Many firms, however, emphasize performance criteria without establishing cost limits. Under these conditions, XYZ engineers might design an excellent product that meets or exceeds all essential specifications. Unfortunately, the cost ends up at $3,500, dictating an OEM price of $7,000. This price significantly reduces market demand and potential profits, in effect negating the financial data generated in the preliminary business analysis. In other words, the information that indicated the project should move forward is no longer valid. Now, instead of enjoying the fruits of their labor, the firm will expend wasted effort to determine who was "wrong."

Market Testing   Market testing of new business products typically centers on the product evaluation of *major potential users.* Salespeople must identify these firms and then interact with individuals who make the buying decisions as well as the technical personnel who will actually evaluate the product. Given the oligopolistic nature of most industries, acceptance of a product by relatively few users can often assure its success. For example, if Apple, Compaq, IBM, and Packard-Bell all approved the use of a new disk drive in their computers, the disk drive manufacturer would have no worries about keeping the production line running. In fact, limited production capacity might become the primary problem.

Acceptance of a new product by major users, as pointed out in Chapter 10, is neither automatic nor a rapid process regardless of the product's merits. A new component, for example, may require redesign of the end equipment to make full use of its cost or performance advantage. The equipment manufacturer (OEM) may not have personnel immediately available to do the redesign work. The production manager may convince other decision makers that it would be unwise to disrupt the smooth-running production line, since potential cost savings might be offset by lower product quality or reduced yields (as a result of the impact of change on production workers). Even if the OEM decides to make the necessary changes on a limited quantity basis, final approval may rest on the results of field tests. In other words, market testing of the component could hinge on market testing of the customer's end equipment.

The foregoing comments do not imply a gloomy prospect for new products. Rather, if a product addresses an important need and satisfies it well, market acceptance will probably follow. The time delay, however, can easily stretch into months. Hence, the new product supplier may face an extended period during which production capacity is in place but no sizable demand develops. Since some customers will have purchased limited quantities for evaluation purposes, the subsequent delay gives the impression of a market failure, that is, a very brief growth followed by decline. Actually, the growth phase of the product life cycle has not yet begun.

COMPLETING THE BUSINESS PLAN

Through the prototype development and product testing stages, the firm has determined both technical and production feasibility along with current market demand and time/volume projections. A formal business plan can now be established. This plan should include quantification of all relevant financial criteria to determine whether the physical product can be manufactured and marketed profitably.

Controlling the Product Introduction   In addition to a financial plan, marketing must develop a plan that spells out and coordinates all the tactical programs that lead up to and include commercial introduction. (After major customers have been identified and sampled during the market testing stage, marketers may have to make adjustments to the final plan.) Pricing must be established, an advertising program developed, the sales force trained, distributor inventories put in place, and so forth.

Table 11-8 depicts a planning checklist for new product introduction. While such a list will vary appreciably with product, industry differences, and variations in company policies, it focuses on two important factors. First, the product planner must coordinate a broad range of activities extending *outside* the marketing department. Second, the planner must establish a sequencing of activities, time requirements, and individual responsibilities. Some firms refer to these checklists as "What, When, Who" or "W³" forms. Companies use this information to create a control mechanism that tracks the sequence of activities and calls attention to potential delay problems.

Critical Path Method (CPM)   Coordinating the activities of multiple, independent departments and staying on schedule presents one of the most challenging tasks in new product introduction. For example, the sales force cannot be trained to sell the new product until a data sheet has been developed by engineering, but the engineers will not finalize specifications before they receive yield information from the production department. Pricing also depends on this yield information, and without pricing, distributors will not place orders for their initial inventories.

As Figure 11-5 shows, CPM graphically displays the various sequences involved in the introduction process along with the time estimated for completion of each task. The critical path is that sequence of tasks or activities that consumes the *greatest*

		Area/Person Responsible	Prior Task	Time (weeks)
Manufacturing Process				
M1	Order production equipment	Mfg/Purchasing	None	13
M2	Hire production workers	Mfg/Human resources	None	3
M3	Install production equipment	Manufacturing	M1	2
M4	Start pilot production run	Manufacturing	M2, M3	2
M5	Determine production yields	Manufacturing	M4	1
M6	Compute production costs	Cost accounting	M5	1
M7	Begin volume production	Manufacturing	M6, S4	1
Product Engineering				
E1	Analyze production yields	Product engineering	M5	2
E2	Evaluate product quality	Quality control	M5	5
E3	Finalize product specifications	Product eng/Product mgr	E1, E2	2
E4	Provide data sheet information	Product engineering	E3	1
Sales Force				
S1	Hire required salespeople	Sales manager	None	3
S2	Complete product training	Product manager	S1, E4	2
S3	Contact major customers to determine demand	Sales force	S2, A6	3
S4	Prepare initial sales forecast	Sales force	S3, P4	1
S5	Establish annual sales quotas	Sales manager	S4	1
Advertising/Promotion				
A1	Establish promotional budget	Product manager	None	2
A2	Complete space ad layouts	Advertising manager	A1	4
A3	Select appropriate media	Product/Adv managers	A1	1
A4	Set space ad scheduling	Product/Adv managers	A1	2
A5	Run initial ads	Advertising manager	A2-4	1
A6	Prepare and print data sheets	Product/Adv managers	E4	3
A7	Prepare and mail direct mailers	Product/Adv managers	A6	2
Distribution				
D1	Compose distributor agreement	Marketing manager	None	1
D2	Determine distribution needed	Sales/Product managers	S3	3
D3	Select and sign distributors	Sales manager	D1, D2	2
D4	Obtain initial stocking orders	Sales force	D3, P5	2
D5	Ship stocking orders	Manufacturing	D4, M4	1
D6	Train distributor personnel	Sales force	D5	3
Pricing				
P1	Analyze competitors' pricing	Product manager	None	1
P2	Analyze production costs	Product manager	M6	1
P3	Estimate demand elasticity	Product manager	S3	1
P4	Establish OEM pricing	Product manager	P1-3	1
P5	Establish distributor pricing	Product manager	P4	1

TABLE 11-8 Checklist for New Product Introduction

amount of time. Other paths, requiring less total time, could incur some slippage without affecting the introduction date. With CPM, program coordinators know which tasks must be monitored closely and who is responsible for their completion.[40]

More recent studies take issue with the classical concept that the critical path is defined as that which consumes the most time. An argument is made that the *probability*

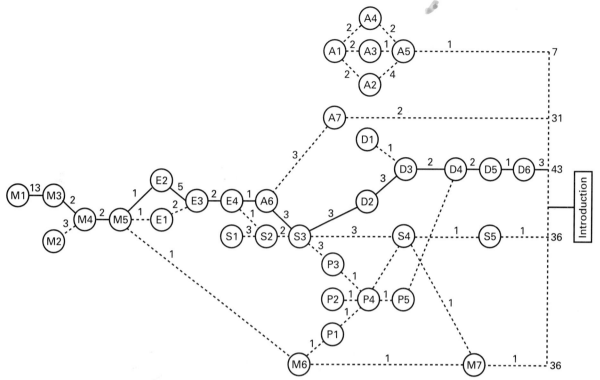

Note: Circles represent the activities listed in Table 11-8. Uncircled numbers are the weeks required to complete the preceding activity. The solid line indicates the critical path.

FIGURE 11-5 A critical path network.

of performing on time must also be taken into consideration. Thus, a path predicted to consume less time may become critical as a result of a low probability of performance.[41]

Other Control Techniques   Depending on the complexity of the scheduling task facing the firm, control mechanisms can range from a simple bar chart to a complex computer program. Program Evaluation and Review Technique (PERT) is an example of a sophisticated, computerized control system designed to monitor a complex development process. The U.S. Navy originated PERT to monitor the design and development process of the Polaris missile and submarine. No other scheduling system in use at the time could satisfactorily track the thousands of interrelated activities.

Companies do not commonly use programs as complex as PERT to monitor commercial products. In essence, the firm must weigh the cost of performance delays against the cost of the system designed to prevent them.

COMMERCIAL INTRODUCTION

A product becomes a commercial entity when formally introduced to a target market. Viewed from another perspective, commercialization is the implementation of a tactical marketing program. This implies that all the action items associated with market communication, product distribution, and customer support activities will be triggered. Weaknesses, or failure to act, in any of these areas can undermine the entire program. An untrained or uninformed sales force, lack of introductory advertising, failure to stock distributors adequately, or an understaffed customer service organization can trigger a commercial disaster.

Looking Back

No manufacturer can enjoy continued market success without continually improving the cost effectiveness and performance capability of its product line. Such improvement, unfortunately, often obsoletes existing products. But the firm has only two choices: obsolete its own products or be obsoleted by competition.

New product ideas can come from the market (either customers or competitors) or from various sources within the firm—top management, R&D personnel, the production or marketing department, or intrapreneuring individuals. When the idea originates externally, the firm must determine whether it has the technology, resources, and motivation to respond. Not all business opportunities justify product development. When the idea originates internally, the firm must verify that identifiable needs, capable of generating sufficient volume, exist in the market. Otherwise, a product idea that is very exciting technologically may become a commercial failure.

Innovation does not end with the creation of a new product. Creative firms can and do lose market share to imitators who find more effective and less costly methods of production, distribution, and marketing.

The criteria used to decide which product ideas to pursue should stem from the marketing strategy, which in turn, must support corporate objectives. Thus, the product development process becomes an organized, logical extension of strategic planning rather than a haphazard, expedient response to changes in either market conditions or the firm's technological capability.

Various alternative structures exist through which the firm can carry out the NPD process. The complexity and focus of the structure coincides with the complexity and investment risk of the development project.

Regardless of the organizational structure chosen, top management should be guided by three primary principles: (1) creativity thrives only in an atmosphere that encourages risk-taking and innovation, (2) every product idea needs a champion who is committed to its success, and (3) successful development depends on a coordinated team effort involving all relevant business functions.

A modern, effective NPD process involves all relevant functional departments at the outset (concurrent engineering) and brings chosen suppliers into the decision making (partnering). During this process, the firm will sequentially answer three critical questions. Is there a market for the idea? Can the idea be transformed into a physical product? Can the physical product be manufactured and marketed profitably? Thus, successful commercialization will depend on customer needs, market conditions, technological feasibility, and profit potential. Although concerned individuals within the firm (top management, engineers, manufacturing personnel, financial analysts, and marketers) must decide how to answer the three questions, both customers and competitors will act as prominent decision influencers.

Questions for Discussion

1. A major manufacturer of medical equipment approaches one of its suppliers with specifications for a precision switch that has been tentatively designed into a new blood analyzer. The switch supplier thinks existing technology can be used but has not previously produced

a device with such close tolerances. What information and assurances should the switch supplier have before embarking on a full-scale development program?

2. If the idea for this precision component had originated within the switch manufacturer's product development group, how would this origin alter the need for information? Does this change the likelihood that the product can be successfully and profitably marketed?

3. "A firm is much better off if the majority of its new products originate internally. As long as the technology is 'state of the art,' and the products are priced aggressively, there is bound to be a ready market." Respond to this statement.

4. Which is more important: creating a constant flow of new products or continually updating and improving the current product line? Explain your answer.

5. Given the challenge American electronic firms face in trying to regain market position, what specific tasks would you assign to the marketing department; to R&D; to manufacturing? Would you have them work independently or collaborate? Why?

6. Describe the major strengths and weaknesses of new product committees and new product departments. Which is your personal preference and why?

7. What generalized but significant comments should be made about all forms of new product development organizations?

8. Explain the relationship between new product development and strategic planning. Should one precede the other? Why?

9. We discussed an agreement that should be reached between marketing and engineering personnel before the product idea is converted into a physical entity. What elements or factors should be included in this agreement? Why is an agreement necessary?

10. "Price should drive cost instead of cost dictating price." Explain the meaning and implications of this statement.

Endnotes

1. Robert G. Cooper, "New product success in industrial firms,"*Industrial Marketing Management* 11 (1982):215-23.

2. C. Merle Crawford, *New Products Management,* 5th ed. (Burr Ridge, Ill.: Richard D. Irwin, Inc., 1997), p. 4.

3. C. Jackson Grayson, Jr., and Carla O'Dell, *American Business: A Two-Minute Warning* (New York: The Free Press, 1988).

4. *New Product Management for the 1980s* (New York: Booz, Allen, and Hamilton, 1982).

5. Austin K. Pryor and Michael Shays, "Growing the business with intrapreneurs," *Business Quarterly* 57 (Spring 1993):42-47+; also Erik G. Rule and Donald W. Irwin, "Fostering intrapreneurship: The new competitive edge," *Journal of Business Strategy* (May/June 1988), pp. 44-47.

6. Donald F. Kuratko, Jeffrey S. Hornsby, and Douglas W. Naffziger, "Implement entrepreneurial thinking in established organizations," *Advanced Management Journal* 58 (Winter 1993):28-33+.

7. "Intrapreneurship at Bell Atlantic," *Business Quarterly* 57 (Spring 1993):46-7.

8. William E. Halal, "The transition from hierarchy to—what?" *Technological Forecasting and Social Change* 45 (February 1994):207-10.

9. See Leigh Lawton and A. Parasuraman, "The impact of the marketing concept on new product planning," *Journal of Marketing* 44 (Winter 1980):19-25; also Eric von Hippel, "Successful industrial products from customer ideas," *Journal of Marketing* 42 (January 1978):39-49.

10. See Robert G. Cooper, "New products: What distinguishes the winners?" *Research Technology Management* 33 (November-December 1990):27-31; also Robert G. Cooper and Elko

J. Kleinschmidt, "Screening new products for potential winners," *Long Range Planning* 26 (December 1993):74-81.

11. C. Merle Crawford, "The dual-drive concept of product innovation," *Business Horizons* 34 (May-June 1991):32-8.

12. Roland W. Schmitt, "Successful corporate R&D," *Harvard Business Review* 63 (May-June 1985):124-8.

13. Eric von Hippel, "Successful industrial products from customer ideas," *Journal of Marketing* 42 (January 1978):39-49

14. Robert G. Cooper, "Predevelopment activities determine new product success," *Industrial Marketing Management* 17 (1988):237-47.

15. "Technology gives the U.S. a big edge," *Business Week* (June 30, 1980), p. 102+.

16. William J. Spencer and Deborah D. Triant, "Strengthening the link between R&D and corporate strategy," *Journal of Business Strategy* (January-February 1989):38-42.

17. "How to teach old plants new tricks," *Business Week* (June 16, 1989):130.

18. "Trucks set pace in so-so year," *Automotive News* (January 8, 1996), p. 1+.

19. "Pssst! Want a secret for making superproducts?" *Business Week* (October 2, 1989), pp. 106+; also "Smart factories: America's turn?" *Business Week* (May 8, 1989), pp. 142+.

20. Donald L. Mitchell, "Reducing cycle time," *Across the Board* 31 (May 1994):56-7.

21. "Nurturing those ideas," *Business Week* (June 16, 1989):106-7.

22. See David A. Boag and Brenda L. Rinholm, "New product management practices of small high-technology firms," *Journal of Product Innovation Management* 6 (1989):109-22; also Cooper, "Predevelopment Activities . . . ," p. 239; and Peter L. Link, "Keys to New Product Success and Failure," *Industrial Marketing Management* 16 (1987):109-18.

23. "Beyond sourcing teams," *Purchasing* 116 (June 16, 1994):14-15.

24. P. Ranganath Nayak and Bruce M. Thompson, "Technology must be managed: A focus on strengths and multifunction teams are two keys," *Industry Week* 242 (December 20, 1993):57-8.

25. Peter E. Drucker, "The discipline of innovation," *Harvard Business Review* 63 (May-June 1985):67-72.

26. Ilkka A. Ronkainen, "Criteria changes across product development stages," *Industrial Marketing Management* 14 (August 1985):171-78.

27. See C. Merle Crawford, "New product failure rates—facts and fallacies," *Research Management* (September 1979), pp. 9-13; also C. Merle Crawford, "New product failure rates: A reprise," *Research Management* (July-August 1987), pp. 20-4.

28. "R&D in 1988," *Business Week* (June 16, 1989):178-9.

29. Thomas J. Peters and Robert H. Waterman, Jr., *In Search of Excellence* (New York: Harper & Row, 1982), p. 208.

30. Theodore Leavitt, "Ideas are useless unless used," *Inc.* (February 1981), p. 96, as cited by Peters and Waterman.

31. Alok K. Chakrabarti, "The role of champion in product innovation," *California Management Review* 17 (Winter 1974):58-62.

32. Erik W. Larson and David H. Gobeli, "Organizing for product development projects," *Journal of Product Innovation Management* 5 (September 1988):180-90; also Erik W. Larson and David H. Gobeli, "Matrix management: Contradictions and insights," *California Management Review* 29 (Summer 1987):126-38; and C. Merle Crawford, "The role of the general manager in the R&D/marketing interface," *Advances in Telecommunication Management* 1 (1990):93-8.

33. Ken Murphy, "Venture teams help companies create new products," *Personnel Journal* 71 (March 1992):60+.

34. Erik W. Larson and David H. Gobeli, "Organizing for product development projects," *Journal of Product Innovation Management* 5 (September 1988):180-90.

35. Crawford, *New Products Management,* 5th ed. (Homewood, Ill: Richard D. Irwin, Inc., 1997).

36. Robert G. Cooper and Elko J. Kleinschmidt, "Screening new products for potential winners," *Long Range Planning* 26 (December 1993):74-81.

37. Murray R. Millson, S. P. Raj, and David Wilemon, "Strategic partnering for developing new products," *Research Technology Management* 39 (May-June 1996):41-9.

38. Ashok K. Gupta and David Wilemon, "The credibility-cooperation connection at the R&D-marketing interface," *Journal of Innovation Management* 5 (January 1988):20-31.

39. Robert G. Cooper and Ulrike de Brentani, "Criteria for screening new industrial products," *Industrial Marketing Management* 13 (1984):149-56.

40. See, for instance, Glenn R. Dundas and Kathleen A. Krentler, "Critical path method for introducing an industrial product," *Industrial Marketing Management* 11 (1982):125-31.

41. H.M. Soroush, "The most critical path in a PERT network," *Journal of the Operational Research Society* 45 (March 1994):287-300.

Bibliography

Cooper, Robert G., and Ulrike de Brentani, "Criteria for screening new product ideas," *Industrial Marketing Management* 13 (1984):149-56.

Cooper, Robert G., and Elko J. Kleinschmidt, "Screening new products for potential winners," *Long Range Planning,* 26 (December 1993):74-81.

Chakrabarti, Alok K., "The role of champion in product innovation," *California Management Review* 17 (Winter 1974):58-62.

Crawford, C. Merle, *New Products Management,* 5th ed. (Homewood, Ill.: Richard D. Irwin, Inc., 1997).

Grayson, C. Jackson, Jr., and Carla O'Dell, *American Business: Two-Minute Warning* (New York: The Free Press, 1988).

Gupta, Ashok K., and David Wilemon, "The credibility-cooperation connection at the R&D-marketing interface," *Journal of Innovation Management* 5 (January 1988):20-31.

"Innovation in America," *Business Week,* Special issue (June 1989).

Kurato, Donald F., Jeffrey S. Hornsby, and Douglas W. Naffinger, "Implement entrepreneurial thinking in established organizations," *Advanced Management Journal* 58 (Winter 1993):28-33+.

Larson, Erik W., and David H. Gobeli, "Organizing for product development projects," *Journal of Product Innovation Management* 5 (September 1988):180-90.

Millson, Murray W., S.P. Raj, and David Wilemon, "Strategic partnering for developing new products," *Research Technology Management* 39 (May-June 1996):41-9.

Pryor, Austin K., and Michael Shays, "Growing the Business with Intrapreneurs," *Business Quarterly* 57 (Spring 1993):42-7+.

Schmitt, Roland W., "Successful Corporate R&D," *Harvard Business Review* 63 (May-June 1985):124-8.

Soroush, H.M., "The most critical path in a PERT network," *Journal of the Operational Research Society* 45 (March 1994):287-300.

Spencer, William J. and Deborah D. Triant, "Strengthening the link between R&D and corporate strategy," *Journal of Business Strategy* (January-February 1989):38-42.

CHAPTER **12** Business Services Marketing

Business services marketing have become a very large slice of the total business sector environment. More than 70 percent of America's employment, including government employees, was in the service sectors compared with approximately 23 percent employment in manufacturing, as seen in Figure 12-1. Services contribute 67 percent of GNP, an increase of 33 percent since 1950.[1] The U.S. economy features an increasingly professional services sector, which currently leads the world with 12.7 percent of the international services export market.[2]

Business services, including technical, managerial, delivery and transportation, financial, and engineering consulting, have grown appreciably since 1980 and now constitute one of America's most significant exports. Much of this growth has been the result of the specialization of labor and increases in production output as well as in economic activity. In addition, the quantum leaps in the advancement of the state-of-the-art technology involved in each of these fields, further emphasizes the importance of business services. These state-of-the-art advancements include data and information transmission; computer advancements, such as CAD-CAM, wonder chips that can store more data, increased memory and data storage; optical data scanning; computer image enhancement in the fields of manufacturing, medicine, meteorology, cartography; and quantum jumps in the use of data in the information superhighway. All of these advancements have enhanced the demand for many of the business services, but particularly for technological communication business services.

Another growth area that has exacerbated the rapid change in the demand for business services has been business's propensity to move toward more outsourcing of many of the technical services, previously performed by the company's in-house employees. The practice of newer managerial concepts such as concurrent engineering, total quality management, forming horizontal organizations and the drive to down-size an organization have provided further strength to the demand for outside experts in business services. Therefore, the objectives of this chapter are to cover the following areas:

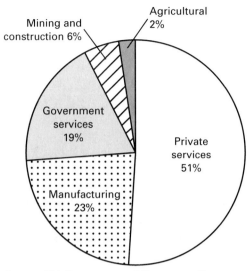

Source: U.S. Department of Commerce, Bureau of Economic Analysis.

FIGURE 12-1 U.S. workers by industry. NOTE: Fractions have been rounded off; hence the sum is greater than 100%.

1. The magnitude of the size of business services and its importance to the other sectors of business marketing
2. The differences between business services and product services
3. The major problems associated with marketing business services
4. Marketing strategy in the business service industry

Magnitude of Business Services

Business services can be defined as "any act or performance that one party can offer to another that is essentially intangible and does not result in the ownership of anything. Its production may or may not be tied to a physical product."[3]

Business services are often overlooked in their dominance and importance because they are often taken for granted. Without reviewing all the listed services, shown in Table 12-1, an inspection of just one service field—transportation—can show the importance of business services to both business organizations and their customers. Transportation modes—rail, air, water, and motor—carry the products used in business and commerce. Business services marketing has become an essential element in the normal course of running a business; however, business services marketing has not received the coverage in academic literature it deserves. A review of Table 12-1 will show that many of these services are indispensable when running a business of any type.

It is important to distinguish the differences between the two distinct types of services. First, a **business service industry** exists that includes transportation, advertising, management consulting, marketing consulting, engineering consulting services, and lawyers, to name a few. Second, there are **product service functions,** which are associated with manufacturing firms and include high product quality, on-time product delivery, proper installation, personal follow-up, and so on. The first area encompasses all the marketing acumen necessary for a stand alone business to be the successful. The second area is more isolated and is associated with tangible products.

TABLE 12-1 A Partial List of Business Services	
Accounting services	Marketing consulting
Advertising services	Marketing research
Architects	Medical and dental services
Building and real estate management	Meeting facilities
Car rental	Moving services
Communications and speech writing	New product testing services
Computer programming	Office equipment rentals
Construction design services	Office layout design
Credit reporting	Overnight letter service
Data processing services	Party services
Educational and training services	Personnel services
Employment agencies	Petrochemical design services
Engineering services	Printing services
Entertainment services	Private aircraft service
Excavation services	Public relations
Factory layout design	Records management
Fax service	Recreational services
Financial information	Restaurant services
Food and catering services	Retailing
Health and hospital services	Sales promotion services
Helicopter service	Satellite services
Hotel services	Store window design
Industrial equipment leasing	Taxi service
Insurance	Technical inspection services
Interior design services	Technical research
Investment banking	Telecommunications services
Janitorial services	Telemarketing services
Landscaping/lawn services	Telephone service
Laundry and cleaning	Traffic management services
Legal and law firm services	Transportation (all kinds)
Limousine service	Veterinary services
Mailing and delivery	Videotaping service
Maintenance services	Warehouse and storage
Management consulting	Wellness clinics
Market reports	Wholesaling

Professional Business Service Marketing: Problems and Strategies

A few years ago, most providers of professional services—consultants, lawyers, health care providers, and so on—relied on their country club connections and reputations to obtain contacts with prospective clients in business. Times have changed. Today's professionals have to be actively involved in the marketing of their services because of increased competition[4]:

> Newsletters, press releases, and other public relation tools are widely used by accounting, law, architectural, engineering, and management consulting firms. And, in a less

visible way, professional service firms of all types and sizes are employing marketing research and strategic planning with increasing frequency.

The marketing of professional services presents a unique set of problems which require a different marketing approach from the marketing of tangible products.

Differences Between Business Goods and Business Services

Business services marketing is more complex than business goods marketing.[5] Obviously a service is not the same as a tangible product, but the awareness that business services require a much different marketing strategy is not as obvious as it should be to many practitioners and academicians. Service knowledge and product knowledge are not the same.[6] The major difference between the two offerings, besides the obvious intangibility versus tangibility, is the difference in customer perception of a service versus a product.[7] When marketing a service, it is critical that the firm be able to determine what traits of the service are valued most highly by the individual customer. The successful marketer will be the firm that can develop and market services which provide maximum long-term value to their customers.[8] A tangible object can be described, examined, and quantified. A business service, which is often intangible—with such exceptions as a consulting report, an engineering design, an architect's drawings, or a software program—is frequently difficult to quantify or to even visualize by the prospective customer.

THE ISSUE OF TANGIBILITY

As seen in Figure 12-2, it's not always easy to distinguish a business service as either a purely tangible product or a purely intangible service. A continuum exists, starting with a very tangible product, such as a drop forge, to a very intangible service, such as an executive management seminar. Obviously, a drop forge used in the production process for stamping out hoods for automobiles is a very tangible product. Executive management seminars are very intangible, except for the take-home materials a seminar might produce. In the center of the continuum would lie convention hotels, where the offering is basically a service, since meeting rooms are provided, along with sleeping accommodations, and hotel meals are a very tangible product associated with the total convention hotel service.

Although establishing the difference between goods and services can be a bit difficult, the dichotomy that *goods are produced* and *services are performed* establishes the major reason to separate the different marketing strategies used for each activity. Services marketing people cannot simply take existing product marketing strategies and "nip and tuck" them to fit their services needs. The significance of this statement is substantiated by the analysis of the six differences between products and services that follows. Six significant differences set services apart from tangible products. Table 12-2 shows the first four differences; the remaining two are contributed by Jackson and Cooper[5]:

1. The *intangibility* of the service
2. The *inseparability* of a service's production and consumption
3. The *heterogeneity* or greater degree of variability
4. The *perishability* of a service that can't be inventoried

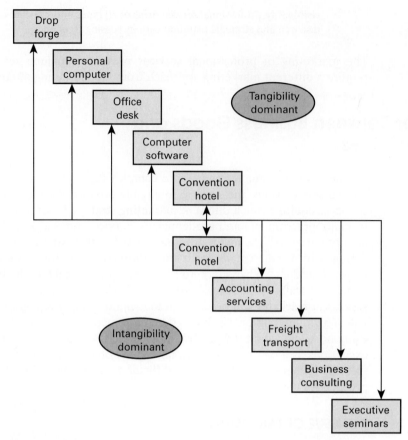

Source: Adapted from G. Lynn Shostack, "Breaking free from product marketing," *Journal of Marketing* 41 (April 1977):77. Reprinted by permission of the American Marketing Association.

FIGURE 12-2 Business services versus products, based on the degree of tangibility.

5. The *specialization* that requires customization for customers
6. The *technology* required because services can contain greater complexities

INTANGIBILITY

Services are physically intangible, in most instances, since they cannot be touched, tasted, smelled, or seen as can physically tangible products. *Knowledge* is the cornerstone of most business service providers and this constitutes the most difficult concept for most people to grasp. Services such as life insurance or health insurance coverage, management and marketing consulting, technical and engineering inspections and consulting, and auditing are essential functions. Each area comprises many abstract concepts, as perceived by the potential buyer, yet it is difficult for the buyer's mind to grasp the intricacies and the significance of three major concepts: (1) When are the services needed? (2) When are the services completed? (3) When do the services performed meet the expected quality set by the buyer or buying center center?

Buyers do not always have the expertise to be able to make a quality judgment. For example, organizational buyers who may be searching for employee medical coverage for the first time may find it difficult to judge which HMO is best for the

TABLE 12-2 Unique Service Features, Resulting Marketing Problems, and Suggested Marketing Strategies		
Unique Service Features	*Resulting Marketing Problems*	*Suggested Marketing Strategies*
Intangibility	1. Cannot be stored. 2. Cannot be protected through patents. 3. Cannot be readily displayed or communicated. 4. Prices are difficult to set.	1. Stress tangible cues. 2. Use personal sources more than nonpersonal sources. 3. Simulate or stimulate word-of-mouth communications. 4. Create strong organizational image. 5. Use cost accounting to help set prices. 6. Engage in postpurchase communications.
Inseparability	1. Consumer involved in production. 2. Other consumers involved in production. 3. Centralized mass production of services difficult.	1. Emphasize selection and training of public contact. 2. Manage consumers 3. Use multisite locations.
Heterogeneity	1. Standardization and quality control difficult to achieve.	1. Industrialize services (standardizing certain common service). 2. Customize service.
Perishability	1. Services cannot be inventoried.	1. Use strategies to cope with fluctuating demand. 2. Make simultaneous adjustments in demand and capacity to achieve closer match between the two.

Source: Valarie A. Zeithaml, A. Parasuraman, and Leonard L. Berry, "Problems and strategies in services marketing," *Journal of Marketing* 49 (Spring 1985): 33-46. Reprinted by permission of the American Marketing Association.

employees and the company, since their expertise is limited. Their lack of expertise in this area may encourage them to duplicate the actions of a competitor or a similar company's choice.

Services Intangibility   Business services are performances rather than produced objects.[9] Services must be evaluated and purchased on either "credence" or "experience" qualities. Credence qualities involve obtaining the service purchasers' faith in the competency of those who sell the services. Experience qualities, on the other hand, refer to the fact that most customers must evaluate service companies on the basis of their personal experience, since they lack the necessary technical skills to otherwise assess a service providers' capabilities.[10]

Credence Levels   Not only are credence and experience attributes needed to assist in the purchase decision, they are also needed after the sale is made. Few nonprofessional organizational buyers are able to determine whether an accounting audit has been performed thoroughly and correctly, or a building has been engineered properly and safely designed, or a court case has been properly pleaded.[11] It is difficult for customers to conceptualize entirely as to what business services are offered or to evaluate the business services they have received. Because of these difficulties the customer tends to look for "tangible evidence of the intangible service" when evaluating the service.

Marketing strategy must take the customer's dilemma of uncertainty and lack of expertise into consideration. Not only must business service marketers clarify their service offering to their customers, but they must also assist customers' attempts to evaluate them by "providing tangible surrogate features whenever possible."[11] An insurance company selling a life policy to a corporate executive produces a tangible folder containing all of the fine print that most people would not read until it becomes necessary. A marketing consultant produces a colorful final proposal as tangible evidence that the recommended plan is workable. Federal Express built its business on customer value through excellence of execution, but its competitor, Airborne, has chosen to create value and competitive advantage through excellence in customer care. Thus, Airborne attempts to make an intangible perception into a tangible advantage.

Some evidence indicates that business organizations attempt to enhance the tangibility of their service offering by carefully selecting and training customer-contact personnel, who encourage their customers to tell others about their services, and by gearing their marketing programs to project a specific company image. One accountant, for instance, states that it is important "to do things like setting out accounts neatly and carefully, answering letters promptly and making sure you look as if you are totally familiar with the client's affairs."[4] A law office exudes legal competence with its law books, leather chairs, and efficient receptionist. An advertising agency consciously projects the fast-paced momentum of creativity in their organization. A janitorial service uses a clean, white truck to project an image of its efficiency. A marketer of a painting service dresses in a suit and tie to project a professional image to the client, rather than show up in painting garb. Service marketers are forced to give physical evidence of their abstract offerings to communicate properly with prospective clients.

Advertising consultants frequently maintain posh offices, drive expensive cars, and entertain lavishly to make what is intangible, tangible to the client. An outward show of success will impress upon the client the service provider's past successes. Many industrial consulting firms insist their sales reps drive Buicks, BMWs, or Mercedes rather than Chevrolets, Hondas, or VWs.

Management consultants market their ability to be able to perform the client's task by displaying advanced degrees, a track record of past accomplishments, and the word of previously satisfied clients. The buyer has to wait and wonder if the consultant knows what he is doing, while the consultant performs his investigation and submits his final report. The report takes on its own personality with graphics, charts, line diagrams, intensive analysis, and adroit conclusions which are designed to impress and convey to the client that the job was well done. The report also is a vehicle used to impress on the buyer that the service provider knew what they were doing and that what is recommended is best for the client.

Overcoming Buyer Uncertainty To overcome buyer uncertainty in the purchase and evaluation of any business service, Bloom suggests that personal contacts, public relations activities, advertising, and service delivery be designed to educate clients about the following[4]:

1. When they should seek professional services
2. Which attributes to consider in evaluating different providers
3. How to communicate their concerns, desires, or other issues to professionals
4. What they can realistically expect providers to accomplish

Competitive Advantage   Professional service firms face a little more difficult task in differentiating their service offering to gain competitive advantage than do product marketers. How does one differentiate an accounting audit, management analysis and advice, or an executive search service from those offered by competitors? Some providers of services attempt to use clever titles such as the Touche Ross Audit Process (TRAP) and Statistical Techniques for Analytical Review (STAR) to differentiate their offerings; the most useful approach is achieved through researching potential market segments needs and then designing the service to meet those segment or niche needs.

When service providers research potential market segments and pinpoint the attributes that clients use to differentiate one service from another, they are in a better position to establish their firm as a possessor of the desired attributes. Once market needs are known, a business service marketer can gain competitive advantage by:

1. Being referred
2. Possessing more experience, specialization, credibility, and contacts
3. Having better solutions to problems and superior procedures
4. Having high-level professionals personally involved
5. Providing easy access to services
6. Gaining on-time completion of work
7. Using state-of-the-art support equipment such as computers, communications systems, and testing devices
8. Writing easy-to-understand reports, presentations, and invoices
9. Frequent follow-up contacts to ensure satisfaction

Intangibility of a business service makes it difficult for the buyer to perceive the true value and quality of a service. The buyer has to draw inferences about the seller's reputation, honesty, integrity, professionalism and their ability to deliver the correct service. Selling business services is very closely associated with the client's image of the service's quality and true value.

INSEPARABILITY OF PRODUCTION AND CONSUMPTION

A product can be manufactured, inventoried, and sold later, but business service and its marketing is a personal, dyadic relationship between the buyer and seller. The seller's production of the service happens simultaneously with the buyer's consumption of the service. Hence, the buyer's perception of both the service firm's capabilities and validity of its integrity and quality of the service depends on the interaction that takes place between the buyer and the seller. (i.e., the face-to-face interactional relationship between a buyer and a seller in a service setting).[12] Not only is the perception of quality of service received dependent on the effectiveness of the person rendering the service; it is determined, in part, by the customer. For example, the quality of tax advice provided depends to some degree on the information provided by the customer. In an attempt to achieve greater control, business marketers must be aware of the importance of effectively managing the human element, namely the buyer's perception of the situation.

Figure 12-3 shows the importance for continuity in the relations between service providers. Firms remain in relationships because of the social and economic benefits they receive, the degree and nature of investment in relationships, the lack of better quality alternatives, the lack of opportunity to change suppliers, and/or the personalization of relationships.[13]

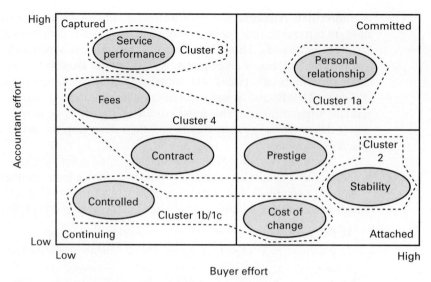

Source: Louise Young and Sara Denize, "A concept of commitment: Alternative views of relational continuity in business service relationships," *Journal of Business and Industrial Marketing* 10 (1995):32.

FIGURE 12-3 Types of relative continuity between business service providers and customers.

Each cluster in Figure 12-3 exhibits one or more different combinations of effort from the accountant and client directed towards developing and maintaining the relationship. It summarizes the variety of different relationship commitments described by the accountants interviewed. For example, if both the buyer's and the accountant's efforts are high, a strong personal relationship, a committed cluster, *1a,* develops. However, if both the buyer's efforts and the accountant's efforts are low, a cluster *1b/1c* develops, which is a controlled relationship. Under these conditions the cost of change becomes a very significant factor. Business service firms cherish the good relationships they have with their customers or clients. These commitments are necessary to maintain both viability and a competitive advantage for the business service provider.

HETEROGENEITY

It is difficult to standardize most services since the service provider is the service. Output, quality, delivery and value can vary widely, per service provider. One psychologist diagnosing an employee's stress level can draw different conclusions compared with another, although both have looked at the same individual and have examined the same data. The results are not equal because biases, educational background, predispositions, and attitudes help to determine each diagnoses. Investment bankers bidding for the right to market a corporation's new stock issue may not offer the same service, although the price per share is calculated down to the sixth or seventh decimal place. One investment banker's service mix could include additional perks to develop a competitive advantage as opposed to the service offerings of other bankers.

Services are not only rendered by different individuals within a firm, but individual performance also tends to fluctuate from day to day.[10] A high potential for variability exists which makes standardization of delivery extremely difficult. Quality in service delivery, however, must be carefully guarded. Word of mouth is an essential ingredient in communicating a professional service firm's reputation and to generate referrals. A bad experience on the part of the provider can severely affect a firm's business future. While consistent quality is difficult to achieve, business service marketers have to be marketing oriented before they can influence their clients favorably. To ensure client satisfaction, a service provider must choose its personnel carefully, and regularly collect information on client's or customer's needs.[14]

PERISHABILITY

Time is money for service people since time is a finite quantity and service providers have only time to sell. Time and knowledge constitutes the only product professional service providers have to sell. Services cannot be stored to be used another day. The demand for a provider's services must be forecast accurately to produce the most lucrative use and most cost-effective allocation of the service provider's time.

If the demand for perishable services is slow or even nonexistent, service time is wasted—never to be available for use again in that lost time slot. In an attempt to cover these periods of down time, the service provider has to charge a higher fee when working. A trend for using outsourcing to satisfy business service needs has reshaped business service's marketing.[15] Nontraditional business services have been created to meet the demand as company growth and newer technology comes on stream. Some of these new business services include PC network management, telecommunications, copier and print rooms, computer systems, nursing services, payroll administration, investment services, collection services, janitorial services, landscaping services, and parking facilities. As companies downsize, it is more apparent that outside sources must be contracted, hence increasing the overall demand for many types of business services.

The most troublesome area in the marketing of business services is the fact that services cannot be mass produced and stored. Thus, strategies for coping with fluctuating demand are difficult to develop. When demand is low, business service firms attempt to increase business by actively calling on customers to create more business. According to Aquila, the major objective in the marketing of a CPA program is to motivate and assist personnel in the development of new business and the retention of current clients.[14] Traditionally, accountants, who develop new business for the firm, tend to become heroes in the eyes of the firm's partners.

Growth is a major objective of most CPA firms. To support and complement this goal, the firm's marketing program has to teach people to be attuned to new business opportunities which present themselves during the normal course of a day. Too often, accountants simply are afraid to ask, or forget to ask, for referrals from satisfied clients, so the marketing staff must groom the accountants to develop empathy for clients, appreciate clients' problems, and ask the clients for referrals.[14]

A perishable, time problem exists for a manufacturer when a temporary increase in demand for products or a surge of increased office work stresses the present company staff and leaves insufficient time to complete all of the necessary tasks. Outsourcing of temporary people is required under these circumstances. Temporary service personnel firms have capitalized on the perishable nature of personnel by being able to supply individuals who have the skills as word processor operators, secretaries, nurses, accountants, lawyers, and a host of other "temps" to fill the people gaps for a client when the client's personnel demand and supply equations do not match.

PURCHASING MANAGER'S PERCEPTIONS OF BUSINESS SERVICES

Little research has been done in how organizational buyers perceive business services, but one study does shed some light in this direction. Jackson, Neidell, and Lunsford[7] conducted a study among 86 members of one chapter of the National Association of

Purchasing Management. Respondents came from a number of different types of firms with 38 percent of the respondents from manufacturing firms. The results of this study show some variances with previous studies. The results are as follows[7]:

1. Three fourths of the buyers agreed or strongly agreed that there is a difference in the purchasing of goods and services.
2. The majority of the respondents indicated that the switching costs for goods was no higher than for services.
3. Respondents indicated that determination of quality of services is more difficult than is for goods.
4. Respondents indicated that at least as many people are involved in the purchase decision for services as there are for goods.
5. Respondents indicated that collaboration between the supplier and the customer is a way to ensure the delivery of a quality service.
6. Buyers believe that fewer brands of services are available than product brands.
7. The majority of buyers believe it is better to outsource services.
8. A third of the buyers agreed that there is little variability in quality over time when purchasing the same brand.

The authors of this study suggest a number of marketing actions be taken. They recommend that service marketers move toward standardizing their service process by establishing a set of benchmarks for customers to use in evaluating the quality of the services. (In other words, provide a cognitive map for the customer to better judge what a good service should look like.) The service provider should act in a professional manner with the customer brought into the process early. Reaching the right people in the buying center is more important than being concerned about verifying the consistency of the services over time. Providers should work more closely with the customers during the specification stage in order to offer a tighter service package. A good relationship with the customer is more important than prices charged if good follow-up and the warranties of the service are fulfilled.

Major Marketing Problems in Business Services

Given the nature of the inherent problems of business services, service providers have to cope with many different kinds of problems. Among these problems is coping with effective marketing strategy: (1) how to differentiate one's service and gain a competitive advantage among various competitive services, (2) how to determine the quality and its evaluation of each service, and (3) how to determine the productivity or cost-effectiveness of each type of service.

DIFFERENTIATION (COMPETITIVE ADVANTAGE)

One of the basic tenets of any marketing strategy is to offer a product or service which is distinct from its competition. This distinctiveness provides the seller an opportunity to position their product or service in the minds of the buyers. Sometimes business services are treated as if they were a commodity, rather than a specialty item. The buyers perceive the purchase of the services from a small landscaping firm, for example, to be as good as from a large firm; use of a small CPA firm is as good as the purchase of accounting services from Arthur Anderson or Coopers & Lybrand. To these buyers, one landscaping firm or CPA firm is as good as any other. Big Six CPA firms must try to overcome this complacency by differentiating their professional expertise and professional level of service. The user's lack of technical knowledge, combined with the service provider's inappropriate or nonexistent marketing skills, have helped to perpetuate the commodity image of service providers among some buyers. Some business service buyers believe a business service tends to be relatively homogeneous and, consequently, price becomes the major decisional factor when contrasting the various CPA services.

The breakup of many long-term advertising/client relationships provides evidence that even creative services, such as advertising, can experience the problem of a lack of differentiation, as many firms merged to maintain their viability in the face of fierce competition on Madison Avenue.[16] As each advertising agency achieved remarkable results, the buyers tended to equate such an output as being normal, making the differentiation among different agencies much more difficult.

QUALITY EVALUATION

The intangibility of companies in the service industries makes it difficult to evaluate each firm's rendered quality of service. The quality of a particular professional service is a subjective matter which can inject a great deal of uncertainty into the client's decision process. This uncertainty is compounded by the prevalent opinion among professional service providers that the layman is incapable of properly judging the abilities and performance levels of a professional service provider.[17] Quality of service problems are further aggravated by the simultaneous production and consumption of the service and the overwhelming proliferation of the number of professionals offering a given service in a specific geographical area. Professionals are aware of these problems and are baffled as to their solutions. As a consulting engineer admitted, in spite of the high level of knowledge of the subject matter as a prerequisite for success as an engineering consultant, it is a daunting task to try to establish distinct competence on the basis of performance only, even between members of the same profession.[17]

In one attempt to overcome these uncertainties, researchers have provided the following help for service providers. Service customers expect fulfillment in at least five areas, according to the research of Berry, Parasuraman, and Zeithaml, and if a service-performance gap develops, the customer's perception of the service's quality is diminished[18]:

Tangibles: the physical facilities, equipment, and appearance of personnel

Reliability: the ability to perform the desired service dependably, accurately, and consistently

Responsiveness: the willingness to provide prompt service and to help customers

Assurance: employee's knowledge, courtesy, and ability to convey trust and confidence to the customer

Empathy: the provision of caring and providing individualized attention to the customer

Gronroos established a conceptual dichotomy that helps also to clarify the service quality problem. Since quality is a comparison between the buyer's expectations and service provider's performance, Gronroos concluded that the client is not only interested in what he receives as an outcome of the production process, the technical quality, but in the service process itself, which he calls functional quality.[19] Technical quality answers the question of what the customer gets, and functional quality answers the question of how he gets it or how the buyer perceives it. In another study of 379 managers, more than 90 percent rated reliability and responsiveness to customer's demands as either generally, or extremely important variables in services marketing. Of equal importance was the vendor's willingness to help customers and provide prompt support.[8]

As seen in Figure 12-4, the service provider's quality of service must match the client's expected level of service or, otherwise, the client can become dissatisfied (develop cognitive dissonance) with the quality of the service. The development of some gaps between the two perspectives are inevitable. The client may perceive various parts of the service may exceed, or meet, or fall below expectation levels. But tolerance among buyers may prevail. If all the service performance falls below the level of the buyer's expectations, it will stimulate buyer dissonance, and perhaps unhappiness, with the service, although the technical aspects of the service may be judged satisfactory by another professional in that field.

Delivering quality service to a client means conforming to the client's expectations of quality on a consistent basis. Similar to any other marketing operation that involves customers, this consistency means the service provider must try to manage the client's perception or image of the service provider's quality level of service. The most important service quality dimension is reliability—doing for the customer what the service provider said he would do and then a little bit more, according to Leonard L. Berry, a leading service marketing expert.[20]

FIGURE 12-4 Perceived service quality model.

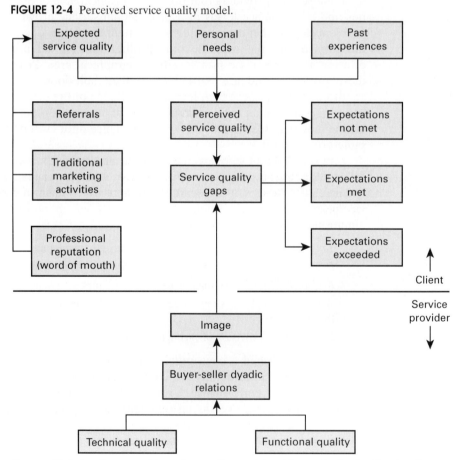

Source: Christian Gronroos, "A service quality model and its marketing implications," *European Journal of Marketing* 18 (4) (1984):40. Reprinted by permission. From A. Parasuraman, Valarie A. Zeithaml, and Leonard L. Berry, "A conceptual model of service quality and its implications for further research," *Journal of Marketing* 49 (Fall 1985):44. Reprinted by permission of the American Marketing Association.

Another study conducted among 379 managers in the telecommunications industry concluded that reliability and responsiveness to customer demands were either generally or extremely, important. Of equal importance to these variables was the vendor's willingness to help customers and provide prompt support.[8]

Managing the client's perception of the service provider's image requires both aggressive and enlightened marketing. John Grapham, president of John R. Grapham, Inc., a marketing management firm, stresses their marketing-driven approach by striving for the long run commitment to demand stimulation.[21] The company mails quarterly newsletters, one of which is called "Good Impression," to about 3,500 businesses to increase the clients' awareness of Grapham's activities.

Many professional doctors, lawyers, and consultants have become experts in marketing their services, and their experience can illuminate some of the black holes in the marketing of services. Gelb, Smith, and Gelb found three actions by top professionals stand out as important in client satisfaction:[22] First, the business service marketer must shape realistic expectations, on the part of the client, or correct those expectations which are unrealistic; second, the business service marketer must vigorously emphasize communications during service delivery and even after the service delivery; and third, the business service marketer must focus on the service rendered to provide a successful outcome in the client's terms, not just the providers terms.

PRODUCTIVITY

Service providers do not require a large investment to enter the business. Economies of scale, so prevalent in successful product firms, are seldom within the grasp of service companies due to high labor intensity and high labor costs. All types of organizations face the need to drastically improve their worker's productivity and technical knowledge. The business environment demands effective and efficient delivery of service, and business processes must be streamlined and networked to support this customer-service orientation. Central to achieving the goal of improved service delivery is an integrated architecture. The three levels of integration which must be supported by the infrastructure are (1) the high performance team, (2) the integrated organization, and (3) the extended enterprise.[23]

Kotler suggests that six alternative approaches to improving service productivity exist[3]:

1. Have service providers work harder.
2. Increase the quantity of service by surrendering some quality.
3. "Industrialize the service" by adding equipment and standardizing production.
4. Reduce or make obsolete the need for the service by inventing a product solution.
5. Design a more effective service.
6. Give clients incentives to use some of their labor in place of the service provider's labor.

Constant innovation in services must be a standard approach to thwart competitive inroads and maintain a firm's competitive advantage. Successful service providers, such as The ServiceMaster Co., emphasize reliability, value and productivity, forcing competitors to constantly play catchup.[20] ServiceMaster, a large manager of housekeeping and maintenance departments in hospitals, industrial facilities and schools, is committed to its employees and conducts time-and-motion studies and other research to understand how people work. The company developed a comprehensive training program based on these data. The company believes that although training may not at first sound like a marketing function, in reality, training and updating skills are marketing essentials in business services.[20]

Rural/Metro, a provider of fire prevention and fire fighting services caters to small communities that cannot afford a full-time fire department. The company took another direction to gain competitive advantage. The company customized its fire-fighting equipment to meet the specific needs of the small communities which its serves, to enhance its effectiveness and customer satisfaction.

To handle peak demand, business service firms cross-train employees, have employees work overtime, hire extra part-time employees, and/or encourage customers to use services during nonpeak periods. While some service firms may take care of their regular customers first and allow new customers to wait (or even turn away the new business), can be a risky business. Timing in meeting the demand for services is very crucial. "Demand for services must be met or lost," or the firm will miss the chance of earning increased revenues.[24]

OUTSOURCING

The world's competitive battles have forced many American firms to downsize and become leaner and meaner. This is another way of saying that competitive firms must cut "fat" or nonessential personnel and procedures to reduce costs. The most opportune area to reduce appears to be middle management positions. Companies have started to realize that to outsource some middle managers jobs, would result in cost savings. The perspective in the nineties is to question whether or not a firm really needs to staff functions better performed by outside professionals. This major shift in attitudes of American firms has benefited business services marketing firms by increasing the demand for outsourcing services. Accounting, advertising, management, marketing, and engineering consulting, child care in organizations, industrial landscaping, temporary professional services, tax services, data processing, human relations, etc. have all increased their professional staffs to meet this greater demand.

According to A.T. Kearney, who surveyed 26 major companies, including DuPont, Exxon, and IBM, about 86 percent of major corporations outsource at least some of their services.[25] The tremendous push to outsource contains some disturbing problems. DuPont signed up Forum, under a 5-year contract, to administer all of the company's training and development operations. Forum immediately shrank DuPont's training and development department from 70 employees to 30, but the employees transferred to Forum wound up with diminished benefits compared with those they had received when employed by DuPont.

Managing Marketing Strategy in Business Services

In marketing business services, the dependence is on people almost exclusively. The lack of ability to achieve production economies of scale and the differing quality of each service offered necessitate the use of many different marketing strategies. Although similar to product marketing strategies in that the same marketing procedures are used, service marketing changes how these strategies frequently are used.

CLIENT ANALYSIS

Marketing services to another business requires the analysis of how the offered services will affect either internal variables (affecting operating efficiencies) of the company or affect external variables (affecting the sales and/or marketing processes) of the company. If internal variables are under consideration, Waddell suggests the following questions have to be answered[26]:

1. What function must the person perform to succeed?
2. What are the various responsibilities needed by the person?
3. What are the key business issues the person must address?

If the service offered involves external variables, Waddell suggests the following approach should be taken:

1. Show the client the service provider is knowledgeable.
2. Describe the service characteristics that constitute the prime decision-making consideration of the client's customers.
3. Help the client envision how he might best influence the purchase decision of his customers.
4. Show how the client's customers could be enhanced with the offered services.

Management consulting firms need to efficiently and effectively promote themselves as competent and conscientious resources and as credible and cost-effective problem solvers.[27] Consultants should practice client-centered marketing, in which all promotion efforts are focused on the client's wants and needs. This type of marketing consists of evaluating the consulting practice and markets to identify strengths, weaknesses, opportunities, and threats; setting goals and objectives for the marketing planning period; establishing activity priorities; identifying and organizing resources required to accomplish the goals; and scheduling activities, proceeding with tasks, and monitoring results.[27] With management consulting firms in great demand, fees are rising as engagements lengthen and clients are demanding more results from their consultants. The following provides a list of factors that clients can use to choose a management consulting firm[28]:

1. Screen before hiring.
2. Research by visiting client sites and asking executives.
3. Join in by insisting the analysis of company issues be done by a client-consulting team with in-house managers outnumbering consultants.
4. Learn by demanding that consultants share their skills and knowledge with the teams.
5. Internalize as the assignment moves into implementation with a greater number of insiders involved in the effort to make sure the changes have staying power.
6. Set limits so as to restrict efforts by consultants to "scale up" a project to all other units of the company.

Executives and clients of architectural and engineering (A&E) firms were surveyed to determine the criteria that clients use in selecting and evaluating architectural and engineering service providers and the factors contributing to clients satisfaction and dissatisfaction. The data were obtained from 20 A&E firms and 17 client firms. The responses indicated that client firms' selection decisions were mainly determined by the provider's skills, the likelihood that the provider would conform to contractual and administrative requirements, and the perceived experience, expertise, and competence of the provider.[29] The strategic goal of the business services marketer is to convince the client, using past experience and the result of other successful applications, that his business will be more successful using the offered service. Table 12-3 lists the 10 most successful management consulting firms in the United States, showing how important some consulting firms have become as indicated by their size.

MARKET SEGMENTATION AND TARGET MARKETING

Professional services (physicians, attorneys, accountants, architects, financial advisors, management consultants, marketing consultants), as contrasted with non-professional services (janitorial services, maintenance, lawn care, painters), are what economists and

| | 1993 Revenue | |
Firm	(millions)	Consultants
Andersen Consulting	$2,876	22,500
Coopers & Lybrand	1,351	7,650
McKinsey	1,300	3,100
Booz Allen & Hamilton	800	4,600
Gemini Consulting	516	1,700
CSC Consulting	470	2,600
Boston Consulting Group	340	1,250
A. T. Kearney	278	950
Mercer Mgmt. Consulting	134	600
Monitor	90	340

TABLE 12-3 Ten Leading Management Consulting Firms

Source: "How ten leading consulting firms stack up," *Business Week* (July 25, 1994), p. 65. Reprinted by permission of *Business Week,* © 1994.

marketers call credence goods. The purchaser has to place great faith in those who sell these professional services. The provider has to be perceived as having experience. Lawyers who have litigated cases similar, or identical to the one the client faces, or architects who have designed buildings similar, or identical to, the building under consideration, provide reassurances to the prospective buyers and raise their level of confidence while adding greater credence to the business professional's position.

Market Segmentation   Market segmentation has been practiced by successful service providers to overcome client uncertainty. A service provider, who specializes in serving specific, niche segments, can build a reputation so intense that a prospective client will not speculate about the business service provider's lack of experience or lack of credence. By specializing, the provider can reap some economies of scale in his purchasing of goods for the service and the professional specialization's economies generated by the "experience curve" effects, which can increase both the buyer's and service provider's self-confidence.

Target Marketing   A national management consulting firm that specializes in only small-to-medium-sized companies in specific industries, or a CPA firm that serves only law firms, epitomizes the use of targeted services marketing.[4] The market specialization enables the provider to position their business services so that competitors would have difficulty in dislodging them from their protected market position. Financial institutions realize that they must target their markets to be successful. A survey by Financial Matters, Incorporated, of 10 financial planners from around the country, found that active marketing will be the sustaining and expanding forces for financial services practices.[30] The study also indicated that target marketing, in one form or another, was cited the most, and that most firms hoped to work with small to medium-sized, closely held businesses and professional practices; namely, physicians.[31]

SERVICES

The public accounting profession has undergone a marketing change. Some accountants have changed from complex accounting technicians to broad-based accounting-marketing generalists. Realizing that marketing was a very necessary part of the business, CPA professionals helped to change this passive perspective into a dynamic perspective. New account development was to be generated by the practicing accounting professionals, and not by non-accounting sales staff members. Prospective clients wanted to deal directly with a practicing accountant from a small accounting firm, but were willing to deal with an accounting supervisor from a large accounting firm. The marketing staff in these firms became trainers and supporters of the practicing accountants. The marketing representative in some firms had to be an accountant to arrest the fears of many potential clients. The strategic marketing plan, personal selling, promotion, and delivery became essential components in the promotional strategy of Big Six accounting firms. One such plan is shown in Figure 12-5.

CPA service offerings were enhanced as competition, a broadening market, and mergers within the industry forced many of the Big Six accounting firms to find ways to increase revenues.

Touche Ross & Co. offered only accounting, auditing, and tax services in 1947. By 1955 they had added management consulting. By 1987 their service offerings had swelled to include separate departments for actuarial and benefits consulting, private companies advisory service, a financial services center, Washington services center, Garr Industries, business interruption services, litigation services, corporate finance group, reorganization advisory services, advanced technology, and international services.[31]

Each new development within the firm required specialized individuals such as management consultants, who could appropriately meet client needs. Subsequently, many of these additions; namely, management consultants, became significant revenue developers, much to the chagrin of some of the more traditional accountants who could not see the firm as a collection of many services, all designed to satisfy clients' needs.

FIGURE 12-5 Professional service marketing and selling process.

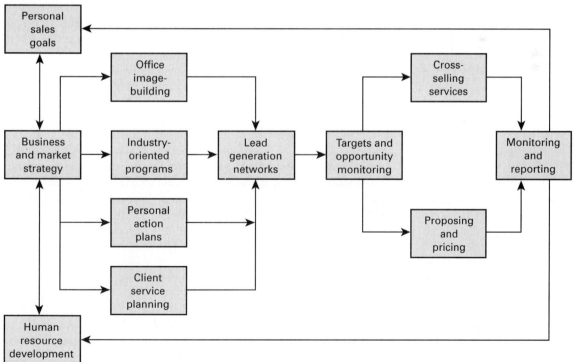

Source: Steven R. Baldwin, "CPAs learn marketing ABCs," *Business Marketing* (October 1981):54. Reprinted by permission of *Business Marketing.* © Crain Communications, Inc.

BUNDLING OF SERVICES

Some services firms have realized that competitive advantage can materialize when they bundle their services. IBM bundled computer hardware, software, and services support for years. *Bundling* means that all buyers are provided with the same package of services, regardless of differences in their needs.[32] By cross-training personnel and more intensive training to meet the needs of clients, such an advantage may be achieved. For example, a landscaping firm might combine garden, lawn, and tree care and also develop outdoor centers for employee recreation, then offer these services as a package to achieve competitive advantage. Marketing consultants might combine one of the following temporary training sessions along with management consulting service: advertising, promotion, personal selling, to gain a competitive advantage.

PROMOTION

Most firms who market professional services are wasting effort because they do not have compelling stories to tell to their marketplace. Five critical factors contribute to a successful professional service marketing campaign.[33] Questions must be asked of customers, suppliers, prospects, and even competitors to determine their underlying concerns. A vision of the company must be developed from the customer's own point of view. The competition must then be identified, along with their strengths and weaknesses. A premise, or statement of belief, and a selling proposition should be developed based on knowledge of the firm and its competitors. Finally, an original story should be crafted to help the professional service firm stand out above the clutter of other professional service firms. Those companies who have compelling stories to tell to their markets are better able to rise above the competition and make effective use of limited marketing resources to increase business.[4]

Professional and nonprofessional business services can offer different types of promotion. In some instances, advertising has been successful. The Michael Baker Corporation, an engineering firm used extensive advertising in coal industry publications and grew from near zero to more than $5 million in billings in that industry between 1977 and 1981. However, advertising by some professionals (lawyers and accountants) was frowned on because of the fear that some advertising would backfire or be unethical. Business customers are still uneasy about seeing or hearing advertising from the many professional services who practice this type of promotion. The conventional wisdom among many professional service providers is that if a firm is good, it should not have to advertise. Conventional promotional techniques would suffice. Rare exceptions to this edict occur, as evidenced by the promotional marketing program that Sotheby's, a fast-climbing auction house, incorporated into its business plans.

Often a service marketer could teach short (noncredit) courses at a university or at the local Chamber of Commerce or community college to persons who would like to increase their knowledge about a particular type of business service. Potential clients could be exposed to the advantages of employing a particular consultant, janitorial service or a industrial day care provider by participating in the course. Professors have for years developed consulting jobs from their students who may be in a position of authority in their respective firms.

Advertising as a Possible Standard   In 10 or 20 years advertising may become the standard promotional fare for business services professionals, but for now, the preferred form of promotion has been newsletters, brochures, desk-top reference handouts, word-of-mouth promotions, referrals, press releases, sales promotions directed to specific industries, and personal selling. Clients prefer to be courted by the persons who actually will perform the services. This approach is not only a personal touch, but also it is one way the client can determine quality of service and any future working relationships with the service provider. Clients may feel uncomfortable buying from people they will never see again or from persons who only sell the service.

Weld Coxe,[34] a management consultant to engineers and architects, believes that clients have demonstrated a clear preference for marketing organizations composed of "closer-doers" (those who close deals or who sell in addition to other work) where the professional making the sale can assure the client that he or she will be personally involved during the execution of the project.[4] The partners in one Big Six accounting firm asked its people to set specific written goals for sales lead generation and the future cultivation of client contacts.[31] Managers can take several steps to ensure that their professionals and workers continuously market the firm's services by establishing recruiting campaigns to gain sales-oriented professionals, setting up sales training programs for these professionals, and making it financially worth the professionals and/or workers' time to bring in new accounts.

Communicating the Service Offering   Although approximately 14 percent of the nation's lawyers and several CPA firms use advertising to reach potential clients, the use of advertising to communicate with potential markets by service providers has two important limitations.[12] First, many service users are unaccustomed to seeing or hearing advertising for professional services, and they may not accept it. They may even interpret it negatively, perceiving that the firm lacks competency if it has to advertise. Second, because professional service firms usually need to reach only a very narrow audience with complicated explanations of their service, advertising is often not worth the expense involved—even if it may appear to be acceptable. For these reasons, most professional service organizations are leery of the results that may be achieved through advertising.

Despite these problems, some professional firms are quite successful in their use of advertising. For instance, one CPA firm that used advertising as its only means of developing business reported an increase in billings from $8,000 to $1.75 million over a 4-year period. When used properly and prudently, then, advertising can be a viable means of reaching potential markets.[4] This success means that the service provider must identify target audiences, reach them through low-cost advertising in specialized publications or direct mail, and monitor the results. Only by carefully tracking the number of inquiries and their receptivity to the professional's sales call can the marketer fine tune the firm's advertising program to achieve the desired results.

PRICING SERVICES

Price-quality relationships are often strong in the marketing of services. This relationship, together with the client's inability to accurately judge the value and quality of the service, places a high premium on the right pricing strategies. If the service is underpriced, the buyer will believe the service is of poor quality. If priced too high, the buyer could perceive the provider could be the very best firm available. Obviously, the pricing strategy is to price high to reinforce the marketing image of high quality service, but a failure to deliver the technical high quality could be inviting a disaster. One of the most common errors made by inexperienced management consultants is to price their services too low in hopes of acquiring a new account, but reinforcing the client's impression that the consultant's work may be inferior to their competitors. Of course, there are always buyers who will try to get the best service for the cheapest price, but these types of buyers are minimal threats.

DISTRIBUTION OF SERVICES

Since service companies do not have a storable product, traditional distribution channels are not feasible, but the need to achieve "place utilities" is very strong. Getting the service, physically, to the client, is an important function. Big Six accounting firms have geographically dispersed their office locations to better serve the largest share of their markets. Law firms, architectural firms, and other non-professional service firms strategically locate their facilities and offices to better service their clientele. Technimetrics, a progressive investors data base services company serving more than 1,100 publicly held companies, including more than a half of the Fortune 500, cannot physically afford multiple office locations because of cost constraints. The firm spreads its output to gain strategic locations via a sales force of eleven domestic and two foreign salespeople to gain distribution.

Freight forwarders have expanded many of their business services beyond transportation. One large German freight forwarder includes packaging, marketing, export management, and foreign market research in addition to all necessary transportation requirements. A domestic service provider could literally distribute his services via a freight forwarder.

Franchising is another way of distributing a service provider's offerings. Telemarketing, mailing lists generation by small offices, and temporary personnel services geared to the business sector are examples of franchising a business service.

THREE MORE *P*s TO SERVICES MARKETING

Straight marketing strategies using the four *P*s—*p*roduct (service in this case), *p*rice, *p*romotion, and *p*lace—may not be enough for business services marketers, according to A.L. Magrath, a market planner for a Fortune 500 company in Canada.[34] He suggests that three more *P*s be added: *p*ersonnel, *p*hysical facilities, and *p*rocess management. Proper personnel is the key to the creation of the service offered and its on-time delivery to the client. Physical facilities are absolutely necessary and very important to enhance marketing believability and delivery of the service. Process management ensures the services' availability and consistent quality in light of the simultaneous consumption and production of the service offered. Emery Air Freight highlights the personnel aspect of its service. Emery maintains an upbeat and enthusiastic environment so that the total of the staff working together is greater than the sum of its individual parts. Computers are used to maintain a workable process between the seller and the buyer of the air freight service.[34] Federal Express also developed an integrated computer system to track a package from its original shipping point to its final destination to provide better customer service and satisfaction.

INTERNATIONAL MARKETING OF PROFESSIONAL BUSINESS SERVICES

Many domestic business service organizations are attempting to increase their market coverage by going into international markets. By entering foreign markets, domestic firms can gain valuable information about their competitors, strengthen their domestic position, and diversify and expand their revenue base.[35] First, new markets may be penetrated by opening offices, making an acquisition, or forming a strategic alliance. When opening an office, marketers must realize that time and patience are required, but this approach is the least risky. The success of opening a foreign office depends on choosing the right type of executive to run the foreign office. Second, if foreign market penetration, by acquisition, is chosen, this approach allows an immediate market impact, but it is probably the riskiest approach. The foreign service acquirers' initial challenge is to determine precisely what they have purchased, in terms of personal, expertise, and market share. The third strategy is to form strategic alliances with clients or complementary service providers. Alliances are less risky than acquisitions as long as alliance participants' business goals and corporate cultures are compatible.[35]

Trade in services is the fastest growing segment of the U.S.–Canada relationship, totaling an estimated $26.4 billion in the early 1990s. Canada's $285 billion services market is highly competitive and potentially lucrative for U.S. business and professional service providers. Removal of tariffs under the North American Free Trade Agreement (NAFTA) agreement continue to spur U.S. exports to Canada, Mexico and perhaps Chile. U.S. exports in the construction services, management consulting services, advertising services, franchising, and software sectors have done well in Canada given the (NAFTA) agreement, passed in 1994.[36] The early reports of NAFTA's success were very encouraging as trade increased among the three partners.

The new GATT agreement passed in December, 1994 created the World Trade Organization (WTO). This event opened many opportunities for U.S. service firms to compete more equally with foreign firms in foreign countries. Although rather disappointing compared with other features of the pact, markets opened in a number of countries for legal services, accounting and software. The U.S. negotiators failed to secure access to foreign markets in Japan and several South-east Asian nations. Many developing countries were largely closed to U.S. banks and securities firms. The new provisions helped U.S. law firms establish a stronger presence in many countries, including France and Japan.[37] Foreign states still do not permit American service firms to operate freely as these countries may fear the importation of too much American culture. The French are irritated by all the American films shown in France. Therefore, the French and many other countries prohibit or limit the entrance of American business banking, insurance, and investment firms.

Products Require Customer Services

The marketing of customer services allied with products have similar facets to the marketing of business services. Customer product services, which can enhance sales and provoke customer satisfaction, can be reduced to two major concerns: (1) actual product quality and commensurate services offered to the customer, and (2) how the customer perceives both the product quality and the commensurate service they receive. E.I. DuPont de Nemours & Co. changed their marketing strategy and, subsequently, reaped huge dividends. Much of DuPont's growth was attributed to a more aggressive, customer-driven approach to marketing.[38] The approach included individual segmenting, relationship marketing, customer management, and prospect databasing. DuPont believed that business customers expect to be dealt with in a way that reflects an understanding of needs, and a one-on-one relationship.

Looking Back

Business services have been the fastest growing sector in the business economic system. As many advanced industrialized countries develop the need for better and more sophisticated business services because of downsizing and increased use of outsourcing, the requirements for marketing of these business services have increased considerably. Although similar in some respects to product marketing, certain business service characteristics require the use of different marketing strategies from those strategies used for product marketing. These characteristics are (1) intangibility, (2) inseparability of production and consumption, (3) heterogeneity, (4) perishability, (5) specialization, and (6) technology. Services can not be stored and inventoried, therefore, business services have to be used as they are developed, or else these services perish.

Business service marketing contains some major problems since differentiating one business service from other to obtain a competitive advantage can be a difficult obstacle to overcome. Two major areas of concern are first, the customer's ability to assess the true quality of the service provided, and second, the delivery or productivity of the business service's output. Many of the solutions to these problems lie in the use of target marketing techniques; improved training and recruiting procedures; and managing the buyer-seller dyadic relationship by up-front buyer conviction. The seller knows the buyer's problems and can effectively resolve them even beyond the buyer's level of expectation. Marketing a business service requires technical expertise, functional expertise, and the ability to properly market the business service.

Marketing strategies are tied into the service, via bundling their services, enhancement, promotion, distribution via freight forwarders and franchising, pricing, personnel, physical facilities, and process management. The service provider must become market-driven and attempt to know and to placate the client's needs if the business service firm expects to remain viable and to continue to grow. The international market for services has been growing and offers a great challenge for many service firms in so many countries.

Questions for Discussion

1. If truck transportation services were stopped or reduced to a slow crawl, what possible effects would the general economy incur? Why?

2. Discuss the six inherent service characteristics that differentiate services from products and prevent services from using the same product marketing strategies. Of the six, which is the most predominate difference?

3. What is meant by the inseparability of a business or industrial service, and why is this characteristic possibly very debilitating to the service provider?

4. Besides differentiating a service, projecting a high quality to the prospective buyer, and increasing the service's productivity in order to reduce costs, what are the service industries' major problems? How can each major problem be resolved?

5. Gronroos and others have identified the need to project a service's level of quality to the buyer by controlling the dyadic buyer-seller relationship. What does this statement mean and why aren't the technical aspects of the service sufficient to sell it?

6. How can a service marketer use market segmentation and targeted marketing concepts and techniques?

7. If service marketers really understood what their product represented in the buyer's mind, why would it be necessary to remind many service employees that they should participate in the marketing effort?

8. How can pricing strategies affect the sales of business services?

9. If services cannot be inventoried or stored, why even consider the distribution of a service?

10. Why are some countries reluctant to allow American banking and insurance firms to enter their markets?

Endnotes

1. Ronald K. Shelp, "The service economy gets no respect," *Across the Board*, New York: The Conference Board. In Christopher H. Lovelock, *Managing Services, Marketing Operations, and Human Resources* (Englewood Cliffs, N.J.: Prentice Hall, Inc., 1988), p. 2.

2. "Innovation in professional services: Potential productivity and trade improvement," *Technological Forecasting and Social Change* 42 (August 1992).

3. Philip Kotler, *Marketing Management, Analysis, Planning, Implementation, and Control*, 8th. ed. (Englewood Cliffs, N. J.: Prentice Hall, Inc., 1994, p. 464).

4. Paul N. Bloom, "Effective marketing for professional services," *Harvard Business Review* (September-October, 1984, pp. 102-110).

5. Ralph W. Jackson and Philip D. Cooper, "Unique aspects of marketing industrial services," *Industrial Marketing Management* 17 (1988):111-18.

6. Lynn Shostack, "Breaking free from product marketing," *Journal of Marketing* 41 (April 1977):73-80.

7. Ralph W. Jackson, Lester A. Neidell, and Dale A. Lunsford, "An empirical investigation of the differences in goods and services as perceived by organizational buyers," *Industrial Marketing Management* 24 (1995):99-108

8. Geoffrey L. Gordon, Roger J. Calantone, and C. Anthony di Benedetto, "Business-to-business service marketing: How does it differ from business-to-business product marketing?" *Journal of Business and Industrial Marketing* 8 (1993):45-57.

9. See John E. Bateson, "Do we need service marketing?" In *Marketing Science Institute Report,* (Coral Gables, Fla.: Academy of Marketing Science in cooperation with the School of Business, University of Miami, 1977), pp. 77-115; and O.C. Ferrel, S.W. Brown, and C.W. Lamb, Jr., eds., *Theoretical Developments in Marketing* (Chicago: American Marketing Association, December 1979) pp. 131-46.

10. Valarie A. Zeithaml, A. Parasuraman, and Leonard L. Berry, "Problems and strategies in service marketing," *Journal of Marketing* 49 (Spring 1985):33-46.

11. Angela M. Rushton and David J. Carson, "The marketing of services: Managing the intangibles," *European Journal of Marketing* 19, 3 (1985):19-39.

12. Michael R. Solomon, Carol Surprenant, John A. Czepiel, and Evelyn G. Gutman, "A role theory perspective on dyadic interactions: The service encounter," *Journal of Marketing* 49 (1985):99-111.

13. Louise Young and Sara Denize, "A concept of commitment: Alternative views of relational continuity in business service relationships," *Journal of Business & Industrial Marketing* 10 (1995):22-37.

14. August J. Aquila, "Marketing of accounting services hinges on referrals, service expansion, communications," *Marketing News* (April 27, 1984):3.

15. B.G. Yovovich, "Outsourcing trend reshapes marketing," *Business Marketing* (May 1994):36.

16. "Can Young & Rubicam keep the crown?" *Business Week* (April 4, 1988), pp. 74+.

17. Kent Wheiler, "Referrals between professional service providers," *Industrial Marketing Management* 16(1987):191-200.

18. Leonard L. Berry, A. Parasuraman, and Valarie A. Zeithaml, "The service-quality puzzle," *Business Horizons* (September-October 1988), pp. 35-43.

19. Christian Gronroos, "A service quality model and tts marketing implications," *European Journal of Marketing* 18 (1984):36-44.

20. Kate Bertrand, "Service marketers thrive on innovations," *Business Marketing* (April 1988), pp. 52+.

21. John R. Grapham, "Traditional sales approach leaves him 'cold,'" *Marketing News* (March 14, 1988), p. 4.

22. Betsy D. Gelb, Samuel V. Smith, and Gabriel M. Gelb, "Service marketing lessons from the professionals," *Business Horizons* (September-October 1988), pp. 29-34.
23. Art Caston, "Surviving the paradigm shift," *CMA Magazine* 67 (1993):20-3.
24. Kenneth P. Uhl and Gregory D. Upah, "The marketing of services: Why and how is it different?" *Research in Marketing* 6 (1983):231-57.
25. "Has outsourcing gone too far?" *Business Week* (April 1, 1996), pp. 26-8.
26. Robert T. Waddell, "Marketing business services depends on customer's internal, external needs," *Marketing News* (May 8, 1987), p. 28.
27. Peng S. Chan, "How to market your professional services: A strategic approach," *Management Decision* 30 (1992):46-53.
28. "The craze for consultants," *Business Week* (July 25, 1994), pp. 60-66.
29. Ellen Day and Hiram C. Barksdale, Jr., "How firms select professional services," *Industrial Marketing Management* 21 (May 1992):85-91.
30. Francis D. Burke, Jr., " The marketing of financial services," *Journal of the American Society of CLU & ChFC* 46 (July, 1992):13-14.
31. Steven R. Baldwin, "CPAs learn marketing ABCs," *Business Marketing* (October 1987), pp. 42+.
32. Michael E. Porter, *Competitive Advantage* (New York: The Free Press, 1985, p. 425).
33. Michael Cucka, "A good story improves professional services marketing," *Marketing News* 27 (June 7, 1993):7.
34. A.L. Magrath, "When marketing services, 4Ps are not enough," *Business Horizons* (May/June 1986), pp. 44-50.
35. Micheline Bouchard, "International marketing of professional services," *Business Quarterly* 56 (Winter 1992):86-89.
36. Reginald Biddle and Toni Dick, "Selling services to Canada," *Business America* 114 (May 31, 1993):2-5.
37. "GATT Rules could make it easier for U.S. firms to succeed abroad," *The Wall Street Journal* (December 2, 1994), pp. A8 and B5.
38. Kim Cleland, "DuPont takes new approach," *Business Marketing* (June 1994), p. 38.

Bibliography

Benjamin, Gerald A, "Building a profitable business development strategy. Part Two," *Journal of Professional Services Marketing* 6 (1991):3-34.

Bostrom, Gert-Olof, "Successful cooperation in professional services," *Industrial Marketing Management* 24 (1995):151-65.

Coxe, Weld, "For professionals, the bottom line is not always the bottom line," *Journal of Management Consulting* 7 (Spring 1992):35+.

Driver, John C., "Marketing planning in style," *Quarterly Review of Marketing* 15 (Summer, 1990):16-21.

Filiatrault, Pierre and Jean-Charles Chebat, "How service firms set their marketing budgets," *Industrial Marketing Management* 19 (1990):63-7.

Harrell, Gilbert D. and Matthew F. Fors, "Internal marketing of a service," *Industrial Marketing Management* 21 (1992):299-306.

Larson, Jan, "Getting professional help," *American Demographics* 125 (July 1993):34-8.

Lovelock, Christopher H., *Managing Services, Marketing, Operations, and Human Resources* (Englewood Cliffs, N.J.: Prentice Hall, Inc., 1988).

Mayo, Edward J. and Lance P. Jarvis, "Excessive growth in the service firm: A strategic marketing planning challenge," *Journal of Services Marketing* 6 (Spring 1992):5-14.

McDonald, Malcolm H.B., "Strategic marketing planning: A state-of-the-art review," *Marketing Intelligence and Planning* 10 (1992):4-22.

Parasuraman, A., Valarie A. Zeithaml, and Leonard L. Berry, "A conceptual model of service quality and its implications for future research," *Journal of Marketing* 49 (Fall 1985):41-50.

Shelp, Ronald K., "The service economy gets no respect," Across the Board (New York: The Conference Board). In Christopher H., Lovelock, *Managing Services, Marketing, Operations, and Human Resources* (Englewood Cliffs, N.J.: Prentice Hall, Inc., 1988), p. 2.

Thomas, Edward G. and Bob D. Cutler, "Marketing the fine and performing arts: What has marketing done for the arts lately?" *Journal of Professional Services Marketing* 10 (1993):181-99.

PART

V

Channel Strategies

One of the oldest and least disputed business principles holds that success in the marketplace depends on having the right product in the right quantity in a place, at a time, and under conditions that prospective customers find satisfying. This statement sounds quite simple and logical. However, it raises a series of questions that producers must answer which are not so simple, and at times, result in seemingly illogical decisions. The answers reached and decisions made form the heart of the firm's channel strategy as well as its customer service policy.

In Chapter 13, we will study the issues that impact the type of channel structure selected. For example, should a manufacturer hire its own sales force or contract the direct selling effort to one or more independent sales organizations (manufacturers' reps)? Further, should this direct selling effort be supplemented by strategically located independent distributors or a network of company-owned regional warehouses? If distributors are chosen, what criteria should the producer use to select the most appropriate ones?

Chapter 14 deals with the logistics of a physical distribution system-warehousing, shipping, and material handling-and the aspects of customer service that can either enhance or harm the firm's sales effort.

CHAPTER 13 Managing Business Channel Members

The business firm seeking a distributor or manufacturers' representative will face decisions and pitfalls similar to those encountered by a lonely single person in search of a mate. For even though channel members remain independent of the manufacturer, free to seek their own goals and profits, both parties agree to work together for common goals and greater profits than either could achieve independently. And, as is true of individuals, these business partners will have a greater likelihood of success the more their values, priorities, and "lifestyles" are similar.

In this chapter we will discuss the following:

1. The internal and external factors that indicate a manufacturer's need of distributors

2. The services that business customers require of distributors

3. The characteristics that a manufacturer must consider when choosing a distributor

4. The circumstances that dictate the use of manufacturers' reps (or other sales agents) instead of an employee sales force

5. The steps that the business marketer must take to ensure that indirect channels are effective

Just as manufacturers can be large or small, innovative or traditional, venturesome or conservative, and oriented toward quality or price, distributors and manufacturers' representatives (also referred to as sales agents or simply reps) can be differentiated by these same characteristics. The stereotypical image of a large, innovative, well-managed manufacturer being forced to use small, unimaginative, poorly run channel intermediaries, who sell primarily on price, is just that—a stereotype that does not reflect modern realities.

In this chapter, then, we will attempt to establish a realistic profile of channel intermediaries as they exist and function in today's marketplace. Distributors will be examined first, followed by manufacturers' representatives and several specialized forms of channel members.

337

Why Use Distributors?

Most manufacturers ask this question at some point, particularly when struggling with a strategic marketing decision involving profitability, growth, market share, or competition. Regarding profits, manufacturers often view distributors as a cost rather than a profit contributor. Distributors demand a profit margin, which means that the manufacturer must sell to them at a price lower than could be used if selling direct. In addition, it is "common knowledge" that distributors only serve markets that the manufacturer has developed and make no effort to aid manufacturers in developing either new markets or new product applications in current markets. The worst situation concerns market share and competition. Distributors traditionally sell both complementary and competing products. So indeed, why use distributors?

CRITICAL FUNCTIONS AND WEAKNESSES

A manufacturer should logically ponder the use of distributors when structuring an overall marketing strategy, but not before considering several other significant questions. First, the manufacturer should ask what functions—such as quick delivery, local inventory, or tailored services—will be critical to the success of the marketing strategy. Such functions require special attention to achieve superb performance. Second, which of these functions represents a weakness in the firm either in the form of scarcity (for example, financial resources, manpower, expertise, or time) or opportunity trade-offs (such as assets that could be better utilized elsewhere)? Finally, regardless of whether internal weaknesses exist, can an outside agency perform these critical functions more efficiently and profitably?

If manufacturers view distributors in this context, they will make channel decisions with greater objectivity and realism. Distributors will be evaluated for their contribution, not their cost. This assumes, of course, that they can indeed make a valuable contribution.

CUSTOMER EXPECTATIONS

Both formal academic research and less formal industry surveys indicate that business buyers are very concerned with customer service. A 1976 academic study by Perreault and Russ concluded that business buyers consistently rate distribution service second only to product quality as a factor influencing their buying decision.[1] A 1993 survey of readers by *Industrial Distribution* indicated that this mind-set has not changed over time.[2] More than 72 percent of respondents cited product quality as their reason for choosing a distributor, 53 percent noted services as most important, and 50 percent chose product availability as the most important asset. Price ranked fifth in importance, cited by only 32 percent of respondents.

Electronic Buyers' News ran replicate surveys of their readership (1980 and 1981). The results of the surveys are shown in Table 13-1. Responses are ranked by the percentage of 1981 responses. Where responses could have multiple implications, they are included in two categories. Again, the replies agree with other research findings. Buyers clearly value service higher than price, and they gauge the quality of service by prompt and accurate communications coupled with adequate inventories. They do not expect distributors to be the primary source of technical assistance. A manufacturer's sales force fulfills this role.

These replicate surveys are particularly helpful in showing the effect of market conditions on buying-decision priorities. In 1980, demand exceeded the supply of electronic components. Buyers struggled to obtain enough products to keep their produc-

TABLE 13-1   Why Business Firms Choose Their Distributors

Reason Stated	Percent of Respondents		
	1980	*1981*	*Category*
1. Dependable local service	30	40	1
2. "One-stop shopping" for most needs	23	27	2, 3
3. Keeps an inventory for us	19	25	2
4. Prompt telephone responses	34	25	1
5. Immediate availability on many products	22	22	2, 3
6. Consistently low-priced	14	22	4
7. Keeps in-depth inventory of specialized parts	20	20	2, 3
8. Expedites factory for us	25	20	1
9. Good technical support	13	18	5
10. Offers blanket (total volume) contracts	18	16	4
11. Always ships accurately	12	14	1
12. Can suggest cost-effective substitute items	7	14	4, 5
13. Carries more inventory than others	15	13	2
14. Ships faster than others	12	8	1
15. Consistently ships complete orders (no back order)	5	8	1, 2
16. Liberal credit policy	5	5	4
17. Consistently supplies proper quantities	5	5	1
18. Various services offered	1	3	6
19. Gives premiums with orders	1	1	4
Responses Grouped by Category (percent)			
1. Dependable service	43.0	39.2	
2. Inventory level	37.0	37.6	
3. Product line breadth	23.1	22.5	
4. Price	16.0	19.0	
5. Technical capability	7.1	10.5	
6. Variety of services	0.4	1.0	

Source: Special Report, *Electronic Buyer's News* (December 1981).

tion lines running. However, within a year, demand fell off significantly, resulting in excess inventories. Note the impact of this swing on the weighting of the six categories.

In times of excess supply, customers experience little difficulty in getting timely shipment of products. Prompt phone replies (item 4) diminished in importance as did the need to expedite factory shipments (item 8). The seller who could not provide prompt price information or ship from stock simply lost the order to a more nimble competitor. As expected, price pressures increased (category four) but did not become dominant. Also, in times of soft demand, buyers seek alternative products that might reduce overall cost (item 12) or improve the performance of their end-products. Hence, the value of technical assistance rose (category five). Overall, consistent and dependable local service remained the primary reason that buyers did business with a particular distributor.

DISTRIBUTORS AS MIDDLEMEN: CHANGING RELATIONSHIPS

Sellers of components and equipment along with industry observers tend to view distributors primarily as customer agents. In other words, distributors allegedly care more about the customers they serve than the producers of the goods they sell. Indeed, the dramatic industrial downsizing that started in the 1980s and continues in the 1990s changed this three-way relationship in several important ways.

Buyers have increasingly turned to distributors for help in reducing their procurement costs. A joint survey by *Plant Engineering* and *Purchasing* magazines found that 78 percent of responding engineers and 67 percent of purchasing personnel depended on distributor recommendations for specific brands of products.[3] Sellers who franchise the distributors fear that this developing bond may weaken their own relationship. They visualize an ominous scenario wherein distributors operate as purchasing arms for their customers rather than as extensions of the seller's marketing force.[4] Thus, they fear that distributors will lack the commitment to carry out critical marketing tasks.

Meanwhile, both buyers and sellers in some industries (groceries, mass merchandising, pharmaceuticals, and industrial supplies) have questioned the value of distributors. Sellers wonder why they should allow their market competitiveness to be hindered by the markups that distributors add to the cost of their products, whereas end users perceive their bargaining power being reduced when they do not deal directly with the manufacturer.[5]

As a consequence, the more creative distributors have sought ways to increase both the actuality and perception of their value-added functions. Some of the steps taken to enhance their customer-satisfying ability include hiring personnel with technical expertise and training others, adding selected assembly operations, computerizing for greater speed and accuracy, and providing consigned inventories for special customers.[6]

Table 13-2 lists the traditional functions that distributors perform. We can view these functions as two sides of a coin. One side benefits the seller (product manufacturer), while the other side benefits the buyer (product user). Thus, each time distributors serve a customer well, they further the cause of the product manufacturer. All three parties would benefit by recognizing their interdependence. The Japanese model of long-term buyer-seller relationships would improve the results of this interdependence by increasing the quality and consistency of product, inventory handling, and intermediate services.[7] For optimal results, all three members must eliminate redundant and inefficient operations. For example, multiple inventories often serve no useful purpose, nor do redundant assembly centers.

Successful distributors may seem customer oriented because of their emphasis on service. They, too, read the conclusions of industry surveys and act to satisfy customer priorities. However, distributors also recognize that their strength mainly stems from the products they carry. They neither create nor produce these products. They cannot survive without desirable franchises. Therefore, only a naive distributor would ignore the necessity to satisfy suppliers as well as customers.

TABLE 13-2 Distributors Serve Buyers and Sellers

Seller Benefit	Buyer Benefit
1. Carry local inventory	Provide fast delivery
2. Combine supplier outputs (synergy)	Provide product assortment
3. Share the credit risk	Provide local credit
4. Share the selling task	Assist in buying decisions
5. Forecast market needs	Anticipate buying requirements
6. Provide market information	Provide product information
7. Enhance customer service	Enhance customer service

Manufacturers who view distributors as being too customer oriented often fall into one of two categories. Either their product lines have failed to generate customer interest, or their own commitment to customer service is suboptimal.

Dual-Channel Strategies

Most manufacturers serving business customers utilize both direct and indirect channels; that is, they sell through their own sales force as well as through distributors and/or manufacturers' representatives. As with any generalized statement, this one has exceptions. For example, some firms use reps exclusively rather than their own sales force for reasons discussed later.

To view the quantitative aspects of this dual-channel strategy, we have selected nine industry segments with associated data from 1972 through 1992. These data shown in Table 13-3 will serve as background information for our analysis. United States GNP data (in current year dollars) is also included as a benchmark of overall economic growth during these two decades.

The nine segments listed in Table 13-3 were chosen for specific reasons:

1. They include both "smokestack" and high-tech industries
2. They cover capital equipment as well as component parts
3. Their growth rates are considerably different
4. Business customers provide the majority of sales dollars

Regarding the fourth reason, various other industries sell a portion of their output to business customers, but the bulk of their sales goes through the wholesaler-retailer channel to consumers. This is true, for example, of motor vehicles (SIC 5012), furniture (SIC 5021), electrical appliances (SIC 5064), and hardware (SIC 5072). Including such segments in our analysis would bias the data in favor of indirect distribution, since the majority of consumer-directed products flow in this manner.

INDIRECT VERSUS DIRECT DISTRIBUTION

Most research concludes that both suppliers and customers prefer the distributor channel when (1) the product is relatively simple and inexpensive, (2) purchases are made frequently and in small quantity, (3) the customer's total buying power is modest, and (4) the overall market consists of many customers geographically dispersed.[8] This conclusion is correct to the extent that the conditions listed actually favor distributors. However, it does not follow that the opposite conditions—complex or expensive products, infrequent or large purchases, buyers with large potential, or concentrated markets—automatically exclude the indirect channel.

Smokestack industries (basic metals, industrial supplies) primarily involve products of less technical complexity than high-tech products. Hence, theory would indicate that distributors should sell the greater portion of these products.

Capital equipment involves a much higher average price than do components or supplies, and purchases are made less frequently. This suggests that purchasers of construction or mining equipment are more likely to buy direct than are buyers of industrial supplies.

The occasion of an industry slump (such as occurred during 1982-1987 in most industries, particularly in SIC codes 5084 and 5085) can affect the indirect channel both positively and negatively. On one hand, some producers will try to reduce costs by cutting the fixed overhead of a sales force in favor of the constant cost-to-sales ratio of

TABLE 13-3   Wholesale Sales and Growth Rates for Selected Industries: 1972-1992

Industry	SIC Code	Sales (billions of dollars)					Annual Growth Rate (%)			
		1972	1977	1982	1987	1992	1972-1977	1977-1982	1982-1987	1987-1992
All metals	5051	40.5	70.1	87.8	101.1	105.8	11.6	4.6	2.9	0.9
Electrical equipment	5063	28.4	36.5	54.0	65.9	74.7	5.1	8.1	4.1	2.5
Electronics	5065	8.3	15.6	40.4	71.1	106.2	13.5	21.0	12.0	8.4
Commercial and office equipment	5081	12.7	27.4	64.5	121.9	180.8	16.6	18.7	13.6	8.2
Office equipment	5044*	—	—	—	27.8	28.9	—	—	—	0.8
Computers and peripherals	5045*	—	—	—	84.5	140.7	—	—	—	10.7
Commercial equipment	5046*	—	—	—	9.6	11.2	—	—	—	3.1
Construction and mining equiptment	5082	8.0	17.7	19.3	24.0	26.1	17.2	1.7	4.5	1.7
Industrial equipment	5084	17.1	40.3	68.6	64.9	86.6	18.7	11.2	–1.1	5.9
Industrial supplies	5085	16.5	28.9	39.8	41.8	56.7	11.9	6.6	1.0	6.3
TOTAL	—	131.5	236.5	374.4	490.7	636.9	12.5	9.6	5.6	5.4
U.S. GNP	—	1,212.8	1,990.5	3,166.0	4,515.6	5,961.9	10.4	9.7	7.3	5.7

*SIC code 5081 was subdivided into codes 5044-46 in 1987. The SIC 5081 data are shown in 1987 and 1992 for growth comparison.

Source: Adapted from U.S. Department of Commerce, Census of Wholesale Trade for 1972, 1977, 1982, 1987, and 1992 (Washington, D.C.: U.S. GPO, 1976, 1981, 1984, 1989, 1995).

indirect distribution. On the other hand, the critical need to increase market share to maintain volume may convince some manufacturers that they require the greater control and commitment of direct sales.

ACTUAL MARKET CIRCUMSTANCES

Table 13-4 presents the distribution of wholesale trade across the three major channels: manufacturers' sales offices (direct sales), distributors, and manufacturers' representatives. This information allows a comparison of theory and intuition against actual market data.

These nine industries have as many differences as commonalities; nevertheless, distributors have held their share of the sales volume in all industries and

TABLE 13-4   Distribution of Wholesale Trade by Channel in Selected Industries, 1972-1992 (percent)

Industry	SIC Code	Channel	1972	1977	1982	1987	1992
All metals	5051	Direct	56.6	51.1	45.4	34.7	32.9
		Distributor	35.0	41.3	49.0	59.3	60.7
		Mfr. Rep	8.4	7.6	5.6	6.0	6.4
Electrical	5063	Direct	31.3	40.6	45.4	29.3	23.0
equipment		Distributor	60.7	46.7	40.8	54.3	57.1
		Mfr. Rep	8.0	12.7	13.8	16.4	19.9
Electronics	5065	Direct	38.9	38.1	39.9	32.6	36.1
		Distributor	31.3	25.9	32.0	47.1	44.0
		Mfr. Rep	29.8	36.0	28.1	20.3	19.9
Commercial/office	5081	Direct	67.4	65.8	63.3	51.7	43.6
equipment		Distributor	27.3	29.7	32.8	44.9	53.3
		Mfr. Rep	5.3	4.5	3.9	3.4	3.1
Office	5044*	Direct	—	—	—	34.6	36.0
equipment		Distributor	—	—	—	61.7	61.2
		Mfr. Rep	—	—	—	3.7	2.8
Computers and	5045*	Direct	—	—	—	62.1	47.9
peripherals		Distributor	—	—	—	35.8	49.8
		Mfr. Rep	—	—	—	2.1	2.3
Commercial	5046*	Direct	—	—	—	10.0	9.5
equipment		Distributor	—	—	—	77.0	76.3
		Mfr. Rep	—	—	—	13.0	14.2
Construction	5082	Direct	23.6	27.9	27.4	25.3	29.3
and mining		Distributor	73.4	69.8	70.3	72.5	67.8
equipment		Mfr. Rep	3.0	2.3	2.3	2.2	2.9
Industrial	5084	Direct	36.2	33.0	29.4	23.4	20.6
equipment		Distributor	47.9	51.9	57.3	62.7	64.8
		Mfr. Rep	15.9	15.1	13.3	13.9	14.6
Industrial	5085	Direct	45.4	46.0	42.6	35.5	35.6
supplies		Distributor	47.1	45.6	49.5	57.9	57.0
		Mfr. Rep	7.5	8.4	7.9	6.6	7.4
TOTAL	—	Direct	45.0	44.9	43.7	36.0	33.7
		Distributor	45.1	44.2	45.9	54.3	55.9
		Mfr. Rep	9.9	10.9	10.4	9.7	10.4

*SIC code 5081 was subdivided into codes 5044-46 in 1987. The 5081 data are shown in 1987 and 1992 for continuity.

Source: Adapted from U.S. Department of Commerce, Census of Wholesale Trade for 1972, 1977, 1982, 1987, and 1992 (Washington, D.C.: U.S. GPO, 1976, 1981, 1984, 1989, 1995).

gained notably in some. Even the 10-year decline in SIC 5063 (electrical equipment) was reversed. Two market conditions during 1982-1987 probably contributed to this result. First, a slower market growth threatened sales revenues and prompted manufacturers to reach as broad a customer base as possible. Simultaneously, severe price competition caused lower profit margins and necessitated cost reductions wherever possible, including sales expenses. Many manufacturers saw distributors as a logical solution to this two-pronged problem. Note that additional sales also flowed through manufacturers' reps during this period and increased further during 1987-1992. The straight commission rate paid to reps, which results in a fixed and predictable sales expense ratio, replaced the semi-fixed expenses of a sales force.

It is interesting to compare the electronics industry (5065) with industrial supplies (5085). Both industries had fairly constant direct and indirect sales ratios from 1972 to 1982 and then exhibited significant increases in distributor shares. This phenomenon certainly does not result from industry similarities. Electronic components and equipment underwent a series of major technological changes during this period, while the supplies industry remained relatively unchanged and unsophisticated. Moreover, the growth in electronics almost doubled the GNP rate: the supplies industry stagnated before resuming average growth.

A special situation developed in electronics. Note the significant decline in sales through reps. Many small manufacturers—the ones more likely to engage reps—found that they needed more than the technical expertise and market contacts of reps to hold or gain market share. They also required the local inventory and services that only distributors could offer. Hence, their emphasis on reps declined in favor of distribution.[9] The increased dependence of buyers on the brand recommendations of distributors also prompted the change.[3] Reps cannot make alternative brand recommendations since their contracts forbid them to carry competing lines.

The industrial supplies data (5085) present a "textbook" story. Distributors theoretically gain their greatest importance in a slow-growth, mature market for unsophisticated products.[10] However, the electronics data clearly indicate that customers do not discard distributors solely on the basis of product complexity, technological change, or market growth. This fact is further supported by SIC 5081, which includes computers and peripheral hardware, software, photocopy and microfilm equipment. In this composite industry, the distributor share actually increased as products became more complex. One can reasonably assume, however, that the lower indirect channel share in both 5065 and 5045, compared with other industries, correlates to greater product complexity and changing technology.

Thus, market data substantiates theory regarding (1) less use of direct sales given product simplicity and (2) increased use of distributors in mature markets. However, the data for SIC 5082 opposes the theory that the largest portion of high-priced equipment is sold directly. For example, Caterpillar sells the bulk of their road-building equipment, which costs $250,000 to more than $1 million, through a network of exclusive distributors. When a contractor wins an award to rebuild ten miles of an interstate highway, the firm normally requires new equipment immediately. They also require fast response to the need for repairs and spare parts. When the contract is finished, they usually want to sell off some or all of the equipment. Caterpillar distributors handle all of these services from the original purchase to the trade-in.

The interrelation of sales through a firm's sales force and reps will be discussed later, at which point we will again refer to the appropriate data in Table 13-4.

Creating an Effective Channel

When a manufacturer decides to use independent distributors, this initial decision prompts several associated choices. The manufacturer must also decide (1) which marketing functions to assign to or share with distributors; (2) what portion of the product line to sell through this channel; (3) what size and type of distributor to select; (4) whether to use exclusive or multiple distribution; (5) how to divide the selling function between distributors and the company sales force; and (6) what policies to adopt that will ensure an effective, profitable, mutually satisfying relationship.

ASSIGNING MARKETING FUNCTIONS

Almost invariably, a manufacturer expects a distributor to carry local inventory sufficient to serve the market. In addition, the manufacturer usually divides existing and potential customers into two broad categories: those whom the manufacturer will serve directly, except for emergency shipments from the distributor, and those whom the distributor will serve almost entirely, except for occasional technical support provided by the manufacturer.

As one might expect, customers served directly tend to be larger and fewer in number. In effect, most manufacturers "high spot" target markets with their sales force. The distributor is expected to serve the mass market of small- and medium-sized accounts.

Along with inventory and sales responsibility, distributors assume credit liability for those customers who buy from them. This often relieves the manufacturer of a problem disproportionate to the sales volume involved. Although sweeping generalizations have exceptions, smaller firms are more likely to pay invoices slowly or to default entirely.[11] This situation leaves distributors with the larger share of potential bad-debt writeoffs.

Distributors assume other functions, such as repairs, in-warranty service, local advertising, trade show participation, and new product sampling, but these duties tend to be product specific. Inventory maintenance, selling, and credit risk assumption are universal.

PRODUCT LINE COVERAGE

Fragmented Channels   Manufacturers sometimes fragment the channeling of their overall product line. This decision usually stems from the premise that portions of the product line are aimed at different market segments served by different distributor groups. For example, distributors in SIC 5065 sell TI semiconductor products, but TI computers move through distributors in SIC 5045, whereas calculators and educational products for children are marketed most effectively by distributors who deal primarily with retailers.

As a general rule, manufacturers try to minimize such fragmentation. Within the bounds of practicality, customers will more likely buy the complementary products of a manufacturer (products that are used jointly) when these products are available from a single source. As shown in Table 13-1, one of the primary benefits customers seek from distributors is "one-stop shopping."

Specialized Products   Custom-designed and single-customer products are the major exceptions to sourcing a complete product line through distributors. The average distributor lacks the technical expertise to negotiate unique specifications with industrial users. Thus, the manufacturer should handle these matters directly. Moreover, engineering departments redesign special products more than once. The second redesign leaves the distributor with a useless inventory of expensive parts that no one wants, including the manufacturer. Therefore, for better control, communication, and relationships, most specialized products flow through the direct channel.

DISTRIBUTOR SIZE

Some manufacturers treat this topic as a minor decision, whereas others make the decision traumatically and subjectively. If all distributors were indeed the stereotypical $1 to $2 million, ten-employee, single-location type of operation, this decision would be relatively simple. But as shown in Table 13-5, such is not the case.

The data in Table 13-5 are based on eight of the nine industries previously analyzed in Tables 13-3 and 13-4. Unfortunately, data for industrial supplies (SIC 5085) are not broken out for the largest 50 distributors. The remaining industries included 72,171 distributors in 1992. If these firms were analyzed as one group, we could correctly state that the "average" distributor had sales revenue of approximately $4.5 million, employed 13.5 people, and did business from a single stocking location (1.2 locations, to be precise). When we purposely segregate the 50 largest distributors in each industry (or a total of 400 for the eight industries), several facts emerge that are critically important to any marketer setting up a distribution channel.

These top 400 distributors averaged $289 million in sales, employed 441 people and operated in 16 stocking locations, which averaged more than $18 million in sales. As Table 13-5 shows, all these numbers dwarf the comparable figures for the remaining distributors. Of even greater importance to manufacturers, these top distributors enjoyed 35.7 percent of the total distribution business and had a significant productivity advantage over their smaller competitors. Each employee generated more than $654,000 in sales compared to $262,000 for the smaller firms.

This combined volume and cost-effectiveness raises several relevant points. First, these firms can afford to carry a larger and more complete inventory for better cus-

TABLE 13-5 Comparison of Fifty Largest Distributors per Industry Versus Others: Eight Selected Industries; 1992

Factor	Top Fifty	Others
Number of firms	400	71,771
Number of locations	6,342	82,488
Locations per firm	15.9	1.1
Employees/firm	441.3	11.1
Employees/location	27.8	9.6
Average Sales ($ 000)	$288,692	$2,903
Average Sales/location ($ 000)	$18,208	$2,526
Average Payroll ($ 000)	$16,140	$344
Sales/payroll (ratio)	17.9	8.4
Sales/employee ($ 000)	$654.3	$262.2
Relative productivity*	100.0	40.1
Percent of firms	0.5%	99.5%
Percent of sales	35.7%	64.3%

*Comparative sales/employee

Source: U.S. Department of Commerce, *Census of Wholesale Trade, Establishment and Firm Size: 1992* (Washington D.C.: U.S. GPO, April 1995), pp.194-211.

tomer service. Second, with lower selling costs, they can either generate higher profits to support complementary services or pursue increased sales with more aggressive pricing. In addition, given their size and relative success in their market, they can regularly attract franchises for those product lines most in demand by business users.

These strengths, however, offer a mixed blessing to any manufacturer that seeks to establish a distribution channel or to improve on an existing one, particularly when the manufacturer's product line commands only a weak market share. Although the distributor's strengths, conscientiously applied, could undoubtedly increase that market share, the manufacturer must question whether these strengths will indeed be applied to a new line. Or, more likely, will the distributor's sales force continue to emphasize products that are easy to sell? Also, if this dominant distributor puts a total effort behind the product line and succeeds in building a significant sales volume, how much control will the manufacturer have over channel strategy?[12]

Manufacturers have the alternative of selecting one or more of the many smaller distributors. Perhaps such firms will, through solid effort, commitment, and enthusiasm, produce outstanding results. Some customer surveys indicate that the largest distributors have forgotten about customer service in their battle for market supremacy.[13] Moreover, by concentrating on smaller distributors, the manufacturer has a better chance of retaining strategic control.[14] Two smaller firms battling together against the industry giants might generate greater compatibility and effectiveness. Although this is a promising scenario, these smaller firms may lack the strength to offset or compensate for each other's weaknesses and can also fail together. As suggested earlier, the selection of distributors can cause emotional trauma.

DISTRIBUTOR TYPE

All distributors perform the same primary functions (carrying inventory, selling, and providing credit), but the relative importance and effort each assigns to these tasks will vary. The types of customers pursued, the emphasis placed on price, the number of product lines carried, and the relative amount of time spent on creative versus maintenance selling also vary considerably. Thus, manufacturers must choose distributors not only on size (assuming options are available) but also on operational strategies.

This latter choice harks back to the basic questions that marketers must answer before establishing a channel strategy, namely: "What marketing functions are critical to the success of strategy?" and "Which of these functions can best be performed by an outside agency?" Obviously, if a marketer sacrifices some degree of control by shifting responsibilities outside the firm, there should be reasonable assurance that the contracted functions will be well performed. And, since the manufacturer can categorize distributors by their specific strengths and areas of concentration, there is no reason to make this choice by flipping a coin.[15]

Why a Particular Distributor Is Chosen

In 1979, the American Supply and Machinery Manufacturers' Association (ASMMA) hired Frank Lynn and Associates to perform a landmark survey. ASMMA includes those manufacturers whose products flow through distributors in SIC 5084 and 5085. These firms wanted distributors to provide information pertinent to several important issues: (1) Which type of distributor sells products most effectively? (2) What amount and type of market coverage do they provide? (3) How much sales effort and inventory support can manufacturers realistically expect from distributors?[16] Table 13-6

		TABLE 13-6 Profile of ASSMA Distributors (SIC 5084, 5085)		

Issue	Technical Specialists	General-Line Distributors	Inventory Specialists
1. Number of Product lines	<40	≥100	<20
2. Sales percent from top three lines	≥70%	<40%	≥80%
3. Selling percent of total expenses	37%	32%	26%
4. Inventory percent of total expenses	42%	42%	63%
5. Sales effort percent put on primary/secondary/ tertiary lines	45/45/10%	72/27/1%	90/10/0%
6. Revenue percent obtained from primary/sec- ondary/tertiary lines	55/40/5%	64/26/10%	90/10/0%
7. Selling role and market coverage	a. Primary lines sold on repeat buys to large and medium customer b. Secondary (new) lines used to create markets c. Ignore small customers	a. Primary/secondary lines both for repeat buys to large/medium customers b. Limited effort to sell to small customers c. Some small customer "call-in" orders	a. Emphasis on large customer contract business b. Aggressive pricing policy c. Ignore small and medium customers
8. Attitude toward high-volume/low-profit contract business package	Only 10% of total volume; not usually the low bidder	About 30%; mostly in multi-product "system" sales	About 50%; actively pursue with price/ inventory

Source: Frank Lynn & Associates, Inc., *Profile of Industrial Distribution 1979; Summary Report* (Cleveland, Ohio: American Supply and Machinery Manufacturers Association, Inc., 1979).

shows the summary results of this survey, which include several important implications for marketers who use or plan to use distributors.

MARKET/CUSTOMER COVERAGE

Manufacturers who concentrate their direct sales effort on major customers would like to see distributors actively soliciting business from the smaller accounts in a given geographic market. The ASMMA survey reveals, however, that both technical and inventory specialists expend most of their sales effort on larger customers, ignoring the smaller ones. Only general-line distributors put any effort in this area, and that effort is spotty at best.

Clearly, a small manufacturer with resources too limited to hire a sizable sales force, and with an equally limited market acceptance, will have to consider space advertising in trade or business publications, direct mail, and other communication techniques to generate a broad base of customers. Manufacturers' reps might present another viable alternative.

Another survey, which studied the buying habits of more than 300 OEM firms in the electronics industry, might help to explain a distributor's concentration on larger customers. Customers in this survey were asked to quantify their total purchases and the percent bought from distributors. Their answers were grouped into six dollar ranges, as shown in Table 13-7.

The data supports a basic channel theory that distributor participation decreases as the customer's buying potential increases. However, the increase in *dollar potential*

TABLE 13-7   Distributor's Participation in OEM Purchases

Customer's Total Buying Potential ($ 000)	Distributor Participation		
	Percent of Total	Dollars ($ 000)	Midpoint ($ 000)
<250	75-100	<250	125
250-499	50-80	125-400	262
500-999	30-60	150-600	375
1,000-2,499	15-35	150-875	512
2,500-4,999	5-15	125-750	437
5,000-10,000	0-5	0-500	250

Source: E.G. Brierty, "Survey of Midwest industrial OEM customers: Purchases of electronic components through distribution," (unpublished report, September 1976).

of larger accounts, up to some level, more than offsets the falloff in *percentage.* As a consequence, distributors can realize greater sales volume and potential profit—for the same amount of effort and inventory investment—by concentrating on larger customers. Given the data in Table 13-7, a distributor can average twice the sales by servicing customers who purchase in the range of $1-2.5 million compared with the same amount of effort expended on those who buy less than $500,000.

The percentages and related dollar potentials shown in Table 13-7 will vary considerably with product, economic conditions, customer buying philosophy, distributor service image, and various other factors. But the same general results are likely to occur across a range of products and markets, as indicated by the ASMMA survey.

Informal conversations with distribution executives indicate to the writer that the findings of both surveys still apply in the 1990s. If anything, the largest distributors spend even less effort on small accounts.

MARKET DEVELOPMENT

The findings of the ASMMA survey also indicate that most distributors do not regularly engage in market development activity. They prefer to direct their sales effort toward product markets that have already been developed. If this implication is accurate, manufacturers cannot rely on distributors to help in this important function. Fortunately, this is an area wherein change has occurred.

During the 1980s, a combination of diminished customer demand, increased competition, and the necessity to penetrate broader markets both at home and abroad led major producers to present their distributors with an ultimatum—either support market expansion efforts or lose the franchise. This meant that distributors would have to increase their technical support, contact small, developing customers as well as the large ones, tailor special services for individual accounts, and in general, move beyond the simple stock-sell-ship formula. Some distributors, particularly those with more ambitious market share goals, revamped their strategies to encompass these new responsibilities.[17]

These demands were not without potential rewards. As a notable example, Motorola's semiconductor division cut their North American distribution network from 36 to four distributors.[18] The four remaining members could now split up a sales potential in excess of a billion dollars. Because of network streamlining by other producers plus a flurry of mergers among distributors and some business closures, the total number of electronic parts distributors shrank from approximately 1,800 in 1980 to less than 1,100 in 1993. However, the survivors shared a U.S. market of almost $13 billion compared with a 1980 market of less than $3 billion.

As a further reference to the relative size and strength of some distributors, the top five in the electronic parts industry held 63 percent of the U.S. market in 1993. This share rose from 48 percent in 1985 and 39 percent in 1980.[18]

PRODUCT CONCENTRATION

Smaller manufacturers who have not yet established a reputation within their target market face a serious challenge when they try to build demand for a new product. Unless the product exhibits extraordinary capability, technical specialists hesitate to take it on as a market development tool. Inventory specialists view it as a secondary product at best and give it less than ten percent of their effort. General-line distributors might be interested, but the product line then becomes only one of more than 100 separate lines vying for attention and sales effort.

The manufacturer faces an apparent no-win situation. Potential users will not adopt the product unless it is supported by local distributor inventory and service. Distributors, however, do not want to stock the product before they see an established market. No wonder that manufacturers must use both direct and indirect channels to establish their markets. Distributors can and do perform certain marketing tasks quite well. Other tasks they perform poorly or not at all.

Exclusive or Multiple Distribution

Manufacturers usually let the size and dispersion of a given geographic market determine the number of distributors that they franchise in that area. Distributors often begin as market specialists, but over time become product specialists. For example, electronic parts distributors in the 1950s obtained more than half their sales from radio and TV service dealers. The replacement of defective vacuum tubes alone accounted for 25 to 35percent of total sales dollars. With the advent of new technologies, particularly semiconductors and computers, two significant changes took place.

First, because of the dramatic increase in component reliability (transistor failure rates were only 1/100 that of vacuum tubes), the replacement market dwindled. Second, component reliability combined with electronic systems capabilities converted many industrial applications from mechanical components to electronics. Nonetheless, relatively few industrial equipment and supplies distributors (SIC codes 5084 and 5085) carried electronic components. Rather, distributors in SIC 5065 found themselves serving a much broader and more diversified group of customers with the ready encouragement of both suppliers and product users. For example, when a steel company needed replacement parts for its computer-controlled rolling mill, it went to a hardware distributor for mechanical parts and an electronics distributor for electronic components and subsystems. It was a natural evolution that all parties accepted readily.

Therefore, the number of franchised distributors depends primarily on the size of a market and the market share held by the various firms. If one distributor is clearly dominant in a market with a relatively low potential, exclusive distribution would seem logical. However, in major market areas (usually coinciding with major population centers), multiple distribution is a common strategy.

PROBLEMS TO AVOID

A manufacturer should try to avoid two potential problems. First, franchising too many distributors in any market simply makes the product line undesirable to all. There is no magic answer as to how many is too many.[19] This will depend on industry norms and the distributor's expectation of sales from this product line. For example, if most manufacturers in a given industry use three to five distributors to serve the greater Los Angeles market, then one is probably insufficient and seven too many.

From the distributor's standpoint, primary product lines should generate $100,000 to 500,000 annually depending on the geographic market. A manufacturer would be imprudent, therefore, to franchise four distributors in a $200,000 product market, unless the firm was willing to accept a secondary position (with secondary attention) for an indefinite period. A manufacturer can normally determine the average sales volume generated by any product in the distribution channel from industry association reports, government documents (e.g., Census of Wholesale Trade and U.S. Industrial Outlook), or by surveying distributors.

The second potential problem involves the mixture of distributors in multiple distribution markets. For example, a manufacturer might prefer the mix of a general-line house and an inventory specialist, feeling that this combination would ensure the broadest possible market coverage. The generalist could cover smaller customers with a comprehensive product package, whereas the specialist would pursue major potentials on a concentrated, price-aggressive basis. On the surface, this strategy makes sense and can work according to plan. However, if the two distributors find themselves competing too often for business at medium-sized accounts, and the specialist consistently undercuts the generalist's prices, there will surely be trouble at the OK Corral. A manufacturer cannot always prevent such problems or even foresee them, but the potential headaches certainly warrant careful analysis during the channel formation stage.

Distribution Policies

The formulation of an effective and workable distributor franchise agreement represents a formidable challenge to the manufacturer. Some firms sin by excess, trying to cover every last detail and contingency that might occur over the next decade; others sin by defect, leaving too many important variables to chance. A happy compromise will accomplish three tasks: it will (1) spell out the respective duties of both parties to each other and to their common market, (2) recognize the rights of both parties and show how these will be protected, and (3) by virtue of the points elaborated, attempt to foresee major potential conflicts and resolve them beforehand.

Since many important topics are product or market specific, one cannot compile an all-inclusive list of items to address in a distributor agreement. However, Box 13-1 sets forth some issues that will probably affect manufacturer-distributor relationships in most industries.

DUTIES AND GOALS

A manufacturer must consider a broad range of marketing activities that can be performed in-house, assigned to distributors, or shared. Given the wide difference of opinions regarding delegation of these activities, marketers must detail, quite clearly, who is responsible to do what. Besides a clarification of duties, the marketer must also explain the major elements of the marketing strategy as they pertain to the distributor, such as the principal

---

BOX 13-1

Issues to Address in Distributor Franchise Agreements

DUTIES OF BOTH PARTIES

Distributor

1. Carry sufficient inventory to meet market needs.
2. Disseminate new product information and samples to assigned accounts.
3. Extend competitive credit terms to credit-worthy customers.
4. Use price to stimulate market growth, but maintain reasonable profit margins.
5. Participate in co-op advertising programs to enhance market share.
6. Relay market information regarding business opportunities and/or problems.
7. Provide manufacturer with a list of customers by product segment.
8. Follow up on all customer leads forwarded by the manufacturer.

Manufacturer

1. Supply products with a level of quality and innovation necessary to meet market penetration plans.
2. Make these plans known to distributor in order to coordinate joint efforts and minimize conflict.
3. Establish distributor buy prices (costs) that permit competitive resale pricing plus a reasonable profit margin.
4. Devise promotion programs to stimulate market demand.
5. Provide distributor personnel with adequate training, guidance, information, and support.
6. Handle all stocking orders accurately and on schedule.
7. Refer to the distributor all customer orders that fall within "protected quantity" levels.

8. Keep the distributor informed regarding activity at major accounts that might require distributor support or represent a business opportunity.

RIGHTS AND PROTECTION OF BOTH PARTIES

Distributor

1. Right to return obsolete inventory provided the inventory mix and quantity was previously approved by the manufacturer.
2. Protection against the manufacturer's arbitrary decision to make any distributor customer a "house account."
3. Protection against the arbitrary addition of new distributors in this geographic area as ling as market penetration goals have been met.
4. Inventory cost protection whenever the manufacturer reduces market price so that distributor's new profit margin is inadequate for sales within the protected quantity level.

Manufacturer

1. Any proprietary information given to distributor for guidance of coordination purposes will be safeguarded (particularly from competition).
2. Distributor will not use price in a manner that disrupts normal market activity (e.g., continually soliciting business at a price below cost).
3. Protection against the distributor arbitrarily adding competing product lines.
4. Distributor will not use co-op advertising funds to promote products other than those supplied by the manufacturer (unless special permission is given beforehand).

---

target markets, the approximate market share desired, the relative emphasis on price, the degree of product innovation to be expected, and the level of customer service required. These strategic positions cannot be left to inference or individual interpretation.

A large portion of channel conflict stems from ambiguity and incompatibility between the goals of the manufacturer and those of the distributor. For example, a skimming price strategy will be subverted by a distributor who emphasizes low prices instead of superior service. A broad customer base will not accrue through distributors who concentrate on the same key customers that the manufacturer serves directly. A manufacturer seeking increased market share requires distributors equally dissatisfied with their own competitive position. There is no reason for ambiguity, and potential incompatibilities should surface during initial negotiation, when compromise is possible, rather than later, when they can disrupt the entire strategy.

RIGHTS AND PROTECTION

Channel participants remain independent business organizations, even though both parties recognize the benefits of working together. Although this might sound like an elaboration of the obvious, some manufacturers give disproportionate attention to their own needs and goals. On the other side, some distributors see customers as their reason for existence but treat suppliers as a necessary evil. Therefore, the wise and prudent marketer will try to prevent false assumptions by exhibiting an understanding of both sides of the proposed relationship.

For example, by stressing product innovation, manufacturers often engage in self-obsolescence. This means that portions of a distributor's inventory can suddenly become worthless. Unless the manufacturer assumes some financial liability, the distributor must choose between carrying too little inventory for proper customer service and running the risk of severe profit erosion resulting from inventory writeoffs. [12] As a consequence, many manufacturers agree to accept the return of obsolete inventory for full credit, provided the distributor has exercised reasonable judgment by carrying an appropriate inventory volume.

As pointed out earlier, manufacturers commonly use multiple distributors in major markets. This practice stems from a desire to achieve market acceptance through increased selling effort. By similar reasoning, distributors regularly carry competing product lines to satisfy a broader range of customer preferences. Although neither party is completely satisfied with these conflicts of interest, they both tend to accept the situation as a market reality. Nevertheless, each wants some control over potential alterations after the franchise agreement is in effect. Manufacturers want "veto power" over a distributor's desire to add competing lines, and distributors want the same prerogative regarding the addition of distributors within the served market. [12]

Franchise agreements commonly include a 60- or 90-day cancellation clause, with either party having the right to cancel for "just cause." The addition of distributors or competing lines is a frequent reason for this clause being exercised. In the 1960s and earlier, manufacturers wielded the greatest power. They added and deleted distributors for a variety of self-serving reasons. However, as distributors grew in size and importance, the power struggle became more equal. In addition, some states have enacted legislation that puts greater pressure on both parties to prove alleged misdeeds and disservice by referencing written contracts that clearly delineate partnership expectations. Maryland's Fair Distribution Act of 1993 is a notable example.[20]

Manufacturers' Representatives

REPS COMPARED WITH DISTRIBUTORS

Reps share relatively few characteristics with distributors aside from both being independent entrepreneurs primarily engaged in selling. Beyond this commonality, differences abound. Distributors buy and stock inventory, which they resell at prices of their own choosing. Reps, as sales agents, do not buy the products they sell, rarely carry inventory, and sell at prices dictated by the manufacturer. Distributors also regularly sell competing products, whereas reps handle only complementary products. Although both emphasize the selling function, reps are more likely to engage in market development through a combination of established contacts and technical competence. Part of this technical competency stems from the fact that reps usually handle only five to eight product lines that they understand fairly well. Distributors, however, who handle 50 to 100 different product lines, cannot provide a customer with much more than catalog information. Finally, a product manufacturer will frequently use more than one distributor in a geographic market. With rare exception, reps operate under an exclusive franchise in their assigned territory.

Although reps are usually viewed as an indirect marketing channel, this designation can be misleading. Distributors are indeed an indirect channel, because they purchase the products of a manufacturer and resell them to various customers. The products do not flow directly from maker to user. A manufacturer selling part of its output directly to other customers may use sales employees, independent reps, or a combination of both to serve these customers. In this context, reps are not really an indirect channel, but a substitute or surrogate for a direct sales force. It is more important to understand the marketing roles performed by distributors and reps rather than their semantic definitions.

WHAT TO EXPECT FROM A REP

Reps have been described as the purest form of sales practitioner. Indeed, since they operate with few assets other than personal skills, exist on straight commission (no sales, no income), and are subject to the whims of both suppliers and customers, they must certainly possess a high level of self-confidence and unwavering motivation. In addition, those who succeed also possess product and market knowledge, have the customer's trust, and the ability to compete.[21] In short, the rep appears to offer all the traits that a corporate sales manager seeks in prospective employees but cannot always find or afford. Firms tend to choose reps instead of a company sales force when they suffer from some type of constraint or limitation. The constraint may be financial, such as limited resources, disappointing expense/sales ratios, or a depressed market potential. The limitation may center on a lack of experience in a particular market. Since reps are paid a straight commission and cover all of their operating expenses, the marketer will not encounter fixed personnel expenses without sales; and once sales start to flow, the expense/sales ratio will be predictable and fixed at the commission rate.

Dartnell's 1992 survey of sales compensation contained some interesting comparisons between the cost of maintaining a sales force compared with the commissions paid to reps.[22] Table 13-8 contains the relevant highlights on this issue. As one might expect, smaller firms use reps to a greater degree, but larger companies also recognize their value. The fact that commission rates paid are substantially above the expense-to-sales ratios reported by firms with sales of $100 million would indicate that reps are not selected solely as a cost-cutting measure.

Even though companies might have the resources to hire and support their own sales force, they can still benefit from a rep's established market presence and customer rapport. In addition, the presence of the rep's other lines often serves as an indirect door-opener, an advantage the manufacturer would not have selling directly. Finally, an established rep firm can provide a level of experience, professionalism, and cohesiveness that the manufacturer would have difficulty matching with new hires.[23]

TABLE 13-8 Sales Force Expenses Compared With Rep Commission Rates

	Sales Force Expense/Sales*	Manufacturers' Rep Commission (%)	Percentage Who Use Reps
Company Size			
<$5 million	14.7	13.3	20.2
5-25 M	10.5	11.1	34.9
25-100 M	7.9	6.1	24.5
100-250 M	3.5	12.0	10.0
>250 M	6.8	15.3	14.3
Business			
Office products	9.4	15.3	20.6
Office services	8.1	15.9	13.2
Consumer products	5.4	11.4	26.8
Consumer services	7.9	12.8	11.3
Industrial products	4.1	9.1	33.0
Industrial services	6.4	13.2	14.6
Customers			
Retailers	6.9	9.9	19.5
Industrial firms	6.4	10.5	23.4
Distributors	5.5	11.0	25.5
Consumers	3.6	14.7	19.0

*Includes total compensation, travel and entertainment expenses paid, and fringe benefits but *excludes* the cost of support personnel necessary in a sales office.

Source: Dartnell Corporation, *Sales Force Compensation Survey,* 27th ed. (Chicago: Dartnell Corporation, 1993), pp. 109, 171.

These factors prompt many firms to begin their sales efforts with reps, even though they intend to hire a sales force eventually.

POTENTIAL PROBLEMS IN DEALING THROUGH REPS

Lack of Control   A reason frequently given by manufacturers who do not use reps, and a common complaint by some who do, concerns operational control.[24] No one suggests the possibility of open rebellion, but independent entrepreneurs exist primarily to meet their own goals. Some manufacturers go on to state that reps are also more difficult to motivate.[25]

Not all manufacturers, however, lay blame for these problems completely on their reps. One firm, which has had notable success selling through reps, stated, "Too many of us expect the rep to do all the work in return for his commission."[26] This spokesperson could have meant that manufacturers often expect more from reps than they would from their own sales force.

For example, reps often complain about being loaded down with excessive missionary sales, market research, credit and collection problems, and similar tasks that subtract from their productive selling time and do not generate commissions. Yet if the offending firm had a company sales force, one of their primary interests would be keeping sales people relatively free of nonselling tasks. For instance, product managers would perform the preliminary missionary work and market research, a credit department would worry about delinquent payments, and customer service personnel would take care of routine paperwork and follow-up. Moreover, the rep's sales skills and customer contacts cannot substitute for desirable products, competitive prices, and effective advertising. Without these prerequisite tools, the world's greatest salesperson will be ineffective.

Competing Product Lines   Marketers must also remember that they face competition at two levels when selling through reps.[26] Not only do they face competing product lines in the market but also compete with other firms selling products through the same reps. In this instance, the products do not compete for the same customer dollar. However, they do compete for the rep's time and effort. Theoretically, a rep with five complementary product lines devotes 20 percent of time and effort to each line. In reality, this rarely occurs. Like any logical and goal-oriented individual, the rep allocates time and effort in proportion to results obtained. If one supplier generates an increasing share of the rep's sales, this firm will demand more time and attention, and the rep finds it very tempting to oblige. Thus, a supplier must provide products, prices, promotion, and supportive services not only to attract customers but also to motivate reps who sell to those customers.[27]

FRANCHISE AGREEMENTS FOR REPS

Many of the previous comments regarding distributor franchise agreements apply equally to rep agreements. Since the functions of a rep and a distributor differ, however, the agreements will emphasize different operational details. For example, since the rep acts as the duly authorized sales agent of the manufacturer, the laws of agency apply. Therefore, if only for legal purposes, the manufacturer must have an agreement that clearly delineates the range and limitations of the rep's delegated authority. However, in addition to legal considerations, the critical need to articulate shared responsibilities as well as individual rights and protections still exists.

PARTICIPATION OF REPS IN THE BUSINESS MARKET

In 1984, an estimated 45,000 to 50,000 U.S. manufacturers, plus some unknown number of foreign suppliers, were selling through reps.[26] According to the 1992 Census of Wholesale Trade, 38,556 manufacturers' reps in the United States sold more than $351 billion in both domestic and imported goods and services.[28] As with distributors, one must be careful not to group all reps into a single stereotype. Table 13-9 shows that these channel intermediaries also range from rather small organizations to very sizable ones. The thirteen largest rep firms averaged more than $2.4 billion in sales during 1992.[29]

As Table 13-9 indicates, reps sell for both large and small companies, although anecdotal evidence indicates that their tenure with smaller firms tends to be somewhat uncertain. As the sales volume increases, some companies "grow out of" the relationship and hire their own sales force. However, sizable companies like National Semiconductor, ITT, Corning Glass, Monsanto, Teledyne, and Mobil Oil have been using reps for decades.

THE IMPACT OF MARKET FACTORS

Table 13-4 data provide a more definitive picture of the role reps play in U.S. wholesale trade. As a weighted average across the nine selected industries, reps control approximately ten percent of total volume with little variation since 1972. The data for all wholesale trade in 1987 and 1992 track very closely at 10.5 percent and 10.8 percent respectively.

These figures do not, however, signify a uniform participation across all industries. Table 13-4 indicates rates varying from less than five percent in office equipment,

TABLE 13-9 Wholesale Trade through Manufacturers' Reps by Size of Firm; 1992

Number of Employees	Number of Firms*	Percentage of Total	Sales (millions of dollars)	Percent of Total	Sales/Firm (millions of dollars)
1-19	36,508	94.7	200,231	5 6.6	5.5
20-99	1,854	4.8	73,402	29.6	39.6
100-249	151	0.4	27,256	6.5	180.5
250+	43	0.1	44,183	7.3	1,027.5
Total	38,556	100.0	345,072	100.0	8.9

*Firms in business through the entire year.

Source: U.S. Department of Commerce, *Census of Wholesale Trade, Establishment and Firm Size: 1992,* (Washington D.C.: U.S. GPO, April 1995), p.175.

computers, and construction/mining equipment to more than 20 percent in electronics. Although no research has been published to explain this variability, one can infer several plausible reasons.

Reps enjoy their highest participation rate in electronics (SIC 5065). Several factors associated with this industry caused both the high participation rate as well as the decline during the 1980s. First, this industry contains more than 10,000 U.S. manufacturers, many of them small, specialized entrepreneurial organizations. A significant portion of these firms were founded by technologists with little or no marketing experience. In order to penetrate their target markets ahead of competition and before limited financial resources ran out, they contracted with marketing specialists (reps) to sell their products.

A second factor involves the hundreds of foreign companies, particularly Asian semiconductor producers, who wanted to penetrate the world's largest market in the 1970s. Not only did these firms lack contacts here, but also major U.S. producers threatened to disenfranchise distributors if they took on the foreign product lines. The foreign producers thus had to sell directly to end users, but "directly" in this instance meant through reps. Eventually, the largest distributors, not willing to lose significant sales opportunities by default, challenged the stand of U.S. producers and signed franchises with firms such as Toshiba, NEC, and Hitachi. They argued successfully that the strength of these firms lay in products (high-volume memory chips) that U.S. semiconductor makers were phasing out. This redistribution of wholesale trade resulted in a greater share for distributors and a declining share for reps. But note that total sales volume in SIC 5065 (review Table 13-3) grew from $15.6 billion in 1977 to $106 billion in 1992. Thus, despite a declining share, sales through reps grew from $5.6 to $21.1 billion.

One sees an entirely different picture in the construction/mining equipment industry (SIC 5082). As discussed earlier, the preponderance of sales in this industry flows through distributors. Manufacturers like Caterpillar handle most of what remains, primarily major buys involving customer-specific performance and negotiated pricing.

Other Channel Participants

Distributors and reps are by far the predominant channel members in the business market. Several other categories of intermediaries play lesser roles. Brokers and value-added resellers are two examples.

Brokers   These commissioned agents may represent a seller or buyer or both. The term of service is usually shorter than that of the rep; it may only be a "one shot" relationship. Brokers often handle the buying and selling of surplus inventory. For example, a manufacturer of government equipment may have its contract cut short and be left with a useless stock of component parts. The contracting agency will usually reimburse the firm for the unusable parts, but only after the firm has made a reasonable effort to recover some part of the cost. A broker is then commissioned to "find a home" for the surplus inventory. The broker may know of another manufacturer who can use the parts or a distributor who normally sells this type of product. The broker then negotiates a deal that is mutually satisfactory to buyer and seller.

Value-Added Resellers (VARs)   This category is not new but has gained greater prominence since the 1970s because of the computer industry. Computer manufacturers also refer to VARs as OEMs to differentiate them from business end-users. Many VARs specialize in the needs of a particular market segment (e.g., retailers, banks, accounting firms, medical labs, etc.). They gather together the separate products of individual producers and design an operating system tailored to the needs of their specialty market. With computers becoming increasingly pervasive, peripheral equipment more diversified, and specific applications more demanding, VARs provide a very valuable service to both buyer and seller.

Import and Export Agents   The need for effective channel members increases in importance when a company decides to sell beyond its domestic borders. Many of the issues discussed regarding distributors and manufacturers' reps still hold but become more critical. The term "local inventory" implies not only a warehouse thousands of miles away from the factory but also the possible imposition of tariffs, taxes, and unfamiliar laws. In addition, business customs change significantly from one country to another. Just as Asian and European firms need marketing guidance in the United States, so too, American firms going international cannot use their past experience without alteration.

Import and export agents (some agents do both) provide a handy solution. Put simply, these intermediaries know how to get products in and out of countries and into the hands of prospective buyers with a minimum of hassle and an optimal profitability. As with distributors and their operating profit margins, some firms begrudge paying a commission to these agents. However, after one or two very costly fiascoes on their own, they quickly learn the meaning of the phrase "you get what you pay for."

Some of the physical distribution changes taking place in the 1990s (and discussed in Chapter 14) also help to simplify international sales. Worldwide carriers are opening public warehouses in many industrialized countries. Major U.S. distributors have opened branches in Europe and Asia. Other international sales and distribution companies are forming that will act as multinational rep organizations. Even nations are looking for ways to simplify the flow of trade between them. Nonetheless, doing business on an international scope confronts both buyers and sellers with additional product-flow challenges.

Maintaining Indirect Channel Effectiveness

Manufacturers do not always dominate a marketing channel. Specific industry situations bear this out. For example, the 23 largest electronic parts distributors each had 1994 sales volumes in excess of $100 million. The two largest, Arrow Electronics and

Avnet, sold $4.5 billion and $3.7 billion respectively. An "average" manufacturer with total sales, direct and indirect, of $10 to 20 million cannot dictate strategies and tactics to distributors of this magnitude. Yet every manufacturer, regardless of size, must assume the responsibility for its own marketing strategy, including the choice of channels. Unless the firm can produce a desirable product that satisfies some target market, there is no need for a channel of distribution. Once the product and market exist, the firm must select a channel that enhances a customer's perception of the product's value. To ensure that channel participants provide this enhancement, the firm must supply several essential ingredients.

ESSENTIAL INGREDIENTS FOR SUCCESS

Realistic Goals   Inferior or uncompetitive products do not entice an experienced distributor or rep. A manufacturer with unrealistic goals for a desirable product, either in terms of market share or potential profitability, appears equally unattractive.

Therefore, any successful channel strategy requires realism and objectivity. The objectivity should encompass not only quantitative goals, but also the level of commitment expected from channel members and the factory support provided to earn it.

Two-Way Communications   Virtually every survey aimed at identifying and eliminating channel problems places poor communications at or near the top of the list.[29] Ironically, manufacturers and intermediaries express the same sentiment with equal vehemence. Distributors and reps complain, for example, that manufacturers do not clarify their goals or intended level of support, whereas manufacturers bemoan the unwillingness of channel members to discuss their customer plans and results.

Like the chicken-and-egg dilemma, this one must also have a beginning. The manufacturer who recognizes the channel member as a full marketing partner usually enjoys equal treatment. A sharer of proprietary information tends to receive similar information in return. Treating constructive criticism with respect and corrective action increases the flow of positive information (and may even reduce the amount of trivial complaints).

The establishment of a distributor or rep council provides an excellent first step in creating an effective two-way communication flow.[30] These councils allow executive personnel to meet informally, on an equal footing, to discuss mutual goals and problems. Proprietary information flows more readily in such settings.

Necessary Training   The word *necessary* indicates both importance and variability. Reps do not require sales training, but they certainly require training in new products and benefit from greater knowledge of competition and industry trends. Distributors often require help in providing their new salespeople with effective selling techniques and product knowledge. In addition, smaller distributors can use (and, if presented properly, will appreciate) business training. This may include controlling inventory, managing accounts receivable, pricing for profitability, or analyzing customer potentials.

The central point is that marketers can either sit back and bemoan the lack of capability and professionalism they perceive in distributors, or they can take constructive steps to remedy deficiencies. Obviously, only the latter approach improves channel effectiveness to the benefit of the manufacturer.

Compatibility   We suggested earlier that the compatibility of channel partners is critical. This includes compatible attitudes regarding growth, pricing, target markets, and customer service levels. Incompatibility in size may prove necessary, depending on the availability of channel members in a particular geographic area. The other issues transcend size, and the marketer willing to devote sufficient time and energy to the search can usually find a suitable partner.

Compensation and Support   Too often manufacturers worry more about the cost of their selected channels than the benefits provided. A controller once said to the writer, "A six percent commission is okay for the rep selling $100,000, but suppose he lucks out and sells $1 million. What do we do then?" He was advised, "Don't worry about the rep, just have fun counting your $940,000!"

A manufacturer must again use objectivity when evaluating the functions performed by channel members. Presumably, they can perform both effectively and efficiently; otherwise, the manufacturer has made a poor choice. If the choice is correct, their compensation should realistically reflect the costs and benefits involved. Unless this is true, the distributor will sell competing products, and the rep will concentrate on the complementary lines.

Channel members, even when compensated fairly, do not perform all the functions necessary to make the channel strategy a success. For example, product innovation, quality control, advertising, and competitive pricing are still required. These responsibilities, along with a segment of customer service and inventory maintenance, fall on the manufacturer. Thus, the manufacturer's overall image in the market depends on the service provided by channel members, but their ability to serve customers depends on the manufacturer's support. It is truly a partnership.

Looking Back

Most manufacturers, after evaluating their own capabilities and the service demands of customers, decide to channel at least part of their product sales through distributors. Although using this indirect channel costs the manufacturer some degree of control, the loss is offset by the benefits of localized service and inventory, plus the synergy of associated product lines that the distributor can offer.

Distributors vary widely in size, market coverage, and operating philosophy; thus, they may differ greatly with the manufacturer regarding pricing strategy, the attention paid to smaller customers, or the importance of developing new markets. Although manufacturers commonly use multiple distributors in major markets, problems can also arise if these distributors prove to be more adversarial than compatible. Thus, partial lack of control may be the least challenge facing a manufacturer in the process of establishing an indirect channel.

To prevent some of these problems, both distributor and rep franchise agreements should clearly define the primary duties and responsibilities, as well as the rights and protection, of both parties. If marketers expect to gain optimal cooperation from channel members, they must first prove their willingness to accept these intermediaries as full strategic partners.

Manufacturers' representatives bear greater resemblance to a corporate sales force than to distributors. Given clear operating roles, responsibilities, and authority by the manufacturer, these two types of channel members can operate quite compatibly with each other. Their historical modes of operation indicate the division of activities that can logically be assigned to each channel when both are utilized.

The primary responsibility for channel success lies with the manufacturer, who must recognize which marketing functions cannot be delegated and then perform these at a level that will motivate the other channel members.

Questions for Discussion

1. "The typical manufacturing firm is neither organized nor motivated to perform the tasks normally assigned to distributors." Explain why you agree or disagree with this statement.

2. If you were the general manager of a distributorship, given the customer demands and supplier expectations discussed in this chapter, what goals and objectives would you establish for the firm? How would you rank them?

3. Assume you are the marketing manager for a manufacturer. The product and target market may be any you choose. Describe the characteristics and strengths you would most desire in a distributor and the weaknesses you would want to avoid.

4. Given the product/market scenario you chose for the preceding question, cite the issues you would include in your distributor franchise agreement and explain their importance.

5. What, in your opinion, are the primary advantages and disadvantages of a company sales force compared with manufacturers' reps or other sales agents?

6. If, as a marketing manager, you have chosen to sell through a combination of distributors and reps, explain how and why you would subdivide the marketing duties between these two groups.

7. With reference to the preceding question, would the combination of a company sales force and distributors make the division of responsibilities easier or more difficult? Explain your answer.

8. In what functional areas and operating philosophies should manufacturers be compatible with their distributors? with their reps?

Endnotes

1. William D. Perrault, Jr. and Frederick A. Russ, "Physical distribution service in industrial purchasing decisions," *Journal of Marketing* 40 (April 1976):3-10.

2. Susan Avery, "Distributors ask 'How are we doing?' Buyers tell all," *Purchasing* 115 (December 16, 1993):48.

3. George M. Fodor, "Buyers solicit distributor input," *Industrial Distribution* 83 (May 1994):42-4.

4. John R. Johnson, "Manufacturers and distributors must make amends," *Industrial Distribution* 83 (May 1994):44-6.

5. Joseph V. Barks, "Squeezing out the middleman," *Distribution* 93 (January 1994):30.

6. John R. Johnson, "Making something out of nothing," *Industrial Distribution* 82 (April 1993):20-2.

7. John E. Rice, "Build long-term relationships." *Industrial Distribution* 83 (September 1994):42.

8. Donald M. Jackson, Robert F. Krampf, and Leonard J. Konopa, "Factors that influence the length of industrial channels," *Industrial Marketing Management* 11 (1982):263-8; see also Donald M. Jackson and Michael F. d'Amico, "Products and markets served by distributors and agents," *Industrial Marketing Management* 18 (February 1989):27-33.

9. Paul Herbig and Bradley S. O'Hara, "Industrial distributors in the 21st century," *Industrial Marketing Management* 23 (July 1994):199-203.

10. See Jackson and d'Amico, "Products and markets served," p. 33; see also Gul Butaney and Lawrence H. Wortzel, "Distributor power versus manufacturer power: The customer role," *Journal of Marketing* 52 (January 1988):52-63; also Frank V. Cespedes, "Control vs. resources in channel design: Distribution differences in one industry," *Industrial Marketing Management* 17 (August 1988):215-27.

11. James A. Narus, N. Mohan Reddy, and George L. Pinchak, "Key problems facing industrial distributors," *Industrial Marketing Management* 13 (1984):139-47.

12. David Ford, "Stability factors in industrial marketing channels," *Industrial Marketing Management* 7 (1978):410-22. See also Butaney and Wortzel, "Distributor power vs. manufacturer power," pp. 60-1.

13. James P. Morgan, "Distribution 2000: Is this the age of the super distributor?" *Purchasing,* 116 (February 17, 1994):38; see also Bernard Levine, "Distributors mull mega-neglect issue," *Electronic News* 40 (January 17, 1994):42.

14. Peter R. Dickson, "Distributor portfolio analysis and the channel dependence matrix: New techniques for understanding and managing the channel," *Journal of Marketing* 47 (Summer 1983):35-44. See also Cespedes, "Control vs. resources," pp. 222-6.

15. See Thomas L. Powers, "Industrial distribution options: Trade-offs to consider," *Industrial Marketing Management* 18 (August 1989):155-61; also Louis W. Stern and Frederick D. Sturdivant, "Getting things done," *Harvard Business Review* 65 (July-August 1987):34-41.

16. Frank Lynn & Associates, Inc., *Profile of Industrial Distribution 1979: Summary Report* (Cleveland, Ohio: American Supply and Machinery Manufacturers Association, Inc., 1979).

17. William C. Copacino, "The changing role of the distributor," *Traffic Management* 33 (February 1994):31; see also H. Holt Cason, "Distribution's future: Integrated supply," *Industrial Distribution* 82 (June 1993):132.

18. *Standard & Poor's Industry Surveys,* 162 (June 9, 1994):E36.

19. "J & J Tears a Strip off," *Sales and Marketing Management,* (May 14, 1984), p. 32.

20. John R. Johnson, "Distributor termination: You can fight back," *Industrial Distribution* 83 (February 1994):20-2.

21. Harold J. Novick, "The case for reps vs. direct selling: Can reps do it better?" *Industrial Marketing Management* 11 (March 1982):90.

22. Dartnell Corporation, "27th survey of sales compensation," (Chicago: Dartnell Corporation, 1993), pp. 109, 171.

23. "Strategy: reps or sales force?" *Inc.* 13 (December 1991):154.

24. "Why we don't use sales reps," *Sales and Marketing Management* 131 (July 9, 1979):32; see also Edwin E. Bobrow, "Suddenly, an urge to boost their potential," *Sales and Marketing Management* 134 (June 7, 1982) Special Report; also John W. Grant, "More feet on the street," *Small Business Reports (Monterey, CA)* 18 (April 1993):20-4.

25. Edwin E. Bobrow, "Suddenly an urge to boost their potential," *Sales and Marketing Management* 134 (June 7, 1982) Special Report.

26. Earl Hitchcock, "What Marketers Love and Hate About Their Manufacturers' Reps," *Sales and Marketing Management,* 136 (September 10, 1984):60-65.

27. Edwin E. Bobrow, "Reps and recognition: Understanding what motivates," *Sales and Marketing Management* 143 (September 1991):82-86.

28. U.S. Department of Commerce, *Census of Wholesale Trade, Establishment and Firm Size: 1992* (Washington D.C.: U.S. Government Printing Office, January 1995), pp. 175.

29. Christine Forbes, "Creating the super supplier," *Industrial Distribution* 82 (September 1993):30-2; see also Jack Keough, "The forces of change sweep through distribution," *Industrial Distribution* 82 (April 1993):11.

30. John R. Johnson, "Promoting profits through partnerships," *Industrial Distribution* 83 (March 1994):22-24.

Bibliography

Bobrow, Edwin E., "Reps and recognition: Understanding what motivates," *Sales and Marketing Management* 143 (September 1991):82-6.

Bobrow, Edwin E., "The question of reps," *Sales and Marketing Management* 143 (June 1991):32-4.

Butaney, Gul, and Lawrence H. Wortzel, "Distributor power versus manufacturer power: The customer role," *Journal of Marketing* 52 (January 1988):52-63.

Cespedes, Frank V., "Control vs. resources in channel design: Distribution differences in one industry," *Industrial Marketing Management* 17 (August 1988):215-27.

Fodor, George M., "Buyers solicit distributor input," *Industrial Distribution* 83 (May 1994):42-4.

Herbig, Paul and Bradley S. O'hara, "Industrial distributors in the 21st century," *Industrial Marketing Management* 23 (July 1994):199-203.

Hitchcock, Earl, "What marketers love and hate about their manufacturers' reps," *Sales and Marketing Management* (September 10, 1984):60-5.

Levine Bernard, "Distributors mull mega-neglect issue," *Electronic News* 40 (January 17, 1994):42.

Morgan, James P., "Distribution 2000: Is this the age of the super distributor?" *Purchasing* 116 (February 17, 1994):38.

Stern, Louis W., and Frederick D. Sturdivant, "Getting things done," *Harvard Business Review* 65 (July-August 1987):34-41.

14

The Logistics of Physical Distribution and Customer Service

Regardless of the channels used, unless a supplier delivers products in the right amount, at the right time, and in proper condition, buyers do not hesitate to find another source. However, suppliers must provide this service at a competitive cost that still allows them a satisfactory profit margin. Thus, manufacturers invest substantial resources in physical distribution systems that provide a satisfying level of customer service at an affordable cost.

In this chapter we will discuss the following:

1. The importance of logistics in a marketing strategy
2. The role of physical distribution and customer service
3. Methods used to optimize customer service levels and reach desired profit goals
4. Difficulties involved in optimizing customer service
5. The expansion of services provided by third-party transporters and warehousers

Customer service is a crucial element in any marketing strategy. Business customers depend on consistent deliveries to maintain production flow. Shutting down a production line because of a parts shortage results in a sizable financial loss. Thus, as mentioned in Chapter 13, business buyers rank dependable service second only to product quality and more important than price when selecting suppliers.

Logistical marketing activities—transportation, inventory availability, warehousing, materials handling, and order processing—can also have a significant impact on customer costs and operations. Poor service in any area can cause delayed or inconsistent deliveries, forcing customers to carry larger safety stocks, to develop secondary sources of supply, or to use another source entirely to ensure a smooth running, cost-effective operation.

Thus, the typical firm finds that the most effective logistical system is one that balances overall performance against total cost. Rarely will either lowest total cost or highest service performance be the best logistical strategy.[1]

The Relationship Of Logistics and Physical Distribution

The term *logistics* originated in the military. In fact, Webster's dictionary defines the term as "the aspect of military science dealing with the procurement, maintenance, and transportation of military material, facilities, and personnel." The unprecedented problems faced by Allied armed forces during World War II led to the development of distribution systems that were quite remarkable for their time. Today, manufacturers use modern revisions to serve worldwide product markets.

In the business arena, logistics refers to the interrelation and management of all the activities (Table 14-1) required to make components and raw materials available to manufacturers and finished products to end users when, where, and how they are desired. This requires the management of two primary product flows: physical supply and physical distribution. *Physical supply* (also called materials management) includes all those activities necessary to make *production inputs* (raw materials, component parts, and supplies) available to the manufacturing process. *Physical distribution* encompasses those tasks necessary to deliver the completed product to end-users or channel intermediaries. The two flows must be coordinated. However, physical supply is more the responsibility of production and purchasing. Thus, the focus of this chapter is physical distribution, which is a responsibility of marketing. Physical distribution

---

TABLE 14-1   Typical Logistical Activities and Decision-Making

Key Elements	Supporting Activities
Transportation Mode and carrier Carrier routing Vehicle scheduling	*Warehousing* Determine space and configuration Stock layout and placement
Inventory Management Stock-level policies Short-term sales forecasting Stocking locations and product mix	*Materials Handling* Personnel and equipment required Order picking process Stock storage and retrieval system
Customer Service Determine customer needs and service priorities Set customer service levels	*Protective Packaging* Protect product Simplify handling and storage
Order Processing Sales order-inventory interface Order information transmittal Order terms and conditions	*Production Scheduling* Aggregate volume forecasts Product sequencing and timing *Information Maintenance* Collection and storage Data analysis

Source: Adapted from Ronald H. Ballou, *Business Logistics Management: Planning and Control*, 2nd ed. (Upper Saddle River, N.J.: Prentice Hall, Inc., 1985), pp. 7-8.

must mesh smoothly with a customer's physical supply system to support a manufac-turing process or provide resale inventory in a timely fashion. Failure to do so can cost thousands of dollars in lost production time or lost sales.

Evolution Of Modern Physical Distribution Systems

Dramatic changes in physical distribution strategy, practices, and methods have taken place in the last 30 years. Ever-changing customer wants and technological innovations have forced suppliers to refocus their attention on the elements and objectives of an effective distribution system.

EXPANDED CONSUMER NEEDS

Resellers required a wider assortment of goods as consumers broadened their tastes and desires. Product brands proliferated and expanded. Coca-Cola, for example, had only one product item for almost a century; but by the mid-1980s, the brand encom-passed a half dozen items. The same type of brand proliferation occurred across the entire spectrum of consumer products. Manufacturers and wholesalers became aware of the major impact that their physical distribution systems had on both customer sat-isfaction and corporate profits. Systems that had remained virtually unchanged since the 1950s were now inadequate.

TECHNOLOGICAL CHANGES

Innovations evolved in product packaging, handling, and transporting. Computeriza-tion yielded dramatic improvement in order processing, inventory control, customer service and communication, and warehousing efficiency. For example, in 1977 the typ-ical food producer had 14 regional warehouses, shipped to these warehouses by boxcar, and reshipped to retailers by truck. Customers received products about 7 days after order placement. Today, producers operate only five to seven warehouses, ship via intermodal (rail piggyback) carriers and truck, and deliver customer orders overnight or on the second day.[2]

When dealing with major retailers, producers often use a process called **cross-docking.** This process refers to any system that provides direct flow between producer and retailer, avoiding intermediate storage. Cross-docking eliminates the labor cost and time involved in loading, unloading, storing, and retrieving products. It also elimi-nates inventory carrying costs. Thus, customer service improves while costs decline.[3]

INTEGRATED PHYSICAL DISTRIBUTION

The physical distribution system used to be viewed as a series of individual steps, per-formed by separate organizational bodies, with only a loose bond uniting the whole. For example, products moved from a production line to finished goods inventory in the fac-tory. An independent carrier transported the products to a corporate warehouse, then to an independent wholesaler (distributor), and in the case of consumer goods, on to a retailer and eventually to the consumer. Some producers now recognize the need to inte-grate this process into a *holistic total-flow system* that optimizes customer satisfaction, stimulates overall demand, and reduces a dangerous escalation of marketing costs. In 1992, total U.S. logistics costs (warehousing and transportation of all business inventory) amounted to $647 billion, or 10.9 percent of GDP. On the positive side, the U.S. percentage was second only to Japan's 10.1 percent. European costs ran 12.2 percent, and other Pacific Rim countries experienced costs at 13 percent of their composite GDP.[4]

Physical Distribution and Marketing Strategy

Marketers can use logistics proactively to create a competitive advantage in the marketplace.[5] For example, Whirlpool, a leading producer of household appliances, has developed a joint venture system of transportation and logistics called ERX Logistics. Whirlpool enlisted warehouser Elston Richards Corp. and trucker Missouri-Nebraska Express to provide a regional distribution system that delivers products to dealers within 24 hours of order. The system works so well that a number of other durable goods suppliers have adopted Whirlpool as a benchmark firm in the category of physical distribution.[6] Numerous other companies across industries are bundling logistics activities with other marketing functions to offer customers tailored solutions to their physical supply needs.[7]

Most organizations have become more sophisticated and effective in their problem-solving techniques, thanks to the computer. For example, both producers and resellers have inventory control systems that can analyze demand trends, recalculate minimum and maximum quantity levels, and automatically issue necessary purchase orders or cancellations.

Faced with the necessity of reducing costs wherever possible, many businesses are utilizing the integrated distribution systems mentioned earlier to lower their inventory carrying costs, to get better utilization of their facilities, and to become more efficient in handling product flow. By establishing an efficient distribution system capable of providing quick, reliable delivery, the business marketer can pass on substantial savings to customers and gain a competitive advantage.

The importance of physical distribution and its ultimate impact on marketing objectives, however, depends on the type of product being marketed, the needs of the customer, and the structure of the distribution channel. When products are inputs to manufacturing, buyers normally face a wide range of problems, including storage, stock control, order processing, and traffic management. Thus, suppliers of component parts must use physical distribution systems that comprehend and resolve these supply problems. Suppliers of capital equipment, on the other hand, are more concerned with meeting a scheduled delivery date than maintaining a finished goods inventory and, therefore, have relatively low logistical service requirements.

The effectiveness of physical distribution also has a dramatic impact on the ability of resellers to serve end markets. When a manufacturer's delivery schedule is extended or erratic, resellers must carry higher inventory levels to prevent stockouts and the potential loss of customers. Thus, the manufacturer's distribution capability directly influences resellers' costs and their ability to provide adequate service.

The Total-Cost Approach

An efficient physical distribution system minimizes the costs of storing and transporting products from the point of production to the point of purchase while providing a satisfactory level of customer service. Management of logistical activities, then, focuses on two essential variables: (1) total distribution costs and (2) the level of service provided to customers. The system should result in a combination of cost and service level that optimizes profits and market demand for the producer and channel members. Logistical costs in business markets vary considerably, depending on the nature of the product and the level of service required. On average, total logistical costs for all manufacturers ran 8 percent of sales in 1993, according to the consulting firm, Herbert W. Davis and Company.[8]

INTERACTIVE COSTS

The total-cost approach to logistics management is based on the premise that a firm should combine all the costs of moving and storing finished goods when it attempts to establish specific customer service levels. The costs of these activities often interact in an inverse manner. For instance, a policy of maintaining low inventory levels to reduce holding costs can result in stockouts and backorders, special production runs, costly airfreight shipments, or even lost customers. When a company evaluates logistical activities individually on their ability to achieve a given management objective, suboptimization often occurs. The total-cost approach seeks to achieve efficiency *across the entire system,* not within one specific activity. Thus, all cost items should be considered simultaneously, and the total should include the cost of lost sales resulting from inadequate service levels.

Unfortunately, even when dealing with composite costs, too many executives concentrate myopically on accounting ledger figures. One survey of twenty-seven CEOs at Fortune 500 manufacturing and service companies revealed a clear and consistent tendency to evaluate corporate achievement on profit margins rather than customer satisfaction or quality of performance. Profit improvement came from cost reduction rather than increased market share.[9] In another survey, only 35 percent of the CEOs included logistics in their evaluation of sales and marketing performance, and only 57 percent saw the potential for improvement in the area of transportation services.[10]

EVALUATING COST TRADE-OFFS

Cost trade-offs are not limited to any specific activity. As part of their corporate downsizing and restructuring, some firms have closed warehouses and switched to public warehousing and distributors to handle their regional storage activities. Others have concentrated on using faster transportation modes to minimize the level of intermediate inventories. Still others have employed third parties to act as overall logistics providers. These third-party firms can provide transportation, warehousing, inventory management, and other associated activities.[11] More will be said later about the emergence of contract logistics firms along with their strengths and limitations.

Customer Service

Customer service presents a supplier with a classic *cost/benefit trade-off* decision. An improved service level will probably increase sales revenue, but it will most likely increase costs also. Customer service can also impact pricing. For example, from the customer's perspective, a reduction in order-cycle time (the elapsed time between order placement and delivery) justifies a lower buffer inventory and reduces holding costs. Consistent, on-time delivery performance by a supplier permits a routine, lower-cost purchasing process and greatly reduces the danger of production shutdowns. As discussed in earlier chapters, business buyers determine the value of a product not by its invoice price, but by its *total use-cost.* Therefore, when customers receive a higher level of service, resulting in lower use-cost, they are more receptive to paying a higher price.

In effect, a supplier should view customer service not as a generated cost per se, but as an essential and contributory part of the total marketing mix. Economists like to remind us that there is no free lunch. Likewise, there are no free marketing benefits.

DETERMINING CUSTOMER SERVICE LEVELS

Determining the level of customer service requires consideration of all those activities involved in processing orders and keeping customers happy. The service elements most frequently cited as important to buyers are shown in Table 14-2. Note the obvious similarity among the items shown here and the reasons given by industrial buyers for their use of distributors. This similarity suggests two associated ideas: (1) distributors play a vital role in providing ultimate customer service levels, and (2) customers perceive the service provided by distributors as more consistent and effective than what they would obtain directly from the manufacturer.

Customer service has traditionally been a frustrating area to analyze because of the difficulties involved in establishing an all-inclusive statement of standards. As noted by a National Council of Physical Distribution Management task force, "No apparent means exist to specifically measure customer service performance in a total sense. Therefore, individual 'elements' must be defined and measured."[12] Customer service elements actually occur in three stages: (1) before the transaction (preaccount servicing, assistance in problem solution and product specifications), (2) as part of the transaction, (the speed and efficiency with which a supplier fills and delivers orders), and (3) after the transaction has been completed (the provision of technical services, training, and support materials).[12]

The customer's prioritized needs should help to establish customer service levels. Not all customers require the same level nor the same areas of emphasis. As discussed previously, purchasers of capital equipment generally have lower service needs than do those who buy component parts. The level of service also depends on the aspects of ser-

TABLE 14-2 Relative Importance of Customer Service Elements

Element	Description	Importance to Customers of Manufacturers	Importance to Customers of Resellers
Product availability	Most common measure; percent of units shipped from stock	42.7	43.1
Order cycle time	Time from order placement until receipt of shipment	19.4	25.5
Information support	Timely/accurate answers regarding inventory levels, order status, etc.	12.4	11.8
System flexibility	Ability to handle unusual situations, emergencies; expedite and substitute	11.6	10.1
Malfunction handling	Ability to rectify problems quickly (errors, delays, damage, claims, etc.)	8.0	7.2
Postsale support	Efficiency in providing technical support, repairs, spare parts, etc.	5.1	2.3
All other		0.8	0.0
Total points		100.0	100.0

Source: Adapted from Bernard J. LaLonde and Paul H. Zinszer, *Customer Service: Meaning and Measurement* (Chicago: Council of Physical Distribution Management, 1975), p. 118; also Bernard J. LaLonde, *The Distribution Handbook* (New York: The Free Press, 1985), p. 244.

vice that are most important to the customer; however, service levels cannot be set on customer desires alone. Management must also consider the nature of the competitive environment and its own profit goals.[12]

The Competitive Environment   The competitive environment relates to industry service standards. Customers form expectations based on what they view as "normal" within their industry. When a supplier provides a lower level of service than that offered by competitors, sales will suffer unless some other element of the marketing mix offsets the deficiency. On the other hand, when customers neither expect nor value a given service, a supplier would be foolish to offer it.

When there are many competing products that perform basically the same task, good service is an essential competitive tool. However, when the product is a highly desired innovation with minimal competition, a high level of customer service may not be required.

Profitability   The major criteria for evaluating the appropriate customer service level are profitability and customer priorities. The higher the level of service, the greater the costs involved. Rapid air freight to ensure fast delivery increases transportation rates. Therefore, the sales and cost impact of various service levels must be analyzed, both from the firm's and the customer's perspectives.

Information must be developed on alternative service levels and resultant sales revenues. Figure 14-1 shows that profit contribution varies with the level of service. In the graph, sales are suboptimal at the present level of service, approximately 73 percent. Between 73 and 85 percent service levels, marginal sales remain above marginal costs, generating additional profits. Beyond 85 percent, marginal costs exceed marginal sales, with a resultant loss of profit. Thus, in this case, the optimal service

FIGURE 14-1 How much should a firm spend on customer service to gain extra sales? The graph shows how a typical firm can increase its sales volume by spending more to improve its overall service level. Note the point of diminishing returns, at which additional expenditures will exceed the value of greater sales. The graph suggests an optimal point of 85 percent service level, but this will vary with product, market conditions, transportaion, and other factors.

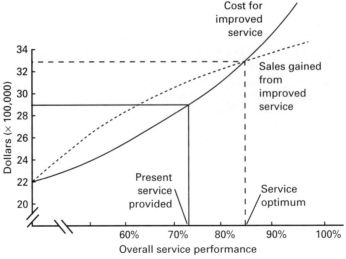

Source: From *Traffic Management* (September 1982), p. 55. Reprinted by permission.

level is at 85 percent. How much a firm should invest in customer service, however, can be determined only by studying the specific conditions in its industry and by assessing customer expectations.

ASSESSING AND OPTIMIZING CUSTOMER SERVICE REQUIREMENTS

The effectiveness of customer service policies depends on the customer's definition of satisfactory service. Firms often set service levels higher than customers require. Thus, customer service levels can be optimized by (1) researching the customer's needs, (2) setting service levels that realistically balance revenues and expenses, (3) making use of the latest order-processing technology, and (4) measuring and evaluating the performance of individual logistical activities.[13]

Customer Service Audits   Quantitative and qualitative information pertaining to the target market's perceptions of and desires for service can be obtained through an audit.[13] Not only does an audit evaluate existing services, but it also provides a benchmark for establishing effective customer service policies. Shifts in inventory policies, transportation modes, and warehouse locations have a direct effect on both channel members and end users. Customer service audits provide a viable means of assessing and, where necessary, revising customer service strategy to emphasize those aspects important to customers or to improve uncompetitive performance.

This is another area in which distributors and manufacturers' reps can provide valuable information. Since they handle other product lines, they are in a better position to evaluate the various service levels available to customers and to assess the impact that each level has on sales volume.

THE IMPACT OF LOGISTICAL SERVICE ON CHANNEL MEMBERS

Logistical service levels affect the relationship between the manufacturer and customer as well as the operations of channel members. Inefficient service to middlemen either increases their costs, by forcing them to carry more inventory, or causes stockouts and lost business. Poor logistical support in the channel negates the marketing effort of the firm by constricting potential sales and antagonizing middlemen. When Harley-Davidson set out to regain market share in the United States and Europe, their marketing priorities included an integrated distribution process, with a just-in-time inventory system to improve customer service and enhance dealer relationships.[14] Both the length and consistency of the order-cycle period affect the level of dealer inventories, which generally represent their largest asset investment and largest distribution expense. Dealers will not remain loyal when logistical service adversely affects their service to end users. To ensure an adequate level of logistical service to middlemen, information systems should provide realistic sales forecasts, and where possible, inventory control systems should be linked to the manufacturer's management information system (MIS).

Identifying Cost Centers

Logistics management includes the integration of relevant cost centers so that the level of logistical service desired by customers and middlemen can be provided at the lowest possible cost. Management must consider both the operating costs and investment level associated with each level of customer service.

Total-cost analysis begins with the identification of relevant cost centers (i.e., transportation, warehousing, inventory, materials handling, and order processing). Depending on the firm's environment and customer needs, individual cost centers will vary in importance. Thus, total-cost analysis aims to (1) identify the costs by activity center, (2) evaluate these costs in terms of a desired level of customer service, and (3) seek trade-offs between and among the various activity centers so that a possible cost increase in one activity is more than offset by a reduction in another.[1]

COST TRADE-OFFS REVISITED

Cost trade-offs are possible within a single activity center. For instance, there are modal alternatives in transportation (rail, truck, water, air, or pipeline.) Trade-offs can occur at two levels. The first concerns the type of mode selected, such as truck over rail. Once a mode has been selected, further trade-offs may exist within that mode, such as the use of leased versus company-owned trucks.

Of equal importance is the trade-off between and among activity centers. The number and location of warehouses, for example, affect inventory levels, transportation, materials handling, and order processing. Table 14-3 shows the results from several studies of logistical costs. Although the distributions vary, transportation, inventory carrying costs, and warehousing consistently account for the major portion.

Although trade-offs within an activity center are relatively easy to identify, measuring trade-offs between and among centers is more difficult. Therefore, total-cost analysis begins with the identification of relevant cost centers.

TABLE 14-3 Examples of Logistical Cost Distribution (by percent)

	Transport	Inventory Carrying	Warehousing	Other
1. Composite 1976[1]	35	28	18	19
2. Composite 1984[2]	45	20	20	15
3. Composite 1992[3]	40	22	25	13
4. Electronics[4]	24	19	24	33
Machinery and tools	45	10	20	25
Chemicals and plastics	44	11	23	22
All manufacturers	46	10	26	18
Industrial resellers	22	45	11	15
Consumer resellers	33	35	17	15

Sources:

[1]Herbert W. Davis & Co., "Survey of selling costs," *Sales and Marketing Management* (April 1976).

[2]Adapted from *Davis Database,* a newsletter published by Herbert W. Davis & Co., Englewood Cliffs, N.J. (October 1984); as cited in Johnson and Wood, *Contemporary Physical Distribution and Logistics,* 3rd ed. (New York: Macmillan Publishing Co., 1986), p. 106.

[3]Survey by Cass Logistics as reported by Thomas A Foster, "Logistics costs drop to record low levels," *Distribution* 92 (July 1993):6.

[4]Ronald H. Ballou, *Business Logistics Management,* 2nd ed. (Englewood Cliffs, N.J.: Prentice Hall, Inc., 1985):16-17.

Transportation

The single most important (and generally the most expensive) activity function in physical distribution is the shipment of goods to customers and/or middlemen. Depending on the factors of speed, dependability, availability, and cost, product movement may be accomplished via air freight, rail, motor carrier, water, and, for some products, pipeline. Table 14-4 indicates how the five primary transportation modes have changed over the past five decades in terms of their relative shares of intercity freight.

AIR FREIGHT

Air freight is the most expensive mode (Table 14-5). It is also the fastest from airport to airport, although this time advantage is often decreased by weather delays, terminal congestion, and/or the need to use other modes between airports and points of origin and destination. Its use is determined by unique circumstances rather than product categories.

Highly perishable goods (fresh seafood, cut flowers) require air shipment, as do emergency shipments of other products. The use of air freight to ship products with a high value per density or weight can reduce overall logistical costs. For a few hundred dollars, microprocessors worth thousands of dollars can be delivered overnight, reducing the backup inventory level from days to hours.

TABLE 14-4 Distribution of Intercity Freight by Transportation Mode (by percent)

Year	Railroad	Truck	Waterway	Pipeline	Air	Ton-miles (billions)
1940	61.3	10.0	19.1	9.5	<0.1	618
1950	56.2	16.3	15.4	12.1	<0.1	1,063
1960	44.1	21.7	16.8	17.4	<0.1	1,314
1970	39.8	21.3	16.4	22.3	0.2	1,936
1980	37.5	22.3	16.4	23.6	0.2	2,487
1985	36.4	24.8	15.5	22.9	0.3	2,458
1991	37.4	26.3	16.0	20.0	0.4	2,886

Source: Adapted from Frank A. Smith, *Transportation in America,* 10th ed. (Washington, D.C.: Eno Foundation for Transportation, 1992), p. 10.

TABLE 14-5 Domestic Intercity Modal Costs (in cents per ton-mile)

Year	Railroad	Truck	Waterway	Pipeline	Air Freight
1970	1.4	8.5	0.3	0.3	21.9
1975	2.0	11.6	0.5	0.3	28.2
1980	2.9	18.0	0.8	1.3	46.3
1985	3.0	22.9	0.8	1.6	48.6
1991	2.7	24.8	0.8	1.5	44.5

Source: Adapted from Frank A. Smith, *Transportation in America,* 10th ed. (Washington, D.C.: Eno Foundation for Transportation, 1992), p. 14.

TRUCK

Since 1940, the trucking industry has increased its share of total intercity freight shipments (in terms of ton-miles) from 10 percent to 26 percent. Trucks transport more than 75 percent of all agricultural product tonnage, plus a variety of manufactured products, including most consumer goods.

Trucks compete favorably with air carriers for any size shipment transported up to one thousand miles. They also outperform railroads on shipments under 10,000 pounds transported 500 miles or more. The 3.8 million miles of highway in the United States allow trucks to reach many locations not served by other transportation modes. Although only one percent of total highway mileage, the 42,500 miles of the interstate system provides access to more than twenty percent of all auto and truck traffic.[12]

RAIL

Railroads specialize in transporting raw materials, such as metallic ores, coal, and gravel; unprocessed agricultural products; scrap; and automobiles. The bulk of rail shipments is in carload (CL) quantities, usually 30,000 pounds or more. In 1991 the average rail shipping rate was 2.7 cents per ton-mile, reflecting the efficiency of transporting commodities in bulk quantities. However, although railroads transported about 40 percent more tonnage than trucks did in 1991, the trucking industry received nine times more revenue.[15]

PIPELINE

Pipelines are a limited but highly specialized mode of transportation. Petroleum products and natural gas are the primary products shipped by this mode. Almost 90 percent of all petroleum products are shipped by this method.[12] By means of "slurry pipelines," other products such as coal, sulfur, iron ore, limestone, and waste commodities can also be shipped. To accomplish this, the product is ground into a powder, then mixed with water to form a "slurry," and sent through the pipeline.[12]

INTERMODAL TRANSPORTATION

In addition to the individual transportation modes, some transportation systems use a combination of two or more modes. The major feature of intermodal transportation is the free exchange of equipment between modes. For example, transoceanic shipping containers can be transferred to domestic airlines or from truck trailers to railroad flatbed cars.

Intermodal is the fastest growing segment of the rail industry. In 1993, seven million trailers and containers traveled via this method, an eight percent growth rate compared to no growth in conventional rail shipments. Unfortunately, this growth created equipment shortages and rail yards clogged with shipments awaiting transfer. Experts suggest the need for a national equipment pool and improved management systems at terminals.[16]

Despite current difficulties, trucking firms want to increase the amount of traffic moved over rail from a current 10 to 15 percent to as much as 35 percent. They cite lower costs, the convenience of door-to-door service, and competition from firms such as UPS as primary reasons. But first, trucking firms need changes in the Teamsters Union contracts that give priority to over-the-road traffic.[17]

FREIGHT FORWARDERS

Freight forwarders are considered transportation middlemen because they consolidate shipments to get lower rates for their customers. Transportation rates on less-than-truckload lots (LTL) or less-than-carload lots (LCL) are often twice as high on a per unit basis as are TL or CL shipments. Freight forwarders charge less than the higher rate but more than the lower rate. In many instances, freight forwarders provide faster and more complete service than does a carrier.

CRITERIA FOR SELECTING THE MODE OF TRANSPORTATION

Transportation costs are directly affected by the location of the firm's warehouses, plants, and customers and the level of customer service goals. The selection of individual carriers, however, is based on delivery performance—speed of service, dependability of delivery, and capability in accommodating the goods to be shipped—as well as the cost of the service.[1] Table 14-6 compares the five transportation modes on important operating characteristics.

Speed and Availability of Service   As mentioned previously, speed of service (i.e., the elapsed time to move products from one facility to another) often outweighs the cost of service. Slower modes cost less, but may result in lower service levels, and often, larger inventories. Thus, a firm must evaluate not only individual transportation modes but also various intermodal combinations.

Availability refers to a carrier's ability to serve a given pair of locations. This factor will necessitate, in many instances, intermodal combinations, particularly the use of local trucks (in addition to rail, air, or water transport) for pickup and final delivery.

Dependability of Service   Dependability of service refers to the delivery of a product on time and in good condition. Dependability is a form of performance quality and at least as important as speed.

Carrier Capability   The ability of the carrier to physically accommodate the size and weight of the product being shipped must also be considered. Although barges can transport items as large as space rockets, trucks are limited by state and federal weight restrictions.

TABLE 14-6   Comparison of the Five Modes of Transportation

Operating Characteristics	*Transportation Mode*				
	Rail	Highway	Water	Pipeline	Air
Speed	3	2	4	5	1
Availability	2	1	4	5	3
Dependability	3	2	4	1	5
Capability	2	3	1	5	4
Frequency	4	2	5	1	3

Source: Donald J. Bowersox, David J. Closs, and Omar K. Helferich, *Logistical Management,* 3rd ed. (New York: Macmillan Publishing Co., 1986), p. 166.

Frequency of Service   Frequency refers to the number of scheduled movements. Pipelines are best because of their continuous operation between two points. Trucks and air freight are next in line.

Final Decisions   Transportation decisions usually depend on several interrelated factors: unit value of the product, predictability of demand, transit time, the cost of the transport mode, related impact on inventory costs, and desired customer service levels. Table 14-5 shows the trend and magnitude of modal costs per ton-mile. The significant difference among the five modes is obvious. However, this difference cannot be analyzed properly except in the context of total logistical costs and customer service.

Shippers typically select transportation modes and specific carriers on the basis of overall efficiency—the lowest rate for a desired delivery performance. Perhaps five percent of the time, customer orders require speedier handling to meet unexpected changes in production rates or to replace defective parts. More frequently, higher transport cost offsets even larger inventory carrying cost.

Warehousing

Warehousing provides significant opportunities for cost savings without lessening customer service. The location of warehouse facilities can have a tremendous impact on a firm's sales volume and distribution costs. When warehouses are properly deployed, customer service can be improved or transportation costs reduced, or both. The major problem in determining the number and location of warehouses is that the important factors to be considered—markets, customers, sources of supply, transportation, and other distribution costs—change continually.

Warehouse location decisions coincide with attempts to improve customer service and/or reduce costs. Thus, warehouse locations should provide a more efficient and timely flow of goods to the market. For instance, if short order-cycle time is crucial (as is usually true for repair, maintenance, and operating supplies), suppliers locate their warehouses in key markets to avoid long-distance communications and premium air freight transportation.

The *channel* of distribution also impacts both the number and location of warehouses. When manufacturers employ reps, their selling function must be supported with strategically located inventories. In contrast, when distributors are used, their stocking function eliminates or greatly reduces the need for company-operated warehouses.

PRIVATE OR PUBLIC FACILITIES

A firm may own, rent, or lease warehouse space. Owned or leased space is classified as "private warehousing." Rented space is referred to as "public warehousing." Private warehousing offers the advantage of total control of operations and personnel. Thus, from a customer service perspective, private warehousing generally provides a higher level because specialized equipment and facilities can be used, and company personnel are more familiar with the firm's products, customers, and service goals. Although the capital investment can be substantial, private facilities also provide operating cost advantages when they are used close to capacity. The main disadvantage of private warehousing is its inflexibility. When sales fluctuate, or demand shifts to another market area, they must either be operated at a loss or closed.

Public warehousing minimizes the firm's financial risk. Since no fixed investment is required, a firm can increase or decrease usage in a given market or move into or out of any market quickly. Thus, when faced with an erratic demand or seasonal sales, the firm can benefit from public warehousing. These public facilities can also supplement or replace distributors in a market. However, public warehouses tend to require higher operating costs due to the inclusion of a profit factor, selling and advertising costs, and a premium to cover unused space. Box 14-1 lists factors to consider when choosing a public warehouse.

WAREHOUSE SITE LOCATION

The selected warehouse location should provide the desired level of customer service at the least cost of distribution. This location decision involves both a macro and micro perspective. Macro considerations involve geographical choices of location, whereas micro considerations examine economic and legal factors within specific geographical areas.[13] From the macro perspective, warehouses may be (1) market positioned, (2) production positioned, or (3) intermediately positioned.

BOX 14-1

Factors Influencing the Choice of a Public Warehouse

How do you go about selecting a public warehouse? In a technical paper recently published by the Warehousing Education and Research Council, William R. Folz, senior vice president of Tri-Valley Growers, offers some tips on finding the right facility. The following recommendations are excerpted from his paper.

1. First, review the reasons for your requirement. Examine why you want to use a public facility.
2. Develop a list of warehouses you want to contact.
3. Contact each warehouse by phone and set up a personal visit. Consider the following points during the visit.
   a. *Housekeeping.* Develop a perception of what the facility looks like every day. Is there an ongoing plan for good sanitation.
   b. *Equipment.* Review equipment age, maintenance, number of makes, and equipment selection. A high percentage of old equipment may mean increased downtime and maintenance costs. A good maintenance program is a must. Keep in mind that the existence f a high number of makes may indicate a lack of purchasing strategy. Also, note

whether the kind of equipment you require is readily available.
   c. *Operations control.* Study the procedures that the warehouse uses to control costs and improve efficiency.
   d. *The facility.* The building should be well maintained and meet your needs in terms of sprinklers, rail siding, dock doors, etc.
   e. *Management clerical procedures.* Review administrative and clerical controls and procedures for inventory management, customer service, claims, shipment logs, etc.
   f. *Insurance.* Know your insurance needs and inquire about the operator's coverage.
   g. *Proximity to rail yard/major highways.* Study the facility's transportation access.
4. Obtain outside references. Talk to other users of a facility and ask their opinions of the services provided.
5. Ask about the warehouse's financial condition. If you're potentially a large customer, you can demand financial information and the operator probably will provide it.

Source: "How to choose a public warehouse," *Distribution* (September 1984). Reprinted by permission.

Market-Positioned Warehouses   Market-positioned warehouses are located close to final customers to maximize customer service levels. This type of warehouse location strategy is influenced by factors such as order-cycle time, order size, and the cost and availability of transportation.

Production-Positioned Warehouses   These warehouses are located near production facilities or sources of supply. Although this type of location strategy does not provide the same level of service that can be offered through market-positioned warehouses, the warehouses serve as collection points for products that are manufactured at a number of different plants. Factors influencing this strategy include product perishability, a very broad product line, multiple production sites, and advantageous transportation consolidation rates (TL and CL shipments).

Intermediately Positioned Warehouses   When a firm must offer a relatively high level of customer service and has a variety of products being produced at several plant locations, warehouses can be located somewhere between customer and producer. Customer service levels for intermediately positioned warehouses typically fall between those afforded by the other two types.

Site location strategies, however, should also include consideration of local economic and legal aspects. When a firm leans toward private warehousing, the following factors must be considered[13]:

1. Quality and variety of transportation carriers serving the site
2. Quality and quantity of labor
3. Labor rates
4. Cost and quality of industrial land
5. Potential for expansion
6. Tax structure
7. Building codes
8. Nature of the commodity environment
9. Cost of construction
10. Cost and availability of utilities

Inventory

The quality of inventory management has a significant impact on a firm's ability to serve customers well, but at a reasonable cost. Inventories act as a buffer against supply and demand uncertainties and as an economic trade-off to transportation, production, and other conflicting costs. Production and demand are rarely in perfect balance. Operating deficiencies, such as delayed shipments or inconsistent carrier performance, occur. Business customers cannot always predict their requirements with certainty because of machine breakdown or a sudden surge in their own market demand. Therefore, finished goods inventories are an essential part of any customer service system.

Determining the level of inventory that optimizes customer service while minimizing cost requires full knowledge of *inventory carrying cost* and total system cost. Inventory carrying cost impacts both the number of warehouses used and the choice of transportation mode. Low carrying cost leads to more warehouses and slower, cheaper modes of transportation. A dramatic fall in *interest rates,* such as occurred in 1993, have a significant impact on the cost of inventory.

INVENTORY CARRYING COST

Inventory carrying cost usually represents a major factor in the logistical system and includes a number of different elements. These elements are subtle and difficult to comprehend, however, since they are not grouped together but are spread throughout the firm's accounting system. In fact, many firms do not calculate carrying cost directly, but use estimates or traditional inventory benchmarks.

Inventory carrying cost is usually stated as a percentage of the total inventory value. For example, a carrying cost of 25 percent means that the cost of carrying one unit in stock for one year is 25 percent of the unit's value. This cost can range from 13 to 35 percent, depending on the type of product, and can be considerably higher when all relevant inventory-related costs are included.[18] Thus, it is dangerous to use inventory trends or averages to compute carrying cost. Instead, each firm must determine its own percentage and attempt to minimize it.

Inventory costs should include only those costs that vary with the level of inventory, and these can be grouped into four basic categories: (1) inventory *acquisition* costs; (2) inventory *service* costs, such as property taxes and insurance; (3) *storage space* costs; and (4) inventory *risk* costs, including damage, pilferage, obsolescence, and relocation costs.

OPTIMIZING INVENTORIES

Being out of inventory can be costly. Customers grow disenchanted and turn to competitors. But carrying an inventory large enough to fill every order from stock can also be very costly. There is no hard-and-fast rule governing the percentage of orders that should be filled from stock. Most business marketers who deal with a broad, diversified product line accept the *80/20 axiom*. This generalized principle states that approximately 80 percent of all sales will be generated by only 20 percent of the product line. Therefore, those products should represent a disproportionate share of the inventory to ensure a minimal loss of orders because of poor availability.

ABC Analysis This technique identifies those items with the largest sales payoff. It sorts inventory into three groupings: high dollar volume (A), moderate dollar volume (B), and low dollar volume (C).

By listing the annual usage of inventory items in descending order of dollar volume, as shown in Table 14-7, one can readily perceive how few items account for the preponderance of sales volume. The average sales price of an item does not automatically determine its classification. Many low-priced items will be classified A because of their high volume usage, whereas expensive items may generate very low volume. Through ABC analysis, suppliers can reduce inventory costs by cutting back on slow-moving items, while concentrating inventory dollars in fast movers. For example, when Kaman Bearing & Supply Corporation discovered that over half its assets were tied up in inventory, it overhauled the entire inventory system. With the assistance of ICPMG Peat Marwick, a cost-effective, computerized inventory control system that used ABC analysis was installed. Through accurate status reports on inventory levels plus improved sales forecasts, Kaman can now set product-by-product service levels that eliminate unnecessary inventory.[19]

DETERMINING INVENTORY LEVELS

Inventory planning serves the same purpose as warehouse location, namely, a deslired level of customer service at the least total cost. To accomplish this end, physical distri-

| | | Percentage | Percentage | Item |
Item	Sales	of Sales	of Items	Category
		TABLE 14-7 ABC Analysis		
1	$25,000			
2	22,000			
3	20,000			
	$67,000	55.4	25	A
4	15,000			
5	10,000			
6	8,000			
7	6,000			
	$39,000	32.2	33	B
8	5,000			
9	4,000			
10	3,000			
11	2,000			
12	1,000			
	$15,000	12.4	42	C

bution managers, using sales forecasts and movement analyses, must determine how much inventory to keep on hand and when those stocks should be replenished to optimize cost. To obtain the lowest overall cost, managers strike a balance between order processing costs and inventory carrying costs.[12] The cost of restocking field warehouses typically includes (1) the cost of transmitting and processing the inventory transfer, (2) the handling costs at the shipping and receiving points, (3) transportation costs, and (4) the cost of associated documentation.[13]

Two basic approaches have been used traditionally to determine the best inventory policy. One is the **economic order quantity (EOQ) model,** which is used under conditions of continuous, constant, and known rates of demand. The other is the **fixed-order quantity model,** which is used when demand is uncertain.

The EOQ Model   The cost trade-offs involved in determining the most economical order quantity, given demand certainty, are shown graphically in Figure 14-2.

After determining the EOQ and dividing the annual demand by this quantity, both the size and frequency of the minimal-cost order will be known. The EOQ can be found through the following formula where P = the ordering cost (dollars per order); D = annual demand or usage (number of units); C = annual inventory carrying cost (as a percent of product value or cost); and V = average value or cost of one unit of inventory. If P = $40; D = 4,800 units; C = 25 percent; V = $100 per unit, then

$$EOQ = \frac{\sqrt{2\,(\$40)\,(4800)}}{(.25)\,(\$100)}$$

$$= \frac{\sqrt{384,000}}{25}$$

$$= 124 \text{ units}$$

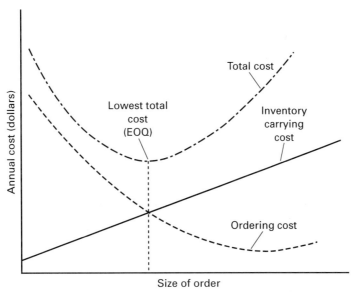

FIGURE 14-2 Cost trade-offs required to determine the most economic order quantity.

Although the EOQ model has received widespread attention and is broadly used in industry, its application under conditions of uncertain demand is restricted by its underlying assumptions:

1. The rate of demand is continuous, constant, and known.
2. Lead time is a constant or known.
3. Price is constant and is independent of order quantity or time.
4. All orders are filled (no stockouts permitted).
5. There is no inventory in transit.
6. There is no interaction among different items in inventory.
7. The planning horizon is infinite.
8. Capital funds are unlimited.

Use of the traditional EOQ model can also be misleading with respect to bulky, inexpensive, low-risk items that occupy large amounts of warehouse space. Unless space cost is factored into inventory carrying cost, the model will recommend ordering because of the low unit cost, ignoring the high space cost.[20]

Fixed-Order-Quantity Model   Rarely does a firm know with certainty what demand to expect for its products. Order-cycle and transit times are not consistent. As a result, suppliers normally maintain additional inventory as safety stock, particularly for fast-moving products, to avoid lost sales. Fixed-order-quantity models (also called **min-max inventory** models) enable the manager to concentrate on when to order. Through previous analysis of demand rate and necessary lead time (order cycle time for replenishment stock), the manager knows the inventory level necessary for customer demand and the point at which replacement stock should be ordered.

For example, assume that a distributor sells an average of 1,000 gizmos per month, carries a maximum inventory equal to 2 months' demand, and does not want inventory to drop below 2 weeks' demand. In addition, the supplier's quoted delivery time is currently 2 weeks after receipt of order (ARO). From these data, we know the min-max inventory points are approximately 500 and 2,000 units, respectively. With lead time running 2 weeks, an order will have to be placed when the inventory level drops to 1,000 units (four weeks before stockout, or 250 units/week $\times$ 4). But what quantity should be ordered? Not 1,000. By the time delivery is made 2 weeks later, inventory will be down to 500 units. So the manager orders 1,500. If lead time changes to 3 weeks, the replacement order will still call for 1,500 units, but will be placed when the inventory level reaches 1,250. (Think it through. . .)

Computer Simulation   Computer simulation or statistical techniques, such as IBM's inventory management program and control technique (IMPACT), are used to determine the amount of safety stock necessary to satisfy a given level of customer demand. IBM's IMPACT model is used by firms that are mainly concerned with the distribution phase of their production/distribution systems, such as wholesalers, retailers, and suppliers of basic materials. The primary objective of IMPACT is to provide inventory control rules that minimize cost. Its main advantage is that it forces management to (1) forecast demand, (2) determine the required safety stock for a specific level of customer service, (3) determine the order quantity and time for reorder, (4) consider the effects of freight rates and quantity discounts, and (5) estimate the expected results of the inventory plan. Users of the IMPACT system claim that it:

1. Reduces inventory costs because inventory size is reduced with no loss in service to customers, or conversely, service levels are increased with no additional inventory

2. Improves overall management control because the specific rules and objectives are consistent and easily revised, the effectiveness of the system can be measured, customer service is more stable, unprofitable product lines and slow-moving items are readily identified, and the cost output from the program is valuable for profit analysis and planning

Whatever system is applied, it must be applied cautiously and will depend on the cost and service trade-offs involved. Inventory decisions must be based on cost/service and transportation/warehousing trade-offs. Analysis of product turnover and customer usage dictates the specific inventory, transportation, and warehousing policies to be implemented.

The use of computers and analytical models provides two other important benefits. First, even in companies with traditional vertical structures, personnel from multiple functions must collect accurate data and share this information with others to arrive at mutually acceptable objectives and to define important costs and constraints. Marketers learn to view production planners and buyers as collaborators rather than adversaries. Second, managers are brought closer to operational realities, giving them a greater feeling of involvement and responsibility.[21] In short, everyone involved sees more vividly the importance of meeting customer demands and expectations in addition to company goals. Both corporate cooperation and market awareness increase substantially.

The Overall Contribution of Marketing Logistics

An effective logistics system plays an essential role in the overall marketing strategy, particularly in maintaining a favorable customer perception of the firm's service capability and attitude. Effective logistical activities form the foundation for the level of customer service. For example, the availability of products stems from inventory level and storage policies, whereas on-time delivery results from efficient order processing and proper carrier selection. Thus, when used effectively, a well-designed logistics system enhances the overall marketing effort. Further, a supplier cannot maintain long-term customer relationships without meeting their service needs.

The actual effectiveness of marketing logistics, however, depends on four basic factors. First, the marketer must recognize that the ability of the firm to provide a high level of customer service is of great concern to many customers, and those customers should be informed of the firm's ability to meet their needs in a straightforward, realistic manner. Specific information pertaining to product packaging, material handling, order processing, transportation modes, and normal delivery times and their variability must be transmitted to customers. Second, sales people must listen to customers to determine their service needs, demonstrate an understanding of those needs, and advise customers of the firm's capabilities in relation to those needs. Third, procedures to meet emergency situations, such as the shipment of rush orders or critical parts, must be developed and communicated to customers. Fourth, sales people must be capable of explaining any available service options and their price differentials to customers. The crucial point is that the marketer be fully aware of the capabilities of the distribution system, integrate these capabilities into the overall marketing strategy, and communicate the results to customers.

Emerging Trends: Domestic and International

Many companies and executives now view physical distribution—once the most mundane, unglamorous, and largely ignored segment of marketing—in a new light. Both organizational and environmental trends have spurred this change and should be recognized by marketers who wish to lead rather than follow competitors into the next century.

TOTAL QUALITY MANAGEMENT

For an increasing number of firms, TQM has become the new battle cry. Customer satisfaction now ranks on a par with corporate profits. In reality, marketing practitioners and academics have advocated TQM for decades, except that they have referred to it as "the marketing concept." Both concepts, simply put, state that all business functions must concentrate on satisfying customers. To do so, every organizational entity must be geared to minimize errors, seek continual improvements, and respond to market shifts quickly and effectively. Profits stem from these abilities. If performance deteriorates, profits do likewise.

All logistical activities aim to provide customers what they want, when and where they want it, with minimum cost and confusion. The best product at the most competitive price loses its value when the customer cannot obtain it. All the effort expended in the design and production of the product can be negated by a late shipment sent to the wrong address.

Vertically structured firms are particularly vulnerable when products move from the product management stage to introductory sales and then to ongoing customer service. Studies indicate that up to half of new product failures stem from a poor transition across these three stages.[22]

RISING COSTS AND SHRINKING PROFITS

Stagnant markets and increased competition caused many firms to downsize and restructure during the 1980s and early 1990s. All assets not contributing to current profits became potentially expendable, including warehouses, material handling and transportation equipment, and associated personnel. Manufacturers as well as resellers analyzed every activity in an attempt to reduce costs, particularly marketing costs in relation to declining contribution margins. Although 85 percent of U.S. manufacturers prefer in-house distribution systems, a growing number of firms are moving to third-party logistics providers. Paradoxically, the reasons given for staying in-house—cost, control, flexibility, and better customer service—are the same benefits emphasized by the marketers of third-party services.[23] However, one expert cautions that third-party providers may promise more than they can deliver, particularly in the areas of customer service, inventory control, and order processing.[24]

EXPANSION OF PUBLIC SERVICES

Suppliers of logistical services, particularly transporters and public warehousers, view the situation as an opportunity to increase their own markets. To do so, they have not only upgraded their base business activities, but have expanded into a broader range of services.

For example, public warehouses have added computerized inventory control systems, inbound and outbound shipment tracking, even carrier selection and rate negotiation.[24] Major trucking firms and package delivery services, including Roadway, UPS, and DHL, have formed air freight divisions to enhance and expand their domestic and international capabilities. UPS and DHL have focused on the European Economic Community and the Pacific Rim markets.[25]

PENETRATION OF INTERNATIONAL MARKETS

Successful market penetration has always required knowledge of and ability to serve a target market. Rarely does a supplier have the ability to move into foreign markets unaided by local alliances. Physical distribution is one area where a strong local presence provides invaluable enhancement. When Apple Computer revised their European penetration strategy in 1992 to reduce costs and improve customer service, third-party transporters and warehousers played a major role.[26] However, several global areas that represent major business opportunities for American firms also lack the sophisticated storage and transport systems that have been discussed in this chapter. Eastern Europe, Central and South America, and major portions of Asia are just three examples. Firms that intend to penetrate these markets must also be prepared to collaborate in the establishment of an effective logistical infrastructure.

Looking Back

Marketing logistics alone do not determine the success of a marketing strategy, but a highly effective and competitive system will improve any strategy, and an inefficient system will reduce a brilliant strategy to mediocrity.

A logistics system is the interrelation of all those activities—inventory control and storage, order processing, material handling, transportation, and customer communications—that move products from a point of manufacture to the end user. The combination of these activities forms the foundation for customer service.

Every activity has a cost, but not every one has a value to every customer in every market. Therefore, a firm will wisely survey its target markets to identify those services with the highest value to the majority of customers, thus providing some reasonable assurance of optimizing the return on its logistics investment.

Optimizing the return involves cost trade-offs not only within functional activities but also across activities. Therefore, strategic logistical decisions should be made at middle to upper management levels. These decisions will include the level of customer service, normal and emergency transportation modes, number and type of warehouses, and overall inventory level.

Given the increasing complexity of modern logistics systems and the broadening of product lines, a firm that has not already done so should give serious consideration to computerizing the entire distribution system. The inaccuracies, slow response, cost, and relative inflexibility of a manually controlled system make the cost/benefit trade-off rather obvious. The firm should also compare the relative advantages of performing various logistical activities in-house versus contracting them out to third-party service providers.

Questions for Discussion

1. Marketing logistics entails a variety of activities, all aimed at providing products to customers on a timely basis. Describe these activities and show how they are all interrelated.

2. Each logistical activity has associated costs, but a purposeful cost increase in one area might actually reduce the cost of the entire system. Explain this apparent contradiction.

3. Certain market conditions increase the pressure on a supplier to maintain a competitive logistics system. Describe some of these conditions and explain why they have such an impact.

4. What factors should a firm evaluate in determining what level of customer service to offer and which elements to emphasize?

5. What modes of transportation would best serve the following situation and why?
   a. Shipping iron ore from the Mesabi Range in northeastern Minnesota to steel mills in Gary, Indiana
   b. Shipping $100 microchips from a semiconductor plant in Texas to distributors in New York, Chicago, and San Francisco
   c. Shipping auto air conditioners from a factory in Ohio to an automotive assembly plant near Los Angeles
   d. Shipping head lettuce from the San Joaquin Valley to markets in the Midwest? to Seattle

6. What factors should a firm consider in deciding the following?
   a. Where to locate warehouses
   b. Whether to operate its own or use public facilities

7. How can a firm determine "the right amount" of inventory to carry in stock?

Endnotes

1. Donald J. Bowersox, David J. Closs, and Omar K. Helferich, *Logistical Management,* 3rd ed. (New York: Macmillan Publishing Company, 1986).

2. Jay Gordon, "In warehousing, speed is king," *Distribution* 91 (July 1992):84.

3. Lisa Harrington, "Cross-docking takes cost out of the pipeline," *Distribution* 92 (September 1993):64-6.

4. Jean V. Murphy, "State of logistics," *Traffic World* 234 (June 14, 1993):4.

5. H. Jay Bullen, "New competitive selling weapon—physical distribution management," *Sales and Marketing Management* (May 8, 1985), pp. 41-42.

6. Nanette Byrnes, "Transportation and logistics: whirlpool," *Financial World* 162 (September 28, 1993):61.

7. William C. Copacino, "Moving beyond 'just say yes' logistics," *Traffic Management* 32 (September 1993):35.

8. Jim Thomas, "Distribution costs take the plunge," *Distribution* 93 (January 1994):56-7.

9. Ronald Henkoff, "CEOs still don't walk the talk," *Fortune* 129 (April 18, 1994):14.

10. "Tough issues face shippers," *Transportation and Distribution* 35 (May 1994):75.

11. Julie Candler, "You make it, they distribute it," *Nation's Business* 82 (March 1994):46.

12. James C. Johnson and Donald F. Wood, *Contemporary Physical Distribution and Logistics,* 5th ed. (New York: Macmillan Publishing Company, 1993).

13. James R. Stock and Douglas M. Lambert, *Strategic Logistics Management,* 2nd ed. (Homewood, Ill.: Richard D. Irwin, Inc., 1987).

14. Lawrence Richter Quinn, "Harley-Davidson integrates its distribution," *American Shipper* 34 (May 1992):16-18.

15. Adapted from Frank A. Smith, *Transportation in America,* 10th ed. (Washington, D.C.: Eno Foundation for Transportation, 1992), pp. 8, 10.

16. William McKee, "Intermodal: bursting at the seams," *Distribution* 93 (July 1994):46-8.

17. John D. Schulz, "Truckers embrace line-haul savings, seek greater flexibility in use of Intermodal," *Traffic World* 238 (April 18, 1994):40.

18. Dennis Davis, "Distribution warehousing," *Distribution* 83 (June 1984):65-6.

19. Lisa Harrington, "Better management means lower costs," *Traffic Management* 21 (November 1982):43.

20. Kailash Joshi, "Storage Space costs and the EOQ model," *Journal of Purchasing and Materials Management* 26 (Summer 1990):37-41.

21. Marc Goetschalckx, "Why use computers to design your distribution network," *Transportation and Distribution* 34 (August 1993):34.

22. Frank V. Cespedes, "Industrial marketing: managing new requirements," *Sloan Management Review* 35 (Spring 1994):45-60.

23. Lori Meek Lockman, "Outsourcing logistics," *Global Trade and Transportation* 114 (February 1994):45-6.

24. "Third-party Logistics: Cozy up, but stay tough," *Purchasing* 116 (March 17, 1994):47.

25. See Phillip Hastings, "The express route to contract logistics," *Accountancy* 109 (February 1992):68-9; also Paul Page, "Roadway global air plans aerial assault on world air freight market," *Traffic World* 235 (August 9, 1993):16-17.

26. "Apple takes a bite out of logistics costs," *Traffic Management* 31 (December 1992):84.

Bibliography

Bullen, H. J., "New competitive selling weapon—physical distribution management," *Sales and Marketing Management* (May 8, 1985):41-2.

Cespedes, Frank V., "Industrial marketing: managing new requirements," *Sloan Management Review* 35 (Spring 1994):45-60.

Candler, Julie, "You make it, they distribute it," *Nation's Business* 82 (March 1994):46.

Gooley, Toby B., "To outsource or not to outsource," *Traffic Management* 31 (December 1992):84A.

Gordon, Jay, "In warehousing, speed is king," *Distribution* 91 (July 1992):84.

Harrington, Lisa, "Cross-docking takes cost out of the pipeline," *Distribution* 92 (September 1993):64-6.

Henkoff, Ronald, "CEOs still don't walk the talk," *Fortune* 129 (April 18, 1994):14.

Joshi, Kailash, "Storage space costs and the EOQ model," *Journal of Purchasing and Materials Management* 26 (Summer 1990):37-41.

McKee, William, "Intermodal: Bursting at the seams," *Distribution* 93 (July 1994):46-8.

"Third-party logistics: Cozy up, but stay tough," *Purchasing* 116 (March 17, 1994):47.

VI

Communication Strategies

A 1995 survey conducted for the American Marketing Association found that firms concentrating on the business market spent an average of 3.5 percent of revenue on marketing. Personal selling received the lion's share, or 61 percent, of that budget. Only 25 percent was allocated to other forms of market communication (media advertising, direct mail, trade shows, etc.), and another 11 percent to marketing support activities.

These figures show the significant difference between business market communication strategies and those normally employed in the consumer market, where advertising and sales promotion activities represent the preponderance of marketing expenditures. However, this difference does not indicate a significant weakness of either personal selling or advertising, but rather, reemphasizes the importance of carefully constructing a communication strategy that best suits the target market.

As a general statement, personal selling provides greater flexibility plus the opportunity for buyer-seller dialogue. Both of these attributes enhance a salesperson's ability to close orders in the one-on-one selling situations common to the business market. However, advertising saves both time and money when communicating with a mass consumer market spread across a wide geographic area. There are notable exceptions in both markets. Avon, Mary Kay Cosmetics, and Encyclopedia Britannica emphasize personal selling to consumers, while Dell Computer and Gateway 2000 communicate with their business customers primarily through mass media and direct mail.

Chapters 15 and 16 explain how successful firms hire, train, motivate, and deploy their salespeople. These activities are studied from the viewpoint of a sales manager. Chapter 17 covers the other areas of market communication.

Endnote

Cyndee Miller, "Marketing industry report: Who's spending what on biz-to-biz marketing," *Marketing News* 30 (January 1, 1996):1+.

15 Planning and Developing a Sales Force

Willy Loman died long ago, and with him, the myth that sales hinge on a smile and a shoeshine. Sales success today requires an impressive range of skills—to analyze the buyer's problem or need, to communicate the firm's offering effectively, to interact with diverse personalities, to negotiate areas of differences, and eventually, to devise a mutually satisfying solution.

Stanton, Buskirk, and Spiro[1] view modern sales professionals as ones who "work to relay consumer wants back to the firm so that appropriate products may be developed. They engage in a total consultative, nonmanipulative selling job and are expected to solve customers' problems, not just take orders."[1] Ingram and LaForge[2] consider this process "a customer-oriented approach that employs truthful, nonmanipulative tactics to satisfy the long-term needs of both the customer and the selling firm."[2] The purpose of this chapter, then, is to discuss how sales managers can develop and direct a force of such professionals by:

1. Selectively recruiting and hiring potentially successful salespeople
2. Employing a training program designed to maximize the potential of these individuals
3. Directing the sales force to produce the most favorable results
4. Developing compensation packages and other incentives to achieve the greatest amount of motivation

A Promising Career

Most successful salespeople view selling as a personally rewarding career opportunity. It offers the career salesperson a lucrative income and challenging career path, and it provides a springboard for those who wish to advance into top management positions (Figure 15-1).

Graduating seniors always feel pangs of doubt about the value of their degree in the job market. In the 1990s these doubts have not been alleviated. Corporate down-

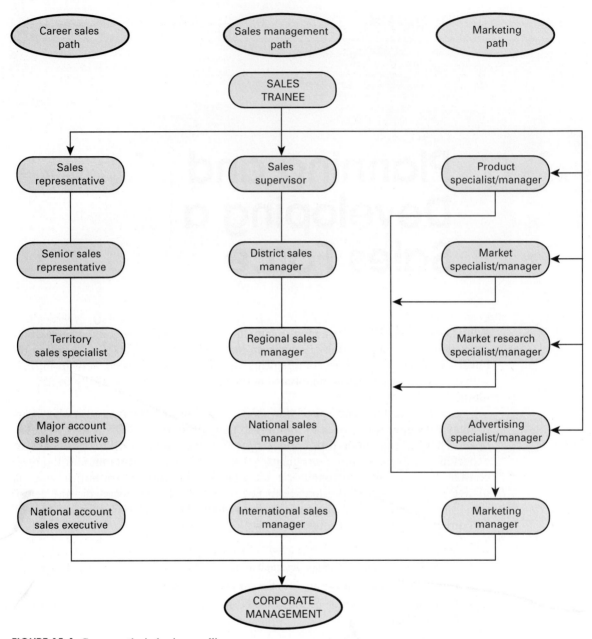

FIGURE 15-1 Career paths in business selling.

sizing, increased worker productivity, and the loss of sales and jobs to international competition combine to make the job market very competitive. However, marketing majors can take heart from several pieces of information.

Table 15-1 shows the career paths for the CEOs of *Business Week*'s 1,000 leading firms. Almost one in four rose through a sales and/or marketing background, a close second to those who came from finance or accounting.[3] It is worthwhile to note that in the 1950s, the sales/marketing path was in fourth place behind finance, engineering, and production. Since then, firms have become increasingly aware that even quality products produced at a competitive cost can and do fail without an effective marketing

TABLE 15-1 Career Paths of the Corporate Elite, 1991: CEOs of *Business Week's* Top 1000 U.S. Firms

Business Specialty	No. of CEOs	Percentage of Total
Finance/accounting	294	25.6
Sales/marketing	270	23.6
Engineering	184	16.1
Production/operations	170	14.8
General administration	135	11.8
Legal	71	6.2
Founder/entrepreneur	18	1.6
Human resources	4	0.3
TOTAL[1]	1146	100.0

[1]Total includes some multiple paths among 1000 individuals.
Source: Data compiled from "Corporate elite," *Business Week* (November 25, 1991), pp. 185+. Reprinted by permission of *Business Week,* © 1991.

program. Executives with an appropriate background are more likely to appreciate and sponsor such programs.

In the experience of a leading executive-search firm, more CEOs follow the sales/marketing path than any other, and this lead has been widening since 1979.[4] Their data do not contradict the *Business Week* findings but rather extend them beyond the top firms.

According to a projection by the Bureau of Labor Statistics, the major occupational groups that require the most education—professional specialties (including business sales and marketing), managerial, and technical—are also among the four groups that will provide the most new jobs between 1994 and 2005.[5] This statistic equates well with estimates that two thirds of marketing graduates begin their careers in sales.[6]

Dartnell Corporation's Twenty-seventh Sales Force Compensation Survey also reveals that the educational level of salespeople continues to rise. In 1992, *62 percent of salespeople were college graduates,* a significant increase over 1982, when only 20 percent of salespeople in the United States held a college degree. These data provide two insights: (1) companies prefer to hire individuals who are better educated and better prepared to sell complex products in sophisticated markets, and (2) the sales profession has clearly become a more accepted career path for college graduates.[7]

WOMEN IN SALES

Several decades ago women found the business market a hostile environment in which to begin a sales career. Consequently, many entered the sales profession through direct selling of consumer products.

Firms such as Avon, Mary Kay Cosmetics, and Tupperware offered women the opportunity to sell products that they used and understood to their peers. Other multilevel sales organizations, such as Amway, stressed the prospect of being one's own boss and earning an impressive income. In actuality, 5 million people (90 percent of them women) worked as direct-sales representatives in 1992. More than 90 percent of these reps, both men and women, earned less than $20,000 annually, with a surprising *50 percent below $2,500.*[8] For those seeking only a part-time, special-purpose income, these figures might be satisfactory. As a steady income for a female head of household, however, they range from marginal to inadequate.

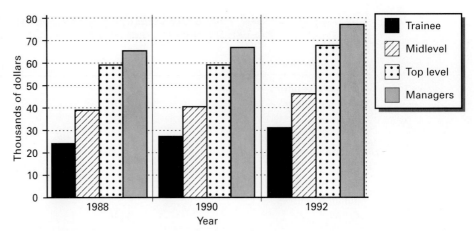

Source: "Salespeople's average annual compensation," *Sales & Marketing Management,* (June 28, 1993), p. 63.

FIGURE 15-2 Annual compensation by salesperson's rank (includes any bonus or commission but excludes travel and entertainment allowance).

By comparison, Figure 15-2 shows the current range of income earned by salespeople based on their rank or time in position. As a brief explanation, trainees have less than 1 year on the job; midlevel salespeople 1 to 3 years; top-level individuals have progressed to positions such as major account executive; managers have attained at least the first level of sales supervision (e.g., branch manager).

Comparative Compensation   Unfortunately, as is true in other business functions, the compensation of saleswomen lags beyond that of men. A 1994 Bureau of Labor Statistics survey confirmed that women in executive, professional, technical, and sales positions earned less than their male counterparts. A comparable relationship held true for educational backgrounds ranging from less than a high school diploma to attainment of a master's degree. The summary data are shown in Table 15-2.

The comparison of women's incomes to that of men across occupations and educational levels holds fairly constant between 70 percent and 80 percent—with the glaring exception of sales. Here, women earn only 57 percent as much as their male counterparts. There is a major fallacy in this comparison, however. Women have made the greatest penetration into those industries that pay their salespeople below national average (e.g., retail trade, hotel/motel, and health services). Men still dominate the higher paying industries. This point is substantiated by comparing the median income of salespeople with that of executives and technical personnel for both men and women (see Table 15-2). The percentages for salesmen are 71.2 and 95.9 percent respectively; for saleswomen, only 58.7 and 68.4 percent.

Valuable Personality Traits   Women stand to benefit, even in male-heavy industries, from the increasing popularity of **consultative selling.** Women tend to excel at such selling because they are "relationship builders." Within this broad term lie particular characteristics that women frequently possess to a greater degree than men do. Included are the ability to listen carefully and objectively, a close attention to detail, a natural tendency to follow through on commitments, and the ability to convey the perception of genuine caring for another's needs. These attributes are also the hallmarks of successful consultative salespeople.[9]

	Men ($)	Women ($)	Women (%)
TABLE 15-2 Comparative Median Incomes for Men and Women by Occupation and Education, 1994[1]			
Occupation			
Executive and managerial	41,184	28,600	69.4
Professional	42,172	32,448	76.9
Technical	30,576	24,544	80.3
Sales	29,328	16,796	57.3
Sales as percent of executive income	71.2%	58.7%	—
Sales as percent of technical income	95.9%	68.4%	—
Education			
Less than high school	18,460	13,364	72.4
High school graduate	25,480	18,408	72.2
Some college (associate's degree)	29,952	21,892	73.1
Baccalaureate degree	39,156	31,980	81.7
Master's degree	49,920	39,260	78.6

[1]Third quarter 1994 survey data annualized; full-time workers only.

Source: U.S. Bureau of Labor Statistics, *Current Population Survey* (November, 1994).

Women have made significant penetration into the sales forces of some industries and only minimal penetration into others. Table 15-3 provides data for some industries along with information by product and service classification. All three *service sectors*—consumer, industrial, and office—seem to offer greater promise for employment at both the representative and managerial levels.

Recruiting and Selecting Salespeople

Professional salespeople, particularly those who make selling an extended career, are unique individuals. They have drives and desires that set them apart from other employees. For example, they seek out challenging situations, they prefer to function with a minimum of supervision, and they thrive in a highly competitive environment. Such individuals are not easy to find.

Thus, conventional methods of personnel selection often lead to suboptimal choices. Commonly used hiring techniques fail to attract outstanding prospects. However, sales managers need not rely solely on "gut feelings" to hire qualified candidates. They can approach the task logically by developing an accurate job description and a related list of personal aptitudes that this job requires.

To find people with the right skills and attributes from among dozens or hundreds of applicants, sales managers must develop procedures and criteria that correctly differentiate based on potential ability to succeed. The definition of success will vary with the goals, strategies, and culture of the organization. So, too, must skills and attributes vary. Then, to enhance the full potential of newcomers, sales managers must create training programs that develop the skills essential to the formation of long-term customer relationships.

RECRUITING DESIRABLE CANDIDATES

Sales professionals can be recruited from six generic sources:

1. Salespeople working for direct competitors
2. Salespeople working for noncompeting firms in the same industry

TABLE 15-3 Women in Sales: Selected Industries, 1992		
	Percent of Sales Reps	*Percent of Sales Managers*
By Industry		
HIGHEST		
Hotels/motels	73.0	64.2
Communications	51.2	23.2
Health services	49.8	12.5
Office equipment	39.0	31.0
Retail trade	36.9	0.0
Business services	36.3	14.2
Insurance	33.2	19.3
Printing/publishing	32.3	18.9
Trucking and warehousing	26.5	25.0
Paper and allied products	25.7	26.1
Educational services	23.0	40.0
Electronics	22.3	0.0
LOWEST		
Machinery	2.8	10.0
Instruments	3.8	0.0
Chemicals	11.0	1.3
Manufacturing	12.9	12.5
Wholesale (consumer goods)	14.6	3.3
Wholesale (industrial goods)	14.5	0.0
By Product or Service		
Consumer products	24.4	11.4
Consumer services	40.4	20.9
Industrial products	13.5	8.2
Industrial services	26.9	13.2
Office products	30.4	9.6
Office services	41.0	18.1

Source: Adapted from Dartnell Corporation, *Sales Force Compensation Survey,* 27th ed. (Chicago: Dartnell Corporation, 1993), p. 157.

3. Salespeople working for firms in other industries
4. Customer employees with supplier contacts (purchasing, production, or engineering personnel)
5. Employees in this company (similar to customer employees)
6. New college graduates

Sales managers differ in their priorities, but virtually all seek candidates with three primary qualities: *empathy, ego drive,* and *creativity.* Empathy allows them to view their product or service in terms of customer benefits. Ego drive engenders a strong need to close sales and achieve assigned goals. Creativity provides the ability to solve problems by looking beyond the obvious for solutions. Flexibility and the desire to learn serve as further enhancement.

In addition to these attributes, successful salespeople require a variety of skills and knowledge. These include technological knowledge, communication skills, effec-

					Knowledge of			
Source	*Technical Skills*	*Communication Skills*	*Interpersonal Skills*	*Negotiation Skills*	*Product*	*Competition*	*Customer*	*The firm*
1. Direct competition	G	G	G	G	G	G	G	F
2. Within the same industry	G	G	G	G	F	F	G	P-F
3. Outside the industry	F	G	G	G	P-F	P-F	P-F	P-F
4. Customers	F-G	G	G	F-G	F-G	F-G	P-F	F-G
5. This firm	F-G	G	G	F-G	G	P-G	F-G	G
6. College graduates	P-G	G	G	P-G	P	P	P	P

TABLE 15-4   Matrix of Desired Sales Abilities Versus Sources of Candidates

tive interpersonal relations, problem-solving ability, and negotiation skills. Managers also give preference to applicants knowledgeable of the products, competitors, and customers in a relevant market. Finally, a salesperson becomes effective more quickly if he or she understands the goals and workings of this specific company. Obviously, only the salespeople already employed could have all of these skills and experience to an adequate degree. Whenever skills or experience is lacking, new hires require training from a minimal to extensive level.

Table 15-4 provides a range of abilities (poor, fair, good) that might be anticipated from the six sources. It is assumed that only candidates with good communication, interpersonal, and problem-solving skills will receive further consideration. Recent college graduates must recognize that they compete not only with each other but with people already in the business world who want to improve their career opportunities.

SELECTION PROCESS

Companies use a variety of selection tools to choose the most promising sales candidates. Table 15-5 lists these tools and the frequency with which large and small firms employ them. Personal interviews, education and work experience, and reference checks are the tools most commonly used.[10]

PERSONAL INTERVIEWS

The primary method used to determine a candidate's personal characteristics, attitude, skills, and experience is the personal interview. Numerous studies, however, have shown that its *validity* (ability to determine what it is being measured) is lower than other selection techniques. However, the problem often lies with the interviewer rather than the process. Some managers look for a mirror image of themselves. Others fail to treat and question all applicants the same. In short, properly conducted interviews can and do regularly yield the desired information about an applicant.

Multiple and Panel Interviews   To overcome the weakness in the personal interview, many companies employ multiple or panel-type interviews. Multiple interviews involve a variety of company employees who talk to the candidate at different times from their individual perspectives. In the panel interview, the candidate appears before a diverse group on just one occasion. Both techniques help to reduce the biases of any

TABLE 15-5	Selection Tools Most Commonly Used	
Selection Tools	Percent of Small Firms	Percent of Large Firms
Personal interviews	91	96
Application forms	73	70
Personal reference checks	70	62
List of job qualifications	34	45
Job descriptions	30	51
Psychological tests	22	32
Credit reports	15	36

Source: From Alan J. Dubinsky and Thomas E. Barry, "A survey of sales management practices," *Industrial Marketing Management* 11 (1982):133-41. Copyright © 1982 by Elsevier Science Publishing Co., Inc.

one interviewer. They also provide a broader determination of an applicant's strengths and weaknesses.

Patterned or Structured Interviews   An increasing number of firms believe that the most successful interviewing method is the patterned or structured format. This technique uses questions constructed beforehand and directed to all candidates.[11] Interviewers can then compare responses. During the interview, for example, candidates can be asked open-ended questions that prompt them to reveal more of their thought processes. Open-ended responses are usually more valuable than the simple "yes" or "no" elicited by closed-ended questions.

Problem-solving questions aid the interviewer in determining a candidate's reasoning abilities and technical knowledge. Such questions place the candidate in a hypothetical situation that requires a fast analysis and response. For example, the candidate might be asked: "What would you do if a buyer made repeated appointments to meet with you but was never available when you arrived?"

APPLICATION BLANKS

An application blank provides a synopsis of the applicant's personal history and is the second most commonly used selection tool. However, laws that protect civil rights and/or prohibit discrimination in hiring—such as the Civil Rights Act of 1964, the Age Discrimination in Employment Act of 1967, the Fair Employment Opportunity Act (1972), and Americans with Disabilities Act (1990)—have reduced the range of information that can be legally sought. For example, a firm cannot ask the applicant's age, marital status, race, height or weight, or property ownership. Questions in sensitive areas may be asked during the interview only if they relate to *bona fide occupational qualifications* (BFOQs).[1] For example, the ability to speak a certain foreign language or to carry demonstration equipment may be essential to the job. Thus, only information that is *job relevant* may be sought.

REFERENCE CHECKS

Reference checks have restrictions similar to those that limit the usefulness of application blanks. By law, former employers can provide only three pieces of information about their former employees: length of employment, job title (or titles), and eligibility (or lack thereof) to be rehired. Given this limitation, we have found it very helpful during the interview to ask applicants with sales experience for the names of five customers who could attest to their effectiveness. Our experience has shown that most salespeople answer readily; those who do not usually have other areas of questionable strength.

TESTING

Many companies are ambivalent regarding the testing of applicants. On one hand, the increasing complexity of the business market requires salespeople with greater skills, broader knowledge, and more stable characteristics. Psychological and aptitude tests can provide an additional source of information. On the other hand, poorly designed tests can be either discriminatory or unreliable. One study concluded that traditional tests rarely succeed because they analyze interests rather than ability, favor group conformity rather than individual creativity, and look at specific traits rather than the whole person.[12]

One company, Advanced Network Design, uses two tests to screen sales applicants. The first checks for honesty, goal orientation, and persistence. The second indicates the individual's selling style. This combination helps to eliminate weak candidates and uncover those who have desirable attributes but lack selling skills.[13]

Training for Professionalism

Referring again to Table 15-4, one can see that very few new salespeople come to the job with all the required skills and knowledge in place. Consequently, some amount of training is required. In 1992, industrial firms spent an average of $6,200 training inexperienced new hires; $3,300 was spent on the ongoing training of experienced salespeople.[14] Although the second figure may appear to be a "bargain," it must be recognized that hiring experienced people may be equivalent to recycling marginal performers or those who must "unlearn" bad habits. On the other hand, recent college graduates may require extensive technical and market training, but they may also possess boundless enthusiasm, creativity, strong interpersonal skills, and unique problem-solving capability. They have also been exposed to the latest theories and concepts being taught in academia.

Given the range of skills and attributes required, it is not surprising that companies such as Motorola, Hewlett-Packard, Xerox, and Merck, whose sales forces are continually ranked among the best, also have the most comprehensive training programs. One extensive study identified the areas of training provided by the greatest number of companies.[15] These are shown in Table 15-6. It is interesting to note that several other aspects essential to sales success are not among the top twenty training areas: negotiating skills (49 percent), ethics (43 percent), and creativity (42 percent). Perhaps the latter two figures bear out the thought that firms cannot successfully impart personality traits that are not already native to the individual.

Another study commissioned by the National Paper Trade Association sought to determine the factors most important to selling effectiveness. Both salespeople and sales managers provided input. The five factors identified as most critical were sales teamwork, sales training, buyer-seller relations, hiring practices, and sales manager traits.[16]

Fortunately, the two studies indicate a fairly strong relationship between skills required and the training being provided. Moreover, the training areas stressed in the past—product knowledge, company policies and procedures, and the "mechanics" of

TABLE 15-6 Areas of Training Most Frequently Provided by Companies	
Training Area	*Percentage of Companies That Provide Training*
New employee orientation	91
Handling performance appraisals[1]	79
Leadership	75
Interpersonal skills	73
Listening skills	71
Time management	71
Personal computer applications	69
Team-building[1]	68
Goal setting	66
Product knowledge	66
Problem solving	66
Motivation techniques	64
Conducting meetings	62
Quality improvement	62
Stress management	61
Public speaking/presentations	59
Writing skills	57
Management/marketing information systems	56
Tactical planning	55
Strategic planning	51

[1]Primarily for new managers.
Source: "What employers teach," *Training* 29 (October 1992):43-55. © 1992, Lakewood Publications, Minneapolis, Minn. All rights reserved.

selling—did not prepare individuals well for the "soft" or interpersonal aspects of selling. So again, the listing in Table 15-6 is encouraging.

TRAINING AS AN ONGOING PROCESS

To keep salespeople from becoming outdated, stale, or demotivated, sales training must be an ongoing process. Business markets have always been dynamic and hard to predict, but the dramatic growth of international markets plus the increased threat of global competition have caused changes with even greater frequency and impact. Moreover, changes that might begin thousands of miles away from a salesperson's territory may become a competitive crisis before this individual can devise an effective offsetting strategy. Therefore, training must also impart knowledge—about economic conditions, new sales opportunities, technological trends within and outside the firm, and competitive threats—that salespeople might otherwise lack because of their territorial constraints.[17]

Recurring training can also rejuvenate a person's self-confidence, self-motivation and effectiveness.[18] New product training provides a prime example. Salespeople unquestionably sell more of what they know best. The more they sell, the better they feel about themselves, the greater the level of confidence they exude, and the more positive the image they portray to customers (Box 15-1).

In the same vein, we tend to fear most what we understand the least. When a salesperson understands a competitor's strategy well enough and soon enough to take effective counteraction, the probability of success rises substantially.

Training Isn't Micro at IBM

The importance of education to IBM shows up clearly in some simple numbers. On any given day, 18,000 of its 390,000 employees take part in some kind of formal education event—in a classroom, through self-study, or via computer-based training. IBMers around the world complete a staggering 5 million student days per year, giving each one an average of about twelve days. The yearly education budget of $900 million includes the costs of the people, equipment, and facilities needed to deliver the training but does not include the salaries of the people being trained.

Source: Patricia A. Galagan, "IBM gets its arms around education," *Training and Development Journal,* January 1989, pp. 34-41. Copyright © 1989, American Society for Training and Development. All rights reserved; reprinted by permission.

WHO SHOULD TRAIN?

To a large degree, successful training depends on the capabilities of the trainers. Training is a specialized skill, and those who train should be chosen carefully. The three most popular types of sales trainers are (1) the sales manager, (2) an experienced salesperson, and (3) training specialists.

Sales Managers as Trainers   When sales managers train new salespeople, several advantages accrue: (1) the trainee learns what factors this immediate supervisor will emphasize when evaluating performance, (2) the trainee also gains the advantage of preparing a sales presentation and meeting a prospect in the company of an experienced sales manager, and (3) the sales manager's firsthand observation can pinpoint the trainee's strengths and weaknesses to determine areas for further development.

However, sales managers have busy schedules, are often afraid of diminishing the formal supervisor/subordinate relationship, and may lack knowledge of learning theory. Trainees also tend to worry more about impressing the supervisor than about learning.[19]

Experienced Salespeople as Trainers   Some organizations with limited formal training programs place new salespeople in the hands of more experienced peers who provide additional on-the-job training. Although experienced sales personnel have the ability to provide excellent guidance, they often do not for several reasons. For one, experienced salespeople tend to view the additional training load adversely because to them, it represents responsibility without compensation. They may also view the trainee as a potential in-house competitor for rewards and promotion. In addition, trainer and trainee may have different backgrounds or personalities that would favor dissimilar sales techniques. Most important, though, is that salespeople do not always possess training skills, regardless of their sales experience.[19]

Training Specialists   Although more expensive and often resented by sales managers, training specialists from within or outside the firm frequently provide the training service. These individuals more likely have greater teaching capabilities than the sales practitioners, but on the other hand, they may lack knowledge of the goals and strategies employed by a given company or those common to a geographical area or product market. In addition, they often lack realistic field selling experience.[19]

Combinations of Trainers   By combining training methods, many of the foregoing problems can be avoided. For example, training specialists might impart knowledge regarding time management and interpersonal relationships. Sales managers might then concentrate on local market conditions including customer opportunities and competitive threats.

Training specialists can also enhance the ability of sales managers to carry out their training assignments. Of course, company size, the quality and number of sales personnel, and the cost of the various alternatives will influence such decisions. For example, IBM found in 1989 that it cost $350 per day to train an employee in one of its educational institutes, $150 in a class at a plant site, $125 taught by satellite in a plant site, or $75 if the learning involved only self-study.[20]

Areas of Sales Training

As discussed earlier, areas of sales training and the emphasis given to each depend on the company, its goals, the products involved, the marketing environment, and the skills and experience of the sales personnel. Table 15-6 provides greater detail. Despite greater attention being paid to the interpersonal aspects of selling, two potential dangers still exist. One involves the difference between what the company promises to candidates during the initial interview and what it subsequently provides. The other danger stems from the assumption of many companies that they know what their customers expect from salespeople without actually going out to gather the facts.

In the first instance, the most promising of inexperienced applicants usually recognize their own limitations and seek an employer who will help them grow in knowledge and capability. They know this will involve extensive training. In order to hire them, the interviewer "tells them what they want to hear." However, numerous surveys indicate that at least one-third of all business firms have no training program and many others depend on peer training or "hands on" experience to prepare new salespeople.[21]

Another exhaustive study compiled buyer opinions over a seven year period to determine those characteristics of salespeople that had the greatest positive impact on buying decisions. Table 15-7 shows the results of that study. Conversations between the authors and former industry colleagues indicate that these preferences have changed very little over the past decade. The desirability of these characteristics seems obvious;

TABLE 15-7   Sales Attributes Preferred by Buyers

Attribute	*Percentage of Mentions*
1. Thoroughness and follow-through	65.0
2. Knowledge of the product line	58.9
3. Willingness to go to bat for the buyer within selling firm	54.3
4. Market knowledge and willingness to keep buyer posted	40.6
5. Imagination in applying products to the buyer's needs	23.1
6. Knowledge of the buyer's products line (and business)	18.3
7. Diplomacy in dealing with operating departments	16.3
8. Preparation for well-planned sales calls	12.4
9. Regularity of sales calls	8.7
10. Technical education	7.4

Source: From Alvin J. Williams and John Seminerio, "What buyers like from salesmen," *Industrial Marketing Management* 14 (1985):75-8. Copyright © 1985 by Elsevier Science Publishing Co., Inc.

but unless care is taken to hire people who already possess them or to train those who do not, business will be lost to competitors who better fit the desired image.

COMPANY KNOWLEDGE

A salesperson will probably perform better on points one and three in Table 15-7—thoroughness/follow through and buyer advocacy—when properly educated in the policies, goals, and capabilities of the company. This is particularly true with reference to those factors involving customer-oriented services. Such training alerts salespeople where to go within the organization for specialized information or support. They are also kept informed of improvements and additions—new products, longer warranties, improved market share—that enhance their competitiveness. This type of knowledge builds company loyalty, increases confidence and morale, and leads to reduced turnover. It also enhances the salesperson's ability to deal with the increased paperwork and bureaucratic systems that usually accompany corporate growth.

PRODUCT KNOWLEDGE

Table 15-7 indicates that buyers rank product knowledge second in importance and implies that this attribute will affect their overall judgement of the salesperson. Because of the importance of product knowledge, magnified by the acceleration of technological change, firms must provide continuous product training. Product knowledge also enhances point five, "imagination in applying products to buyer's needs."

Product training programs should cover product features and applications, but equally important, translate this information into customer benefits, including how products might improve the quality, reduce the cost, or increase effectiveness in the buyer's end products, production process, or distribution system.

Product training must also impart knowledge of competitors' products, including their relative strengths, weaknesses, pricing structure, and market acceptance.

INDUSTRY AND MARKET TREND KNOWLEDGE

To be effective, salespeople must stay abreast of current business conditions within their industries and markets. Such knowledge includes trends in customer practices, such as reducing inventory levels in response to higher interest rates, or conversely, increasing their purchases before an anticipated price increase.

This area should also include knowledge of specific customers, such as who make buying decisions, who influence these decisions, and what criteria shape the decisions. Sales managers who insist that salespeople identify and document customer information for their own effectiveness also end up with a valuable database with which to train new hires.

With regard to customer preferences (see Table 15-7), industry and specific customer knowledge will certainly increase a salesperson's attractiveness on points four, five, six, and eight. In addition, self-confidence and effective decision-making will also be enhanced. Further, when salespeople are aware of downward trends industrywide, they are less discouraged by their own decline in sales.

COMPETITIVE KNOWLEDGE

In addition to the product knowledge mentioned earlier, salespeople must be aware of the distinctive organizational competencies and strategic goals of their competition. One sales manager exhorted his sales force to "know the capabilities, limitations, strategies, and goals of your major competitors as well as you know your own, because these firms are your customer's alternative choices." He sought to emphasize that knowledge of competition also provides a greater knowledge of the customer.

Referring again to Table 15-7, competitive knowledge helps the salesperson to "keep the buyer informed," the fourth-ranked attribute.

Ethics Are Important   Ethics, or moral standards of conduct, must not be ignored. A nationwide survey of CEOs indicated that 71 percent "put integrity at the top of a list of sixteen traits most responsible for enhancing an executive's chances for success."[22] For example, salespeople must know the acceptable limits of criticizing competition. Buyers view the criticism of competitors as one of the least desirable sales techniques.[23] Put another way, buyers want salespeople to concentrate on their own strengths, not the perceived weaknesses of competition.

Given this strong opposition by both CEOs and buyers to tactics viewed as unethical, the absence of ethics in the training agenda of more than half of U.S. firms is even more surprising and unfortunate. The importance of training in ethics increases when firms enter the international marketplace, because the definition of ethical behavior also depends on culture and traditions. For example, despite its widespread use in the United States, comparative advertising—naming names and describing faults—is illegal in many countries and frowned on virtually everywhere else. Thus, the open criticism of a competitor, even when based in fact, will almost certainly result in lost business.

SALES SKILLS KNOWLEDGE

Selling activities in the business market can range from closing a repeat order for office supplies to orchestrating the design, construction, and mechanization of an automated production facility. The repeat order might consume only minutes, while the sale of a production facility could take months, even years to finalize. Regardless of product or situational complexity, an effective sales presentation stems from a series of related goals and techniques. Table 15-8 provides one compilation of these efforts.[24]

TABLE 15-8   Elements of a Good Sales Presentation

Element	Technique
Presentation has to be believed, agreed with, and acted on.	Personalize the presentation for this buyer.
Gain the prospect's attention by dramatizing the product value.	Choose impact words with motivational strength.
A presentation produces orders when it is built around buyer benefits.	Direct the presentation toward the prospect's self-interest and priorities.
Sales are seldom closed unless the prospect has confidence in the proposition.	Achieve credibility. Support claims with evidence and testimonials.
Speak the prospect's language. It's a sure way to build buyer confidence.	The ideal presentation contains both emotion and logic.
Take the initiative in motivating the prospect to take action and place the order.	Be an assistant buyer; stay ahead of the decision makers with a strategy you trust.

Source: Adapted from Roger Staubach, Jack Kinder Jr., and Gary Kinder, "Secrets of making good presentations," *Marketing Times* (March/April 1983), pp. 20-3.

Professional Selling Styles   Depending on the product, customer need, and circumstances, one of several selling styles will be appropriate. These styles are commonly referred to as technical, consultative, negotiating, systems, and team.

- *Technical styles* require the ability to solve customer problems through the use of the salesperson's technical background and knowledge. In actuality, technical selling involves the selling of a service—problem solving—as well as a product. For this reason, many technical salespeople have degrees in engineering or some physical science.

- *Consultative styles* require excellent written and verbal communication skills as well as analytical ability to reach and solve problems for decision makers at higher organizational levels. Consultative selling frequently involves services such as management consulting, executive search, or the design of a corporate pension plan. Thus, people involved in this type of selling must be capable of understanding the client's business operation, the exact nature of the problem, and the range of solutions that might be acceptable to this particular company.

- *Negotiating styles* involve the ability to maximize benefits for both the buyer and seller during the transaction period so that both parties reach a mutually beneficial arrangement.

- *Systems styles* require the ability to analyze a prospect's operational or information needs and make recommendations that involve a package of goods and services to fulfill those needs. The need could be a training program for new employees, a redesigned production process, or an equipment maintenance program.

- *Team-selling styles* involve the ability to work with other functional experts within the selling firm who are more capable of matching the specialized knowledge or requirements of the buying firm.

HUMAN RELATIONS SKILLS

Business selling often requires considerable time to identify and build relationships with key influencers and decision makers. This task often involves a series of calls over an extended period (perhaps a year or two). During these calls, salespeople strive to identify and reach key influencers and gain the respect and confidence of these individuals.

This process requires the display of skills and attributes that will favorably influence professionals who have become skeptical of the claims regularly put forth by salespeople eager to please. Sincerity, objectivity, creativity, and empathy are among the personal traits that the salesperson must possess and portray. An ability to "read people" and adapt to their perspectives is essential.

As Stumm emphasized, the major difference between success and failure in selling depends on the salesperson's ability to deal with the different personalities encountered[25]:

> People do not react to an objective world, but to a world they have fashioned for themselves out of their own unique, individual perceptions and assumptions about the world. Salespeople, like all the rest of us, can readily be trapped by these assumptions into misleading, misdirected, and ineffective selling efforts.

The decisions that buyers make stem from their personalities (which include their motivations, attitudes, knowledge, and skills), the environment within which they work, the nature of their job, and the rewards associated with their performance. In attempting to uncover buying motives, then, the salesperson must also recognize "that there is always a relationship between the variables of the individual's total, if faulty, awareness and the variables of his environment."[25] Rarely are buying decisions made on cold logical reasoning. In fact, studies have shown that people often make decisions based on their personal perceptions and then use logic and reasoning to justify those decisions. Therefore, sales success depends on the ability to perceive and relate to the emotional needs of the customer. Sales training, then, must also teach the arts of questioning effectively, listening carefully, and responding empathetically.

NEGOTIATION SKILLS

Negotiation requires an emphasis on *mutual dependence* rather than self-interest. Effective selling emphasizes customer benefits. This approach does not ignore the salesperson's need to close an order or reach a quota, but rather recognizes the truth that a sale requires a satisfied customer. In short, both parties must see the transaction as a desirable event.

Not too long ago, training in negotiations included such rules as "Never be the first party to concede," "Make your concessions smaller than the other party's," and "Make several small concessions and immediately strive for a major concession in return."

The Japanese buyer-seller interface helps to explain the current perspective of mutual interdependence. A Japanese buyer typically relies on only one firm to supply all quantities of a particular input. Thus, supplier and buyer must work together, and the buyer expects the supplier to deliver a quality product, on time, to minimize inventory. Consequently, Japanese buyers and sellers interact as though they were divisions of a common enterprise, working for their mutual well-being. In fact, the term *partnering* stems from this close interrelation.

As more American businesses adopt the concepts of partnering, just-in-time delivery schedules, and materials-requirement planning to meet increased domestic and international competition, their negotiating relationships will also reflect this concern for common needs. Banting and Dion have found that exploitative and adversarial negotiating strategies are becoming the exception rather than the rule. Adversarial strategies impede negotiation and the development of productive buyer-seller relationships.[26] Thus, negotiation strategies should center on developing a synergy between firms by combining the distinctive competencies and comparative advantages of each for mutual benefit.

Successful negotiation consists of three important stages: (1) preparing for negotiation, (2) establishing fundamental attitudes, and (3) conducting the negotiation.

Preparing for Negotiation[27]   As a first step, the salesperson should develop an appropriate strategy. This entails gathering as much information as possible on the matter to be negotiated. During this stage, the seller's strengths and weaknesses, along with those of competition, are evaluated in the context of this buyer's needs. The seller must be prepared to discuss the relevant issues under consideration so that the basic interests of both parties can be served. When salespeople understand their organization's position on issues, they can more readily decide when to make any necessary concessions or to pursue an alternative course of action.

To provide a favorable atmosphere for negotiating, the buyer should make arrangements to hold negotiations in a suitable, distraction-free location with a seating arrangement that reflects equal status, and at a time that is mutually convenient. This assumes that most sales negotiations are conducted at the buyer's place of business. A businesslike atmosphere accompanied by formal conduct by both parties tends to reflect mutual respect and is beneficial to the individuals involved. Negotiators usually bring written material and sometimes experts in a particular field to reflect the importance of the negotiations.

Establishing Fundamental Attitudes   The establishment and continuation of favorable attitudes is essential to successful negotiation. Buyers and sellers often spend considerable time defining a problem or a product's application to establish areas of agreement before discussing points of conflict. This effort sets the stage for cooperation and mutual benefit. Salespeople should make known their company's strong desire and commitment to resolve the conflicting issues.

Conducting the Negotiations   During the negotiations, salespeople should focus on the buyer's decision-making priorities rather than on positions taken or individual personalities. By asking questions instead of making statements, the seller learns more, gives the buyer the satisfaction of being heard, and usually progresses toward an area of mutual satisfaction. Breaking major issues into smaller, less troublesome subparts increases the likelihood of reaching agreement without the necessity of compromises.

Salespeople should be prepared with an alternative method of resolving a problem—or be ready to break off negotiation to find a suitable alternative when the discussion degenerates below a level of mutual benefit. For example, when the buyer insists on a price that is incompatible with product specifications under discussion, it is better to offer an alternative product than to argue over price.

Because negotiating is such an important aspect of business marketing, the subject of price negotiation will be covered further in Chapter 19.

DIRECTING (MOTIVATING) THE SALES FORCE

Many salespeople experience considerable stress because their jobs seem to have very few "average" days; instead, they have days that are either very good or very bad. The solitude of on-the-road days and in-the-motel nights can become depressing. Further, given their commitment to customer satisfaction, they can become frustrated when customer needs and corporate goals seem to conflict. Because of these issues, many sales managers find that their most challenging responsibility is renewing and maintaining sales force motivation.

MOTIVATION THEORIES

Directing "is concerned with stimulating members of the organization to undertake action consistent with the plans."[28] As a function performed by sales managers, *directing* is generally synonymous with *motivating*. Motivation theories fall into two groups: content theories, which describe the internal drives or needs of individuals, and process theories, which describe the reasoning processes involved in motivation.

Content Theories   Two popular content theories are those developed by Abraham Maslow and Frederick Herzberg. Maslow developed a hierarchy of needs and hypothesized that individuals progressed through physiological, safety and security, social, and self-esteem needs to self-actualization.[29] The hierarchy's ultimate need, self-actualization, is defined as fulfilling one's true potential and growth, that is, being all that one can be. Herzberg theorized that salary, work conditions, job security, and other external considerations do not provide motivation; instead, people are motivated by achievement, recognition, responsibility, advancement, and growth, that is, feelings of self-accomplishment.[30]

Process Theories   One popular process theory is *expectancy theory,* which is expressed by the formula[31]

$$\text{Motivation} = (E-P) \times (P-O) \times \text{Valence}$$

where

   E−P = A person's perceived probability of being able to perform a task if he or she expends the *effort* to do so

   P−O = A person's perceived probability of obtaining a desired *outcome* if he or she performs the task

Valence = The anticipated *value* (satisfaction or dissatisfaction) of what will be obtained from an outcome

Another process theory, *attribution theory,* holds that individuals are motivated or demotivated as a result of their perceptions regarding who is in control or responsible for their actions. It stipulates that those who perceive themselves to be in control tend to be motivated, whereas those who perceive someone else to be in control are not motivated.

Implications for Sales Management   Expectancy theory implies that sales managers must seek ways to increase a salesperson's perception of being able to perform assigned tasks and receiving a desired reward as a result of performance. Studies have shown that improved communications, training, helpful co-workers, and previous successful experiences do convince people that appropriate efforts result in rewards.[31, 32] The model also implies that various considerations motivate different people. Some people need more training and assurance than others to believe that their efforts will indeed lead to accomplishments. Others, with higher levels of self-confidence, require less training.

The outcomes that individuals seek also vary considerably. While one salesperson may work harder to receive a promotion to impress a spouse, another may simply want recognition from a sales manager. This variability in desired outcomes indicates that the sales manager who develops closer job relationships with his or her salespeople provides more meaningful leadership.

Attribution theory relates well to the theories of Maslow and Herzberg. Individuals who believe that they are personally responsible for their accomplishments have, in the Maslow framework, an increased sense of self-esteem and a greater feeling of self-actualization. According to Herzberg, individuals who believe that they are personally responsible for accomplishments have an increased sense of achievement, recognition, plus the opportunity to advance and grow.

It seems logical that salespeople, who spend so much time working without supervision, are not only motivated by their perception of being in control, but also resent any attempts to deprive them of that personal control. A marketing vice president at Du Pont indicated the firm's application of this concept when he said, "The company's salesperson ... may bring in the director of production or even a vice president when he makes a sales call, but the salesperson is the one who calls the shots. Nothing happens at that account without his say-so."[33]

Trust, Subtlety, and Intimacy   The foregoing motivational theories relate well to current popular theories regarding Japanese management. One Japanese management theorist maintains that American managers must be more trusting, subtle, and intimate in regard to their subordinates.[34] In discussing trust, he suggests that American managers should more closely approach the Japanese practice of placing great trust in subordinates. Subtlety suggests that managers should become more astute in recognizing the differences and peculiarities of their subordinates. By intimacy he means that managers should encourage the development of personal friendships in the workplace.

New Theories and Old Principles   During the 1980s authors wrote innumerable books dedicated to the proposition that American managers have lost their ability to direct organizations and motivate subordinates. These authors put forth a variety of explanations for this deterioration of leadership. Some placed the blame on a growing desperation triggered by the accelerated loss of business to foreign competition. Labor unrest, deterioration of product quality, uncompetitive pricing, and a loss of customer orientation were all laid at the feet of uncaring, if not incompetent, managers.

Among the various solutions offered, many centered on manager/worker relationships. However, on careful analysis, most solutions had a very familiar sound. For example, Tom Peters and Nancy Austin wrote that workers need to be liberated, involved, accountable and allowed to reach their potential. They further stressed that a supervisor should be more of a leader than a manager and should use symbols, drama, and vision.[35] These are excellent points and were equally valuable when offered earlier by Maslow, Herzberg, Lawler, Vroom, and countless other behavioral theorists.

Elsewhere in this text, we suggest that customer satisfaction should precede profits as a company's primary goal. Satisfied customers produce profits; dissatisfied customers prevent profits. By the same token, *only motivated and appreciated employees achieve optimal organizational returns.* This concept originated long before the 1980s; unfortunately, many firms forgot it in their attempts to survive or to increase profits.

EFFECTIVE USE OF SALES COMPENSATION

During the early years of the twentieth century, many managers viewed money as a primary motivator. Since then, considerable research has indicated that money is important but not as a direct motivator. For example, Herzberg's dual-structure theory,[36] accepted by many managers although rejected by others, proposes that work factors should be subdivided into motivation factors and hygiene factors. Motivation factors—including achievement, recognition, responsibility, and growth—deal with the job itself and motivate individuals when present. Their absence, however, does not cause demotivation, but only a neutral attitude. On the other hand, hygiene factors—including pay, working conditions, and company policies—deal with the work environment and demotivate when absent, but result in a neutral attitude when present. Thus, motivation factors can be said to range from zero to some positive value, hygiene factors from zero to some negative value.[36]

Regardless of any theory, the median salary for senior salespeople reached $53,300 in 1992, exceeding $50,000 for the first time. This level represented an 8.8 percent rise over 1990. Hence, companies must still feel a need to compensate experienced salespeople quite well.[37]

MONETARY COMPENSATION

Differences of opinion regarding the ability of money to motivate can be partially reconciled if we acknowledge that money can motivate an individual to work in one of three different ways. First, a sufficiently high salary can motivate someone to *accept* a job offer. Many people who believe that money motivates them to work may only be motivated by a need for money; they may feel little motivation to work once employed.

Second, money may motivate an individual to *keep* a job. People so motivated, however, usually perform only the minimum amount of work necessary to keep from being fired. The exception occurs when they are also motivated by some other consideration, such as a work ethic conditioning, which causes them to believe that they should contribute an "honest day's work for an honest day's pay."

Straight salaries can provide this basic motivation, and some companies use this type of compensation plan to give salespeople a sense of security. In addition, such plans are easy to understand and administer, remain constant (to the benefit of the company) as sales increase, and reduce a salesperson's resistance when asked to perform nonselling tasks—customer surveys or missionary sales calls—that offer no promise of immediate return. The important realization is that money without some additional form of motivation will not encourage individuals to excel.[36]

As a third point, money may motivate an individual to *perform above* minimal level if the amount of pay depends on the volume or quality of work performed. Such a relationship between work effort and compensation received is characteristic of most sales compensation programs.

Herzberg's contention that people are not motivated by salary can be weighed against these three types of motivation. Most U.S. workers are paid straight salaries that motivate them only to accept jobs and display some minimal performance level to retain those jobs. However, the majority of U.S. firms employ sales compensation plans that intend to provide the third type of motivation.

Straight Salaries, Commissions, and Bonuses   Table 15-9 depicts the tendency of most companies to compensate sales personnel with a base salary plus either a bonus or commission tied to the salesperson's accomplishments.

As the data further indicates, less than 20 percent of business firms use a straight salary plan, and this portion drops below 14 percent for companies with annual sales of $25 million or more. Straight commission is employed by 13 percent of all firms and about 10 percent of larger companies. This leaves two-thirds to three-fourths who prefer a combination plan.

Commissions and Bonuses as Motivators   Both commissions and bonuses are used to motivate salespeople. Commission rates can be adjusted to provide greater or less motivation depending on the activity involved. For example, a company might pay a 10 percent commission on sales received from current customers but increase the commission to 15 or 20 percent on first-order sales to new accounts. The same approach could be used for old and new products, or low and high profit items.

As these examples indicate, combination plans provide a sales manager with increased motivational flexibility. Inducements can be offered wherever greater sales

TABLE 15-9   Sales Compensation Plans by Size of Firm, 1992

Size of Firm/Revenue (in millions of dollars)	Firms Surveyed (%)	Straight Salary (%)	Straight Commission (%)	Combination Plan (%)
Under $5 M	38.4	20.8	18.1	61.1
$5-24.9 M	27.2	24.5	11.0	64.5
$25-99.9 M	21.1	13.9	10.6	75.5
$100-249.9 M	4.3	13.8	0.0	86.3
$250 M	9.0	13.3	11.2	75.4
Weighted Average	100.0	19.4	13.1	67.5

Source: Sales Force Compensation Survey, 27th ed. (Chicago: Dartnell Corporation, 1993), pp. 29, 179.

effort is desired. In addition to providing increased incentive for the salesperson to excel, the base salary also acts as a "safety net" to protect the individual against unexpected and uncontrollable market disasters. For example, a major customer might move to another part of the country or go bankrupt. The base salary remains fixed despite this unexpected sales reduction.

Sales managers can usually explain commission rates more easily than bonuses. Since commissions are also paid more frequently than bonuses, they strengthen the perceived relationship between increased performance and reward (expectancy theory).

Bonuses often depend on the sales manager's subjective judgment and may be based on the accomplishment of several related tasks, such as improved customer relations, new account penetration, feedback reports on market conditions, and an improved sales to expense ratio. Bonuses thus encourage the performance of *nonselling* tasks.

Although widely used, bonus systems have drawbacks. When the manager's subjectivity is obvious, salespeople question the system's fairness. Moreover, the infrequent payment of bonuses obscures the relationship between performance and reward.

INCENTIVE PROGRAMS AS MOTIVATORS

Sales managers often use the term *incentive program* to describe an array of motivational schemes other than those involving monetary compensation. Such incentive programs often involve contests. Because of the strong American spirit of competitiveness, contests can induce strong motivation; they can also provide an aura of excitement and "treasure hunting." However, while sales contests can produce desirable results, the authors also experienced downsides when attempting to motivate salespeople beyond their normal level of performance. In short, incentive programs must be carefully designed to yield positive results.

Elements of a Successful Sales Contest   First and foremost, the contest must strive for realistic goals that can be achieved by a majority of the sales force with appropriate effort. If, however, only two out of ten or fifteen salespeople eventually win some reward, the sales manager will have a group of frustrated individuals who will describe in detail the unfairness of the contest. It will be twice as difficult to energize them for the next competitive event.

Second, the contest should have clear, focused, and limited goals. For example, rewards might be given for percentage increase in sales over a previous time period (same month last year), first orders from new accounts, first orders for a new product line, overall increase in market share, etc. However, the contest should not be a shotgun approach aimed at anything that increases sales volume. Sales managers face this temptation in times of severe market downturns.

Third, contests should last long enough to reach a goal but end before they become ineffective. One to 3 months is usually a reasonable time frame. If, for example, the normal customer order cycle is 4 to 6 weeks, a 2-week contest is too short. In this instance, with prior notification of the contest duration, salespeople may induce customers to delay orders that would have been placed earlier and to accelerate others. Subsequent analysis of the sales curve would reveal an intriguing peak surrounded by unusual declines.

Fourth, rewards must definitely include widespread recognition and a feeling of personal accomplishment. For example, winning a family trip to corporate headquarters where the entire family could see mom or dad being congratulated by top management is worth far more than the monetary value of the trip. But if the headquarters is located in Crabgrass Junction, a trip to Hawaii might be even more effective.

Fifth, the contest should improve customer relations, not jeopardize them. Salespeople should hone their selling skills and develop more creative, effective problem-solving techniques. When managers overemphasize the need to reverse a downward sales trend, however, salespeople may be sorely tempted to increase their own performance at any cost. If this temptation results in selling products that poorly fit the buyer's needs, or dropping price for a quick sale, the company and salesperson both lose in the long run.

Finally, sales contests should be fun. The sales manager should sense a revitalized atmosphere at the weekly sales meeting. The sales force should be talking about their successes and ongoing plans, even making friendly wagers. The job has become an exciting attempt to excel.

Contemporary Compensation Challenges   As business firms face more aggressive competition, increased litigation, higher costs, input shortages, and a plethora of other contemporary problems, they also discover the need to fine-tune compensation packages so that they harmonize with marketing goals and objectives.

One writer found that some companies increase the commission rate on one product line if the specified goal for a second line is met; others increase total commissions if goals are met in two (or more) product lines; still others base commissions on the achievement of multiple product/market quotas.[38] Companies also *segment volume;* that is, they vary commissions to encourage the development of more desirable market segments, either by increasing sales in new industries or attracting new customers in the same industry.[39]

Pitney Bowes, for example, runs a two-tier program that involves a trip to Hawaii for those in the top tier and various smaller incentives for those in the second tier. To qualify, salespeople meet quotas for both existing and new customers. Additionally, Pitney Bowes bases compensation for sales managers on the achievement of an overall sales goal plus the motivation of a given percentage of their reps to achieve superior performance.[39] Some companies tailor their compensation to boost the quality of sales effort. USAA, for example, bases 35 percent of its commissions on how well sales reps handle correspondence, conduct phone conversations, and accurately quote prices. In an effort to quell litigation and enhance customer rapport, Dun & Bradstreet now uses customer satisfaction surveys to establish a portion of its sales compensation.

Corporate America expends considerable effort to develop compensation plans that enhance the achievement of corporate goals and objectives. These efforts do not occur haphazardly, but stem from a need to improve performance in markets increasingly unforgiving of mistakes.

Looking Back

Selecting and hiring salespeople involves more than the usual selection procedures. Because of the nature of business sales, sales managers must look for technical, human relations, and negotiating skills. Several interviewing methods, such as multiple, panel, patterned, or structured interviews, as well as realistic job previews enable sales managers more effectively to find those uniquely different individuals who make the best salespeople.

Once selected, salespeople must be given the opportunity to develop to their full potential through company, product, competitive, and industry and market specific training. In addition to training in selling techniques, business salespeople must also be trained in human relations and negotiating skills. Such training enhances the salesperson's ability to understand and meet the needs of both buyers and sellers. Care, however, must be taken in selecting those who are to do the training. Marketers may choose sales managers, experienced salespeople, or training specialists as sales force trainers. While each choice will have advantages, the disadvantages must also be considered. Whoever is chosen to supervise sales force training must be aware of learning theory, which emphasizes that people learn best when motivated, involved, and given immediate, positive feedback.

Directing the sales force involves both content and process theories of motivation. Since salespeople spend much of their time working without supervision, a sales manager might want to consider using trust, sympathy, and intimacy, as well as ambiguity and indirection, in directing the sales force. Both monetary and nonmonetary forms of compensation can be used effectively as a motivator when they are tied directly to selling as well as nonselling objectives.

Questions for Discussion

1. In hiring and selecting salespeople, the sales manager should remember this: "About 80 percent of business buyers are male, and the sex-role stereotypes that are common in our culture may work to the disadvantage of saleswomen." Do you agree that this is true? Why or why not?

2. Traditional measures are inadequate to evaluate the short-term productivity of the sales process, because many nonselling activities that are necessary to the job may not result in any measurable sales output for months or years. Discuss.

3. "The manager gave me specific instructions on how to handle a particular customer. I did as instructed. But when the customer contacted my boss, he made a turnabout and handled the situation quite differently." In this situation, was the sales manager a good motivator?

4. Older workers have greater pride in job accomplishment, understand the moral importance of work, and embrace the work ethic. Thus, older people make better salespeople. Do you agree with this conclusion?

5. Some suggest that the practice of sales management resembles the medicinal practices of tribal witch doctors. Both employ large doses of folklore, tradition, and personal experience to direct and motivate those in their care. Would the use of Herzberg's theory improve on this practice? Explain your viewpoint.

6. How can a sales compensation plan be designed to consider the objectives of both management and the sales force? Describe its critical features.

7. In many organizations, salespeople do not know whether rewards are performance based, because they do not know how their peers are evaluated and rewarded. Is this a logical conclusion? If true, how can it be corrected?

8. What special skills or attributes can explain how a college dropout might earn more as a salesperson than we pay the president of the United States? Can any of those skills be obtained through training?

Endnotes

1. William J. Stanton, Richard H. Buskirk, and Rosann L. Spiro, *Management of a Sales Force,* 9th ed. (Chicago, Ill.: Richard D. Irwin, Inc., 1995).

2. Thomas N. Ingram and Raymond W. LaForge, *Sales Management: Analysis and Decision Making* (Hinsdale, Ill.: The Dryden Press, 1989), p. 21.

3. "The corporate elite," *Business Week* (November 25, 1991), pp. 185+.

4. "Marketing newsletter," *Sales and Marketing Management* 139 (February 1987):27.

5. U.S. Department of Labor, Bureau of Labor Statistics, *1996-1997 Occupational Outlook Handbook* (Washington, D.C.: U.S. GPO, 1996).

6. Louis E. Boone and David L. Kurtz, *Contemporary Marketing*, 7th ed. (Chicago: Dryden Press, 1992), p. 595.

7. "Willy Loman, where are you?" *Supervision* 54 (July 1993):5.

8. Laurel Touby, "Direct selling: Behind the hype," *Executive Female* 17 (March/April 1994):33-4.

9. Nancy Arnott, "It's a woman's world," *Sales and Marketing Management* 147 (March 1995):54-9.

10. Alan Dubinsky and Thomas Barry, "A survey of sales management practices," *Industrial Marketing Management* 11 (1982):133-141; also "Selecting Salespeople," *Training* 29 (July 1992):12+

11. "Selecting Salespeople," *Training,* 29 (July 1992):12+

12. David Mayer and Herbert M. Greenberg, "What makes a good salesperson?" *Harvard Business Review* 70 (January-February 1992).

13. "Test-driving job applicants," *Inc* 14 (May 1992):148.

14. *Sales Force Compensation Survey,* 27th ed. (Chicago: The Dartnell Corporation, 1992), p. 131

15. "What employers teach," *Training* 29 (October 1992):43-55.

16. Adel I. El-Ansary, Noel B. Zabriskie, and John M. Browning, "Sales teamwork: A dominant strategy for improving salesforce effectiveness," *Journal of Business and Industrial Marketing* 8 (3) (1993):65-70.

17. W. David Gibson, "Fielding a force of experts," *Sales and Marketing Management* 145 (April 1993):88-92.

18. John P. Kirwan, Jr., "Training can help sales reps feel comfortable with new technology," *Marketing News* 27 (May 10, 1993), p. 18+.

19. Mary Jane Gill and David Meier, "Accelerated learning takes off," *Training and Development Journal* (January 1989), pp. 199-200.

20. Patricia A. Galagan, "IBM Gets Its Arms Around Education," *Training & Development Journal* (January 1989), pp. 34-41.

21. S. Joe Puri, "Where industrial sales training is weak," *Industrial Marketing Management* 22 (May 1993):101-8.

22. "Profiles in leadership," *Management Review* 76 (May 1987):8.

23. Larry Giunipero and Gary Zenz, "Impact of purchasing trends on industrial marketers," *Industrial Marketing Management* 11 (1982):17-23.

24. Roger Staubach, Jack Kinder, Jr., and Garry Kinder, "Secrets of making good presentations," *Marketing Times* (March/April 1983), pp. 20-3.

25. David Arthur Stumm, *Advanced Industrial Selling* (New York: AMACOM, 1981), p. 1.

26. Peter M. Banting and Paul A. Dion, "The purchasing agent: Friend or foe to the salesperson," *Journal of the Academy of Marketing Science* 16 (Fall 1988):16-22.

27. This section based on David D. Seltz and Alfred J. Modica, Negotiate Your Way to Success (New York: The New American Library, Inc., 1980).

28. R. Wayne Mondy, Robert E. Holmes, and Edwin B. Flippo, *Management: Concepts and Practices* (Boston: Allyn & Bacon, Inc., 1980), p. 13.

29. Abraham Maslow, *Motivation and Personality* (New York: Harper & Bros., 1954).

30. Frederick Herzberg, "One more time: How do you motivate employees?" *Harvard Business Review* 65 (September-October 1987):109-20.

31. Lyman W. Porter and Edward E. Lawler, *Managerial Attitudes and Performance* (Homewood, Ill.: Richard D. Irwin, Inc., 1968), pp. 329-31.

32. Fred Luthans, *Organizational Behavior* (New York: McGraw-Hill Book Co., 1985), pp. 211-12.

33. "At Du Pont everybody sells," *Sales and Marketing Management* 136 (December 3, 1984):33.

34. William Ouchi, *Theory Z* (Reading, Mass.: Addison-Wesley Publishing Co., 1981), pp. 5-10.

35. Tom Peters and Nancy Austin, *A Passion for Excellence* (New York: Warner Books, Inc., 1985).

36. Frederick Herzberg, Bernard Mausner, and Barbara Snyderman, *The Motivation to Work* (New York: John Wiley & Sons, Inc., 1959); revisited in Frederick Herzberg, "One more time: How do you motivate employees?" *Harvard Business Review* 65 (September-October 1987):109-20.

37. Sandra Pesman, "Salaries in sales rise despite recession," *Business Marketing* 78 (May 1993):78.

38. Stockton B. Colt, Jr., "Improving sales productivity: Four case studies," *Sales and Marketing Management* 141 (May 1989):10-12.

39. Leslie Brennan, "Promoting quality sales through incentives," *Sales and Marketing Management* 141 (May 1989):64-72.

Bibliography

Bertrand, Kate, "The 12 cardinal sins of compensation," *Business Marketing* (September 1989): 51-8.

Brennan, Leslie, "Promoting quality sales through incentives," *Sales and Marketing Management* (May 1989):64-72.

Cardozo, Richard, and Shannon Shipp, "New selling methods are changing industrial sales management," *Business Horizons* (September-October 1987): 23-8.

Hendrickson, John, "Getting close to the business," *Training and Development Journal* (February 1989):68-70.

Herzberg, Frederick, "One more time: How do you motivate employees?" *Harvard Business Review* 65 (September-October 1987):109-20.

Linkemer, Bobbi, "Women in sales: What do they really want?" *Sales and Marketing Management* (January 1989):61-8.

Mayer, David, and Herbert M. Greenberg, "What makes a good salesperson?" *Harvard Business Review* 70 (January-February 1992).

Puri, S. Joe, "Where industrial sales training is weak," *Industrial Marketing Management* 22 (May 1993):101-8.

Twenty-seventh Sales Force Compensation Survey (Chicago: Dartnell Corporation, 1992).

CHAPTER **16** # Organizing and Controlling the Sales Force

Although some firms successfully reach their markets through advertising alone, personal selling constitutes a major force in the marketing of business goods and services. The knowledge and skills of well-trained salespeople link the company's offering to the needs of customers. Advertising and sales promotion help to communicate a firm's image and capability, but rarely do they close a sale or create a competitive advantage.

In this chapter, we will discuss the importance of the following:

1. The sales force in business marketing strategy
2. Planning and organizing the selling effort to produce an effective and efficient sales force
3. The use of control methods to ensure that the selling effort achieves the desired results

Chapter 15 demonstrated that companies may choose to market their goods through their own sales force, manufacturers' representatives, distributors, value-added resellers, or through some combination of these groups. The optimal choice depends on the nature and composition of the market, the type of product or service sold, and the company's goals and financial resources. Regardless of the channel selected, personal selling is the principal option by which business marketers reach potential customers. The salesperson personifies the corporate image, presents the company's products and service, and handles the lengthy transactions characteristic of commercial sales. Two circumstances account for this heavy reliance on personal selling.

First, compared with the consumer market, most business market segments contain relatively few customers, each easily identified and located, with a relatively large buying potential. Second, many buyers prefer to deal with salespeople who represent the selling organization and have the ability to generate solutions. Business problems often require a complex combination of technical, financial, and service solutions plus specialized activity before and after the sale. Consequently, most buyers weigh decisions heavily on their perceptions of the salesperson.[1] Among buyers who nominated salespeople for *Purchasing* magazine's Top 10 in 1994, 63 percent listed the *willingness to fight for customers* as the quality they most sought in a salesperson; 59 percent cited *thoroughness* and *follow-through* as essential attributes.[2]

Personifying the Marketing Concept

Salespeople in the business market play a greater role in personifying the marketing concept than they do in the consumer market. This emanates from the need to make countless adjustments and compromises while working through long, involved decision processes. With customers facing greater competition and shorter deadlines, suppliers must provide more than just physical products. A salesperson, with the support of engineers and production personnel, can effectively portray how the supplier can become an interactive partner to the customer. Creative salespeople continually use their products and services to increase a customer's productivity, to reduce excess inventory, to enhance the quality of an end-product, and to lower the overall cost of doing business. When unable to act independently, they communicate specific customer needs to the various functional areas of their own organization for appropriate action.

SALES FORCE AUTOMATION (SFA)

Sales Force Automation (SFA) has had a major impact on selling for many of the same reasons that in-plant automation (or mechanization) has revolutionized engineering, manufacturing, and accounting. Thirty years ago, salespeople traveling from one customer to another were isolated from all other business activity. Until they could reach a telephone, they operated on opinions and data that were sometimes incorrect or outdated. Today, with portable computers, fax modems, and cellular phones, they have the latest information almost as soon as it develops.[3]

Given their vital intermediate position between two dynamic organizations—their firm and a customer—salespeople cannot be knowledgeable and productive if forced to operate with outdated information or obsolete communication tools.[3]

Sales Force Efficiency   Table 16-1 compares the tasks that sales managers consider the most important and their perceptions of how well the sales force performs these tasks. Three of the most important—serving major customers, finding new ones, and improving profits—suffer from the greatest deficiency. Yet all three can be significantly improved with SFA.

Customer service hinges on knowing what actions were promised to a customer, when these must occur, and the likelihood of on-time performance. Instant access to appropriate databases makes the salesperson a key source of information. Unless customers receive such information accurately and regularly, the probability of retaining their business is low, particularly in the face of capable and "hungry" competitors.

With modern electronic tools, salespeople are prepared for a variety of tasks from the creation of an impressive presentation to prioritizing sales leads. Salespeople can use computers to send e-mail to the factory, access the corporate database from anywhere, enter new customer orders or check the status of an open order, generate instant price quotations, or analyze numbers for their latest sales forecast.

TABLE 16-1	Sales Task Importance and Achievement				
Task Importance	*Very Important*	*Somewhat Important*	*Important*	*Not Important*	*Overall Weight[1]*
Retain current accounts	83.8%	11.4%	3.5%	1.3%	93.3
Sell to major accounts	69.0	21.4	7.9	1.7	87.3
Find new accounts	64.8	25.2	8.3	1.7	85.9
Improve profits	55.3	31.6	10.1	3.1	81.8
Sell new products	32.6	32.1	27.1	8.3	66.7
Reduce selling costs	18.5	35.2	35.2	11.0	58.3
Integrate new technology	15.9	35.0	35.8	13.3	56.1

Current Effectiveness	*Very Effective*	*Somewhat Effective*	*Not Effective*	*Overall Effective*	*Weight[1]*	*Deficiency*
Retain current accounts	37.8	50.0	10.8	1.4	77.3	−16.0
Sell to major accounts	17.3	43.6	33.8	5.3	61.9	−25.4
Find new accounts	9.9	42.2	43.0	4.9	57.1	−28.8
Improve profits	8.6	38.7	45.5	7.2	54.6	−27.2
Sell new products	9.1	36.4	42.6	12.0	52.8	−13.9
Reduce selling costs	9.1	33.0	44.7	12.8	51.4	−6.9
Integrate new technology	8.3	31.5	42.6	17.6	49.2	−6.9

[1]Scale = 10-100. Preceding four columns weighted 100, 70, 40, and 10, respectively.

Source: Adapted from *Sales Force Compensation Survey,* 27th ed. (Chicago: Dartnell Corporation, 1993), p. 149.

Finding new (and suitable) customers depends, in great part, on knowing their business, their decision-makers, and their priorities. Much of this information exists in industry reports, the business media, and company publications. In turn, a large percentage makes its way into the ubiquitous and all-knowing Internet. Once again, salespeople with appropriate communication tools have this data at their fingertips and can place ill-equipped competition at a distinct disadvantage.

Increased profits logically flow from happier customers, greater market share, and salespeople who can spend more productive time accomplishing their goals. As proof that SFA can deliver results, a 1993 survey by *Sales & Marketing Management* (their seventh annual) provided some impressive data. More than 60 percent of the respondents said that they recouped their investment in eight months or less. Eighty percent enjoyed sales-force productivity gains in double digits, with a median value of 20 percent.[4] However, a subsequent survey indicated not all users of SFA systems are satisfied with the results. In this instance, the dissatisfaction centered on certain packaged software programs rather than on the hardware or the basic concept of SFA.[5]

Technological Laggards   The founder of a leading market research and consulting group, Howard Anderson, stated in 1989 that SFA includes "everything from software to cellular phones to voice mail to artificial intelligence. It means using these tools to make the salesperson more productive, help the manager manage the sales force more effectively, and make relations with customers more profitable." He concluded that ". . . selling will never be the same."[6] His declaration was visionary but not surprising.

Of greater surprise is the number of business firms that do not supply electronic equipment to their salespeople or even encourage its use through partial payment of expenses. Table 16-2 contains the SFA information provided by the 250 firms

	Firms	Firms	Percentage of
Tool	Pay All (%)	Pay Part (%)	Part Paid (%)
Car phone	52.9	11.6	34.1
Home fax machine	46.2	2.9	50.0
Laptop computer	43.7	4.9	51.5
Home photocopier	29.1	4.7	50.0

TABLE 16-2   Percent of Firms Paying for Sales Productivity Tools, 1992

Source: Adapted from *Sales Force Compensation Survey,* 27th ed. (Chicago: Dartnell Corporation, 1993), pp. 123-6.

that answered Dartnell's twenty-seventh biennial survey of sales compensation. In fairness, some of the laggards in SFA may have been among the first to hop on the PC bandwagon in the early 1980s only to discover that a computer placed on someone's desk does not automatically increase productivity. To the contrary, by simplifying mundane tasks, computers sometimes encourage the output of excessive trivia to the detriment of more creative efforts. Likewise, firms should carefully assess how their salespeople conduct business and what tasks will benefit most from SFA before rushing out to buy hardware and software.[7] True gains in sales force productivity come from a well-planned combination *of automation and management techniques* that allow salespeople to manage themselves and their territories in a more businesslike fashion.[8]

The Business Selling Environment

Business salespeople toil in a multifaceted environment. To cope with this environment, they organize their efforts to coincide with the habits and expectations of the customer. An effective salesperson must perform three fundamental tasks: (1) identify the buying center members and their priorities, (2) present the product or service in the context of these priorities, and (3) develop and maintain the customer's trust and respect.

IDENTIFYING BUYING CENTER MEMBERS

Figure 16-1 indicates the need to create an aura of professionalism and credibility. The customer must believe what is said about the company and the product line. This requires *trust* in the salesperson. However, individuals tend to perceive professionalism and credibility in the framework of their own experience and priorities. Thus, the seller must describe the product and its associated services to each person in a way that emphasizes that individual's priorities.

Different Priorities   As a simple example, a buyer might prioritize the importance of price and dependable delivery. The engineer wants to be convinced of quality and durability. The production line supervisor worries about the ease of assembly and its impact on production costs. Thus, the salesperson must probe to discover these influential issues and tailor separate communication strategies. Each strategy addresses not only the individual's needs but also the needs of the relevant department and the overall company. All three sets of needs must be considered concurrently in making a sales presentation. The first task in the selling process, then, is identification of buying center members, their individual behavior patterns, and personal priorities.[9]

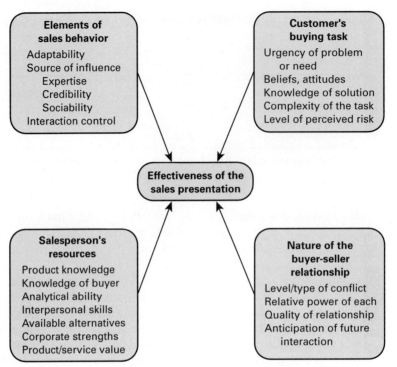

Source: Based on Barton A. Weitz, "Effectiveness in sales interactions: A contingency framework," *Journal of Marketing* 45 (Winter 1981):85-103.

FIGURE 16-1 Elements of the sales environment.

Company Influence   As discussed in Chapter 5, the needs and expectations of buying center members stem from a variety of influences, including the basic orientation of their company. Some companies emphasize the development of innovative technologies, others concentrate on mass production, still others focus on the specific requirements of a target market. Each emphasis places a different functional department in the limelight—engineering, manufacturing, or marketing. Sometimes this functional emphasis brings the entire organization closer together with a common focus. In other instances, interfunctional conflict occurs with each department concentrating on its own goals and glory. Salespeople must recognize the specific organizational atmosphere and adjust their strategy accordingly. The section on conflict resolution in Chapter 5 covered this subject in detail.

ORGANIZING THE SALES PRESENTATION

An effective sales presentation requires considerable planning and effort. Prospective firms must be identified, buying center members contacted, and the sales presentation tailored to address specific needs. Selling begins with prospect identification and continues until a long-term relationship has been established.

Identifying Prospects   An essential part of the selling process (see Table 16-1) involves identifying prospective customers. A supplier cannot rely on a static customer base to sustain its market share let alone achieve growth objectives. Thus, prospecting represents a future-oriented task that provides both the company and the salesperson with (1) future sources of sales revenue, (2) a more productive selling environment, and (3) better use of the limited time available for selling.[10]

A wide variety of sources, along with personal observation and referrals, can provide customer prospects. These include company-generated efforts such as media advertising, trade shows, direct mail, and telemarketing. However, not all firms that respond to promotional efforts are viable prospects. Business firms make purchases to save money, to make money, or to improve their operations, but need alone does not qualify a firm as a potential customer. The operating philosophies of the two firms must also "fit well together," or put another way, the supplier's strengths and the customer's expectations should coincide.

Salespeople must establish and follow an orderly procedure for identifying potential customers. This entails (1) setting quantitative objectives for prospecting (such as the number of qualified new accounts to identify); (2) allocating time for prospecting (for example, setting time aside from other selling tasks and administrative duties); (3) systematizing the prospecting plan (such as classifying accounts by geography, sales volume potential, type of business, and type of product they might purchase); and (4) evaluating the results (for example, analyzing which prospecting techniques worked best and discarding the least productive).[11]

Getting to Know Buying Center Members   A salesperson should learn as much as possible about the buying organization and its decision makers before developing a specific sales approach. Serious problems (including a lost sale) can result from a presentation based on assumptions and generalizations. To avoid unnecessary blunders, most salespeople plan several preliminary calls before making a formal sales presentation. The majority of business sales result from the cumulative effort of many calls.[12] The selling task is complicated further because the seller must work through an initial contact, normally a buyer, to gain access to decision makers in other functional areas. As discussed in Chapter 4, buyers will sometimes act as "gatekeepers," preventing the salesperson from reaching the right people.

The Sales Presentation   The presenter should provide prospects with specific information, educate them about the firm's product or service offer, answer questions, and solve problems. The key to successful selling rests on the salesperson's ability to *recognize and respond to customer priorities and expectations.* This requires a sensitivity to the differences between buying organizations and individuals within a buying center. Before a sale can be made, the decision-makers must believe that they will individually and collectively benefit from doing business with the supplier. This means that the corporate, engineering, production, and purchasing priorities will be satisfied. Such confidence rarely exists after a few calls, but rather, requires numerous contacts with many individuals over an extended period of time.

DEVELOPING AND MAINTAINING CUSTOMER RAPPORT

The importance of developing and maintaining customer rapport varies considerably in the business market and depends on the nature of the buyer-seller relationship as well as the type and magnitude of transactions that take place. For some sales, this rapport is relatively unimportant. For example, if the sale involves office supplies readily available from a number of sources, the buyer may simply scan a catalog and make a phone call to a local source. If price and delivery meet the buyer's expectations, an order is placed. However, this type of transaction does not describe the buyer-seller relationship increasingly encountered in the business market.

Partners, not Adversaries   The buyer-seller relationships becoming more common in the 1990s were detailed in Chapter 4. Concepts such as partnering, concurrent engineering, and relationship marketing involve two organizations virtually working as one. Both firms anticipate benefits from this arrangement. Buyers enjoy a more reliable supply, improved delivery schedules, lower component and production costs, and speedy conflict resolution. Suppliers achieve price and production stability, greater marketing efficiency, optimal capacity planning, and closer customer ties.[13] Such profitable partnerships have convinced many companies to move away from the adversarial, tough-negotiating type of relationship to one based on collaboration. Primarily, both firms seek to eliminate any traditional barriers that frustrate effective communication and cooperation.[14]

Thus, a long-term buyer-seller relationship depends on *mutual dependence and trust.* Each firm sees a greater opportunity of reaching its organizational goals by utilizing the capabilities of the other. Outsourcing, for example, results in greater efficiency for the buying firm while reducing demand uncertainty for the seller. Both firms enjoy the potential of greater return on their respective investments.[15]

Dyadic Interaction   At the heart of business selling is a dyadic interaction between the buyer and the salesperson.[16] In return for the sale, the salesperson provides the buyer with information and assistance. The confidence and trust that each party places in the other determine the boundaries of their interaction.[15]

In some instances, buyer and seller exchange roles in what can be termed *reverse marketing or selling.* The buyer tries to convince the seller to solve a new problem or provide services previously unavailable. When a creative salesperson can orchestrate actions that satisfy the buyer's unique needs, a stronger, longer-lasting relationship ensues that benefits both firms.[17]

Managing the Business Sales Force

Competitive survival in the business market depends on a confident, proactive, well-trained and well-supported sales force. Today's marketplace requires salespeople keenly sensitive to customers' needs, technically proficient, and capable of effective communication. Sales managers must then ensure that these professionals are directed and deployed in a fashion that generates maximum profits to the firm.

For purposes of our discussion, sales management is subdivided into two elements: strategy and administration. *Strategy* includes planning, organizing, and controlling; *administration* involves recruiting, selecting, training, compensating, motivating, and directing the sales force. Chapter 15 covered administration. The balance of this chapter deals with strategy. We will consider how to determine sales potentials for geographic areas, how to establish reasonable and workable sales territories, and how to assign duties to the sales force for maximum efficiency and effectiveness.

Planning for Sales Force Deployment

A company cannot expect optimal profits unless it utilizes its sales force in the most cost-effective manner. This includes a judicious control of sales expenses. In 1992 the cost of maintaining an experienced salesperson in the field reached an average of $76,900. Pay (including any commissions or bonuses) averaged $56,700, fringe benefits added $7,000, and field expenses (travel, entertainment, lodging, communication

TABLE 16-3 Average Distribution of a Business Salesperson's Time

Activities	Weekly Hours	Percent of Time
Selling Activities	23.3	51.2
Face-to-face	13.8	30.3
On the phone	9.5	20.9
Nonselling Activities	22.2	48.8
Travel	9.0	19.8
Administration	7.7	16.9
Service, follow-up	5.5	12.1
Total Effort	45.5	100.0

Source: Adapted from *Sales Force Compensation Survey,* 27th ed. (Chicago: Dartnell Corporation, 1993), p. 163.

tools, etc.) reached $13,200.[18] Adding to the challenge of controlling costs, the average salesperson worked 45.5 hours per week, but *only 51 percent of this time was spent in direct contact with customers.* The remaining 49 percent was consumed by paperwork, travel, meetings, and general follow-up. Table 16-3 shows the breakout of time by activity.

Traditionally, sales managers have attempted to improve sales effort effectiveness through administrative functions, tending to neglect efforts to improve sales force deployment strategy.[19] Perhaps this neglect stems partly from the complex nature of sales deployment analysis. Deployment refers to decisions regarding the size of the sales force, territorial design, and the organization and allocation of the selling effort. David Hughes noted, "Sales managers should not be recruiters and cheerleaders but business managers of territories, districts, and regions."[20]

Several sales force decision models have been developed that make the deployment task more systematic. However, these models have several problems. They require the collection and analysis of large amounts of data, usually applied to specific types of selling, and lack the support of top managers who question the ability of computers to handle the mathematical formulations required for proper analysis.[19]

Regardless of the method chosen, effective deployment decisions require:

1. Estimation of total market potential by geographic regions and customer type
2. Conversion of this estimate into total sales potential
3. Sales forecasts for specific customers
4. Analysis of trends that may affect potential sales
5. Determination of how many salespeople will be required to achieve the sales forecast (such as workload analysis)
6. Assignment of salespeople to territories and customers

ESTIMATION OF COMPANY SALES POTENTIAL

When regional sales managers forecast sales for their areas, the total market potential has usually been determined by individuals—such as corporate planners, product managers, or market development managers—who have broader responsibilities and perspectives within the company. For example, the product manager might utilize Department of Commerce data showing a trend of national sales for a particular product category (based on SIC codes). Working from this information, regional managers construct forecasts for their areas based on the number of customers who use the product,

		TABLE 16-4 A Regional Sales Projection	
(1) Customer Group	*(2)* Total Sales Potential ($)	*(3)* Maximum Company Share (%)	*(4)* Projected Maximum Sales ($)
A	1,000,000	50	500,000
B	500,000	80	400,000
C	250,000	100	250,000
D	75,000	67	50,000
TOTAL	1,825,000	65.7	1,200,000

their potential purchases, the presence and strength of competition, and the market share that can be achieved.

The product manager then totals the several regional forecasts. This "sum of parts" total may differ from the macro estimate made for the national market. This difference often requires negotiation and debate to reach a company total and regional distributions acceptable to all.

Regional Sales Forecasts   In developing their forecasts, sales managers usually depend heavily on the people most aware of the market dynamics—their sales force. For example, a salesperson may know that certain firms with large buying volume are strongly committed to their present suppliers. Consequently, other smaller prospects may represent a more promising sales opportunity, at least for the short-term.

To illustrate how regional managers convert a market potential, let's assume that a component manufacturer wants to increase sales by penetrating new accounts whose purchases have been estimated (column 2 of Table 16-4). These *purchases* are equivalent to the supplier's *sales potential.* The salespeople indicate the maximum *share* (column 3) that can be obtained from the sales potential of four different customer groups. As Table 16-4 indicates, each customer group's total potential multiplied by anticipated company share, (column 2 × column 3), yields a maximum sales projection. However, the *probability* of obtaining this sales level must also be considered. This can be done through the use of expected sales analysis.

Expected Sales Analysis   An expected sales volume results from applying a probability factor to the maximum sales potential of each customer group. This requires an additional estimation by the sales force and results in a sales forecast with a higher likelihood of occurrence. Table 16-5 shows this extension of the data contained in Table 16-4.

Evaluating Strategy Choices   The expected sales total does not always translate into a sales forecast. A manager may decide, for example, that some sales will be lost because of insufficient salespeople, inadequate promotional funds, or an entrenched competitor. In other words, the product line may warrant higher sales volume, but other factors prevent that from happening. Thus, the actual sales forecast may be something less than the expected sales.

Expected sales analysis is a useful tool for comparing alternative courses of action. For example, analysis of Table 16-5 indicates that customer group B may be the best prospect. Even though group A's total purchases are the highest, the expected sales volume from group B (and even group C) is greater. Therefore, the sales manager would develop a program to pursue groups B and C rather than A or D. Firms that

(1) Customer Group	(2) Total Sales Potential ($)	(3) Maximum Company Share (%)	(4) Projected Maximum Sales ($)	(5) Probability Factor	(6) Expected Sales ($)
A	1,000,000	50	500,000	.35	175,000
B	500,000	80	400,000	.60	240,000
C	250,000	100	250,000	.75	187,500
D	75,000	67	50,000	.20	10,000
TOTAL	1,825,000	65.7	1,200,000	.51	612,500

TABLE 16-5   Expected Sales Analysis

have operated in specific industries for some time take this approach because of previous experience and sales force knowledge.

The Heavy Half   In the business market, a small number of customers often buy the bulk of a supplier's product or service. Hence, the terms *heavy half* and the *20/80 phenomenon* have sprung up. The latter term implies that 20 percent of a firm's customers purchase 80 percent of its output.

Expected sales analysis helps in identifying these major prospects who constitute the largest portion of a company's potential sales. Once identified, these prospects usually become the major targets of the supplier's selling effort, unless, as indicated earlier, smaller accounts make better prospects for the near or foreseeable future.

Purchasing power should not be the sole criterion for selecting sales prospects. This approach tends to ignore smaller accounts. However, other things being equal, higher buying power suggests that a greater return can be realized for the same amount of time and effort. One effective strategy has outside salespeople concentrating on the larger accounts, while phone salespeople service the smaller potentials until they reach a level that requires face-to-face service.

WORKLOAD ANALYSIS

After estimating the geographic sales potential, the sales manager must decide how many people will be required to service the area properly. Workload analysis determines the amount of work required within a given time period. To determine the workload, the sales manager estimates how many sales calls each salesperson can and should make in a given period of time, for example, one year. This requires an estimate of the following:

1. Number of selling days available during the period
2. Number of days that must be devoted to nonselling activities
3. Average number of daily calls that can be made given the travel time involved
4. Desired call frequency per customer per period

The manager can determine the number of selling days rather easily by starting with the number of potential working days available for the time period (for example, 52 weeks per year × 5 days per week = 260 days). This gross total is adjusted for holidays, vacation time, estimated sick days, plus the days set aside for sales meetings, trade shows, paperwork and other nonselling activities.

Typically, at least 4 weeks or 20 working days will be lost to vacation, holidays, and sick time, leaving 240 potential selling days. Another 50 days, or approximately 20 percent of the remaining time will be spent on nonselling activities. Thus, only *190 days* remain for actual selling effort.

Number of Sales Calls That Can Be Made   After determining the actual selling days available, the manager must estimate the number of calls that can be made daily. This estimate considers travel and waiting time, which can vary significantly from one territory to another. The average length of time that the salesperson will spend with each account is also an important variable. The daily number of calls in 1992 across industries was approximately four.[18] Given 190 selling days, this means that a salesperson could make 760 calls during the year. We will use this number for further analysis.

Desired Call Frequency per Customer   As previously discussed, most industries are oligopolies, wherein relatively few firms constitute the majority of the buying power. In view of their relative importance to suppliers, these firms expect and receive a greater share of a salesperson's time and effort. Call frequency per customer, therefore, usually reflects that firm's buying power. Although this frequency varies by industry, many salespeople call their largest customers weekly. They usually check with purchasing on each visit but contact other buying influencers less frequently or as required. Table 16-6 provides a hypothetical selling schedule for one salesperson's territory.

PROFITABILITY ANALYSIS

Establishing a viable selling schedule is primarily a "cut and fit" process, wherein the service level required for a customer group and the number of firms in the territory must fall within a salesperson's available time. However, merely setting a schedule that accomplishes this quantitative goal does not assure optimal profits. Further analysis of the schedule in Table 16-6 will clarify this point.

Assume that the product line involved and the supplier's reputation and capability can capture ten percent of the potential in each customer group. Given a combined potential of $15.7 million, the salesperson would end the year with sales of $1,570,000—a very substantial figure. But is this the most profitable use of the limited selling time?

Expense-to-Sales Ratio   The profitability of a salesperson's efforts depends on both the amount of sales generated and the expenses incurred. Assume now that this individual is a typical experienced salesperson with the income and expenditures referenced earlier in the chapter. Thus, the sales would entail a selling cost of $76,900, or

TABLE 16-6   Territorial Selling Schedule (50 weeks/year)

Customer Group	Number	Average Potential ($ 000)	Group Potential ($ 000)	Call Frequency	Calls/ Customer	Total Calls	Potential Sales/Call ($)
A	10	1,000	10,000	1/wk	50	500	20,000
B	15	300	4,500	1/mo	12	180	25,000
C	20	60	1,200	1/qtr	4	80	15,000
TOTAL	45	NA	15,700	NA	NA	760	20,658

an expense-to-sales ratio of 4.9 percent—again, a satisfactory ratio. Table 16-7 shows how this ratio was derived.

The first step in determining the expense-to-sales ratio requires an allocation of expenses to the customers involved. The sales call serves as a unit of expense. In other words, the sales manager assumes that each of the 760 calls should carry a proportionate share of the $76,900. This results in a cost per call of $101.18 in this particular territory.

In scenario A, which includes the customer distribution set forth in Table 16-6, the overall expense-to-sales ratio is 4.9 percent, but this figure is not consistent across the three customer groups. Put another way, the salesperson spent 10.5 percent of time and effort on Group C to garner only 7.6 percent of the territory sales.

Scenario B shows one possible way of redistributing this time and effort. Assume that other firms in this territory do not currently buy from the supplier for various reasons, including the salesperson's decision not to call on them regularly. If the sales person could successfully penetrate only one account in group A and three in group B by using the time presently devoted to group C, sales would *increase by $70,000 with no additional expenses*. The time saved by not having to serve 45 group C accounts would permit six additional calls per year. Not only has the sales volume increased, but also the cost per sale and overall expense-to-sales ratio have declined. The territorial profit has obviously increased.

Relative Importance of Territory Variables   Sales managers continually debate the best choice of variables to use for territorial analysis. Some feel that the number of calls made has the greatest impact on territorial success, since this figure indicates not only the level of effort expended but also the exposure customers have to the product and the company. Others emphasize the relationship of expenses to sales. Still others believe that market share is more important than either the effort or expenses required to achieve it.

TABLE 16-7   Territory Profitability Analysis

Scenario A

Customer Group	Number	Total Sales ($ 000)	Total Calls	Cost/ Call ($)	Total Expense ($ 000)	Expense-to-Sales Ratio (%)
A	10	1,000	500	101.18	50.6	5.1
B	15	450	180	101.18	18.2	4.0
C	20	120	80	101.18	8.1	6.7
TOTAL	45	1,570	760	101.18	76.9	4.9

Scenario B

Customer Group	Number	Total Sales ($ 000)	Total Calls	Cost/ Call ($)	Total Expense ($ 000)	Expense-to-Sales Ratio (%)
A	11	1,100	550	100.39	55.2	5.1
B	18	540	216	100.39	21.7	4.0
TOTAL	29	1,640	766	100.39	76.9	4.7

Scenario C

Customer Group	Number	Total Sales ($ 000)	Total Calls	Cost/ Call ($)	Total Expense ($ 000)	Expense-to-Sales Ratio (%)
A	5	500	250	97.34	24.3	4.9
B	15	450	180	97.34	17.5	3.9
C	90	540	360	97.34	35.1	6.5
TOTAL	110	1,490	790	97.34	76.9	5.2

All of these factors help to determine the relative success of a territorial strategy—if they are put in proper context. No salesperson in a dynamic market can rest on past achievement or previous customer acceptance. There is always a competitor hungrier for success and willing to work harder to achieve it. However, effort must be founded on sound planning and effective research; otherwise, it simply qualifies as "wheel-spinning."

Scenario C in Table 16-7 illustrates that *profitability criteria* can also mislead. This scenario assumes that the territory representative decided to concentrate on a broad spectrum of smaller accounts that demand less time and coverage. Consequently, the number of (shorter) calls jumped to 790 and the resultant cost per sale fell to $97.34. Both figures seem to indicate an improvement over the other two scenarios. However, the sales volume declined and the expense-to-sales ratio rose.

This result could stem from two factors. First, too many of the major accounts have been forsaken to achieve a broader customer base. Second, the salesperson may be dashing madly from one account to the next without giving proper service to any of them.

Market share seems like an unquestionable criterion of success, but only if its *cost of attainment* receives appropriate attention. The current corporate strategy may place emphasis on growth. Growth usually comes at the expense of short-term profits. However, only profitable firms survive over the long haul, and profit achievement must begin with the sales force.

In short, regional sales managers and their territorial personnel must balance and occasionally adjust a variety of factors—some of which may be diametrically opposed.

Organizing the Sales Force

When one views sales organizations across industries and in the various channels of the business market, they appear infinitely diverse and in a constant state of flux. Indeed, a company's sales force should be structured to achieve the optimal mix of two simultaneous goals, *customer satisfaction* and *corporate profitability.* As customer needs and priorities change and competitive pressures build, sales force structure must either adapt or become less effective.

For example, when mainframe computers represented the bulk of its sales, IBM organized its salespeople by geographic territories, with each sales rep handling the entire product line. As the computer market became more diverse in both product and application, the geographic sales force could no longer handle this diversity as well as specialized competitors. Consequently, in 1994 IBM restructured their worldwide sales organization into thirteen vertical industry groups. Sales specialists now contact specific industries with information-processing products and services tailored to their needs. The industries include communications, distribution, finance, government, health, insurance, manufacturing, petroleum, process, transportation, travel, utilities, and cross-industry segments.[21]

Hewlett-Packard restructured their sales force into industry specialists in 1992. While IBM and DEC sales floundered, HP sales increased 14 percent in 1992 and grew another 26 percent in the first half of 1993.[22]

When George Fischer took over the CEO role at Kodak, he decided that the professional products sales force should be subdivided by industry. Following a significant sales increase in this division, the consumer-imaging products sales force was similarly restructured.[23] Fischer's experience as CEO at Motorola convinced him that broad, complex markets cannot be satisfactorily served by sales generalists.

STRUCTURAL ALTERNATIVES

The broad variety of sales force organizations can be distilled into four basic structures: organization by geography, by product, by market or industry, and by national accounts. The structure chosen by a particular firm depends on (1) the nature and length of the product line, (2) the diversity of market segments served, (3) the role of intermediaries in the marketing program, (4) the structure of competitors' sales forces, and (5) the nature of buying behavior encountered in each market segment.

ORGANIZATION BY GEOGRAPHY

Despite the examples cited above, more firms use geography to structure their sales forces than any other method. Geographic territories can range in size from several states to one or more highrise office buildings in downtown Manhattan. These territories are easy to form, relatively inexpensive to control, and allow the salesperson to act as a local presence with total customer responsibility. On the downside, salespeople must understand the entire product line, however broad, and be able to sell successfully across diverse industries.

ORGANIZATION BY PRODUCTS

Companies that use product-structured sales forces subdivide them into groups that specialize in only one product or a narrow spectrum of the total product assortment. As a consequence, salespeople tend to become *product experts* with greater ability to analyze and satisfy customer needs for that product segment.

Product-oriented sales forces cost more to develop, and this cost must be justified by greater market penetration and profitability. When the firm has a very broad product line, two or more representatives may be responsible for calling on the same account. This can result in costly overlap as well as the frustration of buyers who feel their time is being monopolized.

ORGANIZATION BY MARKETS OR INDUSTRIES

Market-structured sales forces concentrate on customers who produce similar end products or utilize the supplier's product in similar applications. The IBM, Hewlett-Packard, and Kodak scenarios are all examples of this organizational strategy. The diversity of customers in the business market creates the need for *market specialists,* with group categories determined by the customer's industry and/or end market (for example, industrial, commercial, government, or consumer). Salespeople so organized become particularly attuned to the trends and opportunities in their markets, the strategies of specific competitors, and the operational nuances of major customers.[24] For this type of organizational structure to be profitable, market segments must be *large enough* to warrant a specialized focus. Market specialists, like those organized by geography, face the task of selling the entire product line.

Product/Market Specialists   When a company attempts to serve large markets with a broad, complex product assortment, it may choose to segment its sales force by both product and market (industry). Kodak provides one example of this approach. They had already subdivided their sales force by professional and consumer products before further subdividing by market. Motorola also has separate sales forces to handle mobile communication products, semiconductors, and computers, with each force made up of major market specialists.

ORGANIZING TO SERVE NATIONAL ACCOUNTS

Since the early 1980s, the emphasis on serving national accounts has increased. Customers no longer seek only product, price, and basic delivery service but seek *value-added factors* such as training, compatible MIS systems, joint product design, integrated planning, and so on.[25]

The designation of "national account" varies among sellers, but this generally means major customers, with a centralized purchasing function that either buys or coordinates buying for decentralized units operating in more than one geographic location. Selling to such firms frequently involves[26]:

1. Obtaining acceptance or specification of the company's products at the customer's headquarters
2. Maintaining relations at various levels in the customer's organization
3. Negotiating long-term sales contracts
4. Ensuring superior customer service

Such activities require a wide range of selling effort that often involves other company personnel besides the salesperson. Thus, many organizations serving national accounts employ team selling.[25]

Team Selling   Team selling combines the effort of salespeople with that of other personnel to provide a specialized, but unified, sales and service coverage. For example, engineers from both the selling and buying organizations may jointly create component specifications; joint logistics teams devise inventory levels, locations, and shipping schedules; and market researchers combine their talents to ensure market acceptance of the buyer's end product. Thus, team selling not only *creates synergy* through the combined efforts of multiple departments but also forms the basis for *partnering with customers.*

Span of Authority   How the efforts of a national account program are organized and structured varies. In some firms, sales managers have line authority over a large, geographically dispersed sales and support team; in others, they may simply coordinate the efforts of sales and support personnel. Regardless of the type of organization, the objective of a national account program is to become the preferred or sole supplier of large, complex accounts.[27] To be successful, national account programs must overcome the "who got the order" orientation by developing a compensation system that recognizes and rewards the efforts of all team members.[25]

ORGANIZATION MUST FOLLOW STRATEGY

Organization represents an arrangement of activities aimed at achieving company objectives. The fundamental objectives of customer satisfaction and company profitability do not change. The strategies required to achieve these objectives, however, must change when they no longer relate to external conditions or internal capabilities. When a firm changes its strategies, it often becomes necessary to redesign the sales force structure.

For example, IBM faced a new set of challenges in the late 1980s from what they had experienced over the previous 25 years. Mainframes—IBM's major product strength—declined as the market's computer of choice. Microcomputers and workstations freed users from the inconvenience and delays associated with central memory banks and did so at lower cost. Moreover, competition multiplied and strengthened as new firms entered the industry, many of them targeting specific markets with tailored products. The IBM sales force, despite excellent training and support, could not compete effectively when organized by geographic territories. Thus, as described earlier, the company eventually changed to a market-structured sales organization.[21]

ASSIGNING THE SALES FORCE TO TERRITORIES

If all individuals were of equal ability and all territories of equal potential, salespeople could be assigned to territories on the basis of random selection. However, salespeople vary in their ability, and territories often differ in their potential. These differences can be offset by assigning territories of lower potential to the more capable salespeople, thus increasing the likelihood that sales volumes and incomes will be more equal. Unfortunately, the better salespeople become discouraged and quit under this arrangement.

When territories with greater potential are assigned to the more capable representatives, they usually achieve considerably higher incomes, which discourages their less capable peers. The best solution lies in creating territories of *equal potential,* recognizing the differences in human capability, and letting more capable individuals stand out as models for others. Although this strategy may result in lower short-term profits, it generates higher long-term profits, since it elicits the best efforts of the entire sales force, rather than overrewarding some and frustrating others.[28]

Personalities Affect Customer Relations   When assigning sales territories to individuals, the sales manager should consider the effect that a salesperson's personality has on customers. Territories differ in their distribution of large and small accounts. Some salespeople handle smaller accounts very well, whereas others excel with large accounts. Territories also differ in their mix of industries, which the manager should try to match with the knowledge and experience of the salesperson. Because of education, cultural background, and experience, some salespeople achieve greater results in one region of the country than in another. For these reasons, sales managers should look beyond average sales data and a territory's potential to determine individual assignments.[28]

Relationship Selling   The need to consider the personal characteristics of salespeople stems from the factors that influence the buyer-seller relationship. Sheth theorized that two elements strongly affect the quality of interaction between a seller and a buyer: the content of information and the style in which that information is exchanged.[29]

Content refers to the points of interest that brought the two parties together, such as a set of product-performance attributes or the expectations of the parties relative to those attributes. Content of communication centers on both the attributes and an individual's needs and expectations. *Style* refers to the format, ritual, and mannerisms that buyers and sellers use in their personal interactions.

According to Sheth, three types of interaction may be adopted: (1) *task-oriented,* which is highly purposeful; (2) *interaction-oriented,* which involves socializing and interpersonal relations; and (3) *self-oriented,* which is a preoccupation with one's own self-interest. Successful interaction occurs only when buyer and seller are compatible in both content and style of communications.[30]

Subsequent research, building on Sheth's concepts, determined that buyers who forsook hard-nosed, adversarial negotiations in favor of collaborative efforts gained greater cooperation and more profitable results from their suppliers.[13] Similarly, sellers who treated the buyer as a person as well as a prospect and gave clear evidence of a desire and ability to solve problems generally became a preferred supplier.[30]

Some researchers have hailed relationship selling as the "new paradigm" of marketing. One observer notes, however, that the ideas of developing a customer-focused approach and tearing down hierarchies that prohibit effective customer service are as old as the marketing concept.[31] Perhaps competition has simply forced more companies to recognize what the marketing concept really means.

Controlling Sales Force Activities

Controlling means regulating activities. Once planning and organizing have been accomplished, the sales manager must establish criteria that will indicate whether objectives have been reached. If significant variances exist between planned and actual results, adjustments must be made.

Effective sales managers do not attempt to control all activities, given their number and varying importance. Rather, they focus on strategically important activities and give less attention to those that are inconsequential. Managing a group of salespeople demands considerable time and effort, even when inconsequential activities are ignored. Management by exception provides an effective solution to this problem.

MANAGEMENT BY EXCEPTION

Management by exception (MBE) means that the manager will note and analyze only those results that are *unusually* favorable or unfavorable. For example, if 95 percent of the time each salesperson sells between $10,000 and $20,000 per week, the manager would analyze only those situations when sales fell below $10,000 or rose above $20,000. The former result indicates a problem requiring correction. Market conditions may have deteriorated, or the salesperson could have a personal problem, need retraining, or just lack motivation. The latter situation may indicate only a one-time bonanza, or possibly, a new opportunity also available to the other salespeople.

Control Charts   Managers customarily set their MBE range by first finding the average and the standard deviation of sales, and then adding and subtracting two standard deviations from the average. The resultant interval represents the 95 percent range. For example, if sales over the last six months averaged $15,000, and the standard deviation was $2,500, management can construct a control chart, as shown in Table 16-8, to

TABLE 16-8 Management by Exception Control Chart		
Upper control limit	$20,000	· ✕ · · · · · ·
plus one standard deviation		· · · ✕ · · · · · · · · · ✕ ·
Average	($15,000)	· · · · · · · · · · · · · · · · · · · ✕ · · · · · ✕ · · · · · · · · · · · ✕
minus one standard deviation		· · · ✕ · ✕ · · · · · · · ·
Lower control limit	$10,000	· · · · ✕ ·
	Week ⟶	1 2 3 4 5 6 7 8 9 10 11 12 13 14

track the performance of each salesperson. Control charts enable managers to track individual sales on a regular basis (weekly or monthly). Appropriate action can then be taken when sales fall above or below the control limits.

Management by exception may involve various statistical methods, ranging from simple tests that determine differences between means to more complex methods such as regression or variance analysis. Any of these approaches provide better decision-making than one's intuition. Many managers prefer control charts, since the mathematical computations are straightforward, and the chart can be easily understood by both the sales manager and the salesperson involved. A graphic display invariably provides easier comprehension than a column of numbers.

Control charts can track whatever sales managers consider to be important: number of new customers added, volume of new products sold, or magnitude of sales expenses.

MANAGEMENT BY OBJECTIVES

The effectiveness of both planning and organizing depends on *sales force involvement. Management by objectives* (MBO) serves as an excellent tool for involving salespeople and evaluating them.

MBO includes superior-subordinate interaction in the establishment and evaluation of objectives. Allowing salespeople to participate in setting goals, such as the level of market penetration or the number of new customers to develop, increases not only their involvement but their motivation to achieve the objectives. MBO as a control tool affects the preplanning and implementation of the task; control charts become effective only after some measurable work has been performed. In this sense, a properly utilized MBO can reduce the number of problems that would be reflected later in the control charts.

Key Elements of MBO   MBO programs include two key elements: (1) *specific objectives,* best expressed in quantitative terms with target due dates, and (2) *subordinate participation* in the process of goal setting and review.[32]

The formulation of objectives requires considerable thought to develop realistic company and individual objectives. Objectives should be ranked in order of importance, be mutually consistent, be quantified whenever possible, and have specific completion dates. The sales manager, assisted by individual salespeople, should formulate objectives that are quantifiable and accurately represent both company and individual objectives. Table 16-9 lists the characteristics of well-formulated objectives.[32]

Making MBO Work   Although managers of sales as well as other business functions use MBO, it does have limitations. First, it requires a definite time commitment. Second, unless the sales manager takes the program seriously and adheres to the objec-

---

TABLE 16-9   Characteristics of Well-Formulated Objectives

1. Related objectives should be prioritized and mutually consistent.
2. Each should be quantified whenever possible and have specific completion dates.
3. The total set of objectives should be limited in number.
4. Objectives should be described in terms of results, not processes.
5. Each should be challenging, yet attainable.
6. Objectives for one project should be coordinated with those of related projects.

Source: Adapted from Edwin B. Flippo and Gary M. Munsinger, *Management,* 5th ed. (Boston: Allyn & Bacon, Inc., 1982), p. 94.

tives, salespeople will become skeptical of the program. Third, quantitative objectives for some selling tasks are difficult to establish (such as market share for a previously unserved market or for an innovative product).

MBO works best when objectives are put in writing, when control mechanisms (such as control charts) are regularly updated, and when sales managers constantly reaffirm their support and interest in the program. To build and actuate an effective program, sales managers must exercise a participative management style so that salespeople will feel that the objectives are theirs and strive to achieve them.

The Future of Sales Force Strategy

Increasing international competition, rapid technological change, soaring costs, and the partnerships between suppliers and customers are four factors causing significant changes in the sales force of the 1990s. The former governor of Colorado, Richard Lamm, illustrated increasing competition by pointing out that when he graduated from high school in 1953, the United States produced 80 percent of the world's automobiles and 90 percent of its TV sets, and "made in Japan" meant "junk." However, when his son graduated in 1986, the United States was producing less than 30 percent of the world's automobiles and TV sets, and "made in America" meant "poor quality" to many Americans.[33]

Technological improvements in products and processes have begun to stem the loss of market and image. Although Zenith is the only remaining U.S. manufacturer of TV sets, U.S. automotive nameplates have increased their share of the world market throughout the 1990s. In 1994 and 1995, the Big Three produced seven of the ten best-selling models in this country. Programs designed to improve overall quality and productivity (such as TQM) have reduced costs to at least a competitive level.

Changed attitudes among managers and salespeople have resulted in an increased sensitivity toward customer desires. The tools of SFA have made salespeople more capable of satisfying these desires. In short, given the closer alliances between customers and suppliers and the need for constant communication and interaction between the companies, the role of salespeople will certainly grow in importance.

INTRAPRENEURIAL PHILOSOPHY

Many marketers are beginning to view the S.W.O.T. (strengths, weaknesses, opportunities, and threats) approach to strategy as primarily reactive. They see it as one that emphasizes a response to environmental change rather than proaction. On the other hand, the entrepreneurial approach encompasses the dimensions of innovativeness, risk-taking, and proactivity. One authority describes the entrepreneurial firm as one that "engages in product-market innovation, undertakes somewhat risky ventures, and is first to come up with 'proactive' innovations, beating competitors to the punch."[34]

Gifford Pinchot III developed the word "intrapreneurship" as a shorthand for "intra-corporate entrepreneurship."[35] An intrapreneur is a person within a large organization who plays the role of an entrepreneur and asks, "What would I do in this situation were I an entrepreneur?"

Intrapreneurship attempts to inspire and maintain a decision-making spirit and commitment in corporate employees. For this to occur, top management must advocate and continuously support the intrapreneurial philosophy. Once instilled, the philosophy can be maintained by installing a system that (1) solicits creative/innovative ideas and provides a means to screen them; (2) frees innovators from traditional organization constraints that stifle creativity; and (3) rewards the innovators.[36]

SALES FORCE STRUCTURE

Research studies clearly indicate (1) that increased specialization of sales personnel has reduced the number of sales generalists; (2) that the several functional departments within companies interact more (concurrent engineering, platform teams, horizontal organizations, and so on); and (3) computers and technology have aided this specialization and improved communications.[37] Cardozo and Shipp interpret these changes to mean small accounts will increasingly be handled through phone sales, as will medium-account prospecting, qualifying, servicing and reordering. They further envision national account managers coordinating more with other functional areas in order to improve the servicing of large accounts. They predict a much smaller role for the generalist salesperson—that of selling to and servicing medium-sized accounts.[37]

As these structural changes occur and are coupled with increased intrapreneuring, both marketing managers and salespeople must alter their roles accordingly. National account managers will require stronger interpersonal skills both inside and outside their companies. Sales managers will have to become more supportive, participative, and flexible. Salespeople, in turn, will become more involved with their customer's inner workings and require greater flexibility, creativity, thoroughness, and overall business knowledge. Overall, the contribution of the sales/marketing function to the company's strategic planning process will assume even greater importance.

Looking Back

The role of the sales force in personifying the marketing concept makes it the primary emphasis in the business marketer's promotional mix. The leading role that the sales force plays in promotion demonstrates a major difference between business and consumer marketing; it also requires sales managers to understand the selling environment and their role in creating an effective sales effort. The effectiveness, efficiency, and professionalism of a sales force mostly depends on the quality of their management.

Sales management consists of two primary functions: sales force strategy and administration. Administration—including the hiring, training, and motivation of salespeople—was discussed in Chapter 15. Strategy includes the functions of planning, organizing, and controlling the selling effort.

Planning is the process whereby a manager chooses among alternative courses of action that the sales force might pursue. It involves the determination of sales potentials and forecasts, service requirements for individual customers within a target market, and the deployment of sales personnel to achieve optimal customer service and corporate profitability. Proper sales deployment requires the sales manager to analyze expected sales, workload, and profitability to ensure that both sales revenues and expense-to-sales ratios meet predetermined targets.

Organizing is the creation of relationships and structure that will allow the sales force to achieve company objectives. A sales force must not only be structured in relation to its target market but also must have a logical relationship to other functional entities within the company.

Controlling involves regulating activities according to the objectives and strategies of the firm. Since the detailed activities of individual sales personnel cannot and should not be micromanaged, management by exception allows the sales manager to focus on those situations that represent unusual losses or gains. Managing by objectives brings sales personnel into the strategic process, increasing both their involvement in the plan and their commitment to the objectives. This is a means of control that enlists the support of sales personnel in the self-control of their activities. MBO increases the likelihood of spotting potential problems before they become exceptional situations.

Questions for Discussion

1. What result would occur if members of the marketing department and the sales force considered themselves to be on different teams? How would this result affect achievement of the marketing plan?

2. To be most effective, a salesperson must understand the nature of personal selling and how it relates to organizational buying behavior. One common sales method used in the consumer market is AIDA; that is, first attract the buyer's attention, then develop interest, create desire, and induce action to buy. Given the environment of business selling, does this approach work?

3. Important but difficult questions for many sales organizations are: "Does the current deployment of the sales force work well?" "Would sales improve if a formal deployment analysis were used?" and "Where are the best opportunities for increasing sales?" Discuss the various aspects of sales deployment and how they would impact the answers to these questions.

4. How can sales managers measure the productivity of nonsales activities and use these measures to evaluate overall job performance?

5. During her tenure in the New York/New Jersey area, Sarah Jones was a top-notch salesperson who consistently exceeded her quota. However, shortly after her transfer to the Kansas/Oklahoma territory, her performance fell considerably, and within 6 months, she left the company. Discuss the factors that could have contributed to Sarah's downfall.

6. Was IBM wise to change the structure of a sales force that had been highly successful for years? Discuss whether you would have chosen to organize by industry rather than product? What tradeoffs (pros and cons) would be associated with such a change?

Endnotes

1. Howard Upton, "The best equipment sales reps sell integrity and trust," *National Petroleum News* 85 (August 1993):12.

2. James Morgan, "Are your supplier reps proactive, knowledgeable?" *Purchasing* 116 (June 2, 1994):43.

3. Emily Kay, "Selling enters the information age," *Datamation* 41 (May 1, 1995):38-42.

4. Thayer C. Taylor, "Computers bring quick return," *Sales and Marketing Management* 145 (September 1993):22.

5. "Sales automation: Short on satisfaction," *Inc.* 17 (March 1995):110

6. Thayer C. Taylor, "'Selling will never be the same,'"*Sales and Marketing Management* 141(March 1989):48-53.

7. Tony Seideman, "Computers to go," *Sales and Marketing Management* 146 (June 1994):25-26.

8. K. Bruce Koepcke, "Automating your sales force," *Small Business Reports* (Monterey, Calif.) 19 (March 1994):14-17.

9. Richard H. Buskirk and Bruce D. Buskirk, *Selling: Principles and Practices,* 13th ed. (New York: McGraw-Hill, Inc., 1992), p. 150.

10. Gordon Storholm and Louis C. Kaufman, *Principles of Selling* (Englewood Cliffs, N.J.: Prentice Hall, Inc., 1985), p. 94.

11. Danny N. Bellenger and Thomas N. Ingram, *Professional Selling*, (New York: Macmillan Publishing Company, 1984), pp. 139-42.

12. Clifton J. Reichard, "Industrial selling: Beyond price and persistence," *Harvard Business Review*, 63 (January-February 1985):127-33.

13. Sang-Lin Han, David T. Wilson, and Shirish P. Dant, "Buyer-supplier relationships today," *Industrial Marketing Management* 22 (November 1993):331-8.

14. Malcolm Wheatley, "Partners in purchasing," *Management Today* (October 1991):84-6.

15. Shankar Ganesan, "Determinants of long-term orientation in buyer-seller relationships," *Journal of Marketing* 58 (April 1994):1-19.

16. Thomas V. Bonoma and Wesley Johnston, "The social psychology of industrial buying and selling," *Industrial Marketing Management* 7 (July 1978):213-23.

17. David L. Blenkhorn and Peter M. Banting, "How reverse marketing changes buyer-seller roles," *Industrial Marketing Management* 20 (August 1991):185-91.

18. *Sales Force Compensation Survey,* 27th ed., (Chicago: The Dartnell Corporation, 1992), pp. 3, 19.

19. Raymond LaForge and David W. Cravens, "Steps in selling effort deployment," *Industrial Marketing Management* 11 (1982):183-92.

20. G. David Hughes, "Computerized sales management," *Harvard Business Review* 63 (March-April 1985):102-12.

21. Jan Jaben, "IBM stages bold marketing drama: Sales aligned by industry," *Business Marketing* 79 (June 1994):1.

22. Thayer C. Taylor, "Hewlett-Packard: Best sales force winner," *Sales and Marketing Management* 145 (September 1993):59.

23. Wendy Bounds, "Kodak reorganizes its sales force at imaging group," *Wall Street Journal* Eastern Edition, (January 24, 1995), p. B3.

24. Norton Paley, "Cut out for success," *Sales and Marketing Management* 147 (April 1994):43-4.

25. Kerry Rottenberger-Murtha, "National account management: the lean and the green," *Sales and Marketing Management* 145 (February 1993):68-71.

26. Roger M. Pegram, *Selling and Servicing the National Account,* (New York: The Conference Board, 1972).

27. Benson P. Shapiro and Rowland T. Moriarty, *National Account Management: Emerging Insights,* Report No. 82-100, (Cambridge, Mass.: Marketing Science Institute, 1982).

28. Philip Kotler, *Marketing Decision Making: A Model Building Approach,* (New York: Holt, Rinehart and Winston, 1971), p. 378.

29. Jadish N. Sheth, "Buyer-Seller Interaction: A Conceptual Framework." In B.B. Anderson, ed., *Advances in Consumer Research,* Vol. III (Cincinnati: Association for Consumer Research, 1976), pp. 133-44.

30. Barry J. Farber and Joyce Wycoff, "Relationships: Six steps to success," *Sales and Marketing Management* 144 (April 1992):50.

31. David Morris, "What's old is new in relationship marketing," *Marketing News* 28 (February 14, 1994):4.

32. Edwin B. Flippo and Gary M. Munsinger, *Management,* 5th ed. (Boston: Allyn & Bacon, Inc., 1982), p. 91.

33. Richard D. Lamm, "Crisis: The Uncompetitive Society." In Martin K. Starr, ed., *Global Competitiveness,* (New York: W.W. Norton & Co., 1988), pp. 12-42.

34. D. Miller, "The correlates of entrepreneurship in three types of firms," *Management Science* 29 (1983):770-91; cited in Michael H. Morris, Duane L. Davis, and Jane Ewing, "The role of entrepreneurship in industrial marketing activities," *Industrial Marketing Management* 17 (1988):337-46.

35. "Secrets of intrapreneurship," *Inc.* 7 (January 1985):69-76.

36. Erik G. Rule and Donald W. Irwin, "Fostering intrapreneurship: The new competitive edge," *The Journal of Business Strategy* 9 (May/June 1988), pp. 44-7.

37. Richard Cardozo and Shannon Shipp, "New selling methods are changing industrial sales management," *Business Horizons* 30 (September/October 1987):23-8; also Andrew Parsons, cited by Thayer C. Taylor in, "How the game will change in the 1990s," *Sales and Marketing Management* 141 (June 1989):52-61.

Bibliography

Blenkhorn, David L. and Peter M. Banting, "How reverse marketing changes buyer-seller roles," *Industrial Marketing Management* 20 (1991):185-91.

Bonoma, Thomas V., and Wesley Johnston, "The social psychology of industrial buying and selling," *Industrial Marketing Management* 7 (1978):213-23.

Cravens, David W., and Raymond W. Laforce, "Sales force deployment analysis," *Industrial Marketing Management* 12 (1983):179-92.

Falvey, Jack, "Compare football to selling? Nonsense," *Sales and Marketing Management* 141 (1989):15-17.

Ganesan, Shankar, "Determinants of long-term orientation in buyer-seller relationships," *Journal of Marketing* 58 (1994):1-19.

Han, Sang-Lin, David T. Wilson, and Shirish P. Dant, "Buyer-supplier relationships today," *Industrial Marketing Management* 22 (1993):331-8.

Jaben, Jan, "IBM stages bold marketing drama: Sales aligned by industry," *Business Marketing* 79 (1994):1.

Kelley, Bill, "Ideal selling jobs," *Sales and Marketing Management* 140 (1988):26-31.

Laforge, Raymond, and David W. Cravens, "Steps in selling effort deployment," *Industrial Marketing Management* 11 (1982):183-92.

Reichard, Clifton J., "Industrial selling: Beyond price and persistence," *Harvard Business Review* 63 (1985):127-33.

Rottenberger-Murtha, Kerry, "National account management: the lean and the green," *Sales and Marketing Management* 145 (1993):68-71.

Rule, Erik G. and Donald W. Irwin, "Fostering intrapreneurship: The new competitive edge," *Journal of Business Strategy* 9 (1988):44-7.

Suarez, Edward A., "Results will sell marketing," *Business Marketing* 74 (1989):52-4.

Taylor, Thayer C., "Computers bring quick return," *Sales and Marketing Management* 145 (1993):22.

Wortman, Leon A., "Meet the hot shot," *Business Marketing* 73 (1988):62-8.

CHAPTER

17

Business Advertising, Sales Promotion, and Public Relations

Although personal selling is the dominant tool in most business communication strategies, advertising, sales promotion, and public relations also play important roles. Properly planned and implemented, these elements can enhance the company's image, build recognition for its products and services, reach unknown or inaccessible buying influencers, and generate new sales prospects.

The purpose of this chapter is to discuss the following:

1. How promotional variables other than personal selling enhance the effectiveness of the firm's overall communication strategy
2. Business advertising media options
3. What decision factors are crucial in the effective development of advertising, sales promotion, and publicity programs in the business market

The Role and Objectives of Business Advertising

Advertising can be defined as *a nonpersonal, persuasive form of communication by an identified sponsor.* To differentiate advertising from sales promotion, advertising usually employs traditional media such as trade journals, magazines, television, direct mail, and newspapers.

In 1994, the leading 100 business advertisers spent $2.4 billion promoting their products and services through print and electronic media.[1] Advertising lays a foundation for the sale by providing information on the company and its products. Rarely does advertising serve as the sole promotional element in the business market. Product complexity and the buyer's need for extensive information requires personal contact. However, studies indicate that salespeople typically reach only three or four out of every ten purchase-decision influencers. Specifically, business advertising seeks to accomplish seven goals:

1. Disseminate information throughout the market to reach unknown and inaccessible prospects
2. Stimulate direct and derived demand by increasing the buyer's knowledge and propensity to purchase a product
3. Presell the customer by creating a favorable climate for the sales rep
4. Enhance the corporate image
5. Generate sales leads
6. Provide the most cost-effective promotional tool by combining low-cost per contact advertising with sales
7. Provide promotional support for the marketing efforts of a producer's distributors

The Use of Advertising in the Business Market

REACHING BUYING INFLUENCERS

Salespeople may be unaware of some individuals who exert influence on purchasing decisions. This is particularly true of a new salesperson or one calling on a new prospect. For various reasons, including the reluctance of buyers to allow salespeople beyond the purchasing department, key influencers remain hidden. Executive turnover compounds this problem. Key influencers frequently move to other areas of responsibility, get promoted, or change jobs. However, these individuals do read trade magazines and general business publications, making them available through advertising. Some influencers identify themselves through requests for additional information, making it possible for salespeople to contact them.

The importance of business advertising can be seen in the following example. An industrial salesperson from Burroughs Corporation, now Unisys, called on a new account. After introducing himself to the office manager and naming the company he represented, the office manager shot back, "We don't need any drugs." Shocked, the Burroughs sales rep proceeded to inform the office manager that Burroughs was a computer company, not a drug producer. The interview deteriorated rapidly after that, and the sales rep excused himself gracefully by leaving some literature and promising to call back. This sales call was not successful because of a lack of presale advertising. The buyer confused the seller with Burroughs Wellcome, a drug manufacturer. If Burroughs had expended sufficient promotional efforts to educate this customer, the sales rep would not have wasted his expensive time.[2]

CREATING AWARENESS

Advertising effectively creates awareness of both the company and its offerings. As discussed in Chapter 4, buyers normally select a supplier after moving through several phases of the purchasing decision process. These phases include (1) recognizing a need, (2) determining characteristics and quantities of a needed item, (3) describing those characteristics and quantities, (4) searching for and qualifying sources, (5) acquiring and analyzing proposals, and (6) evaluating proposals and selecting suppliers. Effective advertising can create awareness or alert potential purchasers to problems within their operations (phase 1) and identify the supplier's company and its products as possible solutions to those problems (phases 2 and 4), which helps to assure that the advertiser receives favorable consideration when specifications are written and suppliers are selected (phases 3 and 6).

A 1993 survey found that advertising generates more sales leads for business marketers than any other promotional vehicle. Advertising generates 30 to 35 percent of all leads compared to 22 to 24 percent through public relations, the next best source.[3]

ENHANCING THE SALES CALL

Well-planned advertising programs that promote the name, image, and reputation of a company are gaining increased favor, particularly in industries with ever-shortening product life cycles. The institutional messages identify the company with a set of general benefits that it promises to deliver to its customers.[4] When buyers recognize a company, its reputation, its products, and its record in the industry, salespeople are more effective.

INCREASING OVERALL SALES EFFICIENCY

For producers of undifferentiated products such as industrial supplies, advertising may be the only way to reach broad groups of buyers. Moreover, when little or no product differentiation exists, marketers need to remind customers and potential users of any unique corporate capabilities (e.g., dependable delivery or fast reaction time).

The cost of reaching large numbers of buyers through personal contact can be not only prohibitive, but also unjustifiable. In 1992, the average cost of maintaining one senior salesperson in the field exceeded $80,000, including total compensation (salary and incentives) plus operating expenses and benefits.[5] Given a typical working schedule that generates 750 to 850 sales calls per year, the average cost per call is approximately $100. Comparing this cost per call with an advertisement that can reach thousands of influencers at a cost of $.50 to $.60 each, one can readily see how advertising efficiently supplements personal selling.

SUPPORTING CHANNEL MEMBERS

Manufacturers who use distributors to share the marketing effort must support these distributors by ensuring that customers are aware of their products as well as the existence of local inventory and special services. Distributors, in one sense, can only be as effective as their product franchisers allow. They want assurance that the producer will provide not only reliable products at competitive prices but information and promotional support to augment their selling efforts.

Technical Management's Misunderstanding of Advertising

Marketing people understand the importance of advertising, but not all business executives hold this view. Some technically trained industrial managers lack a full appreciation of marketing, advertising and promotional tools. As a consequence, their inactions lead to lost sales and decline in market share. Too many technical people have a distorted view of marketing and promotion. As a result, many of these individuals tend to be ultraconservative, fearful of change, and willing to copy the lead of their competitors. They market space-age products with a low-tech mentality.[6] Although 12 to 15 percent of all engineers eventually end up in marketing positions, many engineering schools, with the exception of engineering management programs, have refused to include marketing and sales courses in their undergraduate curriculum. As a result, many industrial firms managed by technical people misuse their advertising because they fail to understand the factors that influence their markets.[7]

Business Advertising Media

Manufacturers whose revenue stems primarily or totally from the business market employ a variety of advertising media. Firms that target both the business and consumer markets find the choice of a media strategy particularly difficult. In 1995, the top 100 business advertisers spent more than $2.7 billion in various media. Table 17-1 outlines the distribution of these dollars. As one might expect, trade journals received the most dollars, approximately 36 percent of total. However, media that are more consumer-oriented (television, consumer magazines, and Sunday supplements) were also widely used. As we will examine shortly, some of the largest business advertisers also target the consumer market. Thus, they must use print and audiovisual media that reach both markets.

TABLE 17-1   Media Expenditures by Top 100 Business Advertisers, 1994-1995 (in millions of dollars and percent)

Media	1994($)	1994(%)	1995($)	1995(%)
Trade journals	$950.4	39.8%	$974.4	35.9%
Television	808.9	33.9	925.0	34.1
Network	453.3	19.0	514.0	18.9
Spot	228.2	9.6	242.6	8.9
Cable	108.2	4.5	138.7	5.1
Syndicated	19.2	0.8	29.7	1.1
Consumer magazines[1]	318.0	13.3	476.0	17.2
Newspapers	228.5	9.6	248.2	9.1
Local	119.4	5.0	117.4	4.3
National	109.1	4.6	130.8	4.8
Radio	76.7	3.2	87.1	3.2
Spot	59.8	2.5	54.9	2.0
Network	16.9	0.7	32.2	1.2
Outdoor advertising	6.7	0.3	13.0	0.5
TOTAL	2,389.2	100.0	2,715.8	100.0
Print media	1,496.9	62.6	1,690.7	62.2
Electronic media	885.6	37.1	1,012.1	37.3
Outdoor media	6.7	0.3	13.0	0.5

[1]Includes Sunday magazines.

Source: Special Report: "Top 100 business-to-business advertisers," *Business Marketing* 81 (September 1996):9.

GENERAL BUSINESS AND TRADE PUBLICATIONS

General business and trade publications are classified as either horizontal or vertical. *Horizontal publications* deal with specific functions, tasks, or technologies and cut across industry lines. *Vertical publications* aim at a specific industry and may be read by almost anyone from the production line supervisor to the company president. The choice of one or both types depends on a firm's desire to penetrate a particular industry, reach common influencers across industries, or optimize the goals of reach and frequency.

General business publications (e.g., *Fortune, Business Week,* and *The Wall Street Journal)* are read by business professionals in all industries because of their broad coverage of the business market. Specialized business publications, such as *Advertising Age, Purchasing,* and *Chemical Week* are targeted to individuals across industries who either have responsibility for a specific function (e.g., advertising or purchasing) or are interested in a particular technology such as chemicals. Industrial publications such as *Consulting Engineer* address the information needs of readers with specialized knowledge in technical areas. Other specialized business publications (e.g., *Iron Age, Steel,* and *Electronic News*) are targeted to individuals in a specific industry.

DIRECTORY ADVERTISING

Every state publishes directories of its local manufacturers, resellers, and service providers. Private firms publish dozens more with most of these aimed at specific industries or product/service categories. The oldest and most widely used industrial directory is the New York-based *Thomas Register of American Manufacturers,* which has been published since 1910. The 1995 issue consists of 27 volumes and contains both manufacturers and resellers subdivided by more than 50,000 product categories. To maintain its dominance, the *Thomas Register* has continued to change over time. Since 1991, for example, subscribers have been able to obtain updated information by fax inquiry or a 1-900 phone call,[8] and today such inquiries can also be made by e-mail. Despite the addition of a CD-ROM version, many of its subscribers insist that the Thomas Register continue as a printed publication.[9]

Directories such as the *Thomas Register* offer the advantage of a highly credible medium, and for many buyers, serve as their basic purchasing tool. At the same time, advertising in these directories is wasted unless buyers purchase the directory for regular use.

CONSUMER MEDIA

As Table 17-1 indicates, consumer media are heavily used by the leading business advertisers. There are several reasons for this. First, as mentioned earlier, many of these firms sell products or services that are intended for both the business and consumer markets. Second, this advertising tends to reach buying influencers away from the office, when there is less distraction from other business duties. According to Sarah Lang, an account executive for Wight, Collins, Rutherford, and Scott, a London-based advertising agency, "TV is the medium for reaching small businessmen, who are a mass audience. . . . It is also the most effective for shifting attitudes, which is the job we have to do."[10] Third, most consumer media (e.g., network TV and radio, consumer magazines) provide a broad national coverage, reaching into secondary and tertiary markets that are not well-covered by a manufacturer's sales force or even regional distributors. However, the value of such broad coverage must be weighed against the high cost involved.

One of the most successful industrial advertising campaigns in recent years has been the "Intel Inside" campaign, which began in 1991. Intel launched the campaign to differentiate itself from several other microprocessor producers entering the market. At the same time they sought to convince computer buyers that not all PCs had the same components inside and should not be purchased based on price alone. Intel formed co-branding agreements with well-known PC manufacturers, allowing these producers to attach the "Intel Inside" logo to their computers and computer packaging. In turn, Intel provided co-op funding for the manufacturers' advertising and, of course, supplied the microprocessors.[11]

Two aspects of the campaign stand out. First, a significant portion of Intel's promotion dollars went into consumer media—television, consumer magazines, and point-of-purchase promotion. Second, they used a classic **"pull" strategy** to make consumers aware of a product that had previously been out of sight and out of mind. By 1994, Intel was judged to be the third most valuable brand in America, according to *Financial World,* behind Marlboro and Coca-Cola.[11] For the producer of an industrial product, this acclamation is unprecedented.

DIRECT MARKETING

In addition to the various media, business marketers use other promotional tools, including direct mail, telemarketing, catalogs, and data sheets. In fact, with the increasing sophistication of desktop publishing, business marketers are "turning to direct mail as never before."[12] For example, Xerox more than tripled its sales for low-end products through the use of direct mail. Numerous industrial marketers also see telemarketing as a means of enhancing the efficiency of their overall communications program.

Direct Mail   Direct mail is an especially useful tool that is frequently employed in conjunction with, or as an alternative to, trade publication advertising. When carefully conceived, direct-mail advertising can provide a greater impact than other print advertisements because of its ability to gain the reader's full attention.

Direct mail offers the advertiser advantages over business or trade publications. Messages can be targeted toward a precisely defined audience to introduce a new product, promote the corporate image, or announce the addition of new services. Direct mail—properly directed—is relatively low in cost, highly selective, and flexible with regard to timing. It also offers considerable space for telling the "full story."

Direct mail, however, also presents potential disadvantages. Prospects must be clearly identified to prevent significant waste. Many recipients think of direct mail as "junk mail" and toss it aside without reading the message. A secretary may have instructions to perform the discard. To avoid these problems, direct-mail programs should be carefully conceived and directed toward a specific target audience whose names, job titles, and functions are known.

Advertisers can obtain specific mailing lists with relative ease from trade publications, industrial directories, or mailing list houses such as Dun & Bradstreet's Marketing Services Division or National Business Lists. Lists can be developed from trade show leads and the company's own marketing information system. When obtaining mailing lists from outside sources, however, care should be taken to ensure that the lists are up to date.

Telemarketing   Telemarketing parallels direct mail in several aspects. It is another fast-growing segment of marketing communication and for the same reasons as direct mail. It is also used more in the consumer than in the business market, although the activity referred to as "phone sales" has been a mainstay of distributor selling for decades.

Used in an ethical and professional manner, outgoing phone calls can effectively substitute for face-to-face selling at a substantially reduced cost. As mentioned above, wholesale distribution houses as well as manufacturers of commodity products have successfully used phone sales (telemarketing) for years. In this context, phone sales refers to a *proactive, organized selling effort* rather than the reactive process of answering a ringing phone and providing the caller with requested price and delivery information.

This type of telemarketing works best when an inside phone salesperson and an outside sales representative coordinate their efforts. For example, the phone person initially advises major customers regarding a new product introduction, a price revision, or some service enhancement. The outside rep follows up with a personal visit, but now it is a call anticipated by the customer, not a "cold call." The phone person also maintains regular contact, perhaps weekly or biweekly, with customers that the outside rep sees infrequently.

The phone approach can also be used to survey and solicit accounts that are not regular customers. For this coordinated effort to succeed, both the sales manager and outside rep must give their wholehearted support. If the manager feels that phone contacts should be primarily reactive, or the outside rep guards customers too jealously, the process will fail.[13]

Marketers who use phone selling view it as a means of *complementing,* rather than replacing, face-to-face selling. In a study of 249 industrial sales and marketing managers, the primary reasons given for its use were (1) to qualify sales leads, 73.6 percent of respondents; (2) support field sales representatives, 73.2 percent; (3) generate sales leads, 73.1 percent; and (4) to handle marginal accounts, 70.0 percent.[14]

Telemarketing can enhance the effectiveness of publication and direct-mail advertising. When a toll-free number is included in the ad, prospects can easily respond and get immediate information while the advertised message is still fresh in their minds.

Telemarketing also has a negative image similar to direct mail. Due to the unscrupulous activities of some telemarketers in the consumer market, the entire field has become suspect. Some buyers will not converse over the phone with firms or individuals not already known to them. The curt response is, "Talk to my secretary for an appointment." Fortunately, in the business market, the use of telemarketing by highly respected companies has kept the overall reputation of this medium at an acceptable level and permitted a remarkable growth rate.[14]

CATALOGS AND DATA SHEETS

Catalogs and data sheets add an important element to a firm's promotional effort by directly supporting the salesperson. Business customers use catalogs regularly to compare the products and prices of potential suppliers, although catalogs alone rarely determine a purchasing decision. They provide buyers with a basis of comparison among competitors once a decision has been made to purchase a specific product.

When properly prepared and effectively distributed, catalogs can amplify the purchasing process by providing information, creating vendor recognition, and increasing business opportunities. Catalogs also enhance the efforts of distributors who do not always carry a manufacturer's complete product line in stock. The catalog alerts customers to a product's existence and its source of supply.

Data sheets provide detailed information on product dimensions, performance data, and unique characteristics. Salespeople cannot memorize all the information that buyers and design engineers may require. Moreover, buying decisions are often made without a salesperson present. A clear and complete data sheet, containing key sales features in additional to technical information, can be powerful sales tools.

The Use of Sales Promotion in the Business Market

Sales promotion, in the form of trade shows, premium incentives, and specialty advertising, plays an important part in the overall communication strategy of a business advertiser.

TRADE SHOWS

For many business firms, trade show exhibits play a major role in their advertising strategies. These exhibits support both the selling effort and other marketing activities.[15] Depending on the size of the firm and its budget, trade show participation can range from six to more than twelve per year. Caterpillar, for example, exhibits at more than forty-five conventions and expositions annually.[16] According to one source, some companies allocate as much as 35 percent of their annual promotional budget to trade show expenditures.[15]

Trade shows offer manufacturers, distributors, and service providers an opportunity to display their products or describe their services to business customers, channel members, suppliers, consumers, and the media (Box 17-1). In addition to increasing market awareness of the firm and its products, trade shows can also enhance field sales effectiveness.

One study, conducted for the Trade Show Bureau, found that *less than one* sales call (0.8 average) will close a trade show lead, since more than half of such purchases are made either by phone or mail after the show. In contrast, according to a McGraw-Hill study, it takes an average of 5.1 sales calls to close an industrial sale.[17] The 1992 Dartnell compensation survey found very similar results with an average of 4.7 calls to close in the industrial sector. Office products and services required 4.9 calls, and the consumer sector average was 4.0 calls.[18]

Setting Trade Show Objectives   The relative effectiveness of trade shows depends on the objectives assigned to this segment of the overall communication strategy. These objectives can range from creating awareness of new products, to enhancing the technological image of the firm, to closing actual orders. Market research and customer stimulation play an important part in the establishment of appropriate objectives. Several actions can improve this process:

BOX 17-1

The Largest Industrial Trade Show in the Western Hemisphere

With self-advertisement reminiscent of Barnum's claim to "the Greatest Show on Earth," the International Manufacturing Technology Show '94 (IMTS) took over Chicago's vast McCormick Place in September 1994, as it does every 2 years.

More than 1,000 exhibitors covered 960,000 square feet of exhibit space with more than $350 million worth of metalworking and production equipment weighing in at almost 14,000 tons. Attendance set a record at more than 117,000 people made up of management, engineering, sales, and R&D personnel from industrial firms around the world.

Source: Adapted from Tim Keenan, "Manufacturing mecca," *Ward's Auto World* 30 (September 1994):93; also Flora Ling, "IMTS hums along, year after year," *Business Marketing,* 79 (October 1994):4.

1. Check the typical *attendance mix* of previous shows. Do the registration lists indicate personnel normally involved in the "buying center" (design engineers, production supervisors, senior buyers, etc.)? Does the show attract upper management?[19] Without attendance data, marketers run the risk of bringing inappropriate products, sending the wrong personnel, or even setting up the wrong-sized exhibit.

2. Try to determine *how much business* typically takes place during the show? Evidence has shown that some international companies generate as much as 70 percent of their annual sales at international trade fairs.[20] The typical figure for domestic U.S. shows is considerably less.

3. *Promote* the upcoming show to customers and prospects. Exhibitors have come to realize that they should not depend on show management to handle all the promotion.[21]

4. Have the *appropriate individuals* in the exhibit booth. Salespeople are not always best prepared to discuss new products, manufacturing techniques, or projected pricing. Some firms bring credit managers to open new accounts, raise credit limits for customers in good standing, and counsel others who are having a difficult time with their finances.[22]

PREMIUMS, INCENTIVES, AND SPECIALTY ADVERTISING

Promotional contests and giveaways are common elements in consumer marketing; they are used, but less frequently, in business marketing. In contrast to premiums, which are items of value closely related to the products they are intended to sell, specialty advertising consists of useful, low-cost giveaways such as calendars, ballpoint pens, key chains, baseball caps, or similar items given to prospects by salespeople. Since the item normally has the firm's name and address imprinted on it, it also serves as an advertisement.

Care must be taken in the distribution of specialty items, so that the offering will be neither misunderstood nor offensive.[23] For example, an item can be included as part of a proposal (the memo pad on which it is written, or the binder in which it is contained) or offered to several members of the buying firm (desk calendars or pens). When offered to a prospect, they should be presented in a way that does not appear to apply pressure or obligate the individual.

The Use of Publicity in the Business Market

Publicity, because of its high credibility and minimal cost, is a very effective promotional tool. Favorable editorial material placed in the media about a company or its products can generate sales leads and create better customer perceptions. Evidence indicates that industrial customers rate technical editorial material in trade journals as an important source of information in the buying process. Thus, technical articles are excellent vehicles for reaching business customers. While the term "technical article" includes all types of technical publicity (e.g., feature articles written by the publication's staff and interviews with key industry personnel), an article signed by a respected author (referred to as a "signed article" in trade publications) gives added authenticity to the product.[24]

Sophisticated buyers engaged in new task purchasing projects do considerable research to find potential suppliers who appear capable of providing products with suitable specifications, desired quality level, and competitive prices. Part of that search involves information gathered from trade publications—information perceived to be accurate and current. Editors of trade journals are viewed as being technically competent in their field and able to evaluate the usefulness of information. Thus, when buyers read about a product in an editorial or featured article, they tend to accept the information as credible and worthy of their consideration.[24] The benefits of using signed articles are outlined in Table 17-2.

TABLE 17-2 Four Good Reasons for Using Signed Articles in Business Promotion

1. Signed articles improve a firm's technical image and presell products.	An effective and inexpensive way to demonstrate technical competency.
	Approaches customers with credibility.
	Stimulates customers with education and a fresh awareness of the firm's capabilities.
2. Signed articles extend the reach of sales engineers.	Reach buying influencers not usually contacted or accessible.
	Publication serves as a third-party reference.
3. Signed articles serve as a valued source of information to customers.	Only handbooks are considered a more valuable source. Articles rank ahead of catalogs, ads, and other promotional elements.
4. Signed articles appear in publications that are well read by potential customers.	Almost all buying influencers read one or more articles in issues of interest. High probability of reaching top executives.

Source: Adapted from Jerome D. Williams, "Industrial publicity: One of the best promotional tools," *Industrial Marketing Management* 12 (1983):207-11.

Although many view publicity as "free advertising," there are some costs associated with the creation of an article, the preparation of a news release, and the efforts to convince influential editors to run the article. However, these costs are minor compared with the creation, production, and space costs associated with paid advertising. In general, publicity constitutes less than 10 percent of a firm's promotional budget.

Developing the Advertising Program

Economic factors force marketers to consider carefully the elements used in a company's promotional program. Promotional variables must be artfully integrated to achieve communication objectives in a cost-efficient manner.

Many advertising principles serve the consumer and business markets equally well. Business advertising, for instance, should communicate something favorable and attractive about the company or its products. It should thus be designed to attract the attention of current and potential customers, to convey specific information about the capabilities of a product line, to enhance the selling effort of the sales force, to motivate and support distributors, and to reach those who directly or indirectly influence the buying decision.

To develop an effective advertising program, the business marketer must carefully integrate the program's objectives, the budget, the target audiences to be reached, and the message strategy.

ADVERTISING OBJECTIVES

Any effective advertising plan begins with the formulation of objectives. These objectives, however, cannot be developed in isolation. They must support the firm's overall business and marketing objectives.

For example, a corporate objective to increase growth rate (e.g., from 5 to 10 percent growth per year) would require strategies aimed at either greater penetration of slower growing markets or entry into previously unserved markets. In turn, marketing inherits an objective of increasing sales annually by 10 percent. Associated marketing strategies might include increased market share in certain segments, a more aggressive

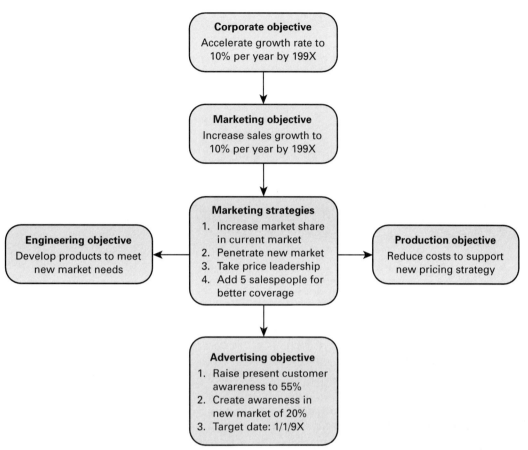

FIGURE 17-1 Interrelated objectives and strategies.

pricing strategy, added salespeople for broader coverage, and increased advertising to create greater customer awareness.

Customer feedback might indicate that a broader product line is required. This information would necessitate an engineering strategy of product development. Similarly, the aggressive pricing strategy could trigger the need for cost reductions in manufacturing—another strategy. Figure 17-1 depicts this interrelation of objectives and strategies.

With the corporate objective of accelerated growth, the marketing objective of increased sales requires greater market penetration. The advertising objective, then, would be stated in terms of *increased customer awareness* or the generation of *more sales leads*.

Advertising objectives should not be stated in terms of increasing sales. Although increased revenue may well be the ultimate corporate objective, it is difficult, if not impossible, to link sales directly to advertising. Personal selling, price, product performance, competitors' tactics, customer preferences, and a myriad of other factors affect sales levels. Thus, pinpointing the impact of advertising on sales is a difficult task at best.

Whatever the marketing objective, advertising objectives must identify definitive goals related to the marketing objective and stated in specific, measurable, realistic terms that delineate what is to be accomplished within a defined period of time, for example:

> Increase the awareness of Acme's product line benefits among current customers from 35 percent to 55 percent within 18 months beginning January 1, 1998. Create an awareness of 20 percent among unserved accounts during the same period.

ADVERTISING APPROPRIATIONS AND BUDGETS

Since business advertising accounts for 15 to 20 percent of all American advertising expenditures, it is an important element in the marketing budget. Research suggests, however, that business marketers tend to rely on arbitrary methods for developing their advertising budgets.[25] The *appropriation of funds* for advertising must consider the cost of purchased space or time in advertising media plus the cost of producing these advertisements. An *advertising budget,* on the other hand, details how the dollars appropriated will be spent for individual campaigns by media, by time periods, by market segments and audiences, and by geographic areas.[25]

To ensure that expenditures budgeted for advertising can be effectively monitored, advertising appropriations should exclude trade shows, catalogs, or other promotional outlays. These other outlays should be monitored separately to evaluate their individual effectiveness and to prevent the advertising appropriation from becoming a "catch-all" for other promotional expenses.

As Table 17-3 shows, advertising appropriations are approached in a variety of ways depending on the philosophy of the particular company. In addition to the "what we can afford" method, industrial advertisers also use the rule-of-thumb and the objective-and-task techniques.[26]

Rule of Thumb   A rule of thumb relates advertising expenditures to some other measure of company activity in a consistent way. For instance, funds can be allocated as a percentage of past sales or on the basis of industry averages. Such rule-of-thumb methods for appropriating advertising dollars are quite common in business marketing, particularly when advertising is a relatively small percentage of the total promotion budget.

Allocating funds on the basis of *past* sales contradicts the basic principle that marketing activities should *stimulate* sales. If marketers insist on relating advertising expenses to sales generated, they should at least use *projected* sales volume, not past history.

Another problem exists when advertising expenditures are directly correlated to sales volume. This suggests that the advertising budget will decline when sales fall. In reality, the advertising effort, along with all other marketing activities, should probably rise to halt or diminish the sales decline. Conversely, there is less need to spend heavily in a booming market.

Objective and Task   Market studies indicate that the popularity of the "objective-and-task" method for setting the advertising budget has increased, moving from a fourth or fifth ranking in the 1970s to second in the 1980s.[25] This technique applies logic

TABLE 17-3   Methods Used to Create Advertising Budgets (n=560)

Method	Use Regularly (%)	Have Tried (%)	Know About But Never Used (%)	Never Heard of or No Reply (%)
What we can afford	54.1	15.7	9.5	20.7
Objective and task	39.8	13.0	17.7	29.5
Percentage of expected sales	33.0	15.4	29.1	22.5
Experimentation	7.3	17.9	37.7	37.1
Desired share of voice	5.7	10.9	31.1	52.3
Match competition	4.3	13.7	48.7	33.2

Source: Adapted from James E. Lynch, "Advertising budgeting practices of industrial advertisers," *Industrial Marketing Management* 16 (1987):63-9.

to the advertising appropriation by determining the tasks that must be performed to achieve the advertising objectives and assigning costs to these tasks. Table 17-4 depicts a hypothetical example.

In developing the required appropriation, the marketer must also consider the company's financial capability. If the appropriation seems too high, the objectives may have to be scaled down and the strategies adjusted accordingly. Program results play a key role in the determination of appropriations and budgeting for the next planning period.

The objective-and-task method forces the firm to think in terms of objectives and the probability of their attainment. The major drawback of this method, however, lies in the difficulty of forecasting the amount of funds required to reach specific objectives. Further, while techniques for measuring advertising effectiveness continue to improve, many still consider them inadequate. However, "horseback guesses" and reflections on the past are even more dissatisfying.

DEVELOPING A MESSAGE STRATEGY

Message strategy defines the *theme* for the advertising program and the desired company *image or position* in the market. When industrial and commercial buyers make their purchase decisions, they are seeking problem-solving benefits and economic advantages. Thus, business advertisers must convince the buyer of their ability to provide such benefits or advantages. Emotional issues do not equal technical and financial criteria in level of importance.

Unlike the consumer marketplace, where products, services and even the ads themselves often must promise satisfaction for strong emotional desires, the context of business advertising is the reader's work. He needs to make correct decisions heavily dependent on performance and value facts. Although emotions such as fear, anxiety, frustration and status attainment can play a large role in a business buyer's mind, those desires to achieve are best served and those fears are best assuaged by the performance and value benefits attached to a business decision.[27]

Advertising messages must focus on the ability of a supplier's product or service to *solve customer problems* and *improve business operations*. However, as indicated earlier in this chapter, some firms seem oblivious to the power and purpose of advertising.

TABLE 17-4 The Objective-Task Method of Appropriating Advertising Funds

Steps in the Process	*Examples*
1. Determine marketing objectives.	Introduce new product; increase market share or sales volume.
2. Determine advertising objectives.	Increase product awareness; generate sales leads.
3. Determine target audiences.	Engineers, purchasing, key executives.
4. Determine reach, frequency, and continuity needs (communication objectives).	How broad is the market; how often message must be repeated for impact; how long to continue ad campaign to achieve goal?
5. Determine appropriate media to reach target audiences.	Which print media; should TV or radio be used?
6. Establish other promotional needs.	Publicity, catalogs, trade shows, etc.
7. Establish control measures.	Pretesting and posttesting; appropriate ratios.
8. Estimate funds necessary to achieve media and communication objectives.	Computer simulation of media costs.

Identify Audience Needs   The requirements of the audience should provide the central focus of the message strategy. However, as discussed in earlier chapters, a buying committee with members from various operational departments frequently make important purchasing decisions. Each of these members has a unique set of criteria and priorities. As Table 17-5 indicates, information needs and responses vary with an individual's social or interaction style. This tempts some advertisers to develop a "one story tells all to all" type of advertisement. Unfortunately, these ads usually sink under the weight of their complex and confusing message. A more effective approach involves the development of individual messages appropriate to each key audience. In short, advertising should exhibit the same message flexibility that a successful salesperson would employ when addressing these diverse individuals.

Stick to Important Specifics   Many business advertisers attempt to cover too much in their advertising messages. On the other hand, buyers usually base their purchases on several criteria. Thus, advertising messages should be developed around those issues that represent the *major concerns* of the audience.[28]

In developing the advertising message, marketers should remember that buyers tend to screen out messages inconsistent with their attitudes and experiences. They also tend to "translate" information so that it conforms to their beliefs. Thus, market research should include the task of determining customer's beliefs and attitudes in addition to their needs.

DEVELOPING THE MEDIA PLAN

The primary elements to consider when developing a media plan include (1) the number of different target audiences (*reach*), (2) the number of times to repeat the message for optimal impact (*frequency*), (3) the length of time to run the campaign (*continuity*), (4) the most appropriate media (*selection*), and (5) *scheduling*.

Reach   Many industrial purchases involve multiple influencers, each with unique information needs and interests, who read different types of publications. To reach these diverse individuals with a message that addresses their needs, multiple message strategies must be developed and delivered through media that focus on their interests.

Frequency   One-time ads are rarely effective; several exposures are necessary before a message has a sufficient impact. As the number of message exposures increases, both the *number* of individuals who remember it and the *length of time* they can recall it increases. However, overexposure of a message can be wasteful. When an audience experiences wear-out effects, it tends to tune out the message. To justify the choice of frequency, media planners must assume some response function that correlates to the number of exposures.

Continuity   When a message has both long continuity and high frequency, wear-out effects can be severe. In developing message strategy, the advertiser should build in variety while maintaining the overall theme and positioning strategy. For example, the Borg-Warner campaign in Figure 17-2 ran for more than five years. The theme "Watch Borg-Warner" was continuously maintained, but each advertisement featured a different product category with an appropriate message. Determining the best mix of reach, frequency, and continuity is directly related to media selection and scheduling.

TABLE 17-5   Adjusting the Message to the Social Style of the Audience

Message Element	Driver[1]	Expressive[2]	Amiable[3]	Analytical[4]
Approach should be	Structured, clear	Creative, imaginative	Very people oriented	Detailed, orderly
Copy style should be	Concise, to the point	Stimulating, arousing	Friendly, conversational	Precise
Product or service emphasis should be	Ability to reduce cost; profit improvement; avoid excess details	Innovation; recognition or more status; "sell the sizzle, not steak"	Reduce uncertainty and risk; improve safety; help people	Proof of performance; process integrity
Impress them with	Short-term results; bottom-line improved	Expert testimonials; short-term results	Partnership; proof of claims; services	Logic and proof; short- and long-term results; authority testimonials
Induce action with	Choices, options, chance to customize	Incentives, personal recognition, speed of results	Guarantees, assurances, service, and support	Detailed proposals, good service, proof of claims

[1] High on assertiveness (task orientation), and low on responsiveness (people orientation).
[2] High on assertiveness (task orientation), and high on responsiveness (people orientation).
[3] Low on assertiveness (task orientation), and high on responsiveness (people orientation).
[4] Low on assertiveness (task orientation), and low on responsiveness (people orientation).

Source: Adapted from Robert A. Kriegel, "Does your ad talk the way your prospect thinks?" *Business Marketing* 69 (July 1984):86-98. Reprinted by permission of *Business Marketing.* © Crain Communications, Inc.

Source: Courtesy Borg-Warner Corp., Chicago, Ill.

FIGURE 17-2 An excellent example of how continuity of theme can be carried out while maintaining the same positioning strategy: "Watch Borg-Warner."

Want to see the Father of our country around for your grandchildren?

Borg-Warner air conditioning systems keep the temperature and humidity constant to help preserve the historic paintings at the National Gallery of Art. That's today's Borg-Warner. Diversified for financial stability. A company worth watching.

Watch Borg-Warner

For an annual report call 312-322-8680.

FIGURE 17-2—Cont'd See p. 452 for legend.

Want to see water where it almost never rains?

Borg-Warner submersible pumps help bring vital irrigation water 5000 feet, almost a mile, straight up from beneath arid desert sands. That's today's Borg-Warner. Diversified for financial stability. A company worth watching.

Watch Borg-Warner

For an annual report call 312-322-8680.

FIGURE 17-2—Cont'd See p. 452 for legend.

MEDIA SELECTION

Selection of the appropriate media depends on the target audience to be reached, the ability of the media to reach that audience, and the efficiency with which the media can be used to maximize reach, frequency, and continuity goals within budgetary constraints.

Media selection also depends on whether the advertiser wishes to penetrate a particular industry or cut across industries. It would be unwise to pay the higher insertion costs of publications aimed at multiple industries rather than the lower costs charged by publications directed at the one or few industries in which the advertiser's product is used. On the other hand, when potential users exist in many industries, and the functional areas of key buying influencers are not well defined, publications that cut across industries and functional areas will probably produce the best results.

Table 17-6 shows the media choices of the top 20 business advertisers in 1995. This list offers some very interesting comparisons and observations. As one observation, we have obviously entered the Age of Information. Sixteen of the top 20 advertisers manufacture computer hardware, software, associated components such as semiconductors and peripheral equipment, or they provide telecommunication services. In fact, 19 of the top 25, 33 of the top 50, and 56 of the top 100 business advertisers are in these same industries.

Nineteen of these 20 firms directed over 50 percent of their media advertising dollars at the business market, although the percentage by firm varies as does the distribution of dollars across the media. The only exception was AT&T, which spent over 80 percent trying to keep consumers from switching to MCI or Sprint. Federal Express and UPS spent even more of their budget on television plus consumer magazines, 98 and 93 percent respectively. However, the largest portion of their ads addressed the needs and concerns of business firms. Apparently both of these shippers subscribe to Sarah Lang's strategy that was referenced earlier in the chapter, "TV is the medium for reaching small businessmen, who are a mass audience. . . ."

Intel, because of the consumer-oriented thrust of their "Intel Inside" campaign, spent 50 percent of their budget on consumer media. However, they still recognized the fact that equipment manufacturers purchased their products, not consumers, so 48 percent of the budget went into trade journal advertising.

Circulation, Editorial Content, and Cost   Selection also depends on circulation, editorial content, and the cost of advertising space. To define the audiences of particular publications accurately, media planners use the circulation audits of the various publications. Three organizations—*Audit Bureau of Circulation, Business Publications' Audit of Circulations,* and *Verified Audit Circulation Corporation*—also audit circulation, via the SIC codes of their member businesses. Business publications are also listed by such services as the *Standard Rate and Data Service's Business Publications* and the *Business Publication Rates and Data Directory,* which provide information on editorial content, advertising rates, closing dates for ad placements, and circulation figures.

Controlled Circulation   Business and trade publications are circulated on a paid or controlled basis. When a publication is available on a paid basis, the *recipient pays* the subscription price to receive it. Controlled circulations are *free* and are mailed to a selected list of individuals, chosen by the publisher on the basis of their unique position to influence purchase decisions. To qualify, recipients must designate their profession or occupation, their job title, function, and purchasing responsibilities. Thus, users of controlled circulation publications can more accurately evaluate which target markets their publications reach and whether their advertising dollars are being properly expended.

TABLE 17-6 Media Choices of Top Twenty Business Advertisers, 1995 (in millions of dollars and percent)

Rank 1995	Rank 1994	Company	Total Ad budget	Trade Journals	Consumer Magazines	Network TV	Other TV	Newspapers	Radio
1	1	AT&T Corp.	$248.3	$22.6	$24.5	$76.0	$82.1	$27.2	$15.8
2	2	IBM Corp	228.1	87.4	50.7	50.4	15.7	21.8	1.6
3	5	Microsoft	124.2	50.6	34.9	22.0	7.4	8.1	1.2
4	3	MCI Communic.	108.2	0.5	2.5	58.7	31.5	3.0	11.7
5	4	Hewlett Packard	84.2	46.9	15.2	5.7	9.1	6.0	1.3
6	7	Sprint Corp.	77.3	5.1	4.8	31.0	29.1	7.2	0.1
7	8	United Parcel (UPS)	66.8	0.7	10.3	41.6	10.0	3.2	1.0
8	6	Compaq Computer	59.2	33.8	10.8	10.5	0.5	3.5	0.0
9	9	American Express.	58.4	4.2	4.8	20.0	23.5	5.0	0.9
10	13	Canon	55.1	11.5	19.5	11.3	5.2	6.1	1.5
11	12	Apple Computer	52.3	18.9	12.2	9.9	5.5	4.7	1.1
12	10	Digital Eqpt. Corp.	52.1	28.6	7.3	7.7	1.2	6.8	0.3
13	11	NEC Corp.	49.8	32.4	11.5	4.2	0.8	0.9	0.0
14	19	Gateway 2000	49.7	36.7	11.4	1.1	0.3	0.2	0.0
15	18	Dell Computer	45.8	39.2	6.3	0.0	0.0	0.2	0.0
16	14	Federal Express	45.4	0.4	2.7	23.1	18.7	0.1	0.5
17	17	Xerox Corp.	45.4	5.7	10.4	7.3	0.9	11.0	10.1
18	15	Intel Corp.	38.3	18.4	5.5	11.2	2.4	0.8	0.0
19	23	Toshiba America	35.5	20.8	12.5	0.0	0.3	1.6	0.1
20	16	Nat'l. Assoc. of Security Dealers	32.6	0.1	0.0	29.6	2.9	0.0	0.0
		TOTAL	1,556.8	464.6	257.9	421.5	247.0	117.4	47.2
1	1	AT&T Corp.	100.0%	9.1%	9.9%	30.6%	33.1%	10.9%	6.3%
2	2	IBM Corp.	100.0	38.3	22.2	22.1	6.9	9.6	0.7
3	5	Microsoft	100.0	40.7	28.1	17.7	6.0	6.5	1.0
4	3	MCI Communications	100.0	0.5	2.3	54.2	29.1	2.8	10.8
5	4	Hewlett Packard	100.0	55.6	18.1	6.8	10.8	7.2	1.5
6	7	Sprint Corp.	100.0	6.6	6.2	40.1	37.7	9.2	0.1
7	8	United Parcel (UPS)	100.0	1.1	15.4	62.3	14.9	4.8	1.6
8	6	Compaq Computer	100.0	57.0	18.2	17.8	0.9	5.9	0.0
9	9	American Express	100.0	7.2	8.3	34.3	40.2	8.6	1.5
10	13	Canon	100.0	20.9	35.4	20.6	9.4	11.0	2.8
11	12	Apple Computer	100.0	36.2	23.3	18.9	10.5	9.0	2.1
12	10	Digital Eqpt. Corp.	100.0	55.0	14.1	14.8	2.3	13.1	0.6
13	11	NEC Corp.	100.0	65.0	23.0	8.4	1.6	1.8	0.0
14	19	Gateway 2000	100.0	73.9	23.0	2.1	0.5	0.4	0.0
15	18	Dell Computer	100.0	85.7	13.9	0.0	0.0	0.4	0.0
16	14	Federal Express	100.0	0.9	5.9	50.8	41.2	0.1	1.1
17	17	Xerox Corp.	100.0	12.6	23.0	16.0	1.9	24.2	22.2
18	15	Intel Corp.	100.0	48.1	14.4	29.2	6.3	2.0	0.0
19	23	Toshiba America	100.0	58.7	35.3	0.1	0.9	4.6	0.2
20	16	Nat'l. Assoc. of Security Dealers	100.0	0.2	0.1	90.8	8.8	0.0	0.0
		TOTAL	100.0	29.8	16.6	27.1	15.9	7.5	3.0

Source: Special Report: "Top 100 business-to-business advertisers," *Business Marketing* 81 (September 1996):10.

Scheduling Scheduling in publications depends on whether they are monthlies, weeklies, or dailies. If the media plan incorporates the use of a daily, a weekly, and a monthly publication, scheduling of advertising inserts might, for example, require six inserts per year in the monthly, twenty-six inserts per year in the weekly, and fifty-two inserts per year in the daily.

TABLE 17-7	Primary Elements of Advertising Evaluation	
Element	*Pretesting*	*Posttesting*
Markets	Test advertising message strategy against various target audiences to measure their reaction.	Determine how well campaign reached target market. Measure changes in awareness.
Motives	Determine reasons for buyer behavior and what product benefits appeal to them.	Measure effect of motives (i.e., did purchase occur?).
Messages	Determine what the message says and how well it is said—includes copy, headlines, illustrations, and typography.	Determine whether ad was seen, remembered, believed.
Media	Determine best combination of media to reach target market; includes space and time factors; usually done by computer simulation.	Evaluate how well the chosen media reached audience.
Scheduling	Determine the optimal aspects of reach, frequency, and continuity.	Evaluate the effectiveness of scheduling.
Budgeting	Determine the optimal level of expenditures; usually done by computer simulation.	Evaluate the return on budgeting strategy.
Overall results		Evaluate whether objectives were achieved. Determine whether to continue, what to change, and how much to spend in the future.

Scheduling also depends on the objectives of the advertising program. If the objective is to achieve recognition, scheduling might call for a steady year-round campaign. Recognition takes time to achieve. If the advertising involves a new product introduction, scheduling might call for heavier advertising at the beginning of the campaign with periodic pulsing throughout the year to remind influencers of the product's existence.

EVALUATING THE ADVERTISING PLAN

An advertising strategy must be continually evaluated to ensure the achievement of objectives and the wise expenditure of money. Various elements of the strategy can be measured before and after the tactical advertising plan is implemented. Measuring the effectiveness of the message before it is implemented is called *pretesting*. By pretesting particular elements of the plan, the advertiser can discover what is or is not effective, correct the ineffective elements, and avoid costly errors.

Determining the effectiveness of the plan after it has been implemented is known as *posttesting*. While posttesting is generally more costly and time consuming than pretesting, it can provide useful guidelines for future advertising programs. It also permits the advertiser to measure the effectiveness of the plan under actual market conditions. The effectiveness of an advertising plan depends on how well it reaches the intended market and whether the message had an impact on the market. Thus, advertisers are generally concerned with the areas shown in Table 17-7.

The Need for Preplanning   To evaluate an advertising plan effectively, the evaluator must carefully consider which *elements* to evaluate, what *data* to gather, and the *method* of data analysis.

For example, although IBM finds it difficult to measure whether advertising goals have been attained, because their name washes over all their advertising, the company develops its advertising program by first researching specific market areas, then establishing advertising objectives based on this research, and finally, pre- and posttesting the effectiveness of the overall program.[29]

The choice of advertising evaluation method depends on the specific objectives of an advertising campaign. The quality of campaign conception and execution, however, hinges on the sophistication of responsible individuals. Frequently, outside research professionals are hired to develop field studies. Many industrial firms have found that advertising agencies can help significantly in planning the campaign as well as conducting advertising research.

Business Advertising Agencies An increasing number of advertising agencies are either specializing in business advertising or pursuing this segment as a major portion of their own business plan. These agencies assist the business advertiser with various aspects of the communication plan. In addition to preparing advertisements and conducting research, they help to coordinate the advertising program with other promotional elements by assisting in the design of sales promotion material and publicity releases. The leading business advertising agencies, ranked by 1994 billings, are listed in Table 17-8.

The Integrated Promotion Plan

The basic elements essential to a well-conceived business promotion plan have thus far been discussed individually. However, these elements must be artfully integrated to achieve communication objectives most effectively. Once the various strategies have been conceived, action plans must be developed *in writing* so that the individuals involved can carry out their assigned tasks in a coordinated manner.

The advertising departments of firms in the business market typically participate more in the actual creation and placement of promotional strategy than do those in consumer organizations. This is true because much of the promotional package is developed in-house (e.g., direct mailers, catalogs, data sheets, trade show exhibits, etc.).

TABLE 17-8 Leading Business Advertising Agencies, 1994 Billings (in millions of dollars)

Agency	Business Billings	Total Billings	Percentage of Business
Ketchum Advertising	$ 156.2	$1,200.0	13.0%
Bronner, Slosberg, Humphrey, Inc.	155.9	333.5	46.7
Valentine Radford, Inc.	122.6	122.6	100.0
Anderson & Lembke, Inc.	122.0	141.6	86.2
Dahlin, Smith, White, Inc.	110.1	111.3	98.9
Harrison, Star, Wiener & Beitler	102.6	102.6	100.0
Clarion Business Communications	94.0	242.0	38.8
Hill, Holiday, Connors, Cosmopulos	93.2	296.7	31.4
Corbett HealthConnect	90.4	90.4	100.0
Rumrill-Hoyt, Inc.	87.6	116.8	75.0
TOP TEN SUBTOTALS	1,134.6	2,757.5	41.1
121 OTHER AGENCIES	1,710.9	3,837.1	44.6
TOTAL: 131 AGENCIES	$2,845.5	$6,594.6	43.1%

Source: Survey conducted by *Business Marketing*; as cited in Marla R. Maslanka, "Business-to-business 43% of agency billings," *Business Marketing* 66 (May 1995): pp. 3, 22, 44. Reprinted by permission of *Business Marketing*. © Crain Communications, Inc.

Moreover, the technical aspects of business advertising demand greater involvement in the creation of copy, charts, and graphs.

A well-written action plan, as developed in Table 17-9, covers specifically what is to be communicated, when, and through which media. It should also include all promotional plans (publicity, trade shows, giveaways, and data sheets) that are part of the overall promotional strategy.

The communication action plan, complete with research data, coordinated activities, a detailed budget, and stated objectives makes it much easier to secure management's approval of the strategy. Once funding has been approved, the plan serves as an effective control mechanism.

TABLE 17-9   Anatomy of a Marketing Communication Plan

Marketing objective	Increase Acme's market share from 12% to 18% over the next 12 months, beginning January 199X.
Advertising objectives	Increase current customer awareness of Acme Widgets from 35% to 55% over the next 12 months. Create an awareness of 20% among unserved accounts during the same time period.
Target market and audience	Firms that design widgets into their products: design engineers, production engineers, buyers, and influential managers.
Communication strategies Advertising	Prepare copy to emphasize the benefits of having one proven source for widgets. Develop headline and illustrations that draw attention to the problems of having multiple sourcing.
	Run six two-page, 4-color ads every other month in *Widget World.*
	Run a half-page, black-and-white ad monthly in *Widget Product News* offering free technical manual "Cross Sectional Dimensionality of Widgets."
	Insert 1-800 toll-free number.
	Run four 4-color ads in June, July, September, and October issues of *ABC Monthly Roundup* and *ABC Process Times* to announce a "breakthrough" in widget cost superiority without a sacrifice in quality. Emphasize the breadth of Acme product line, technical superiority, and cost leadership. Also free offer of widget technical manual.
Direct Mail	Rewrite "The Acme Widget Advantage" product brochure, stressing new broader line. Complete the rewrite, get approval, and start production by March 20.
Telemarketing	Hire telemarketing consultant in January to set up an outgoing telephone program. Start calls by March 1.
Sales promotion	Schedule trade show participation in July at Cleveland Widget Expo. Promote trade show through invitations mailed with technical manual to new market sales leads. Mail invitations by April 31. Complete exhibition booth and assign personnel for booth duty by June 15.
	Offer free "Widgeting Versatility" manual in nine fractional ads to run April through December in *Production Unlimited* and *Factory Engineering* along with 1-800 phone number. Run same ad in *Perfect Plant* postcard mailing in September.
Publicity	Prepare and mail press release and product brochure to *Widget Industry*'s editorial department in January, emphasizing the customer benefits of Acme's newly expanded product line.
	Distribute technical manual and press release with a short synopsis to *Factory Engineering* editorial department in June.
	Research and write application case history, emphasizing the flexibility of the broad product line available from single-source Acme. Present to editor of *Widget World* for possible June-July publication.

Source: Adapted from Robert A. Kriegel, "Anatomy of a marketing communication plan," *Business Marketing,* 68 (July 1983):72-8. Reprinted by permission of *Business Marketing.* © Crain Communications, Inc.

Looking Back

Advertising, sales promotion, and publicity play an important part in the communication strategy of business marketers. These variables, however, must be carefully coordinated with personal selling if they are to contribute to the overall effectiveness of communication strategy.

Business advertising is used to reach unknown or inaccessible buying influences, to create awareness of the company, to enhance the sales call, to increase the overall effectiveness of the selling effort, and to support distributors' effort. While media usage generally differs from that used in the consumer market, the same principles apply in developing advertising and other promotional strategy.

The various reasons for using sales promotion and publicity and their enhancement of advertising as well as the selling effort were pointed out. Effective use of these variables, however, requires a well-devised, integrated communication program. That program begins with carefully developed advertising objectives that must be formulated from corporate and marketing objectives so as to set the direction for creating, coordinating, and evaluating the entire promotional program. Unless target markets are carefully identified, it is unlikely that communication and media strategy will attain the results desired. Once strategies are developed, based on the desired objectives, marketers can then decide on the necessary appropriations.

Questions for Discussion

1. In an attempt to measure the impact of advertising on the firm's sales force, Motor City marketers surveyed the sales staffs of several midwestern manufacturers. Although the majority of respondents were apprised of advertising objectives and programs, only 31 percent had their advice solicited during the creation stage. Express your opinion, pro or con, about the involvement of salespeople in the formulation of advertising programs.

2. The chief marketing executive of a major industrial firm had the habit of consistently cutting advertising budgets, even when presented with evidence indicating a strong link between advertising, market awareness, preference, share of market, and profit. He staunchly maintained his skepticism—even in the face of studies showing that the average industrial firm can increase its market share by 30 percent when it supports the sales force with advertising. He would simply lean back, reflect on the range of his product/market situations, and say, "That's only true sometimes." Can you come up with some arguments to change his mind?

3. Most companies spend the greater part of their promotional effort in developing direct mail, trade shows, and advertising. The lowly data sheet is often created as an afterthought. Should this be the case? Explain your position.

4. Sales and profitability are the measures of effectiveness that advertisers ultimately seek, but sales volume depends on so many factors that it is difficult to isolate the unique effect of advertising while controlling for other extraneous variables. Discuss possible ways to measure the specific effectiveness of advertising.

5. What can the business marketer do to get important technical information published in several competing publications that reach the markets of interest?

6. The strategy to promote a product to an audience of middle managers should be different from one aimed at operating engineers. Explain why you agree or disagree with this statement.

7. Business buyers usually make decisions based on specific use and profit-oriented factors; therefore, technical wording is common. However, will well-chosen technical language alone produce an effective advertisement? Why or why not?

8. Many marketers look forward to trade show participation but come away feeling dissatisfied. Often their dissatisfaction stems from a failure to develop a suitable measure of effectiveness. Develop a plan for evaluating the benefits of a trade show.

Endnotes

1. "The top 100," *Advertising Age* 67 (April 15, 1996):S1-S36.

2. Adapted from Robert W. Eckles, *Business Marketing Management* (Englewood Cliffs, N.J.: Prentice-Hall, Inc., 1990), pp. 282-3.

3. "Advertising scores high in lead generation," *Sales and Marketing Management* 147 (April 1994):25.

4. B.G. Yovovich, "Image ads transmit value to customers," *Business Marketing* 79 (August 1994):20.

5. *Sales Force Compensation Survey,* 27th ed. (Chicago: The Dartnell Corporation, 1992), pp. 19, 110.

6. George Black, "Why most engineers market space age technology with low-tech mentality," *Business Marketing* 72 (May 1987):124+.

7. Gordon McAleer, "Do industrial advertisers understand what influences their markets," *Journal of Marketing* 38 (January 1974):15-23.

8. "New *Thomas Register* service offers company and product information via telephone number and fax," *Online* 15 (March 1991):12.

9. Kate Bertrand, "Catalog choices: DEC and Apple go on-line, while Thomas remains paper powerhouse," *Business Marketing* 77 (May 1992):43-5.

10. "Ad rates," *Business Marketing,* 73 (April 1988):38.

11. Nancy Arnott, "Inside Intel's marketing coup," *Sales and Marketing Management* 146 (February 1994):78-81.

12. Chuck Paustian, "Direct's star on the rise," *Business Marketing* 79 (October 1994):31+; also Peter Finch, "The direct marketing data base revolution," *Business Marketing* 70 (August 1985):34+.

13. Judith J. Marshall and Harrie Vredenburg, "The roles of outside and inside sales representatives: Conflict or cooperation?" *Journal of Direct Marketing* 5 (Autumn 1991):8-17.

14. Judith J. Marshall and Harrie Vredenburg, "Successfully using telemarketing in industrial sales," *Industrial Marketing Management* 17 (February 1988):15-22.

15. Thomas V. Bonoma, "Get more out of your trade shows," *Harvard Business Review* 61 (January-February 1983):75-83.

16. Edward Roberts, "Training trade show salespeople: How Caterpillar does it," *Business Marketing* 73 (June 1988):70-3.

17. Richard K. Swandby and Jonathan M. Cox, "Trade show trends: Exhibiting growth paces economic strength," *Business Marketing* 70 (May 1985):50-6.

18. *Sales Force Compensation Survey,* 27th ed. (Chicago: The Dartnell Corporation, 1992), p. 165.

19. Daniel C. Bello and Ritu Lohtia, "Improving trade show effectiveness by analyzing attendees," *Industrial Marketing Management* 22 (November 1993):311-18.

20. Brad O'Harra, Fred Palumbo, and Paul Herbig, "Industrial trade shows abroad," *Industrial Marketing Management* 22 (August 1993):233-7.

21. William W. Mee, "Working together to promote trade shows," *Association Management* 46 (December 1994):78-80+.

22. Carolan Trbovich, "Try a new approach: Credit at the trade show," *Business Credit* 96 (November/December 1994):5.

23. George M. Zinkham and Lauren A. Vachris, "The impact of selling aids on new prospects," *Industrial Marketing Management* 13 (1984):187-93.

24. Jerome D. Williams, "Industrial publicity: One of the best promotional tools," *Industrial Marketing Management* 12 (1983):207-11.

25. James E. Lynch and Graham J. Hooley, "Advertising budgeting practices of industrial advertisers," *Industrial Marketing Management* 16 (1987):63-9.

26. Vincent J. Blasko and Charles H. Patti, "The advertising budgeting practices of industrial marketers," *Journal of Marketing* 48 (Fall 1984):104-10.

27. "Our Choice: 1984's Best Business/Industrial Print Ad," *Business Marketing* 70 (January 1985):114-28.

28. Joseph A. Bellizzi and Julie Lehrer, "Developing Better Industrial Advertising," *Industrial Marketing Management* 12 (1983):19-23.

29. Byron G. Quann, "How IBM Assesses Its Business-to-Business Advertising," *Business Marketing* 70 (January 1985):106-12

Bibliography

Arnott, Nancy, "Inside Intel's marketing coup," *Sales and Marketing Management* 146 (1994):78-81.

Bello, Daniel C. and Ritu Lohtia, "Improving trade show effectiveness by analyzing attendees," *Industrial Marketing Management* 22 (1993):311-18.

Lynch, James E. and Graham J. Hooley, "Advertising budgeting practices of industrial advertisers," *Industrial Marketing Management* 16 (1987):63-9.

Marshall, Judith J. and Harrie Vredenberg, "Successfully using telemarketing in industrial sales," *Industrial Marketing Management* 17 (1988):15-22.

Marshall, Judith J. and Harrie Vredenberg, "The roles of outside and inside sales representatives: Conflict or cooperation?" *Journal of Direct Marketing* 5 (1991): 8-17.

Mee, William W., "Working together to promote trade shows," *Association Management* 46 (1994):78-80+.

O'Harra, Brad, Fred Palumbo, and Paul Herbig, "Industrial trade shows abroad," *Industrial Marketing Management* 22 (1993):233-7.

Paustian, Chuck, "Direct's star on the rise," *Business Marketing* 79 (1994):31+.

Yovovich, B.G., "Image ads transmit value to customers," *Business Marketing* 79 (1994):20.

Ziegenhagen, M.E., "When management doesn't 'believe' in advertising," *Business Marketing* 69 (1984):81-4.

P A R T **VII**

Pricing Strategies

A fellow marketing practitioner once observed that of the "four *P*s," three generate costs (product, promotion, and place), but only one, price, generates profits. He based this observation on the fact that the better the product, the greater the promotion, and the more widespread the distribution, the higher the cost to achieve these ends. On the other hand, only price can generate a level of income high enough to offset the other costs. He went on to berate those marketers who consider the height of creativity to be a price set ten percent below that of competition instead of using the other three *P*s to justify a price high enough to generate a reasonable profit.

Although one might argue with this individual's mind set, one cannot debate the overarching role of price in a marketing strategy. Aside from being a major element in the profit equation, price establishes an image for both a product and its producer. It also suggests a value to a buyer that must be justified by the the elements of the marketing mix. Another way of looking at price, no matter how attractive, it is what the buyer must give up in order to obtain the seller's promised benefits.

In the next two chapters, we will study the three factors that must underpin any effective pricing strategy: customers (market demand), competition, and costs. We will also look at the pros and cons of setting an aggressive, proactive pricing policy versus a more passive "follow the lead" approach. The aspects of pricing under conditions of uncertainty and the factors that impact price negotiations are also covered.

CHAPTER 18

Price Determinants: Costs, Competition, and Customers

Business buying decisions are typically more pragmatic and "fact oriented" than similar decisions made by consumers. This does not imply that business decisions are completely emotionless, nor that consumers base decisions solely on ego and social needs. However, business products have a direct impact on the profits of both buyer and seller. Price becomes a pivotal issue, with each party weighing multiple factors to determine the relative importance of price in a specific negotiation.

The goal of this chapter, then, is to clarify:

1. The impact of costs and competition on pricing strategy
2. The importance of determining what customers value before setting price
3. The experience curve and its affect on costs, pricing, and profits
4. Variations in pricing strategy and the need to change over the product life cycle
5. The impact of price on profitability

Assuming that price acts as a catalyst for the marketing mix, it must be carefully integrated with the firm's product, channel, and communication strategies. The marketing manager faces the challenge of balancing these four elements to ensure that the total offering not only satisfies the market's needs but also provides a profit consistent with the firm's objectives. This is not an easy task.

E. Raymond Corey cautions, "Price is a key element in an overall business strategy, and to make strategic pricing decisions one should know what objectives are being served. . . . In setting pricing objectives, therefore, it is important to ask a range

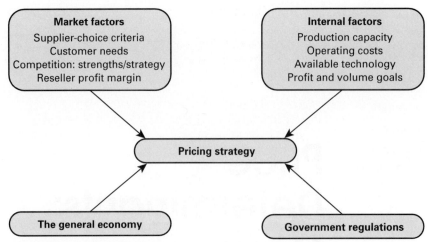

FIGURE 18-1 Constraints on pricing strategy.

of questions: What is do-able? Where will sales volume come from? How will my competitors react? What will be the impact of the pricing strategy for one product on other products in the line? How will potential customers react? But the most important question of all: What are we trying to do?"[1]

Price must agree with the value a customer places on a product or service, but different customers perceive different values. They may also place different priorities on various product attributes, such as durability, warranty, innovative design, or ease of use.[1] In addition, price setters must consider costs, market demand, competition, governmental regulations, the profit margins of distributors, and the commissions of manufacturers' representatives. Figure 18-1 depicts these multiple and conflicting price constraints.

Once the price setter understands the goals to be met, the first decision entails the element to be used as the triggering mechanism for price—cost, competition, or customers. Each choice involves advantages, disadvantages, and further decision-making. We will consider each in turn.

Cost-Driven Pricing

Cost-driven pricing is the simplest to devise but also the most simplistic. For example, retailers like to resell their merchandise at double their "buy price." However, this choice ignores what customers are willing to pay as well as the price charged by competing retailers. Many professional service organizations bill clients at an hourly rate equal to three times the hourly wage of the individual providing the service. Salary, overhead, and profit are each allocated one third of revenue.[2] Again, neither market demand nor competition are part of the equation.

The predicted cost to produce a new or significantly revised product, however, represents a "moving target." This prediction is a form of circular logic: the predicted cost dictates a price, the price drives demand, and demand affects cost. In other words, within a reasonable range, larger volume will result in lower cost, smaller volume in higher cost. Continuing the same logic, the revised cost should result in an altered price, which will alter volume, which will change cost—and so on ad nauseam.

This latter point indicates the paradox of cost-driven pricing in a changing market. Intuition suggests that pricing should be more competitive (lower) in a depressed market, but higher costs prohibit this strategy. Likewise, in a booming market replete with shortages, higher prices can be charged, but lower costs dictate price cutting. Thus, the ease of setting price comes at the cost of mediocre profits.[3]

Perhaps the greatest limitation of cost-driven pricing stems from what is *not* considered. This process essentially ignores the following[4]:

- Market conditions
- Competitive prices
- Available substitutes and their prices
- The relative stability of other prices
- Product differentiation
- Phase of the product life cycle
- Growth rate of the market
- The firm's market share
- Excess productive capacity
- The market's ability to buy
- The market's expectations about prices
- Competitors' typical responses to price changes

Virtually none of Corey's questions are answered.

Competition-Driven Pricing

Texas Instruments (TI) trains its new sales engineers broadly and thoroughly. One point always emphasized in the training sessions is "know your competition almost as well as you know TI. They represent your customer's *alternative choices*." Price-setting marketers must also know their competition, particularly their approach to pricing.

Two related strategies that have gained in popularity are *value marketing* and *value-based pricing*. To employ either strategy successfully, a marketer must understand how competitors try to create a perception of value in the minds of customers (their strategy) and the attributes they emphasize in promotion (their strengths). "Value" implies the provision of greater satisfaction at a given price or equal satisfaction at a lower price. Unfortunately, too many marketers feel that they must stress lower price rather than strive for greater satisfaction.

When Compaq entered the personal computer market as a virtual unknown, they had the opportunity to join the other IBM clones in stating, "We are almost as good as IBM, and our prices are lower." This approach can work well in market segments seeking the lowest possible price. However, it also creates the image of being less than the best. Compaq, wishing to be viewed as an industry leader in all respects including product quality and innovation, declared that they were better than IBM and had a competitive price—equal to IBM and above the clones. Within a few years, they became the recognized volume leader.

Even though price cuts can increase market share more quickly, emphasis on issues such as product superiority, extended warranty, or superior after-sale service creates longer-lasting results and has a more favorable impact on profits.[3] Moreover, competition may be unable to duplicate nonprice attributes, but they can readily match or exceed any price reduction. Consequently, marketers who are concerned about near-term profits should cut price only when they see no other way to create or maintain a competitive value image. The use of price leadership as a proactive strategy to generate greater long-term profits will be discussed later in this chapter.

COMPETITORS' REACTION TO PRICE CHANGES

Marketers must also anticipate the reactions of competitors to pricing decisions and factor these reactions into any contemplated change. Competitors usually meet price reductions on undifferentiated products immediately; as a result, everyone keeps the same market share but at a lower profit for all. However, various factors can alter a competitor's ability or willingness to duplicate a price reduction. Table 18-1 outlines these factors.

Competitors may also decide not to respond to a price increase. When this occurs, the firm that initiates the price increase usually loses market share, unless some customer-valued benefit accompanies the increase. For competitors to follow a price increase, they must believe that (1) total market demand will not be reduced by the increase, (2) other major suppliers will also follow the increase, and (3) the initiator of the price increase is acting intelligently and in the best interest of all suppliers.

Most major industries are oligopolistic. A smaller firm in such an industry normally cannot induce its major competitors to follow a simple price increase. On the other hand, a price reduction often brings swift reaction, even an undercutting. Smaller firms can impact pricing levels by developing superior products or innovative marketing programs that impact the perceived value offered by their competitors. Compaq took this approach.

Market leaders (those with the highest market shares) can usually induce their competitors to follow both price increases and reductions.[4] Since the derived demand for business goods is often inelastic, total market volume does not increase because of a price reduction, but any company's market share will certainly decline unless it remains price competitive. Even market leaders cannot always dictate prices; the general price level tends to reflect both supply and demand pressures. However, the market leader does act as the dominant reference point among competing sellers.

TABLE 18-1 Factors That Influence a Competitor's Reaction to a Price Reduction	
Costs	When the profit margin is relatively low, a further reduction in price could eliminate profit. If business is scarce, a reduction may be met as long as variable costs are covered. Having a fairly accurate idea of competitors' costs is very important. This provides a gauge of their willingness to meet reductions as well as to initiate them.
Time to react	In general, competitors can react immediately. However, when a price reduction stems from a major product redesign or increased production efficiency, the competitor may need time to affect the same changes. The short-term impact on sales volume for the price cutter may be substantial.
Existing commitments	Even when a firm sells under terms of "price in effect at time of order placement," major customers will not allow a supplier to cut market price without adjusting the price on their open orders. Thus, the supplier may face a backlog reduction of thousands of dollars with only a slight chance of offsetting that loss through increased business.
	Another limiting circumstance is the effect a price cut on one product will have on the sale of other products in the line. The end result could be a massive inventory of unsalable goods.
Relative sales volume	A firm with low market share can often reduce price without reaction from market leaders. They feel that the potential profit lost from lower sales is less than the profit lost from a price change.
Current production capacity	When operating at full capacity (or with large backorders as mentioned above), firms have little to gain by meeting a price reduction. In fact, when market demand taxes current capacity, a firm is more likely to raise price.

Source: Adapted from E. Raymond Corey, *Industrial Marketing: Cases and Concepts,* 3rd ed. (Upper Saddle River, N.J.: Prentice Hall, Inc., 1983), p. 319.

Customer-Driven Pricing

This pricing strategy can be far more effective and profitable than pricing based on either cost or competition; it is also more difficult and subjective. Referring again to value-based pricing, customers form their value perceptions from three perspectives: what they *receive,* what they *give up,* and what they *forsake.* They receive a product or service, they give up an amount of money, and they forsake the offerings of other suppliers. In short, they choose a "bundle of benefits" that offers the most satisfaction for the money. This seems simple enough. Where is the difficulty?

DIFFERENT BUYERS, DIFFERENT PERCEIVED VALUES

Several aspects create the difficulty. First, not all customers value the same product attributes or associated services. In fact, not all users within the same company will see the same value in a given product. Consider, for example, a company planning to buy a new computer system complete with desktop PCs, workstations, printers, network servers, upgraded software, and so on. Engineering might put a priority on three-dimensional graphics for computer-aided design (CAD), plus the speed and memory necessary to solve complex mathematical equations. The sales department wants the latest in relational databases to track customers, products, and territories; advertising also wants graphics, but coupled with multimedia capability. Accounting needs . . . manufacturing prefers . . . Attributes and services are not benefits unless a prospective buyer places a value on each. Otherwise, they are simply cost generators that trigger an uncompetitive price.

Second, the supplier must be able to provide the desired benefits at a profit; that is, the buyer's perceived value must exceed the supplier's costs. A buyer's perception presents another hurdle for the price setter. Will prospective buyers place a realistic value on a new product that has capabilities beyond their past experience? Probably not. This raises the distinction between *perceived value* and *potential value.* The prospect sees the former but must be educated regarding the latter.[1] For example, a more expensive laser printer capable of printing in monochrome, grayscale, and color can be interconnected to multiple users with varying needs. In actual use, it is much cheaper than three printers each dedicated to a single user. A buyer accustomed to seeing a printer sitting alongside a computer would not consider the economies of a network unless helpful suggestions are made.

ANALYZING CUSTOMER BENEFITS

The computer system example indicates that various buying and decision influencers within the firm view different product attributes as primary benefits. Benefits may be functional, operational, financial, or personal.[5]

Functional benefits involve product design characteristics, aspects particularly attractive to technical personnel. *Operational* benefits involve attributes such as reliability and consistency, issues of importance to manufacturing and quality control people. *Financial* benefits include favorable credit terms and cost-saving opportunities that are valued by purchasing managers and comptrollers. *Personal* benefits stem from factors such as reduced risk, greater peer respect, and the personal satisfaction of doing a job well. These benefits affect the decision of any influencer.

Analysis of potential customer benefits can begin with the performance capabilities of a physical product as well as the elements of the augmented product (delivery, financing, technical support, or warranty). By analyzing all potential benefits, the marketer can see the product from the customer's perspective, evaluate competitive strengths more objectively, and identify unique sales opportunities. This analysis also provides the insight to price a product at its true value.

Although physical product benefits are seen rather clearly, augmentation benefits may be more difficult to define. However, given the similarity of many business products, particularly those sold to customer specifications, the type of services offered may provide the only means of differentiation. Thus, as a very helpful sales manager once suggested, "Learn how to describe your total offering in 101 ways—each aimed at pleasing some customer."

ANALYZING CUSTOMER COSTS

As discussed earlier, business firms weigh the expected benefits against the costs associated with obtaining and using a product. Marketers must recognize that the invoice price is only one segment of end-use cost. Acquisition costs will also include freight, order handling costs, and possible installation charges. Less obvious costs stem from defective material, lower production efficiencies, and even production line shutdowns caused by nondelivery or receipt of defective material.[5]

Too many sellers in the business market react instantaneously to a competitor's price cut. They feel there is no defense against such a situation. However, a less emotional analysis may show that the competitor's 5 percent price reduction does not offset end use costs that are 10 percent higher. Of course, such an analysis requires an informed knowledge of the customer's operating conditions.

Some creative marketers offer to share or assume some customer costs in lieu of price-cutting. A consigned inventory reduces the customer's inventory carrying costs substantially. A computer terminal in the customer's purchasing department, connected by a dedicated phone line to the supplier's inventory database, minimizes the time and effort required to place and expedite orders. This arrangement also greatly increases the likelihood of orders being placed with that supplier at market prices.

PRICE SENSITIVITY

Basic economic theory indicates that buyers will always choose the supplier's offering that provides the greatest value or benefit. However, we have already seen that perceptions of value differ with the individual. Moreover, most buyers do not make purchase decisions based solely on economic value. For example, a time shortage, pressure from supervisors, ignorance of existing alternatives, or inability to assess a product's capabilities may result in suboptimal decisions. As outlined in Table 18-2, a number of specific factors may impact a buyer's sensitivity to price.[3]

THE IMPACT OF DERIVED DEMAND

As Table 18-2 indicates, the concepts of price sensitivity and derived demand are interrelated. Derived demand means that sales to an original equipment manufacturer (OEM) ultimately depend on the level of customer demand for the OEM's products. These customers can include wholesalers, retailers, and consumers. Any increase in the OEM's demand for component parts, raw material, capital equipment, and ancillary services hinges on increased purchases of the OEM's output. Eventually, all business purchases depend on demand in the consumer market. Because of the usual distance, physical as well as attitudinal, between an industrial supplier and the ultimate consumer, the expected relationship between price and quantity demanded becomes less obvious and sometimes even reversed. For example, when product reliability becomes a significant

TABLE 18-2	Factors That Influence Price Sensitivity
Perceived substitutes	Price sensitivity increases the more a buyer is aware of satisfactory substitutes at a lower price. Sensitivity can be decreased by positioning the product in relation to high-value substitutes rather than low-price versions.
Unique value	Price sensitivity decreases the more a buyer values a product's attributes not offered by competing products. Buyers must first recognize the attributes and then be convinced of the value.
Difficult comparison	Price sensitivity decreases when the buyer cannot easily compare the value of an unknown substitute to that of a proven supplier. However, information that eases this comparison reduces the weighting of a supplier's past performance.
Price-quality ratio	Price sensitivity decreases the more a buyer perceives a higher price as an indicator of better quality or assured performance. The "Intel Inside" campaign seeks to provide such an indicator for the participating PC makers (while sustaining Intel's dominant share of the microprocessor market).
Expenditure level	Price sensitivity decreases the lower the total expenditure and/or the greater the effort required to reduce it. Relativity is involved two ways: more profitable firms can better afford to absorb unexpected price increases; larger firms are in a stronger position to negotiate smaller increases.
End benefits	Price sensitivity for supplies and components is directly proportional to the price sensitivity of the demand for the buying firm's end product. In addition, the buyer will be more sensitive to the pricing of items that represent a major portion of the end-product's total costs.
Shared cost	Price sensitivity decreases the more the buyer can pass along a portion of the purchase price. The "pass-along" can either be forward to the buying firm's customers (higher prices) or backward to a supplier (consigned inventory).
Fairness	Price sensitivity decreases the more the buyer views a price as fair or reasonable. For example, a firm that has just negotiated a labor contract that includes higher wages is more likely to accept a supplier's price increase based on higher labor costs.
Inventory	This factor is transitory and depends on the buyer's ability to buy and hold inventory for future use. The opportunity to purchase additional quantity before an anticipated price increase is more likely to be exercised the greater the expected price increase compared to inventory carrying costs.

Source: Adapted from Thomas T. Nagle and Reed K. Holden, *The Strategy and Tactics of Pricing,* 2nd ed. (Upper Saddle River, N.J.: Prentice Hall, Inc., 1995), pp. 78-93. Adapted by permission.

buying criterion, increased price (leading to the perception of higher reliability) may result in higher demand. Compaq again serves as an excellent example of this result.

COST AND PROFIT RELATIONSHIPS

We have analyzed how competition sets the upper limits on price, costs set the lower limits, and customer perceptions determine the focal point in between. As Table 18-3 indicates, the total cost of a product is made up of multiple elements that change differently with variations in the quantity produced. Properly identifying and classifying these separate costs is an essential step toward making profitable pricing decisions. The price setter should determine which costs are volume dependent, which market factors generate the costs, and where opportunities for additional profits might exist.

When **fixed costs** make up a large portion of total cost, price should be set to maximize the use of operating capacity. Until fixed costs are covered, a firm is losing money. Once covered, each incremental sale can contribute to profits. On the other hand, when **variable costs** are relatively high, pricing to maximize the contribution margin (selling price minus variable costs) is crucial to profitability. **Break-even**

analysis, a method of determining quantity levels of production that are necessary to cover fixed and variable costs, is covered in Chapter 19.

Under certain conditions, a firm may elect to price at less than full cost. For example, during a recession a firm may set a price that covers variable costs but makes only a partial contribution to fixed costs so that the plant keeps running. This is often called *survival* pricing. This pricing strategy may also be used in the short run to secure an exceptionally large order, to penetrate a specific customer, or to gain market share. In these instances, it is *preemptive* or *predatory* pricing, and may be illegal. If an irate competitor were to allege, and subsequently prove in court, that the price cutter's primary purpose was the reduction of competition, the offending firm could be found in violation of the Sherman Antitrust Act, the Clayton Act, and/or the Robinson-Patman Act (depending on the exact nature of the preemptive pricing).

Over the short run, when a firm has excess capacity, management tends to ignore allocated costs as long as the revenue received from an additional order covers more than its direct cost and makes a contribution to overhead. However, over the long run, all costs must be covered if the firm is to survive.

MARGINAL COSTS AND REVENUE

To develop a profitable pricing strategy, the price setter must also understand the concept of marginal revenue and cost. Theoretically, the firm should continue to increase sales and production volume as long as the total cost of producing the last unit does not exceed its selling price. (As shown in Table 18-3, the variable component of unit cost will bottom out at some production level and then begin to rise, sometimes rather steeply, because of decreased efficiencies.) In practice, it is difficult to measure actual cost trend lines, as opposed to spurious aberrations, and even more difficult to main-

TABLE 18-3 Cost Classifications

Fixed costs	These costs are stable over a considerable variation in output. Rent, insurance premiums, and managerial salaries are examples. As volume increases, the average fixed cost per unit will decrease, since the total cost is amortized over a greater number of units.
Variable costs	These costs are volume-dependent because they vary in direct proportion to output. The average variable cost per unit is usually quite high for a low production level and decreases as volume and efficiencies increase. At some production level, the average variable cost will minimize. This is the optimal short-term production level. As volume increases beyond this point, variable costs also rise.
Semivariable costs	These costs fluctuate with changes in volume but not in direct proportion, since they have both a fixed and a variable component. Equipment repair and maintenance costs are typical examples.
Direct costs	Both fixed and variable costs that can be attributed to a specific product or market are considered direct costs (e.g., advertising, production wages, selling expense, freight).
Indirect costs	Both fixed and variable costs that are associated with and indirectly assigned to some product or market (e.g., production overhead, quality control, customer service, and application engineering).
Allocated costs	These are costs for activities that serve many aspects of the business and must be assigned to some revenue-generating element by arbitrary criteria. The criteria chosen usually involve production or sales volume, inventory level, or generated workload. Costs generated at the corporate and administrative levels are normally allocated.
Sunk costs	These are costs of resources already acquired whose total will not be affected by alternative decisions. They must be absorbed one way or another.

tain sales at the optimal level. Moreover, the marginality theory must be balanced against the experience curve concept, which holds that the firm's variable costs will decline as output accumulates over time. If the firm forsakes business opportunities based on current costs, and these opportunities are seized by a more aggressive competitor, the competitor will drive its costs down more quickly and eventually be in a position to dictate industry pricing and profits.

ESTIMATING COSTS

Price setters can use two different sources of information to estimate costs: accounting records or engineering and manufacturing estimates. Accounting records provide actual data of previous costs relevant to the pricing decision. Engineering and manufacturing estimates are used when no cost precedent exists. Based on the production technology involved and the product specifications set by engineering, cost estimators can determine the optimal input combinations to produce any given output. Multiplying each input by its price provides a reasonably accurate cost estimate. Engineering estimates help determine the costs of new products when historical data is lacking.

COST ANALYSIS

The cost of producing and distributing a product establishes the floor for the contemplated price. If these costs are not at least covered, losses will be incurred. But which costs should the price setter consider? We have already identified fixed and variable costs as the major concerns, but care must be exercised to consider only *relevant* costs, that is, those costs that bear directly on the decision at hand.[3] Perhaps an example will show how such costs change with circumstances.

Assume a manufacturer is contemplating the development, production, and sale of a thermoforming mold (a mold used to make plastic containers). We will call the firm Thermo-Molds, Inc., or simply TMI. This proposed addition to the product line requires that TMI purchase new production machinery and hire a production supervisor, several machine operators, and one more salesperson to call on distributors. Since there is executive slack, no addition to the TMI management core is foreseen— a situation that might change if yearly volume exceeds 150,000 units. The firm will spend $50,000 on promotion, plus $10,000 to train the production supervisor and salesperson. Table 18-4 shows the purchase of new machinery for $120,000, plus the promotion and training costs, or a total investment of $180,000 to be written off by straight-line depreciation over 5 years at $36,000 a year. (The discrepancy between this approach and standard accounting procedures will be discussed shortly.) Table 18-5 shows the fixed expenses, direct and indirect, as well as the variable expenses per unit for estimated yearly volumes of 75,000, 100,000, and 150,000.

TABLE 18-4 TMI's Capital Investment and Start-up Costs	
New machinery	$120,000
Initial promotional expense	50,000
Training of supervisor	5,000
Training of sales people	5,000
	$180,000

	Volume		
	75,000	*100,000*	*150,000*

TABLE 18-5   Average Unit Costs at Several Yearly Volumes

Fixed Expense			
Supervisor's salary	$0.26	$0.20	$0.13
Salesperson's salary	.20	.15	.10
Tax and insurance	.03	.02	.01
Depreciation	.48	.36	.24
Cost of capital	.36	.27	.18
Total fixed unit cost	$1.33	$1.00	$ .66
Variable Expense			
Direct labor	$ .45	$ .45	$ .45
Direct materials	.35	.35	.35
Factory supplies	.05	.05	.05
Inventory carrying cost	.09	.09	.09
Total variable unit cost	$ .94	$ .94	$ .94
Average Total Unit Cost	$2.27	$1.94	$1.60

Difficulties in Cost Estimation   An examination of Table 18-5 raises a question regarding which total unit cost is appropriate: $2.27, $1.94, or $1.60? Obviously, there is no single, "natural" cost. Total unit cost depends on the predicted volume of sales. However, this prediction is only one of three difficulties encountered in determining a relevant cost for pricing purposes.

Another difficulty is the estimation of variable and semivariable costs as a function of volume. Although Table 18-5 shows these costs to be constant between 75,000 and 150,000 units per year (roughly 6,000 to 12,000 per month), variable costs are usually not constant over the full range of output. Instead, they first decline, then reach a low point, and finally increase as output is expanded, exhibiting the U-shaped **economy-of-scale** curve. Figure 18-2 displays this phenomenon.

A third difficulty in the determination of relevant cost involves the inclusion or exclusion of certain items. Should depreciation include non capital items, and should cost of capital be included in Table 18-5? In our TMI example, total investment amounts to $180,000. To raise these funds, investors or lenders must receive a return on their investment, either through dividends or interest. Assuming a 15 percent rate of return, as was done in Table 18-5, the cost of capital is $27,000 ($180,000 × .15), or 36, 27, and 18 cents per unit at the three production levels. Obviously, this rate of return can and will change significantly with a rise or fall in the national economy.

Consider also the promotional expense and training cost that were included in Table 18-4. The accountants at TMI would not capitalize such expenses. However, the attention and goodwill that the promotion creates with distributors continues to bring in revenues over the long run just as the machines do. The cost of training invested in "human capital" also produces returns over the long run. Therefore, these investments should be treated as depreciation charges to provide a better estimate of the true profitability of the project, even though they may not be entered in the formal accounts of the firm.

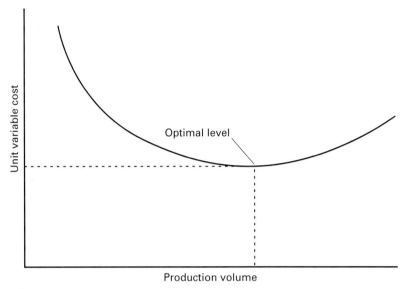

FIGURE 18-2 Economy-of-scale curve.

Consideration of Fixed Costs   Whether fixed costs should be included in the pricing decision depends on the situation. Suppose that TMI is successfully marketing 100,000 units per year at an average price of $2.85, and sales begin to fall off. If the opportunity arose to sell an additional 20,000 units to a foreign buyer for $1.35 each, should the offer be accepted? The answer lies in an analysis of fixed and variable costs. The fixed costs will exist whether or not this particular order is accepted. As long as the variable costs associated with the order are covered, any excess revenue can be applied to fixed costs, thereby increasing net profits (or decreasing net losses if the firm is currently unprofitable). The **contribution margin** (i.e., sales revenue minus variable costs) of the proposed offer is

$27,000	20,000 units @ $1.35
–18,800	Minus total variable cost
$ 8,200	Contribution margin

In the TMI example, the price decision involves a new product introduction. Unless the firm can recover all costs incurred, including fixed costs, there is no point in going through with product development. None of the costs should be incurred. Thus, in the long run, all the costs are variable in the sense that they can be avoided or incurred.

In ongoing, short-run situations, fixed costs will be incurred whether or not a particular decision is made. For example, a decision to increase plant capacity would involve the variable costs of doing so, whereas the fixed costs of the existing plant would be unaffected by the decision. Thus, the test of relevance hinges on whether a cost is changed by the contemplated decision. If the decision does alter a cost, this cost is relevant to the pricing decision.

Cost Behavior Over Time: The Experience Curve

The **experience curve** (E-C) has become an extensively researched and analyzed strategic concept since it was originally championed by the Boston Consulting Group in 1972.[6] Day and Montgomery state that few strategic concepts have gained wider acceptance than the notion that value-added costs (excluding inflation) decline systematically with increases in cumulative volume.[7] Lieberman says it has become a central concept in corporate strategic planning.[8] Even Alberts, an acknowledged critic, accepts the basic concept of production volume rising and costs falling concurrently, while rejecting the idea that the former is the primary cause of the latter.[9] Although accepting the premise that costs can decline with an accumulation of volume, Nagle explains why certain circumstances would prevent a pricing strategy based on the experience curve from being profitable.[3] In short, there is an ongoing debate as to whether the experience curve is a valuable strategic tool or a flawed source of misdirection.

THE BASIC E-C CONCEPT

Before considering the opposing schools of thought, we need a more precise definition of the experience curve. The phenomenon was first recognized in the early 1950s by Boeing. They discovered that the number of hours required to build aircraft decreased about 20 percent each time cumulative production doubled. Many other firms that have actively employed the E-C concept (including General Motors, General Electric, IBM, and Texas Instruments) found that not only labor hours decreased but also other volume-related cost factors (for example, scrap materials, defective parts, machine down-time, procurement costs, distribution costs, and even marketing expenses). The Boston Consulting Group found similar results in such diverse industries as chemicals, paper, steel, electronics, knitwear, and mechanical goods.

Hence, it was postulated that variable or volume-dependent costs (in constant dollars) decline by a predictable and constant percentage each time cumulative volume is doubled. This percentage will vary among product categories from 10 to 30 percent, with 15 to 20 percent the most common range. It should be noted that one of the authors, while using the E-C concept to make some very effective and profitable pricing decisions, witnessed a fairly constant decline in variable costs of a semiconductor product line from a cumulative volume of less than 100,000 units to more than a billion. This increase took place over a multiyear period and represented a doubling of cumulative volume *more than thirteen times.* Figure 18-3 depicts the impact of the experience curve on variable costs with three different rates of decline over four doublings of cumulative quantity.

IMPORTANT DISTINCTIONS

Three additional points are significant. First, the experience curve is a *volume-dependent,* not a time-dependent, phenomenon. Thus, as a product line matures and cumulative volume increases, it will take *longer* to double the cumulative volume again unless the production *rate* also increases. This fact has led some observers to erroneously surmise that the rate of cost reduction actually declines. Others profess that the E-C does not apply in mature industries. This is not so; it simply takes longer to achieve the same percent reduction.

Second, cost savings are definitely not limited to the production process. Managerial decision-making, product and process designs, distribution systems, as well as marketing programs and tactics, can all become more cost effective.

Third, the E-C concept should not be confused with **economies of scale.** The former deals with the accumulation of quantity and is independent of the rate of production. In effect, the E-C shows the trend of variable costs over time. Conversely, economies-of-scale show the impact that different levels of production have on unit costs at a specific time.

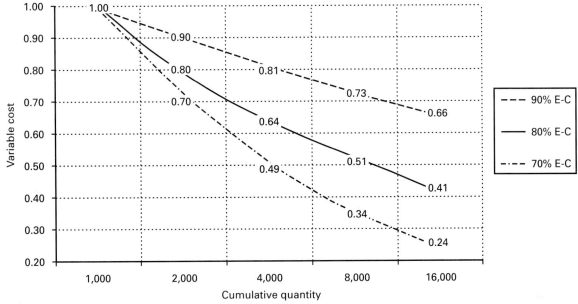

FIGURE 18-3 Impact of experience curve on variable costs at slopes of 90, 80, and 70 percent.

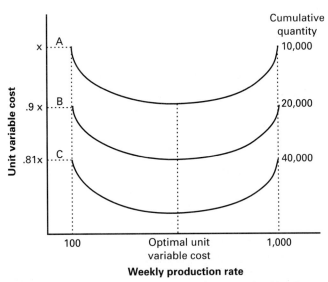

FIGURE 18-4 Experience curve impact on economies of scale.

Figure 18-4 should help clarify this last point. Curves A, B, and C each show a variation of unit costs over a range of production rates (hypothetically, from one hundred to one thousand units per week). Curve A shows the level of these costs after a cumulative output of 10,000 units. Curve B spans the same range of production rates, but shows how the entire curve falls after cumulative output reaches 20,000 units (double the level for curve A). The number of weeks required to reach this cumulative quantity is irrelevant. Curve C repeats the story after 40,000 units, or double the level of curve B. In short, the *shape* of the curve shows the economies of scale, whereas the *distance* between the curves shows the impact of experience.

STRATEGIC USE OF THE EXPERIENCE CURVE

The experience curve frequently plays a major role in a market penetration strategy. A company, aiming for a dominant position in a new product-market, adopts an aggressive pricing policy. Theoretically, this price will speed up market growth as well as discourage some potential competitors from entering the market. However, it is false to assume that all firms using the E-C concept as a strategic tool do so in the form of predatory pricing.

If a firm feels confident that the target market will grow at a satisfactory rate and its position in this market will be strong without aggressive pricing, the E-C cost reductions can be used for other desirable purposes:

1. To recover sunk costs more quickly
2. To enhance marketing efforts in the target market
3. To develop new market opportunities
4. To increase R&D expenditures
5. To raise needed working capital
6. To expand production capacity

It is also important to remember that an effective pricing strategy, as discussed earlier in this chapter, must be based on external factors in addition to costs. The ratio of demand to supply, the number and strength of competitors, the relative impact of pricing on derived demand, and the ability of the product to satisfy market needs must all be part of the pricing decision. Firms that myopically base their pricing solely on costs plus some magic multiplier rarely survive in today's competitive international markets.

THE CURRENT DEBATE

Part of the controversy regarding the usefulness and reality of the experience curve stems from the problems researchers face in trying to develop empirical evidence, either pro or con:

1. Researchers have difficulty getting specific volume-cost data from business firms, who zealously guard such proprietary information. Hence, most research depends on overall industry pricing, computer-simulated cost data, or limited samples from individual firms.
2. Industry-wide information has limited value for several reasons. First, published small-quantity prices bear little relationship to the prices quoted on large contracts. Second, competing firms use a variety of pricing strategies with different time horizons and profit margins.
3. So-called average prices usually involve a relatively heterogeneous mix of products. If the higher-end products begin to command a greater volume than the less expensive counterparts, the overall mix price will increase regardless of cost trends. For example, independent of inflation, the average price of automobiles has increased as car makers strive to sell more upscale models with their coincident higher profit margins. At the same time, costs have been reduced substantially.
4. As outlined in the preceding section, businesses can use cost savings for various purposes other than price reduction. Thus, there is no "automatic" relationship between costs and current pricing. This last point alone makes the analysis of individual firms, without their explicit cooperation, very questionable.

Barring specific product-firm volume and cost data, one is left with the apparent consistency of price-volume trends across a variety of American industries. During the 1980s, Japanese manufacturers provided clear evidence that they, too, recognize and use the E-C concept. When asked about the apparent "dumping" of memory chips by

Japanese producers, Paul Ely, president of Convergent Technologies, said, "We don't have any right to complain about the Japanese companies using tactics [such as experience-curve pricing] that we invented." Unfortunately for American producers, the Japanese can use these tactics even more effectively because they run their manufacturing operations more efficiently. This leads us to a significant factor associated with the E-C concept.

OPPORTUNITIES MUST BE CAPITALIZED

In rebutting what he terms the "experience curve doctrine," Alberts makes several incisive and accurate observations:

1. *Innovations* (involving the operator, management, and processes) are a significant source of cost reductions
2. Most innovations do not "just pop up" as the result of volume increases, but must be *recognized and exploited* by a perceptive management
3. The degree to which opportunities for innovation are recognized and exploited within the firm depends on *volition* (the desire to innovate), *imaginativeness* (or creative intelligence), and *drive* (the ability to pursue goals effectively)[9]

Whether these observations actually rebut the E-C concept or simply add a very important qualification is less important than the caveat they present to managers. As a reasonable paraphrase, one can say that experience makes it easier to spot opportunities, but the firm and its managers must want to seize the opportunity. As discussed in Chapter 10, the Japanese provide an excellent example of this issue. In countless instances, they have taken products that were invented elsewhere and, by innovating the product, the process, or the marketing strategy, have gained market dominance. The originating firm had equal, if not greater, opportunity to innovate but failed to do so. While we debate strategic concepts, international competitors capitalize on them.

Price was identified in Chapter 11 as one of the critical design criteria for any new product. A firm must determine what customers want in terms of product performance, as well as the price they are willing to pay, before it begins the physical development phase of the new product development process. A target resale price then establishes the upper limit for costs, rather than allowing uncontrolled costs to dictate a resale price well beyond the market's willingness to pay.

Many products that fail because of uncompetitive pricing do not reflect inferior engineering design or inefficient production techniques. Instead, either marketers do not specify price-performance relationships, or other managers ignore this vital input. As a consequence, the value perceptions of customers are essentially omitted from the design equation. High-technology firms that place undue emphasis on a product's physical attributes are particularly prone to make this fatal mistake.

GOVERNMENT INFLUENCE ON PRICE

Government influences pricing strategy primarily through legislation. Sections 1 and 2 of the Sherman Antitrust Act specifically forbid agreements among suppliers to fix industry prices. The Clayton Antitrust Act (Section 2) and the Robinson-Patman Act also prohibit price discrimination among similar buyers of identical products. Sections 2(a) through 2(f) of the Robinson-Patman Act specifically relate to price differences and price concessions being offered to competing manufacturers and distributors.

Pricing to drive out competition, geographic and general price discrimination are also prohibited by the Bonah-Van Nuys Amendment, Section 3, of the Robinson-Patman Act.

Price setters in the business market face more constraints than their counterparts in the consumer market. For example, an auto dealership might sell four identical models on a given day to different buyers at various prices. Regulators would view these transactions as the result of a free market and varying degrees of negotiation. However, the four consumers *do not compete* with each other. Therefore, the Robinson-Patman edict that says all customers who buy "like goods and quantity" must receive the same price does not apply to most transactions in the consumer market.

On the other hand, if this same dealership were to sell like vehicles to four competing wholesalers for use by their sales people, Robinson-Patman would apply, and all four wholesalers would have to receive the same price to prevent a claim of price discrimination.

Pricing Strategies

Marketers must develop pricing strategies that support overall business objectives and marketing strategy. The success of any business depends on a blend of long-run profit, growth, and survival objectives. Price, because of its impact on unit sales volume and profit margins, affects long-run profits. By contributing to a positive cash flow, price helps to finance growth. And maintaining profitability through sound pricing practices is necessary to ensure the firm's survival over time. It should be recognized, however, that a diversified firm with multiple product lines can have several pricing strategies in operation at one time. They should be consistent with one another as well as with overall marketing strategy.

NEW PRODUCT INTRODUCTION

The new product development process represents a substantial investment that the firm must eventually recover. How quickly a firm should try to recover this investment depends on the nature of the product and its projected life span, the strength of potential competition, the type of demand, and the financial strength of the company. Generally, two broad strategies are available: (1) market skimming—setting an artificially high price that will not be sustained in the long run—and (2) market penetration—setting price at or near the level it would eventually reach after competition developed.[10]

Market Skimming Strategy   This strategic approach, charging an artificially high price and then gradually reducing it over time, has the advantage of generating greater profits per unit earlier than would be possible with a lower price. If development and marketing costs can be recovered before competitors enter, surplus earnings can be used for product improvement and expansion into additional markets, thus increasing volume and reducing the average cost of production. Unless late-arriving competitors achieve a genuine breakthrough in product design or processing, they will be at a cost disadvantage relative to the innovative firm.

The greatest disadvantage to market skimming is that the high margins attract competition. A price skimming firm with a successful product can expect competitors to introduce similar products. Therefore, skimming is more effective when strong patent protection, complex technology, high capital requirements or other barriers to market entry exist. Other conditions that favor price skimming are listed in Table 18-6.

Market Penetration Strategy   Penetration pricing is particularly effective when demand for the product is highly elastic. By setting a relatively low price, the firm hopes to stimulate market growth and capture a major share. Penetration pricing also

TABLE 18-6   Conditions Favorable to Market Skimming

1. Product has a strong patent protection or other barriers to entry exist.
2. Product innovation is likely to represent substantial value to potential users.
3. Buyers will pay a premium to receive product's benefits.
4. Costs must be recovered over a short expected life span.
5. Potential competitors are relatively weak or distant in time.
6. Price sensitivity is uncertain. Price can be cut later, but raising it may be difficult.

TABLE 18-7   Conditions Favoring Market Penetration

1. Market appears to be very price sensitive.
2. An opportunity exists to enjoy economies of scale.
3. Potential competitors are strong and may enter the market quickly.
4. Firm's primary goal is market share instead of optimal short-term profits.
5. Product has subtle benefits that will not be obvious until it is used.
6. The sale of complementary products will also increase.

tends to discourage competition, who perceive a lesser opportunity to reap profits. Penetration pricing may also generate economies of scale. By seeking a dominant market share, a firm will move down the experience curve more quickly, achieving greater cost advantage over competitors as well as higher long-term profits.

Penetration pricing has two primary disadvantages. First, the firm must sell a larger volume before recovering start-up costs. Thus, short-run profits are sacrificed in favor of market share and long-run profits. Second, although total profits may be higher than those achieved with a skimming strategy, the profit ratio (i.e., the return on assets or investment, or profit as a percent of sales) is usually lower. Firms that use these ratios to gauge their success usually avoid a penetration strategy. Conditions favorable to penetration pricing are outlined in Table 18-7.

Introductory Pricing Variations   Skimming and penetration pricing strategies are only guides that cannot be applied in all situations. Certain instances may require that price be set at some intermediate level. The choice of an appropriate pricing strategy for new products depends on the firm's objectives, the relevant customer segments, the anticipated reactions of present and future competition, cost considerations, and appropriate distribution strategies.

In Chapter 3, we looked at the variance of introductory pricing strategies with product category-components, capital equipment, business services, and so on. Marketers can also devise pricing strategies to create value perceptions in the mind of potential buyers. A matrix of nine strategies is shown in Figure 18-5. Each of these strategies positions a product so that the target market will perceive a specific price-quality relationship.[11]

These strategies are not mutually exclusive. For example, Sears Roebuck used a "good, better, best" approach in their catalog for years. In effect, they employed strategies 1, 5, and 9 simultaneously by showing the same generic product in three different quality levels, each priced accordingly. This approach helped to create an aspect of "fairness" and to reduce price sensitivity.

Price

	High	Medium	Low
High	1. Premium strategy	2. High-value strategy	3. Super-value strategy
Medium	4. Overcharging strategy	5. Medium-value strategy	6. Good-value strategy
Low	7. Rip-off strategy	8. False economy strategy	9. Economy strategy

(vertical axis label: Product quality)

Source: Philip Kotler, *Marketing Management: Analysis, Planning, Implementation, and Control,* 9th ed. (Upper Saddle River, N.J.: Prentice Hall, 1997), p. 496. Reprinted by permission.

FIGURE 18-5 Price-quality positioning strategies.

Strategies 2, 3, and 6 combat the diagonal strategies. Wal-Mart has used this approach to proclaim that they offer greater value than Sears by selling comparable products at a lower price. Strategies 4, 7, and 8 are examples of overpricing that will probably create negative customer perceptions under most market conditions.[11]

PRODUCT LIFE-CYCLE CONSIDERATIONS

During the course of a product's life cycle, the competitive situation and market demand level will vary greatly. The product itself, along with promotion and distribution, must also change. Likewise, for price to remain an effective marketing tool, a marketer must constantly monitor and adjust it appropriately.[3]

Growth During the product growth stage, when more customers adopt the product and competitors offer substitutes, price has greater impact on the purchasing decision. However, in an expanding market, suppliers tend to emphasize nonprice factors as their primary selling points rather than cutting price severely. The exceptions are those firms that set price on the experience curve to achieve a dominant market share. During this stage, business buyers look for multiple sources of supply as a hedge against the potential dominance of a single supplier. In general, these conflicting supply and demand factors result in price falling below the introductory level.

Maturity By the time a product enters the maturity stage, the level of competition has peaked, and product differentiation has decreased. Consequently, even though buyers still prioritize product quality and service dependability, price weighs heavily on their buying decisions. Since a supplier can increase volume in a flat market only by cutting into the market share of competitors, price wars become commonplace.

Decline Many suppliers leave a market before its decline, particularly those who emphasize growth strategies. The decline stage can thus be a fairly profitable one for the remaining suppliers. If a firm has developed a positive image by providing quality products, competitive prices, and dependable service, profits need not erode completely in the decline stage. Business firms, both sellers and buyers, recognize the relationship between production volumes and incurred costs. Within reason, a respected supplier can increase prices during the decline stage and maintain an acceptable profit level, as long as some segments of the market still need the product and adjust their value perceptions to match the higher selling price.

FLEXIBLE PRICING STRATEGY

Most large firms maintain a rather rigid pricing structure. They establish their pricing structure by adding a traditional markup to costs, by following the industrial leader, or by aiming for some predetermined return on investment.[12] However, since the early 1970s, American firms have faced a pricing environment that included several recessionary periods, price controls introduced by the federal government, double-digit inflation, stagnant demand, and intense competition from abroad.

The need to adapt to such a dynamic environment has brought about flexibility in pricing and a willingness to cut prices aggressively to hold market share. Smaller firms do not consistently play "follow the price leader." IBM maintained price leadership in the mainframe and minicomputer markets for years. However, in the 1980s, companies like Dell Computer and Packard Bell seized price leadership in the PC market, whereas DEC challenged IBM pricing in the minicomputer market. Flexible pricing strategy—the willingness to adjust prices or profit margins when market conditions change—has become common in business marketing. However, price flexibility does not always mean a reduction in list prices. Escalator clauses to protect against inflation, quantity discounts to entice major users, and emphasis on nonprice factors can each contribute to strategic flexibility.

Pricing Policies

Because business customers buy products in different quantities and are located in different geographical regions, pricing policies normally include list price adjustments to account for these differences. Organizational buyers focus on their net price. *Net price* means the list price less allowances made for various cost-saving or cost-transfer factors, such as volume purchases by the buyer, prompt payment of invoices, or distributor sales efforts on behalf of a manufacturer. *List price* is the published figure distributed to all customers, regardless of their type or classification. Manufacturers use list pricing for two primary reasons. First, the wide variety of products contained in a typical catalog preclude the printing of a new catalog each time the price of one or more items is adjusted. Second, list pricing provides a common base from which a variety of discounts can be subtracted.

DISCOUNT PRICING

Discount pricing involves a deduction from the list price to (1) account for the cost and benefits of dealing with different classifications of customers, (2) encourage customers to buy in large volumes, and (3) encourage rapid payment by customers.[11]

Trade Discounts   Trade discounts are used by manufacturers to account for the benefits derived from the services provided by certain customer groups. The difference between a distributor's "buy price" and the resale price, for example, should cover the costs incurred in providing a sales effort and associated services (local inventory, customer credit, and technical support) plus allow for a reasonable profit margin. Discounts to OEMs are justified on the basis of their high-volume purchasing and lower marketing expense/sales ratio. Care must be taken in establishing trade discounts. A variance in discounts offered within the same customer group can amount to price discrimination, a violation of the Robinson-Patman Act. In addition, discounts that cannot be justified by a cost savings are usually viewed as either predatory or discriminatory. Trade discounts, therefore, must be nondiscriminatory and cost-justified as an economic trade-off for the benefits they induce.

Quantity Discounts   To encourage volume purchasing and maintain buyer loyalty, quantity discounts are given for the volume of goods purchased either on individual orders or a series of orders over a longer period of time, usually one year. These discounts are termed *noncumulative* and *cumulative,* respectively. Cumulative discounts have the effect of "locking in" a customer's purchases for an extended period, thus reducing both marketing expense and competitive pressure, while providing a smoother, more cost-effective production flow. Noncumulative discounts tend to encourage larger individual orders, which reduce costs of storage, order processing, and delivery for the seller.

So long as quantity discounts are available to all customers and are cost-justified, they do not constitute a violation of the Robinson-Patman Act. However, if the discount granted is not offset by an equal or greater cost savings, both buyer and seller can be charged with violation of the act.

Cash Discounts   To encourage rapid payment and allow for a better cash flow, cash discounts are typically granted in the business market. A discount of "2/10, net thirty" means the customer may deduct 2 percent if payment is made within 10 days of the invoice date; otherwise, the gross bill is due and payable within 30 days. Cash discounts, however, can present a problem for the marketer when large buyers pay their bills well beyond the 10-day period, but still deduct the cash discount. This practice is especially prevalent during periods of high interest rates. The customer essentially "borrows" the supplier's money at a below-market interest rate. Whether a supplier can correct this problem depends on the power of the firm in the buyer-seller relationship. The Robinson-Patman Act compounds the problem by stipulating that the same terms must be offered to all buyers, large and small.

GEOGRAPHICAL PRICING

Geographic factors can have a significant impact on pricing decisions. For example, cross-country shipping cost may constitute a large portion of the invoice price. If the seller absorbs this cost, profits are reduced. If the cost is passed on to the buyer, the seller's composite price may not compete with local suppliers. Thus, a decision must be made on how these costs will factor into the price structure.

A supplier has three options in handling shipping costs as shown in Table 18-8. When the seller concentrates on local markets or sells products where shipping charges are minimal compared with product value (precious metals and microprocessors), these costs are a minor issue. However, unlike consumers buying at various local retailers, business buyers often utilize multiple suppliers located at varying distances from the delivery point. Moreover, many products (basic metals, unsophisticated capital equipment, and shelving) have a high weight-to-value ratio so that shipping charges represent a significant part of the combined product-transportation cost.

The seller must weigh the advantage of passing costs on to the customer against the need to be competitive in distant markets. If a significant product differentiation exists, the seller may gamble that buyers will ignore a difference in shipping charges. Without such differentiation, this strategy will probably fail.

TABLE 18-8 Alternative Means of Handling Shipping Costs	
F.O.B. factory	Buyer selects mode of transportation and pays all costs. Seller's invoice price is the same to all customers, regardless of location. However, more distant customers pay a higher total product cost.
F.O.B. destination or uniform-delivered pricing	Seller ships via the most economical mode and absorbs all shipping costs. (Buyer can dictate a premium mode but must pay the difference in cost.) The invoice price and total product cost are the same for all customers. This is not a viable strategy when the shipping cost per unit is significant compared to the product price, since the seller's profits are reduced proportionately. Uniform-delivered pricing is legal as long as all customers are charged the same product price for like goods and quantity.
Freight-absorption	Seller absorbs part of the shipping cost to distant customers depending on the competitive environment in that area. Seller evaluates the strategy of major competitors in specific markets, including their method of handling shipping costs, and acts competitively. The seller stays within the bounds of Robinson-Patman legal limits by remembering the phrase "OK to meet—but not beat—competition."

PRICING FOR PROFITS

Although some firms might operate differently, most business organizations seek to maximize long-term profits[13]:

> Profit maximization has many dimensions, and one of the most important of these is time. The firm must decide when to realize profits. Maximizing current-period profits is seldom the same as maximizing the present discounted value of a stream of profits over time. If a firm discounts future profits at a very high rate, then the firm's managers will choose to wring the highest possible profits out of the market in the current period, perhaps by a policy that emphasizes high product prices in price-inelastic markets. Such a policy will induce entry by competitors and will reduce profits in future time periods. Alternatively, a longer time horizon and lower discount rate will often lead to a policy of greater market penetration and lower prices. This strategy will not maximize current-period profits, but can increase the size of the future profit stream and discourage potential competitors. Which strategy the firm chooses will depend on management's beliefs regarding the magnitude and regularity of future profits as well as on the firm's rate of discount.

Koch's observations reemphasize the point that neither market-skimming nor market-penetration pricing is suitable for all times and circumstances. Market skimming reduces risk when the lifetime of a product is unpredictable or of estimated short duration compared with the projected payback period. However, this risk is offset by the likelihood of more intensive competition and slower market growth. Market penetration usually reduces competitive intensity but at the cost of reduced near-term profits.

As a result of these uncertainties and tradeoffs, it is not surprising that many pricing decisions stem from present circumstances, either a competitive threat or a unique and irresistible sales opportunity. Long-term consequences receive less consideration. Until American business managers and investors apply greater patience to the achievement of strategic goals, short-term perspectives will probably remain in vogue.

Looking Back

Setting a pricing strategy is arguably the most difficult task that a marketer faces. First, price must blend with the other elements—product, promotion, and distribution—so that the entire marketing mix presents a clear and desirable package to the target market. Second, the factors that have the greatest impact on the pricing decision—costs, competition, and customers-often suggest conflicting strategies. Third, a strategy that favors short-term success, either in terms of profitability or market share, may cause long-term failure, and vice versa.

Historically, most business firms used costs to drive price and concentrated on short-term results. They ignored the fact that costs vary with market demand, which also varies with price. Neither customer value perceptions nor the offerings of competition received serious consideration.

Modern global marketers recognize that pricing strategy must begin with the external factors of demand and competition. Only when customer needs and their alternative choices are understood can the firm realistically evaluate the internal costs of competing for that business. Thus, market-oriented companies do not ignore costs and profits in setting price, but they allow a target price to drive costs rather than the reverse. This holds true not only when establishing an introductory price but also throughout the life of the product.

The experience curve, debated by many and misunderstood by even more, plays a central role in the pricing strategies of a growing number of firms here and abroad. In essence, this concept holds that volume-dependent costs will steadily decline with the accumulation of output. Without question, organizations must recognize and capitalize on cost-saving opportunities if they want to take full advantage of their experience.

Factors to consider when revising pricing structures over time and for different customer classifications were also discussed.

Questions for Discussion

1. Of all the factors that influence pricing strategy, which ones do you consider the most important? How would they impact your price decisions?

2. What factors or situations make it difficult for competitors to react to a price change?

3. The proper identification of costs is the first step toward making a profitable pricing decision. Do you agree or disagree with that statement? Why?

4. How might a firm use the experience curve in setting price? How else might E-C cost reductions be applied other than price cutting?

5. Discuss the various ways a manufacturer's pricing strategy can impact an industrial distributor.

6. In introducing a new product, price may be set high or low. Under what circumstances should price be set high? When should it be set low?

7. Price should only be changed as a reactionary measure. Do you agree with that statement? If so, why? If not, how would you initiate a proactive pricing strategy?

8. What factors make it difficult to determine cost?

Endnotes

1. E. Raymond Corey, *Industrial Marketing: Cases and Concepts,* 3rd ed. (Englewood Cliffs, N.J.: Prentice-Hall, Inc., 1983).

2. Peter R. Dickson, *Marketing Management* (Fort Worth: The Dryden Press, 1994), p. 470.

3. Thomas T. Nagle and Reed K. Holden, *The Strategy and Tactics of Pricing,* 2nd ed., (Englewood Cliffs, NJ: Prentice-Hall, Inc., 1995).

4. Seymour E. Heymann, "Consider other factors and cost when pricing industrial products," *Marketing News* (April 4, 1980), p. 11.

5. Benson P. Shapiro and Barbara B. Jackson, "Industrial pricing to meet customer needs," *Harvard Business Review* 56 (November-December 1978):119-27.

6. Boston Consulting Group, *Perspectives on Experience,* (Boston: Boston Consulting Group, Inc., 1972).

7. George S. Day and David B. Montgomery, "Diagnosing the experience curve," *Journal of Marketing* 47 (Spring 1983):44-58.

8. Marvin B. Lieberman, "The learning curve, diffusion, and competitive strategy," *Strategic Management Journal* 8 (September 1987):441-52.

9. William W. Alberts, "The experience curve doctrine reconsidered," *Journal of Marketing* 53 (July 1989):36-49.

10. Joel Dean, "Pricing policies for new products," *Harvard Business Review* 58 (November 1980):45-53. See also: David V. Lamm and Lawrence C. Vose, "Seller pricing strategies: A buyer's perspective," *Journal of Purchasing and Materials Management* 24 (Fall 1988):9-13.

11. Philip Kotler, Marketing Management: *Analysis, Planning, Implementation, and Control,* 8th ed., (Englewood Cliffs, N.J.: Prentice-Hall, Inc., 1994), pp. 489-90.

12. E. Jerome McCarthy and William D. Perreault, Jr., *Basic Marketing: A Global Managerial Approach,* 11th ed., (Homewood, Ill.: Richard D. Irwin, Inc., 1993), p. 506.

13. James V. Koch, Industrial Organization and Pricing (Englewood Cliffs, N.J.: Prentice-Hall, Inc., 1974), Chap. 3.

Bibliography

Alberts, William W., "The experience curve doctrine reconsidered," *Journal of Marketing* 53 (July 1989):36-49.

Day, George S., and David B. Montgomery, "Diagnosing the experience curve," *Journal of Marketing* 47 (Spring 1983):44-58.

Lamm, David V., and Lawrence C. Vose, "Seller pricing strategies: A buyer's perspective," *Journal of Purchasing and Materials Management* 24 (Fall 1988):9-13.

Lieberman, Marvin, B., "The learning curve, diffusion, and competitive strategy," *Strategic Management Journal* 8 (September 1987):441-52.

Nagle, Thomas T. and Reed K. Holden, *The Strategy and Tactics of Pricing,* 2nd ed., (Englewood Cliffs, NJ: Prentice-Hall, Inc., 1995), particularly Chapters 4 and 11.

19 Pricing Decision Analysis

The business marketer cannot make intelligent price decisions without analyzing costs in relation to projected sales volume and long-term profit goals. Also, the marketer must study the needs and buying power of the customer, as well as the strengths and weaknesses of competition, and develop an effective negotiating or bidding strategy. In some situations, a leasing program might be more appropriate than an outright sale. After reading this chapter, you should understand:

1. The use of break-even analysis and experience curves to determine the effect of price on volume, cost, and profit
2. The importance and application of return-on-investment pricing
3. The use of expected payoff analysis when initiating or responding to price changes
4. The development of strategic models for competitive bidding
5. The factors that determine a firm's negotiating position
6. The role of leasing in pricing strategy

Pricing decisions should balance the impact on short-term profits against the impact on market share, long-term volume, and subsequent cost reductions. Business marketers should analyze these impacts at several crucial decision points: (1) during the development of a new product, (2) when initiating a price change, and (3) when responding to a competitor's action. Profitability analysis, frequently referred to as break-even analysis, is an important first step.

Break-Even (or Profitability) Analysis

An appropriate pricing strategy should generate satisfactory profits at various combinations of unit volume and selling price. A financial tool commonly used to determine the level of sales required to cover all relevant fixed and variable costs is break-even or profitability analysis. This process also indicates the impact of different pricing schedules on profit margins and identifies the minimum price below which losses will occur.

Obviously, to employ break-even analysis, the marketer must know the fixed and variable costs of producing and marketing a product. As discussed in Chapter 18, these costs are not always easily determined. Although fixed costs generally remain constant as volume increases, this is true only so long as output can be expanded without associated increases in administrative personnel, plant size, depreciation, debt-service costs, and other fixed costs. Also, the distinction between fixed and variable costs is not always clear. To compound the problem, the economies-of-scale curve shows that variable costs do not change linearly with production volume.

Break-even calculations are often heavily weighted by historical data, but such data does not always reflect current realities. Projected rather than historical costs should provide the foundation of the pricing decision process, and the business marketer should expend the effort necessary to forecast future costs by drawing on experience curve patterns. Marketers must also constantly monitor the level of market demand and the pricing strategies of competition. Even though these are uncontrollable variables, they can have a significant impact on the firm's break-even point and pricing flexibility.

Break-Even Quantity and Contribution Margin

A firm's *profitability* can be expressed by the equation

$$Y = PX - VX - F$$

where

$$F = \text{total fixed costs}$$
$$P = \text{price per unit}$$
$$V = \text{variable cost per unit}$$
$$X = \text{number of units produced/sold}$$
$$Y = \text{profit}$$

By calculation, the *break-even point* occurs where total revenues equal total costs, or

$$PX = VX + F$$

By solving for X, we find the break-even point,

$$X = \frac{F}{P - V}$$

Note that the expression P – V is the *contribution margin,* that is, the amount (if any) by which the selling price of a unit exceeds its variable cost and contributes toward fixed costs. Therefore, at the break-even point, the contribution margin multiplied by the unit volume equals total fixed costs.

With an estimate of demand at various price levels, the price setter can develop a break-even chart showing total revenue, costs, and profits across a range of production volumes. Table 19-1 exhibits such a chart, and Figure 19-1 shows the information graphically.

In the TMI example used in Chapter 18 (see Tables 18-4 and 18-5), the company's fixed costs equaled $180,000, and unit variable costs (UVC) remained constant at $.94 per unit. More realistically, UVC will change with volume, so that all three unit finan-

TABLE 19-1 TMI Break-Even Analysis (in thousands)

Unit Price	Market Demand	Revenue	Unit Variable Cost	Total Variable Cost	Fixed Cost	Total Cost	Profits	
$3.80	60	$228.0	$1.10	$66.0	$180.0	$246.0	$−18.0	
3.50	70	245.0	1.05	73.5	180.0	253.5	−8.5	
3.25	80	260.0	1.00	80.0	180.0	260.0	0	*Mimimum B/E quantity*
3.05	90	274.5	.97	87.3	180.0	267.3	7.2	
2.85	100	285.0	.94	94.0	180.0	274.0	11.0	
2.65	110	291.5	.90	99.0	180.0	279.0	12.5	
2.58	115	296.7	.90	103.5	180.0	283.5	13.2	*Optimum quantity*
2.50	120	300.0	.90	108.0	180.0	288.0	12.0	
2.40	130	312.0	.94	122.2	180.0	302.2	9.8	
2.30	140	322.0	.97	135.8	180.0	315.8	6.2	
2.20	150	330.0	1.00	150.0	180.0	330.0	0	*Maximum B/E quantity*
2.15	160	344.0	1.05	168.0	180.0	348.0	−4.0	
2.10	170	357.0	1.10	187.0	180.0	367.0	−10.0	
2.05	180	369.0	1.15	207.0	180.0	387.0	−18.0	

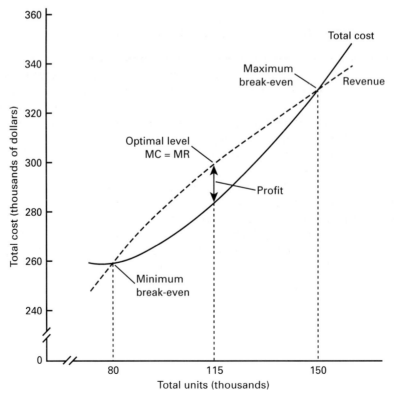

FIGURE 19-1 Break-even and optimal profit analysis graph.

cial quantifiers (fixed cost, variable cost, and price) will be "moving targets" in the analysis to determine optimal price-cost-volume level.

To simplify the analysis, we assume that production volume is equal to market demand. This assumption eliminates the need to compute the number of produced units that would go into inventory awaiting orders, the cost of carrying the inventory, and the associated costs of double-handling these units. The assumption admittedly belies what occurs in the day-to-day world.

In Table 19-1, UVC is $1.10 at 60,000 units; it drops to $0.90 between 110,000 and 120,000 units and increases again above 120,000 units. Note that two break-even points occur. The *minimum* point represents the "critical mass" quantity necessary (at the price the market is willing to pay) to generate revenue dollars equal to total fixed and variable costs. This point occurs at 80,000 units sold at $3.25 each. The *maximum* point occurs where revenue and total costs are again equal—at 150,000 units and a sales price of $2.20.

An analysis of contribution margin verifies the dual break-even points. At 80,000 units, the contribution margin (price-variable cost) is $2.25, which generates $180,000, the exact amount of fixed cost. At 150,000 units, the contribution margin is only $1.20, but multiplied by the larger quantity, this margin again produces $180,000. Thus, we can see that internal and external factors conflict in the establishment of pricing. A price that generates a larger contribution margin also restricts market demand. Lowering the price to increase demand also reduces the contribution margin.

The break-even data indicate an optimal selling price of $2.58. At this price, estimated sales volume is 115,000 units, generating $296,700 revenue at a total cost of $283,500, leaving a profit of $13,200. At any volume above or below this level, profits decline. This leads to the concept of marginality.

MARGINAL COSTS AND REVENUES

In the next increment of market demand—between 115,000 and 120,000—marginal costs exceed marginal revenue. For these 5,000 units, variable cost increases $4,500, or $0.90 per unit, whereas revenue goes up only $3,300, or $0.66 per unit. Profit necessarily declines. The 5,000 units below 115,000 also cost $4,500 but generate $5,200 in revenue. Total profit increases by $700. Therefore, we can state that a firm should strive to increase volume as long as marginal revenue exceeds marginal costs, in other words, as long as *total profit increases*. Thus, the total profit column in Table 19-1 contains the most relevant analytical data.

Where the marketer eventually sets price depends on the marketing objectives of the firm. If TMI wants market penetration, it can set a price as low as $2.20, still cover current costs, but capture a larger portion of the market than it would at $2.58. This result shows the primary significance of **penetration pricing**. On the other hand, if the firm wants to maximize short-term profits, it should employ a **market skimming price**. Hence, assuming market response to price (i.e., demand elasticity) has been correctly analyzed, a price of $2.58 would be the optimal choice.

Return-on-Investment Pricing

A widely used method of setting price in the business market is return-on-investment pricing (sometimes referred to as target return or capital asset pricing). To understand return-on-investment pricing, it is helpful to examine the concept of return on investment (ROI), which refers to the amount of profit earned on the dollars invested by the firm during a finite time period, usually one year. It is expressed as

$$\frac{Profit}{Investment} = Return\ on\ investment$$

We can derive this same equation by combining the equations for profit margin and investment turnover, which are

$$\frac{Profit}{Sales} = Profit\ margin$$

and

$$\frac{Sales}{Investment} = Investment\ turnover$$

When these two equations are combined, we get

$$Profit\ margin \times Investment\ turnover = Return\ on\ investment$$

In the TMI example, capital investment totals $180,000. If the firm chooses to charge $2.58 on an expected demand of 115,000 units, expected profit will be $13,200. With these figures, the firm's return on investment can be determined by using equation 19-1:

$$Return\ on\ investment = \frac{\$13,200}{\$180,000} = 7.3\% \tag{19-1}$$

or by developing equations 19-2 and 19-3, and then combining them into equation 19-4:

$$Profit\ margin = \frac{\$13,200}{\$296,700} = 4.45\% \tag{19-2}$$

$$Investment\ turnover = \frac{\$296,700}{\$180,000} = 1.65 \tag{19-3}$$

so that

$$Return\ on\ investment = 4.45\% \times 1.65 = 7.3\% \tag{19-4}$$

These last three equations illustrate not only that ROI is a direct function of profit and investment level but also that ROI depends on sales volume. Both sales volume and profit hinge on price. Hence, ROI pricing sets a price level that will generate some target return, given the demand curve and costs previously estimated.

Returning to the TMI example, perhaps management decides before the start of production that the molds should generate at least a 12 percent ROI. Given the investment of $180,000, this means an annual profit goal of at least $21,600. Table 19-1 shows that no sales volume between the two break-even points will generate this much profit.

The TMI marketing manager now has an option of being conservative and recommending a price around $3. This approach would provide the opportunity to double check demand elasticity while keeping production commitments low. The manager can also "go for broke" with a price of $2.40 or less, hoping that market demand will at least equal the forecast. A third option calls for a price of $2.58, which would maximize short-term profits as well as the return on investment—assuming that all the estimates and forecasts are correct.

The type of price determination described above is one of the oldest and most common methods used by industrial organizations operating in oligopolistic markets.[1] Several points provide justification for this widespread usage. First, a large industrial firm typically has multiple profit centers, each with its own ROI goal, which depends on the relative degree of risk involved in its particular business. Investments involving greater risk must project a higher rate of return to obtain approval. The projected ROI will later serve as a yardstick for gauging success over the life of the business. In turn, the projected ROI directly affects the price of the products to be marketed, thus adding internal consistency to pricing strategies.[1]

The computations for ROI pricing, however, involve sales volume and customer price sensitivity in addition to profits and total investment. Thus, the market-oriented decision maker resists judgments based solely on internal financial criteria, but rather, adds in customer value perceptions and competitive offerings. Attempts to improve profits by raising prices or cutting costs, while ignoring market demand, usually prove counterproductive.[2]

Finally, ROI pricing suits industrial firms particularly well, since it is based on standard costs and volumes estimated for longer time periods. Over a year, actual costs may fluctuate considerably; but by using estimated cost as a standard, firms are able to hold prices relatively constant. Such stability is conducive to oligopolistic markets where firms customarily want to avoid price competition. It is also conducive to the long-term buyer and seller interface that characteristically exists in the industrial market.

Experience Curve Impact on Price Analysis

The basic elements of the experience curve concept were described in Chapter 18. Restated simply, for products manufactured and sold on a continuous basis, unit variable costs decline as cumulative quantity increases. These costs will logically decline more rapidly if the rate of production is greater. It should be reemphasized that fixed costs normally do not decline, only those costs that are volume dependent or variable.

As stated earlier, experience curves with slopes of 85 percent are quite common. This means that variable costs will decline 15 percent each time cumulative volume doubles. Table 19-2 illustrates this decline, using slopes of a conservative 90 percent and a more optimistic 80 percent.

For example, Table 19-2 assumes that the 94 cent unit variable cost shown for an annual production rate of 100,000 molds resulted from the "experience" gained during the production of the first 100,000 units. It also shows the UVCs for several production

TABLE 19-2   Change in Unit Variable Cost vs. Annual Production Rate (80% and 90% experience curves)

					Production Rate					
	80K		100K		115K		130K		150K	
					E-C Slope (%)					
Cumulative Quantity (000)	90	80	90	80	90	80	90	80	90	80
100	1.00	1.00	.94	.94	.90	.90	.94	.94	1.00	1.00
200	.90	.80	.845	.75	.81	.72	.845	.75	.90	.80
400	.81	.64	.76	.60	.73	.575	.76	.60	.81	.64
800	.73	.51	.685	.48	.655	.46	.685	.48	.73	.51
1600	.655	.41	.615	.385	.59	.37	.615	.385	.655	.41

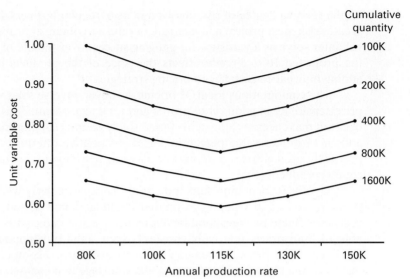

FIGURE 19-2 Graph of unit variable cost versus annual production rate at 90 percent experience curve.

rates after the cumulative production of 200,000, 400,000, 800,000, and 1,600,000 units with experience curves of 90 and 80 percent.

Note first that costs decline at a *constant percentage.* Therefore, the absolute decline is steadily *decreasing* (the result of a constant percentage being applied to an ever-smaller number). Second, keep in mind the difference between the experience curve and economies of scale as discussed in Chapter 18. Economies of scale refer to the relative production efficiency at different quantity levels at any point in time. The experience curve shifts the EOS curve *downward* with the accumulation of quantity. This relationship is shown graphically in Figure 19-2 for a 90 percent slope only.

Finally, note here that the *entire* EOS curve shifts downward. In short, "experience" helps the firm in three ways:

1. For any given price, profits are increased.

2. The minimum break-even quantity is reduced, giving the firm greater protection against major market erosions.

3. The maximum break-even quantity is increased, allowing the firm to capitalize on major market expansions.

This leads us to reconsider TMI's pricing options and the importance of market share. Our previous break-even analysis showed that TMI would maximize short-term profits by establishing a $2.58 selling price and producing at an annual rate of 115,000 units. This analysis ignores time-related factors. For example, if TMI reduces its price to $2.20, and annual volume increases to 150,000 units, the firm would only break even by current cost standards. But in two years, the cumulative output would equal 400,000, and the UVC unit variable cost would drop from $1.00 to $.81 even with a conservative 90 percent experience curve. Table 19-3 shows that at 400,000 unit accumulation, profits from 150,000 annual production would rise to $28,500 per year, more than double the firm's current optimal profits at the 115,000 unit run rate. Return on investment will also rise to 15.8 percent, exceeding management's target.

TABLE 19-3 Impact of the Experience Curve on Profit (90% slope)

Cumulative Quantity (000)	Market Demand (000)	Unit Price	Total Revenue (000)	Variable Cost per Unit	Total Variable Cost (000)	Fixed Cost (000)	Total Cost (000)	Profit (000)	Break-even Price
100	80	$3.25	$260.0	$1.00	$80.0	$180.0	$260.0	$0.0	$3.25
	100	2.85	285.0	.94	94.0	180.0	274.0	11.0	2.74
	115	2.58	296.7	.90	103.5	180.0	283.5	13.2	2.47
	130	2.40	312.0	.94	122.2	180.0	302.2	9.8	2.32
	150	2.20	330.0	1.00	150.0	180.0	330.0	0.0	2.20
	180	2.05	369.0	1.15	207.0	180.0	387.0	-18.0	2.15
200	80	3.25	260.0	.90	72.0	180.0	252.0	8.0	3.15
	100	2.85	285.0	.845	84.5	180.0	264.5	20.5	2.65
	115	2.58	296.7	.81	93.2	180.0	273.2	23.5	2.38
	130	2.40	312.0	.845	109.9	180.0	289.9	22.1	2.23
	150	2.20	330.0	.90	135.0	180.0	315.0	15.0	2.10
	180	2.05	369.0	1.035	186.3	180.0	366.3	2.7	2.04
400	80	3.25	260.0	.81	64.8	180.0	244.8	15.2	3.06
	100	2.85	285.0	.76	76.0	180.0	256.0	29.0	2.56
	115	2.58	296.7	.73	84.0	180.0	264.0	32.7	2.30
	130	2.40	312.0	.76	98.8	180.0	278.8	33.2	2.14
	150	2.20	330.0	.81	121.5	180.0	301.5	28.5	2.01
	180	2.05	369.0	.93	167.4	180.0	347.4	21.6	1.93
800	80	3.25	260.0	.73	58.4	180.0	238.4	21.6	2.98
	100	2.85	285.0	.685	68.5	180.0	248.5	36.5	2.49
	115	2.58	296.7	.655	75.3	180.0	255.3	41.4	2.22
	130	2.40	312.0	.685	89.1	180.0	269.1	42.9	2.07
	150	2.20	330.0	.73	109.5	180.0	289.5	40.5	1.93
	180	2.05	369.0	.84	151.2	180.0	331.2	37.8	1.84
1600	80	3.25	260.0	.655	52.4	180.0	232.4	27.6	2.91
	100	2.85	285.0	.615	61.5	180.0	241.5	43.5	2.42
	115	2.58	296.7	.59	67.9	180.0	247.9	48.8	2.16
	130	2.40	312.0	.615	80.0	180.0	260.0	52.0	2.00
	150	2.20	330.0	.655	98.2	180.0	278.2	51.8	1.85
	180	2.05	369.0	.755	135.9	180.0	315.9	53.1	1.76

TMI also wants to maintain a leadership position in its market. If it can hold the largest market share, it will obviously move down the experience curve faster than any competitor. Therefore, all other things being equal (technology, production techniques, and efficiency), its variable costs will be lower than those of any competitor.

Competition might decide to "buy into" the market by cutting price. If this should happen, TMI will be in a strong cost position to compete on price. Alternatively, given its leadership position, it can shift emphasis to nonprice factors (product quality, technical assistance, promotion, and delivery dependability) to retain market share. As we have stated repeatedly, a firm will not rise or fall on price alone. The entire marketing mix must be optimized for customer satisfaction. But the faster a firm moves down the experience curve, the more profits it will generate at any given volume and price, and the more discretionary dollars it will have to develop the most effective marketing mix.

An important cautionary note must be added regarding the experience curve. To take full advantage of the cost-saving opportunities, the firm must have a steady production flow uninterrupted by shutdowns, major technology changes, or personnel turnover. Therefore, products manufactured in a "job shop" type of output do not benefit from the maximum effect of experience and learning.

Expected Payoff Analysis

Pricing decisions are not over when a firm sets its original schedule. As discussed in Chapter 18, a number of circumstances can force the firm to reconsider its pricing decisions. Before initiating a price change, however, the reactions of buyers, competitors, distributors, and government must be carefully weighed. Unfortunately, these reactions cannot be accurately predicted. The price setter must somehow integrate expectations and uncertainties into a logical pattern for decision making. Expected payoff analysis lends itself well to decision making under uncertainty, since it requires predictions of the possible outcomes and forces knowledgeable executives to assign subjective probabilities to those outcomes.[3]

INITIATING A PRICE CHANGE

We can return to TMI to see how expected payoff analysis is used in making pricing decisions for established products. Suppose that the molds were introduced at $2.58 and this price induced a demand of 115,000 units. Suppose further that one year later another firm offers a similar product at the same price. The sales manager of TMI estimates that the potential market demand during the next year could reach 200,000 units because of the presence of dual sources plus movement of the product into its growth stage.

To hold market leadership, TMI is considering a price cut. From previous break-even analysis (Tables 19-1 and 19-3), the product manager knows that price can be reduced to $2.20 before the firm will begin to lose money. The product manager narrows the decision set to three options: (1) maintain price at $2.58, (2) reduce price to $2.40, or (3) reduce price to $2.20. Given these options, a team of experienced sales, engineering, and production personnel reach agreement on the probabilities of potential reactions by the competitor to each of these prices. Table 19-4 outlines the three options along with the team's forecast of competitive reactions and the probability of their occurrence. The expected payoffs for the proposed prices are outlined in Table 19-5.

Since the expected payoff for option 2 is $13,940 and only $7,480 for option 3, maintaining the current $2.58 price yields the greatest profit ($23,500) and appears to be the obvious choice. However, TMI must weigh the benefits of short-term profit against growth potential, market share, and long-term profit. They must also consider whether the higher price will attract other competitors into the market.

The use of expected payoff analysis requires assumptions regarding the probable reactions of competition, the effect on market demand, subsequent production output, unit variable costs, and profit. Once the price setter determines the anticipated change in sales volume, revised production costs and profit evolve logically.

The qualitative aspects of price changes are usually more difficult to assess. Will competition view the move as the logical result of lower costs or as the start of a price war? Will lower price actually generate a higher market volume, or will sales be constrained by an unchanged derived demand for the end products? Will the Justice Department view the proactive move of an industry leader as an illegal attempt to restrain competition? These potential outcomes must also be weighed but are not easily quantified.

TABLE 19-4   Decision Options for Proposed Price Change

Option 1: Maintain Price at $2.58
If $2.58 is maintained, sales volume will remain at 115,000 units, unit variable cost (UVC) will stay at 81 cents, and profit will be $23,500.

Option 2: Reduce Price to $2.40
a. A 40% probability that competition will not react; sales should increase to 130,000 units; unit variable cost (UVC) will rise to $0.85.
   Revenue = $312,000; total cost = $290,500; profit = $21,500
b. A 30% probability that competition will match $2.40; sales should increase to 125,000 units; UVC will rise to $0.84.
   Revenue = $300,000; total cost = $285,000; profit = $15,000
c. A 30% probability that competition will undercut to $2.30; sales would stay at 115,000 units; UVC will stay at $0.81.
   Revenue = $276,000; total cost = $273,150; profit = $2,850.

Option 3: Reduce Price to $2.20
a. A 20% probability that competition will not react; sales should increase to 150,000 units; UVC will rise to 90 cents.
   Revenue = $330,000; total cost = $315,000; profit = $15,000.
b. A 30% probability that competition will reduce to only $2.30; sales should increase to 145,000 units; UVC will rise to $0.89.
   Revenue = $319,000; total cost = $309,000; profit = $10,000.
c. A 40% probability that competition will match $2.20; sales should increase to 140,000 units; UVC will rise to $0.87.
   Revenue = $308,000; total cost = $301,800; profit = $6,200.
d. A 10% probability that competition will undercut to $2.10; sales would still increase to 125,000; UVC will rise to $0.84.
   Revenue = $275,000; total cost = $285,000; loss = $10,000.

TABLE 19-5   Expected Payoffs for Price Change Options

Possible Reactions	Sales Volume (000)	Revenue ($ 000)	Revised UVC	Total Cost ($ 000)	Estimated Profit ($ 000)	Probability of Outcome	Expected Payoff
Option 1: Maintain $2.58 Price and Profit of $23,500							
Option 2: Reduce Price to $2.40							
No reaction	130.0	$312.0	$0.85	$290.5	$21.5	.40	$8,600
Match $2.40	125.0	300.0	.84	285.0	15.0	.30	4,500
Cut to $2.30	115.0	276.0	.81	273.2	2.8	.30	840
							$13,940
Option 3: Reduce price to $2.20							
No reaction	150.0	$330.0	$0.90	$315.0	$15.0	.20	$3,000
Go to $2.30	145.0	319.0	.89	309.0	10.0	.30	3,000
Match $2.20	140.0	308.0	.87	301.8	6.2	.40	2,480
Cut to $2.10	125.0	275.0	.84	285.0	−10.0	.10	−1,000
							$7,480

The important aspect of payoff analysis is that it generates a pragmatic, quantitative analysis of alternative choices in the face of uncertainty. Managers can apply the tools of logic and experience rather than "shooting from the hip."

Competitive Bidding

In the business market, buyers purchase a significant volume of goods through competitive bidding rather than from a price list. Government agencies and most public institutions must purchase through the bidding system. Private sector buyers also use competitive bidding to explore price levels when purchasing nonstandardized materials, complex fabricated products, and items made to their specification that do not have an established market price.[4]

Competitive bidding may be either closed or open. Closed bidding starts with a formal invitation to potential suppliers to submit written, sealed bids. At a preestablished time, all bids are opened and reviewed. Open bidding is more informal. Suppliers may make a series of oral or written offers up to a specified date. When products or services of competing suppliers vary substantially, or when specific requirements are hard to define precisely, open bidding is commonly used.

Potential suppliers can expend a great deal of time and money developing bids. The profit derived from an awarded contract will depend on the firm's technical expertise, competitive knowledge, and past bidding experience.[4] Price plays a major role in contract awards, but the low bidder does not always win. Some awards go to the "lowest responsible bidder." This means that the award is based on the bidder's ability to deliver as promised, the purchaser's past experience with the bidder, or an assessment of the bidder's technical, financial, and management capabilities.[5] Successful bidders learn to develop an effective bidding strategy. This strategy consists of two stages—prebid analysis and bid determination.

PREBID ANALYSIS

Prebid analysis requires a precise definition of company objectives, an analytical approach for screening alternative bid opportunities, and a method for assessing the probability of success for a particular bidding strategy.

Company Objectives   The decision to bid or not begins with an assessment of company objectives at the time of a bid invitation. Objectives may focus on profit maximization, gaining market entry, or keeping the plant operating and the labor force intact. Whatever the objectives, they influence the types of business to pursue, when to bid, and the level of pricing to quote. For example, to keep its labor force intact for the short run, a firm may bid at a level close to its variable costs.

Screening Bid Opportunities   Many business firms improve their bidding success by using a carefully designed screening process.[6] This process has three stages: (1) an identification of the decision criteria, (2) a measure of their relative importance, and (3) an evaluation of the bid opportunity.

To assess the value of various bids, the marketing manager must consider factors such as plant capacity, competition, delivery requirements, and profit. Although the nature and number of criteria will vary by firm and by industry, plant capacity is usually a very important factor in deciding whether to respond to a bid invitation.[7] For instance, if a company is at 95 percent capacity, it may not welcome a bid that would require 20 percent more capacity. The firm might bid regardless, but its figures would reflect the costs of the additional production capacity. On the other hand, if production facilities were underutilized by 50 percent, the firm would most likely want the contract at virtually any price above variable cost.

Knowing the number of potential competitors and the probable range of their bids plays a crucial role in effective prebid analysis. However, such information may be quite difficult to obtain, particularly by a firm that is relatively inexperienced in the bidding process. A firm should also consider its degree of experience with this or similar products and the likelihood of follow-up business opportunities.

BID DETERMINATION

Having decided to submit a bid, the marketer must now choose a price that has a high probability of winning the bid and producing a profit. The optimal bid price will hinge on (1) the belief of how competitors will bid, (2) the expected profit from a successful bid, and (3) the probability that the contract will be won. A high bid with a large expected profit has a low probability of being accepted. Conversely, a low bid that provides little or no profit has a high probability of being accepted.

The use of a probability model is the most common approach to price setting in a competitive bidding situation. These models provide the bidder with an objective procedure for evaluating potential profits and the likelihood of success at different price levels by drawing on historical data and competitive assumptions. Such models also force bidders to quantify what otherwise might be only vague intuitive feelings.

In using probabilistic bidding models, the bidder seeks to determine the optimum level of profit (or the contribution margin) if a bid is accepted and the likelihood of its acceptance. An optimum bid offers the highest expected payoff. It would maximize $E(X)$ as expressed in the equation[8]

$$E(X) = P(X)\ Z(X)$$

where

$$X = \text{amount of the bid}$$
$$E(X) = \text{expected payoff from a bid of } X$$
$$P(X) = \text{probability of a bid of } X \text{ being accepted}$$
$$Z(X) = \text{profit from a bid of } X \text{ if accepted}$$

Suppose that company A wants to bid on a contract that will probably go to the lowest bidder. The firm expects three other competitors to bid—companies B, C, and D—and wants to determine the probability of its bid being the lowest. To accomplish this, company A must first gather historic information on the relationship between its estimated direct costs and B, C, and D's bids on similar projects. This information appears in Table 19-6. The firm then analyzes the data to determine the probabilities of its competitors submitting bids at various levels above A's estimated direct costs. Table 19-7 depicts these results.

Since the contract will go to the lowest bidder, if company A's bidder views each potential bid as a percent of A's estimated direct costs, the probability that competitors will submit a bid *higher than* this figure is also the probability that A will be awarded the contract. Accordingly, from Table 19-7 the bidder can determine the probability that a bid will be successful based on the number of times competitors bid higher in

		B's Bid		C's Bid		D's Bid	
Project	A's Direct Cost	Amount	Percent of A's Direct Cost	Amount	Percent of A's Direct Cost	Amount	Percent of A's Direct Cost
1	$59,000	$73,750	125%	$74,930	127%	$70,800	120%
2	28,000	41,160	147	39,200	140	39,760	142
3	30,000	43,200	144	45,000	150	43,800	146
4	36,000	47,520	132	48,240	134	46,080	128
5	21,000	34,440	164	34,020	162	33,180	158
6	15,000	23,250	155	24,000	160	24,300	162
7	20,000	29,800	149	30,400	152	30,000	150
8	30,000	39,900	133	38,100	127	37,500	125
9	42,000	60,900	145	58,800	140	59,640	142
10	22,000	29,700	135	28,600	130	28,160	128
11	70,000	99,400	142	102,200	146	98,000	140
12	32,000	53,760	168	52,480	164	53,120	166
13	8,000	12,080	151	12,160	152	12,000	150
14	47,000	64,860	138	61,100	130	62,980	134
15	10,000	12,000	120	12,200	122	11,500	115
16	50,000	72,500	145	71,500	143	69,000	138
17	25,000	33,750	135	35,000	140	33,000	132
18	40,000	62,800	157	64,000	160	61,600	154
19	65,000	88,400	136	89,700	138	88,400	136
20	15,000	19,800	132	19,500	130	20,100	134

TABLE 19-6 Relationship of B, C, and D's Bids to Company A's Direct Cost

Source: Adapted from Wayne J. Morse, "Probabilistic bidding models: A synthesis," *Business Horizons*, 18 (April 1975):67-76.

the past. (Company A assumes, by the way, that they will be awarded at least part of the contract if a competitor ties their low bid.)

Table 19-7 shows that if A submits a bid of 125 percent of its estimated direct costs, they have a 72.7 percent probability of bidding lower than B, C, or D's bid (.90 × .95 × .85 = .727). If A submits a bid of 115 percent of estimated direct costs, its bid would almost certainly be lower than its competitors. However, a bid of 115 percent contributes little to profit and overhead.

As previously stated, the optimum bid provides the highest expected payoff. Expected payoff is a product of the contribution margin of each bid multiplied by the probability of that bid being accepted. Thus, the optimum bid for company A, assuming a desire to maximize profit, is 125 percent of direct cost:

$$(.855)(20\%) = 17.1\% \text{ payoff for } 120\% \text{ bid}$$
$$(.727)(25\%) = 18.2\% \text{ payoff for } 125\% \text{ bid}$$
$$(.472)(30\%) = 14.2\% \text{ payoff for } 130\% \text{ bid}$$

A bid of 125 percent of estimated direct costs has the highest expected payoff—18.2 percent. As the number of competitors increase, the probability that a given bid will be accepted decreases. However, aside from the unpredictable actions of inexperienced bidders, the mere presence of additional competitors does not necessarily result in a lower optimum bid.

TABLE 19-7   Probability of Underbidding Competitors B, C, and D

Bid as Percent of A's Estimated Direct Project	No. of High Bids			Probability of Underbidding[1]			Probability of Winning[1]	Contribution Margin (%)[2]	Expected Payoff (%)[3]
	B	*C*	*D*	*B*	*C*	*D*			
110	20	20	20	1.00	1.00	1.00	1.000	10	10.0
115	20	20	19	1.00	1.00	.95	.950	15	14.2
120	19	20	18	.95	1.00	.90	.855	20	17.1
125	18	19	17	.90	.95	.85	.727	25	18.2
130	18	14	15	.90	.70	.75	.472	30	14.2
135	13	13	12	.65	.65	.60	.254	35	8.9
140	11	9	9	.55	.45	.45	.111	40	4.5
145	7	8	7	.35	.40	.35	.049	45	2.2
150	5	6	4	.25	.30	.20	.015	50	0.7
155	3	4	3	.15	.20	.15	.004	55	0.2
160	2	2	2	.10	.10	.10	.001	60	0.1
165	1	0	1	.05	.00	.05	.000	65	0.0

[1]The probability of winning (underbidding all three competitors) is found by multiplying the probabilities of underbidding each one.

[2]The contribution margin is the difference between the bid price and the estimated direct costs.

[3]The expected payoff, or optimum bid, is found by multiplying the contribution margin by the probability of winning.

Source: Adapted from Wayne J. Morse, "Probabilistic bidding models: A synthesis," *Business Horizons,* 18 (April 1975):67-76. Reprinted with permission.

When a firm is unfamiliar with the past strategies of specific competitors or lacks historical data that is applicable to a given bid situation, it may have no choice but to make the best possible intuitive guess. Published information of awards made on similar projects sometimes provides helpful guidance. Trade association information regarding industry profitability and/or capacity utilization can also suggest a ballpark price. Obviously, relevant quantitative data provides the greatest level of assurance.

Experienced bidders tend to fear inexperienced ones the most. Lack of experience, when coupled with a strong desire to win the contract, frequently causes the bidder to overestimate the severity of competition and to undercut the price.[9] Hence, the actions of such firms or individuals defy normal attempts to predict them.

Price Negotiation

Business marketing commonly involves price negotiation, particularly in complex buying situations where buyers and sellers make a number of proposals and counterproposals before agreeing on a price. In this sense, negotiation and open bidding are virtually synonymous. These negotiations include not only price but also service, delivery, technical assistance, product characteristics, and quality.

The process of negotiation may begin with a price quotation that is later modified to reflect the particular requirements of the buying firm and the special strengths of the seller. In the case of open bidding, negotiations are often carried on simultaneously with a number of suppliers until enough information has been exchanged to allow for a competitive bid.

Negotiation regularly occurs in the sale of a new product because of unknown factors involved. Sellers, faced with uncertain manufacturing and marketing costs, often prefer to negotiate rather than volunteer a fixed price. Buyers, lacking assurance that the product will fill their needs, prefer to negotiate in the belief that negotiated prices are closer to the "right" price than original quotations. The successful negotiation of a contract requires skill, experience, and preparation. Like a good trial lawyer, the seller must analyze the firm's strengths and weaknesses compared with potential competition, the factors that the buying firm will prioritize, the opportunities for future business, and projected profitability.

Negotiation involves some form of bargaining strategy that is influenced by the relative strengths of the parties. In general, there are four types of negotiating strategies[10]: (1) a *negotiated* strategy in which buyer and seller have a close match of strengths and negotiate a price that would be fair to both parties; (2) a *dictatorial* strategy in which the buyer is weak relative to the seller, and the seller will attempt to set a price that is most favorable to his or her firm; (3) a *defensive* strategy in which the seller is weak relative to the buyer; and (4) a *gamesmanship* strategy in which both parties are weak and play "hide and seek" to arrive at price. Figure 19-3 illustrates the relationship among these four strategies.

MEASURING BUYER AND SELLER STRENGTH

To determine the appropriate type of negotiating strategy, the strength of the seller's bargaining power relative to that of the buyer must be measured. These relative strengths can arise from a number of factors. For instance, a buyer's strengths can stem from the size of the organization, the volume of past purchases, its future buying power, or its length of time in business. The seller can derive strength from a favorable corporate image, notable product quality or uniqueness, proven delivery capability, strong technical assistance and post-sale services. The strengths of the buyer and the seller must be measured in relative terms. Once the strengths of each have been evaluated, an overall measure of strength/weakness can be derived. This can be accom-

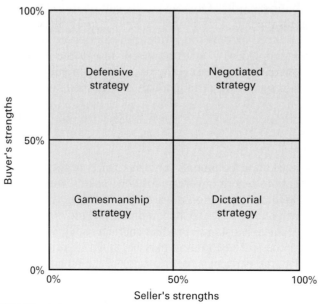

FIGURE 19-3 Pricing strategy quadrangle.

plished by rating the strength of criteria on a scale of 1 to 10 (weak to strong) and then assigning weights to each criterion based on its importance in the negotiating situation. The score for each criterion is the product of its strength multiplied by the weight. Total strength is the summation of all scores. Table 19-8 illustrates this method.

One must recognize that the buyer and seller will each evaluate the situation. Thus, the buyer may estimate his or her strengths as greater than those of the seller and try to put the seller on the defensive. However, the seller may perceive an opposite scenario and launch a dictatorial strategy.

In this hypothetical situation, the buyer enjoys a somewhat better bargaining position with a total strength score of 66.4 percent compared to the seller's 52.3 percent. The large buying firm represents desirable future business, even though their past purchases have been small. The seller's strength stems from a favorable company image, competitive price, and an attractive trade-in policy. However, weaknesses exist in delivery capability and product quality. Unfortunately for the seller, delivery is more important than trade-in policy.

The two overall scores, 66.4 and 52.3 percent, are used to determine where the seller stands relative to the buyer in the pricing strategy quadrangle, Figure 19-3. In this situation, both scores fall in the northeast quadrant, indicating that a negotiated strategy is most appropriate.

Comparing Buyer and Seller Needs   When the negotiation strategy has been identified, both firms must choose their tactical maneuvers. In the illustrated situation, both buyer and seller will attempt to set a price, but their tactics will depend on the buyer's need for the product compared to the seller's need for the sale.

A buyer's product need can be acute, moderate, or marginal. If the proposed purchase involves the immediate replacement of a defective machine critical to the manufacturing process, the buyer would be ready to pay any reasonable price for the equipment, and the seller would classify the buyer's need as acute. A seller who took undue advantage of this situation through price gouging, however, might suffer from retaliation in future negotiations. The buyer would have a moderate need if sufficient time

TABLE 19-8   Measurement of Buyer's and Seller's Strengths

Measurement of Buyer's Strengths				*Measurement of Seller's Strengths*			
Criteria	*Strength (1 to 10)*	*Weight*	*Total Score*	*Criteria*	*Strength (1 to 10)*	*Weight*	*Total Score*
1. Organization size	9	3	27	1. Delivery	4	3	12
2. Potential	7	2	14	2. Company image	6	3	18
3. Past purchases	3	4	12	3. Product quality	3	2	6
4. Future purchases	8	5	40	4. After-sale services	5	2	10
				5. Trade-in policy	6	1	6
				6. Price	8	2	16
TOTAL		14	93	TOTAL		13	68
Total possible score			140	Total possible score			130
Percentage score = 93/140 × 100 = 66.4%				Percentage score = 68/130 × 100 = 52.3%			

Source: Adapted from Subhash C. Jain and Michael V. Laric, "A framework for strategic industrial pricing," *Industrial Marketing Management* 8 (1979): 75-80. Copyright © 1979 by Elsevier Publishing Company, Inc.

existed to engage in a supplier search before finalizing the equipment order. If a buyer was casually searching for alternative suppliers before replenishing office supplies three months later, the need would be marginal, because the buyer has ample time to locate and obtain a satisfactory price from an acceptable supplier.

The seller's need to make the sale can also be acute, moderate, or marginal. An acute sale need exists, for example, when a company is operating well below capacity, needs working capital, or desires to secure a prototype order that will lead to sizable repeat business. On the other hand, if operating at or near full capacity, or unsure of repeat orders, the seller would probably view the need for this sale as marginal.

Figure 19-4 illustrates the pricing tactics matrix. When the buyer's need exceeds the seller's, the buyer will probably yield to the seller (cells 4, 7, and 8). If the seller's need for the sale exceeds the buyer's need, then the buyer will have the upper edge in negotiation (cells 2, 3, and 6). However, when both have the same degree of need, neither can dictate price (cells 1, 5, and 9).

DETERMINING KEY NEGOTIABLE FACTORS

The seller must determine the buyer's stance with respect to all negotiation factors. Some factors will be clearly irrelevant (such as import tariffs when buyer and seller are in the same country). Other factors will fall into one of three categories: *nonnegotiable* factors, *prime trade-off* candidates, or *nonvalue* factors.

For example, a buyer may require 6-week delivery to support a planned production schedule, but the seller cannot supply the component to complete specifications in that time. In this instance, the delivery date cannot be negotiated. However, suppose that the buying firm's engineers indicate that a product in the seller's warehouse, differing from the specified component in only minor details, is acceptable, particularly when combined with a price reduction. The coupling of specification revision and price reduction becomes a major trade-off item. Neither party puts a value on the fact that the substitute product is slightly smaller than the original component.

This simple example illustrates that most business negotiations aim at a win-win result, not a win-lose (or zero-sum) outcome. Experienced negotiators realize that any worthwhile transaction must yield something of value to both buyer and seller. The key lies in open-minded and flexible investigation of alternatives when the initial desires of either party cannot be satisfied exactly. Naturally, either party can initiate creative action. Since this text emphasizes the seller's perspective, we

FIGURE 19-4 Pricing tactics matrix.

	Buyer's need		
Seller's need	Acute	Moderate	Marginal
Acute	1. Neutral ground	4. Buyer has leeway	7. Buyer in control
Moderate	2. Seller has leeway	5. Neutral ground	8. Buyer has leeway
Marginal	3. Seller in control	6. Seller has leeway	9. Neutral ground

Source: Adapted from Subhash C. Jain and Michael V. Laric, "A framework for strategic industrial pricing," *Industrial Marketing Management* 8 (1979):75–80. Copyright © 1979 by Elsevier Publishing Company, Inc.

suggest that marketers develop such capability, if only from the standpoint of making their own jobs more productive and satisfying.

THE IMPACT OF ALTERED BUYER-SELLER RELATIONSHIPS ON BIDDING AND PRICE NEGOTIATION

The concepts of partnering, just-in-time purchasing, and total quality management have significantly altered buyer-seller relationships which, in turn, have changed the amount and type of price negotiations.

Historically, buyer and seller negotiated at arm's length in an almost adversarial relationship. As soon as one supplier designed and quoted on a product, the buyer solicited bids from multiple sources in an attempt to drive the price down. The original supplier either met the lowest alternative bid or was threatened with the loss of all business.[11] Today, business firms, manufacturers in particular, have reduced the number of qualified suppliers to a minimum. Buyer and seller collaborate on the design of components with both parties striving for optimum performance at minimum cost. The buying firm recognizes that it cannot realistically practice total quality management unless it can control the quality of its production inputs, such as the components and materials provided by suppliers. The buyer evaluates suppliers on both product quality and the value of associated services. Continuous improvement becomes a mutual goal. Once a satisfactory relationship has been established, both parties work to maintain it over the long-term.[11]

Just-in-time purchasing requires a degree of interrelated planning and exchange of proprietary information that also prompts firms to reduce their suppliers to one or a very few. Consequently, the resultant relationship between buyer and seller favors mutual trust and stable pricing.[12] As a result, potential suppliers who want to share in the buying potential of large manufacturers find the barriers to entry greater than ever.

Leasing

Leasing in the business market serves as an alternative to buying capital equipment. Between 1986 and 1993, leasing transactions in the United States increased from $85 billion to nearly $130 billion according to the Department of Commerce.[13] However, lessors of sophisticated computing and telecommunication equipment face problems that were not recognized a decade ago. Instead of having long-term assets of predictable value that provided profit at minimal risk, they now have to worry about unexpected obsolescence caused by short-lived technologies. For example, networks of inexpensive desktop computers have greatly diminished the mainframe market and devalued its equipment. Lessors must now monitor more closely the dynamics of their target industries as well as the emerging technologies aimed at these industries.[13] Despite the potential dangers, leasing offers an attractive alternative to the marketer of capital goods who might not otherwise be able to make an outright sale.

New technologies also affect equipment users in several ways. Leasing allows firms to utilize the latest equipment without weakening their cash or credit reserves.[14] The lessees escape the danger of technological obsolescence by upgrading the equipment at the end of the lease period.[15] Leasing has also created a used equipment market. Independent leasing and remarketing firms offer a variety of flexible programs to smaller companies that need to conserve cash flow and can meet their computing needs without the very latest equipment. There is the added advantage of being able to "mix and match" components from several manufacturers.[16]

When contemplating the purchase of capital goods, buyers examine the cost/benefit trade-offs of various financing alternatives; if the benefits of leasing outweigh the benefits of owning, they lease rather than purchase. The main difference between leasing and purchasing is that lease-related payments can be deducted as business expenses each month, whereas purchases can only be deducted as an expense once a year at tax time. By leasing, a company can save cash while using the equipment it could not afford to purchase up front.[15]

Leasing provides other benefits to the lessee such as minimizing equipment disposal problems and avoiding the accumulation of debt or equity dilution. For example, profitable airlines have little difficulty obtaining equity or debt financing to support their equipment needs, but smaller carriers are less fortunate because many financiers are reluctant to enter this failure-plagued industry. Consequently, operating leases involving new or used aircraft provide the only potential solution to this funding impasse.[17]

LEASING ARRANGEMENTS

As indicated in the foregoing coverage, business firms can lease equipment through either the original manufacturer, authorized resellers, or independent marketers. In turn, the lessor can carry the financing contract within an operating division or through a credit subsidiary. The lessee might prefer to arrange credit through one of many banking institutions that finance commercial leasing agreements.

Types of Leases   The two basic types of business leases are (1) *operating* leases and (2) *financial,* or full-payout leases. The operating lease is usually short term and cancelable, the lessor owns what is leased and takes the depreciation, and the lessee can treat the lease cost as an expense that does not appear on the balance sheet. The lessee generally must cover operating expenses, but the lessor provides maintenance, service, and sometimes, technical updating. Since an operating lease primarily provides customers with equipment for a limited time, contracts usually do not contain a purchase option.[14]

A financial lease typically runs longer with total payments that often exceed the original value of the equipment. The lessee capitalizes this cost and also takes the depreciation. Contracts usually contain a price for optional purchase at the end of the contract.[14]

Successful leasing strategy requires a careful assessment of its role in the overall marketing program, an understanding of the benefits and costs of leasing from the customer's perspective, and well-developed financial proposals that show potential customers the economic benefits of leasing. As with all other products and services, the lessor who identifies and promotes customer benefits will enjoy a strong market position in a growing industry.

Looking Back

The impact of price on subsequent sales volume and cost must be analyzed before introducing a new product, initiating a price change, or responding to a competitor's action. This analysis should include the combined concepts of marginal profit and experience-curve cost reduction.

Break-even analysis and return-on-investment pricing facilitate the interrelation of market demand, production levels, and costs, which jointly determine company profits.

Expected payoff analysis allows the price setter to quantify various market uncertainties and substitute these figures for pure intuition when making price decisions. However, certain qualitative factors must also be weighed.

Developing an effective competitive bid consumes time and expenses. Marketers must develop a bidding strategy that includes an analysis of company objectives, evaluation of alternative bidding opportunities, and an assessment of the probability of success for a particular bid.

Price negotiation, common in business marketing, is a bargaining process aimed at reaching agreement between two parties. The successful negotiation of a contract requires skill, experience, knowledge of the major relevant factors, and an objective appraisal of the seller's and buyer's relative strengths. Methods for measuring that strength and for determining tactical maneuvers during negotiation were discussed.

Leasing has become a major alternative strategy to outright selling, particularly in the capital equipment market. Lessors face both attractive opportunities and potential dangers. Lessees can realize various advantages by leasing capital assets, especially those with an uncertain life span.

Questions for Discussion

1. Finding the optimal level for prices is a difficult task in business marketing. Outline specifically the approach that Prentice Hall should take to find the optimal price for this textbook.
2. What factors make it difficult to use break-even analysis? Can they be overcome?
3. Why is return-on-investment pricing common in oligopolistic business markets?
4. When and how should expected payoff analysis be used in establishing price?
5. Discuss how the experience curve provides a broader perspective of available pricing options.
6. To enhance the odds of winning contracts, a building contractor bids on every potential contract in his market area. Evaluate this bidding strategy.
7. Buyers and sellers spend a lot of time negotiating price and other related factors during the exchange process. What steps can sellers take to improve their negotiating strategy?
8. Leasing is becoming increasingly important in the marketing of capital goods. What factors should a buyer consider in the lease versus buy decision?

Endnotes

1. Otto Eckstein, "A theory of the wage-price process in modern industry," *Review of Economic Studies* 31 (October 1964):267-87.
2. David Fagiano, "Are we in business to make money?" *Management Review* 81 (January 1992):4.
3. See Adam Brandenburger, "Knowledge and equilibrium in games," *Journal of Economic Perspectives* 6 (Fall 1992):83-101. Also Jacob Hornik and Joseph Cherian, "Data-use in marketing: a normative analysis from an artificial science perspective," *Journal of Business Research* 27 (July 1993):229-38.
4. Thomas T. Nagle and Reed K. Holden, *The Strategy And Tactics Of Pricing,* 2nd ed., (Englewood Cliffs, NJ: Prentice Hall, Inc., 1995), p. 199.
5. "NASA rejects low-ball bids for data system," *Aviation Week and Space Technology* 137 (August 17, 1992):24.
6. Robert A. Garda, "Use tactical pricing to uncover hidden profits," *Journal of Business Strategy* 12 (September-October 1991):17-23.

7. Robert W. Staiger and Frank A. Wolak, "Collusive pricing with capacity constraints in the presence of demand uncertainty," *The Rand Journal of Economics* 23 (Summer 1992):203-20.

8. Wayne J. Morse, "Probabilistic Bidding models: A synthesis," *Business Horizons* 18 (April 1975):67-74.

9. Michael H. Rothkopf and Ronald M. Harstad, "Modeling competitive bidding: a critical essay," *Management Science* 40 (March 1994):364-84.

10. See Subhash C. Jain and Michael V. Laric, "A framework for strategic industrial pricing," *Industrial Marketing Management* 8 (1979):75-80.

11. Ernest Raia, "Quality wins out: the shrinking supplier base," *Purchasing* 116 (January 13, 1994):93.

12. Paula J. Haynes and Marilyn M. Helms, "An ethical framework for purchasing decisions," *Management Decision* 29, 1 (1991):35-8.

13. Richard Parkes, "Equipment leasing: an industry in transition," *Business Credit* 96 (February 1994):12-13.

14. Richard B. Elsberry, "Leasing equipment has its advantages," *The Office* 114 (July 1991):60.

15. Kate Evans-Correia, "Buyers find savings by leasing equipment," *Purchasing* 115 (August 19, 1993):73-4.

16. Kenneth A. Bouldin, "Flexible leasing options: the growing market for used equipment," *Information Systems Management* 9 (Summer 1992):68-70.

17. Ian Verchere, "Lessors come to airlines' rescue," *Interavia* 46 (December 1991):23-4.

Bibliography

Brandenburger, Adam, "Knowledge and equilibrium in games," *Journal of Economic Perspectives* 6 (1992):83-101.

Fagiano, David, "Are we in business to make money?" *Management* Review 81 (1992):4.

Garda, Robert A., "Use tactical pricing to uncover hidden profits," *Journal of Business Strategy* 12 (1991):17-23.

Hornik, Jacob and Joseph Cherian, "Data-use in marketing: a normative analysis from an artificial science perspective," *Journal of Business Research* 27 (1993):229-38.

Jain, Subhash C., and Michael V. Laric, "A framework for strategic industrial pricing," *Industrial Marketing Management* 8 (1979):75-80.

Morse, Wayne J., "Probabilistic bidding models: A synthesis," *Business Horizons* 18 (1975):67-74.

"NASA rejects low-ball bids for data system," *Aviation Week and Space Technology* 137 (1992):24.

Rothkopf, Michael H. and Ronald M. Harstad, "Modeling competitive bidding: a critical essay," *Management Science* 40 (1994):364-84.

PART VIII

Competing, Controlling, and Expanding

This section deals with certain market realities. First, competitors invariably exist who can subvert the best of strategies. Another strategy must be formed to minimize the negative affects of existing and/or expected competition. Chapter 20 elaborates on such strategies. Second, in dynamic markets, changes occur that may obsolete a strategy or render it ineffective. A firm must closely monitor its market activity and make prompt adjustments to keep its substrategies appropriate and effective. Chapter 21 deals with controls aimed at improving efficiency, profitability, and market penetration. Finally, Chapter 22 enumerates steps a company can take to recognize and capitalize on opportunities that constantly arise in an ever-changing global market.

CHAPTER 20

Competitive Strategies

In the previous chapters, product, price, promotion, and distribution strategies were discussed, with the emphasis on the use of these variables to achieve a company's desired marketing objectives. This chapter uses these variables and covers some of the useful competitive strategies used to develop competitive advantage and to survive the battles of business marketing.

In this chapter we will discuss the following:

1. Marketing strategy and how this strategy can be used to achieve company objectives
2. An explanation of what is competitive advantage
3. An analysis of the business market leader strategies
4. A discussion of which business market strategies are available to the market challenger
5. A discovery of what a market follower can do to maintain market position
6. An investigation of niche marketing strategies
7. A discussion of the high market share risks involved in the competitive struggle to survive in business marketing
8. The importance of business time cycles and competitive advantage

The Ever-Present World of Competition

The omnipresent competitive business marketing struggle has to be considered serious business when an increase of 1 percent in market share means millions of dollars in added revenue, or, conversely, a loss of 1 percent in market share could mean the loss of millions of dollars in revenue. Company viability can be achieved by capturing a market segment or a portion of the existing market and then maintaining this market share against all kinds of competitive attacks. These competitive attacks, which are designed to unseat the industry leader, incorporate much thought, product and campaign design, and engineering to create workable competitive marketing strategies.

The rate of market change has accelerated dramatically over the past decade. Products that were state-of-the-art a decade ago are now obsolete, particularly in the computer field. Rapid change has become the rule, and the requirements for competitive advantage have shifted.[1] Although price, promotion, and distribution are compet-

511

itive weapons, new products provide one of the most effective items in the on-going competitive marketing struggle. For example, the DRAM of 1993, with a capacity of 16 megabits, speed of 150 megahertz, that can feature the smallest size of 0.5 microns, will be bested by the computer DRAM of 1999, with a capacity of 256 megabits, a speed of 400 megahertz, and can feature a smaller 0.25-micron chip.[2] A PC with a 100-mega-hertz Pentium microprocessor or a Macintosh PowerPC chip provides the processing power of a 1988-vintage Cray Y-MP supercomputer from Cray Research Inc., plus a lot more, including a CD-ROM disk drive and stereo speakers.

Not only are innovative products an important ingredient of successful competitive strategies, but timing, or how soon a company acts or reacts to a marketing opportunity, also can be of great importance (Box 20-1). IBM, Apple, and Motorola combined resources to develop the PowerPC chip. Three years after forging this alliance around the ultrafast PowerPC chip, IBM and Apple were not close to an agreement to create a single hardware "platform" around the PowerPC chip. Apple introduced its Power Mac using the PowerPC chip. Many experts believed that IBM made a mistake when it decided its PowerPC chip should be used in its OS/2 system, but the project to rewrite that software bogged down, delaying IBM's market introduction.[3]

Before the widespread use of fax machines, Federal Express spent millions of dollars on a new venture called Zap mail service, by which it could send a customer's letter in minutes to a given destination via a fax, rather than wait for the overnight letter service it had successfully pioneered. The Zap mail venture proved to be an embarrassment to the highly successful company, and Fed Ex's expected profits fell short of the firm's profit goal as a result of cultural lag. Fed Ex had simply entered a

---

BOX 20-1

Bill Gates's Vision at Microsoft

Microsoft Corporation had achieved total success by anyone's definition. With the corporation at its peak power; its fiscal year ending with revenues of $4.5 billion; after tax margins of 25 percent, and $3 billion in cash placed the company in an inevitable position. William H. Gates, CEO, was not happy as he looked into the future for business markets. Microsoft was the king of the PC market, but Gates wanted to be in the markets of the future: high-speed networks, both within companies and across the Internet. Eventually, these networks would shift the computer industry's "center of gravity" away from the desktop.

Gates saw, from looking at the past, that great powers in one era of computer technology could not extend their dominance into the next. Determined not to fail as others had, Gates set Microsoft's future vision on the Internet. Developed programs to control computers and other gadgets were used to tap into the network; developed software to run the net, and the content and services that flowed across the system were the major focus for Microsoft. Gates stated, "Our software will be used in the home, in the pocket, and in the car." The new business pitted Microsoft against a whole new array of competitors. Many, especially cable TV and telephone companies, were far more powerful than any software rivals. Subsequently, Microsoft allied itself with several cable-TV companies.

Gates' biggest worry became AT&T, which wanted to be the kingpin in the internet era. AT&T allied with Microsoft's most bitter rivals Novell Inc. and Lotus development Corp. AT&T and Microsoft became significant competitors as computers and communications converged. The new center in the competitive computer-communications market became the Internet. Future strategies must cultivate and nurture a competitive advantage for both a company's growth and survival.

Source: "Bill Gates's vision," *Business Week* (June 27, 1994), pp. 56-62.

field that was rapidly taken over by the proliferation of numerous fax machines in the hands of its customers.

Four premises underlie successful marketing strategies. Two management consultants offer the following[4]:

1. Companies can no longer raise prices in lock step with higher costs; they have to try to *lower costs* to accommodate rising customer expectations.

2. Companies can no longer aim for less than hassle-free *service.* Their customers enjoy effortless, flawless, and instantaneous performance from one industry and want it from every other.

3. Companies can no longer assume that good basic service is enough; customers demand *premium service* and raise their standards continuously.

4. Companies can no longer compromise on quality and product capabilities. They must build products to deliver nothing less than *superiority* and eye-popping innovation.

Competitive Marketing Positions

Hopefully, in search of a winning strategy or a set of winning strategies, business marketing firms may chose from a variety of offensive and defensive strategic positions, depending upon the firm's present competitive position. Figure 20-1 depicts these various positions of competitiveness as (1) *market leader,* (2) *market challenger,* (3) *market follower,* and (4) *niche marketer.*

Market leaders are usually well-known companies who have been recognized as market leaders by their competitors. Frequently, a large physical size, dominance in most of its markets, strong distribution systems, and stable pricing are hallmarks of this type of leader. Other firms in the same industries use the leader as a yardstick to measure their own successes, but more important, they target the leader for developing competitive strategies. Some of these market leaders are IBM, Nucor, Xerox, GE, Du Pont, Weyerhaeuser, Microsoft, Norfolk & Southern, Dell Computer, Compaq, Intel, and Caterpillar. Befitting this lofty position, the leaders know that every industry in which they hold leadership, competitors are anxiously waiting for market opportunities to wrest away the leader's **market share,** and their **market power.**

To maintain their leadership positions, the companies must (1) take forceful actions in viable markets (2) exit markets that are not commensurate with a leadership position, or (3) pursue other marketing opportunities they have recognized to enhance their market leadership positions. Some of these leaders may chose to become very conservative in their marketing and product activities, which tactic may plant the seeds of their

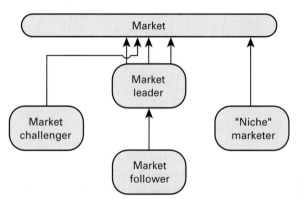

FIGURE 20-1 Competitive product market strategic positions.

own destruction, e.g., IBM's market slide in the 1990s when, the company's PC business had difficulty in revitalizing itself.[5] Digital fell because Kenneth Olsen, its founder, lost sight of the potential power of the PC and refused to enter the market thinking the PC was only a toy. To stay ahead, the market leader has to get better and better.[4]

Market challengers are the next level of power in a given market hierarchy and accept the challenger position by attempting to unseat the market leaders. Companies such as Digital, Apple, Compaq, Bethlehem, Ricoh, Phillips, Dow, and Boise-Cascade are runner-up firms who are fighting for increased market share, usually at the expense of the market leaders. Challengers stress new products, superior services, and better engineering, coupled with promotion and innovative distribution systems to gain more market share. Often market challengers spur the market development by taking the lead in new product introduction. Compaq Computer took the PC lead away from IBM by following aggressive product development and high quality production techniques.[4]

Market followers are best known for their lack of overall aggression in the market and are best known for being willing to take a portion in the market that the leaders either do not want, or allow the follower to take, knowing that the follower is neither a threat or a serious competitor. Many of these companies are very successful in their own right but frequently do not challenge the market leader. Firms which tend to be in this category are Unisys, Wheeling-Pittsburgh Steel, Mead Papers, Monsanto, and Hewlett Packard. The watch-words of the market followers are their willingness to maintain their profitable market share and not to "rock the boat." Hewlett Packard has reversed its role and has become more aggressive entering the PC wars. New products, superior service, lower prices, and status quo promotions are used to retain the followers' gains without disturbing the wrath of the leaders and challengers. Those with "live-and-let-live" strategies tend to be the peacemakers in the industry, but in their quiet way followers can make slow inroads into the leader's market share without the leaders panicking. Disturbing the leader usually accompanies more radical shifts in market share as the leader reacts to the threats of the market challenger. If the follower precipitates panic for the leader, similar reactions and threats may ensue.

Niche marketing is the most common competitive form. This strategy is used most by all the smaller firms in industry, or by smaller components of larger companies. The major forte of the niche marker is to specialize in a given market segment where its defense can prohibit other competitors from gaining a foothold. Companies which display such tendencies are Prime with CAD-CAM, Allegheny-Ludlum with stainless steel, Cummins with diesel engines, and Gould with pumps. These firms are not really small in size, but are highly specialized in given markets because of either abeyance to a niche strategy or because of technical limitations self-imposed by the firm. Frequently many markets are protected from larger predators by existing in small market niches which larger firms have either overlooked, would not pursue, or can not match the specialized strength of the niche marketer. The major thrust of the nichers is to be the best in a specific market segment which provides easy entry into the market, easy defensiveness of that niche, and protects its market longevity.

Market Leader Strategies

Usually every industry has one company which controls the largest market share and is considered the market leader. This leadership is frequently expressed in price, products, and/or promotional leadership. The top firm must bear the brunt of attack from market challengers who are trying to unseat the market leader, while other firms may try to either imitate the leader, or circumvent the leader, and follow their own market desires.

Compaq's taking over the number one spot in PC sales in 1994 from IBM propelled Compaq into a powerful position within the computer industry. Microsoft's leadership in the software industry materialized as a result of progressive marketing, leading software, adventurous alliances, and business deals with other leaders in the computer industry. Microsoft is also intent on maintaining its leadership in the software industry by writing the software that runs many of the machines used on the internet.

The dominant, leading company must practice three different game plans, at the same or different times, to retain its leadership[6]:

1. *Expand* total market demand via new users, new uses, and more usage
2. *Protect* its present market share from competitors through good defensive and offensive strategies
3. *Increase* its market share at the expense of competition if increasing the total demand is not possible

INCREASE TOTAL MARKET DEMAND

Total market demand can be increased by developing new users, finding new product uses, and encouraging present users to use the product more often. Because of the business market's derived demand features, to expand markets is not always easy or even possible for some companies, unless the company uses foresight and some technological transfer methods. OEM manufacturers selling to end users may be in the best position to expand total market demand since they can visualize more practical technological transfer techniques and/or invade new markets with completely new products, existing products, or modified product designs. Caterpillar developed a sleek, new $100,000 all-purpose farm tractor. Instead of tank-like steel tracks, the new Cat had wide rubber treads that preserved the soil and let the operator take the 15-ton workhorse onto the highway without tearing up the pavement.[7] The new development was Caterpillar's attempt to enlarge the market. When you are the market leader and own most of the pie, it is better to try to increase the whole pie rather than just increase your slice. This strategy can soothe and possibly placate the anxious challengers by also expanding their market share, but a more important factor is that you are thus increasing the future viability of the entire industry.

Likewise, if disaster strikes one company in the industry, the entire industry may feel the repercussions. The commercial airframe market has drastic sales ups and downs. Every time a commercial plane crashes, whether it is carrying passengers or is being flight tested, the repercussions affect the future sales of that company and the entire industry. Europe's Airbus Industrie, and the airlines which fly its planes, suffered when a test plane crashed when it was on autopilot, right after take off from a Paris airport. Some critics claimed that Airbus's propensity to push technology to the "cutting edge" may have fostered the crash. An official of the International Airline Passengers Association believed that Airbus may have gone too far. Airbus had been dogged with this issue since 1988 when it delivered the industry's first "fly-by-wire" airliner—an electronically controlled jet whose computer could overrule pilot maneuvers it considered dangerous.[8] But critics claimed this safety system may cause accidents, if it malfunctions or if ill-trained pilots tried to override it. This feature became a problem for Boeing, as well, since Boeing's 777, introduced in 1995, was the first of its jets to be computer run or "fly-by-wire."[9]

New Users   Attracting potential users who are unaware that a product exists, or are uninformed about the product's efficacy and cost-effectiveness for their company, constitute the development of new users. Examples of new users include desktop conferencing, with software that now permits people in separate locations to work together as if they were in the same room, thus eliminating the use of a stream of E-mailed spreadsheets, faxed transparencies, and harried phone calls.[9] Microsoft's invasion of the Internet was to spread the use of software to new users.

New Uses   Present users increase their usage of the product by finding new uses. Du Pont's multiple purpose Nylon started as a synthetic fiber for parachutes; then new uses for the product opened new vistas in women's hosiery, women's blouses, men's shirts, automobile tires, seat upholstery, and carpeting; jet engines have been used as an auxiliary power supply for when a manufacturing plant suffers a power black-out; petroleum jelly used as a lubricant in machine shops, until factory workers found it was also beneficial in curing skin irritations and relieving stuffy noses.

Many new business product's uses are suggested by customers rather than developed by the company's R&D department, which highlights the need for good marketing research services.[7] Silicon Graphics, Inc., an advanced image-technology company, had specialized in three-dimensional images for Hollywood by producing plausible dinosaurs for the movie "Jurassic Park" and by creating images of President John F. Kennedy and John Lennon "meeting" actor Tom Hanks in the movie "Forrest Gump." Using the same imaging graphics technology, SGI moved into image-making for car designs—similar to CAD, but with much more detail and clarity—to check anything from airflow to aesthetics without any detailed design other than on the computer. This progressive company purchased Cray Research, the supercomputer firm, to broaden its market coverage and generate new uses for its products.

More Usage   Increased usage means having current users use the same product more often. Records and storage management companies, legal, and management and marketing consulting companies frequently have repeat jobs given them by their satisfied customers. Product quality, quality service and attention to customer needs and the little details that make up these customer's needs are important ingredients for increased product and/or service usage. CAD computer programs have been one of the new fountain-heads for new and more uses as they are being used in the design of everything from new cars and aircraft to new valves, oil refinery piping systems, and children's toys.

SUSTAINING COMPETITIVE ADVANTAGE

Being a market leader can be a very dangerous position to sustain. Competitive advantage may be a fleeting experience, and sustainability may be a target that never is actually reached.[10] Michael Porter, the father of the competitive advantage concept, advocates: (1) market leadership requires a firm to possess a strong cost advantage, (2) stress product differentiation, (3) offer buyer value and differentiation contrasted to competitors, (4) have the latest technology, (5) improve the companies' competitive position by increasing its current industry structure, (6) focus on segments in the market that have the best matches, and (7) be market driven in all the companies' endeavors.[11]

Stanley Slater provides a more detailed approach to sustaining competitive advantage and market leadership.[11] The requirements for *competitive advantage* are first that the basic foundation must be a product or service that provides value to the business customer. Value is the difference between the benefits realized by the customer from using the product or service and the costs they incur in finding, acquiring, and using it. The price of the individual product is not as important as the overall costs associated with its purchase, including its price, its operating and maintenance costs, and an acceptable rate of return on its investment.

The key to this value concept is the customer's perception of this value. The seller determines what the customer wants, develops and makes the product, then adds up its costs of production and puts a standard margin on top. This not as important as what the customer perceives as a product's value. Price should not be at the center point of competitive contention. Competing on price often leads to destructive price wars, as witnessed by the airline industry. Value-driven companies have a fundamental understanding of their customer's businesses and of their current and latent needs to determine which product features really provide customer benefits and which features merely add to the product's cost, without any benefits. Cost-benefits, as determined by the customer, is the best benchmark.

Second, delivering superior value may not be enough. Excellent quality matched by a company's competitors isn't enough differentiation. The Japanese share of the chip market shrink because American firms bested their efforts. Competitive advantage comes to a market leader who gives the customer the lowest or shortest *life cycle cost,* discussed later in this chapter. Lowering life cycle costs means helping the customer reduce start-up, training, and/or maintenance costs, as well. Total value is perceived by the customer as the total of all associated product costs. IBM was the first computer company to offer augmented service (hardware, software, training and service) which drove many of its competitors from the market.

SOURCES OF COMPETITIVE ADVANTAGE

A firm can't expect to retain its leadership role without constant improvement in its capabilities and output. Successful companies can't rest on their laurels; to maintain competitive advantage, they must have a plan to what constitutes value to their customers.

Six components can fulfill the firm's drive to sustain competitive advantage. First, the products they produce must be of *highest quality* because customers expect it. To do otherwise is courting disaster.

Second, *excellent service* is the basis for customer loyalty which will help to sustain a firm when business may be tough to get. Executives should spend some time with their customers so that they may identify with their customers needs and their problems.

Third, *cost control* is imperative. Good companies "reengineer" themselves through understanding the business processes that are necessary to deliver customer value. Processes that do not engage in customer value become prime candidates for reduction. If any process measured against a benchmark of the "best-in-class" companies' process, doesn't measure up to this standard, then either reengineer the process or outsource the process to a company that does measure up to the standard. GE's aircraft engine group reengineered its jet engine manufacturing process and reduced its new engine order time from 24 months to 6 months, making it the lowest cost producer in the business.[12]

Fourth, speed or *time to market* is so critical for profit considerations, given the shorter life cycle durations. How much time it takes for a company to get a product into customer's hands could make the difference between a successful or unsuccessful product. Hewlett Packard develops a new printer in 1 1/2 years when the time spread use to be 4 1/2 years. McKinsey & Company found that high-tech products that come to market 6 months late but on budget will earn 33 percent less profit over 5 years. For products that come out on time but are 50 percent over budget, profit cuts are only 4 percent over the same period.[11] Time is also important when solving customers' problems. It is expected to have the right solution at the right time.

Fifth, product *innovation* is a necessity. Many companies survive on products that have been in their lines 5 years or less. In progressive firms, mistakes are forgiven when attempting to innovate. Market failures are tolerated in these companies if the products introduced were based on sound marketing concepts. Playing it safe will no longer work in a competitive market.

Sixth, a leader must have a business culture that enhances a set of values and beliefs that provides for individual behavior. A market-driven, learning-oriented *organizational culture* that provides the insights necessary to understand the importance of customer relations and encourages risk-taking that forces competitors to scramble will benefit, regardless of the length of its products' life cycles.

Protect Present Market Share

Because market leaders have to bear the brunt of the constant onslaught from market challengers as well as from cash-rich companies from other industries who attempt to gain a piece of the pie in their industry, the leader is forced to practice different defensive strategies. As depicted in Figure 20-2, Michael Porter suggests three major defensive categories[11]:

1. Raise structural barriers for any challenger.
2. Increase challengers expected retaliation from the leader.
3. Lower inducement for the challenger to attack.

FIGURE 20-2 Defensive strategies.

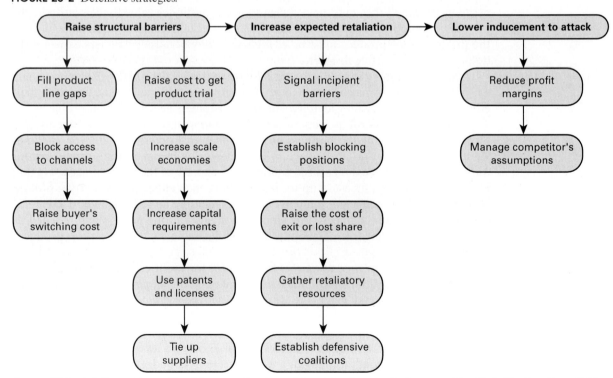

Source: Michael E. Porter, *Competitive Advantage: Creating and Sustaining Superior Performance* (New York: The Free Press, 1985), pp. 487–99. Adapted by permission of The Free Press, a division of Simon & Schuster.

RAISE STRUCTURAL BARRIERS

To build an impregnable fortification around one's marketing territory and intimidate or deny success to any attacker requires strategies that can take many forms. This category includes the following twelve actions, which could make it difficult for a challenger to invade the leader's markets. Cincinnati Milacron, for example, long known as one of the world's premier machine tool manufacturers, was forced to expand into robotics, numerical control machines and software to maintain its market position as it lost its number one position in machine tools to Giddings and Lewis.

Fill Product Line Gaps   Filling product line gaps shuts off any market weakness the leader may have and thwarts the challengers opportunity to expand into the leader's territory. Japanese companies have exploited market leaders who did not fill product line gaps. The Japanese sought out unfilled market niches from which they could fill and could maintain a base for future operations. The Japanese electronics industry challengers outflanked many American electronics company leaders by hitting the Americans where they were least defensible. Small copiers and small fax machines blasted American firms where the Americans did not have a product, hence, no defense.

Navistar International (formerly International Harvester) was started as a farm implement company that rapidly grew into trucks and construction equipment. The construction equipment was an outgrowth of the farm tractor. In 1952, IH purchased the Frank G. Hough Company, a manufacturer of payloaders (large earth-moving equipment) that competed directly with Caterpillar. IH's poor showing in the payloader market and other related markets was a reflection of weak support and poor management, resulting in the company's bankruptcy and the subsequent creation of Navistar International.[13]

Block Channel Access   Blocking a competitors access to a channel may require loading the industrial distributor with so many products that the challenger can not acquire space in the distributor's warehouse. Bundling of services and providing customers with superior after sales service are useful.

Raise Buyer's Switching Costs   One approach is to offer free or low cost training for buyer personnel in the use of and maintenance of the seller's equipment. Another approach is to participate in joint product development projects with the buying firm, which can help the leader to raise structural barriers. Airline engine manufacturers work closely with the airframe manufacturer in the development of new aircraft. Just-in-time delivery systems and buyer-seller concurrent engineering programs are good illustrations of this strategy.

Raise the Cost of Gaining a Product Trial   Price reductions can be effective as competitors stand to lose money if they enter the market. The competitive bidding process can encourage a competitor to literally "buy the order" by bidding very low to force a challenge out of the market.

Increase Scale Economies   By increasing its spending rate for R&D to produce more new products increases the competitor's need to match the leader in new product development to maintain its competitive position. Greater economies of scale resulting from increased quantities at lower costs per unit via improved processes are the most effective.

Increase Capital Requirements   Raising the amount of financing given to buyers and distributors and practicing JIT deliveries can preclude unwanted competitors.

Secure Patents and Licenses   Patenting product features, as Apple did on the Macintosh operating system and then licensing the use of the system as IBM did so adroitly helps to keep out unwanted competitors. However, in the case of Apple's delay in licensing its operating system helped lead to its financial predicaments.

Tie Up Suppliers   Signing long-term contracts, making exclusive contracts with the best suppliers, and purchasing in excess of needs can stymie competitors.

INCREASE THE CHALLENGER'S EXPECTED RETALIATION

The second type of defensive tactic is any action that increases the perception by the challenger that retaliation will come forth if the challenger takes offensive actions. Both the perceived threat and expected threat are equally effective as both will force the challenger to accept greater risk, hence greater costs, if they enter the market. Tactics that indicate that a firm intends to vigorously defend its position raises the level of expected retaliation. Zenith Electronics announcement that they had developed a workable cable modem for computers put potential competitors on notice to think twice about entering the field. Zenith, better known for television sets, developed the cable modem 6 years before the market was ready for its use. The cable modem has greater capacity than telephone lines used by more conventional computer/modems systems.

Signal Incipient Barriers   A firm may achieve exclusiveness in a given market by making a large initial investment. This signals competitor that the stakes are high. However, announcing planned moves, new products, and making partial investments can give many of the same signals.

Establish Blocking Positions   Maintain defensive positions that can block a competitor's entry by using price cutting and other such tactics. Blocking positions may be less risky than a direct retaliation, a maneuver that has a greater likelihood of triggering escalation and spilling over into more damaging activities.

Raise the Penalty for Exiting   Increase any activity that demonstrates to competitors the seriousness of the leader's retaliation. Long-term contracts with suppliers, increased vertical integration, and interrelationships with other business units in the leader's firm demonstrate an overall corporate commitment to succeeding in the industry.

Accumulate Retaliatory Resources   The threat of retaliation is increased when a firm has all the retaliatory resources in place needed to make an effective effort. Two viable resources are maintaining excess cash reserves or liquidity and holding new product models in reserve, but then leaking their existence so potential challengers can take note.

Establish Defensive Coalitions   A coalition with other firms may help to provide an increased threat to challengers by providing blocking positions and providing retaliatory resources the leader does not already have.

LOWER THE INDUCEMENT TO ATTACK

The third and last defensive tactic is actions that lower the challenger's desire to attack by raising their costs. Profit is the major inducement for a challenger to attack the leader. Lowering the inducement to attack tactic reduces the profits expected by a potential or present challenger.

Reduce Profit Margins   Squeezing profit margins and accepting lower profit goals are two ways to lower a challenger's profit expectations. Many firms have invited attacks by being too greedy. Lower profit expectations and lower cost structures may encourage the challenger to look elsewhere. Many firms have reengineered and downsized their firms as a defensive measure. GE's Aircraft Engine Group extracted huge concessions from its suppliers, dropped its employment from 20,000 to 8,000, asked customers how it could redesign its engines to reduce costs, practiced reverse pricing in that it asked customers what they were willing to pay, and then lowered its costs accordingly to maintain its profit. GE became the most profitable company in the highly competitive jet engine business. Despite the pain, the results were impressive.[12] GE captured two thirds of worldwide orders for large commercial aircraft engines. GE's GE90 engine powers the Boeing 777. Besides GE, Pratt & Whitney and Rolls-Royce are selling high-thrust turbines for up to 75 percent below list prices—too little to earn a paycheck on a total industry investment of more than $4 billion.[14] However, all three engine manufacturers made a lot of money. GE's jet-engine division had an operating income rise of 26 percent in 1995; Pratt & Whitney, a unit of United Technologies, saw a 39 percent increase; and Rolls-Royce PLC's jet engine unit posted a 92 percent gain. The war over the 777 engines forced all three manufacturers to bring down costs to eventually earn a return on its share of this huge market.

Managing Competitor Assumptions   A challenger will attack if it assumes that a given industry possesses explosive growth potential, despite any high barriers that may exist. Public announcements of realistic forecasts, discussing realistic interpretations of the industry in public forums, and sponsoring independent studies that will question unrealistic assumptions held by the competitors are counteracting strategies.

The semiconductor business is one of the world's great growth industries, with global sales expected to leap from $50 billion in 1990 to more than $100 billion by the late 1990s.[15] Semiconductors drive all other electronic industries. Electronics are the major source that makes workers of the world more productive. Japan owned the semiconductor business in the eighties with seven of the world's ten largest computer-chip makers, but failed to manage the assumptions of its competitors. With stiff competition and intensive research and development by the United States, Korea, and Europe, coupled with a worldwide recession in the early 1990s, a fatal Japanese weakness was exposed—an inability to make midcourse corrections. Japanese computer companies had an obsession with cutting prices to increase market share at the expense of profitability. By cutting prices, these Japanese companies lost money and could not find the funds to invest enough in newer high-tech products to compete. America grabbed the leading share of the world market in high-end chips from Japan, and the gap continued to grow.[17] American companies tapped what they believed to be a tremendous growth market with superior products to increase their market share. This movement announced to the world that America could be in a good economic position as the twenty-first century unfolds.[17]

Strategies of the Market Challenger

Champion Spark Plug Co. lost business when American cars reduced the number of cylinders per car and improved engine design, requiring fewer tuneups. Champion trimmed management, revamped factories, changed sales and marketing staffs, added new product lines that included air filters, ignition cables, batteries, and fuel additives, and invaded the international field.[16] Champion was forced to practice the market aggressor or assume the **challenger role** in different markets as a result of both environmental and competitive changes.

Market challengers have to have at least one prerequisite before they can start a successful challenge strategy. Market challengers have to have a sustainable, long-term competitive advantage with which to neutralize the leaders advantages. The challenger must recognize and create defenses against the leader's possible retaliation. The challenger must find a different strategy that can develop a sustainable competitive advantage. **Sustainable competitive advantage** can become effective when potential competitors either cannot or will not take action required to close the competitive gap. The challenger has to determine the leader's weakness and attack on as narrow a front as possible to maximize both **resources concentration** and **economy of force.**[18] According to Michael Porter, challenger attack strategies, as displayed in Figure 20-3, are aimed at the desired target firm or market segment. Challenger strategies include: (1) reconfiguration, (2) redefinition, and (3) pure spending.[19]

RECONFIGURATION

Reconfiguration implies a reengineering of many of the firm's resources. The more value-added activities or improvements made, the more the firm's ability to challenge the leader will be enhanced. One successful challenger attack that was largely ignored

FIGURE 20-3 Challenger strategies.

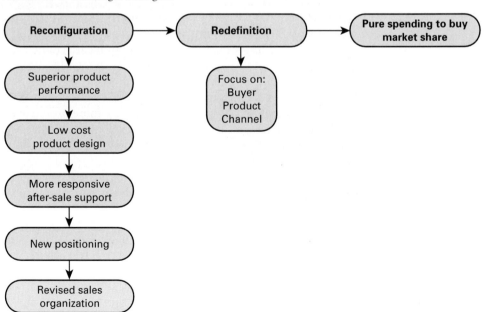

Source: Michael E. Porter, *Competitive Advantage* (New York: The Free Press, 1985), pp. 519-30. Adapted by permission of The Free Press, a division of Simon & Schuster.

by IBM was a small IBM-compatible company called Gateway Computing (not to be confused with the mail-order computer firm by the same name). Its name was changed to Compaq Computer on the recommendation of consultants. Known for its high-quality PCs because the company tested or "burned" each unit before shipment, Compaq struggled against all competitors until it reached the preeminent position of the number one seller in the PC market.[21]

Superior Product Performance   Rather than compete in the highly competitive airframes market by improving existing airframes, Boeing bypassed its competitors and developed the 777 to meet the needs of the twenty-first century. This required Boeing to dive into new technologies and unrelated processes and diversify into new markets. The 777 was the first aircraft to be developed by Boeing entirely through the use of CAD-CAM techniques.

Low-Cost Product Design   Japanese loss of leadership in the semiconductor market resulted from the strong attack by aggressive American firms who developed new products with lower costs. American chip makers were in a stronger position because they invested more heavily in research and development. This preparation in advanced R&D gained the lead in this high-tech market. Experts predicted that in low-tech color television, where Japan excels, a 5 percent annual growth in sales might be expected; but in advanced, multimedia personal computers, where the United States has the edge, a 35 percent annual growth was expected.[15]

More Responsive After-Sale Support   Vetco, a division of Combustion Engineering that sells off-shore drilling equipment, gained more customer favor by providing excellent training materials and other after-sale support to help its buyers master the complex underwater drilling task.[23]

New Positioning   The challenging battle for position on the Internet has forced innovation. Netscape's Navigator browser can be downloaded for free. Navigator was usually bundled with Windows95 PCs. This is a standard procedure that gave Navigator the number 1 browser position. Microsoft went a step father to best rival Netscape and achieve a new market position: it brought out a free program for running a Web site that could be downloaded from the Net and became part of Windows NT.[20]

A Changed Sales Organization   A new type of sales organization with different salespeople can be the basis for a successful attack on a leader. Rather than have its salespeople sell only one or two lines, Crown Cork and Seal's sales force sold the complete line of Crown's cans, bottle caps, and packaging machinery to canners on the same sales call. This move helped Crown to succeed against American Can and Continental Can.[11]

REDEFINITION

Despite the previous activities, which are usable for the market challenger, a harder hitting set of strategies and actions are created by redefining the scope of competition. A broadening of the scope can allow the construction of interrelationships or the benefits of integration. Narrowing the scope permits the tailoring of the challenger's activities focused on a particular target market.

Focus on the Buyer, Product, and/or Channel   A focused strategy is difficult for the leader to defense or to retaliate against without compromising its own strategy.

Specific attention is given by the challenger to a narrow range of buyer, product and/or channel objectives. This concentration of the challenger's strengths can be directed at weak spots in the leader's strategy, which may place the leader in a compromising position of not being able to respond without incurring sizable costs.

Geographic Redefinition   A leader may be successfully operating in a few countries, but can be attacked by the challenger with a regional or global strategy. The challenger broadens the geographic market to gain cost of competitive advantage through geographical interrelationships. The globalization of an industry has occurred in the construction equipment (Caterpillar), banking (CitiCorp), oil exploration (Exxon), and computer (IBM, Compaq), and semiconductor (Atmel), to name a few. By broadening the geographic markets forces the leader to spread their defenses, making it more vulnerable to attack.

PURE SPENDING TO BUY MARKET SHARE

The final and riskiest way to attack a leader is through pure spending without using any of the previous two strategies covered above. This involves investments to buy a market share, increase volume through lower prices, or use heavy product promotion. Although the least preferred approach by many firms, pure spending, is often costly and frequently fails.

Airbus invested much money in the development of the 340 to gain leadership in the business. Boeing developed the 777, which was a costly venture, to maintain its leadership. Boeing started to investigate the development of new jetliners, namely, the 747-500X/600X to keep the challenger, Airbus, at bay in the future. This anticipated event precipitated a battle between the aircraft engine manufacturers. A new aircraft engine typically costs $1 billion to $1.5 billion to design and produce, as opposed to redesigning an existing engine. General Electric and Pratt & Whitney, vigorous rivals in the aircraft engine business, agreed to jointly develop a new engine for the proposed Boeing jetliner. This 50-50 venture was discussed with Boeing who urged them to proceed.

Market Follower Strategies

The leader, challenger or attacker must commit financial funds, personnel, and extra executive time to initiate a new or modified product (product design, engineering, and product testing) and the new product's implementation (distribution, packaging, promotion, and pricing). These activities require the seller to develop overt competitive marketing strategies. Much sweat, time, stress, and uncertainty surround these undertakings. Some companies are not willing to accept or encumber all of these risks and the allocation of company resources, so they accept the less glamourous strategy as a market follower, a role that can provide high profits, to avoid the high cost and trauma associated with market leadership and offensive competitive challenger strategies. The follower can make a reasonable copy (an exact copy would be a counterfeit) or offer an improved product, and still stay out of trouble.

The follower firm may appear not to have a strategy, but, on the contrary, the follower's strategy is to remain close to the leaders it is imitating and to retain its customers by charging a lower price, offering better service, or being nicer to deal with than the sales reps with the leader firms.

Imitation and *conscious parallelism* is common in steel, chemicals, fertilizer, oil, coal, iron ore, aluminum, timber, soybeans, corn, and a host of other relatively homogeneous, standardized commodity markets that require capital intensive product refinement, mining, or product processing. From the customer's perspective, the difference in a commodity product versus a specialty product may rest with the place of extraction, the purity of the product, its price, its location of its resale, the services offered with the sale, any financing by the seller, and the amiability of the seller-buyer personalities involved.

Some commodity manufactures attempt to differentiate their products by customizing a product's engineering, shape, size, package, or price. One coal producer, for example, segmented its market and positioned itself by shaping its coal in standard sized briquettes for exclusive use in coke ovens for steel making, and in bake ovens (kilns) for drying ceramics products. In this case a commodity product was literally changed into a specialty product by some ingenuous marketing strategy along with market segmentation, target marketing and product retro-engineering.

Niche Marketing Strategies

A *niche marketer* specializes in one (or a few) narrow market segments whose needs fit those characteristics of that firm's particular set of capabilities and assets. Small companies, a small division of a larger company, or the large division of a large company can practice niche marketing. By its very size, any company can organize and dedicate its resources to the needs of a single market. A niche marketer survives and prospers if the niche is of sufficient size to justify a profitable operation, has growth potential, and sometimes may be so small as to be of little or no interest to larger, full-line marketers. A market niche may consist of an end user with specific needs (a records management consultant to bankruptcy cases), customer size (caters to only small customers), geographic location (sells only in a certain region or city), a job shop (customized decorative plastics for car and computer manufacturers), a product (produces semiconductors only), and channel specialty (purchases soybeans for resale to processors)

Successful niche marketers have been Dell Computer, a firm that specialized in mail-order sales, which affected Compaq's sales until the latter changed its strategy; business consultants who specialize in small accounts; Visioneer, a firm that makes only scanners for small operations; Quantum, which makes only disk drives for OEM and after market customers (one product, but two different markets); and Allegheny-Ludlum Steel, which only makes stainless steel.

Not having the experience and cash flow of a Xerox Corp., the Japanese companies Ricoh and Canon followed a niche strategy to hit the small office or home office copier market where Xerox didn't offer any products. They considered this niche to be Xerox's "Achilles heel." If a home office person needed copies at that time, he went to PIP or Kinkos, costing him both time and money. Xerox ignored this market, which was a bad defensive strategy for Xerox, but the company was number one in the industry and ignored any small, insignificant entrant. Xerox's revenue stream was from large machines for large corporations, universities, and libraries. Xerox was either unaware of the small office market or choose to ignore its existence. A growing market void existed. The Japanese saw this market and immediately pounced on it with inexpensive machines. Once the market was captured and secure, providing the Japanese firms with a good cash flow, these firms invaded the larger copier market and competed "head-to-head" with Xerox. The blow to Xerox was almost fatal. But with hard work and a changed marketing strategy ("the document company"), Xerox weathered the storm and survived to prosper in the nineties.

In a replay of their many invasions of the U.S. market, Japanese manufacturers invaded the fax market with convenient low-priced fax machines selling well below the current prices for larger American and European machines. This invasion spurred the widespread use of fax machines in the United States as Sharp, Canon, Brother, and Ricoh cashed-in by making the affordable small fax machines for small businesses and offices in the home. To fit these two market niches, the Japanese firms eliminated some features of the higher priced, larger machines.[21] The market grew rapidly as more and more companies acquired fax capability. More fax machines meant more use and hence, more fax sales. The market got so "hot" that dealers were unable to keep fax machines in stock. Customers placed orders for the machines, sight unseen.[22]

Once a strong market position was established in the small fax machine market, the Japanese used the lower-priced fax machines as a wedge to invade the higher-priced market once they had secured a good cash flow, name recognition, and a reputation for producing quality machines. The Japanese saw a further opening on their competitor's flank; they exploited it with large, improved fax machines and attempted to crush their competitors with a frontal assault by moving into the large, expensive machines market. The higher-priced Japanese fax machines could send multiple-page documents after hours, when the rates were cheaper; with the aid of feeders and more memory chips these fax machines could store phone numbers and instructions for automatic dialing. Canon and Ricoh launched even higher-priced machines that transmitted over digital networks rather than phone lines. The fax craze cost Federal Express about 30 percent of its overnight letter delivery business, although Fed Ex had been one of the first companies to try to make the business fax concept workable.

Niche marketing can be very profitable, given the lack of competition, high price, and the customer goodwill build-up over time, if the seller offers quality service, quality products and emphasizes a value-added product cluster. In other words, the seller has to give the customer more than what the customer expects. Some niche marketers find their niche by accident, but many find their niche by design and remain in the niche by preference.

Many commodity types of product marketers could take a lesson from the successful niche marketers who have differentiated their commodity by changing its characteristics to meet the needs of a small, but viable, market. Sometimes it is better to be number one in a small market with a 50 or 75 percent market share than it is to be way down the pack with a 1 or 2 percent market share in three larger markets.

High Market Share Risks

The classic **Profit Impact of Marketing Strategies** (PIMS) studies identified the most important variables that have an impact on profit. Of the twelve major components isolated in this giant study, high market share was highly correlated with high profitability. One study found that, on average, a difference of ten percentage points in market share is accompanied by a difference of about five points in pretax ROI.[23] These findings have prompted some companies to adopt strategies that ensured high market shares. GE sold off its small consumer appliance lines (irons, toasters, knife sharpeners, etc.) to Black and Decker because GE wanted to keep only companies that could and would maintain a first or second place market share position.

Richard Hamermesh and others have found that companies such as Unisys Corporation, Crown Cork & Seal Co., and Union Camp Corporation have been very profitable, although none of them enjoyed a dominant market share in their respective industries. Each company earns very respectable returns on its equity, each has healthy profit margins and each continues to maintain strong sales growth every year.[24] Woo and Cooper studied 40 successful low-share businesses and found that not being a market leader did not impair a company's financial results. The study concluded that high-performing, low-share businesses compete in particular environments and that their competitive strategy is reflected by their emphasis on prices, quality, product-line breadth, new products, and advertising and selling efforts. High performers normally offer superior products at prices lower than competition.[25]

Existing evidence shows that profitability actually falls after a company has increased its market share percentage beyond a point of diminishing returns as a result of higher costs, government regulations, and ineffective strategic and managerial implementation. As market share increases, and the experience curve materializes, profitability will increase up to the point of diminishing returns. But which companies are foolish enough to operate at or beyond diminishing returns? One company made semiautomatic tire changers for garages and service stations. The firm grew so fast that it was unable to produce a quality product because of the cost of new construction, a situation exacerbated by a great deal of mismanagement. The company was out of business within 7 years and could not understand why.

Managing the Total Business Cycle Time

Another competitive weapon that is useful for increasing a company's competitive impact has been called the *business cycle time advantage*. A company's total business-cycle time (Figure 20-4) is measured from the time a customer's need is identified to receipt of payment from the customer for the finished product. The total business cycle time includes any or all of the following subcycles or loops[26]: (1) the *make/ship loop,*

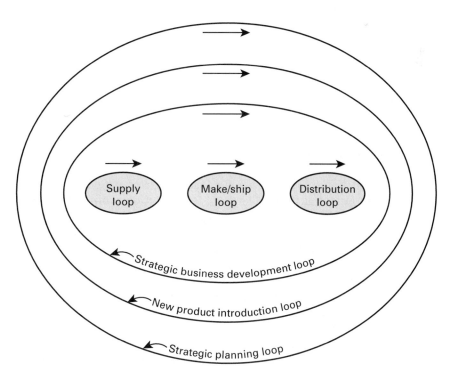

FIGURE 20-4 A seller's total cycle time with component loops.

(2) the *distribution loop*, (3) the *supply loop*, (4) the *new product introduction loop*, and (5) the *strategic business development loop*. As the manufacturing cycle time decreases, the cycle time for processing a customer's purchase order becomes greater than the time it takes to manufacture the product.

PRODUCT LIFE CYCLES AND COMPETITIVE ADVANTAGE

Reducing total cycle time is also beneficial for the seller. In Figure 20-4, the total life cycle cost is represented by the outside loop, the strategic planning loop. The next inside loop, the new product introduction loop starts with the identification of the need for the product, to the final delivery of the product to the customer. The new product introduction loop has four loops within (not shown in the figure) which are (1) new product strategies, (2) new product research, (3) product development, and (4) launch activities. The third inside loop is the strategic business development loop includes the time required to develop a new strategy, make the decision to adopt the strategy, and then to implement the strategy. The final inside loops are the supply loop, make/ship loop, and the distribution loop. (This discussion will be treated in greater depth later in this chapter.) A significant point here is that life cycles throughout the company must be reduced to better serve the customer and to maintain a competitive advantage.

Of all the different loops, the strategic business development loop is probably the most poorly managed of all the loops as a result of the people in this loop's lack of understanding of the high financial returns to be gained from improving the loop's cycle time.[26]

VARYING LENGTHS OF LIFE CYCLES

Life cycle durations for many business products have become shorter and shorter, as firms cut costs and reach the market in as short a period as possible. Whoever reaches the market first usually has the best competitive advantage and the greatest defense against their competitors. Business life cycle durations can be characterized as long, moderate, or short.

Long life cycle products such as pharmaceuticals, machine tools, installation equipment, construction equipment, and plant and office construction, are protected by the lengthy engineering time and/or by patents and brand names. Intel made its brand a household name with "Intel Inside," but an individual can not buy an Intel chip. The company has captured market segments in both the industrial OEM market and the consumer market providing some demand pull in this latter market. This is the best position from which to operate, because many of the product bugs can be worked out before the completion of the project as evidenced by Intel's initial problems with its Pentium chip.

Moderate life cycle products have less time to turn around. Computer software, once thought to have a long life cycle has been reduced as a result of competitive activity. Once customers hear of a new computer application, they frequently want the new application tomorrow. With moderate life cycle products the barriers to imitation and innovation are much lower; therefore, managers must be alert to constantly changing customer tastes and vicissitudes of competitive pressures.

Short life cycle products have the greatest competition and the shortest time to turn for any aspect. Engineers and marketers are running to maintain their present position in the market. As soon as engineers release a product for production, they have to start designing its replacement. Scanners, CD-ROM drives, fax machines, industrial hand tools, and lubricants tend to fall into this category.

MISGUIDED USE OF THE CYCLE TIME CONCEPT

In the 1980s most companies trying to make improvements focused on the make/ship loop. As long as customers tolerated the long wait, the system worked; the manufacturing process was enhanced because "economical batch sizes" was the driving force at the time. When customers demanded shorter delivery time (as we moved to just-in-time deliveries), companies who followed the make/ship loop responded in the following, unhealthy ways. First, the manufacturing department was persuaded to commit to unrealistic delivery times. Sales departments soon found they were forced to break promises to customers when production/operations failed to meet the delivery schedule, which also increased tension with the production people.

Second, the increased factory orders for finished goods and distribution inventory increasingly put more pressure on manufacturing, further exacerbating some of the mistrust between manufacturing and marketing. As a result, the already uncertain sales forecasts had to be projected even further into the future so that material supplies for manufacturing could be ordered and delivered on time. As the forecast times were extended, the potential for error and disagreement increased. Competitors stole market share with a shorter strategic-business-development loop, since they were producing at lower costs as a result of smaller inventories and less waste of time and materials.

To succeed in the coming decades, firms will have to dramatically reduce their new product-introduction time. The keys to success will be to integrate (1) new product strategies, (2) new product research, (3) product development, and (4) launch activities into one effective short-cycle capability that can respond consistently to ever-increasing market demands.[26] In addition, firms who expect to be competitive must integrate their strategic-business-development loops into the other loops by eliminating non-essential tasks, improving the communications flows, and basically reengineering all the critical loops to improve the company's competitive advantage and offer a superior customer service.

Looking Back

In the continuing struggle to increase or maintain market share in the face of stubborn competition, competitive marketing strategies have become a necessary study for many executives. Since a small increase in market share can often mean a sizable increase in revenue flow, marketing wars among firms have become intense.

Four major types of competitive strategies exist: market leaders, market challengers, market followers, and niche markers.

Market leaders attempt to increase the size of the market pie by increasing total market demand, by protecting present share, and by increasing market share at the expense of competitors. The leader's defensive strategies include raising structural barriers, increasing expected retaliation, and lowering the challenger's inducement to attack.

Market challenger's attacks include reconfiguration, redefinition, and pure spending to buy market share. The market challenger attempts to unseat the market leader by employing one or a combination of these strategies. If not performed just right, the market challenger could suffer immense damage, which could restrict some company's future operations.

Market follower and niche marketing strategies can be very profitable, for these strategies appeal to smaller firms who do not wish to engage a larger firm in open combat. Both strategies seek smaller market segments where their market shares can balloon without attracting the attention of the market leader and/or the market challengers, for larger market shares in much smaller markets can be very profitable.

In spite of the PIMS study that suggested a high market share can enhance a company's profit potential, other studies have shown a lower market share can also provide satisfactory profits. As market share increases, a point of diminishing returns may set in and higher costs incurred beyond this point could tax a company's profit picture.

Managing and shrinking the total business-cycle time concept, which stresses better management, reduced timing for all company functions, and improved customer service appears to offer a more promising future as efficiencies gained through better management of the existing resources can provide greater profits and greater service through a better competitive advantage.

Questions for Discussion

1. Discuss in detail why the size of a company's market share is so important to the business marketing firm.

2. Throughout the discussion on competitive strategy, why is the concentration of company resources so important?

3. How can a return to a firm's basic line of business be used to enhance a firm's profitability?

4. Why should the market leader stress enlarging the total market pie as opposed to enlarging its slice of that pie? Discuss all the ramifications of this situation.

5. Does practicing a market follower strategy mean the firm does not have a strategy and simply wishes to save money in market research and promotion? Explain, in detail.

6. Why is niche marketing the most opportunistic for the smaller producer with limited resources? Why may niche marketing be suitable or unsuitable for a larger marketer?

7. Why is business life cycle timing so important to the satisfaction of the customer and to the seller's profitability?

Endnotes

1. Stanley F. Slater, "Competing in high-velocity markets," *Industrial Marketing Management* 22 (November, 1993):255-63.

2. "Wonder chips, how they'll make computing power ultrafast and ultracheap," *Business Week* (July 4, 1994), pp. 86-91.

3. "Are IBM and Apple a day late?" *Business Week* (October 24, 1994), pp. 34-5.

4. Michael Treacy and Fred Wiersema, *Discipline of Market Leaders* (Reading, Mass.: Addison-Wesley Publishing Co., 1995), p. 9.

5. "IBM: There's many a slip . . . ," *Business Week* (June 27, 1994), pp. 26-27.

6. Philip Kotler, *Marketing Management, Analysis, Planning, Implementation, and Control,* 8th ed. (Englewood Cliffs, N.J.: Prentice Hall, Inc., 1994), pp. 383-4.

7. "Product design, another breed of Cat," *Business Week* (January 11, 1988), p. 148.

8. "That sinking feeling at Airbus," *Business Week* (July 18, 1994), pp. 49-50.

9. "Here comes the bicoastal desktop," *Business Week* (July 18, 1994), p. 16.

10. Stanley F. Slater, "The challenge of sustaining competitive advantage," *Industrial Marketing Management* 25 (1996):79-86.

11. Michael E. Porter, *Competitive Advantage* (New York: The Free Press, 1985), Chapters 3-5 and 7.

12. "Just imagine if times were good," *Business Week* (April 17, 1995), pp. 78-9.

13. John B. Clark, *Marketing Today, Success, Failures, and Turnarounds* (Englewood Cliffs, N.J.: Prentice Hall, Inc., 1987), pp. 152-4.

14. "Defying the law of gravity," *Business Week* (April 8, 1996), pp. 124-6.

15. "Chipping away at Japan," *U.S. News & World Report* 119 (July 18, 1994):47.

16. "Champion is starting to show a little spark," *Business Week* (March 21, 1988), p. 87.

17. Kevin P. Coyne, "Sustainable competitive advantage—what it is, what it isn't," *Business Horizons* 29 (January-February, 1986):58.

18. Al Reis and Jack Trout, *Marketing Warfare* (New York: McGraw-Hill Book Co., 1986), Chapter 8.

19. Many of the ideas in this section have been adapted from Michael E. Porter, *Competitive Advantage* (New York: The Free Press, 1985), pp. 519-30.

20. "Browsing for a bruising?" *Business Week* (March 11, 1996), pp. 82-4.

21. "Its a fax, fax, fax, fax world," *Business Week* (March 21, 1988), p. 136.

22. Personal communication, 1985.

23. For more details, see the definitive study by Sidney Schoeffler, Robert D. Buzzell, and Donald F. Heany, "Impact of strategic planning on profit performance," *Harvard Business Review* 52 (March-April 1974):137-45, or Robert D. Buzzell, Bradley T. Gale, and Ralph G. M. Sultan, "Market share—a key to profitability," *Harvard Business Review* 53 (January-February 1975):97-106.

24. R.G. Hamermesh, M.J. Anderson, Jr., and J.E. Harris, "Strategies for low market share businesses," *Harvard Business Review* (May-June 1978), pp. 95-102.

25. Carolyn Y. Woo and Arnold C. Cooper, "The surprising case for low market share," *Harvard Business Review* 60 (November-December 1982), pp. 106-113; see also Robert Jacobson and David A. Acker, "Is market share all that it's cracked up to be?" *Journal of Marketing* 49 (Fall 1985):11-12; and Robert Jacobson, "Distinguishing among competing theories of the market share effect," *Journal of Marketing* 52 (October 1988):68-80.

26. "The cycle-time advantage," *Industry Week* (July 19, 1993), pp. 11-12.

Bibliography

Calantone, Roger J., and C. Anthony di Benedetto, "Defensive industrial marketing strategies," *Industrial Marketing Management* 19 (1990):267-78.

Cardozo, Richard N., Shannon H. Shipp, and Kenneth J. Roering, "Proactive strategic partnerships: A new business markets strategy," *Journal of Business and Industrial Marketing* 7 (Winter 1992):51-63.

Cooper, A., and D. Schendel, "Strategic responses to technological threats," *Business Horizons* 19 (1976):61-9.

Fogg, C. Davis, "Planning gains in market share," *Journal of Marketing* 38 (July 1974):30-38.

Hauser, John R., and S. Shugan, "Defensive marketing strategies," *Marketing Science* 2 (1983):319-60.

Onkvisit, Sak, and John J. Shaw, "Myopic management: The hollow strength of American competitiveness," *Business Horizons* 34 (January-February 1991):13-19.

Paley, Norton, "A strategy for all ages: Basing strategies on product life cycle can give you a vital competitive edge," *Sales and Marketing Management* 146 (January 1994):51-2.

Popper, Edward T., and Bruce D. Buskirk, "Technology life cycles in industrial markets," *Industrial Marketing Management* 21 (February 1992):23-31.

Ramaswany, Venkatram, Hubert Gatignon, and David J. Reibstein, "Competitive marketing behavior in industrial markets," *Journal of Marketing* 58 (April 1994):45-55.

"The cycle-time advantage, an integrated approach delivers the greatest competitive impact, contend the authors of a new book on managing the total business cycle," *Industry Week* (July 19, 1993):11-12.

Woo, Carolyn Y., "Market-share leadership—not always so good," *Harvard Business Review* (January-February 1984):50+.

CHAPTER 21

Strategic Control

Up to this point, throughout the text we have emphasized proper planning, product strategies, product-market matching and efficiently promoting, pricing and distributing business products and services. All these activities, of course, eventually focus on the "bottom line" or on a product's net profit or profit contribution. Marketing managers often can get caught up in the day-to-day activities of running the firm's marketing operations and sometimes overlook their product and marketing activities evaluation and control responsibilities.

Some business firms actually are unaware of some of their important marketing costs that may rob the company of profitability for a given product, profit center, division, plant, and so on. "Only 40 percent or so of cost information is now reliable," says Bala Balachandran, director of the Accounting Research Center at Northwestern University's Kellogg School of Management. "The rest is stupid allocation. The degree of error has risen to the point where companies do not know whether they are losing or gaining on any particular product. . . .One major multinational tried cutting its unprofitable lines in the 1990s. The result: Losses tripled. It turned out that the company inadvertently outsourced production of its best moneymaker and greatly increased production of its unprofitable lines."[1]

Some firms believe that sales and marketing organizations should investigate some innovations in the area of cost management instead of only product and service revenues. Possible innovative cost strategies include containment, transformation, sharing, piggybacking and substitution.[2]

This chapter investigates the strategic control factors and procedures useful for the control enhancement of business marketing activities. This chapter covers the following strategic control factors:

1. The annual plan control including sales analysis, market share analysis, marketing expense-to-sales analysis, financial analysis, and customer-attitude tracking analysis

2. The profitability control including full costing versus contributory costing, full costing, net profit approach, contribution margin, activity-based costing, and semifixed costs

3. The efficiency control for the sales force, sales promotion, advertising, and distribution

4. The strategic control using the marketing effectiveness rating review, and the marketing audit

5. The concept of a marketing controller

The Need for Control

In a private study of 75 companies of varying sizes in different industries, the following was found[3]:

1. Smaller companies have poorer controls than larger companies and do a poorer job of setting clear objectives and systems to measure performance.
2. Fewer than half of the companies know the profit for individual products, and about one-third have no regular review process for identifying and deleting weak products.
3. About half of the companies fail to compare their prices with competition, analyze their warehousing and distribution costs, determine advertising's effectiveness, or review sales force call reports.
5. Many companies do not have control reports ready until 4 to 6 weeks later, and many are inaccurate.

As discussed in Chapter 18, the experience curve doctrine holds that causation runs from market share building to cost advantage. The driver for any particular business unit is the combination of volition, imagination, and cost-effective expenditure of effort that the unit brings to bear on the task of decreasing the average total cost schedule. However, the impact of *economies of scale* on efficiency is modest over time in comparison with the impact of innovation. Cost management is a push game where a business unit attempts to push its average total cost schedule below that of its rivals to obtain a primary competitive cost advantage. Therefore, an opportunity exists to increase profits by either holding the price and increasing the firm's return on equity or by cutting price and increasing the firm's market share, if the market is expandable.

The Control Process

As illustrated in Figure 21-1, the control process, is a closed loop system that represents a feedback system where the term *control* means to take corrective actions to ensure that planning results have been achieved. The strategic planning phase initiates the plan and gives direction to the organization. The plan is implemented, resulting in the system's output or results. The results are measured against the plan's predetermined evaluative criteria, and any variances between the plan's anticipated results and the actual results are then corrected with marketing actions or costs modification.

Business marketing control contains a number of entities. Philip Kotler, distinguishes four distinct areas of marketing control that are critical to a firm's success and its future viability[3]:

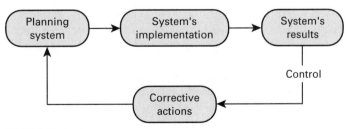

FIGURE 21-1 The control process.

1. *Annual plan control:* check ongoing performance against the annual plan and take necessary corrective actions to attain the plan's expected results.
2. *Profitability control:* determine actual profitability of different products, territories, end-use markets, and channels as best it can be done.
3. *Efficiency control:* search for ways to improve the impact on profitability of different marketing tools and expenditures.
4. *Strategic control:* determine whether the company's basic marketing strategies are well matched with market opportunities.

Annual Plan Control

The annual plan control mechanism must be built into the plan when it is developed to facilitate control of all activities. After the plan has been activated, these mechanisms used for control are (1) the quantitative-qualitative analysis of sales and marketing goals, (2) the plan's time-frame horizons, and (3) the necessary procedures for measuring the progress of the plan's implementation. Business marketing managers have found that *management by objectives* (MBO) tenets are profitable, if properly used.[4] Under an MBO plan, the manager, in conjunction with each member of the unit, jointly plan the tasks to be accomplished by each member. Three distinct phases of this planning are involved. First, the manager and participant establish common task goals; second, they develop the procedures to be followed to achieve these goals; and third, they estimate the approximate costs that would be involved in the procedural phase of the process. Periodically during the implementation of the plan, the manager and each participating member evaluate the progress made up to that point by each participant toward achieving the planned tasks or goals. The member's degree of progress is then evaluated against the planned goals. These events and accomplishments are used as the basis for recommendation of any corrective actions which should be taken to assist the participant in their quest to attain the planned goals.

MBO planning techniques highlight the manager's need to achieve results. This situation occurs when managers desire to accept responsibility for achieving these results, and their right to exercise a high degree of self-control in their job performance. The underlying assumption is that the manager should be directly involved in the planning, organizing, and controlling of their job while working with their subordinates. Making these things happen at the same time requires establishing monthly or quarterly review benchmarks to alert marketing managers to take early action, if necessary, to correct any variance between the planned goals and the progress achieved so far. The key to the whole system is to isolate the cause of the variance and to take the corrective actions as soon as possible to minimize any further damage.

Five useful tools are available for managers to measure, evaluate, and control their annual plans: (1) sales analysis, (2) market share analysis, (3) marketing expense-to-sales analysis, (4) financial analysis, and (5) customer-satisfaction tracking.[3]

SALES ANALYSIS

Sales analysis, or micro-sales analysis, typically measures actual sales against the planned sales goals and calculates the variance or difference between the two. This analysis helps marketers evaluate the strengths involved and helps marketing managers to determine which corrective actions have to be taken. For example, a manufacturer planned to sell 840 filtration units in the first quarter of the fiscal year at $75 per unit (total of $63,000), but at the end of the first quarter, 768 units averaging $64 per unit (total of $49,152) were sold. A negative variance of $13,848 or 22 percent of expected sales existed. This negative sales performance resulted from one of two things. Either the price declined per unit of sale, hence producing lower revenues, or a sales decline transpired because of numerous other factors that are not always obvious, as marketers would like them to be.

$$\text{Variance resulting from price decline} = (\$75 - \$64)(768)$$
$$= \$8.448 \ (61\%)$$
$$\text{Variance resulting from volume decline} = (\$75)(840 - 768)$$
$$= \$5,400 \ (38.9\%)$$

Almost two thirds (61 percent) of the sales variance in this example is the result of the price decline, suggesting the company should reevaluate its price of filtration units, given the market response, if it expects to achieve its planned dollar sales volume.

Micro-sales analysis can take another approach. Marketers can look at products and territories to ascertain discrepancies that would alert managers to study the problems further. As seen in Table 21-1, if four sales territories were expected to sell 17, 14, 23, and 7 units respectively, but after 6 months produced 18, 12, 8, and 10, respectively, micro-sales analysis would show these discrepancies expressed as percentages. Territory 1 had 106 percent of quota, territory 2 had 86 percent, territory 3 had 35 percent, and territory 4 had 143 percent.

Further analysis of Table 21-1 would isolate additional pertinent facts. Territory 4's quota (143 percent) may appear to have the best performance, but on closer inspection of the data, territory 4's sales quota may have been set too low, or territory 4's sales potential may have increased immeasureably, because of the arrival of new industries after the sales quotas were set. Under these circumstances, it is possible that the sales rep in territory 4 could have been coasting in a growing territory and simply reaped the benefits. Thus, territory 4 may have been one of the worst territories, as determined by micro-sales analysis, in contrast to a cursory examination of the available statistics. Territory 2's sales rep achieved only 86 percent of sales quota and may need assistance and a little prodding if an investigation does not turn up either a drastic change in economic sales potential in the territory or the realization that an incorrect sales quota was assigned. Territory 3, with only 35 percent of quota, appears to have serious problems, which may suggest inexperience, sickness, or even personal problems. The sales manager should take corrective actions in territory 3 as soon as possible, since the present territorial resources are not being used properly. The manager should investigate recent economic growth or decline in the territory, the fairness of the sales quota, and any personal problems that may exist beyond the sales rep's control.

It may seem rather strange that marketing managers must investigate the existence of any personal problems, but one should realize that sales are made by human beings, and this relationship includes all the successes and failures experienced by any human.

TABLE 21-1   Sales Territory Performance Analysis

Territory	Sales Quota (budget)	Actual Sales	Variance	Percent
1	17	18	+1	106
2	14	12	−2	86
3	23	8	−15	35
4	7	10	+3	143

Any distraction, such as a divorce or sickness, which interrupts or reduces the rep's sales production, becomes significant cost factors for the firm and must be investigated.

MARKET SHARE ANALYSIS

Tracking market share provides a different perspective than sales data analysis in that it can show how well, at a given point in time, a company or product is doing against competitors. Simple market share analysis (company sales divided by industry sales) may not be good enough, however. Some Japanese companies may sacrifice short-term profits to capture a larger market share to better control the market. Subsequently, after the degree of market control is achieved, these firms raise prices to increase their profits (Figure 21-2). Apple reduced many prices to maintain its number two market share position in personal computers, only to find that profits shrank appreciably. The company's financial troubles forced many buyers to postpone purchases of Apple computers, thus exacerbating the situation.[5]

Many factors have to be considered to arrive at a reasonably accurate market share analysis. The impact of outside forces on the different companies; the industry segment used to judge market share; the entrance of new firms into the industry; forced profit enhancement by a competitor who may have dropped unprofitable customers to show a higher profit; and unusual shifts in market share because of an unusually large order have to be taken into consideration, or else the market share analysis could produce faulty results.[6]

Kotler believes a more correct way to analyze market share is expressed in the following relationship[3]:

$$\frac{\text{Overall market}}{\text{share}} = \frac{\text{Customer}}{\text{penetration}} \times \frac{\text{Customer}}{\text{loyalty}} \times \frac{\text{Customer}}{\text{selectivity}} \times \frac{\text{Price}}{\text{selectivity}}$$

where

Customer penetration is the percentage of all customers who buy from the company.

Customer loyalty is the purchases from the company expressed as a percentage of their purchases from all other companies.

Customer selectivity is the size of the average customer purchase expressed as a percentage of the average purchase from an average company.

Price selectivity is the average price charged by this company expressed as a percentage of the average price charged by all the companies.

FIGURE 21-2 Impact of effort to increase market share on price and quantity.

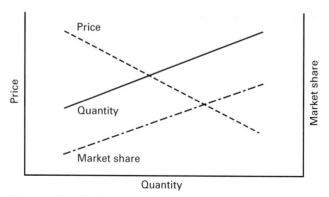

(Assumption: all other variables remain unchanged)

If a company's market share falls in a given period, this equation can provide four possible explanations:

- The company lost some of its customers (lower customer penetration).
- Existing customers are buying a smaller share of their supplies from this company (lower customer loyalty).
- The company's existing customers are smaller (lower customer selectivity).
- The company's price has slipped relative to that of its competition (lower price selectivity).

By tracking these factors over time, marketing management can make a better diagnoses of the underlying market share changes. By comparing each of the four factor's series' trend lines, strengths and weaknesses can be spotted easily. If the customer selectivity series is down, the company's share is on a serious slide compared with other companies in the industry.

MARKETING EXPENSE-TO-SALES ANALYSIS

When a marketing expense-to-sales ratio exceeds the planned boundaries, collection of data is necessary to isolate the inherent strengths, weaknesses and the possibility of potential problem(s). Illustrating how these ratios can provide significant information useful for making intelligent decisions, Table 21-2 compares sales revenue and sales expenses in two different sales territories. Territory 1, shown in Table 21-2, has an ME-S ratio of 15:1; that is, for every $15 of sales revenue, expenses represent $1. Territory 2's ME-S ratio is 13:1, which indicates a higher total expense. Territory 2 has more travel and entertainment expenses, but fewer sales calls and other factors, not disclosed by these data. The fact that these data do not tell the whole story is significant. However, the ME-S ratio for territory 2 alerts the sales manager that a problem may exist.

The variances in travel between the two territories may indicate the differences in the size of each territory, given the $16,700 travel expense of territory 2 versus the travel expense of $11,500 for territory 1. This overall conclusion may well be right, but until the size of the territories is determined, no absolute decision can be made. Assuming that the two territories are approximately the same size, then territory 2 could be wasting company gas and automotive expense. Again, these data may only alert the sales manager to the possibility that a problem may exist. On further investigation, the sales manager finds that territory 2 is experiencing a rapid period of growth (relative to territory 1) and is stimulating the territorial manager to make more fre-

TABLE 21-2   Marketing Expense-to-Sales Analysis

		Territory 1	*Territory 2*
Sales revenue ($)		1,250,000	1,175,000
Sales expenses ($)	Salary	35,000	35,000
	Travel	11,500	16,700
	Entertainment	7,800	13,800
	Auto repair	700	2,700
	Insurance	2,000	2,000
	Sales commission	26,000	17,500
	TOTAL EXPENSE	83,000	87,700
Marketing expense-to-sales ratio		15:1	13:1

quent trips to the field to investigate the newly arrived industries. Territory 1's travel activity illustrates a more stable, less dynamic territory. But fewer sales calls are registered in another report (daily call report).

How can this discrepancy between total marketing expenses and sales calls be interpreted? One could conclude that the territory manager has been wasting time and has not been as productive. Certainly the marketing expense-to-sales figure offers some explanation, particularly the exorbitant entertainment expense incurred in territory 2 relative to territory 1. The rapid growth of territory 2 and the fact that more industries are moving into the territory may justify the higher entertainment expense as the territory manager seeks to become acquainted with the new arrivals. This theory sounds good, but the experienced sales manager knows that new accounts do not require higher entertainment expenses in the early stages of generating a sale, whereas older, more established accounts require more entertainment expenses, such as lunches and baseball tickets, as the possibility of a sale reaches a close, or competitive actions require more expenditure to maintain a competitive advantage. Therefore, the territory 2 manager should investigate the higher entertainment expenses to determine the cause.

Electronic or E commerce has become an essential part of doing business; it can reduce the costs of order procurement and hence reduce the marketing expence-to-sales ratio. The widespread use of computers allows a company to display an electronic catalog on the Internet from which a buyer places an order by computer. The seller brings up the customer's profile and the order is approved after a check of the customer's credit. If the items ordered are in inventory, the order is sent electronically to the warehouse with delivery instructions. The order is shipped and the customer receives an invoice via computer. Hence, the computer has radically altered the way business buys and sells by eliminating much of the paperwork and giving the customer more choices.[7]

FINANCIAL ANALYSIS

Financial analysis is used to determine the factors that affect the company's rate of return on net worth. As can be seen in Figure 21-3, the financial model of return on net worth is the result of two ratios: return on assets (asset turnover times net earnings) and financial leverage (assets divided by net worth). To increase net profits, a company must either increase its ratio of net profits to assets or increase the ratio of assets to net worth, or both.

The return on assets is derived by the percentage that net profits represent total assets, or profit margin multiplied by asset turnover. The business marketing executive can improve performance by either increasing net sales, decreasing costs, increasing asset turnover via an increase in net sales, and/or reducing total investment by carrying smaller inventories and faster moving goods. These relationships follow accepted accounting practices but do not provide the best answers, relative to asset allocation or making a choice in marketing strategy. The concept of *activity-based costing* (ABC) has provided many answers and it links the performing of particular activities with the demand those activities make on the organization's resources.[8] The ABC helps marketing managers focus their attention and energy on improving activities that will have the biggest impact on the bottom line. This matching process can give managers a clear picture of how products, customers, or distribution channels both generate revenues and consume resources. Marketing managers should refrain from allocating all expenses to individual products and instead separate the expenses and match them to the level of activity that

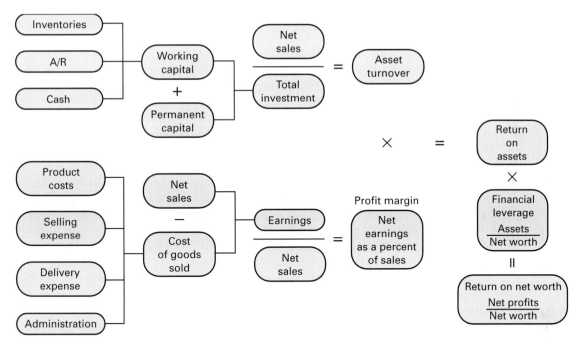

FIGURE 21-3 Financial model of return on net worth.

consumes the resources. In other words, managers should separate the expenses incurred to produce individual units of a particular product from the expenses needed to produce different products or to serve different customers, regardless of how many units are produced or sold. Then the managers should explore ways to reduce the resources required to perform various activities and transform these reductions into profits.

CUSTOMER SATISFACTION TRACKING

Customer satisfaction tracking is a qualitative method to monitor and assess customer's attitudes toward a company's products or professional services, product service before and after the sale, and the quality of its marketing personnel. The system is an early warning alert to management of impending or forthcoming market share changes. Marketers, once forewarned, can take early actions to cope with any pending negative market share change before such market changes can damage future sales. Surveys, telemarketing follow-ups, and sales rep's reports are usually used to generate the data that are funneled into a marketing management's intelligence system. Violating the cardinal sin of not being on top of market variables and being manipulated by these same market variables personifies poor management and, perhaps, a complete absence of control by the marketing management.

Projection of the company's market orientation, as perceived by customers, helps to build company goodwill and strengthen customer relations. This phase of the annual plan control process should be an ongoing operation as the company continually seeks to gain insights into its market's needs, subsequent forecasts of these needs, and then translation of these needs into marketable products/services and marketing programs. Without monitoring its customer's satisfaction levels and subsequent needs, control could be an anathema.

Profitability Control

Since the "bottom line" is so important, it is mystifying to know that anywhere from 20 to 40 percent of a company's products, and up to 60 percent of its accounts, can generate losses. A mere 15 percent of a company's relationships with its customers produce the bulk of its profits.[3] An earlier study that surveyed industry's use of cost accounting found that only 51 percent of the firms surveyed monitor contribution costs after direct marketing expenses have been accounted, and fewer than half of the firms (44 percent) examine net profit by product lines.[9]

The infrequent use of common accounting ratios and financial analysis by business marketers is also the result of a lack of understanding of both accounting practices and financial analysis (Box 21-1). This oversight can produce heavy cash outlays for projects unworthy of the expenditure. For example, one high-tech company with an operating profit of 4.5 percent, half the operating percentage average of its main competitors, responded by pouring in different types of resources to increase the company's sales volume. The company hired more sales reps, spent more money on advertising, and culminated its strategy to become more profitable by offering price reductions. These moves had some advantageous outcomes: the company experienced an increase in its growth rate by 10 percent and reduced operating profit from the original 4.5 percent to 2.3 percent. After making all these changes, however, the profit problem still existed. The company reversed itself by performing some simple ratio analysis, which showed that cost and pricing were causing the profit problem, not sales volume.[10] Figure 21-4 shows a number of accounting and financial ratios that can be useful to business marketing managers to eliminate the error in the previous example. Note that the *return on assets* (ROA), sales/assets, and gross profit/net profit can offer the business manager some of the best insights for control of the operation.

BOX 21-1

Accounting to the Rescue?

If equal proposals were made by the controller and the marketing vice president for the same return at the same cost, a president of a firm would choose the controller's proposal because this analysis is based on sound facts that have a track record. The marketing vice president's proposal would lack the solid promise that what is proposed will be delivered. Therefore, according to Charles W. Stryker, president of Trinet Inc. (Parsippany, N.J.), an information products and services subsidiary of Control Data Corp., companies should have a marketing P&L so he can offer solid, analytical proposals.

The marketing P&L could display all companies in a given industry, companies of a given size, or companies which have placed orders in excess of a specific dollar amount. Using the P&L format, an aging report could show how quickly a company gets its money from customers. Marketers could examine the relationship between the time they spend marketing dollars and the time when revenues come in. The rate of return concept could show the cost of establishing a new account and the resulting revenue produced from that account expressed as a rate of return. Some good food for thought.

Source: Charles W. Stryker, "Take a cue from accounting . . . yes accounting," *Business Marketing* 71 (November 2, 1986):144.

ROE =	$\dfrac{\text{Net earnings (after taxes)}}{\text{Owner's equity}}$	Return on earnings, best for investors
ROA =	$\dfrac{\text{Net earnings (after taxes)}}{\text{Total assets}}$	Return on assets, best for marketers
NP to sales =	$\dfrac{\text{Net profit (before taxes)}}{\text{Net sales}}$	Testing sales volume to be compared with competitors
Sales/assets =	$\dfrac{\text{Net sales}}{\text{Total assets}}$	How well assets are used
Sales/employees =	$\dfrac{\text{Net sales}}{\text{Number of employees}}$	Indication of sales volume problems
Collection period (CP) and inventory turns CP (days) =	$\dfrac{\text{Accounts receivable}}{\text{Net sales}} \times 365 \text{ turns}$	
=	$\dfrac{\text{Cost of sales}}{\text{Inventory}}$	Compare collection period, and stock turns with industry average
Gross profit % =	$\dfrac{\text{Gross profit}}{\text{net sales}} \times 100\%$	Pricing problems are indicated when problems with gross profit percentage exist

FIGURE 21-4 Accounting and financial calculations useful for business-industrial marketing managers.

FULL COSTING VERSUS CONTRIBUTORY COSTING

The reason that known accounting techniques are not used more often to determine product costs frequently relates to the complexities of accounting techniques and the higher costs their use would incur.

As illustrated in Figure 21-5, a comparison is made of two widely used costing techniques: (1) the full costing, in which all fixed and variable costs are allocated to a product regardless of the cost's relationship with the product, and (2) contributory costing, in which only relevant variable and fixed costs that are directly traceable to the product are allocated to the product's cost structure.

FULL COST (NET PROFIT) APPROACH

The full cost approach mandates that costs be separated according to function, such as cost of goods sold and operating costs. Marketing cost analysis relates the cost of marketing activities to sales revenues to measure profits. Hence, a profit and loss statement must be constructed for any marketing component.[11] Relating the sales revenue and marketing costs to a particular market segment greatly improves the company's ability to make the right control decisions for segmenting markets and designating which activities should be entered into a given segment. The administrative and general expenses, such as accounting, corporate headquarters expense, public relations expense, consulting expense, and sales administrative expense, would be arbitrarily assigned, using acceptable cost accounting practices, to the operating expense of the marketing department to derive net income, as shown in Figure 21-5.

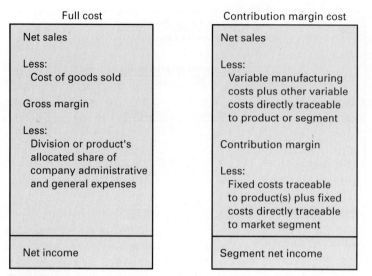

FIGURE 21-5 Full cost versus contribution margin cost approaches income statement.

CONTRIBUTION MARGIN (DIRECT) COSTING

Contributory margin costing eliminates some of the tedium and costs experienced in full cost allocation since it deals only with variable and fixed costs that are directly traceable to the product or market segment under examination. Contribution margin costing allows separation of costs by behavior into variable and fixed costs, rather than by functions, as in the case when full costing is used.[12] Variable costs are those costs that vary predictably with some measure of production or sales activity during a given period of time. For example, variable costs are sales commissions that vary by the amount of sales made, and materials cost that vary depending on how many units are produced. Fixed costs are the costs which do not change in the short run, as exemplified by a sales manager's salary, plant insurance, and mortgage payments for a company's property indebtedness. The economic term *short run* implies the absence of a change in plant, whereas *long run* suggests the plant size has been changed.

THE PROBLEM OF SEMIFIXED COSTS

Many expenses normally encountered in business marketing decision making are neither totally fixed nor totally variable costs, but they may fall into a semifixed cost category. An increasing fixed expense level may occur on some items, regardless of a product's sales volume. These types of expenses are semifixed costs, which include advertising, telephone, utilities, office salaries, bonuses, training, inventory and warehousing costs.[13] These semifixed costs may stir some consternation among marketing cost analysts, but for control purposes, the costs are pertinent if, and when, they are traceable to the activity under scrutiny. Having a better grasp of the actual product costs can provide better control over pricing strategies and general allocation of a firm's scarce resources. For years, accountants have used a traditional system to determine how much a particular product costs to produce: Add together the cost of raw materials, direct labor cost of manufacturing and the overhead; the first two are relatively easy to figure out but the third—overhead—is the killer.[1]

Reengineering and automation have reduced labor costs to between 5 percent and 10 percent of the total, whereas raw materials have held steady at 35 percent. Margins have shrunk to between 5 percent and 15 percent. But the number of overhead items has increased with environmental impact studies and the cost of compliance with federal regulations ranging from occupational safety to pension equity. The need for a better costing approach is long overdue.[1]

The number one attempt at this noble objective has been the movement of many of the large Fortune 500 companies toward using activity-based costing (ABC) in which product costs are traced to the activities, value-added or not, that produced them. The method assumes activities consume resources and products consume activities; therefore, managers must strive to identify all cost drivers.[14] ABC forces a company to scrutinize what it actually does. This can lead to efficiencies. If the answer to "What would happen if we stopped doing X?" is "Nothing," then you can stop doing X. More important, managers can make better decisions when they know the costs associated with a given decision. Once activity-based costing has been established, *activity-based management* (ABM) must follow. Both of these techniques developed because of accusations that traditional cost accounting systems produce bad numbers, bad numbers beget bad business decisions, and bad decisions beget failure.[15] These techniques are more related to TQM techniques which attempt to lower costs of work groups in the factory and do not directly affect the costing of products, *per se*. The concept of shared activity, associated with activity-based costing, has showed that some money-losing product lines should be kept alive since the decrease in cost they generate on related products, through shared activities, actually increases the margins of these related products.[16]

Strategic management based on ABC can provide gratifying results. Hewlett Packard's North American distribution organization moves $7 billion of product through five depots to more than 300 resellers nationwide. It hired Arthur Andersen in 1994 to implement an ABC program to cover its operation from front-end order taking to back-end assembly and distribution costs. There were 527 activities in 81 functional areas identified in the investigation. Those 527 activities were pared down to 27 activity drivers that were used to create models for both customer profitability and product profitability. Three pilot studies revealed more than $2 million of potential savings for Hewlett Packard. HP management also gained priceless insights as 51 customers accounted for more than 85 percent of all orders.[16]

Efficiency Control

All of the components of the marketing mix are subject to varying levels and degrees of efficiency, which can greatly affect a company's ultimate profitability. In the highly competitive global marketing environment of the 1990s and the twenty-first century, most companies find that operating efficiency has taken on a more significant character. During periods of high demand and few suppliers, efficiency was not always widely practiced. Those days appear to have ended for some time. Technical and instrumental suppliers to oil companies offered less than perfect products during the oil boom of the late 1970s and early 1980s. However, after the oil bust in the middle 1980s, the companies scurried to improve their product quality and the efficiency of their customer service.[17] It is unknown how much money was actually wasted during these boom days, but the entire oil industry and its suppliers drastically changed direction when the bust occurred.

The world's semiconductor market lies at the base of a country's economic future, since chips drive the machines that increase manufacturing and marketing efficiency. American chip makers heavily invested in chip research and development in the early 1990s and eventually took a large share of the world's market share away from the

Japanese manufacturers. As such, the United States has a clear edge in the lead for chips in the latter 1990s and well into the next century.[18] Companies need to be aware of the need for increased efficiency and be capable of adopting better and more efficient ways to operate their marketing research, marketing management, sales forces, sales promotion, advertising, and distribution functions. To do otherwise is courting a disaster.

SALES FORCE

The following are all necessary accounting data that are very useful to sales supervisors, at all levels: accounting for the number of sales calls, per person, per day; the average of sales per call; the average time per sales call; the average cost per sales call; entertainment costs, per sales call; percentage of orders per sales call; percentage of orders per 100 sales calls; number of new customers per period; and sales force cost, as a percentage of total sales. These data would indicate whether the sales rep is spending too much time on a particular function at the expense of other functions; whether he is incurring too many sales expenses compared with sales productivity; and whether he needs to prospect for new sales, and perhaps new customers, with more tenacity and sincerity. For many sales positions, this statistical analysis would suffice, but for salespeople who sell large ticket items—such as major installations, computers, construction, and so on—maintaining an appearance of control would take a very different tack. Control people desire as much data as possible to make their jobs easier, but the reporting of all these data by the outside sales rep places an undue burden on the rep. Many progressive companies do not collect all these data but are concerned with the sales rep's future prospect list, sales made, and the total cost per sales rep. All the other data are collected and analyzed by the field sales managers who are closer to the field of action and in a better position to control. Too many reports required of the sales rep can affect sales force morale, sales productivity, and conflict between the sales force and the home office. Actual sales could fall if the sales rep is burdened by too much paper work. Figure 21-6 illustrates this problem. Managers have to realize that nothing happens of significance to the "bottom line" until a sale is made. Actual sales must become the basis for determining the true benefits of a cost analysis. Cost cutting is most appropriate as a control over the firm's resources. Too much control of the sales force can, and will backfire, as disgruntled sales people leave the company to seek better working conditions elsewhere.

Increased efficiency among sales reps occurs with their receiving increased product quality, better engineered products, better advertising campaigns and sales promotion activities, improved supervision and sales leadership. The accounting data can highlight inefficiencies and indicate directions that management should take, but productivity increases occur with the improvement in field sales support. Companies

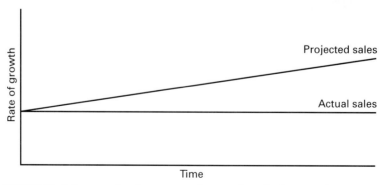

FIGURE 21-6 Impact of undue paperwork on projected sales growth.

have achieved greater cost efficiency by replacing ineffective sales reps and using distributors, manufacturer's reps, National Account Management teams, demonstration centers, industrial stores, catalog selling, trade shows, and telemarketing.[19] Sales managers who hide behind accounting data and attempt to manage their people by using statistics only could be negating their leadership responsibilities.

SALES PROMOTION

Sales promotion efficiency can be improved by data analysis, but also a down side exists. Useful data for mapping the future are trade show leads cultivated per show, trade show sales training to enhance efficiency, display costs, and the number of inquires per demonstration. Some companies do not know their costs per trade show and are sadly paying exorbitant fees and display costs that are not justified, relative to the sales leads and sales closes generated by that trade show. Closer supervision of personnel at trade shows, for example, could cut down on waste of a sales rep's time. Many trade shows require sales reps to work the show, thus they have to leave their territories and their customers to do so. Besides a possible morale problem, current customer's needs may go unanswered with the absence of the sales reps.

ADVERTISING

Advertising presents similar problems to sales promotion when determining how to increase efficiency. Much money is lost in ineffective advertising, but tracking the loss is not that easy. Some very good clues include measuring advertising costs per inquiry, the actual number of inquires a specific ad develops, and customer reception to a new ad campaign. Advertising is a support promotion to trade shows and personal selling in business marketing.

Management can increase advertising's efficiency by establishing more precise ad objectives; positioning their ads so that the messages communicate with the best prospects, for example, by using more direct mail; being more analytical in their choice of media; and promoting better coordination among advertising campaigns, the sales force, channel reps, and the total sales promotion effort.

Lilien and Little[20] conducted a series of investigations (called ADVISOR) to determine the practices used by industrial marketers to set their communication budgets. The study sought to establish marketing expenditure norms. The average firm spent only 0.6 percent of its sales on advertising, it budgeted about 7 percent of its sales for the total marketing budget, and it budgeted about 10 percent of its total marketing budget for advertising.

DISTRIBUTION

Quantitative channel and physical distribution data, such as costs of storage, transportation costs per mode, use of distributor and/or manufacturers' sales reps compared with the costs of telemarketing and the sales force can be collected to isolate needed savings to increase a firm's profit margins. Scientific routing of product deliveries, improved storage and materials handling, choice of better and more effective transportation modes, and a reduction of waste on the part of managers and sales reps are areas for increased cost control improvements. Transportation costs, by themselves, are very significant expenses. Any firm that does not monitor transportation costs will suffer the consequences. Transportation costs represent the largest, single area for achieving sizable costs reductions via better managerial leadership and control and empowerment of those who are asked to perform these every day tasks.

Strategic Control

Many companies have found it useful to use portfolio models such as BCG's share/growth matrix, and the PIMS matrix of tactical success models. However, packaged strategic analysis methods are no substitute for insightful strategic thinking.[21] The same thing is true of strategic control. Regardless of the level of sophistication of the planning devices, companies should take a critical view of their overall marketing effectiveness and their approach to the marketplace. An outside auditor or consultant can be employed to shed some light on the obvious biases and prejudices held by internal marketers. Judging the marketing success of a sales or marketing unit based solely on unit sales, profit contribution, percent of quota, and so on, may not really identify all the real truths of that unit's efficiency or lack of efficiency. The sales or marketing unit's sales history may have been strongly influenced by being in the right place at the right time or by being in the wrong place at the wrong time. Rather than judging either superior or inferior marketing management, sales data have to be combined with many of the nuances involved in any strategic control procedure. Exercising better control requires using improved analytical tools. Kotler advocates two tools—a marketing effectiveness rating review and the marketing audit—to help in the resolutions of the many strategic control problems.[3]

MARKETING EFFECTIVENESS RATING REVIEW

Business firms are often guilty of promoting a sales manager with a technical background in engineering, chemistry, or other physical science to the position of marketing manager or VP of marketing because of their technical capabilities, intelligence, and ability to accomplish assigned tasks. In one company where the technical marketing vice president was extremely strong in both spirit and in will, the use of short-run sales-oriented promotions were constantly disrupting the company's production planning and immediate cash flow requirements. One of the company's plants frequently operated at either 50 percent capacity much of the time or at 150 percent the rest of the time, whenever a sales promotion took hold.[22] Obviously, the marketing effectiveness rating for this company was very low.

Good marketing that is both cost and customer effective is reflected in the degree to which managers participate and subscribe to the following five major attributes of a marketing orientation[3]:

1. *Customer philosophy:* includes recognizing the importance of designing the company to serve the needs and wants of chosen markets; developing different offerings and marketing plans for different market segments; and viewing the entire marketing system, including vendors, channels, competitors, customers, and environment, in planning its business.

2. *Integrated marketing organization:* includes a high level of marketing integration and control of the major marketing functions, such as marketing working well with research, manufacturing, purchasing, physical distribution, finance, and accounting and by resolving all issues in the best interests of the company.

3. *Adequate marketing information:* knowing where the best research studies of customers, channels, and competitors can demonstrate the actual sales potential and profitability of different market segments, products, territories, customers, channels, and order sizes so that the cost effectiveness of different marketing expenditures can be measured.

4. *Strategic orientation:* gauging the extent of formal marketing planning, quality of current marketing strategy, and the extent of contingency thinking and planning.

5. *Operational efficiency:* knowing how well marketing information at the top is communicated and implemented down the line; the utilization of marketing resources; and how management shows good capacity to react quickly and effectively to instantaneous developments.

THE MARKETING AUDIT

The second tool, the marketing audit, is a more thorough study of problems uncovered in the marketing effectiveness rating review given previously. The major headings and a brief description of this detailed analysis includes the following[3]:

1. *Marketing environment audit:* analysis of major macroenvironmental forces and trends relative to the firm's markets, customers (both OEM and MRO), end users, competitors, distributors, dealers, suppliers, and facilitators

2. *Marketing strategy audit:* review of a company's marketing objectives, marketing strategy, and how well they are adapted to the current and forecasted marketing environment

3. *Marketing organization audit:* evaluation of the capacity of the marketing organizations to implement the planned strategy

4. *Marketing systems audit:* examination of the quality of the company's systems for analysis, planning, and control

5. *Marketing productivity audit:* examination of the profitability of different marketing entities and the cost effectiveness of different marketing expenditures

6. *Marketing function audits:* in-depth evaluations of major marketing mix components, namely, products, price, sales force, distribution, advertising, promotion, and public relations

At too many companies, the push for quality can be as badly misguided as it is well-intended.[23] The push for quality can dissolve into a mechanistic exercise that proves meaningless to customers. Varian Associates, Inc., a scientific equipment maker, put 1,000 of its managers through a four-day course on quality. The company buzzed with both quality slogans and quality costumes for weeks. Great success was achieved by the company, at first. For example, a unit that made vacuum systems for computer clean rooms boosted on-time delivery from 42 percent to 92 percent. Much of this success was attributed to the new emphasis on total quality management, which would have made W. Edward Deming and J.M. Juran, the leading prophets of quality control management, very proud. However, the emphasis on quality lost its appeal as costs soared in an attempt to maintain the highest quality. Beginning in the 1990s Varian's total sales volume grew by a paltry 3 percent and the company posted a $4.1 million loss.[23]

Another company that invested large sums of money in reaching for a high quality output was Wallace Co., an oil company, which won the Malcolm Baldrige National Quality Award. Two years later the firm filed for Chapter 11 as the cost of its quality programs soared in conjunction with collapsed oil prices. These companies discovered that quality control, which means very little to customers, usually does not produce a payoff in improved sales, profits, or market share. Total quality management devotees have started to concentrate on the product and service quality their customers want, not the statistical benchmarks worshiped by some TQM acolytes.[23]

Business Marketing Controller

General Foods, Du Pont, Johnson & Johnson, TWA, and American Cyanamid have hired inside marketing auditors to police the cost-effectiveness of advertising, promotion, budgets, profit plans, merchandising policies, and a host of other financial control responsibilities. The attempt has been successful since the marketing controllers are trained in finance and marketing and do many of the jobs that many marketing people either dislike or do not have time to complete.

Mead Johnson, a subsidiary of Bristol-Myers, was an early proponent of the marketing controller concept when they hired an accounting major who had strong interests in marketing. This individual's duties included costing products and protecting marketing's interests, concerns, and perspectives when working, sometimes fighting, with the accounting and finance departments.

The real value of the marketing comptroller concept in its early stages of development was to "level the playing field" between marketing and the other departments that tended not to understand the value of marketing concepts and practices. However, in the 1990s, little discord develops among these different functions, since almost everyone within a company appreciates the necessity, value, and worth of the company's marketing effort. Some business firms may even consider that all the employees are in a marketing effort, regardless of the employee's specific job function.

Many computer companies have attempted to emulate a marketing-oriented company. The old adage, "If it doesn't sell, it's no good," still works well among most business people.

Looking Back

Strategic planning develops the plan, but control functions foster the corrective actions to ensure that the plan's objectives are met. The control process in marketing has four major components: the annual plan control, profitability control, efficiency control, and strategic control. Annual plan control entails sales analysis, market share analysis, marketing expense-to-sales analysis, financial analysis, and customer-satisfaction tracking. Variances from the plan's objectives trigger management to take corrective actions and steer the company back on track.

Profitability control uses accounting and finance concepts in costing out products to determine contribution margins, using fixed, variable, and semifixed costs. More firms are moving toward activity-based costing where an attempt is made to directly trace costs to specific activities, whether any value-added takes place during the activity.

Efficiency control tries to unmask the outwardly appearing successful marketing operation to determine whether it is operating as efficiently as it should. Marketing units evaluated are the sales force, sales promotion, advertising, and distribution.

Strategic control is a more profound investigation that utilizes more potent tools: marketing effectiveness rating review and the marketing audit. Both tools, usually used by an outside consultant, are designed to probe in-depth to ascertain whether a company is employing astute marketing concepts, practices, systems, organizational designs, and operations with the proper and sufficient amount of information and personnel.

The marketing audit probes even further into those areas of weakness uncovered by the marketing effectiveness rating review by analyzing the marketing environment, marketing strategy, marketing orientation, marketing systems, marketing productivity, and the marketing functions.

Finally, many of the marketing control functions are assisted by the use of a marketing controller who can perform the duties of an accountant or finance person assigned to the marketing department. A number of progressive companies employ this concept to perform in-house financial-marketing control.

Questions for Discussion

1. Explain the control process and how it may operate in business firms making steel products.
2. Determine the significant differences between annual plan control and profitability control.
3. Analyze the similarities and differences between efficiency control and strategic control and how these two plans might operate in a firm that manufactures plumbing supplies.

4. How can sales analysis be used to detect the culprit causing the difference between planned sales and actual sales in a given sales territory?

5. If two territories experienced marketing expense-to-sales ratios of 13:1 and 14:1, which territory manager (sales rep) would be considered the better producer? Why? What other factors should be considered to make definitive conclusions?

6. Compare the differences between full costing and contribution margin costing. Which is the more appropriate for marketing control purposes? What is the relationship with activity-based costing?

7. Which sales force accounting data method could obscure the truth about its company's true operating efficiency?

8. Ineffective advertising can be quite costly. How can efficiency control measures help alert managers to increase business and industrial advertising's cost-effectiveness?

9. The marketing effectiveness rating review system covers five broad areas of marketing. What are these areas and what are the intentions of each?

10. The marketing audit is a sequential analysis of the marketing functions that concentrates on the weak factors uncovered by the marketing effectiveness review. Why is such a system necessary for a successful company?

Endnotes

1. Srikumar S. Rao, "True cost, activity-based accounting measures costs (and possible savings) far more precisely," *Financial World* (September 26, 1995), pp. 62-63.

2. Allan J. Magrath, "Innovative cost management in marketing," *Sales and Marketing Management* (December 1992), p. 33.

3. Philip Kotler, *Marketing Management, Analysis, Planning, Implementation, and Control,* 8th ed. (Englewood Cliffs, N.J.: Prentice Hall, Inc., 1994), p. 742.

4. Michael J. Etzel and John M. Ivancevich, "Management by objectives in marketing: Philosophy, process, and problems," *Journal of Marketing* 38 (October 1974):47-55.

5. "Apple's bumper crop of bad news," *Business Week* (April 8, 1996), p. 32.

6. Alfred R. Oxenfeldt, "How to use market share measurement," *Harvard Business Review* 47 (January-February 1969):59-68.

7. "Invoice? What's an invoice?" *Business Week* (June 10, 1996), pp. 110-12.

8. Robin Cooper and Robert S. Kaplan, "Profit priorities from activity-based costing," *Harvard Business Review* 69 (May-June 1991):130-5.

9. Dana Smith Morgan and Fred W. Morgan, "Marketing cost control: A survey of industry practices," *Industrial Marketing Management* 9 (1980):217-21.

10. Henry A. Haddad, "Marketing 'profit doctors,'" *Business Marketing* 73 (March 1988):70+.

11. Leland L. Beik and Stephen L. Buzby, "Profitability analysis by market segment," *Journal of Marketing* 37 (July 1973):50.

12. Patrick M. Dunne and Harry I. Wolk, "Marketing cost analysis: A modularized contribution approach," *Journal of Marketing* 41 (July 1977):83.

13. Thomas L. Powers, "Breakeven analysis with semifixed costs," *Industrial Marketing Management* 16 (1987):35-41.

14. Eugene E. Sprow, "The new ABCs of cost justification," *Manufacturing Engineering* 109 (December 1992):27-32.

15. Anne Millen Porter, "Tying down total cost," *Purchasing* 115 (October 21, 1993):38-43.

16. Thomas Durand, "Economy of scope, added value chain and cost dynamics: A tentative optimization model," *International Journal of Production Economics* 29 (May 1993):237-47.

17. Author's personal interviews with many oil industry service suppliers who readily admitted that their products had flaws during the oil boom period. The demand was so strong that the customer wanted immediate delivery and would take almost anything.

18. "Chipping away at Japan," *U.S. News & World Report* 119 (July 18, 1994):47.

19. Benton P. Shapiro and John Wyman, "New ways to reach your customers," *Harvard Business Review* 59 (July-August 1981):103-10.

20. Gary L. Lilien and John D.C. Little, "The ADVISOR project: A study of industrial marketing budgets," *Sloan Management Review* (Spring 1976), pp. 17-31.

21. George Day, "Gaining insights through strategy analysis," *Journal of Business Strategy* 2 (Summer 1983):57.

22. Philip Kotler, "From sales obsession to marketing effectiveness," *Harvard Business Review* 55 (November-December 1977):67-75.

23. "Quality: How to make it pay," *Business Week* (August 8, 1994), pp. 54-9.

Bibliography

Alberts, William W., "The experience curve doctrine reconsidered," *Journal of Marketing* 53 (1989):36-49.

Beik, Leland L., and Stephen L. Buzby, "Profitability analysis by market segment," *Journal of Marketing* 37 (1973):48-53.

Cooper, Robin, and W. Bruce Chew, "Control tomorrow's costs through today's designs," *Harvard Business Review* (1996):88-97.

Durand, Thomas, "Economy of scope, added value chain and cost dynamics: A tentative optimization model," *International Journal of Production Economics* 29 (1993):237-47.

Evans-Correla, Kate, "Big four endorse quality standard," *Purchasing* 115 (1993):97-9.

Farris, Paul W., and David J. Reibstein, "How prices , ad expenditures, and profits are linked," *Harvard Business Review* (1979):173-84.

Filiatrault, Pierre, and Jean-Charles Chebat, "How service firms set their marketing budgets," *Industrial Marketing Management* 19 (1990):63-7.

Haddad, Henry A., "Marketing 'profit doctors,'" *Business Marketing* (1988):70+.

Hulbert, James M., and Norman E. Toy, "A strategic framework for marketing control," *Journal of Marketing* 41 (1977):12-20.

Jackson Donald W., Lonnie L. Ostrom, and Kenneth R. Evans, "Measures used to evaluate industrial marketing activities," *Industrial Marketing Management* 11 (1982):269-74.

Johnson, H. Thomas, "Activity-based management: Past, present, and future," *Engineering Economist* 36 (1991):219-38.

Kirpalani, V.H., and Stanley S. Shapiro, "Financial dimensions of marketing management," *Journal of Marketing* 3 (1973):40-7.

Kotler, Philip, "From sales obsession to marketing effectiveness," *Harvard Business Review* (1977):67-75.

Mayros, Van, and Dennis J. Dolon, "Hefting the data load: How to design the MkIS that works for you," *Business Marketing* (1988):47+.

McConville, Daniel J. "Start with ABC," *Industry Week* 17 (1993):33-6.

Morgan, Dana Smith, and Fred W. Morgan, "Marketing cost controls: A survey of industry practices," *Industrial Marketing Management* 9 (1980):217-21.

Mossman, Frank H., Paul M. Fischer, and W. J. E. Crissy, "New approaches to analyzing marketing profitability," *Journal of Marketing* 38 (1974):43-8.

Porter, Anne Millen, "Tying down total cost," *Purchasing* 115 (1993):38-43.

Powers, Thomas L., "Breakeven analysis with semifixed costs," *Industrial Marketing Management* 16 (1987):35-41.

Rayburn, L. Gayle, "Accounting tools in the analysis and control of marketing performance," *Industrial Marketing Management* 6 (1977):175-82.

Sevin, Charles H., "Marketing profits from financial analysis," *Financial Executive* (1966):22-30.

Selzer, Steven W., "Activity-based system taking hold," *ENR* 231 (1993):35.

Sharman, Paul A., "Activity-based management: A growing practice," *CMA Magazine* 67 (1993):17-22.

Sprow, Eugene E., "The new ABCs of cost justification," *Manufacturing Engineering* 109 (1992):27-32.

Subhash, Sharma, and Dale D. Achabal, "STEMCOM: An analytical model for marketing control," *Journal of Marketing* 46 (1982):104-13.

Turney, Peter B.B., "Beyond TQM with workforce activity-based management," *Management Accounting* 75 (1993):28-31.

CHAPTER **22** International Business Marketing

Businesses have made a drastic change in their treatment of international business marketing. The interfacing of the world's cultures and economies has mandated progressive companies to accept a global, almost a borderless, international marketing perspective by placing a high priority on international markets and by playing their international strategies in concert with the company's domestic marketing strategies.

The importance of international business marketing cannot be minimized. This chapter attempts to convey the importance of global markets and international business marketing strategy by covering the following topics:

1. Providing an appreciation of the inevitability and importance of international business marketing
2. Contrasting the numerous environmental differences and planning changes needed between domestic and international business marketing
3. Showing how cultural, political-legal, economic, and financial environments of each host country affect the success or failure of an international marketing effort
4. Emphasizing the value of having a well-planned and well-executed business marketing strategy
5. Determining how the first step in an international marketing strategy—choosing which foreign market to enter—is so important
6. Determining which practice is best when entering a foreign market and how to develop an international business marketing program

The Lucrative International Business Market

Exports have become the central issue in many companies and account for much of the economic strength of the American economy. Americans produced half of the world's manufactured goods and had about 80 percent of the world's hard currency reserves, following World War II. In the 1990s, America's share of world GNP had shrunk to just near 24 percent, and the U.S. dollar shares the world stage, in importance, with the Japanese yen and the German deutsche mark.[1]

MOST OF THE WORLD'S POPULATION IS OUTSIDE OF THE UNITED STATES

Ninety-five percent of the world's population resides outside of the United States and represents 75 percent of the world's purchasing power. Recognizing this great potential, U.S. exports have increased and account for 11.3 percent of the American GDP, twice what it was 20 years ago.[2]

The export market for American goods is enormous; markets in Europe, Japan, Asia, Canada, Mexico, and Latin America continue to grow and prosper. Besides the stable markets of Europe and Japan, Asia's $5.7 trillion economy and Latin America's $1 trillion economy offer great promise for growing demand for infrastructure, aircraft, and high-tech capital goods—all areas in which the United States has real or potential strengths. Additionally, the entrance into the world economies of Central/Eastern Europe and the countries of the former eastern bloc show great promise as potential markets for U.S. exports.[2]

THE EXPANDING PACIFIC RIM

The entire Asia/Pacific region accounts for 56 percent of the world's population. In 25 years that figure is projected to grow to 62 percent, boosting Asia's population by as many as 2.5 billion additional customers. John Naisbitt believes contacts with the Chinese and their economic holdings will determine the future of the western hemisphere.[3] But according to some economists, the United States is missing the boat by overlooking and not capitalizing on this tremendous market. Japan is the dominant player among industrialized nations active in the Asian region, but Naisbitt believes Japan will soon be surpassed by China. Motorola has placed high stakes in China with several joint ventures and a $560 million semiconductor wafer fabrication plant in Tianjin.[4]

China has become a very serious trader with the United States. U.S. computer makers have eyed the Chinese market because only one computer exists for every 6,000 people compared with one for every four persons in the United States. It is estimated that the Chinese computer market will expand 22.4 percent per year for the rest of the decade. The greatest demand for computers is in fields such as finance, heavy industry, and transportation.[5] By the year 2000, China will need $500 billion to modernize its highways.[6] However, foreign companies are starting to feel the effects of government-imposed credit restrictions, price controls, and and other steps taken by the Chinese government.[7] Although approximately 50 power plant projects are on the drawing boards, the Chinese government has not approved a single joint-venture deal for power plants since 1992.

The Case for International Marketing

International business markets can be attractive for many firms. Global advantages stem from basically four causes[8]:

1. *Conventional comparative advantage:* when a country or countries have significant advantages in factor cost or factor quality used in producing a product, these countries will be the sites of production, and exports will flow to other parts of the world

2. *Economies of scale:* or learning curves extended beyond the scale or cumulative volume achievable in individual national markets, including production, logistics, marketing, and purchasing economies of scale

3. *Advantages from product differentiation:* can give the firm an edge in its reputation and global market credibility

4. *Public good character of market information and technology:* proprietary product technology and mobility of production offer technical advantage in the international marketplace

IMPEDIMENTS TO GLOBAL COMPETITION

The advantages of entering the international or global markets can be blocked by major impediments.[8] Transportation and storage costs may offset the economies of centralized production. Because of differences in culture, income levels, and state of economic development, domestic product varieties may not always be demanded by the host country. The firm may be required to access already established independent distributors to compete successfully, thus negating some of the competitive advantages if direct investment or direct export were possible. When it is necessary to use the local sales force and the local maintenance and repair services, some of economies of scale may diminish. Complex segmentation within geographical markets, compounded by a lack of world demand for a given product, further can reduce a firm's competitive advantages. All of these risk factors must be carefully analyzed when committing a firm's scarce resources to any international venture.

Global competition is extensive and, at times, is very harsh. The intensity and harshness of the competition forces the global player to become more efficient, constantly improve products, constantly develop new products, and be more innovative to gain and maintain competitive advantage in the international market place. Global companies soon receive "wake-up" calls whenever the international strategy pursued is not either appropriate or is insufficient in impact or intensity.

INTERNATIONAL BUSINESS MARKETING—AN OPPORTUNITY OR A THREAT?

International business marketing is both an opportunity and a threat. On the opportunity side, exports to other G-7 nations outside the United States (United Kingdom, Italy, Germany, Japan, Canada, and France) continued to be dwarfed by exports to the rest of the world. In 1991, half of American exports went to the other G-7 nations; but by 1994, that share drifted to 46 percent whereas demand from such nations as Mexico, Brazil, and South Korea soared[9] (see Figure 22-1). As seen in Figure 22-1, the Pacific rim nations of South Korea, Taiwan, and Singapore are now in the top ten nations to which the U.S. exports. In brief, the U.S. international trade in goods and services saw the deficit increase from $75.5 billion in 1993 to $108.1 billion in 1994. However, the trade balance in advanced technology products showed a $22.4 billion surplus in 1994, led by surpluses in aerospace and information and communication products.[10]

The International Business Marketing Environment

When a firm enters the global markets, it encounters a different set of uncontrollable environmental factors. These uncontrollable factors are (1) cultural, (2) political-legal, (3) economic, (4) and financial differences. These differences are illustrated in Figure 22-2.

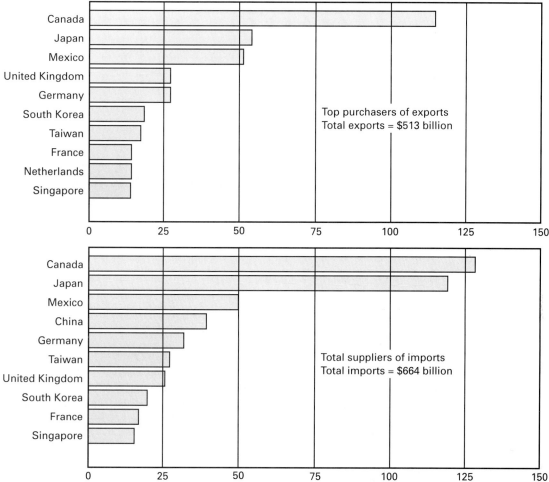

Source: U.S. Department of Commerce, International Trade Administration, *U.S. Foreign Trade Highlights: 1994* (September 1995), Tables 10, 11.

FIGURE 22-1 Top purchasers of U.S. exports and suppliers of U.S. general imports: 1994.

CULTURAL ENVIRONMENT

Among the many mistakes made by inexperienced international marketers is violating a host country's cultural values. Culture is the integrated sum total of learned behavioral traits that are manifest and shared by members of a given society.

Cultural considerations are less concerned with perceptions of products and more concerned with cultural problems in personal selling, personal relationships, advertising, and sales promotion. In part, this concern exists because business products are more homogeneous worldwide. Steel, for example, when purchased by an Englishman, a Japanese, or an American original equipment manufacturer (OEM) is basically for the same purpose—to produce goods. Steel is steel no matter where it is sold, as long as it meets the buyer's standards.

Personal selling or personal relationships, on the other hand, present the international business marketer with special problems because of the differences in cultural attitudes among nations—differences that can critically affect the busi-

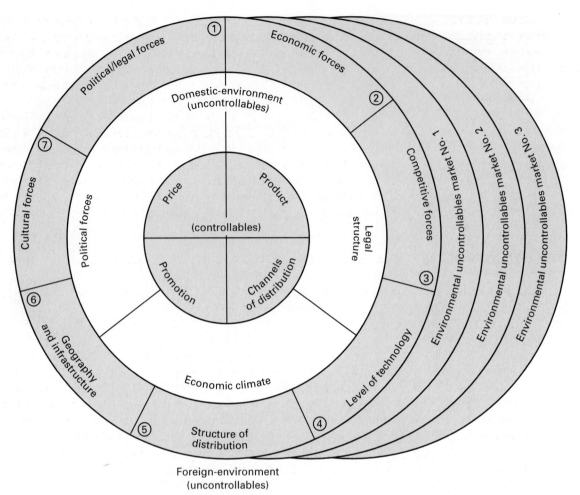

Source: Philip R. Cateora and John M. Hess. *International Marketing,* 6th ed. (Homewood, Ill.: Richard D. Irwin, Inc., 1987), p.9. Reprinted by permission.

FIGURE 22-2 The international marketing environment.

ness marketer's effectiveness whenever cultural norms are violated on an interpersonal relationship.

Cultural Attitudes, Time, Space, Friendships, and Contractual Agreements
These cultural attitudes directly affect the climate for international business. Salespeople, as well as other company representatives going abroad, should be sensitive to these differences and how they influence the behavior of people within international organizations.[11,15]

Attitudes present paramount obstacles to unsuspecting and inexperienced international business marketers. Swiss never discuss business over lunch. Salespeople in Germany must be very respectful of their customers by calling them "Herr Doktor Schmidt," even if it sounds redundant. In Brazil, a salesperson has to dress the same as the customer, whether it's formal or informal. In India, contracts are seldom signed by the third meeting. In Switzerland and Germany, it's rude to shake hands across desks; instead, executives walk around their desks. French business people appreciate it whenever a foreigner attempts to speak French, even if it's only a few poorly spoken phrases. Japanese dislike immodesty, and any salesperson or company official who boasts of or oversells his accomplishments is considered boorish.[12]

Pride and dignity are important any place in the world, but nowhere is this as important as in Asia. To speak or act in a way that may cause an Asian to lose face is tantamount to a physical assault in Western society. "Frank" Americans may complain loudly about the defects they perceive in a host country, hence possibly taking "face" away from the Asian business people who might be listening.[13]

Time perceptions are an important American cultural value. The synthesis of immigrants coming from different cultures and the effects of the Protestant work ethic have led Americans to develop an obsession for doing things on time. A more extreme view was given by one Japanese businessman who said, "You Americans have one terrible weakness. If we make you wait long enough, you will agree to anything."[11]

Spatial perspectives, called *proxemics,* is the use of space in communications or when talking; that is, how far apart persons sit or stand. South Americans, Greeks, and Japanese prefer to conduct business while standing or sitting close to their business associates.[14] In many countries, business acquaintances tend to be more animated in their conversations, even including touching, than do their American counterparts. Even the degree of eye contact between businesspeople varies considerably from nation to nation. Eastern Europeans and some Latin people, for instance, prefer eye-to-eye contact in business dealings. Such differences in spatial perceptions and eye contact often lead to feelings of apprehension and uneasiness on the part of Americans, who fail to respond in kind, according to Latin business people.

Friendship perceptions in most of the world depend more on friendship, trust, and service than is the case in the more pragmatic, case-by-case, basics-oriented United States. In Central and South America, for example, the business buyer prefers to buy from the foreign supplier who has expressed a long-term, genuine friendship and an interest in the buyer's country. Long-term business friendships are perceived as a kind of social insurance.[15]

Americans have separate social rules for business and personal relationships. This division is not true elsewhere. In Saudi Arabia, the same courtesies are provided to a business caller as to a personal friend. In Latin America, a businessperson would never rush a counterpart. In Japan, should a business proposition become unsatisfactory, the Japanese businessperson will never flatly turn it down, but instead will suggest that "there are too many difficulties."[16]

Contractual agreements hold a high place among American businesspeople, because these instruments are based on carefully written contracts that have been negotiated under certain rules, regulations, and laws. However, the rules of contracts and contract negotiation vary from culture to culture. The vice president of international trade operations for AMF Corporation warned, "Beware of contractual sales agreements. In some nations—they're good for life."[17] In Latin America and Greece, the written contract is viewed only as an expression of intent at the time the contract is signed. Much importance is given to personal friendships after the signing. On the other hand, for many Moslems, the written contract is offensive and is perceived as a reflection on their honor.[11]

In the United States, written contracts are usually upheld, whereas oral contracts may be broken. In Japan, however, oral contracts are considered to be as binding as written contracts. This agreement results because relationships between two firms are "always assumed to be continuous." Thus, when problems occur between two companies, the firms' primary interests are to maintain a continuing relationship. And because both firms assume that the relationship will continue, they tend to be conciliatory. These continuing relationships are a type of insurance against the uncertainties of new contracts and they allow firms to renegotiate without litigation; hence, fewer lawyers are found in foreign countries as compared with the United States. In fact, Japanese firms regard these continuing relationships as having a higher value than the economic benefits that might be achieved by changing relationships.[18]

Cultural Elements   In addition to cultural attitudes, cultural elements are very important in shaping the environment of international business marketing. Cultural elements are shaped by an array of causal factors, but cultural elements indigenous to business marketing are language (linguistics), and material culture.

Language has been called the mirror of society. It is one of the basic vehicles of communications used in marketing business products and services. George Bernard Shaw thought the United States and the United Kingdom were two countries separated by a common language. Words like lorry, lift, water closet, and biscuit are used in England, but truck, elevator, restroom, and cookie are used in America. English, now widely recognized and practiced in international transactions, is richly endowed with a commercial vocabulary reflecting both the British and American societies that originated and/or helped to perpetuate the language. Even in industrialized countries where English is not the primary language, many companies have changed to the use of English to enhance business communications. Philips, a Dutch firm, uses English as the official language of the company, partly because of its many businesses in English-speaking countries and because so few people speak Dutch.

Material Culture   Material culture is represented by the tools, artifacts, and technology of a society. Material culture helps business marketers to identify markets and assist in defining and segmenting these markets. For example, Mexico has frequent electrical outages in the rural areas. China's outer provinces conserve electricity by providing hot water for bathing for only a few hours in the morning. When opening a plant in a foreign country, the existence of an adequate supply of raw materials, power, transportation, trained labor, and financing has to be investigated.

POLITICAL-LEGAL ENVIRONMENT

Political and legal elements include laws, government stability, political trade barriers, money and monetary controls. The practice of international business marketing is significantly influenced by the politics and laws of host nations. What takes place in the political/legal environment affects (1) whether a firm will engage in international business marketing in a particular country, (2) its form of international market entry, and (3) how it employs marketing strategies in the chosen country.

Governmental and/or political action can benefit a country's economic situation, and hence, the country's propensity to purchase foreign goods. Italy elected a pro-business government that tried to enhance an economic revival. Rome sold off close to $6 billion in state assets, including two of Italy's largest banks, Banca Commerciale Italiano and Credito Italiano. That move was revolutionary in a country such as Italy, where the traditional centers of economic power could be counted on one hand—namely, the state banks, state industry, Fiat, and two or three other private groups.[19]

Laws   It has been estimated that more than 60 percent of U.S. companies doing business abroad suffered politically inflicted damage in the period from 1975 to 1980. In the 1980s and 1990s, some American firms suffered political fallout in Yemen, Bosnia, Somalia, Haiti, and Rwanda—countries that had endured political and military strife. International law is minuscule compared with domestic law, but two groups, the

TABLE 22-1	Member Countries in the Organization for Economic Cooperation and Development (OECD)
United States	Germany
Ireland	Turkey
Iceland	Greece
Canada	Italy
United Kingdom	Austria
Japan	Switzerland
New Zealand	Netherlands
Australia	Belgium
Norway	Luxembourg
Sweden	France
Finland	Spain
Denmark	Portugal

Source: OECD handout, 2 rue Andre-Pascal, 75775 Paris Cedex 16 France, May 1977.

Organization of Economic Cooperation and Development (OECD) in Paris (see Table 22-1) and the United Nations Conference on Trade and Development (UNCTAD) in New York, have developed codes of conduct for multinational businesses. Although these codes are not law, they have become the norms by which countries can judge the actions of global firms.

All government policy changes do not have equal impact on a given company. Governments will not interfere with companies who offer higher technology and greater ownership share held by host country executives.[20] A change in government policy can be very beneficial to a company, as evidenced by the NAFTA trade pact among the United States, Canada, and Mexico, passed in 1994. This pact phased out all international barriers among the three countries over a 10-year period. The agreement with Canada produced a sharply boosted trade flow, but after an initial trade flurry, Mexico's economy was rocked in 1995 by the Mexican government's devaluation of the peso.[21] An American loan kept the Mexican economy afloat, and the Mexican fiscal crisis was averted by 1996.

Government Stability   Host government instability can affect an exporter's viability in a given country. Signs of instability (Russia, Bosnia, and Cuba) can show frequent regime changes; unrest among the inhabitants can erupt as violence, terrorism, and economic injustices prevail.

Governmental policy shifts can also cause trouble for international business marketers. Beijing Jeep was formed as a joint venture between AMC (Chrysler Corp.) and Beijing Automobile Works to manufacture Jeeps in 1985. Beijing Jeep imported 90 percent of the parts used to assemble its Jeep Cherokee. When the Chinese government restricted joint ventures' foreign exchange purchases, the company did not have enough hard currency to buy supplies and was left high and dry.[22] In the 1990s, China welcomed direct foreign investments enthusiastically in its quest to move as rapidly as possible toward a full-fledged market economy.

Political Trade Barriers   A nation's political and legal actions that normally affect the international business marketer are (1) restricting imports, (2) establishing market and monetary controls, and (3) taking control of foreign-owned assets.

Political trade barriers restrict the inflow of foreign goods when nations use tariffs, quotas, nontariff barriers, and monetary controls. Import restrictions help to protect the national economy. When foreign products are more expensive or inaccessible, jobs and capital remain at home.

Tariff is a tax on imported goods from other countries usually levied on the quantity or the value of the imported good. Some companies skip tariffs with a lower import value by shipping products completely knocked down (CKD) for subsequent assembly in the host market. For years, Unisys imported unassembled machines, manufactured in Scotland, into the United States to reduce the company's tariff expense.

Quotas are quantitative barriers to imports. Japanese semiconductor and microchip manufacturers have been under pressure from the U.S. Congress to restrict their U.S. importation. The Japanese voluntarily placed an import quota on these products to placate the American government and, hopefully, ward off any more restrictive protectionist moves.

Nontariff barriers (NTB) are an effective, invisible tariff and are widely practiced throughout the world. They include customs duties, documentation requirements, marks of origin, labeling laws, safety requirements "buy national" policies, and so on. For example, 26 countries refuse to grant American insurance and financial companies licenses to operate in their countries. These refusals deprive many U.S. manufacturing firms entrance to those countries because they need funding and insurance coverage from these American insurance firms.[23]

All countries practice some forms of NTBs or invisible import barriers, but Japan has had the greatest propensity to do so, and the most success. Japan, which embraces government subsidies, coordination, and protection, hides behind NTBs, such as product specifications, which serve the same purpose as any tariff barrier. Japan concentrates its NTB practices on foreign industries that produce sophisticated products, use few natural resources, and have a potential for fast growth in Japan.[24] Typical of the Japanese's well-organized efforts, Japan's industrial goals are influenced by the various government-supported trade institutes such as the Ministry for International Trade and Industry (MITI). These goals become a national purpose for Japan and are pursued with support from the different companies in a given industry.[25] Japan has many explicit and implicit trade barriers, but most American companies have overcome these and in general are enjoying enormous success.[26]

Barrier remedies are available through the economic organizations that assist free trade such as the World Trade Organization (WTO), started in 1995, and the United Nations Conference on Trade and Development (UNCTAD). The WTO oversees trade agreements and has power to mediate trade disputes between nations. WTO members can not veto the findings of the WTO's three-person panel as was the case in the old GATT agreement. The sweeping WTO trade agreement slashed tariffs globally by roughly 40 percent. The computer, drug, and farming firms in the United States were favored.[27] However, during trade conflicts in 1995 between Japan and the United States, WTO played a rather small role in the final outcome.

Market and Monetary Controls   These controls are instituted to protect a country's home industries. Governments worldwide enact a number of forms of market and monetary control. These include (1) restricting the sale of particular foreign products; (2) levying various types of taxes on foreign-owned production facilities; (3) establishing price ceilings on products produced in foreign-owned plants; (4) requiring foreign-owned companies to employ a certain percentage of local workers; (5) requiring that products produced locally have a specified amount of locally produced components; (6) requiring that local foreign-owned companies be owned in part by local businesses or the local government; (7) limiting the amount of profits that can be remitted to the parent company; and (8) giving direct support to local businesses.

Despite these restrictions, strategies exist to overcome them. General Motors, for instance, was hurt in Argentina when the regime of General Videla placed price controls on assembled vehicles, but not on what were mostly locally made component parts. Canadian Prime Minister Trudeau reduced foreign ownership, mostly United States, of petroleum reserves to fulfill promises to his strong supporters in Canada's eastern provinces.[28] The international marketer should always be cognizant of political decisions, no matter how remote, that could ultimately affect business operations. Table 22-2 indicates the various political/legal environmental forces that should be assessed by a business firm planning to expand into international business operations.

ECONOMIC ENVIRONMENT

Two economic factors that affect international business marketing considerations are exchange rates and the balance of trade. Exchange rates depict how many monetary units (or portions of a monetary unit) of one nation's currency are required to obtain one monetary unit of another nation's currency. When exchange rates change, making one nation's currency more expensive and the other's less expensive, the effect is to change the price of products sold between nations.

TABLE 22-2 Checklist for Analyzing the Political/Legal Environment

1. What is the country's political structure?
2. How do citizens, political parties, and special interest groups participate in political decision making?
3. What is the current government's political philosophy? How is it implemented?
4. What are the philosophies of opposing political forces?
5. What role does the current government see for foreign business?
6. Is foreign business treated differently from local firms in public policy? If so, how?
7. What is the country's history in dealing with different types of foreign businesses?
8. What is the process whereby changes in public policy are made?
9. What are the current and foreseeable trends in relationships between government in this country and in my home country?
10. What general role does government see for private business in this country's economic life?
11. What restrictions on international transfers of resources will affect my firm's operations in this country?
12. What are the major trends in the regulatory environment?
13. What incentives does the government give to private business and foreign investors?
14. What are the trigger points for increased nationalistic feelings in the host country?
15. How does the government assert its economic sovereignty?
16. What are the specific risks of loss of ownership or control of assets?
17. What are the chances of political harassment and what form is it likely to take?
18. What tools can we use to build a mutually beneficial relationship with this country's government? Will they survive a possible change of government?
19. What are the possibilities of a change in government or other expressions of political instability?
20. Are my firm, my industry, and/or my products likely to be politically vulnerable?
21. What is the basis of this country's legal system?
22. Will my firm's activities violate any of the home or host countries' extraterritorial laws?
23. What areas of my marketing strategy will be affected by the host country's legal environment?

Source: Edward W. Cundiff and Marye Tharp Hilger, *Marketing in the International Environment* (Englewood Cliffs, N.J.: Prentice Hall, Inc., 1984), p. 167. Reprinted by permission.

The balance of trade is a monetary summary of the value of exports and imports between nations. For example, the United States balance of trade for 1993 was a negative $115 billion, down from a high in 1987 of $152 billion deficit, meaning that when the values of exports and imports were tallied for 1993, the United States had imported $115 billion more than it had exported in 1993.[29]

Exchange Rates   Since the early 1970s, the values of all currencies in the free world have been allowed to "float" relatively freely; that is, their comparative values have been allowed to change in response to the supply and demand for that money with little governmental interference. When a foreign currency becomes more expensive, compared with the U.S. dollar, (making U.S. products cheaper abroad), the U.S. marketer should consider such options as (1) expanding overseas marketing efforts to increase world market share or (2) raising price to increase profits. When a foreign currency becomes less expensive, compared with the dollar (making U.S. products more expensive abroad), the U.S. marketer should consider (1) reducing price to increase quantities sold, with the hope that learning curve effects will make the price reduction profitable, (2) importing less expensive inputs from overseas, or (3) relocating its production facilities abroad. The United States regained its market share in industry after industry, particularly microprocessors, partly because of the exchange rate advantage from the dramatic rise in the Japanese yen compared with the American dollar.[30]

Balance of Trade   Between nations, one of the major causes for changing exchange rates is the balance of trade. Trade balances are affected by the development of a nation's production facilities, the cost of its inputs (such as labor), and the quality of its products.

Nations that experience long-term trade deficits, along with a decline in their currencies' exchange rates, have little foreign currency in reserve to purchase products from abroad. This dilemma does little to increase a country's standard of living. To counteract the effects of decreasing exchange rates, governments often take severe actions such as (1) devaluing their own currency, which has the effect of making their goods cheaper in world markets and foreign goods more expensive at home, and (2) directing the spending of scarce foreign currencies toward capital goods and away from consumer goods, as practiced in Brazil. In 1971 and again in 1973, the United States devalued the dollar for this very purpose to improve its foreign trade balance.

The economic environment in international marketing is considerably complex. Many economic elements are advantageous, but some of these elements present obstacles in the path for the free flow of products. The global volume of international trade (world exports) is approximately $2 trillion, which is larger than the GNP of every nation in the world except the United States and three times the GNP of South American countries.[31] (See Table 22-3 for the GNP data for the industrialized 24 OECD nations).

FINANCIAL DIFFERENCES

Getting paid in international transactions can be a trying experience. After receiving a signed contract with a Hong Kong or Hanover, Germany firm, the next question is how the seller can be paid. Many domestic American banks do not care to spend the hours required to set up letters of credit, which have a thin profit margin.[32] Many small banks are not sophisticated enough to understand international markets. The resulting financial gap is one of the biggest impediments for thousands of "wannabe" exporters. However, other sources exist besides commercial banks. Table 22-4 provides the definitive answers to financing export sales.

TABLE 22-3 Organization for Economic Cooperation and Development (OECD)—Gross National Product, 1980-1990

| | GROSS NATIONAL PRODUCT | | | | | GNP PER CAPITA | | | | | |
| | Total in Constant 1990 Dollars (bil.) | | | Annual Percent Change | | In Constant 1990 Dollars[1] | | | Annual Percent Change | | Inflation Rate,[2] 1989-1990 (percent) |
Country	1980	1985	1990	1980-1990	1989-1990	1980	1985	1990	1980-1990	1989-1990	
United States	4,182.6	4,757.1	5,465.1	2.7	1.0	19,466	19,948	21,863	1.8	-0.1	4.1
OECD Europe[3]	5,526.7	5,974.4	6,974.1	2.4	2.8	14,505	14,798	16,639	1.7	1.8	5.9
Belgium	158.3	164.4	192.4	2.0	3.5	16,542	16,673	19,953	2.0	3.6	3.5
Denmark	103.3	117.4	123.5	1.8	1.0	22,016	22,975	24,027	1.8	0.8	2.7
France	954.0	1,028.6	1,187.7	2.2	2.5	18,369	18,644	21,044	1.7	2.0	2.7
Germany[4]	1,216.1	1,291.5	1,507.1	2.2	4.2	20,733	21,183	23,885	1.9	2.3	3.4
Greece	57.6	61.6	67.3	1.6	1.2	6,040	6,203	6,697	1.1	1.0	20.1
Ireland	31.2	32.4	37.4	1.8	4.4	9,065	9,153	10,685	1.5	4.8	3.6
Italy	855.1	925.5	1,078.0	2.4	2.6	15,825	16,197	18,696	2.1	2.3	7.5
Luxembourg	6.4	7.2	9.0	3.5	2.6	19,000	19,568	24,270	3.2	5.4	3.4
Netherlands	232.6	243.2	276.1	1.7	3.0	16,470	16,776	18,481	1.1	2.2	3.1
Portugal	44.7	46.7	58.0	2.6	3.9	4,490	4,596	5,505	1.8	3.3	14.2
Spain	364.6	390.4	486.9	2.9	3.5	9,953	10,148	12,497	2.5	3.3	7.5
United Kingdom	753.0	829.3	975.0	2.6	1.6	14,722	14,647	17,004	2.4	0.9	6.1
Austria	126.8	135.5	158.0	2.2	4.5	17,510	17,923	20,493	2.0	3.2	3.4
Finland	99.2	114.6	137.3	3.3	1.7	22,725	23,388	27,518	2.9	1.1	6.0
Iceland	4.4	4.8	5.4	2.1	-0.1	19,458	20,125	21,680	1.3	-0.2	12.5
Norway	75.8	89.4	105.0	3.3	3.0	20,507	21,672	24,764	2.9	2.7	4.0
Sweden	185.1	202.5	224.7	2.0	0.9	23,753	24,251	26,250	1.6	0.1	9.2
Switzerland	192.2	206.0	235.4	2.1	2.5	30,838	31,829	35,081	1.4	1.6	6.5
Turkey	66.6	83.4	109.9	5.1	7.6	1,619	1,660	1,873	2.2	4.1	53.1
Australia	213.5	250.0	294.2	3.3	2.2	15,259	15,833	17,215	1.7	0.6	3.8
Canada	415.1	477.8	558.0	3.0	1.1	18,267	18,990	21,094	2.0	-0.1	3.1
Japan	1,893.2	2,307.4	2,910.4	4.4	6.1	18,319	19,045	23,558	3.8	5.7	1.9
New Zealand	34.5	41.3	41.9	2.0	0.7	11,981	12,708	12,507	1.2	-0.5	2.9

For interpretation of the absolute levels of GNP and per capita GNP, the market exchange rates used in converting national currencies do not necessarily reflect the relative purchasing power in the various countries. As a consequence, it should not be concluded, for instance, that the United Kingdom's individual standard of living in 1990 was only 78 percent of that of the United States, as the statistics may imply. Minus sign (−) indicates decrease. For explanation of annual percent change, see Guide to Tabular Presentation.

[1]National currency values converted into dollars by the average 1989 Market Rate, as published by the International Monetary Fund, Washington, DC. [2]GNP of GDP (gross domestic product) implicit price deflators; totals weighted by 1989 (base year) GNP. [3]See text, section 31. [4]Former West Germany (prior to unification).

Source: U.S. Department of State, Bureau of Intelligence and Research, *Economic Growth of OECD countries, 1980-1990,* Report No. IRR 22 (Washington. D.C.: U.S. GPO).

TABLE 22-4 Financial Options for Exporting	
1. Forfeit financing	This procedure accepts a foreign receivable. When the receivable is backed by a government guarantee, it often converts to commercial paper, which is negotiable. The seller gets paid quickly, minus a small fee.
2. Factoring	Factors also recognize a seller's foreign receivables. Seller receives most of its money quickly. This possibility works best for 30-, 60-, or 90- day transactions.
3. Export trading companies	ETCs take title to a seller's goods and complete the transaction. Seller receives its money and does not handle the shipping. ETC fees are slightly higher.
4. Banks	The traditional route is a letter of credit from a domestic bank, but the best approach is to seek the support of regional and foreign-based banks.

Source: U.S. News & World Report (January 17, 1994), p. 98.

International Business Marketing Strategies

Having in-depth knowledge of the uncontrollable environmental elements in international business marketing is the first prerequisite toward achieving success. Developing the most effective and least costly strategy, is the second most critical step. International strategy determines: (1) which foreign markets to enter, (2) how will the market be entered, either indirect or direct exporting, (3) which products should be included, and (4) how these products should be designed, promoted, priced, and distributed to and within each of the foreign countries chosen. International marketing is more than just exporting to and competing in other markets, however. According to the president of Asea Brown Boveri (ABB), a $29.4 billion company headquartered in Zurich, the strategy also involves having a product development and manufacturing presence in many markets.[33]

To succeed, an international company needs to change from a multidomestic competitor, which allows individual subsidiaries to compete independently in different domestic markets, to a global organization, which pits its entire worldwide system of product and market positions against the competition. Successful global competitors mirror the following characteristics: (1) they all perceive competition as global and formulate strategy on an integrated, worldwide basis by creating innovations to change the rules of the competitive game in its particular industry; (2) they use this innovation as a lever to support the development of an integrated global system that contains a strong market position; and (3) they execute their strategies more aggressively and effectively than do their competitors.[34]

INTERNATIONAL PRODUCT LIFE CYCLE

Foreign markets offer domestic manufacturers an avenue in which to extend their product life cycles—especially when extension of its domestic PLC alternatives have been exhausted. As each international market is entered, a new PLC could be started for each product in each market. PLC extension in an international market is tantamount to initiating the start of a domestic product's PLC rejuvenation, such as product change, different promotion, changed distribution, and/or a price change. Needless to say, "economies of scale" can materialize with additional international sales; hence, lowering a product's cost structure and increasing its profitability.

A COMMITMENT TO FOREIGN MARKETING

Firms have to become boundaryless and focus more on globalization to succeed in the present and future marketplace.[35] Instead of going international to only "beef up" sagging sales, a company must have a well laid out plan that includes goals, policies, and mission statements that mirror the commitment of top management. Financial, marketing, cost goals, and long-term marketing strategies for each foreign market entered must be established.

Determining Which Foreign Markets To Enter

An American company contemplating which foreign markets to enter should first entertain the following internal company analysis to ascertain the best markets to enter by matching the needs of the country with the company's resources[31]:

1. Company size
2. Company's international experience
3. The product and industry
4. Firm's level of involvement in international markets
5. Company's organization for international business
6. Company goals

Second, the company should match the firm's international capabilities with the best foreign market(s) that exhibit product needs, potential sales, and profit returns, as partially represented by population statistics shown in Table 22-5. Such a marketing feasibility study would include marketing intelligence, marketing research, potential sales volume, costs forecasts, and the development of preliminary distribution, pricing, and promotion strategies to determine if the company's capabilities are best utilized in the chosen markets.

Choosing countries cannot always be an obvious decision. China, once thought of as an economically stagnant giant, has become an American corporate bonanza and a leading manufacturing source for American goods.[36] As China's most favored nation (MFN) was renewed in 1994, China became a major player in trade with the United States.[37] Caterpillar had a joint venture to build hydraulic excavators in China, where Caterpillar expected the market to be worth $2 billion by the year 2000. Boeing won a $5 billion order from Chinese Airlines. Apple Computer, Inc., began production of components in China, as part of an effort to grab 20 percent of the Chinese PC market and catch up with IBM, who signed an agreement with China to design and install information-technology networks. China expects to spend $41.4 billion on telecommunications, and AT&T expects to receive a lion's share of this expenditure.[37]

Analyzing How Best To Enter A Foreign Market

After a company has targeted a foreign market, the next step is to determine the best way to enter that particular market, given the company's marketing, financial, and managerial capabilities. As illustrated in Figure 22-3, different modes are available, depending on the market's needs and the marketer's abilities. If a firm does not have any production facilities overseas and has had little or no experience in international marketing, it can indirectly export the product via a local buyer of a foreign manufac-

TABLE 22-5 Population and Density for the Twenty Most Populated Countries, 1993 and 2000 Projection

Country	Population (in thousands)	Projected (year 2000)	Density per Square Mile
1. China	1,177.6	1,260.1	327
2. India	903.1	1,018.1	787
3. United States	258.1	275.3	73
4. Indonesia	197.2	219.5	280
5. Brazil	156.6	169.5	48
6. Russia	149.3	151.5	23
7. Japan	124.7	127.6	818
8. Pakistan	125.2	148.5	416
9. Bangladesh	122.2	143.5	2,365
10. Nigeria	95.1	118.6	270
11. Mexico	90.4	102.9	122
12. Germany	80.8	82.2	597
13. Vietnam	71.8	80.5	571
14. Philippines	68.5	77.7	595
15. Turkey	60.9	69.6	143
16. Thailand	58.7	63.6	297
17. Egypt	58.0	67.5	99
18. United Kingdom	58.0	59.0	621
19. Italy	58.0	58.4	511
20. France	57.6	59.4	273

Source: Statistical Abstract of the United States (1993), pp. 840-42.

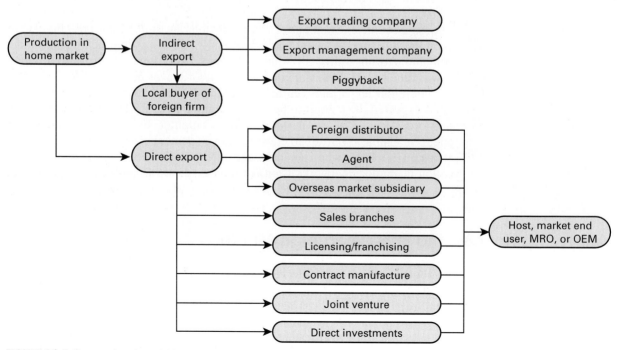

FIGURE 22-3 International marketing, business goods exporting.

turer or distributor or use one of three alternative exporting operations, such as a trading company, export management company, or ship the order by piggybacking the product with another exporter going to the same destination.

INDIRECT EXPORTING

The most common and least risky form of foreign market entry is indirect exporting. Here the firm sells to local intermediaries, who, in turn, sell to the foreign markets. Usually a company becomes an indirect exporter when the firm has no or little expertise and doesn't have any special activity for exporting within the company. The type of sale is handled as a domestic sale to a local buyer from the foreign firm or foreign distributor. In a survey of 139 firms in the United Kingdom (U.K.), the most common type of business relationship with U.S. partners was that of the U.K. firm acting as a distributor. The majority of U.K. firms have formed links with between two and five U.S. companies.[38] Manufacturers in the extractive industries often have U.S. offices to procure equipment and supplies for their foreign operations.

Piggyback exporting develops when one manufacturer uses its overseas distribution facilities (carrier) to sell another company's product (rider) along with its own. GE has been doing it for years, but the concept appears to be new.

Export trading companies (ETCs), permitted in the United States since 1982, were established to emulate Japanese trading companies. ETCs act as the exporting arm for a number of manufacturers, similar to a domestic manufacturer's rep. Major corporations, such as Control Data, Borg-Warner, GE, and GM, have formed ETCs with major U.S. banks, which include Bank of America, First National Bank of Boston, and Citicorp to achieve the efficiencies of economies of scale in market knowledge, transportation, and finance to compete with the better established Japanese trading companies. GE formed a large ETC that had 60 bilingual engineers with MBAs in its countertrade department alone.[31] Countertrade is a composite of a number of different methods. Basically, countertrade is an agreement between two parties where a deal is struck that has strings attached. Barter is widely used; compensation, is the most frequently used form of countertrade[39] (a modern form of barter); counterpurchase (which says if you buy from me, I'll buy from you).[40]

Export management companies are similar to ETCs in that EMCs can become the equivalent of a firm's export department because it can use the letterhead of the manufacturer, negotiate on the firm's behalf, and get the manufacturers approval on orders and quotations. The EMC appears ideal for the medium-sized or smaller exporter.

DIRECT EXPORTING

In direct exporting, a firm's export department takes on all the tasks of marketing intelligence, marketing research, distribution, documentation, promotion, pricing, choice of target markets and the choice of specific products to use in these markets.

Direct exporting can be implemented in several ways: (1) selling direct to the independent foreign distributor or (2) establishing a foreign sales branch or other local representative. Dealing with a foreign distributor can make contact with the end users and/or the OEMs, but some of the exporter's control is decreased. Japan's distribution system is a good example of such a system where channels are so elongated that distributors and/or agents sell repeatedly among themselves before the end user or OEM receives the product. Many distributors employ only three to four people and a manufacturer who chooses this channel may have to go through five or six intermediaries before a customer is contacted. This is one way Japan can inhibit exporters from doing business in their country. Obviously, an exporter would shy away from any involvement in the Japanese distribution system.

Perhaps the alternative that provides the most desirable control over the entire exporting process is the direct foreign sales branch, licensing, franchised distributor, or contract manufacturing.

DIRECT FOREIGN SALES BRANCHES

Perhaps the most expensive form of direct marketing, a foreign sales branch, offers the most control over the sale, distribution, and promotion of a product. Unless the exporter has numerous products to carry the cost load incurred to support factory reps, a sales branch may not be profitable.

LICENSING, FRANCHISING, AND CONTRACT MANUFACTURING

Foreign licensing involves an agreement between a firm in one country (the licensor) and a firm in another country (the licensee) whereby the former permits the latter to use its manufacturing processes, patents, or trademarks in exchange for a royalty fee. Foreign licensing often occurs when an exporter's overseas production facilities have been taken over by a foreign government. The experienced managers are asked to stay on and provide technical and managerial expertise for the operation.

A licensing agreement gives something of value to the licensee in exchange for a specific level of performance and remuneration to the licensor. Such things as patent rights, trademark rights (use of a name), or copyrights (duplicates of the product), and certain product and process know-how could be exchanged. In return, the licensee agrees to produce the product, market it in assigned territories, and to pay the licenser a specified amount of royalty per unit sold or produced. Licensing is an easier way to enter a market, and the exporter does not lose control over the process, so long as the licensee abides by the licensing agreement. A foreign licensee often may attempt to use the licensed technology to manufacture products that are then marketed in the United States or third countries in direct competition with the licensor or its other licensees. U.S. licensors may wish to impose territorial restrictions on their licensees, depending on United States or foreign anti-trust laws and the licensing laws of the host country.[41]

Franchising is a viable alternative for both large and small companies who want to enter a foreign market that will support only a minimal investment. Similar to licensing, franchising does require an extensive amount of standardization to control the franchiser. Business products and services tend to be the most predominate area using business franchises.

Contract manufacturing is simpler, as the exporter contracts a local foreign firm to manufacture the product, after which the exporter markets the product through a subsidiary or turns it over to agents, distributors, or other appropriate intermediaries. Manufacturing locally saves shipping and storage costs and permits the exporter to maintain costs without experiencing international exchange rates, NTBs, and import tariffs.

JOINT VENTURES

When two or more firms share ownership and control over operations and investments, they have entered into a joint venture. Joint ventures provide better knowledge of local markets, a local identity, and a shared risk since one party in the joint venture is in the host country. Sometimes joint ventures may be necessary for political and/or economic reasons because no other arrangement is permitted by the government. The local government may require joint ownership as the condition for entry, such as China will not permit any other kind of relationship with a foreign firm.

Another reason for entering into a joint venture is the firm may lack the essential financial or managerial resources to undertake market entry by itself, so a joint venture would satisfy the exporter's needs. Joint ventures, however, sometimes result in serious conflicts in management and marketing philosophies.

A joint venture agreement often requires manufacturing and distribution by the host country's firm, with the exporter receiving equity in and being able to exercise a voice in management. Equity shares usually range from 25 to 75 percent. Fujitsu, Japan's largest manufacturer of computers, found it difficult to get established in the U.S. market and decided to form a joint venture with TRW to get American market know-how and American distribution. Among the American firms who set up joint ventures in China were Tandem, IBM, Westinghouse, and Pitney Bowes.

DIRECT INVESTMENT

In direct investment, the firm should consider such host country factors as (1) the level of wage rates, (2) the level of employment skills, (3) infrastructure conditions, (4) import restriction on manufacturing inputs and facilitating equipment, (5) market and monetary controls, (6) the likelihood of a government takeover, and (7) costs of shipping products to customers.

An exporter's wholly owned foreign production unit represents the largest investment, with commensurate control, and the greatest test of an organization's will. This route is taken because of cheap labor, closer proximity to the foreign market, and devalued currencies in the host country, making it more profitable to invest directly.

Other considerations must be analyzed when developing the market entry strategy. Competing countries may take a power position in a foreign market that can shut out an exporter. For example, America's exports to China is only about one-third the size of China-bound Japanese exports. America's trade deficit with China of $38 billion is dwarfed by Japan's $12 billion shortfall. Ironically, Japan's investment in China may well exacerbate U.S. trade frictions with the Chinese because many of the products once exported from Japan are now being assembled and shipped from China, widening America's huge trade deficit with China.[42]

The International Business Marketing Program

International buyers of business products are interested in value, performance, reliability, price, delivery, and quality. As long as the seller does not violate the host country's taboos or business customs, the marketing program has to include market research, product, pricing, promotion, and distribution strategies.

INTERNATIONAL MARKET RESEARCH—RESEARCHING TARGET COUNTRIES

Once a firm has established the general export potential of a given product and the information available as determined by intelligence research, the next step is to investigate a number of countries to develop target markets.

In researching target countries, twelve considerations should be analyzed[40]:

1. Economic viability
2. Country's purchasing potential

3. Product demand and suitability

4. Culture (including religion and leisure habits)

5. Legal system and commercial practices

6. Language and climate

7. Ease of access

8. Degree of difficulty and sophistication

9. Economies of scale

10. Political stability

11. Availability of foreign exchange

12. Geography and regional management

The Department of Commerce (DOC) is one of the primary and most readily accessible sources for foreign county information. The DOC has a wide variety of reports on individual countries in terms of economics, demographics, and specific industries. However, because of governmental cutbacks and a computer system that does not work all the time, it is no longer certain that some DOC trade specialists, with sufficient experience to know what reports are available and how to use them, would be available to help the inquirer.[40] The best suggestion is to obtain the most recent edition of the DOC's *Basic Guide to Exporting* and the Small Business Administration's *The World Is Your Market* to compile the needed market information. Hundreds of export-related publications are available through the U.S. Government Printing Office. In addition, the U.N. International Monetary Fund (IMF) and the Organization for Economic Cooperation and Development (OECD) are excellent sources. It is best to do some independent research on each country by visiting the country and collecting more data, first hand, through local people, local reports, and one's general impression of the country using the twelve points listed previously.[40]

For information on the business climate in more than 55 countries, the American Chamber of Commerce has member organizations in those countries that can supply this information. A typical member is either an American company operating in a foreign country or a U.S. citizen who is working there.[43]

The members of the United Nations prepare a report called the Export Information System, which organizes the data according to Standard International Trade Classification (SITC) Revision 2 (1981). Approximately 2,500 products are included in this list. The information is provided on (1) the top 25 import markets for a product, (2) the top 10 U.S. markets by market share, and (3) whether to pursue the export option for a particular product and identifies those country markets that should be investigated further.[44]

Online databases are beginning to supply a considerable amount of information, usually in the form of extracts from foreign publications.[45] Of course, such extracts cannot be expected to explain peculiarities of subtle cultural differences. However, these databases do offer much worthwhile information for the business marketer interested in technical facts. For example, the Japanese do not rely heavily on written communications and contracts in their business operations; thus, their database abstracts do not provide the same range and depth as those on American databases.[46] Foreign databases frequently provide technological information the business marketer can find useful. The World Wide Web Internet, with its many features, such as web pages and faxing capabilities, can be another valuable source of international data and information.

International Business Product Strategies

Although products in the international business market are more homogeneous than consumer products, there are more product variations internationally than domestically because of the greater number of international economic, cultural, technical skills, maintenance levels, labor costs, climatic conditions, standards, available power, and political/legal variables[16] (see Table 22-6). International product strategies depend on the whether an indirect or a direct approach is taken. If a direct approach is taken, exercising maximum control is very essential. Once a domestic product leaves the United States, its future is determined by who controls the market strategies in the host country. Proper pricing, distribution, and promotion strategies can ensure such control.

INTERNATIONAL PRICING STRATEGIES

Pricing strategies have to consider costs, prevailing prices, competition, and the international environment. International pricing strategies encounter unique situations, unlike any other pricing situation. These include the practices of transfer pricing, dumping, scams and bribes and government influence.

Transfer Pricing   Transfer prices are the prices placed on products as they are transferred between business units belonging to the same company. Transfer prices can be used to mitigate the effects of tariffs and taxation. Since tariffs are usually based on the value of imported goods, a producer can charge a low transfer price to a foreign subsidiary, thereby reducing the foreign tariff. It can also charge a high transfer price (making a large profit) as it exports from a country having a low tax rate, and then sells (making little profit) in a country having a high tax rate. Exporters to countries not allowing profit repatriation (the return of profits to overseas parent companies) can charge high transfer prices and make little profit in such countries. Price controls are often based on some markup on cost, so that by charging a high transfer price, the controls can be partially overcome.[47]

TABLE 22-6   Design Implications of Environmental Factors

Environmental Factors	Product Design Implications
Level of technical skill	Product simplification
Level of labor cost	Automation of manualization of the product
Level of literacy	Remaking and simplification of the product
Level of income	Quality and price change
Level of interest rates	Quality and price change (investment in quality might not be financially desirable)
Level of maintenance	Change in tolerances
Climatic differences	Product adaptation
Isolation (repair difficult and expensive)	Product simplification and reliability improvement
Differences in standards	Recalibration of product and resizing
Availability of other products	Greater or lesser product integration
Availability of materials	Change in product structure and fuel
Power availability	Resizing of product
Special conditions	Product redesign or invention

Source: Richard D. Robinson, "The challenge of the underdeveloped national market," *Journal of Marketing* 25 (October 1961):22. Reprinted by permission of the American Marketing Association.

Adjusting transfer prices for the sole purpose of circumventing government regulations is looked on with disfavor by governments and should be avoided. The American IRS carefully watches transfer prices. In a 2-year period the Internal Revenue Service examined 591 cases and decided in 174 of those cases that goods transferred from the United States had been underpriced. Its average settlement with the companies involved was $750,000.[48]

Dumping   Dumping is disposing of goods in a foreign country at less than their full cost or value. Goods will sometimes be exported at prices that only cover direct product costs to dispose of excess inventories. Companies sell their excess inventories overseas to avoid disturbing their own national markets (for example, reducing prices or causing price wars at home). The purchasers of dumped goods may not mind the practice, but firms that produce the same products in nations where these goods are dumped do mind. Such competitors call for protective legislation, as did the U.S. steel industry before the industry's mini-mills became a big hit. Most nations have strong antidumping regulations, and firms must be very careful to avoid any pretense of skirting the local law.[49]

Scams and Bribes   Unfortunately, bribes and political favors figure into international pricing. Some premier European high-tech companies have been involved—including Germany's Seimens, France's Alcatel Alsthom, and the European airframe consortium Airbus Industrie—are among the major practitioners.[50]

Government Influence   Direct government controls over pricing are extensive. Governments can exercise price controls through government-owned firms and government-owned stockpiles. U.S. firms face a growing pressure from China to transfer technology. When Boeing sells a plane to China, the Chinese government insists Boeing spend as much as a third of the money received buying Chinese parts, or handling over the technology to make those parts. Motorola earned a lot of money in the mobile telephone market in China, so the government forced Motorola to build a computer-chip plant in windswept northeastern China.[51]

Many firms throughout the world are taking another look at China and its huge potential markets. Of the world's big traders, China is in a protectionist league of its own. The Chinese government enacted prohibitive duties and arbitrary rules to curb imports of computers and other industrial products. Marcus Noland of the Washington Institute of International Economics says China is the biggest potential threat to the world trade system. Since its application to enter the World Trade Organization has stalled, China may be able to play this game for years.[52]

INTERNATIONAL PROMOTIONAL STRATEGIES

Three major forms of promotion work the best in international business markets. Trade shows, direct mail and personal selling have the most impact. Each promotional form has its unique qualities, but any effective promotional effort includes different quantities of all three forms.

Trade Shows   Sales promotion in the form of a trade fair, mostly held in Germany, is playing an increasingly important role in international business marketing because so many prospects can be contacted in one place and because the fairs enable quick comparisons of products. Trade fairs allow the seller to meet with, talk, and develop long-term relationships with their international customers. Europeans, in particular, want long-term relationships with American firms, and any U.S company that is committed to the longer term should be successful.[53]

Direct Mail   Direct mail is becoming popular, although mailing lists are usually difficult to obtain. The use of publicity, although growing in popularity, is limited because of language difficulties and media coverage. Advertising for business products is given little attention in the international business market, perhaps because of the difficulties in determining media coverage and numerous, widely varying, governmental regulations.

Domestic Versus Foreign Salespeople   In the international business market, the primary element of the promotional mix is personal selling, for only through personal selling can the coordination so essential to the business buyer-seller interface be effectively achieved.

A firm's international sales force may be composed of American or foreign personnel, or both. American salespeople tend to be more knowledgeable about an American company and its products, which is an important industrial criterion. They tend to be better connected to obtain concessions, such as special product adaptations, from the parent company. However, they will likely be more expensive than a foreign sales force. Normally, the parent company pays not only their regular salaries but also a bonus for overseas hardships, as well as various travel and accommodation costs.

The primary disadvantage of having American salespeople working abroad is their lack of familiarity with cultural differences. In many cases, they will need extensive foreign language and other cultural training which is much more difficult than training foreign individuals in American business methods.

Companies that decide to sell abroad must determine which type of sales organization and management techniques will be the most appropriate. To assume automatically that what works in one country will work in any other country is courting disaster. Multinational corporations that have broad product lines, large sales volumes, and/or operate in large, developed markets prefer specialized organizational structures, such as product or customer assignment, or an assignment based on different cultures.[54] Spoken languages may be the deciding factor in a sales force assignment. For example, in the north of Belgium, people speak Flemish, whereas in the south, they speak French.

INTERNATIONAL DISTRIBUTION STRATEGIES

The primary goal of international business marketing is to achieve wider distribution. But distribution involves more than physically moving a product. Distribution involves channel strategy, physical handling, storage, inventorying, sometimes assembling, using protective packaging, extensive paperwork, and sales forecasting. Figure 22-4 shows how distribution channels might look if a firm used either domestic production or overseas production. The domestic firm must distribute through its international offices, then develop channels to move the product from the domestic market to the foreign market using an international carrier, freight forwarder, or its own carrier and then on to the end user or OEM.

Companies with overseas production capabilities would find less circuitous distribution routes to follow. The company could contract the product's manufacturer to an overseas producer, license another overseas manufacturer to make and sell the product, ship the product completely knocked down (CKD) from the domestic market to the foreign market to be assembled by the licensee or contract manufacturer, or establish a joint venture with a host country company to make and sell the product. If the domestic company had sole control of an overseas manufacturing facility, then the export company could distribute directly to the end user, OEM, or distributor in the foreign country.

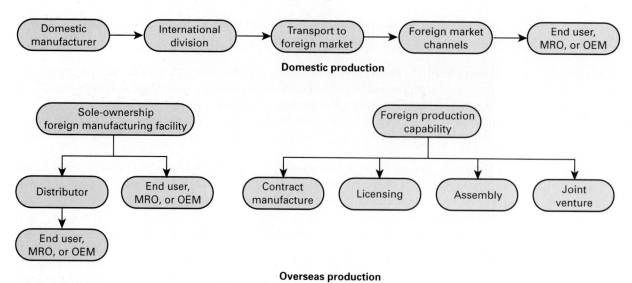

FIGURE 22-4 International distribution channels: domestic versus overseas production.

International Product Standards

In an effort to harmonize quality-management and quality-assurance systems practice, the International Organization for Standards (ISO) established the international series called ISO 9000. Many companies registered their quality systems under ISO 9000 as a way to gain a competitive advantage.[55] To earn ISO 9000 certification, a company must set up and document all procedures that relate to the process to be certified. Certified companies are audited once or twice a year by ISO registrars to make sure that the companies are keeping up with the requirements of the standards of ISO 9000.

The customer of a certified company does not have to visit a plant, saving time and expense and providing the assurance that the products purchased from that firm will be of highest quality.[56] Initially, the motivating force behind gaining ISO 9000 certification was the belief that it was needed to ensure sales to the European Community (EC), but certification later proved to be less important than first thought. This is an important consideration in international business marketing, where customer visits to a seller's plant would incur a great expense to both the buyer and seller. The estimated cost of an ISO 9000 certification costs from $100,000 to $250,000, which includes the staff hours and the procedure, and it often takes from 9 to 28 months to complete the entire registration process.[57] Although only a few hundred U.S. companies have registered for ISO 9000 certification, more than 16,000 companies in the United Kingdom and 5,000 companies in other European countries are certified.[58]

Looking Back

International marketing is primarily business marketing, and the United States has been the principal world advocate of encouraging international marketing through free trade. The emerging Pacific Rim nations and other resurgent economies throughout the world have made international business marketing a necessary venture for many domestic firms. To perform well in the international arena, a firm must be aware of economic, cultural, political/legal, and financial environments.

In the economic environment, major considerations are exchange rates and the balance of trade, both of which have been adverse for the United States in recent years. The world's very different cultural environments cause difficult interpersonal relationship problems in the important industrial interface environment. Political/legal constraints involve import restrictions, market and monetary controls, and foreign entities assuming control of foreign assets in countries. Financial considerations involve solving the question of getting paid after the order has been taken. International firms need to develop unique strategies to handle problems occurring in these international environment areas.

Firms engaging in international business marketing use conventional marketing strategies. These strategies involve product, price, promotion, and distribution strategies. Because of worldwide economic, cultural, and political/legal differences, these conventional marketing strategies encounter many more contingencies and constraints internationally than domestically. The firm that carefully develops these international strategies within a context of the uncontrollable variables can develop competitive advantages, and even distinctive competencies.

Questions for Discussion

1. Respond to Theodore Levitt's claim that multinational companies are in decline and must change themselves into global corporations that view the world as "one vast market rather than as slices of nations."

2. Foreign direct investment in the United States has now reached $329 billion dollars. It has surpassed U.S. investment abroad and is growing much more rapidly than U.S. investment. Should the United States place restrictions on foreign investments in the United States? Why or why not?

3. In efforts to strengthen a long-stagnant economy, Mexico has sharply devalued its currency (the peso) a number of times in recent years. Are these devaluations helping Mexico's economy and what more might be done? Discuss NAFTA involvement.

4. Discuss the cultural obstacles an American business person might have when making a rushed trip to Australia to secure a large contract involving the purchase of a steel mill.

5. Although many Japanese firms have been eminently successful, U.S. firms have invested much more in Italy, The Netherlands, the United Kingdom, and other countries than Japan. What governmental influence may prevail here?

6. The single greatest financial loss in an initial international venture was that experienced by billionaire Daniel Ludwig in Jari, Brazil. What economic, cultural, or political/legal problems might Ludwig have encountered and might they have been overcome?

7. Discuss the role that material culture plays in a foreign buyer's perception of an imported product.

8. When contemplating the export of a high-tech item, should a joint venture be made instead of licensing the manufacture?

9. Why is international market research so difficult to pursue? Be specific.

10. What is dumping and how does this practice raise the host country's anger?

Endnotes

1. "The export imperative, challenge of global change," *America Online* (August 18, 1994), p. 1.

2. "To spur human rights, spur trade," *Business Week* (March 7, 1994), p.138.

3. John Naisbitt, *Megatrends Asia: Eight Asian Megatrends That Are Reshaping Our World* (New York: Simon & Schuster, 1996).

4. "Motorola bets big on China," *Fortune* (May 27, 1996), p. 118.

5. Pete Engardio and Amy Borrus, "What country has a computer for every 6,000 people?" *Business Week* (September 13, 1993), p. 50.

6. "Morgan Stanley's Chinese coup," *Business Week* (November 7, 1994), pp. 50-1.

7. China: One step backward, growth curbs will hurt foreigners," *Business Week* (November 28, 1994), p. 32.

8. Michael E. Porter, *Competitive Strategy, Techniques for Analyzing Industries and Competitors* (New York: The Free Press, 1980), p. 278-98.

9. "Business outlook: The world recovery will lift exports," *Business Week* (July 4, 1994), p. 22.

10. *Statistical Abstract of the United States* (Washington, D.C.: U.S. GPO 1995), p. 799.

11. Edward Hall, "The silent language in overseas business," *Harvard Business Review* 38 (May-June 1960):87-96.

12. Brian H. Flynn, "Homing in on foreign sales customs," *Business Marketing* 72 (June 1987):91-2.

13. John A. Reeder, "When West meets East: Cultural aspects of doing business in Asia," *Business Horizons* 30 (January-February 1987), pp. 69-74.

14. David Ricks, *Big Business Blunders* (Homewood, Ill.: Dow-Jones-Irwin, 1983), p. 16.

15. Larry Garges and Stuart Barrowcliff, *Marketing in Brazil* (Rio de Janeiro: Office of Country Marketing and the U.S. Embassy in Brasilia, 1981), p. 17.

16. Edward Cundiff and Marye Hilger, *Marketing in the International Environment* (Englewood Cliffs, N.J.: Prentice Hall, Inc., 1984), p. 119.

17. Henry Rodkin, "Selling Abroad: 10 Rules to Live (and Sell) by Overseas," *Sales and Marketing Management* (April 2, 1984), pp. 63-4.

18. Yoshi Tsurumi, "Managing consumer and industrial marketing systems in Japan," *Sloan Management Review* (Fall 1982), pp. 41-9.

19. "Italian Renaissance?" *Business Week* (March 28, 1994), pp. 46-8.

20. David A. Schmidt, "Analyzing political risk," *Business Horizons* 29 (July-August 1986):43-50.

21. "The vacuum at the top is getting downright scary," *Business Week* (February 27, 1995), p. 62.

22. Kate Bertrand, "Real-life risky business," *Business Marketing* (January 1987), p. 50.

23. Stephen Barlas, "Service exporters spell relief 'G-A-T-T," *Business Marketing* (January 1987):58+.

24. Clyde V. Presowitz Jr., *Trading Places: How We Allowed Japan to Take the Lead,* (CITY? Basic Books, YEAR?), as reported by Robert Neff, Business Week (April 25, 1988), pp. 12-13.

25. Mark F. McPherson, "When in Tokyo . . . ." *Business Marketing* (September 1987), p. 90; see also "Gene squad: Japanese now target another field the U.S. leads: Biotechnology," *The Wall Street Journal* (December 17, 1987), p. 1.

26. Kenichi Ohmae, *The Borderless World* (New York: Harper Business, 1990), p. 144.

27. "The trade pact's key provisions," *The Wall Street Journal* (December 2, 1994), p. A8.

28. Thomas Shreeve, "Be prepared for political changes abroad," *Harvard Business Review* 28(July-August 1984), pp. 111-18.

29. *U.S. Foreign Trade Highlights,* U.S. Dept. of Commerce, International Trade Administration, 1993, pp. 17, 21.

30. "Is the Japanese dynamo losing juice?" *Business Week* (June 27, 1994), p. 44.

31. Vern Terpstra, ed., *International Marketing* (Chicago: Dryden Press, 1983), p. 24

32. "Congratulations, exporter! Now about getting paid," *U.S. News & World Report* 119 (January 17, 1994):98.

33. John S. McClenahen, "Percy Barnevik and the ABBs of competition," *Industry Week* 243 (June 6, 1994):20+.

34. Thomas Hout, Michael E. Porter, and Eileen Rudden, "How global companies win out," *Harvard Business Review* 60 (September-October 1982), pp. 98-108.

35. Charles R. Day, "It all begins with attitude," *Industry Week* (June 6, 1994), p. 6.

36. "A tidal wave of Chinese goods," *Business Week* (December 12, 1994), pp. 56-57.

37. "China's gates swing open," *Business Week* (June 13, 1994), pp. 52-53.

38. Ian Chaston, "UK/US collaborative exploitation of the European market," *Journal of General Management* 4 (Summer 1993):80-92.

39. Aspy P. Palia and Oded Shenkar, "Countertrade practices in China," *Industrial Marketing Management* 20 (1991):57-65.

40. L. Fargo Wells and Karin B. Dulat, *Exporting, From Start to Finance* 2nd. ed. (New York: McGraw-Hill Book Co., 1991), pp. 391-6.

41. "Beyond exporting," *America Online* (August 21, 1994), p. 3.

42. Gene Koretz, "A marriage made in Asia," *Business Week* (January 29, 1996), p. 20.

43. "Information on business overseas," *America Online* (August 21, 1994), p. 1.

44. "Export information system," *America Online* (August 21, 1994), p. 1.

45. For a partial list of international on-line services, see Tim Miller, "Around the world in forty keystrokes," *Online Access* (May-June 1987), pp. 42-57.

46. Robert Chapman Wood, "Japan online," *Online Access* (September-October 1987), pp. 32-8.

47. Ruel Kahler, *International Marketing* (Cincinnati, Ohio: Southwestern Publishing Co., 1983), p. 264.

48. Vern Terpstra, "Business international." In Vern Terpstra, ed., *International Marketing* (Chicago: Dryden Press, 1983), p. 521.

49. James K. Weekly, "Pricing in foreign markets: Pitfalls and opportunities," *Industrial Marketing Management* 21 (1992):173-9.

50. "A world of greased palms," *Business Week* (November 6, 1995). pp. 36-8.

51. "Price of entry into China rises sharply," *The Wall Street Journal* (December 19, 1995), p. A-12; see also "A chill wind blows from Beijing," *Business Week* (January 15, 1996), pp. 44-5.

52. "Rethinking China," *Business Week* (March 4, 1996), pp. 57-65.

53. Bob Straetz, "U.S. Firms are told how to develop business opportunities in the EC," *Business America* 114 (June 14, 1993):6.

54. Earl D. Honeycutt, Jr., and John B. Ford, "Guidelines for managing an international sales force," *Industrial Marketing Management* 24 (March, 1995):135-44.

55. Steven E. Gazy, "ISO 9000: A common sense approach to quality," *Appliance Manufacturer* 41 (September 1993):33-4.

56. Anne-Marie Roussel, "ISO 9000: A measure of the measurement," *Data Communications* 22 (October, 1993):55-8.

57. Karen Heller, "ISO 9000: A framework for continuous improvement," *Chemical Week* 153 (September 22, 1993):30-2.

58. Donald F. Hastings, "A blueprint to ISO 9000," *Machine Design* 65 (October 22, 1993):226.

Bibliography

"Asia's new giants," *Business Week* (1995):64-80.

Callahan, Madelyn R., "Preparing the new global manager," *Training and Development Journal* (1989): 29-32.

Herbig, Paul A. and Hugh E. Kramer, "Do's and dont's of cross-cultural negotiations," *Industrial Marketing Management* 21 (1992):287-98.

Kaynak, Erdener and Russell D. Wells, "Exporting large capital equipment: A case study of nuclear technology transfer," *Industrial Marketing Management* 19 (1990):173-90.

Koepfler, Edward R., "Strategic options for global market players," *Journal of Business Strategy* 9 (1989):46-50.

Kuttner, Robert, "You could drive a Lexus through the holes in the WTO," *Business Week* (1995):24.

Liesch, Peter W., "Government-mandated countertrade in Australia: Some international marketing implications," *Industrial Marketing Management* 23 (1994):299-305.

Morris, Michael H. and Leyland F. Pitt, "Do strategy frameworks apply in the United States and abroad?" *Industrial Marketing Management* 22 (1993):215-21.

O'Hara, Brad, Fred Palumbo and Paul Herbig, "Industrial trade shows abroad," *Industrial Marketing Management* 22 (1993):233-7.

Onkvisit, Sak, and John Shaw, "An examination of the international product life cycle and its application within marketing," *Columbia Journal of World Business* (1983):73-9.

Okoroafo, Sam C., "Implementing international countertrade: A dyadic approach," *Industrial Marketing Management* 23 (1994): 229-34.

Palia, Aspy P. and Oded Shenkar, "Countertrade practices in China," *Industrial Marketing Management* 20 (1992): 57-65.

Palia, Aspy P., Oded Shenkar, and Heon Deok Yoon, "Countertrade practices in Korea," *Industrial Marketing Management* 23 (1994):205-13.

Weekly, James K., "Pricing in foreign markets: Pitfalls and opportunities," *Industrial Marketing Management* 21 (1992):173-9.

PART

IX

Cases

(P = Primary emphasis, S = Secondary emphasis)

CASE	CHAPTER																					
	1	2	3	4	5	6	7	8	9	10	11	12	13	14	15	16	17	18	19	20	21	22
1. Aberdeen Electronics				P	P		S	S										P	P		S	
2. AMF Wyott, Inc.											S		P	S			P					
3. Calox Machinery (A)									S				P							S		P
4. Calox Machinery (B)									S				P							S		P
5. Coventry Plastics	P								P				S	S		S						P
6. Cumberland Gasket	P	P								S				S								
7. Edward F. Crow								S	S				P	P	S	S					S	
8. F.B.Dunn & Assoc.						P		P	S			S										
9. Hach Co. (A)						S				P	S					P	S			S		
10. Hach Co. (B)															S	S	P					
11. Huntington Electronics							P		S		P											
12. Jet Engine Industry . . .	S	S			P				S													
13. Lewiston-Copeland						S	S	P	P													
14. Mt. Ashland Ski Area							S		P		S										S	
15. P. Reid and Assoc.												P										
16. Phoenix Porcelain Co. (A)						P	P	S												S		
17. Phoenix Porcelain Co. (B)								S	S													
18. Starnes-Brenner Machine																						P
19. Top Plastics Co.				S	S		S	P	P				S	S	S	S				S		
20. Trans-Europa Business Credit	P						S	S								S					P	
21. Zactec Electronics						S	S	S	P		S									P		

CASE 1
Aberdeen Electronics Revisited

The Aberdeen Electronics Corporation was an industrial supplier of small electronic parts, switches, and subassemblies used by a wide variety of other manufacturing firms. The company prided itself on the quality of their products and their ability to manufacture to the precise specifications of their industrial customers. It was not unusual for the firm to design specific machines, sometimes at considerable expense, in order to produce specialized parts for high-volume purchasers. The company's "salesmen" were in reality high-salaried engineers who often acted as troubleshooters and who were greatly respected by Aberdeen's customers.

One of Aberdeen's major customers was a producer of a varied line of electronic equipment and household appliances. This customer, Magnus Manufacturing Corporation, purchased a wide line of Aberdeen products. In the fall of 1991, Magnus had contracted with Aberdeen to purchase an intricate thermostatic switch to be used in conjunction with a government defense contract. The requested item, known as "Model K-50 subassembly," required that Aberdeen develop a specialized stamping machine and allied equipment that could not be readily used for any other purpose. Since the machinery in question required an investment of almost $250,000, including developmental costs, the decision to supply Model K-50 was not undertaken lightly.

At the time the decision was made, Magnus Manufacturing, based on their government contract, agreed to purchase "at least 10,000 units of K-50 yearly at a price not to exceed $16.00 per unit." This purchase agreement was to extend for a minimum of 5 years, from 1992 through 1996.

Aberdeen estimated that the cost of production of K-50, including depreciation on the specialized machinery, would approximate this price. That

Adapted from a case developed by the late Barry J. Hersker, formerly Professor of Marketing, Florida State University.

is, Aberdeen expected to break even at approximately $16.00 per unit. On the other hand, the Magnus account was believed to be so important that Aberdeen undertook to produce this item as a service to Magnus at $16.00.

At the time of this decision, the possibility of selling additional quantities of Model K-50 to other users in an effort to increase its profitability was considered to be "rather remote." On the other hand, it was pointed out that the capacity to dramatically increase output would exist, and such potential increased production would not require any additional investment in machinery or tools. The President of Aberdeen, Mr. Alfred E. Maxwell, who personally entered into the decision, remarked at the time, "You know, the longer I am in this business, the more I am convinced that nothing really goes to waste. If you keep anything long enough, it will find a use and a market. The K-50 may surprise us in the long run."

After 1 year's production of Model K-50, Aberdeen found that Magnus's purchases were slightly higher than their original estimate; they purchased 12,000 units in 1992. Even at this volume, however, Aberdeen estimated that they realized only a $0.49 profit per unit at a selling price of $16.00. At one point management had considered increasing the price to Magnus, but this idea was rejected for two reasons: first, the original sales contract specifically limited the price to an amount "not to exceed $16.00," and second, Magnus threatened that they would revise their product and substitute another device for the assembly requiring Model K-50 if a price increase over $16.00 became necessary.

A few days after the matter appeared to have been settled, an executive from Magnus offered to renegotiate the original sales contract. He said that Magnus might be willing to increase the price paid for K-50 by 10 percent if Aberdeen would remove the volume requirement. That is, Magnus might be induced to pay more for K-50 if Aberdeen would release them from their obligation to purchase 10,000 units yearly until 1996. The Aberdeen executives rejected this offer, stating in a closed meeting that their investment in this product was too great to risk any decline in volume, even at a higher price. The incident began to cause some uneasiness among the Aberdeen executives, especially when Magnus began to reduce their orders during the first 6 months of 1993. However, the total purchases of K-50 in 1993 were ultimately 8,000 units at $16.00 each.

Early in 1994, when Aberdeen attempted to remind Magnus of their agreement under the contract in an effort to guarantee purchase of 10,000 units per year, the entire matter was again opened for discussion. Magnus claimed that they had indeed fulfilled their obligations under the contract since they purchased "an average of 10,000 units in the 1992-1993 2-year period." Furthermore, Magnus contended that certain defective parts were found in the K-50 device, which might necessitate that the contract be voided in its entirety. Aberdeen acknowledged that some defects had occurred in one shipment of the K-50 device in the fall of 1993 but pointed out that these units were replaced free of charge.

Magnus countered that the defects had proven very costly to them, since the devices had already been assembled into a finished product before the error was discovered. They estimated that their direct losses, caused by the defective units, exceeded the cost of the units themselves by $20,000. Aberdeen offered to allow Magnus a credit for $10,000 to reduce this loss, but Magnus countered that they were not willing to accept $10,000 as full payment.

They demanded that Aberdeen should (1) immediately reimburse Magnus for $20,000, (2) improve their quality control to ensure that this problem would not recur, (3) reduce the price of the K-50 unit to $15.50 each, and (4) admit that the contract should be interpreted as 10,000 units average per year over the entire period of 1992 through 1996.

After considerable negotiation and discussion, it was agreed that Aberdeen should meet all of these demands by Magnus. This decision was based to some degree on the ambiguity that existed in the requirements under the sales agreement of 1991, but of greater significance to the Aberdeen executives was their determination to maintain the loyal patronage of the Magnus Manufacturing Corporation. The volume of their other purchases was considerable, and as President Maxwell again pointed out, "The machinery and equipment currently used

on Model K-50 cannot readily be used for other production. It cannot be permitted to remain idle. We'll just have to go along with Magnus in this instance."

Alfred Horn, assistant to the president, pointed out that the new selling price was "dangerously close to actual cost." Table C1-1 presents the cost data at a volume of 10,000 units, as supplied to the Aberdeen management 1 week before the meeting by Fred Shaw, comptroller of Aberdeen Electronics.

"I have done my homework, Al," replied President Maxwell, "but we are not in a strong position on this. It is my decision to sell an average of 10,000 units annually to Magnus at $15.50 until 1996. That is, unless you have a better solution, Al." Horn did not offer any reply.

The price cut to $15.50 per unit became effective February 1, 1994. Purchases of K-50 by Magnus totaled 5,500 units in the 6-month period ending June 1994. It appeared that relations with Magnus once again were quite cordial, and the sale of K-50 was expected to reach 10,000 units by the end of 1994.

In June 1994 the purchasing director of Rigbee Controls, which had not previously been a customer of Aberdeen, contacted the firm about an unusual requirement for a subassembly for a thermostatic switch to be used in aviation equipment. Rigbee had been referred to Aberdeen by Magnus, and it was apparent that considerable executive friendships existed between the Magnus and Rigbee Corporations.

The Aberdeen engineers discovered that if Rigbee would make minor changes in their specifications for the thermostatic device, the Model K-50 subassembly would adequately fulfill their requirements. Rigbee was pleased with the Aberdeen suggestion and did determine that Model K-50 could fulfill their requirements. They asked Aberdeen to quote a price in quantities of 15,000 units annually and assured Aberdeen that they could contract for delivery in these quantities for at least 3 years.

Aberdeen reconfirmed the fact that ample capacity existed to expand production of K-50 to 25,000 units per year. Their comptroller, Fred Shaw, also furnished revised cost information to the Aberdeen management which indicated that production costs would be lower at this increased volume. Table C1-2 presents the cost data supplied by Mr. Shaw for a volume of 25,000 units. The management was pleased that the potential volume increase would permit Aberdeen to make a profit estimated at $3.68 per unit, and it was decided to offer the K-50 to Rigbee at $15.50 each.

TABLE C1-1 Units Costs of K-50 at Production Volume of 10,000 Units	
Labor[1]	$3.18
Material[2]	1.52
Plating[3]	.10
Indirect charges[4]	.48
Depreciation allowance[5]	4.00
Overhead[6]	1.06
Total factory production cost	10.34
Selling and administrative allocations[7]	5.17
Total cost per unit at 10,000 units	$15.51

[1]Combined man-hours of machine time directly allocated to each K-50 unit.

[2]Including some prefabricated parts and metal stock, with allowances for scrap value on residual stampings.

[3]Several components of K-50 are plated to increase resistance to corrosion. The subcontractor charges $0.10 per unit at a volume of 10,000 units.

[4]Indirect charges include supplies, repairs, routine maintenance on specialized equipment, electric power, etc. expressed on a per unit of output basis.

[5]Depreciation is straight line basis over the life of the Magnus contract less residual value, computed per unit of output.

[6]Allocation to cover fixed factory overhead burden, charged or the rate of 33.3 percent of direct labor.

[7]Allocation to cover selling and administrative expenses, charged at the rate of 50 percent of total factory production costs.

TABLE C1-2 Units Costs of K-50 at Production Volume of 25,000 Units	
Labor	$3.18
Material	1.48
Plating	.08
Indirect charges	.48
Depreciation allowance	1.60
Overhead	1.06
Total factory production cost	7.88
Selling and administrative allocations[1]	3.94
Total cost per unit at 25,000 units	$11.82

[1]Allocation to cover selling and administrative expenses, charged at the rate of 50 percent of total factory production costs.

Aberdeen notified Rigbee that they would supply them with the K-50 at a price of $15.50 per unit. Rigbee responded that they could not use the K-50 at any price higher than $11.50 per unit. It appeared that they would be better off to substitute another apparatus entirely if this price could not be met. Although Rigbee admitted that they were unlikely to become a large purchaser of Aberdeen products other than the K-50, they nevertheless urged Aberdeen to lower the price. The Aberdeen engineering staff, after discussions with Rigbee's engineers, confirmed the fact that Rigbee could not afford to use the K-50 at more than $11.50 and furthermore, that Rigbee would probably never require any other items from Aberdeen. Moreover, they also confirmed that Magnus would not use more than 10,000 of the K-50 annually, no matter how low Aberdeen set the price.

At another meeting of Aberdeen executives, the renewed problem of K-50 production was again discussed at length. One vice president thought that the Rigbee price would be acceptable, since the increased volume lowered production costs enough to offset the small loss from the sale the K-50 to Magnus at $15.50. "You're not suggesting that we sell to Rigbee at $11.50 and to Magnus at $15.50, are you?" exclaimed Ernest Bennett, the vice president of sales. "This line of reasoning is out of the question. Rigbee and Magnus are friends—how would Magnus react if we charged them, our good customer, more than we charge Rigbee? This conduct is highly questionable from both a legal and an ethical standpoint!" Maxwell interrupted the dispute and asked Ernest Bennett for his specific suggestions on the matter.

"Well, let's look at it this way," Bennett continued. "K-50 has been an apparent loser since 1991. The reason? Sales volume has been too low! Here we've got the chance to add 15,000 more units, and that's not all. I have reason to believe that we could sell another 25,000 units if this product were priced realistically!"

"What's this? I've never been told of such a potential," said President Maxwell, with surprise and some indignation.

Bennett continued, "The specifications of the K-50 are such that I believe they lend themselves to a wider range of industrial applications than we previously assumed. At least five more of our current accounts could use approximately 5,000 of this device annually, pushing our volume to 50,000 units per year. This is our current productive capacity, but I feel sure we could reach this level within 1 year."

"Mr. Bennett, your job is to sell our products, so I assume you have reason to believe that the business is there," President Maxwell interrupted, "but although I have always felt the K-50 was a good item, may I inquire why we have not exploited this market potential long ago?"

"Well, to hit a capacity volume of 50,000 units, we need to offer the K-50 at a competitive price. If we can sell this item to our industrial customers for $10.00 each, I know this volume can be reached," Bennett responded.

"Pardon the interruption," broke in Horn, "but wouldn't this mean we would suffer a loss of $5.51 per unit?"

Bennett continued, "I have asked the comptroller to bring the detailed cost data with him for capacity volume. While this is admittedly out of my area of responsibility, I do believe that the feasibility of my suggestion deserves your consideration."

Fred Shaw, the comptroller, was the next to speak. "Ernest, I'm sorry that I didn't have time to go over this with you in greater detail before. It's true that we would have a declining cost situation if we reached 25,000, let alone the 50,000 capacity you described. But these savings are not as great as you evidently assumed. I have prepared a detailed cost schedule to make it easier for us to view the situation at capacity volume. This schedule presents our unit costs and charges at the 50,000 unit level of K-50 production.

"We don't expect any labor savings, since this is a machine operation and output varies directly with the time of the run. We can experience some economies on material by purchasing in larger quantities. Our yearly total material charges jump from $15,200 at 10,000 units to $37,000 at 25,000, saving $0.04 per unit at 25,000 and $0.04 more at the 50,000 unit levels. Similarly, plating charges are less in larger quantities; our subcontractor will be able to plate the necessary components at half the price if we hit 50,000 units. But this saves us only $0.05 per unit over what we pay now. And then, too, we must remember that capacity volume will require more frequent servicing. We'll lose some ground here—$0.03 to be exact—between 25,000 and the double machine time required for an output of 50,000 units. But of course, that is only an added expenditure of $1,500."

"You'll have to slow up, Fred, I'm afraid this gray head can't absorb your figures quite so quickly," Maxwell interrupted.

"I'm sorry, Mr. Maxwell, perhaps I'd better distribute the data. If we sell and produce the K-50 at a capacity output, our costs per unit only fall to $10.56. I've itemized this in detail for you at Ernest's request on the cost sheet I've prepared for each of you." At this point, Fred distributed the cost data presented in Table C1-3.

"Perhaps I'd better summarize what Fred appears reluctant to point out," interjected Alfred Horn. "He is saying that Ernest would have us lose $0.56 on every K-50 we sell at this 50,000 volume! Or at least we would, in fact, lose $0.32 per item, if we even sell to Rigbee and hit a total of 25,000 units!"

"But not if we average out—I say sell to Magnus at $15.50 and to Rigbee at $11.50!" added another executive.

"That is out of the question!" interrupted Vice President Bennett.

"Gentlemen, let's have a little order at this meeting," interjected Maxwell.

"Mr. Maxwell has the right idea—I say sell only to Magnus as a favor at $15.50 and let sleeping dogs lie," added Alfred Horn.

"That does it; I'll not preside over a 'free for all!' And stop putting words in my mouth, Al!" President Maxwell angrily exclaimed. "Ernest, we here

TABLE C1-3   Units Costs of K-50 at Production Volume of 50,000 Units

Labor	$3.18
Material	1.44
Plating	.05
Indirect charges	.51
Depreciation allowance	.80
Overhead	1.06
Total factory production cost	7.04
Selling and administrative allocations	3.52
Total cost per unit at 50,000 units	$10.56

at Aberdeen have an obligation to our stockholders as well as to our customers. It appears that perhaps I was the one who made all the decisions on the K-50 from the very beginning. So I'll make this one, too. But first, I want to review all of the facts personally this evening. Gentlemen, I want all of you here in my office tomorrow at 9:00 AM sharp. This meeting is adjourned!"

Questions for Discussion

1. Did Aberdeen adequately handle the dispute with Magnus over contract volume, defective units, and the $0.50 price reduction on the K-50 unit? What would you have done?

2. The Robinson-Patman Act of 1936 primarily protects against unfair pricing by enforcing two conditions: (a) companies must charge the same price to all customers who buy "*like goods and quantity*," and (b) any volume discounts must be justified by proportionate cost savings. Given these conditions, do you agree that Aberdeen must sell the K-50 at the same price to Magnus, Rigbee, and the commercial market? Explain.

3. Suppose that Fred Shaw is incorrect regarding potential cost reductions. Suppose further that both Aberdeen and their parts suppliers, through creative innovations, can benefit from an experience curve effect. As a result, all variable production costs will decline at a constant rate each time cumulative production quantity is doubled. Assume that the data in Tables C1-1, -2, and -3 were effective as of January 1, 1994, at which time a cumulative quantity of 20,000 units had been produced.
   a. Recalculate anticipated costs for the K-50 over the next 4 years (1994 through 1997) with an experience curve of 90 percent. Establish product pricing and profits based on these costs.
   b. Redo the above calculations with an experience curve of 80 percent. Would your pricing change?

C A S E   2

AMF Wyott, Inc.

PUBLICITY AND SALES PROMOTION

AMF Wyott, Inc., produces an extensive line of high-quality food service equipment products that encompasses fryers (french fry, taco, doughnut, corn dog), dispensers (butter, cream, condiment, display), hot dog cookers, griddles, pizza ovens, bun warmers, water filters, lowerators (self-adjusting dispensers for

Jeffrey Beyer, Peter Johnson, Viktor Jonkoff, Ronnie Nickel, and Richard Plewes researched this case.

plates, napkins, cups, or plain shelves, all mobile or installed, heated, unheated, or refrigerated), racks and stand, self-contained snack carts, and trash compactors. Its is a wholly owned subsidiary of AMF, Inc., employing 350 people at its Cheyenne, Wyoming manufacturing facilities.

THE AUTOMATIC OVERHEAD DISPENSER

In line with AMF Wyott's pursuit of competitiveness with quality products, the company developed the automatic overhead dispenser (AOD), designed for use in restaurants, food service areas, or any industrial storage area where materials have to be readily available. As seen in Figure C2-1, the AOD is complementary to the regular lowerators, since it can be hung on a wall rather than the typical floor model lowerators that take up considerable floor space. The AOD is totally new and can be used to store and dispense plates, cups, and glasses in a restaurant or other similar facility.

The prototype of the AOD has a casing built from stainless steel with a transparent plexiglas front dust cover. Inside the casing are two telescoping shelves and a lower stationary shelf. A reversible gear, coupled to a rotating shaft onto which a steel cable is attached, permits the two telescoping shelves to be collapsed one on top of the other to enable loading (Figure C2-2). The electrically driven gear and rotating shaft assembly also allow extension of the two shelves to provide shelf storage space for whatever can suitably fit into the dispenser. The operator has both a "down" and an "up" button that activate the system. The unit is capable of dispensing refrigerated or heated products, depending on the specific configuration of the individualized unit being used.

DISTRIBUTION

On January 1, the company made a significant change to its distribution channel policy. Historically, the corporation dealt with manufacturers' reps who generated approximately 20,000 orders per year, averaging $400 to $500 per order. The reps did not store any of the product and the company experienced a major disruption in sales because its customers did not have product availability where they could see the equipment and have it delivered when they needed it.

The new distribution program was designed to alleviate this situation. Distributors capable of storing the products replaced the reps. The distributorship program reduced the number of purchase orders, which reduced some of the production hang-ups resulting from working only on small orders, negating some of the economies of scale associated with larger orders. As the distributorship program signed more distributors, the company's product availability to its customers was enhanced. Distributors provided some value added and also an opportunity for additional sales promotion via distributor discounts not available when using the reps.

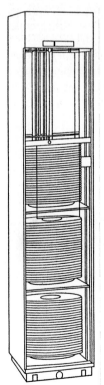

FIGURE C2-1 The automatic overhead dispenser (AOD).

FIGURE C2-2

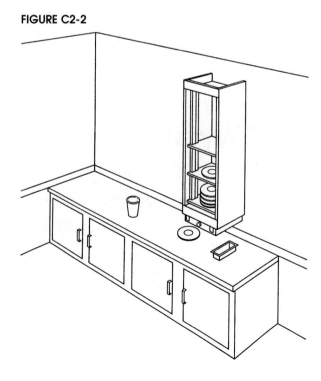

PROMOTION

Little media advertising in trade journals is done by the company, because it prefers to use trade shows, direct mail, and the sales abilities of its distributors to promote its products. Two trade shows are considered a must: the annual National Restaurant Association show and the biannual National Association of Food Equipment Manufacturers are absolutely required trade shows to expose the market to the company's new products and for the company to view competitors' offerings. Trade shows can be very lucrative for producing sales leads and keeping the company name if front of its customers.

The direct mail route for AMF Wyott has proved to be more cost effective than media advertising. The corporation's propensity to consider product availability, quality, and then cost in its hierarchy of importance adds greater emphasis to a "push" strategy by mailing promotion pieces to major restaurant and hotel chains' equipment buyers, cafeteria designers, engineering firms, distributorships, and major dealers.

The promotion for the AOD should follow the same format as previously practiced by the company. Without its own salespeople, the company will experience some market resistance to AOD's reverse lowerator features (see Figure C2-3 for details). The concept of this crucial distinction will take time for the distributors' salespeople to digest and to finally understand its new and expanded applications. As the concept becomes known, distributor's reps will need reinforcement and education on the unit's capabilities—especially engineering specifications on weight limits and cooling/heating temperatures. Therefore, the marketing department recommended that the company use direct mail advertising to educate end users and prepare them for the distributor's sales rep's call.

PRICING

The standard pricing formula will be followed for the AOD. AMF Wyott's pricing formula policy:

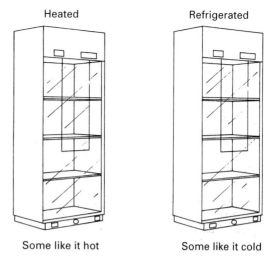

Heated   Refrigerated

Some like it hot   Some like it cold

The AOD can handle the load

FIGURE C2-3

$$\text{Sales price} = \frac{\text{Manufacturing costs}}{60\%}$$

The firm believes this policy allows for the best possible mix of market penetration and investment return without affecting the company's reputation for quality. The price of the new product becomes very important for this industry, which practices the "follow the leader" approach to product innovations.

Questions for Discussion

1. Was it unwise for the company to not use public relations as part of the promotional campaign to introduce the AOD?

2. How could the company better control the distributors' salespeople?

3. What else could have been done to enhance the product's introduction besides using trade shows and direct mail?

4. What other applications besides those discussed in the case would be appropriate to use in promoting the AOD?

Calox Machinery Corporation (A)

Mike Brown, international sales manager, tapped his pencil on the note pad and contemplated his upcoming discussion with Calox's executive committee concerning the distributor situation in New Zealand. The Labor Day weekend break had not been especially conducive to his sorting out the conflicting information and varied opinions concerning the New Zealand predicament. After only 3 months on the job Mike had not expected to be involved in a decision that would have such far-reaching consequences.

On paper the decision looked simple: whether or not to adhere to his earlier decision to replace the original New Zealand distributor, Glade Industries, with a newly formed company, Calox New Zealand, Ltd. Despite his newness to the company, Mike was confident that Calox's executive committee would agree with whatever recommendations he made in this situation, since he had been charged with "solidifying" the International Sales Division. If he decided to reverse his decision to terminate Glade Industries, could he "undo" any damage done so far?

Three previous faxes were spread on his desk along with the brief notes that he had jotted down during Thursday's conference call between Calox's executives and the company's legal counsel. Mike swung back to the PC behind his desk and began to draft what he hoped would be the definitive Calox policy for New Zealand.

THE COMPANY

Calox Machinery Company began in 1946 as a partnership between John Caliguri and William Oxley. The two engineers met during World War II and discovered mutual interests in mechanical engineering and construction. Both were natives of Kansas City, and at the end of the war they established a partnership with the expressed purpose of developing high-quality excavation equipment and accessories. Their first product was an innovative, hydraulically operated replacement blade for a light-duty scraper.

Calox's principal customers were independent contractors engaged in excavation of building sites, and airport and highway construction and maintenance. Calox's products were primarily replacement items for OEM (original equipment manufacturer) parts and accessories. Some OEM sales were achieved; that is, contractors could order new equipment from OEMs with Calox blades and accessories already installed. Growth over the years was slow but steady.

The product line expanded to include payloader buckets, a number of bulldozer and scraper blades, and parts for aerial equipment, including construction forklifts and snorkels. A key to the company's success was their specialty status; their products were used to enhance the performance of expensive equipment produced by Caterpillar, Eaton, International Harvester, Case, and other OEMs. Calox's strategy was simply to provide a better part, often at a premium price, and to have it readily available in the field through a network of strong distributors. Direct competitors in the United States included small specialty producers such as Bobcat, Dresser, and Gradall, as well as the parts divisions of the large OEM manufacturers. Primary competitors in international markets included Terex, Deutsch, Takeuchi, and Hitachi. William Oxley compared Calox with the Cummins Engine Company, which had achieved a superior position in the diesel engine market through a similar strategy.

The partnership was replaced by an incorporated structure in 1970, when Bill Oxley, Jr., became CEO. Despite slow growth of the U.S. economy, both 1990 and 1991 were very good years for Calox; annual sales increases of 12 percent were achieved, and the company set profit records each year. Sales for the 1991 fiscal year broke the $70 million barrier for the first time in the company's history. That year, approximately 280 people were employed at the single location in Kansas City; of these, three out of four were hourly workers engaged in fabrication.

Based on a case written by Lester A. Neidell of the University of Tulsa with the cooperation of management, solely for the purpose of stimulating student discussion. Data are based on field research in the organization. All events and individuals are real, but names have been disguised at the company's re-quest. Copyright © 1993 by the *Case Research Journal* and Lester A. Neidell. Reproduced by permission.

INTERNATIONAL SALES

Calox's first international sale occurred in 1971, when the company responded to an unsolicited inquiry and shipped a small order to Canada. International sales languished throughout the 1970s, when a great deal of construction was put on hold because of the "energy crisis." Channels of distribution for international sales were much the same as for domestic sales. Independent distributors were given nonexclusive rights, although in practice most countries had only one distributor. Forty of Calox's 110 distributors were located outside the United States. In 1991 almost 25 percent of Calox's sales were generated internationally. From 1988 through 1991, aided by the relative decline of the U.S. dollar against most other currencies, international sales grew at an annual rate of 16 percent.

Before Mike's arrival, there had been no uniform procedure by which Calox investigated foreign markets and appointed distributors outside the United States. Bill Lawrence, Mike Brown's predecessor, essentially ran export sales as a one-man operation. Since Calox had very limited international experience and most international markets were relatively small compared with the U.S. market, primary market research was considered to be an unnecessary expense. In those countries "guesstimated" to have large enough markets, Bill obtained a list of potential distributors by advertising in that country's construction journal(s) (if available) and principal newspapers. He then made a personal visit to interview and select distributors. In smaller markets, distributors were appointed through one of two methods. Most commonly, Bill appointed a distributor after receiving an unsolicited request. In a very few cases, distributor applications were solicited via advertisements as in "large" markets, which were then reviewed in Kansas City. In all cases in which personal visits were not made, distributor applicants had to submit financial statements. Efforts to interview distributor applicants by telephone were not always successful because of time constraints and the lack of a suitable translation service.

THE NEW ZEALAND DISTRIBUTORSHIP

In 1986 Calox appointed G.W. Diggers, Ltd., as its agent for New Zealand. This arrangement was a novel one, because G.W. Diggers was also a producer of excavating equipment. Because of some earlier poor experiences in certain foreign markets, Calox had instituted a policy of not distributing through any company that also manufactured excavating equipment. This policy was not followed in New Zealand because of the limited distributorship options available. At the time of the appointment, the owner of G.W. Diggers, Geoffrey Wiggins, assured Calox that the two lines were complementary rather than competitive and that he intended to keep it that way. During 1989, G.W. Diggers purchased $800,000 of equipment and supplies from Calox.

In 1990 an abrupt change occurred in what had been a very successful, if short, relationship. G.W. Diggers was purchased by a large New Zealand conglomerate, Excel Ltd., which gave a new name, Glade Industries, to its excavating facility. The former owner of G.W. Diggers, Geoff Wiggins, was not associated with Glade Industries. Mike Brown's predecessor felt that the acquisition by Glade could only help Calox's position in New Zealand, because the resources available through Excel, Glade's parent company, were so much greater than what had been available to G.W. Diggers.

However, it soon became apparent that working with Glade was going to be very challenging. Glade raised prices on all Calox products in stock. Then they complained that Calox products were not selling well and that a "rebate" was needed to make Calox's products competitive in the New Zealand market. Simultaneously, Glade began production of a line of products competitive with Calox, but of a substantially poorer quality. During 1991 sales to Glade were virtually zero, and market information obtained by Calox indicated that Calox's former position in the New Zealand market was being occupied by Wescot Industries, with products imported from Great Britain. Table C3-1 gives annual sales of Calox products to G.W. Diggers and to its successor, Glade Industries.

Mike Brown began his new job as international sales manager for Calox in June 1992. A few weeks after arriving at Calox, Mike received a long letter from Geoff Wiggins. Geoff suggested that the situation in New Zealand was critical and that he would be willing and able to establish a new distributorship, Calox New Zealand, Ltd., to be exclusive distributors of the Calox product line. Mike then invited Geoff to come to Kansas City the last week of July to discuss the proposal. Mike found Geoff to be very affable, technically knowledgeable, and an excellent marketing person. In the time period since selling his

TABLE C3-1 Annual Sales to G.W. Diggers and Glade Industries (in Thousands of U.S. dollars)

Sales to G. W. Diggers				Sales to Glade		
1986	*1987*	*1988*	*1989*	*1990*	*1991*	*1992 (6 mo)*
21	310	535	801	105	70	10

business to Excel Ltd., Geoff had been working as a general contractor. The 24-month "no-compete" clause Geoff had signed when he sold G.W. Diggers had expired. Geoff provided figures that indicated New Zealand's 1991 imports of excavating equipment were roughly NZ $2 million out of a total domestic market of nearly NZ $3 million. (In 1991, US $1 = NZ $0.62.) He claimed that G.W. Diggers had achieved, at the height of its success, almost a 50 percent share of the New Zealand market. Geoff argued persuasively that with his personal knowledge of New Zealand's needs, Calox could once again achieve a dominant market position. With the blessing of the vice president of marketing, Mike and Geoff shook hands on a deal, with the exact details to be worked out by mail and faxed over the next few weeks. Geoff urged that time was of the essence if Wescot's market advances were to be slowed, and left a $100,000 order for 75 units to be shipped in 120 days, but not later than November 15, 1992.

COMMUNICATIONS WITH GLADE

Mike began to prepare a letter of termination to Glade. However, before this was completed, Calox received three mailed orders from Glade totaling $81,000. This was the first contact Mike had had with Glade, and the first order received from Glade in 5 months. Because the standard distributor's agreement required a 60-day termination notice, Mike felt the Glade orders had to be honored.

A short time later Calox received a letter in the mail from Glade stating that they had heard rumors that another company was going to supply Calox products to Glade's customers and that delivery had been promised within 150 days. The letter continued that this information could not possibly be true because Glade had an exclusive distributor agreement. This was news to Mike as well as to others at Calox headquarters, because it was against company policy to grant exclusive distributorships. A search of Bill Lawrence's files turned up a copy of the initial correspondence to Geoff Wiggins, in which Geoff was thanked for his hospitality and a sole distributorship arrangement was mentioned. However, the distributorship agreement signed with Wiggins was the standard one, giving either party the ability to cancel the agreement with 60 days' notice.

Mike and the other senior Calox executives assessed the situation at length. The letter mentioning the "sole distributor agreement" was in a file separate from all other New Zealand correspondence. It was nothing more than a statement of intent and probably not legally binding in the United States. However, New Zealand courts might not agree. Further, the distributorship agreement should have been renegotiated when Excel purchased G.W. Diggers, but this had not happened. Glade could make a case that the distributorship had endured for 2 years under the existing agreement, which included the letter in which exclusivity was mentioned.

Mike determined that the "sole distributorship" letter also contained "extenuating circumstances" language that Calox could use to justify supplying the new New Zealand distributorship:

[T]here may be occasions in the future when, due to unforeseen circumstances, some entity in your nation refuses to purchase any other way than direct from our factory. We do not want to lose any potential sales; however, we pledge our best efforts to cooperate with you for any such possible sales should they present themselves and provided there is a reasonable profit to be made on such sales by us and cooperation can be worked out.

The letter also specifically stated that all agreements between Calox and G.W. Diggers were subject to the laws of Missouri. Furthermore, Mike felt that Glade had not lived up to the actual signed distributorship agreement in that Glade had not promoted Calox products, had not maintained adequate inventory, and had engaged in activities and trade practices that were injurious to Calox's good name.

Armed with this information, Mike sought legal counsel, both in the United States and New Zealand. After a week, Calox's U.S. attorneys, based on their own investigations and those of a law firm in Christchurch, New Zealand, offered four "unofficial" observations:

1. New Zealand is a "common law" nation, whose commercial law is similar to that of the United States.
2. It was possible to argue that because G.W. Diggers had changed ownership, previous agreements might not be binding. However, the most likely court finding would be that there was an implied contract between Calox and Glade on the same terms as with G.W. Diggers, because numerous business dealings between Calox and Glade had occurred after the takeover.
3. Calox was required to give Glade 60 days' termination notice.
4. There was a possibility that a New Zealand court would agree to assume jurisdiction of the case.

After reviewing these issues, Mike suggested to Calox senior management that Glade be terminated. Mike reasoned that Glade would react in one of two ways. One possibility was that they would accept termination, perhaps suggesting some minor compensation. A second scenario was that Glade would attempt to renegotiate the distributorship agreement. Mike was instructed to draft and fax a termination letter to Glade. This letter, sent by fax on August 20, is reproduced in Exhibit C3-1. The next day the first order for the new distributorship was shipped; the expected arrival date in New Zealand was October 10, 1992.

Glade's faxed reply, dated August 24, was not encouraging (see Exhibit C3-2). It appeared that Mike and the rest of the Calox management team had miscalculated. Despite the tone of the Glade letter, and the expressed request to ship order number 52557, Mike suggested to the executive committee that no additional product be shipped to Glade.

While Mike and the rest of Calox management was deciding how to respond to Glade's initial rejection of the termination letter, a longer fax, one with a more conciliatory tone, dated August 31, was received from Glade (see Exhibit C3-3). In this letter Glade argued that Calox's best interests were served by working with Glade and mentioned an order for approximately ten times the "normal" amount of product. However, the order was not transmitted with the fax letter. Ian Wells offered (for the first time) to come to Kansas City for a visit.

Glade's conciliatory letter created a great deal of consternation at Calox headquarters. Its arrival the week before Labor Day meant that holiday plans would have to be placed on the back burner while a suitable response was formulated. Two distinct camps developed within Calox.

One set of managers, whose position was supported by Mike Brown, felt strongly that despite potential legal risks, retaining Glade as a distributor would be a bad business decision. Although Glade had made promises and was offering to renegotiate, it was still producing a competitive line. Also, Glade's historical performance did not augur well for Calox's long-term competitive situation in New Zealand. The "extraordinary" order was viewed as a ploy to entice Calox into continuing the relationship. It was likely to take more than 2 years for all that machinery to clear the New Zealand market. Cognizant of Glade's earlier price manipulations, many of this group felt that Glade might resort to "fire sale" prices when confronted with a large inventory, further damaging Calox's reputation as a premier supplier.

This camp considered that Calox's long-term interests would best be served by terminating the Glade distributorship and completing a formal agreement with Geoff Wiggins. However, there was concern that outright rejection of the Glade order would add to potential legal problems.

These managers also suggested that any further correspondence with Glade should emphasize that Calox could and would exercise a unique product repurchase option on termination of the distributorship. This provision in the distributorship contract provided that Calox, on proper termination of the distributorship by either party, could repurchase all remaining Calox inventory from the distributor at 80 percent of its net sales price to the distributor. Thus, if Calox did produce and ship the large Glade order, Calox would, if the order were shipped normally via sea freight, be able to buy it back for 80 percent of the price paid by Glade before it ever reached New Zealand.

The alternative camp wanted to forestall any legal battles. Headed by the U.S. sales manager and the comptroller, they argued that Glade had finally "gotten its act together" and that the new Glade team of three sales executives would provide greater market coverage than Geoff Wiggins's "one-man show." This group introduced the possibility of reopening negotiations with Glade, sup-

---

EXHIBIT C3-1

Fax From Calox to Glade

August 20, 1992

Calox Company, Inc .
P.O. Box 21110
Kansas City, MO 64002
U.S.A.

Mr. Ian Wells
Group General Manager
Glade Industries
39 Ames Road
Christchurch, New Zealand 2221

Dear Mr. Wells:

This letter is to inform you that Calox Company terminates any International Distributor's Sales Agreement or other Distribution Agreement that you may have or be a party to as Distributor expressly or impliedly with Calox Co. as Manufacturer. Said termination is effective 60 days from the date of this letter.

During the past year the following have gravely concerned us and effectively shut off our sales to the New Zealand market.

1. Reorganization of G.W. Diggers under Glade has led to continuous loss of personnel who are knowledgeable of the excavation business and made it difficult for Calox to comprehend with whom we are doing business. In June 1990, we were advised by telex that we were dealing with Excel Ltd., not G.W. Diggers or Glade.

2. Only $10,000 in purchases for an 8-month-long period from us, which we clearly found led to a major loss of Calox sales to the marketplace and a complete domination of the excavation business by Wescot Industries, a major competitor.

3. Lack of effort on the part of Glade in promoting our product and maintaining effective selling facilities.

4. Numerous complaints to us from customers in New Zealand about Glade continually changing policies, lack of stock, and wildly increasing prices have clearly pointed out that our reputation, as well as that of G.W. Diggers, has been badly hurt and will impair sales for some time to come.

5. No progress has been made in introducing our heavy industrial line to the New Zealand market despite assurances from Glade personnel that progress would be made.

We have thoroughly investigated the New Zealand market and now have firmly decided that it is time for Calox to make a change in its distribution of products.

For the long term, this will allow us to best carve out a full niche in a market we and you have allowed competitors to dominate for too long. We must guarantee ourselves a consistent, aggressive sales effort in the market, which will not be subject to the effects of major policy changes such as those we have seen from Glade.

While two shipments are already en route to you, order number 52557 has not yet been completed for shipment. Since it will be ready imminently, please let us know immediately whether you wish, under the circumstances, to receive shipment or to cancel this order.

Sincerely,

Michael Brown

Michael Brown
International Sales Manager

EXHIBIT C3-2

Fax From Glade to Calox

24 August 1992

Glade Industries
39 Ames Road
Christchurch, New Zealand 2221

Mr. Michael Brown
International Sales Manager
Calox Company, Inc.
P.O. Box 21110
Kansas City, MO 64002
U.S.A.

Dear Sir:

We acknowledge receipt of your letter dated 20 August 1992.
    We are currently discussing its contents with our solicitors. They are also reviewing the distribution agreement.
    Please proceed with the shipment of order #52557.

Yours faithfully,
GLADE INDUSTRIES, LTD.

Ian Wells

Ian Wells
Group General Manager

---

plying Glade by diverting the order already shipped to Geoff Wiggins, and producing the (yet unreceived) large Glade order.

By Wednesday, September 2, the two sides had hardened their positions. Mike was determined to break with Glade and begin anew in New Zealand. However, he was concerned about legal ramifications, and,on Thursday, September 3,Calox's executive committee and Mike conferred with their Kansas City attorneys via a conference call.

The lawyers agreed that any further business conducted with Glade would be detrimental to a termination decision. They warned that despite the termination letter (see Exhibit C3-1) any further shipments to Glade would likely yield a court ruling that the distributorship was still in effect and, further-

more, that the buyback provision could not be enacted. They also said that if all business with Glade were terminated, and Glade did come to the United States to file, the most they would be likely to receive if they won the court case were the profits on the new sales to Geoff Wiggins, which amounted to $10,000. This sum was probably not large enough to warrant legal action by Glade, especially considering the apparently poor financial situation at Glade and the expense of initiating legal action in the United States.

At the end of this conference call,which lasted about 30 minutes, Bill Oxley, Jr.,turned to Mike and said,"Mike, I'm off to the lake now for the holiday. I'd like your recommendation Tuesday morning on this Glade thing."

EXHIBIT C3-3

Fax From Glade to Calox

31 August 1992

Glade Industries
39 Ames Road
Christchurch, New Zealand 2221

Mr. Michael Brown
International Sales Manager
Calox Company, Inc.
P. 0. Box 21110
Kansas City, MO 64002
U.S.A.

Dear Sir:

I refer to your letter dated 20 August 1992, terminating our agreement which was executed on 28 February 1986. In accordance with this agreement and attached to this letter is our order #A1036, for 600 products and parts. We would be pleased if you would confirm this order in due course.

　　We respectfully ask that you reconsider your termination decision as we believe that it is not in your best interests for the following reasons:

1. Diggers/Glade were not achieving an adequate return on investment until June 1991. An unprofitable distributor certainly is not in your best interests as principal.

2. The individuals that contributed to that unprofitable performance are no longer working for our company. Incidentally, understand that you have appointed Mr. Geoffrey Wiggins to a position as distributor in New Zealand. How can you justify appointing the person responsible for your market share decline over the past three years?

3. Our purchases certainly have been reduced the last nine months due to our need to get inventory down to lift overall return on investment. That situation has now been corrected with the order attached to this letter.

4. We now have a young, aggressive marketing team, all highly experienced in marketing products of a similar nature to yours. When Bill Lawrence was in New Zealand, I advised him that I was restructuring our marketing group. A resume on our three senior marketing men is attached. These men have all commenced in the last 4 months. I am confident that this team will achieve market leadership in New Zealand and selected export markets with or without Calox's involvement. We have already commenced targeting Wescot's customers. Our recommendation is that you renegotiate your distribution agreement with us, with the inclusion of mutually agreed performance targets which will satisfy your objectives in terms of profitability and market share from the New Zealand market. I would like you to advise me a time which is convenient to you, for me to meet with you in Kansas City to commence negotiation of this distributor agreement.

Yours faithfully,
GLADE INDUSTRIES, LTD.

Ian Wells
Group General Manager

These are the three new men who have commenced to work for us:

Sean Cox, Sales Manager
35 years old. Formerly CEO of Sean Cox Industries of Christchurch. SCI was the chief contractor for the Auckland airport, but sold its business to Midland Industries. Mr. Cox has fifteen years' experience in the construction industry.

Joshua Dunn, Sales Representative, North Island
46 years old. Formerly an independent sales representative for various equipment manufacturers, including Hitachi and Ford New Holland.

Brian Muldoon, Sales Representative, South Island
23 years old. Construction engineering degree from New South Wales Institute of Technology (Sydney, Australia). Formerly a management trainee with our parent company, Excel Ltd.

Questions for Discussion

1. What is your opinion of the manner in which Bill Lawrence handled the franchising of G.W. Diggers, Ltd.? Defend any criticisms by pointing out what you would have done differently or in addition to Lawrence's actions.

2. Should Calox have allowed Glade Industries to assume the franchise without any further discussion or negotiation? How would you have handled the changeover?

3. Should Calox have developed a sales target (quota) originally for G.W. Diggers? Should this target have been reanalyzed each year, particularly at the time of the changeover? What useful purpose does a sales target serve? Does it benefit both manufacturer and distributor? How?

4. What actions could Calox have taken (besides setting a sales target) to prevent the deterioration of their relationship with Glade?

5. Setting legalities aside, are your sympathies with Calox or Glade? Explain your position.

C A S E   4
Calox Machinery Corporation (B)

Mike Brown decided that despite the potential legal risks, sound business practice dictated that he follow through with the termination of Glade's distributorship, and his recommendation to that effect was accepted by the Calox executive committee. Mike's letter fax of September 9 (Exhibit C4-1) was very specific. First, he restated that it was in the best interests of both parties to terminate the distributorship. Second, since there was no prospect that the Glade order could be completed and delivered before the termination date of October 20, 1992 (60 days from the first letter; see Case 3, Exhibit C3-1), he made it known that Calox would exercise its buy-back option if Glade did indeed forward the missing order. Following legal advice, Mike added the caveat, "We are open to your comments, of course." The legal reasoning behind this was that if Calox did begin producing the large Glade order and then bought it back while it was on the open seas, it could be interpreted by the courts that Calox was deliberately attempting to damage Glade financially.

Glade's September 14 "hardball" reply (Exhibit C4-2) was discouraging. In it Glade requested an

accounting of sales to other distributors, claiming that they (Glade) were legally entitled to recover all Calox profits from these sales. Several Glade executives began to waffle, and proposed again the solution of diverting the order already shipped to Geoff Wiggins, producing the (still unreceived) large Glade order, and renegotiating with Glade (see Case 3).

Before an acceptable response could be agreed on, another fax (Exhibit C4-3) was received from Glade. In this conciliatory letter, Glade offered to forego any claims if their large order was completed and if Calox agreed not to exercise their buy-back right.

Calox management breathed a huge sigh of relief and instructed Mike to inquire about the specifics of the order, complete it, ship it to Glade, and be done with them! Mike, however, felt it was necessary to obtain additional legal counsel before doing this.

The lawyers were emphatically negative. They felt quite strongly that if Calox shipped the large order, the courts would rule the original agreement binding, despite all the communication about termination. The courts would interpret the correspondence as a ploy by Calox designed to coerce Glade into placing a large order. They reiterated their previous advice that at the current time, Glade could only obtain minimal damages in U.S. courts; it would hardly be worth Glade's time and energy.

Mike and the company's legal counsel agreed that a final letter had to be written to Glade that

---

Fax From Calox to Glade

September 9, 1992

Calox Company, Inc.
P.O. 21110
Kansas City, MO 64002
U.S.A.

Mr. Ian Wells
Group General Manager
Glade Industries
39 Ames Road
Christchurch, New Zealand 2221

Dear Mr. Wells:

Reference your 31 August letter, we must regretfully advise that we feel it is in our best interest to continue with our termination of sales to Glade, Ltd., as we explained. We appreciate the points you made in your letter, but nevertheless remain convinced that working with Glade Industries, Ltd., is not the best way for Calox to achieve its goals in New Zealand.

While we have not yet received your order number A1036 for 600 items referenced in your letter, I should point out that first, Calox is not able to complete an order for all 600 items before the termination date, and second, we would want to exercise our option to purchase back all good outstanding products at 80 percent of our net selling price .

In consideration of these factors, we do not believe it advisable to accept your offer. We feel that this would only affect your situation and we do not seek to take advantage of you in this regard . We are open to your comments, of course.

Sincerely,

Michael Brown

Michael Brown
International Sales Manager

Fax From Glade to Calox

14 September 1992

Glade Industries
39 Ames Road
Christchurch, New Zealand 2221

Mr. Michael Brown
International Sales Manager
Calox Company, Inc.P.O. Box 21110
Kansas City, MO 64002
U.S.A.

Dear Sir:

I acknowledge receipt of your letter of 9 September 1992.

I am very concerned at the position in which Calox Co. has been selling direct into New Zealand to Glade's customers. This is in direct contravention of your obligations and undertakings under the Distributor Agreement between us and in particular in breach of the undertaking contained in your letter of 27 January 1986.

We have clearly suffered loss and damage as a result of these actions on your part in breach of the Distributor Agreement which we would be entitled to recover in legal proceedings.

We therefore seek from you a full account of all sales made by you direct into New Zealand in breach of the agreement and payment to us of all profits made by you in respect of those sales.

Yours faithfully,
GLADE INDUSTRIES, LTD.

Ian Wells

Ian Wells
Group General Manager

EXHIBIT C4-3

Fax From Glade to Calox

September 17, 1992

Glade Industries
39 Ames Road
Christchurch, New Zealand 2221

Mr. Michael Brown
International Sales Manager
Calox Company, Inc.
P.O. Box 21110
Kansas City, MO 64002
U.S.A.

Dear Sir:

I refer to my open letter of 14 September 1992.
    As indicated in that letter we are most concerned at the loss and damage we have suffered by your acting contrary to the terms of the existing Distributor Agreement.
    We are, however, prepared to forego our rights in relation to those breaches in return for your agreeing to supply the 600 items referred to in our order #Al036 and not to seek to exercise any rights of repurchase in relation to those items upon termination of the agreement.

Yours faithfully,
GLADE INDUSTRIES, LTD.

Ian Wells

Ian Wells
Group General Manager

---

would summarize the communications between Calox and Glade and make perfectly clear Calox's position. This letter had to clearly impart that Calox, with the advice of legal counsel, did not recognize as valid Glade's claim that any agreement had been breached. Glade, in fact, had violated the previous distributorship agreement by failing to market Calox's products. As a result of Glade's negligence, Calox had sustained damage to their reputation and good name, so that any legal recompense would be forthcoming to Calox. Calox's intent in the New Zealand market was to repair the damage that Glade had done to Calox's reputation by forging ahead with an aggressive new distributor.

Questions for Discussion

1. If you were Mike Brown, what action would you take at this time? Why this approach?

2. Assuming the Calox legal advisors are correct in their assumption that the potential damages are minimal, how would you view the situation from a marketing standpoint? Is Calox wise or foolish in disenfranchising Glade?

3. What additional information, if any, should Mike Brown have before making a final decision?

Coventry Plastics

INTERNATIONAL BUSINESS MARKETING MANAGEMENT

Coventry Plastics[1] started in 1964 with seven men who were very experienced in their individual skills. The company offered a broad range of molding and decorating methods and facilities where production was augmented by research, engineering, design, marketing, and management in the development of the best ways and means of creating finely designed, quality decorative plastic products for industry. The company offered strong commitment to the customer's needs, which was coupled with high-quality products and customer service.

CUSTOM PRODUCTION CAPABILITIES

The company designed and produced custom molding and finishing of decorative parts for numerous industrial products. It specialized in applications of finishes on front surfaces of opaque molded parts and rear surfaces of clear molded parts or combinations for a host of products: name plates for automobiles, computers, radios, air conditioners, microwaves, and television sets. Simulated wood grain for furniture was created with highly specialized injection molding machines.

Wood grain patterns and textures, in the smallest detail, were produced. The molding process made possible the economical reproduction of intricate carvings, turnings, and other treatments. Furniture finishes were sprayed, brushed, or wiped on, giving striking wood effects at considerable savings, in most cases, over labor-intensive wood construction. Advanced hot stamping techniques also enriched the finish applications.

Structural components, such as office equipment parts, including cases, keyboard tops, and logos, were used in increasing numbers as developed from injection molded and structural foam plastics. These parts were required to maintain strength and the basic nature of the materials being imitated. The plastic parts permitted more design freedom than metals because of plastic's mold-

[1]Fictitious name.

ability, placidity, and innate ability to retain colors. Texture-painted surfaces ensured consistent color and enhanced wearability and cleanability. The structural foam molding and finishing made possible economical production of complex shapes with function and styling advantages. Figure C5-1 illustrates some of the customized plastic parts developed for the company's OEM customers. The parts shown are molded components for office machines that saved tremendous amounts of labor and other costs that would have been incurred if metal was used to assemble these components.

Coventry Plastics offered a complete service from design assistance to dependable delivery.

PRODUCTION TECHNIQUES

The production process provides a glimpse into the intricacies of the company's craftsmanship and fine art capabilities.

1. Expensive metal molds are crafted to meet the rigorous standards of the customer.
2. Clear methacrylate is fed into an injection molding machine and through the forces of friction and shear, combined with high temperatures, the material is liquefied and forced into a mold of the end product's final configuration. Once the acrylic or other material cools, the mold separates and the finished part is removed.
3. The gate material (the liquefied plastic where the material flowed into the mold) is removed.
4. The part is buffed, cleaned, and polished.
5. The part is given a final inspection and compared with established standards and packaged for shipment.

DISTRIBUTION

Coventry Plastics distributes domestically through a series of experienced manufacturers' reps who are strategically located throughout the United States, Europe, and South America. Each rep and his company were trained in the intricacies of obtaining customized production orders from manufacturers of automobiles, electronics, furniture, and computers.

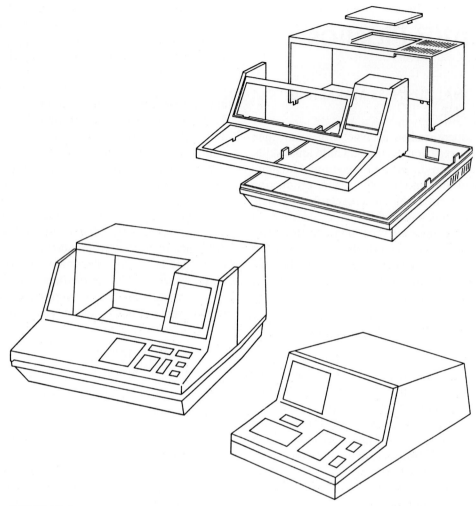

FIGURE C5-1

PROMOTION

Three promotional avenues were pursued by the company. First, the national sales manager and the other top executives of the firm comprised a direct sales force, similar to a National Account Management team, to call on large "named accounts," such as General Motors, Ford, Emerson Electric, and so on. Second, a trained and highly skilled force of manufacturers' reps covered many of the other manufacturing accounts. Third, trade show booths were widely used to disseminate information, generate customer interests, and produce quality sales leads. Fourth, elaborate brochures were used as direct mail pieces sent to prospective customers. The same pieces were used as product literature for handouts by the direct salespeople and the manufacturers' reps.

NEED TO EXPAND AND GROW INTO NEW MARKETS

The company faced the classic case of being a *pessimum firm* or a firm that was too big to be small and too small to be big. Coventry had the production capabilities to handle more business, but not enough cash and financial resources to increase its outside direct sales force to penetrate its market or to utilize an advertising agency or PR firm to compete vigorously with its competitors in a highly specialized, customized market.

INTERNATIONAL MARKETING ADVENTURE

Having been in contact with most of the potential domestic customers, Coventry decided to increase its market penetration abroad. Given its facilities and capabilities, it decided to restrict its overseas ventures to industrialized countries that had the same types of OEM customers it now served. It chose Japan, South Korea, Taiwan, the United Kingdom, France, West Germany, Italy, and Sweden as its likely expansion targets. Western Europe was chosen as its first target, followed by the Pacific Rim nations once the European venture had been consolidated.

The next step was to find how to increase its market penetration in the Western European countries. Although the company had taken orders from many foreign companies, such as Magnavox and Quasar, these firms had sought out Coventry after being referred by other satisfied overseas customers who were aware of Coventry's reputation for product quality, design work, and customer service. Other than this limited experience, the company did not know how to effectively conduct international marketing management.

They called in a marketing consultant, a social friend of the national sales manager, for consultations concerning their desire to expand their markets abroad. The consultant recommended that the company should sell its highly customized services through direct contact with specific industries in the countries in which they wished to operate. These direct contacts would have to be made by either their top executives and the national sales manager or by recruited sales agents in each of the countries. These sales agents would have to be employed in a similar manner to the company's present manufacturers' rep situation.

The president and the national sales manager liked the idea, and within 2 weeks, the two had flown to Frankfurt, Germany to scout out possible accounts and attempt to interview some prospective sales agents to represent the company in Western Europe. Four days later, the pair wearily boarded a plane for the United States, disgusted and angry after being snubbed by the companies they had called on. The pair simply could not understand how the Germans conducted business. First of all, they called on a German computer company, IBM of Germany, and were told they would first have to see the European headquarters people in Paris, France. Second, they called on Daimler-Benz, the manufacturer of Mercedes Benz, and were politely told they would have to wait for an appointment in 2 weeks. Their third call was on the German electronic giant Siemens, who was very interested in the company's capabilities since Siemens was aware of Coventry's work with Quasar, General Electric's RCA division, Zenith Radio Corp., and Sylvania. Siemens asked for the address of the local sales agent and was surprised when the Coventry people stated they didn't have a local rep.

Questions for Discussion

1. What had Coventry done overseas that had violated some of the international business marketing management concepts?
2. Was the advice from the consultant wise, under the circumstances?
3. What cultural, business, and other values had the Coventry representatives violated in Germany?
4. What should they have done? Outline a detailed plan that they should have followed before leaving the United States.

Cumberland Gasket Company, Inc.

"It's my problem and I've got to live with it," said Fred Barlow, vice president and general manager of the Maryland Division of Cumberland Gasket Co., Inc. "There are 30 people out there in the plant working with asbestos, and even with all of the precautions we have taken, some of them may develop symptoms of asbestosis or lung cancer." Barlow went on to observe that the real moral issue for him was related to the fact that most of the scientific evidence of serious consequences from inhaling asbestos dust was based on asbestos miners and other workers around raw asbestos, while only a relatively modest amount of asbestos was used in the Maryland Division. "My trouble is," he said, "that I just cannot be sure how serious it is."

The Maryland Division of Cumberland Gasket Co., Inc., manufactured a wide range of gaskets, washers, and other nonmetallic fittings and parts which were primarily used in petroleum processing equipment such as pumps and valves. Some of these parts and fittings were made of asbestos because of the latter's exceptional resistance to wear and heat. The parts were relatively inexpensive but were unusually critical components of the equipment in which they were used. Failure of one of these small parts could shut down an oil well or cause serious oil spillage, for example. Thus, Cumberland's products were of substantial importance. The parts in question were manufactured in two plants in Cumberland, Maryland. In 1977, the Maryland Division had sales of about $20 million. Cumberland, which in other plants in Michigan and California made parts for the automotive industry, had sales of about $60 million in 1977.

CUMBERLAND AND FRED BARLOW

Cumberland Gasket Co., Inc. had been formed in 1970 by the merger of three smaller companies.

This case was made possible by the cooperation of a business firm that remains anonymous. Prepared by Professors Herman Gadon and Dwight R. Ladd of the University of New Hampshire. Copyrighted by the University of New Hampshire.

While the primary goal behind the merger was to enable the companies involved to better serve an increasingly dispersed nationwide market, the divisions, which were generally equivalent to the predecessor companies, retained a great deal of autonomy. The general managers of each division, who were vice presidents of Cumberland, were primarily responsible for the profitability of their divisions. Thus, Fred Barlow had the authority to decide what was best for his division, although he would also be responsible for the consequences.

Barlow had been vice president at the Maryland Division of Cumberland Gasket for 3 years. His career had been marked by determination to do well and to move on to more challenges when he felt he had come to grips with the ones he faced when he first took a job. Now 34, he had gone to work for a bearing manufacturer after he had finished high school. He worked there for a year to get enough money to get through college, went to college for a year, ran out of money, and went back to the bearing manufacturer and finished his bachelor's degree at night. After completing college, he acquired an MBA in an evening program. When he was 22 he became works manager of the bearing company. At 24 he left that company and joined a larger one that made electromagnetic laminations and stampings. First employed as production control manager, he became manufacturing manager before he left at the age of 27 to manage a division of a company that sold to libraries. At the age of 30 he came to Cumberland Gasket Co., Inc., as manufacturing vice president. Two years later the company merged and he became a corporate officer and general manager of the Maryland Division.

Shortly after he joined Cumberland, Barlow read a book entitled *The Expendable American,* by Paul Brodeur. The book described the hazards of breathing asbestos dust and documented the long struggle to impose maximum exposure standards. The book convinced Fred that working with asbestos could be a major health hazard, and he concluded that dealing with that hazard should be one of his major responsibilities.

THE PRODUCTS

About 15 percent of the Maryland Division's sales were of products containing asbestos. These products ranged from tiny washers and gaskets to relatively large vanes used in air compressors. All of these were parts that had to fit snugly with metal surfaces against which they moved, while also being resistant to heat and having a certain amount of give. The production process began with sheets of canvas and asbestos laminated with resin compounds which were purchased from another manufacturer. At the Maryland plants, the laminated sheets were sawed, cut, or drilled into the desired shapes and sanded as necessary. These operations created the exposure to dust that concerned Fred.

ASBESTOS

Asbestos is a mineral that is impervious to heat and fire and that can be separated into fibers that, like wool, can be carded, spun, and woven or felted. It can also be crushed into powder and mixed with other substances such as paint or patching plaster. These qualities of asbestos mean that it has a multitude of applications in industry and consumer products. Some commonplace applications are brake linings, electrical insulation, washers, gaskets, and shingles.

Asbestos was known and used in ancient times—for lamp wicks, for example—but widespread use began with the Industrial Revolution. For some applications—automotive brake linings, for example—there is no known substitute for asbestos. Unfortunately, it has been generally known since the beginning of this century that asbestos—or more specifically, inhaled asbestos fibers—is a principal cause of certain, almost invariably fatal, diseases. One of these is asbestosis, which is the scarring of the tissues of the lungs, which ultimately results in the victim being unable to breathe. Lung cancer is also a likely result of inhaling asbestos, as is mesothelioma (malignant tumors of the lining of the chest cavity). Asbestos-related diseases are of the sort that, in the absence of regular medical checkups, appear only 20 or 30 years after exposure, at which time they are generally untreatable. As yet, it is not known how much or how little exposure will cause one or another of these diseases, but it is believed that not a great deal of exposure is required and that buildup of fibers in the body is cumulative and irreversible. Further, because asbestos fibers readily cling to other substances such as clothing or the skin, the dust can be widely dispersed. There is incontrovertible evidence that members of the families of asbestos workers have contracted these diseases in an abnormal incidence even though they had never been near places where asbestos was handled. There are hazards other than those related to workers and their families: one estimate holds that 158,000 pounds of asbestos fiber is put into the air each year from the wearing down of automotive brake linings.

REGULATION

Before 1972, the United States had no enforceable standard for maximum exposure to asbestos. In 1969, the American Conference of Governmental Hygienists recommended a minimum exposure standard of not more than twelve asbestos fibers longer than 5 microns in 1 cubic centimeter of air, over an 8-hour period.[1] Despite its name, this organization was a privately funded, nongovernmental agency, and thus adherence to the standard was entirely voluntary.

In 1970 Congress passed the Occupational Safety and Health Act (OSHA), which, among other things, empowered the Secretary of Labor to set safety standards. The act also created the National Institute for Occupational Safety and Health (NIOSH), and during 1970 and 1971 NIOSH publicized a number of earlier studies showing the health hazards associated with asbestos. Trade union officials and independent investigators urged that a minimum exposure standard of two 5-micron fibers per cubic centimeter be instituted by the Secretary. This, incidentally, was the standard adopted by the British government in 1968. However, in early 1972, the Secretary chose to impose a standard of five fibers. After continued controversy and public hearings, the two-fiber standard was promulgated in July 1975, and in 1977 OSHA proposed a new limit of one-half 5-micron fiber per cubic centimeter of air.

---

[1]A micron is equal to 1/5,000 inch. It is about the smallest fiber length that can be measured without an electron microscope. It is estimated that the presence of two 5-micron fibers in a cubic centimeter of air means the presence of up to 1,000 smaller particles. The average person will breathe in about 8 million cubic centimeters of air in an 8-hour period.

NIOSH, at the same time, was urging adoption of a standard of one-tenth 5-micron fiber.

THE FABRICATION DIVISION

The Maryland Division's operations were carried on in two separate plants. One was housed in the original nineteenth century factory where Cumberland began, but the other, in which most of the asbestos processing took place, had been constructed in 1976. In the old plant, only some machines were fitted with dust collectors, and therefore asbestos products could only be worked on those machines—thereby considerably limiting flexibility in scheduling. In the new, one-story, windowless plant, dust was collected from all machines and deposited through a central evacuating system into plastic sealable bags. This meant that products containing asbestos could be worked on any machinery in the plant. Although more costly, the application of dust collection to all equipment in the new plant provided a cleaner total environment as well as more scheduling flexibility. The sealed plastic bags were removed by a small independent contractor and buried within 24 hours in the city landfill dump.

Under OSHA regulations every employee working with asbestos was required to wear a mask. Barlow insisted on rigorous enforcement of the rules by decreeing that the supervisor of any employee working with asbestos without a mask would be immediately suspended for a week. Although Barlow made frequent inspections, no one had ever been found without a mask. In the early days of Barlow's tenure, Cumberland's insurance carrier had made annual surveys of dust conditions. In 1976 Barlow ordered the purchase of testing equipment so that the plant could conduct its own tests every month. In the three inspections by OSHA, particles of asbestos at every machine in the two factories had always been below the OSHA standard of two fibers. In accordance with OSHA regulations, any employee working with asbestos was required to have his pulmonary functions tested and a chest X-ray evaluation performed under the direction of a physician at least once each year. The company was required to keep records of these medical tests of each employee for 50 years.

ATTITUDES ABOUT THE HAZARD

Despite various precautions, Barlow was not sure that enough was being done, or whether any exposure to asbestos was acceptable. Although scientific evidence of the effects of small dosages was still inconclusive, Barlow observed, "If a 5-micron fiber is dangerous, why is a 4.9-micron fiber OK?"

Although his peers were aware of—and concerned about—the dangers of working with asbestos, there were differences of opinion among them about what more could or should be done. Some were resigned to the realization that hazards are all about us anyhow and in some minimum sense unavoidable. Others equated the risk with no more than occasional smoking and raised the question whether tests on animals of massive exposure to substances could really be used to evaluate effects of very small, albeit continuous, exposure of humans to those substances. By and large they had concluded from all the facts as they knew them that Cumberland's precautions provided workers with sufficient protection as well as early warning through regularly scheduled pulmonary inspections. This opinion was strengthened by the results of a study of the medical records of retired Cumberland employees who had died during the preceding 20 or so years. In no case was the cause of death apparently related to asbestos.

Fred Barlow's greatest frustration was with the asbestos workers themselves, who, according to him, "couldn't give a damn." Employees and others, Barlow felt, had seen so many ridiculous government regulations that they assumed that all government regulations were ridiculous.[2] Wiping the white asbestos dust off his finger after he had handled a small, in-process piece of asbestos-laminated sheet, a supervisor, showing the casewriters through the plant, shrugged his shoulders and said he had resigned himself to the exposure as an unavoidable part of his job, though he worried about the effect on his wife and children. He noted the thin layer of dust on all surfaces in the plant despite elaborate dust collection equipment and reflected about the consequences of asbestos particles carried home on his clothes and transferred to the clothes of other family members in the family wash.

---

[2]Barlow believed that contrary to much popular opinion, OSHA was good and effective. He observed that while OSHA had promulgated some silly and widely publicized regulations about the shape of toilet seats and the like, there was incontrovertible evidence that industrial injuries and accidents had declined since OSHA had come into existence. He was confident that these declines would not have occurred without OSHA.

Most customers were primarily concerned that asbestos and asbestos products were becoming more expensive and harder to get, but did not otherwise appear to be overly concerned about the health hazard, since they only installed parts and did not machine, sand, or saw them.

THE MARKET

When Fred Barlow took over management of the Maryland Division, Cumberland Gasket had two competitors for its asbestos-based products. About the time that the two-fiber OSHA standard was introduced in 1975, one of the competitors left the market for reasons not known to Barlow. Thus, in 1978, only Cumberland and one other company were supplying the market. Barlow thought that the other company reflected concern for the hazards of working with asbestos when they stopped selling trimmed asbestos sheets in 1977. (Trimming creates dust.) He had heard rumors from customers and other sources that the last competitor was planning to leave the market.

The market for the asbestos-based products made by Cumberland was dominated by a few large companies. In addition, there were 20 to 30 very much smaller customers. Barlow felt that the primary concern of these customers, especially in the replacement market, was with price and delivery. Early in 1977, the price of asbestos had increased by 16 percent, just 6 months after a 10 percent increase. Because there were now only two producers left, Cumberland and its one competitor, it was becoming increasingly difficult for customers to get timely delivery. Because of the general lack of concern about the hazards of asbestos, very little work had been done on developing a substitute. Nor could Cumberland, a relatively small company, afford to do much pure R&D on its own. Du Pont had developed a substitute that tended to be four to five times more expensive than asbestos, and it was of inferior quality for some applications. The evidence of customer behavior was that they were unwilling to pay more for asbestos substitutes.

COMPANY POLICY AND ALTERNATIVES

In 1978 Cumberland's announced policy was to continue to manufacture as long as it could do so in compliance with OSHA or other standards, and as long as it could do so without further capital invest-

ment—unless the investment had a 6-month or less payback. The investment limitation reflected management's view that standards very probably would be made more restrictive. Products using asbestos were always fully priced, including the costs of the air testing and special cleaning programs. Barlow would not discount products containing asbestos to promote other business. In his visits to and discussions with customers, he regularly tried to get them to try substitutes for asbestos, though with limited success. Barlow stressed the company's obligation to its customers and observed that Cumberland could not leave them without a source. Without Cumberland as a supplier, market demands could not be met. However, if the OSHA standard of one-half of a fiber were introduced, Barlow thought that Cumberland could not continue without major changes.

One possible change would be to move to a complete "white room," space-age environment. This would involve isolating equipment used in making asbestos from the rest of the plant. Employees using the equipment would have to make a complete change of clothing and to shower before leaving the room.. Masks would still be required. In addition to the costs associated with clothing changes and the like, the white room would mean serious underutilization of equipment, since the machines would only be used with asbestos material about 30 percent to 40 percent of the time. A white room would require an investment of $750,000 and would raise operating costs by $100,000 a year. The fabrication division had $6 million in assets. Another alternative would be to process all asbestos under water or other liquid. However since asbestos is absorbent, product properties could change. Thus considerable research would have to go into developing the liquid used and testing the properties of the product after it had been processed in a liquid.

Processing in a liquid would eliminate dust but would substitute asbestos-bearing sludges. Interestingly, neither OSHA nor the state had any regulations preventing the company from dumping sludge containing asbestos into the river. (Eventually, asbestos in the water would be washed up on the banks, dry out, and enter the air.) The new Cumberland plant had a completely enclosed filtration system designed to prevent any discharge into the river. This system had not been required by law, but Barlow had included it when the plant was built, and even though it had added a substantial amount to the cost of the plant, top management had not questioned it.

The final option for Fred and Cumberland was to leave the asbestos business entirely. As noted, this would do irreparable harm to customers and would raise the cost of many goods and services for society generally. Beyond this, there were serious financial consequences for the Cumberland Company and its employees. Unless substitutes developed for asbestos-involved materials and processes which were adaptable to Cumberland's capabilities, jobs in the plant would inevitable be lost. Furthermore, the fabrication division was only marginally profitable, and the contribution of products containing asbestos was considerable. Loss of the asbestos business would place the division in a loss position—and would jeopardize the profitability of other divisions within the company.

Although Fred had given considerable thought to the moral and business issues involved in Cumberland's processing of asbestos materials, he still faced unresolved questions about the extent of the hazards to which Cumberland's workers were exposed and about the ways in which he should respond to them.

If you were Fred Barlow, what action would you recommend to Cumberland's top management? Explain your reasoning.

CASE 7
Edward F. Crow Company

The Edward F. Crow Company is an industrial distributor located in Memphis, Tennessee. Its principal product lines include materials handling equipment such as conveyors and transfer stations, electric motors and controls and power transmissions, and, finally, weighing scales, particularly those used as part of conveyor lines. The firm covers a territory consisting of parts of nine states: Tennessee, Kentucky, Alabama, Mississippi, Louisiana, Arkansas, Missouri, Illinois, and Indiana. Memphis is the hub of a trading area called the mid-South.

The firm was founded in 1937 by the late Edward F. Crow, who had earned his mechanical engineering degree from Case School of Applied Science (now Case Western Reserve University) in the 1920s. Before starting his own firm, he had been a design engineer and then a sales engineer for a major manufacturer of conveyors. When he passed away several years ago, operation of Crow was taken over by one of the lawyers who was handling the estate. There were no heirs interested in or capable of running the firm.

Over this period since Crow's death, annual sales have decreased from slightly less than $3 million to slightly more than $2 million (see Table C7-1). Because of inflation, actual physical volume has decreased even more (about 40 percent). Five years ago the corporation was very profitable, but last year Crow suffered a very small loss.

Five years ago there were five outside sales people. As conditions worsened, the sales force diminished in size. The last outside salesperson quit last week, and only two inside salespersons are left. They are both very competent but are overworked. As a result, the firm lost an opportunity to bid on seven large electric motors for the Tennessee Valley Authority when the closing date was missed.

As of 1983, volume was broken down as follows:

Electric motors and controls and power transmissions	20%
Parts, repairs and service for motors, and so on	25
Materials handling equipment, including parts and design services but not including motors, controls, transmissions, or scales	30
Scales	10
Parts, repairs, and service for scales	15

Over the last 5 years, dollar sales decreased in all five categories. The share of total sales held

Based on a case prepared by Ernest F. Cooke, Professor of Marketing, Layda College, Maryland. Reprinted by permission.

TABLE C7-1 Income Statement, 1978 Versus 1982 (in thousands of dollars)				
	1978		*1982*	
Sales				
Motors and so on	$669		$412	
Parts, repair and service for motors, and so on	642		516	
Materials handling/installations[1]	870		615	
Scales	361		224	
Parts, repair, and service for scales	374		298	
TOTAL NET SALES		$2,916		$2,065
Cost of Goods Sold				
Motors and so on	458		288	
Parts for motors and so on	237		196	
Materials handling	556		406	
Scales	243		155	
Parts for scales	111		94	
TOTAL COST OF GOODS SOLD		1,605		1,139
Gross margin		$1,311		$ 926
Operating Expenses				
Service and repair, labor and overhead[2]	501		412	
Warehouse and distribution expense	212		201	
General administrative and selling expense[3]	318		319	
Basically fixed costs				
TOTAL OPERATING EXPENSE		1,031		932
Operating income (loss)		$ 280		$ (6)
Interest expense less interest revenue		(13)		(4)
Net income (loss) before taxes		$ 293		$ (2)
Income tax (refund)		132		0
Net income		$ 161		$ (2)

[1]Actual materials handling sales are larger than indicated on the income statement because they usually include electric motors and controls, power transmissions, and sometimes scales. When these components are included as part of a materials handling instillation, the sales dollars are shown under the category scales or motors and so on.

[2]About 10% of this is assembly labor and warranty labor associated with material handling sales.

[3]Basically fixed cost and includes the engineer's salary.

according to category has changed, with new motors and scales dropping from 35.3 percent to 30.8 percent, all parts and repair increasing from 34.8 percent to 39.4 percent, and material handling holding steady at 29.8 percent.

In addition to the two inside salespeople, employees include a purchasing agent, a parts manager, a service manager, seven service and repair people, an engineer who designs materials handling systems, some warehouse and delivery people, and clerks who handle bookkeeping, billing, and correspondence. There has been turnover among these employees; consequently,

problems have arisen as a result of being short of help as well as having inexperienced help. For example, there is a 1-month backlog in billing for completed service work because of personnel problems.

The purchasing agent also acts as office manager. The engineer has increased the amount of his customer contact because of a decrease in outside sales people.

The firm is the exclusive distributor in the mid-South for Primax, a foreign manufacturer of electric motors whose East and Gulf Coast port of entry is New Orleans. Primax has a distribution center in

Memphis that serves the entire country. Crow's annual Primax sales 5 years ago totaled 400 units, contrasted with sales last year of 200 units. Its sales quota last year was 200 units. So far this year, sales have been at an annual rate of 200 units, averaging $1,000 per unit.

Crow also represents several divisions of Reliable Electric, a manufacturer of electric motors, controls, transmissions, and so on. Sales of Reliable products this year are running at an annual rate of $300,000 including parts. Almost 10 percent is small power transmission components purchased from Reliable's Lodge Division for materials handling installations.

The firm is the distributor for several different manufacturers of materials handling equipment and scales. These manufacturers are competitors in some of their lines. In these cases, Crow sometimes uses more than one manufacturer for a given installation. For most manufacturers, the firm is the exclusive distributor in the Memphis area even though they carry competitive lines.

In the almost 40 years that Edward Crow ran the firm, he built an excellent reputation among suppliers and customers. Although this reputation has deteriorated somewhat in the last 5 years, the firm still enjoys a good reputation. If the situation continues to deteriorate much longer, it will reach a critical stage and may even become irreversible.

Recently the Fearhank-Moose Scale Company, which manufacturers a line of portable industrial scales, canceled its contract with Crow because it felt that Crow was not doing justice to its line of scales. Subsequently, Fearhank signed up with another Memphis industrial distributor who is in direct competition with Crow.

You have just purchased a controlling interest in the firm and have appointed yourself president, CEO, and chief operating officer. The lawyer who was president is no longer with the firm. There is no doubt that he was ill-equipped to run the business. It requires someone like you, with marketing and management know-how. Describe your intended actions and the reasoning behind them.

CASE 8
F.B. Dunn & Associates, Inc.

BUSINESS MARKET SEGMENTATION

F.B. Dunn & Associates, Inc., an international engineering and construction consulting firm, had extensive experience in Europe, the Middle East, South America, Canada, and Australia, The Houston-based firm believed it had to expand its market coverage to maintain its growth and profitability. Since the company officials were aware they needed some marketing consulting, they enlisted the aid of a marketing consulting firm called Marketing Group II to determine the most appropriate target markets for F. B. Dunn & Associates, Inc.

Richard Cary, Pamela Lockheart, and Allen Webb helped to prepare this case.

COMPANY BACKGROUND

The company was rich in talent, as many of its engineers and inspectors either worked full time or were on call for many years in the construction and petrochemical industries. The president, Ted Dunn, was a veteran construction manager with Fluor, Inc., from 1952 to 1984, where he managed all aspects of both domestic and international construction in the energy industry. As a registered professional engineer (PE), he was responsible for managing and coordinating major projects worldwide. His equally talented vice president, Bob Foster, was an experienced general manager of procurement but was also well versed in traffic, expediting, contracts administration, and inspection.

The firm's corporate staff consisted of Mr. Foster, who was the vice president of sales and marketing, T. McCormack, human resources, W.F. Newman, general manager, quality control, F.A. Fayman, financial, and four sales representatives covering the states of Texas and Louisiana and the Western region of the United States. In addition to the corporate and full-time field staff, quality control representatives and shop expediters lived throughout the United States and could handle nearby inspection jobs, as shown in Figure C8-1.

Project management and engineering inspections were the two major thrusts in the company's consulting mix. The types of industries with which the firm sought consulting contracts were general contractors, municipal, state, and federal governments, insurance companies, bonding companies, engineering companies, oil and gas companies, equipment manufacturers, banks and project lenders, utilities, and petrochemical companies.

MARKETING GROUP II'S ANALYSIS AND RECOMMENDATIONS

The marketing consultants looked at *Sales and Marketing Management's Survey of Industrial & Commercial Buying Power* to determine the existing major four-digit SIC classifications of U. S. industry that showed expansionary trends that would best fit the capabilities of F.B. Dunn. Additional data were extracted from the *U.S. Industrial Outlook* and Standard & Poor's *Industrial Surveys*. Sixteen of the thirty-three SIC codes showed an upward trend between 1986 and 1988.

The areas of expansion were analyzed further to determine which specific segments were either process-oriented or project-oriented market segments. Process-oriented segments would include industries that used refineries, manufacturing, or water treatment processes, for example, in which once the system is started it continues until shutdown. A project-oriented segment, such as construction, in which PERT/CPM analysis is used, has a beginning and an end.

After reviewing and analyzing all the data, Marketing Group II recommended that F.B. Dunn & Associates concentrate its marketing efforts on two specific industries—construction and chemicals—that best matched the company's capabilities and past experiences. Dunn's experience could easily extend to the heavy construction industry where large-scale projects existed, such as:

Petrochemicals

Manufacturing operations

Hospital facilities and other health care facilities
   Research
   Patient care
   Education

Educational institutions

Basic chemical operations appeared to be very suitable to the company's experiences. Chemical operations of all types, including those in Table C8-1, are capital-intensive, high-technology segments characterized by limited R&D needs, and by management's strong emphasis on developing

FIGURE C8-1 Locations of F.B. Dunn & Associates, Inc., quality control representatives and shop expediters.

TABLE C8-1 Selected Industry Segments by SIC Code Demonstrating Expansionary Trends

SIC No.	Chemical and Allied Products	Shipments/Receipts (millions of dollars)		
		1986	1985	1984
2812	Alkalies and chlorines	1,655.1	1,669.6	1,685.2
2813	Industrial gases ▲	2,703.2	1,694.3	1,269.5
2816	Inorganic pigments	1,002.4	1,780.0	2,031.6
2819	Industrial inorganics, nec ▲	17,036.4	12,777.7	13,689.6
2821	Plastics and synthetic resins ▲	21,305.1	19,739.8	20,623.8
2822	Synthetic rubber ▲	6,237.4	3,166.8	3,646.0
2823	Cellulosic man-made fibers ▲	2,142.7	1,602.5	1,786.6
2824	Noncellulosic syn. org. fibers	7,020.1	9,637.8	12,036.3
2831	Biological products	1,534.3	1,702.2	1,597.2
2833	Medicinals and botanicals ▲	3,669.9	3,325.8	3,392.2
2834	Pharmaceutical preparations	21,304.6	21,802.0	19,082.1
2841	Soaps and other detergents	8,646.0	10,281.6	9,556.1
2841	Polishes and sanitation goods ▲	7,369.1	5,096.5	4,615.1
2843	Surface-active agents	826.1	1,758.7	2,081.5
2844	Toilet preparations ▲	12,317.7	10,189.1	9,310.9
2851	Paints and allied products	11,191.2	9,247.5	9,508.2
2861	Gum and wood chemicals	878.8	653.0	731.1
2865	Cyclic crudes and intermediates	7,855.6	8,889.6	8,752.8
2869	Indust. organic chemicals, nec	31,895.0	38,075.9	42,062.5
2873	Nitrogenous fertilizers ▲	6,416.5	4,903.8	4,713.6
2874	Phosphatic fertilizers	4,722.2	4,976.0	5,649.2
2875	Fertilizers—mixing only	2,496.7	2,573.7	2,617.6
2879	Agricultural chemicals, nec	6,193.3	6,218.0	7,093.7
2891	Adhesives and sealants ▲	4,827.9	2,660.0	2,750.4
2892	Explosives	1,162.7	802.9	1,203.0
2893	Printing ink ▲	2,070.0	1,409.7	1,347.4
2895	Carbon black	711.0	1,386.8	905.0
2899	Chemical preparations, nec ▲	10,644.5	6,419.3	6,637.6

▲ Petrochemical

Source: Sales and Marketing Management, Survey of Industrial and Commercial Buying Power, April 84, 85, 86 (April 1987).

engineering process improvements to reduce the use and costs of feedstocks, energy, and labor. Modernization, replacement, revamping, or "debottlenecking" technologies to maintain operating efficiencies, reduce costs, and meet government requirements for pollution abatement mandated the industry's continuous outlay of capital expenditures. Continued high operating rates—more than 80 percent—higher product prices, capacity limitations, and increased demand for exports and specialty products further aggravated the industry's needs to expand its current operating facilities.

The chemical industry was the fastest growing industry in need of construction since its profits were expected to continue their climb due to exogenous market forces that enhanced foreign and domestic demand and the lower crude oil and feedstock costs. Product prices for petrochemicals were forecast to continue firm through 1990 as product demand was barely met through incremental plant expansion and foreign imports. Imports of foreign chemicals, however, were expected to continue their decline as the U.S. dollar remained weak against the British pound, German deutsche mark, and the Japanese yen, consequently raising the price of foreign chemicals.

Questions for Discussion

1. Does the analysis, using SIC codes only, suffice as an analysis to segment to potential market for F.B. Dunn & Associates? What else could the group have recommended to further delineate F.B. Dunn's potential market segment(s)?

2. Were suppositions made concerning the potential building demand in education, health care, manufacturing, and transportation substantiated from the study of growing industries as classified by SIC codes in *SMM's Survey of Industrial and Commercial Buying Power*?

3. What was left out of Marketing Group II's analysis and recommendations that you would recommend should be covered?

CASE 9
Hach Company (A)

PERSONAL SELLING AND SALES MANAGEMENT

Hach Company was founded in 1947 by Clifford Hach while he was a graduate student at Iowa State University in Ames. In working with Dr. Harvey C. Diehl, Professor of Analytical Chemistry, an excellent method for testing water for hardness was developed and first marketed to municipal water works by direct mail. This method was so successful that it was adopted as the standard in the United States and remains the only method in use today. The test is commonly called the Hach test method. The beginning of the Hach Company initiated its association with the largest industrial instrument group of products. Spectroscopy represents 40 percent of the total analytical instrument market, followed by separations at 35 percent, and all the others at 25 percent.

Hach Company, presently located in Loveland, Colorado, developed a general concept that it was beneficial to society to bring analytical chemistry out the laboratory and place it in the workplace and into the hands of the general public. The company's underlying philosophy of simplicity in testing was practiced on a daily basis. They endeavored to develop instruments so a layman could conduct sophisticated testing procedures that previously could only have been performed by a chemist. As such, the Hach goal of simple and accurate test results evolved into the Hach "system for analysis."

Our appreciation to Leroy Bowers, Bernard Cameron, Jim Minchello, and Loren Pritzel for researching this case.

Following this philosophy, Hach company developed the DR/3000 Spectrophotometer, an instrument used to provide direct readouts of concentrations of particular substances in water when the substances react chemically with specific reagents to cause color development proportional to the degree of concentration. The DR/3000 was to replace the company's present spectrophotometer, the DR/2. The DR/3000 was a substantially upgraded instrument over the DR/2, with more sophisticated software and analytical abilities. The DR/3000 is a single-beam instrument that can be operated in three different modes:

1. A best fit program—a linear best fit on any number of standards equal to or greater than two.

2. Manual program—a linear fit using two standards or one standard and a known concentration factor.

3. Stored program—linear or nonlinear Hach procedures for direct measurement of concentration.

PRODUCT RESEARCH

Since the DR/3000 spectrophotometer can measure either light absorbency or light transmittance through a liquid sample to determine concentrations of substances in a liquid, the addition of a microprocessor to do the calculations and provide the readouts greatly enhanced the product. (see Figure C9-1 for details). The strategy of getting U.S. producers to use computer programs was to keep foreign competitors at bay with instruments that reduce data handling and manage lab traffic. Some of the instrument's important features are the microprocessor

A New Generation in Hach Spectrophotometry Is Coming . . . .(Available Fall 1983)

The all new DR/3000 Spectrophotometer integrates microprocessor technology with single beam optics. This bench-top instrument brings greater speed and convenience to laboratory analysis at an affordable price.

FEATURES
- Double-Pass Grating Monochromator
- Full Microprocessor Control
- Prompting Software
- 4-Figure Digital Display
- Auto Zero
- Signal Averaging
- Digital Timer
- Recorder Output Control
- Diagnostics
- Pressure Sensitive Keyboard Operation

IMPROVED OPTICS
Optical advantages such as 340-100 nm wavelength range, ± 1-nm accuracy, 8-nm spectral bandwidth, stray light less than 0.1%, and a 1-3 absorbence range are obtained with the double-pass grating monochromator system.

SIMPLE CONTROLS
The microprocessor ensures precise and rapid control of operations. This reduces analysis time and minimizes user errors. The 4-figure digital display allows accurate readout of photometric values. The operator may select between three readout modes: absorbance, % transmittance and concentration. The instrument can be zeroed simply by pressing the zero key. Other features, such as signal averaging control and decimal place selection, offer more versatility and convenience.

SOFTWARE FOR ANALYSIS
Prompting software provides high performance in colorimetric analysis. Using the manual program mode, a linear calibration may be conducted using two standards, or one standard and a known concentration factor (slope). The best-fit program performs a linear regression analysis on any number of standards equal to or greater than two.

STORED PROGRAMS
Measurements in direct concentration of most parameters found in today's water industry using Hach methods and reagents are possible simply by recalling programs stored in the instrument. Two additional programs assist the user in performing nonlinear calibrations. Stored program 0 is used for point-to-point interpolation between entered standards. Stored program 1 can be used to re-enter the nonlinear calibration data at any time, thereby eliminating the need to repeat the calibration.

OTHER FEATURES
The recorder output of the instrument is jumper selectable. Zero and full-scale settings can be established at the keyboard. The comprehensive manual will include procedures for water analysis parameters. Hach's ROM/manual update plan will allow the user to add new capabilities as they are developed. Verification of instrument calibrations and signal levels are available with the diagnostic software.

FIGURE C9-1

OPTICAL SPECIFICATIONS

Description	Grating	Plain hyperline, 1200 grooves/mm
	Lamp..	Tungsten Halogen (600 hour rating)
	Detector	Blue enhanced silicon photovoltaic
Wavelength	Range	340-1000 nm
	Accuracy....................................	± 1 nm
	Repeatability	± 0.2 nm
	Resolution	0.1 nm
	Bandwidth at 365 nm	8nm
	Stray Light	<0.1%
Photometric	Reproducibility.........................	±0.5% at 1A
	....	±0.7% at 2A
	Linearity at 548 nm	±0.002A at 1A
	....	±0.004A at 2A
	Repeatability (0-2A).................	±0.002A
	Noise Level (Signal avg = 10)	±0.0007A at 1A

PHYSICAL SPECIFICATIONS

Dimensions	H x W x D	18.4 x 43.8 x 47.6 cm (7.25 x 17.25 x 18.75*)
Weight	Basic Unit	12.9 kg (28.5 lbs)
Electrical	Voltage	100/120/220/260 VAC ± 10%
	Frequency.................................	50/60 Hz
	Power	60 VA
	Warm-up Period.......................	15 minutes
Recorder Output	Jumper Selectable...................	0-1.0V (factory set), 0-0.1V, 0-0.01V

ACCESSORIES

- 25 mL square cell/0.953* path length
- Pour-through cell/0.953* path length
- 1 cm cell/0.39* path length
- COD test adapter
- COD test vial/0.58* path length
- I/O peripheral capabilities

In the United States, call toll-free 1-800-525-5940 for current prices (Colorado residents: call collect 669-3050).

 The Analytical Methods Company   Representative

HACH COMPANY – P. O. Box 389, Loveland, CO 80539 U.S.A.
•Telephone 303/669-3050 • TWX: 910-930-9038
U.S. SALES OFFICES – *Ames, Iowa • *Cherry Hill NJ • *Tucker (Atlanta)
GA • Santa Clara, CA • Lake Charles, LA • Loveland, CO • Chapel Hill, NC •
Houston, TX • Palatine, IL • Orlando, FL • Olympia, WA • Cleveland, OH
HACH EUROPE S.A./N.V. – B.P. 51,5000 Namur 1, Belgium * Q81/44.53.81
Telex: 59027
International distributors and sales agents in principal cities world-wide
*Regional Service Centers

control for storing precalibrated Hach test methods, manual procedures, prompting for calibration, error indication, measurement modes of absorbency, transmittance and concentration, recorder output control, digital readout with signal averaging control, printer capabilities, remote control capabilities, and a double grating monochrometer. It is a quality instrument, although the price is moderate at $4,000.

COMPETITION

The competition is very intense, with numerous spectrophotometers on the market. As you will see in Table C9-1, at least thirty-seven instruments exist that range in price from the Bausch & Lomb Mini Spec 20 at $700 to the Perkin Elmer Model 557 at $32,750. This very broad array of products is a function of the instrument's degree of sophistication and use. The

TABLE C9-1 Competitive Pricing	
Model	*Price (dollars)*
1. Bausch & Lomb Mini 29	700
2. Coleman 29	950
3. Hach 2504	790
4. Hach 2582	790
5. Bausch & Lomb Spec PO	675
6. Coleman 41	1,325
7. Sargent Welch SK	1,065
8. Turner 336	830
9. Turner 350	970
10. Bausch & Lomb Spec 21/Vis	1,995
11. Bausch & Lomb Spec 21/UV-Vis	3,500
12. Perkin Elmer Coleman Jr.	1,500
13. Bausch & Lomb Spec 70	1,923
14. Bausch & Lomb Spec 80	2,250
15. Gilford Instrument's Stasar	4,150
16. Bausch & Lomb Spec 100	3,750
17. Bausch & Lomb Spec 710	4,615
18. Perkin Elmer 55B	4,750
19. Hach DR-3000	4,000
20. Kontron UVIKON 710	7,900
21. Beckman Model 42	8,300
22. Sargent Welch Pye Unican 300	8,825
23. Sargent Welch Pye Unican 400	10,925
24. Varian DMS 80	8,100
25. Perkin Elmer Lambda 3	7,200
26. Varian DMS 90	10,750
27. Bausch & Lomb Spec 2000	7,375
28. Perkin Elmer Model 552A	9,950
29. Perkin Elmer Model 559A	15,450
30. Perkin Elmer Model 320	19,400
31. Perkin Elmer Model 330	26,450
32. Perkin Elmer Model 557	32,750
33. Kontron UVIKON	14,450
34. Sargent Welch 8-250 Series	19,450
35. Varian Cary 210	13,450
36. Varian Cary 219	16,450
37. Hewlett Packard 8450A	23,950

DR/300 at $4,000 is well above other instruments in performance at an equivalent price. Although no one company controls the market, Hach's major competitor for market share is Bausch & Lomb.

PERSONAL SELLING

Hach sold both domestically and abroad by emphasizing strong personal selling efforts backed up with strong trade show participation, space advertising in technical periodicals, direct mail advertising, and product literature. The present domestic sales force consists of two sales reps at each of thirteen sales offices distributed throughout the United States (Figure C9-2). These offices are strategically located close to scientific and water resource management areas; namely, Santa Clara and Laguna Beach, California; Loveland, Colorado; Orlando, Florida; Atlanta, Georgia; Chicago, Illinois; Ames, Iowa; Lake Charles, Louisiana; Cherry Hill, New Jersey; Chapel Hills, North Carolina; Cleveland, Ohio; Houston, Texas; and Olympia, Washington.

The company's marketing efforts are designed to create a satisfied customer, and the role of the salesperson is to help ensure the accomplishment of this goal. The sales force fulfills specific duties as it helps to define customer's needs and determines the buying situation for the customer. Relative to the DR/3000, the salesperson will show the customer how the product can contribute to the accomplishment of the customer's objectives. Next, the salesperson provides service where he has important responsibilities relating to the product's application, installation, and maintenance. Additionally, he represents the customer to the factory in all matters including service offerings, credit terms, contract terms, planning, and expediting the delivery.

THE NEED FOR ADDITIONAL SALESPEOPLE

Salespeople will be assigned a very active role in stimulating demand. Corporate office established an annual sales goal of a minimum of ten DR/3000 instruments per salesperson. Given the quality and experience of the present sales force, it was thought that they could handle the additional sales responsibilities. Market research had shown that 36 percent of the present DR/2 customers were in the municipal (water) market, 46 percent were in the industrial market, and 18 percent of the market were classified in many other areas. Of the present DR/2 users, 22 percent foresee upgrading their DR/2s with additional chemistry.

Questions for Discussion

1. Given the present Hach spectrophotometer (DR/2) users' propensity to remain with their present instruments, would the forecast of ten instruments per salesperson be realistic or not? Why?

2. Is the present sales force large enough to attain the company's desired sales goals? Why? What changes, if any, do you believe should be made?

3. Other promotional efforts are to be expended, but is it proper that the sales force shoulder the major burden in the promotional effort? Why? Be explicit.

FIGURE C9-2 National sales offices.

Hach Company (B)

BUSINESS AND INDUSTRIAL ADVERTISING

The DR/3000 Spectrophotometer had been in design for several years. The lines of the overall case were smoothed and the corners rounded to make a much more aesthetic looking presentation. The colors were toned down and the overall size was expanded so that a printer could be easily installed in the future or chips could be added. A jack was added so that a recorder or remote control could be directly hooked into the instrument. An option was the sipper sampler, a special tray capable of holding 100 test samples. The instrument could analyze all of these samples by taking a reading, giving an output, and then going on to the next sample automatically. This instrument laid the groundwork for another generation of newer instruments.

Until recently, the spectrophotometer was considered a mature product. The microprocessor regenerated the product's life cycle into a new product category. The product's PLC will mature in about 3 to 4 years as advances in technology enable competitors to usurp the marketplace lead from Hach. Hach has to plan on redesigning the instrument within this time frame.

ADVERTISING AND PROMOTION

Traditionally, Hach has taken a semipassive role in the marketing of their products. This policy changed with the DR/3000 as an aggressive strategy designed to maximize the marketing effort was employed. The strategy actively explored new markets in an attempt to exceed the predicted sales forecasts.

Trade Show Focus

The primary promotion strategy for the DR/3000 was a coordinated three-prong campaign. The central focus of the campaign was an emphasis on the industrial trade show exhibits. Trade shows were chosen for their relatively low costs, high visibility,

Our appreciation to Leroy Bowers, Bernard Cameron, Jim Minchello, and Loren Pritzel for researching this case.

and high probability of producing quality sales leads. According to industrial sources and the *Wall Street Journal*, a typical industrial field sales rep can make twelve calls per week at a cost of $100 to $200 per call, whereas a trained sales rep at a trade show can make the same number of presentations for a cost of $40 to $50 per call.[1] Trade shows offer the distinct advantage of product demonstrations and "hands on" experience for present and potential customers.

Advertising and the Trade Show Interface

Customer awareness was a vital function that had to be instituted before any effective selling could be promulgated at either the trade shows or through the personal selling efforts of the 26-member field sales force. Trade journals were used to stimulate interest in the product. The ads were one-sixth page space ads placed in fifteen journals with a 20,000 to 40,000 circulation per journal. Direct mail advertising was sent to present and potential customers 2 months before a trade show's occurrence to inform them of the DR/3000's availability for demonstra-

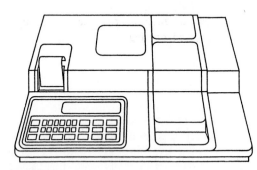

FIGURE C10-1 Microprocessor Grating Spectrophotometer. Our new versatile instrument will analyze any of your water or water base solutions and provide a rapid digital readout. The Hach Company engineers have come up with a sharp instrument for the professional person in your lab, chemist or technician, who wants better results.. The DR/3000 can be programmed for your specific analytical needs. It is one of the most efficient and accurate spectrophotometers on the market. It easily fits into any laboratory.

[1]*The Wall Street Journal* (May 8, 1980), p.3.

tions and operations, and of the times and places of Hach's trade show exhibits. The trade shows included both Hach's traditional and nontraditional shows to generate as many new business and industrial accounts as possible. One direct mail piece appears in Figure C10-1.

The second aspect of the promotional campaign was the trade show itself, where the exhibit was staffed by regional salespeople. The factors that led to a successful trade show exhibit were an appropriate booth size, proper colors, integrating a dramatic, possibly unique, attention getter with traffic control. Booth personnel had to be pleasant and attentive. Demonstrations of the DR/3000 were conducted as often as possible and followed up with product literature, a specification sheet, catalog, and brochures.

Personal Sales Follow-Up

The third aspect of the promotional campaign was a personal follow-up call on prospects who had shown an interest in the machine at the trade show. Here the salespeople could give the customers the personal attention they deserved, and their technical questions could be answered.

PROMOTIONAL BUDGET

The three-part promotional campaign for the DR/3000 spectrophotometer, which consisted of media advertising, regional trade shows, and personal selling follow-ups, was developed to use the company's resources effectively at a minimal cost. Hach's conventional trade journal advertising, in more than 100 types of journals and directories in industries where some type of water analysis is conducted, kept the company's name in a prominent position in buyers' minds. The carryover of this advertising and promotion helped the sale of the DR/3000. Table C10-1 is the promotional budget for DR/3000's first year. Figure C10-2 shows the percentile breakout of

TABLE C10-1 Promotional Budget		
First Year		
Trade shows (two thirds of budget)		$120,000
Show cost × 25 shows	$60,000	
Direct mail	20,000	
Booth set-up	25,000	
Miscellaneous expense and follow-up	15,000	
Space advertising		
Magazine and technical literature		67,000
Catalogs		12,500
Total advertising and sales promotional budget		$200,000

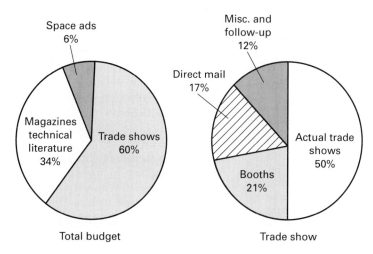

FIGURE C10-2   Percentile breakout of promotional budget.

the company's total advertising budget and the trade show, direct mail, and personal sales follow-up budget breakdown.

Questions for Discussion

1. Why could the three-step promotional plan used by Hach be so effective? Was it the combination of the elements, the sequence of the elements used, or the intensive use of each element?

2. If the salespeople were not trained for trade shows, would the shows be as successful? Why, or why not?

3. Would business and industrial salespeople normally dislike trade shows since it pulled them away from their territories and forced them to talk with customers from other territories? Why?

4. What is the importance of an exhibitor's booth relative to its size, location, colors, design, and function? What is the interface between trade shows and personal selling?

CASE 11
Huntington Electronics

NEW PRODUCT INTRODUCTION

Since the costs of electricity were expected to rise fourfold over the next few years for commercial and industrial users, the search was on for practical ways to cut costs and conserve energy resources. As a leading electrical equipment manufacturer, Huntington had been making a significant contribution to these efforts through the development of new energy-efficient products. The company was currently in the process of developing a new mercury vapor light which was designed to replace recessed incandescent down-lights found in lobbies, conference rooms, and similar public areas of hotels, motels, bank and office buildings, schools and universities, stores, airport terminals, and other facilities.

The problem lay in persuading, or rather, encouraging potential buyers to make the conversion from their existing lamps to Huntington's Superwatt and incurring the initial capital costs involved.

Huntington Electronics had been in existence for about 70 years and had always been active in the lighting business producing such items as fittings and fixtures, searchlights, and signals for traffic control. The firm operated several factories in the United States and abroad and was traded on the New York Stock Exchange.

This case was prepared by Norman A.P. Govoni, Jean-Pierre Jeannet, and Henry N. Deneault, *Cases in Marketing,* 2nd ed. (New York: John Wiley & Sons, Inc. Publishers, 1983.) Copyright 1983 by Grid Publishing, Inc. Reprinted by permission of John Wiley & Sons, Inc.

Huntington was considered one of the top outdoor lighting suppliers in the nation and carried one of the most complete product lines available. Huntington's products were used outdoors to light shopping centers, industrial parks and plants, apartment complexes, aircraft carrier flight decks, streets, malls, billboards, parking lots, and in numerous other situations. The firm had achieved a leading position in the field of aviation as well.

Superwatt was a simple kit that enabled recessed commercial incandescent lighting systems to be quickly converted to more efficient mercury vapor lighting at a relatively low cost and without the use of specialized labor. The advantages were as follows:

A. Energy costs were substantially reduced.
   By replacing an inefficient high-wattage incandescent lighting system with a highly efficient, lower-wattage mercury vapor system, power usage could be reduced by more than 40 percent without sacrificing light levels. The most common conversion would be from a 150W incandescent light to a 70W color-improved mercury vapor.

B. Installation was easy and inexpensive.
   The unit was simply screwed into the existing incandescent socket after the old lamp had been removed.
   1. No expensive rewiring was required.
   2. No specialized labor was required. Anybody could install it.
   3. No special tools were required for installation.
   4. Light levels remained the same.

C. Relamping labor costs were one-twentieth of those of the incandescent system.

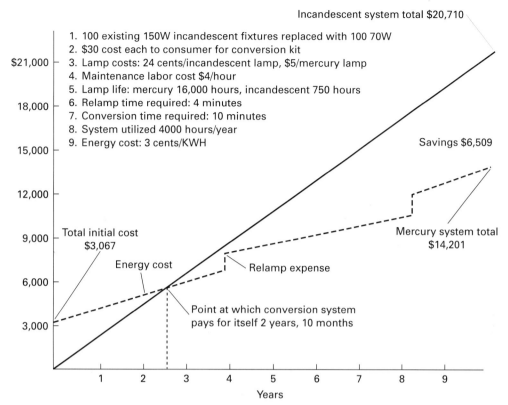

The following notes appear on the figure:

1. 100 existing 150W incandescent fixtures replaced with 100 70W
2. $30 cost each to consumer for conversion kit
3. Lamp costs: 24 cents/incandescent lamp, $5/mercury lamp
4. Maintenance labor cost $4/hour
5. Lamp life: mercury 16,000 hours, incandescent 750 hours
6. Relamp time required: 4 minutes
7. Conversion time required: 10 minutes
8. System utilized 4000 hours/year
9. Energy cost: 3 cents/KWH

Incandescent system total $20,710

Savings $6,509

Total initial cost $3,067

Energy cost

Relamp expense

Mercury system total $14,201

Point at which conversion system pays for itself 2 years, 10 months

FIGURE C11-1 System cost comparison—incandescent versus conversion to mercury.

The mercury vapor source had a lamp life of approximately 4 years (16,000 hours total) compared with that of the incandescent source (rated at 750 hours).

D. Initial cost of Superwatt ($30.00 direct to a large user with lamp) could be recovered by energy and maintenance savings in less than 3 years (see Figure C11-1).

The unit consisted of two aluminum extrusions clamped together around a mercury ballast with top and bottom cover plats completing the basic external housing assembly. The compact mercury conversion kit construction and shallow lamp enable the combination to fit easily into most existing fixture housings and permitted original fixtures hardware to be replaced in its original position so that the overall ceiling appearance remained the same as before.

The fixture housing had numerous fins to provide heat dissipation which ensured that the kit would perform within safe operating temperature limits. A medium base plug body on top of the housing allowed the fixture to be screwed as a unit into the existing incandescent socket. A lanyard-type arrangement was provided with the fixture, which when attached to the existing housing, provided an additional securing device. The down-side of the unit consisted of the socket and reflectory-type lamp which was provided as an integral part of the unit. Two locating clips insured proper positioning of the prong-base lamp.

The market for Superwatt consisted of any existing commercial or institutional building that presently used recessed incandescent lighting in any way for its indoor lighting system. Generally, this type of lighting fixture would be most commonly found in lobbies, hallways, executive offices, conference rooms, or where accent lighting of some kind would be required.

By drawing on several government and industry sources for background information, the market researchers refined this basic information to determine the actual numerical size of the potential market, as shown in Figure C11-2. The study indicated that approximately 7,000,000 fixtures presently in use were mechanically capable of being converted to Superwatt.

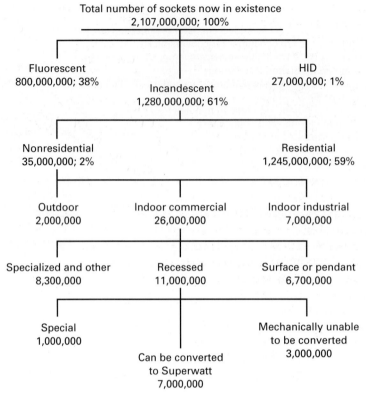

FIGURE C11-2 Market potential—mercury connector kit.

The markets were further divided into segments according to their order of importance as perceived by the product marketing manager who was responsible for the introduction of Superwatt.

1. Office and bank buildings
2. Stores and other commercial buildings
3. Hotels and motels
4. Manufacturing facilities, offices and lobbies
5. Schools and universities
6. Hospitals and health treatment centers
7. Government buildings

Because the target areas were existing installations, the buying influences were expected to be considerably different from those encountered in new project situations.

The most important consideration was locating the individuals within each organization who were concerned with power and maintenance costs since the Superwatt product benefits were heavily weighted in that direction. The researchers estimated that approximately 25 percent of the potential conversion market was controlled by some corporate central organization.

Huntington's most significant competition in the area of interior lighting came from companies such as GTE Sylvania, Westinghouse, and General Electric. Although the industry had by nature been rather blatant in copying one another's product, there had not been any definite indication of competition within this new market thus far. It could be inferred by any means that other industrial firms had ignored the possibilities of manufacturing more energy-efficient incandescent lighting systems. Statistics provided by the U.S. Commerce Department revealed that incandescent lamps had enjoyed the most rapid growth rate of all available lighting sources.

Huntington's Lighting Division, which had been responsible for the Superwatt introduction, distributed its products through about 1,300 electrical distributors as well as approximately 1,000 equipment manufacturers who installed Huntington products in their own products and thus acted as OEMs (original equipment manufacturers).

Huntington's marketing organization was product oriented because of the technical nature of the products manufactured and the resulting differences in methods of use and purchase. The company believed that this organizational structure enabled all parties involved to participate in marketing a product or group of products (from marketing manager to field salesman) and to concentrate on one segment of technology involved with respect to that product and thus become highly expert in it. Huntington believed this resulted in better service to the customer and a more intelligent and effective presentation of the product's benefits on the part of the sales force.

Each division's marketing program was headed by a marketing manager who, based on recommendations of the national sales manager and the product marketing manager, had complete authority in directing the manufacture and marketing of a product or group of products, subject to company policies and overall top management control.

The national sales manager directed six district salesmen and six specialists (usually engineers) who were assigned to the different districts according to their individual level of skill. In addition, there was an original equipment manager who was responsible for the manufacturing companies that Huntington serviced.

The product manager functioned as a source of information about his or her products. The product manager studied the markets, recommended courses of action, planned or assisted in planning the company's operations with respect to products, checked the efficiency of the firm's activities in manufacturing and marketing suggested product modifications, and made other studies and suggestions designed to improve the performance of his or her assigned product. The managers of advertising and sales promotion, market research, and sales analysis lent support to the product marketing manager's decision (see organization chart, Figure C11-3).

Huntington planned to sell the Superwatt kit for $30.00 to its distributors who would in turn sell them at $37.50 to their customers. This price consisted of $24.75 for the fixture (where Huntington earned its profit) and a 70 watt vapor lamp for $5.25. Huntington's gross margin on the entire kit amounted to about 50 percent.

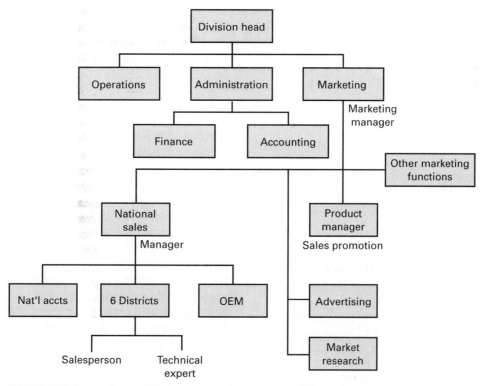

FIGURE C11-3 Huntington Electronics organization chart—lighting division.

From the point of view of the assigned product manager, several favorable and unfavorable factors had to be considered before planning the introductory marketing program. Among the favorable factors were these:

1. Timing for this type of product appeared to be favorable. The shortage of energy which had been developing for several years had created a psychological climate where the conversion of energy was often in the minds of the consumers.

2. The savings that resulted from the lower power consumption realized by converting combined with savings that were realized from lower maintenance requirements, provided a strong sales story. Indications were that electricity rates would increase substantially, especially during peak operating levels, making this an especially important consideration.

3. With the recent improvement of the color rendition of high-intensity discharge light sources, mercury vapor lighting had been gaining acceptance for interior lighting in higher wattages. Superwatt could benefit from this trend by providing a method of utilizing more efficient mercury sources in low-wattage units as well.

There were, however, also some unfavorable considerations:

1. Several easy and inexpensive alternatives were available, including
   a. "Power down" by replacing high-wattage incandescent bulbs with lower-wattage lamps
   b. Remove some lamps completely

2. There was substantial skepticism regarding the validity of the "energy crisis" and many were inclined to take a wait-and-see attitude.

3. Although acceptance might be good, financing might be difficult because the money to convert could be drawn from maintenance budgets which normally required management approval for an expenditure over a minimum amount. Consequently, even though a commitment to convert existed, it would have to be done over a period of several months or years for financial reasons.

With these considerations in mind, it was now up to the product manager to recommend a complete plan to his marketing manager.

C A S E   1 2
The Jet Engine Industry and Its Parts Suppliers

BUYER-SELLER INTERRELATIONSHIPS

In 1978, the United States removed federal restrictions from the commercial airline industry. In effect, this stopped price fixing among the various airlines and caused the carriers to seek immediate cost reductions in their operations and price concessions from their suppliers. The advent of the hub and spoke system was introduced by regional airlines as one of the first cost-cutting steps. The airlines sought reduced prices on new aircraft and on replacement parts which increased competition among the domestic jet engine builders—General Electric and Pratt & Whitney—and among the major suppliers of the engine builders—Cameron Forge, Wyman-Gordon, and Ladish, Inc. The suppliers where whipped into an all-out, competitive war with each other.

A second wave of competitive impact was forthcoming from another governmental action. The Air Force required competition between GE and P&W for F-15/F-16 jet fighter awards. Jet engine builders faced high development costs, shrinking export market opportunities, foreign competition, and U.S. defense budget cuts, which culminated to further intensify the competitive battles being fought. The government's actions to expedite competition among the jet engine builders released Pratt & Whitney's 75 percent stranglehold on the engine market and GE quickly responded by becoming the leading jet engine builder, capitalizing on its ability to offer engines that were more fuel efficient and more powerful. Also, GE was better able to finance the purchases.

We thank Roy Schultz for his contribution to the data and insights in this case.

JET ENGINE SUPPLIERS—INTERNAL FORCES

Since Cameron Forge, Wyman-Gordon, and Ladish, Inc. are the largest suppliers of jet engine component parts, intense competition among the three forced an evenly distributed market share and precipitated a number of organizational consolidations and plant closings. The industry was faced with the realistic admonition that to survive, they had to depend on delivery and product quality to placate their customers. These facts of life motivated the suppliers to upgrade technology, using state-of-the-art forging and machining operations, exotic materials, such as titanium, computerized isothermal forging presses, and completely automated, computer-driven machine shops.

Computerization

Advances in technology brought the suppliers into the computer age. Numerically controlled machine tools, forging presses, and inspection equipment helped domestic suppliers stay ahead of foreign competition. Advances in engineering functions, such as computer-aided design and manufacturing (CAD-CAM) modeling, married engine builders with their suppliers to solve problems before they occurred. As part of their contracts, buyers with the jet engine builders required CAD-CAM, which became a necessity in the jet engine component parts market. This extensive computer modeling technique was very expensive for smaller firms, but allowed parts to be produced that met customer "specs" on the first forging, hence providing a cost savings for both the customer and supplier. Before CAD-CAM was instituted, several trial runs would have been required to reach the acceptable metallurgical and performance specifications.

Customer Orientation

Customers become more involved in the supplier's business by demanding demonstrated innovations to improve productivity, quality, flexibility, response time, and cost reduction. Cameron Forge's statistical quality control system was developed by Pratt & Whitney, who required Cameron Forge to adopt the system and adhere to it in its manufacturing process to continue to supply P&W parts.

Long-Term Contracts

The three major suppliers to both General Electric and Pratt & Whitney had to commit to signing long-term contracts to provide just-in-time deliveries to the customer's designated plants to cut costs and improve product quality. If a shipment contained defective parts, the customer could reject the shipment at considerable expense to itself and either break the supplier's contract or enter the supplier's place of business and oversee the appropriate corrective actions. In either case, the buyer-seller relationships have greatly changed, creating a marriage between the partners whether they like it or not, where the buyer has the supreme rule and the seller must be very customer oriented to supply the customer's needs to the nth degree.

Just-in-Time Deliveries

Just-in-time deliveries placed an additional burden on the suppliers, since their production schedules had to be rearranged to specifically coincide with their customer's needs rather than their own. The suppliers lost some of their freedom of movement and choice when they entered into a contract. However, the relief that the suppliers received from the long business drought offset the loss of freedom. A long-term contract seemed to placate many feelings and helped to justify some loss of freedom and the additional costs of handling the product.

Questions for Discussion

1. How can the suppliers justify the additional burden of the customer's needs being superimposed upon their needs even to the point that the customer can demand that a specific quality control system be used and be able to enter the supplier's plant at will to enforce the quality? What should Cameron Forge do under the circumstances?

2. Is a marriage between a seller and a buyer good for fostering the practice of the marketing concept?

3. What happens to the previous or old buyer-seller relationships that existed before JIT, high product quality requirements, customer demands on specs, and the customer's ability to enter the supplier's place of business to help untangle poor quality problems?

4. What role do you think foreign competition, particularly British, French, German, and Japanese, played in this scenario?

Lewiston-Copeland Company

"We would like to see your division come up with a statement of objectives and strategy that is consistent with that of the corporation as a whole," said Charles Crawford. "In addition, you should lay out both the short-term and the longer-range plans for your division in as much detail as you can within the limited time available to you." Thus, Charles Crawford, president of Lewiston-Copeland Company, summarized his instructions to James Boyd, vice president in charge of the Copeland Paper Division.

Boyd, along with most of the other top executives of the company, had been attending a 3-day long-range-planning session held at a resort motel about 25 miles outside of Evergreen City, headquarters of the Lewiston-Copeland Company, and a community of about 100,000 population located in the Pacific Northwest. This 3-day session, held in the spring of 1971, was the culmination of numerous meetings and discussions extending over a 2-month period during which the company was trying to embark on a formal system of long-range planning. During the 3-day planning session, overall corporate objectives had been agreed on and general strategy guidelines had been set for the company, although none of the specifics of planning had been spelled out.

Toward the end of the planning session, the suggestion was made that rather than launching all of the company's ten divisions on any type of formal long-range planning, one division should be taken first as a "pilot division" and should go through a "complete planning performance." This division was to draw up a statement of divisional objectives and strategy, decide on the appropriate time frame for its plans, consider the roles of division planners versus corporate planners, and draw up some actual plans and programs.

After a relatively short discussion on the matter, the Copeland Paper Division was chosen to

This case was produced with the permission of its author, Dr. Stuart U. Rich, Professor of Marketing and Director, Forest Industries Management Center, College of Business Administration, University of Oregon, Eugene, Oregon. Copyright ©1978 by Dr. Stuart U. Rich. (ICCH CASE #9-373-669)

be the pilot division. The top corporate executives, whose experience had been mainly in timber, lumber, and plywood, felt that the Paper Division was a good one to start with because the complexity of its products and markets was not as great as in other divisions, and because James Boyd had had long-range planning experience at another firm before joining Lewiston-Copeland several years earlier. He also had a reputation as a self-starter and displayed a zest for achievement in whatever job he undertook. Although some of his division executives were a little dubious about this honor bestowed on their division, Boyd tackled the job with accustomed enthusiasm. determined to make his division a showcase of long-range planning during the 3-month period allotted him.

COMPANY BACKGROUND

The Lewiston-Copeland Company was a large manufacturer of forest products with manufacturing, converting, and distribution facilities located throughout the United States as well as in Canada and abroad. Its sales of somewhat over $1 billion were divided among lumber, plywood, particleboard and other panel products, logs and timber, paperboard, containers and cartons, pulp, paper, and real estate and housing. The company was organized along product divisional lines, with ten divisions coming under four different business groups. The Copeland Paper Division, along with the Pulp Division and the Paperboard and Container Division, came under the Fiber Products Group.

All of the divisions were separate profit centers, and some of the product divisions were the raw material sources for other product divisions. For instance, the Pulp Division furnished pulp to the Paperboard and the Paper Divisions as well as selling to outside customers. For its own raw material needs, the Pulp Division bought pulpwood from the Timber Division and wood chips from the Lumber and Plywood Divisions.

The company typically had millsite integration. For example, near one of its large tree farms there might be a manufacturing complex consisting of a lumber and plywood mill and a pulp mill. The latter used logs not suited for lumber and plywood manufacture as well as waste wood in the form of chips from the lumber and plywood mills. AT the same site there might also be a paperboard mill and a paper mill using the output of the pulp mill.

The company also had two nonintegrated paper mills, that is, paper mills located by themselves, not near a pulp mill or a source of timber supply. Such paper mills, which were relatively old compared with the integrated mills, bought pulp from distant company-owned pulp mills as well as from outside sources.

COPELAND PAPER DIVISION

The manufacturing facilities of the Copeland Paper Division consisted of some 25 different paper machines, located in both integrated and nonintegrated mills in the Pacific Northwest, the South, and the Northeast. The company had both on-machine and off-machine coaters used in the manufacture of the higher-quality grades of printing papers as well as some types of technical papers. An on-machine coater was an inherent part of the paper machine and coated only the paper produced on that particular machine, whereas a more flexible off-machine coater stood by itself and could be used to coat paper produced by any paper machine, either at the mill where the coater was located or shipped in from another mill. On-machine coating was a less expensive method of manufacture than off-machine coating.

The average cost of a new paper machine of the type found in the Copeland mills was $30,000,000. A new coater cost $8,000,000. Plant capacity could sometimes be increased at less cost through rebuilding and speeding up old machines, with expenditures of up to $5,000,000. Typically, however, capacity increases in the paper industry came in sizable increments, and depreciation on machinery and equipment, along with other fixed expenses, represented about 30 percent of total product cost for the types of papers made by Lewiston-Copeland. Raw material costs accounted for 50 percent, and variable labor costs the remaining 20 percent.

The division's product line consisted of several hundred different types or "grades" of paper, ranging from standard uncoated offset printing paper to silicone-coated papers with water-repellent and nonadhesive characteristics designed for special industrial uses. As a first step toward simplifying the business of this division, Boyd had recently had the product line classified into 32 product groups, which were then combined into eight product families, based on their marketing and manufacturing affinity. Among these eight product families were premium printing papers, usually with fancy coatings; commodity printing papers, such as uncoated offset paper; converting papers such as envelope and tablet stock; communications papers, including electrographic and other specialized office copy papers; and technical papers such as pressure-sensitive papers.

COMPANY OBJECTIVES AND STRATEGY

The basic corporate objective of the Lewiston-Copeland Company, which had been agreed on during the recent planning meetings, was to "sustain an average growth rate in earnings per share of 15 percent per year over at least the next 5 years." Having set forth this objective, management then analyzed the major strengths of the company, and the nature of the businesses in which the company was engaged, in order to determine an appropriate strategy to achieve its objective.

The company's major strength was its several million acres of timberlands, much of which had been acquired at a cost far below current market value. The timber was a renewable asset, was readily accessible, and could be harvested and sold as logs or could be manufactured into forest products. The company also had extensive and well-integrated manufacturing facilities, a broad product line, and a sound financial condition with a debt-to-equity ratio lower than that of its major competitors.

Management felt that the company was basically in two major businesses: commodities and specialties. Commodities, such as dimension lumber ("two-by-fours" and the like), were manufactured to common specifications, with little or no product differentiation, and were sold on the basis of price and service. The commodity product line had a low rate of technological obsolescence, a low value added by manufacture, and a low profit margin on sales. Markets were large, worldwide, and well established. However, markets were also slow growing, very competitive, and prices might be highly unstable over short periods of time.

Specialties, such as particular types of overlaid paneling, had a high value added by manufacture and often carried a high profit margin, although market size was usually small. There was a real or perceived product differentiation; in fact, some specialties were manufactured to individual customer specifications. Product life was sometimes short because of the rapidly changing technology, and the timing of market entry was often quite important. The successful management of a specialty business required a quite different set of skills than did the management of a commodity business. This was true whether the skills involved marketing, manufacturing, engineering, research and development, logistics, or resource allocation. The relative importance of these various functions also differed in the two types of businesses.

The basic strategy guidelines of the company which were developed at the recent corporate planning meetings were stated as follows:

1. Build a solid commodity business by improving and increasing the utilization of our raw material base and delivering products and required services to market at the lowest unit cost.

2. Use this commodity business as a foundation for supporting investments in higher-risk, higher-return opportunities in present and new markets, by new technologies, and in new businesses.

DETERMINATION OF DIVISION STRATEGY

One of the major strategic issues facing James Boyd was the roles to be played by the Copeland Division's nonintegrated mills and by its integrated mills. In the former were old, slow-running paper machines, suited to the manufacture of specialty papers, which included most of the communications and technical grades. These slow-running machines were also suited for the many trial runs required in the development of new types of specialties. In the integrated mills were large, modern machines designed for high-volume production of commodity papers, including most of the printing grades.

Complicating the nonintegrated versus integrated mill situation was the fact that the more successful specialty papers often developed into commodity papers. This was because their high profit margin and the expanding market demand attracted competitors, and new types of papers were very difficult to patent. As usage developed, their manufacture became more standardized. In order to keep costs down and keep prices competitive, the division then had to shift the manufacture of these paper grades from the old, slow-running machines in the nonintegrated mills to the modern, fast-running

machine in its integrated mills. Technical difficulties sometimes had to be solved in making the shift. After such a shift, the nonintegrated mills often had the problem of filling the gaps in their machine utilization in order to keep the mills profitable.

Another problem that faced all nonintegrated mills, including those of the Copeland Division, was the fact that their raw material costs were about 15 to 20 percent higher than those of integrated mills. This was because in an integrated facility, pulp was fed in slush form from an adjacent pulp mill directly to the paper machines. To supply a nonintegrated mill, pulp had to be shipped in dry form from a distant pulp mill and then reconstituted into a slurry on the paper machines. Because of their location away from any pulpwood supply, it was not feasible to build a pulp mill adjacent to the Copeland Division's nonintegrated paper mills.

About three fourths of the division's sales and four fifths of its profits were from the commodity grades made in its integrated mills, with the remaining percentages from the specialty grades in the nonintegrated mills. Within these two categories, however, there was a wide variation in profit margins, particularly in the specialty papers. Certain grades of copy papers and release papers were the most profitable of the entire product line. Some of the older specialty papers had showed a loss for several years, but were kept as long as they covered their own direct costs and made some contribution to common fixed costs. The most profitable grades were often papers which had recently moved out of the specialty and into the commodity class, and enjoyed a strong market demand.

In working up a statement of strategy relating to the product lines and mills in his division, James Boyd had decided that there were four major strategic alternatives from which to choose. The first was to operate the division's existing businesses without investing additional capital over and above that required for routine maintenance and replacement. If the company ceased to be cost competitive in particular grades of specialty papers, it should withdraw from those particular products and the markets they served.

The second alternative was for the company to shut down and/or divest itself of all nonintegrated facilities. It should emphasize the commodity markets and should retain only those specialties which could be produced in the integrated mills.

The third was to provide adequate capital to modernize and speed up some of the machines in the nonintegrated mills in order to be more cost competitive in the fast-growing fields of copy and release papers. Expenditures would also be made to improve the capability of the integrated mills to produce specialties, including copy and release papers.

The fourth alternative was to close one of the company's nonintegrated mills, to drop all but the most profitable specialties such as copy and release papers, and to increase the emphasis on commodity papers.

SHORT- AND LONG-RANGE PLANNING

In determining the appropriate time frame for his division's planning, Boyd reviewed the type of planning which had gone on in the past. In the Copeland Division, as in other company divisions, planning had been limited largely to an annual sales forecast, production forecast, and financial operating budget, which were drawn up during the fourth quarter of each year for the following year. At the corporate level, although no regular long-term planning had been carried on, special studies were sometimes made extending as far as 15 years ahead. For instance, if the company were considering the acquisition of timberlands, tied in with the construction of production facilities in a new region, a 15-year cash flow analysis was made, and Copeland or other divisions affected might be called upon to contribute data.

Boyd knew that there were many activities in his division that could not be fitted into a 1-year planning cycle, but which did not require a 10- to 15-year look into the future. These included new product development, establishing positions in new markets, and adding new production capacity. As an example of the latter, the typical time required for a new paper machine to be constructed and brought to full production capacity, with operating problems all ironed out, was 3 years.

Regardless of which of the four strategy alternatives under consideration were to be adopted, Mr. Boyd knew that plans would have to be drawn up, built around an appropriate time period for their achievement. The division's annual operating budgets would also have to be made to mesh with any longer-term plans that were adopted.

DEVELOPING PLANS AND PROGRAMS

Before drawing up any long-range plans for his division, Boyd felt that it would be necessary to distinguish between those planning activities which had to

be done at the corporate level and those which were more appropriately left to the division. Obviously the determination of overall company objectives, goals, and strategies was a corporate headquarters responsibility. Major capital investments in new regions or in new lines of business would continue to be planned at the corporate level, although Boyd felt that the divisions should play a larger role in such decisions than merely furnishing data inputs when requested.

The main planning areas in which corporate versus divisional responsibility had not yet been spelled out were as follows:

1. Identification and projection of economic, social, and competitive trends affecting the Lewiston-Copeland Company

2. Identification and study of merger or acquisition candidates

3. Anticipating and securing future resource requirements, and allocating resources to divisions

4. Improving the utilization of raw materials, including raw materials not currently being converted at their highest potential economic return

5. Identification and study of specific new product and market opportunities and of the application of new technology to products and processes

6. Proposal of courses of action to be taken on obsolete, marginal, and unprofitable businesses, facilities, and products

7. Setting of specific targets for such performance criteria as earnings and market share

8. Determination of the particular economic and competitive assumptions on which specific forecasts would be based

9. Determination of the general format in which plans were to be drawn up, and the manner in which they were to be presented, approved, and implemented

James Boyd realized that this list was by no means complete, and he was trying to think of other areas which should be included. Some of the planning areas would apply equally to all Lewiston-Copeland divisions, whereas others would apply particularly or uniquely to divisions in the Fibre Products Group, or perhaps just to the Paper Division.

The role that the Copeland Division market managers should play in planning had yet to be decided. There were eight market managers, one for each of the eight product families. These people, who had all worked up through sales, now occupied these recently created staff positions. In the case of specialty products, several of the market managers still retained some of their old customer accounts. Boyd considered these managers to be sales-oriented but "not well trained in abstract thinking." Their main function was to help to develop the markets in their respective product areas. They studied demand trends and present and future customer needs and tried to determine how the division could better satisfy these needs. They helped the line personnel to balance customer demand with machine capabilities. They also provided "top-down" sales forecasts, which were combined with the "bottom-up" forecasts of the field salesmen and sales managers to arrive at a composite sales forecast which became part of the division's annual operating budget.

Some of the division executives, particularly those in manufacturing, felt that the creation of the new market manager positions had made the division too sales oriented. One of these executives, who had been with the company for many years, remarked, "It's nice to look at the market and see what it wants, but in a capital-heavy industry like ours it may be better to look at the paper machines first and see what they can make, and then ask ourselves how we can sell it. This is particularly true in our big new integrated facilities, where there are machine limitations, pulp mill limitations, and fibre species limitations."

Conclusion

As a start toward carrying out the directions given him at the recent planning meetings, Boyd decided to call his division management staff together and discuss with them what the requirements for success were in the commodity paper business and in the specialty paper business. From such a discussion he hoped there would emerge a consensus as to what division objectives were and what the appropriate strategy should be to accomplish those objectives. The main planning area noted earlier would have to be examined, priorities set, plans developed, and programs launched.

To enlist the full cooperation of his management staff in what seemed to them an awesome undertaking, Boyd knew he would have to show them how planning would help make their daily operating jobs easier. Some of the planning activities he would have to do himself and others he could delegate to his subordinates. One of his most important jobs, he felt, would be to provide everyone with a clear sense of direction as they worked their way through the planning process.

Question for Discussion

1. If you were James Boyd, which of the four alternative strategies would you choose and why? How would you subdivide the nine planning areas as corporate, divisional, or joint responsibilities? What strategic planning duties would you assign to the market managers? Describe your overall strategy.

C A S E   1 4
Mt. Ashland Ski Area

It is an exciting time for the Board of Directors of Mt. Ashland Association as they look to the future opportunities awaiting them. Currently the mountain is in such a good financial position that many feel now is the time to improve and increase the existing facil-

This case was prepared by Sidney J. Bowland and Kelly Sanford Hagele, MBA students, under the direction of Professor Thomas Hitzelberger of the School of Business, Southern Oregon University. The data were gathered with the kind cooperation of the Board of Directors and other personnel of the Mt. Ashland Association. This case is intended only as a basis for class discussion and is not intended to illustrate effective or ineffective handling of an administrative situation.

ities. Others, however, are a little uneasy about jumping into any major expenditures, since they are more than aware of the financial problems the ski area has had in the past. The question on everyone's mind is whether a large expansion project will secure the success of the mountain or usher in its demise.

BACKGROUND

At an elevation of 7,520 feet, Mt. Ashland is a part of the Siskiyou Mountain Range in the Rogue River National Forest in southern Oregon, 12 miles from the Oregon-California border and 20 minutes from the town of Ashland.

In the early 1950s, Mt. Ashland was used by local ski enthusiasts who were in search of fresh powder close to home. Dan Bulkley, director of the Physical Education Department at Southern Oregon University (then Southern Oregon State College), started hauling students up the mountain as part of their physical education program. Soon his enthusiasm spread and the community started to see the need for a local ski area.

In 1963, the Mt. Ashland Ski Area was established by a group of individuals who decided to undertake the construction of the ski area. This was the beginning of a string of short-lived ownerships, which eventually led to the purchase of the mountain by the community who first "discovered" her.

Mt. Ashland Corporation, 1963-1974

The Mt. Ashland Corporation was formed by a group of professional people who invested a total of $52,000 to start the corporation. They received a 20-year permit from the U.S. Forest Service covering 800 acres between the elevations of 5,500 and 7,520 feet. It was estimated that the snow fall on the mountain would allow operations to run from December 1 to May 1 each year.

To raise the necessary capital, 5,000 shares of common stock were offered at $100 per share, but only 2,030 shares were sold. Phase 1 in the development process began in the spring of 1963. A cost of $171,500 was projected to cover the following items:

- A 3,900 square foot lodge
- A pomalift
- Rope tows
- Lodge equipment
- A snow cat and packing equipment
- Sewer and water systems
- Annual operating capital of $41,800
- Contingencies

Later, in 1964, because of a lack of capital the Corporation nearly went bankrupt. At that time, a separate nonprofit corporation (Jackson County, Oregon–Mt. Ashland Winter Park and Recreation Facility, Inc.) was established to allow for complete refinancing of the developments on Mt. Ashland through a bond issue of $1.2 million. Through this agreement, Mt. Ashland Corporation had to transfer its assets to the nonprofit corporation and lease them back. And in turn, the nonprofit corporation obtained approval from the bondholder (Investors Diversified Services,

Inc.) to loan funds to the Mt. Ashland Corporation for continued operation. Therefore, the Mt. Ashland Ski Area was financed, owned, and operated by three separate entities.[1] By early 1965, the area was constructed and the financing arrangement finalized. This was the first time anywhere that a ski resort was financed with bonds.

Partial operations of the ski area started during the 1963-1964 ski season. The first complete season of operations occurred the following year. Local newspapers closely followed the new-found success of the mountain. In fact, many ski experts pronounced Mt. Ashland "one of the most magnificent winter sports areas in the entire West."

Throughout the remainder of the 1960s and into the early 1970s, Mt. Ashland was plagued with poor weather conditions (heavy snow and ice) and little growth in attendance. At first the Corporation was able to secure a few loans, but because of its financial position, it was becoming much more difficult to obtain bank financing. Even though operations were approximately on a break-even basis, the Corporation was unable to cover its lease payments to the nonprofit corporation or debt payments to the bondholders. Throughout all of the financial hardships, the Board of Directors still stated that "the future looks most favorable."

There were two major concerns for the management at that time: (1) "the inability to significantly increase paying skier visits in a good weather season," and (2) the average revenue per skier visit was too low when compared with that of other successful operations. Management realized the need to develop a master plan for the area if it was to realize any growth. A physical analysis was done that suggested that unlimited terrain was available for expansion. The Board felt such expansion was "absolutely necessary" to reach financial success, since the terrain available would add the intermediate[2] skiing that Mt. Ashland needed to become competitive in the industry.

By the 1973-1974 ski season, complaints started coming in about the poor condition of the

---

[1]The three entities involved at this point were the (1) operators–Mt. Ashland Corporation; (2) owners–Jackson County, Oregon–Mt. Ashland Winter Park and Recreation Facility, Inc.; and (3) bondholders –Investors Diversified Service, Inc.

[2]Ski terrain is often classified by skier ability level (beginner, intermediate, and expert).

equipment on the mountain. The lease payments had depleted Mt. Ashland's financial reserves to the point that preventative maintenance had never been adequately performed. The corporation faced two problems: (1) the long-range problem of trying to generate enough income to pay the rent, taxes, and forest service fee and (2) the immediate problem of paying the creditors and preparing for the following ski season.

The Board started pursuing different avenues to generate the capital necessary to open for the 1974-1975 ski season with a full or limited operation. Unable to successfully negotiate a loan for necessary repairs and lift restoration, the Board of Directors recommended to the stockholders on August 19, 1974, that Mt. Ashland not open the following ski season. Soon after, the Mt. Ashland Corporation had to declare bankruptcy and close operations.

Southern Oregon Ski Association, 1974-1977

The news that the Mt. Ashland Corporation was discontinuing operations came as a threat to Southern Oregon State College (SOSC), a major stakeholder. Not only did SOSC own 51 percent of the Corporation's outstanding stock, but the local skiing area had become key to maintaining their enrollment levels. Twenty to 25 percent of current students indicated that Mt. Ashland's close proximity was their reason for choosing to enroll at SOSC. The College realized that if the mountain closed it would probably never reopen.

SOSC President James Sours called on five individuals from the college to form a nonprofit organization to take over Mt. Ashland until an appropriate buyer could be found. This new corporation, the Southern Oregon Ski Association, hired a local attorney to complete the transaction paperwork. Investors Diversified Services, Inc. (IDS), agreed that the College would not have to pay the bond payments during its ownership (which was understood to be of short duration).

At the time of takeover, the Association was faced with several operating issues. To resume operations for the 1974-1975 ski season, they had to address the following:

- Outstanding lease debts to the U.S. Forest Service
- Four years of back taxes
- Permit costs
- Loss of the big t-bar's top terminal from excessive snow buildup

- Lack of rental equipment
- Lack of staff

The Association was able to arrange for financing to cover start-up costs and successfully continue operations. By the end of that year, they paid all the bills, started paying the taxes (1 year at a time), paid the Forest Service, and covered operational costs.

The next couple of years were extremely busy for the Association as they aggressively searched for a buyer. The main problem was that IDS refused to accept any amount less than $500,000 to dissolve its interest in the mountain, which had recently been appraised at $230,000. Another problem sprang up when the City of Ashland started discouraging potential buyers by making accusations that the ski area contributed to their lack of quality water.

During the 1976-1977 ski season, the Association made a pitch to the county commissioners to take over the permit and operation of Mt. Ashland. The City of Ashland opposed this plan, since they wanted the mountain closed. In November of that same year, a plan for the public to buy Mt. Ashland was put on the ballot. If it passed, the ski area would be operated by the public park system. However, the plan was narrowly defeated.

Ski Ashland, Inc. (Richard Hicks), 1977-1983

A local businessman and National Ski Patroller, Richard Hicks, purchased the mountain a week after the November 12 election. He met with the Board of Directors at SOSC and gave them his proposal, indicating that he "didn't know much about running a ski area" but wanted to do what he could to keep a place for skiing in the valley. His one and final offer was accepted.

In the process of taking over the mountain's operations, Hicks sought agreement from the other five entities involved up to this point: Southern Oregon Ski Association; Jackson County, Oregon–Mt. Ashland Winter Park and Recreation Facility, Inc.; Investors Diversified Services, Inc.; Mt. Ashland Corporation; and the Forest Service. He cashed out these five entities at the time of purchase, which included paying off the debts of Southern Oregon Ski Association and getting IDS to forgive the bond payments. By the first of December 1977, Ski Ashland, Inc. was born.

When he bought the Mt. Ashland Ski Area, Hicks indicated he would operate it for about 5 years. His first projects were to install the Windsor chairlift, update the mountain's snow grooming equipment and vehicle service facilities, and open the slopes 7 days a week. In addition, he began building excellent rapport with the community, opening the season pass program to students for $100 and maintaining the popular "Kids Ski Free" program. An avid skier himself, Hicks's desire was to run the area from the skiers' perspective. Hicks put every dime that came in directly back into the mountain without taking a salary for himself. Mt. Ashland saw unparalleled success for six seasons in a row, despite the fluctuating snowfall from year to year. Then, in 1983, the Corporation in its entirety was sold to Harbor Properties.

Ski Ashland, Inc. (Harbor Properties), 1983-1991

Harbor Properties was already operating Stevens Pass, one of the most popular ski areas in the State of Washington, and was looking for additional projects that would bring an acceptable return on investment. This corporation bought Ski Ashland, Inc., with a commitment to upgrade the facilities and lay the groundwork for future expansion. They immediately constructed a new vehicle shop and installed lights for night skiing.

The following year, Ski Ashland, Inc., began the planning stages of a site development project "which would steer the development of the ski area over the next decade." Working under the changing requirements of the U.S. Forest Service, it took 3 years for Ski Ashland, Inc., to develop its first draft of the master plan. This plan covered a wide range of alternatives for development, with the most ambitious version proposing the construction of five additional chairlifts and tripling the present skiable terrain. Whichever alternative was finally selected, the Corporation's primary objective in developing the ski area was to adequately and equally address "the capacities of such planning variables as water, sewers, parking, lodge space, lift capacity, terrain mix, and trail capacities."

With ongoing controversy, Ski Ashland, Inc., continued to work on the master plan. In 1987, with Forest Service approval, they were able to build two triple chairlifts to replace the beginner and intermediate surface lifts. Then, in 1991, the final plan was approved. This plan would allow for three additional chairlifts to be constructed and would increase the permit acreage to 1180 acres with a 238-acre "use" area. Despite the U.S. Forest Service approval, each project would have to be thoroughly evaluated in terms of its environmental impact and be approved, once again, before implementation.

In February 1991, Harbor Properties put the ski area up for sale. Among the reasons given for the sale were "centralization of holdings, two consecutive poor snow years, and frustration in regard to the slow planning process." Harbor Properties stated that if the Mt. Ashland Ski Area did not sell within 1 year, they would remove the lifts and relocate them to Stevens Pass. Once again, the community was faced with the prospect of losing the ski area.

Mt. Ashland Association, 1992-Present

Local businessmen Stephen Jamieson and Bob Matthews began a valley-wide campaign to "Save Mt. Ashland." The community rallied around the idea and soon everyone became involved—even the City of Ashland. Jamieson moved the Mt. Ashland Ski Area toward a nonprofit charitable organization that would allow all donations to be tax deductible. The City agreed to accept ownership of the ski area if the nonprofit group was successful in raising the necessary funds. Through extensive fund-raising efforts, the Rogue Valley raised a total of $1.6 million in 2 1/2 months. The ski area was bought from Harbor Properties for $1.3 million, with $300,000 remaining for an operating fund.

When the fervor of the fund-raising was over, ownership was given to the City of Ashland, and management was transferred to a nonprofit corporation, the Mt. Ashland Association, who leased the assets at $1 per year. The mountain had been "saved" again, but the new Association was faced with the reality of having no additional capital. After the first season, the Board of Directors reported they were ahead of budget in both sales and expenses. Sales of season passes were at an all-time high since 1987, and they were confident with the operation.

During the 1993-1994 ski season, Mt. Ashland was voted "Ski Area of the Year" by the Oregon Ski Industry Association. That same year the Board began discussions about future expansion of the area. Glenn Menzie, ski area manager, started working on a 3- to 5-year plan that prioritized all projects (i.e., parking, sewers, water) as they related to future expansion. Since the current septic system was installed under the parking lot as a temporary solution in 1980, the Board prioritized it as first step in expansion.

At the same time, the Board began reviewing the master plan that was developed and approved by the U.S. Forest Service during the Harbor Properties years. This plan focused primarily on two geographic areas, quite far apart, referred to as "the Knoll" and "the North Side." In 1995, the Board contracted with a firm specializing in ski area planning, design, and financial analysis to determine the feasibility of implementing the master plan. It was hoped that such an analysis would enable the Board and management to have a clearer vision of the direction the ski area will be taking and enable them to make informed decisions and set strategic goals.

THE ALTERNATIVES

There are two alternatives available to the Mt. Ashland Association. First of all, they have the option to continue operating the ski area without expanding, as they have done in the past. However, to remain competitive in the future, the Board does not believe this

is the wisest choice. Mt. Ashland is faced with competition from Mt. Bachelor in central Oregon and Mt. Shasta in northern California. These ski areas are, respectively, a 3-hour and a 1 1/2 hour drive away from the region Mt. Ashland serves. Because of its location, Mt. Ashland has something of a captive audience—but only if it continues to offer a competitive product.

The second alternative is to expand the ski area into "the Knoll" and "the North Side" of the mountain. There are many expensive projects that must be undertaken in this second alternative, but such expansion would also allow opportunities for the ski area to achieve higher returns. The U.S. Forest Service has described the approved aspects of each alternative as follows.

Alternative A: No Change

Alternative A is a no-action alternative (see Figure C14-1). In this case, no action means no change from

FIGURE C14-1

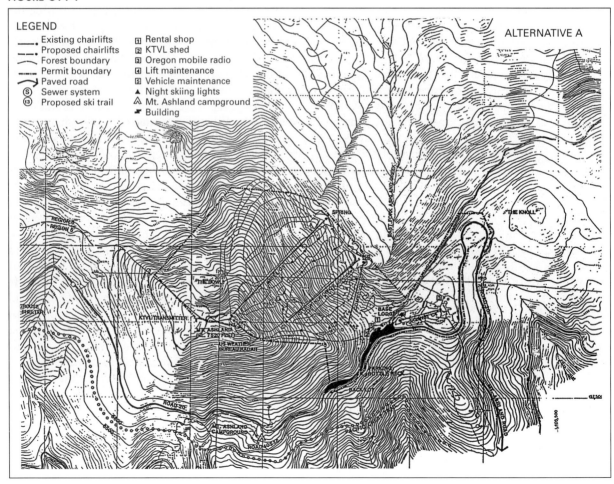

the existing permit and management direction. This alternative would leave the ski area permit boundary at its current location. Developments that are within the current boundary and are within the scope of the current special use permit may be allowed after the required environmental analysis is completed. This alternative includes the following projects.

Projects That Improve Ski Area Management

Project 1: Lodge Modification–Phase 1. This project would include a number of cosmetic repairs to the existing lodge. The objectives of the alterations would be to increase the floor space within the existing building and reorganize the existing space to increase efficiency. The proposal would include a bar and lounge with an outside deck area, dining and food service areas, a retail shop, additional administrative office, expanded ticket sales area, and ski school office.

Project 2: Summer Maintenance Road. This project would access the area west of the Romeo ski run for summer maintenance by constructing approximately 500 feet of road from the bench of the upper terminal of the Comer Lift to the existing road on the west side of Romeo ski run. The road will provide infrequent access to the upper terminal of Windsor chairlift for servicing of the bullwheel and other repairs when necessary.

Project 3: Modification of Ariel Chairlift. This project would modify the Ariel chairlift by moving the upper terminal about 150 feet east and down the slope. The project would prevent the shutdown of the lift because of excessive winds during predominantly southerly storms. During a typical year, this lift may be closed several times. This project would enhance the reliability of ski area operations.

Project 4: Rental Shop and Ticket Booth Modifications. This project would remodel the rental shop and ticket booth to improve their appearance and efficiency. The facility may be slightly enlarged to contain an enlarged Ski Patrol First Aid station. The Ski Patrol First Aid station would be enlarged to a standard of five beds per 1,000 people based on capacity figures. The possibility of combining the rental facilities within the existing ski lodge will also be explored.

Projects That Support the Increased Number of People Using the Ski Area

Project 19: Increased Parking. The amount of additional parking required varies somewhat with capacity. The project would consist of providing access and parking necessary to accommodate the capacity of each alternative. Improvement of access to the "back" parking lot is also considered. For safely purposes, this would include widening the "bottleneck" area to accommodate two-lane traffic.

Project 5: Lodge Modification–Phase 2. This project is within the scope of the current special use permit. However, without additional skiing facilities this lodge expansion is not envisioned. This alternative does not significantly increase the number of skiers at one time. From 1986 to 1989, the average annual growth rate of the Oregon ski industry was over 5 percent. The small parking areas in the vicinity of the lodge would help accommodate this increase in demand. This would provide parking for an additional 50 vehicles.

The downhill ski slopes are currently groomed. Approximately 35 acres on the south side of the mountain has traditionally been used by downhill skiers for the past 27 years, although it is not groomed. Night skiing is also available 3 nights of the week. No snow is made on the ski area because of the lack of adequate water storage area.

Cross-country skiers would continue to use the south side of Mt. Ashland. This use would be unchanged. No cross-country trails would be groomed. Downhill skiers will continue to ski the south side in the vicinity of the Mt. Ashland campground. No developed snow play areas for innertubes would be available.

The lodge would continue to close at the end of the ski season until marketing efforts enhance the summer use of existing facilities. Summer use of the area is predominantly from sightseers who are attracted by the beautiful view along the Siskiyou Crest. Some hikers access the Pacific Crest Trail (PCT) in the vicinity of Grouse Gap for day hikes. Picnicking and camping would continue in the Mt. Ashland campground and on top of Mt. Ashland. Nature study and seekers of solitude would continue. Some rock climbing occurs in the area of "the Bowl." Hunters, especially bowhunters, use the general area in their pursuit of the wily buck.

Alternative B: Expansion

This alternative is in response to public comments for no development on the south side and development on the Knoll (see Figure C14-2). A lift would tie the existing lodge to a new base facility consisting of parking area and lodge. The new lodge would pro-

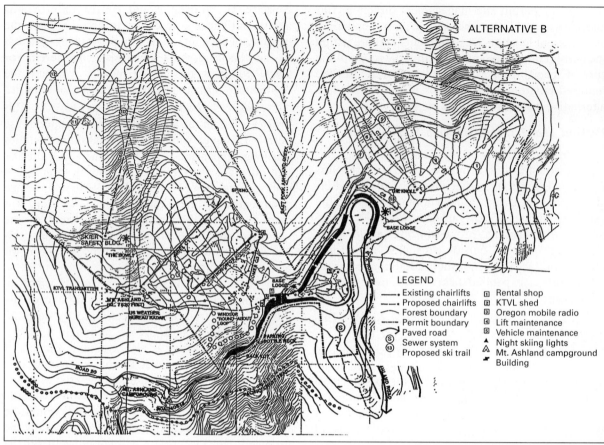

FIGURE C14-2

vide the ancillary facilities to accommodate visitors. Access from the Knoll by skiers would be from a transport lift or, as an interim measure, with a shuttle system from the Knoll to the existing lodge. Construction of the Sonnet parking area would impact the existing sonnet lift. This area would be studied to determine the feasibility of utilizing the Sonnet area for snow play. The following projects would be implemented by this alternative.

Projects That Improve Ski Area Management

Project 1: Lodge Modification–Phase 1. (See description in Alternative A.)

Project 2: Summer Maintenance Road. (See description in Alternative A.)

Project 3: Modification of Ariel Chairlift. (See description in Alternative A.)

Project 4: Rental Shop and Ticket Booth Modifications. (See description in Alternative A.)

Project 5: Lodge Modification–Phase 2. This project would increase the capacity of the ski lodge(s) in a manner that most efficiently serves the calculated capacity of each phase of the alternative. The objective would be to increase the size of the existing lodge and/or construct a new lodge space at the Knoll. Generally, lodge space is based on total capacity with three seat turnovers at 25 gross square feet per seat.

Projects That Increase or Improve Winter Sports Opportunities

Project 6: Windsor Round-About Loop. This project would develop an egress ski trail from the upper terminal of the Windsor chairlift along the southeast side of the mountain. This would provide a long, easy descent with unique vistas to assist the novice and beginning-intermediate skier who might inadvertently use the Windsor lift. Round-trip use of this egress trail will not be encouraged.

Project 11: Cross-Country Ski Facility–Option B. This project would groom approximately 1 mile of cross-country ski trail on Forest Road 20. The permittee would offer cross-country ski lessons on this portion of the trail. The operator would not be required to groom the trail when not in use. The groomed portion of the trail as well as other cross-country opportunities would remain open to the general public at no charge.

Project 12: Chairlift C7A. This project would develop the C7A chairlift. The C7A lift would be approximately 2,600 feet long, originating on the Knoll and extending toward the East Fork of Ashland Creek at a 5,800 foot elevation (see Figure C14-2).

Length:	2,000 feet
Vertical rise:	820 feet
Hourly capacity:	2,400 persons
Seating:	Quad

Project 13: Chairlift C6B. In this option, C6B would originate from a base area within the watershed with an elevation of about 5,900 feet and connect to the terminal moraine below the Bowl at 7,200 feet (see Figure C14-2).

Length:	4,350 feet
Vertical rise:	1,180 feet
Hourly capacity:	1,917 persons
Seating:	Quad

An over-the-snow route would be built for evacuating skiers during a lift failure. This route would extend from the base of C6B to the base of Windsor.

Project 14: Chairlifts C8 and C9. This project would develop two chairlifts and associated ski runs.

The C8 lift would be approximately 850 feet long, originating from the Knoll and terminating below the saddle adjacent to the switchback (see Figure C14-2). The C9 lift would be approximately 2,800 feet long, originating at the Knoll parking and continuing up and over the Knoll, serving as both access to the Knoll skiing and round trip skiing. The ski runs associated with these lifts would cover approximately 25 acres.

These lifts would open the Knoll area, providing skiers with beginner, novice, and low-intermediate skill levels with a natural learning progression in a compact wind-protected sub-ski area with unique vistas (Table C14-1). The development of C8 is contemplated in conjunction with the relocation of the Sonnet lift to the new beginner terrain.

C8:	Length:	850 feet
	Vertical rise:	100 feet
	Hourly capacity:	1,000 persons
	Seating:	double
C9:	Length (total):	2,800 feet
	Vertical rise:	630 feet
	Hourly capacity:	2,400 persons
	Seating:	Quad

Project 16: Summer Use. As with most ski areas, the need exists at Mt. Ashland Ski Area to use established facilities to supplement winter revenues. Most resorts are seeking and finding ways to make use of its assets at times of the year and for purposes other than the skiing season. This project includes a range of opportunities to accommodate year-round use of Mt. Ashland Ski Area facilities. Many of these opportunities are minor in scope; others require additional construction measures, regulation, and/or management requirements. Because of the close, paved access to the Rogue Valley communities and unique subalpine environment with panoramic views, the potential exists to be a summer attraction. Packaging bus tours with theater and lodging components

TABLE C14-1   Downhill Skier Distribution (in percent) by Skier Ability Level

Alternatives	1	2	3	4	5	6	Difference From Ideal (%)
Industry ideal	3	12	27	35	18	4	—
A	0	25	32	15	22	5	47
B	5	21	30	32	11	1	19

Ability levels: 1 = beginner; 2 = novice; 3 = low intermediate; 4 = intermediate; 5 = advanced intermediate; 6 = expert.

would be one such strategy to capitalize on the 300,000 Shakespearean theater visitors to the area per year. Mountain bike rentals or a horseback riding concession could be established. These would be limited to designated roads and trails and be closely regulated. Running or orienteering events, such as races, and specialized music festivals, such as bluegrass, jazz, folk, and classical, have proven successful. Educational seminars such as art, music, photography, and environmental awareness offer the same opportunity for use of existing facilities. If lift service is achieved with chairlifts C10 or C9 (see Figure C14-2), additional opportunities will exist for lift rides and scenic viewing. Observation decks may be located to take advantage of the beautiful scenery. Nature trails and interpretive programs may be developed to increase visitor awareness of the local environment.

Projects That Support the Increased Number of People Using the Ski Area

Project 19: Increased Parking. (See description in Alternative A.)

Project 20: Increased Sewage Treatment. This project would consist of constructing additional sewage treatment capacity. The Forest Service would select the best alternative. The Forest Service, in conjunction with the appropriate county and state agencies, would determine the necessary design requirements. Preliminary studies have identified areas suitable for developing a sewage system.

Project 21: Increased Water Storage. This project would consist of providing additional water storage capacity. This would include a site specific study of all of the alternatives, including any necessary hydrological and geological studies to ensure the safety of the system. The Forest Service would select the best alternative. The Forest Service, in conjunc-

tion with the appropriate county and state agencies, would determine the necessary design requirements.

Preliminary investigations indicate that this project may involve the construction of an approximately 40,000-gallon water storage tank in addition to the current tank. At this time three potential sites have been inventoried: (1) near the present tank above the upper terminal of the Comer lift, (2) in the already existing trench of the present Comer lift bullwheel, and (3) under the off-ramp of Sonnet chairlift. The amount of additional water storage needed varies with capacity.

Project 22: Knoll Access (Transfer Lift). To provide Mt. Ashland skiers with access between the existing base area and the proposed development at the Knoll, two primary techniques have been identified. With limited Knoll development, a shuttle bus concept has been proposed. With more extensive ski development, such as discussed above, a transfer lift would provide a more efficient access option. Depending on the phasing of the Knoll development, a shuttle bus may serve as an interim transfer system.

A DECISION MUST BE MADE

A good year will bring 85,000 skier visits to Mt. Ashland and, at its current size, additional skiers are not projected. The Board of Directors feels that without upgrading the area, they may even be unable to meet the needs of their current skiers. However, everyone knows that changing weather conditions can put financial strain on the ski area. Because of this, the Board feels one of Mt. Ashland's greatest assets is that it has no debt.

In reviewing the alternatives (Tables C14-2 and C14-3), they must be viewed from two perspectives. First, it is important to consider the best investment

TABLE C14-2 Summary of Alternatives		
Element	*Alternative A: No Change*	*Alternative B: Expansion*
Gross area	290 acres	1,180 acres
Use area	120 acres	239 acres
Total capacity	1,658 people	4,795 people
Lifts	Four chairlifts	Eight chairlifts
Lodge	One existing lodge	Two lodges
Square feet	17,695	39,961
Parking	600 vehicles	1905 vehicles
Sewage	9,000 gallons/day	37,000 gallons/day
Water	115,000 gallon storage (existing)	155,000 gallon storage (required)

TABLE C14-3   Capital Cost Estimates by Project

Project No.	Description	Project Cost ($)
1	Lodge modification—phase I	200,000
2	Summer maintenance road	25,000
3	Modification of Ariel chairlift	70,000
4	Rental shop and ticket booth modification	40,000
5	Lodge modification—phase II	1,450,000
6	Windsor round-about loop	25,000
11	Cross-country ski facility—option B	NA
12	Chairlift C7A	936,000
13	Chairlift C6B	1,394,000
14	Chairlifts C8 and C9	1,223,000
16	Summer use	NA
19	Increased parking	900,000
20	Increased sewage treatment	150,000
21	Increased water storage	75,000
22	Knoll access (transfer lift)	150,000

option. How can the Mt. Ashland Association achieve the highest return on their investment? Second, how are they going to pay for those investments?

The Board of Directors have discussed the alternatives over the past season and have not yet decided on a specific plan. Should they take the "safer" alternative and continue to focus only on upgrading the present facility? Or should they step out and adopt an extensive expansion project? Given the span of 10 years and the individual project costs involved, which alternative should the Board choose and how should they implement that alternative?

Questions for Discussion

1. What future goals do the Board of Directors have for Mt. Ashland? Are these goals consistent with the overall mission of the corporation?
2. Review the current position of the Mt. Ashland ski area from a business perspective. What are the important strategic issues for marketing?
3. Review the financial situation of Mt. Ashland Association and evaluate its ability to expand operations in the near future.
4. Given the financial history of the ski area, how should the Mt. Ashland Association arrange to pay for any necessary upgrades or expansion projects without jeopardizing their future existence?
5. Evaluate both alternatives. What would be the best order to implement the given projects, both financially and logistically?
6. What market factors should be emphasized in the development of Alternative B?

Bibliography

"Ski resort purchase assured," The Oregonian (April 15, 1992), p. B06.

Board of Directors' minutes, Mt. Ashland Corporation, 1963-1974.

Board of Directors' minutes, Mt. Ashland Association, 1992-1996.

"County to accept ski facilities by deed of gift," Ashland Daily Tidings (November 25, 1964).

"Early snow brings skiers, hope to long-suffering ski Ashland area," The Oregonian (December 18, 1992), p. D04.

Final Environmental Impact Statement: Mt. Ashland Ski Area, U.S. Department of Agriculture–U.S. Forest Service, Ashland Ranger District, Rogue River National Forest, Oregon, 1991.

Richard, Terry, "$1.7 million fund drive begins to save Mount Ashland ski area," The Oregonian (January 31, 1992), p. E04.

Richard, Terry, "Public rode to ski area rescue," The Oregonian (February 4, 1993), p. C04.

"Roberts routes lottery funds to help Ashland buy ski area," The Oregonian (April 1, 1992), p. B08.

"Ski area purchase extended," The Oregonian (April 8, 1992), p. C02.

APPENDIX A
Mt. Ashland Association Financial Statements

Statement of Activities

Revenues, Gain, and Other Support	1992-1993	1993-1994	1994-1995
Ski lifts	$974,841	$1,059,648	$1,411,136
Ski shop operations	256,357	291,788	354,323
Lodge and bar	156,314	151,312	179,703
Ski school	126,724	134,804	150,895
Other income	3,866	11,378	35,126
TOTAL SKI OPERATIONS	1,518,102	1,648,930	2,131,183
Contributions	343,284	—	—
Interest income	22,697	29,929	82,752
Net assets released from restriction	—	406,548	448,548
TOTAL REVENUES, GAINS, AND OTHER SUPPORT	1,884,083	2,085,407	2,662,483
Costs and Expenses			
Ski lifts	352,297	411,294	575,819
Ski shop operations	78,922	108,030	158,533
Lodge and bar	86,964	97,732	130,461
Ski school	55,486	72,612	118,192
General and administrative	443,601	470,480	395,730
Marketing	42,519	50,649	60,769
Depreciation	1,278	30,671	82,591
Facility lease	—	406,548	406,548
TOTAL COSTS AND EXPENSES	1,061,067	1,648,016	1,928,643
INCREASE (DECREASE) IN NET ASSETS	823,016	437,391	733,840
NET ASSETS—beginning of year	—	823,016	1,260,407
NET ASSETS—end of year	$823,016	$1,260,407	$1,994,247

Statement of Financial Position

Assets	1992-1993	1993-1994	1994-1995
Cash	$ 50,984	$38,496	$5,876
Investments	767,488	1,017,452	1,600,661
Contributions receivable	6,750	1,950	—
Inventories	9,577	13,770	15,421
Deposits	24,585	2,070	9,795
Capital assets	16,611	223,090	417,830
Contributed facility lease	—	—	—
TOTAL ASSETS	$875,995	$1,296,828	$2,049,583
Liabilities			
Accounts payable and accrued expenses	52,979	36,421	55,336
NET ASSETS	823,016	1,260,407	1,994,247
TOTAL LIABILITIES AND NET ASSETS	$875,995	$1,296,828	$2,049,583

APPENDIX B
Mt. Ashland and Oregon Skier Visits

Season Ending	Mt. Ashland Skier Visits	Total Oregon Skier Visits	Mt. Ashland Market Share (percent)	Mt. Ashland Skier Vistis	Mt. Ashland Skier Visits	Mt. Ashland Skier Visits
				Great Year	*Average Year*	*Poor Year*
1964	9,000	498,604	1.81			
1965	48,311	392,208	12.32		48,311	
1966	59,200	476,965	12.41	59,200		
1967	90,207	495,441	18.21	90,207		
1968	57,402	484,479	11.85		57,402	
1969	53,805	499,524	10.77		53,805	
1970	61,706	569,638	10.83		61,706	
1971	62,295	700,170	8.90		62,295	
1972	77,711	720,222	10.79		77,711	
1973	59,595	640,077	9.31		59,595	
1974	81,908	796,006	10.29		81,908	
1975	53,585	859,222	6.24			53,585
1976	59,728	898,126	6.65			59,728
1977	15,041	399,075	3.77			15,041
1978	53,749	962,242	5.59			53,749
1979	24,085	975,334	2.47			24,085
1980	67,875	1,194,614	5.68		67,875	
1981	37,423	868,282	4.31			37,423
1982	67,934	1,260,286	5.39		67,934	
1983	60,401	1,252,939	4.82		60,401	
1984	62,240	1,219,141	5.11		62,240	
1985	78,463	1,457,449	5.38	78,463		
1986	41,184	1,255,132	3.28			41,184
1987	45,619	1,383,423	3.30			45,619
1988	67,136	1,408,192	4.77		67,136	
1989	79,836	1,537,871	5.19	79,836		
1990	39,713	1,517,788	2.62			39,713
1991	49,700	1,564,251	3.18			49,700
1992	30,000	1,610,715	1.86			30,000
1993	87,512	1,452,831	6.02	87,152		
1994	82,594	1,466,244	5.63	82,594		
1995	104,744	1,574,938	6.65	104,744		
Average for 1965-1995	60,023	1,028,801				

C A S E   1 5
P. Reid and Associates

MARKETING PROFESSIONAL AND BUSINESS SERVICES

Many people ask, "What makes a business service company successful?" This question is gaining importance as America moves more and more toward a service-oriented economy. Although manufacturing has enjoyed a healthy resurgence, the significance of the service side of the economy is

Written by John F. Asma of ASMA Seismic Company, a marketing and records management consultant.

apparent. At least part of manufacturing's uprising is due to the weak U.S. dollar. It is certain the service economy in the United States will remain substantial and growing. Perhaps the question people should be asking is, "How do we become successful in professional business services?"

We chose a successful Records and Information Management and Litigation Support Company, P. Reid and Associates, based in Houston, Texas. PRA has enjoyed strong growth and profitability since its inception in 1985. During a time when the Houston economy had been enduring its own recession PRA was active in the utility, oil and gas, petrol, and legal fields. The main reason, among many, for its success is the company's faith, optimism, expertise, and sense of humor in litigation support and records management of the president and founder, Ms. Peggy Reid.

PMA'S MARKETING PLAN

Support of the Trade Associations

At the core of PRA's marketing program is its active support and membership in the relevant trade associations for its industry. Many contacts have been made by Ms. Reid and her staff through regular attendance at the meetings of the Houston chapter of the Association of Records Managers and Administrators (ARMS). These contacts have generated many leads.

Testimonials and Referrals

These leads are second only to testimonials and referrals from satisfied customers. "Word-of-mouth" advertising has proven to be the best form of promotion for any business or professional service organization, but it is the most difficult to activate. Similar to establishing a credit history, a company has to have a second loan before the first loan has been accepted.

Seminars and Speeches

The third element of the marketing program has been seminars and speeches given by Ms. Reid and her staff members for the purposes of educating interested parties around the country in the fundamentals of records management and litigation support.

Strong accrediting, experience, and credentials are the reasons for PRA staffers' invitations to speak throughout the country. PRA has three Certified Records Managers on its staff, more than any other R.M. consultant in its region.

Consultants Market Themselves

PRA does not have a sales staff, per se. They rely on the individual consultants to market themselves while on the job and between jobs. In this way, PRA foregoes the expense of outside sales personnel and ensures that knowledgeable, experienced company representatives describe PRA and its services to potential clients. PRA uses professional marketing consultants for marketing training and identification and discussion of the sales cycle for intangible products and services. In-house seminars are given on many topics that either directly or indirectly affect the marketing effort.

A recent meeting was held to discuss the rise of specific software to improve communications among consulting staff, office personnel, and ultimately, the client. PRA realizes that other service consulting firms may hire outside salespeople, but it believes in-house people can perform well, given proper training, thus saving the expense of hiring a sales force. Other service companies in this market, for example, data storage and micrographics companies, use relatively aggressive sales techniques, including the deployment of full sales staffs.

Professional Team Approach

The fifth element in the marketing program is the *professional team approach,* which uses project management software, teamwork, shared expertise, and the passing on of leads. In addition to a strong presence in ARMA, PRA also associates itself with fringe trade groups and lists its services in many related trade journals. Often, listings in trade journals and directories are free for the asking.

Trade Journal Advertising

The next step in the program is advertising in trade journals and other publications. Printed brochures are distributed annually to clients and potential clients. This keeps PRA's literature current and abreast of changes in the various industries it serves. Quarterly mailings of brochures help to keep the company's name in front of past and potential clients.

Trade Shows

Trade show participation and attendance is also important. A small but well-organized booth can be a worthwhile promotion, especially at regional shows where local or known clients may pass the booth.

Direct Marketing

The promotional program is further enhanced by direct mail campaigns initiated by telemarketing programs organized and implemented by the consultants. Formal telemarketing training is provided to the consultants, who are very thrilled when the records management consultant achieves success after only a few telemarketing training sessions. This type of training also helps improve overall communications effectiveness.

Help From Third-Party Vendors

The last component of the marketing program is the judicious use of third-party vendors, such as filing equipment and storage sales companies, for reciprocal referral and information. It is absolutely imperative to remain impartial and unattached so as not to appear biased. If a consultant, other professional, or industrial service company, can maintain a nonaligned status through third-party vendors, much information can be exchanged to facilitate the gathering of more complete and professional knowledge about any project.

TWELVE-POINT MARKETING PROGRAM

PRA has found success and growth by a dedication to fundamentals and education and by the implementation of the following twelve-point marketing program:

1. Referrals from satisfied customers
2. Trade association membership and support
3. Seminars and speeches by staff members
4. Strong accrediting, experience, and credentials
5. Marketing by staff consultants who receive professional training
6. Professional team approach and sharing of leads

7. Association with fringe trade groups
8. Advertising brochures and quarterly mailings
9. Trade show participation and attendance
10. Direct mail marketing by office staff
11. Telemarketing by records consultants
12. Judicious use of referrals and information on a reciprocal basis with third-party vendors

Marketers of professional and business services can find ways to implement many elements of this comprehensive program to the mutual advantage of the company and self.

Questions for Discussion

1. Does the twelve-point marketing plan, as practiced by P. Reid and Associates, overlook any important marketing points or significant concepts? If so, what are they?

2. Would this type of marketing program work for an engineering consultant, a CPA, or an engineering consulting firm? Why?

3. Can a business/industrial advertising agency use the twelve-point program? Why?

CASE 16
Phoenix Porcelain Company (A)

MARKETING RESEARCH AND COMPETITIVE INTELLIGENCE

The Phoenix Porcelain Company (PPC)[1] is a wholly owned subsidiary of the Phoenix Brewing Company of Phoenix, Arizona. It is the world's largest supplier of technical ceramic products. The company has had a long history of producing and marketing industrial ceramics, beginning operations during World War I.

PPC produces ceramic products that fill critical needs in many industrial fields, namely, energy development and production, transportation, food processing, raw material processing, communications, computers, health care, and recreation. It has produced ceramics primarily from aluminum oxide

[1]Fictitious name. We would like to thank Elsa Angel, W.C. Dickens, Jim Sirko, and Terry Young for their contribution to this case.

(alumina), but in the last 8 to 10 years it has been developing a revolutionary ceramic from zirconium oxide (zirconia). This product's properties are characterized as having greater strength and impact resistance or toughness than the ceramic made from aluminum oxide. The research and development engineers believe this new product may be ready for commercialization.

The engineers speculated that if more truck engine parts were made of ceramic, then higher temperatures could be withstood, the engine would required less fuel and would be more efficient, with fewer breakdowns, and a longer life, and would require fewer replacement parts. Since truck engines were driven for more than 200,000 miles with proper maintenance, an engine that could last longer and require less maintenance would meet a profitable market need. A material that could increase the operating temperatures of a diesel engine would be desirable among professional truckers, truck lines, and others who are concerned with their diesel operating costs and length of engine life. Phoenix Porcelain believes that transformation toughened zirconia (TTZ) has the potential to be that material.

FUTURE TRUCK ENGINE

The company's engineers and product management people speculated that a truck engine made of mostly TTZ could be built. Such an engine would have great promise because of the lightness and greater efficiency of a ceramic engine. It would have no need for a cooling system, because the combustion chamber would be so well insulated with the new ceramic that it could withstand extreme heat. Without the cooling system's radiator, the owner would forget about leaks or drainage. This adiabatic engine is far from final development and commercialization. Additional development is needed before a match between the engine's final design and the properties of TTZ can be determined. The adiabatic engine's cast iron block presents problems for the developer, however.

ENGINEERING AND PRODUCTION PROBLEMS

Transformation toughened zirconia (TTZ) has problems in that its microstructure has been modified by magnesia stabilization to produce a material that is strong, tough, and durable. It possesses good thermal shock resistance, but its newness creates difficulty in maintaining consistent material properties and strength from one production batch to another. PPC had completed a testing program on ten batches of zirconia and achieved the test data shown in Table C16-1.

As shown, with refinement of the product available today, the company stands a 5 percent risk of producing a part with inadequate fracture toughness and a 9 percent chance of producing a part with inadequate flex strength. Much optimism exists that the company will achieve all desired performance criteria in the immediate future as evidenced by the company's ongoing testing program. PPC is currently producing fifteen tappet inserts to be shipped to a truck manufacturer for testing purposes. the results of the test will be used to further improve the validity and reliability of TTZ. The product's use in a diesel engine is illustrated in Figure C16-1.

MARKET RESEARCH

Encouraged by the technical success and the material's great promise, PPC forged ahead with TTZ's market feasibility analysis. Jim Stone, the product manager assigned the task to develop the marketing program for TTZ, was optimistic as he pinpointed the vigorous production compliance of tapped inserts and cam follower inserts to customer specifications before other firms, including the aggressive Japanese firms, beat them to market. Once a firm becomes established in this market as a reliable supplier, its market hold could strengthen to preclude the entrance of any other suppliers.

Stone's use of a decision tree analysis, as illustrated in Figure C16-2, concluded that the market could be segmented among OEM and end user customers who manufacture either internal combustion or diesel engines. If wear on passenger car engines is

TABLE C16-1 Ten-Batch Test Program TTZ	
Parameters	*TTZ*
Flex strength range	70-125 (KPSI)
Mean (x)	94 (KPSI)
Standard deviation(s)	11 (KPSI)
Fracture toughness range	7-12 Meganewtons/meter
Mean (x)	8.5 Meganewtons/meter
Standard development (T)	2.1 Meganewtons/meter
Assumed strength and stability for TTZ use in a tappet insert are	
Flex strength $\quad = 85$ KPSI	
Fracture toughness $\quad = \dfrac{MN}{7\,M^{2/3}}$	

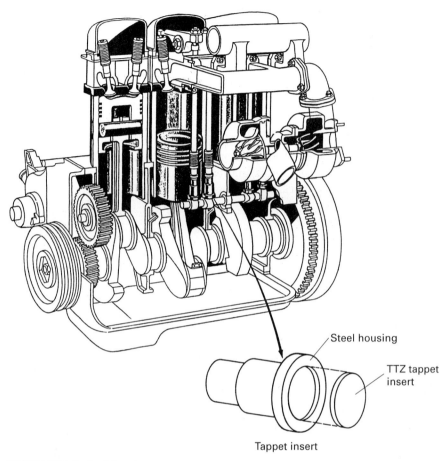

FIGURE C16-1 Steel housing.

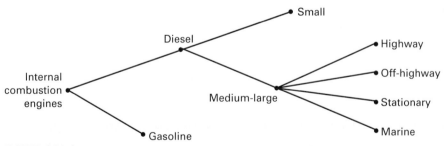

FIGURE C16-2 Decision tree indicating segmentation of potential market and recommended segment for Phoenix Porcelain Company to target.

not as great, because of shorter trips and lower operating temperatures, Stone suggested the company target the medium- and heavy-duty diesel engine manufacturers. Four basic types of diesel engines are produced: highway, off-highway, stationary, and marine engines. All four applications would qualify as medium- to heavy-duty diesel use and be included in PPC's initial target market.

COMPETITIVE FORCES

Compared with its competitors, PPC is in an excellent position. Its good relations with Cummins Engine, which had tested ceramic inserts from PPC before, will provide PPC an advantage in experience and exposure for both the adiabatic diesel and for the tapped inserts. Competitive forces, shown in Exhibit C16-1, are very formidable, with several

================================ EXHIBIT C16-1 ================================

Competitor Profiles

Domestic

Carborundum Co. **(subsidiary of Kennecott Copper Co.)**
Niagara Falls, New York

Manufacturers of silicon carbide, aluminum oxide, grinding wheels, coated abrasives, grains and powders; tumbling media and equipment, abrasive cut-off equipment additives; advanced refractories; heating elements, ceramic fiber in many forms; thermistors, varistors and power resistors; refractories, catalyst carriers, ceramics for electronics; heat exchangers, pumps for molten metals, pollution control equipment, irrigation equipment.

> Employees: 19,641
> Sales and income data not available
> Carborundum is said to be actively working with zirconia at this time.

Norton Co.
Chemical Process Products
Akron, Ohio

Their three major business lines include abrasives, petroleum mining products and services, and diversified products. Diversified products include industrial ceramics, plastic products, tubing and sealants, industrial safety products, and chemical process products.

   Their ceramic business primarily involves alumina, but they are said to be actively working with zirconia also. They are also a manufacturer of ball mills, a piece of equipment used in the process of forming ceramic products.

> Employees: 24,400
> Net Sales in 1986: $1,334,626,000
> Net Income: $95,049,000

Zircoa Products
Ceramic Products Division
Solon, Ohio

Zircoa's primary business is the manufacture of zirconium oxide and zirconium dioxide refractories. Zirconium dioxide is fabricated into standard customer shapes, including nozzles, crucibles, tubes, plates, saggers, brick, and rods.

> Employees: 200

Foreign

Feldmuehle AG
West Germany

> SIC Codes: 6711, 2631, 2641, 3079, 2621
> Employees: 8836
> Known to be working with zirconia and have some products on the market.

Competitor Profiles—cont'd

Kyoto Ceramic Co., Ltd.
Japan

SIC Codes: 3674, 3253
Employees: 5058

Developed a 3-cylinder, 2.8 liter test engine made of silicon nitride and silicone carbide. It was found to be 30 percent more fuel efficient and lighter than a comparable steel engine. Not known to be actively working with or optimistic about zirconia.

NGK Insulators
Japan

SIC Codes: 3264, 3567, 3469
Employees: 4707

NGK's primary business lines are insulating materials and water and sewage treatment equipment. They are also working with Cummins Diesel and zirconia on the adiabatic engine technology. Their engine is also cast iron with zirconia parts insulating the combustion chamber. NGK is, therefore, the most immediate and significant competition for PPC. About 50 percent of the company's output is now exported to the United States in the form of catalytic converters.

NGK Spark Plug Co., Ltd.
Japan

SIC Codes: 3714, 3264, 3251
Employees: 3748

NGK has tested a 50 cc single cylinder, two stroke engine with an alumina crankcase and silicon nitride cylinder head, pistons, rods, and crankshaft. They do not believe that the cast iron zirconia engine is the engine of the future.

Oliver J. Nilsen, Ltd.
Australia

Nilsen is a diversified company involved in electrical equipment manufacturing; powder metallurgy; broadcasting; and porcelain, ceramics, and refractories. They are actively working with and promoting zirconia. Since Australia provides 85 percent of more of the world zirconium used, Nilsen could be a significant threat to PPC. Nilsen is considered the quality leader in zirconia primarily because of their consistent products.

Japanese companies already producing prototype ceramic diesels. Many of these engines are not using the zirconia cast iron concept developed by Cummins Engines. Kyoto Ceramics built a three-cylinder 2.8 liter engine made of silicon nitride rather than zirconia. NGK Spark Plug produced a 50 cc single cylinder gasoline engine made of alumina, silicon nitride, and a few small metal parts. NKG Insulators is working with Cummins Diesel on a diesel engine with a cast iron structure and ceramic components, which poses the greatest competitive threat to Phoenix Porcelain Company's market entrance.

U.S. GOVERNMENT ACTIONS

The U.S. Department of Energy's Oak Ridge National Laboratories has been working on oxides, lumina, and zirconia, and NASA has been examining the nonoxides such as silicon carbide and silicon nitride. These programs were motivated by the great potential of ceramics and the Japanese market encroachment threat. Some of the work was distributed to universities and some was given to the Phoenix Porcelain Company. A lack of federal money stymied further governmental work. The industry feared that the Japanese would become the first to build the first commercially successful adiabatic diesel engine, which could gravely injury the U.S. diesel engine industry.

In contrast to the small amount of federal funds available, the Japanese government had allocated $60 million toward industrial ceramic development over the next 10 years.

Their "moonlight project" is a cooperative effort between private industry and the Japanese government to provide a basic body of knowledge of industrial ceramics. Their intention, as usual, is to dominate the world market by the middle 1990s. This competitive threat is realistic since the Japanese thrive on an export economy, while their domestic consumption and standard of living is below most of the other industrial nations in the free world.

Questions for Discussion

1. Evaluate the company's overall marketing research system.
2. Do you think its competitive intelligence system is adequate? What should be added, if anything?
3. Is the company's market optimism warranted or is it colored by an undue amount of optimism?
4. If you were in Mr. Stone's position, what would you propose as the market research design and the competitive intelligence systems to improve both systems?

CASE 17

Phoenix Porcelain Company (B)

DEMAND ANALYSIS AND SALES FORECASTING

The following week on Monday morning, Jim Stone was to present his sales forecast to top PPC[1] management. He drew the available competitive information and the data collected from the marketing research study conducted in Case 16.

MARKET SEGMENT

Given the properties of transformation toughened zirconia (TTZ), the marketing people believe it may fit a very desirable "marketing niche" as a ceramic insert in the high-wear areas of the valve tappet or cam followers in a diesel engine. All diesel engines have one or the other. Other high-wear applications exist, according to the engineers, within internal

[1]Fictitious name. We would like to thank Elsa Angel, W.C. Dickens, Jim Sirko, and Terry Young for their contribution to this case.

combustion (IC) or gasoline engines. IC engine applications would include valve guides, cylinder liners, lifters, pushrod tips, and valve seats, all high-wear, high-heat engine contact points. These particular parts of an engine are critical to the life of the engine and may wear much faster than other engine parts. Presently, metal components are used in these areas, but they wear much more quickly at temperatures of 850 degrees because metal does not have the property to dissipate or transfer heat as rapidly as does ceramic. This is particularly true when a hot engine is turned off and the operation heat transfer systems become dysfunctional since the engine experiences a reduced volume of air intake.

TARGET MARKETS

After additional analysis, the original target markets were changed as Stone estimated that PPC's target market for TTZ should be the producers of medium- and heavy-duty diesel engines used for

Diesel Engine Producers

Bendix Corporation
Southfield, Michigan

Their business lines include automotive, aerospace electronics and industrial products. Automotive parts are made for cars, light trucks, and medium and heavy trucks. These include air braking systems and components, air compressors, valves and brake actuators; fan clutches, air dryers, foundation brakes; manual and automatic slack adjusters, and friction material.

> Employees: 69,600
> Bendix is already a customer of PPC, so their business would be desirable in the automotive wear parts market.

Dana Corporation
Toledo, Ohio

Their businesses include vehicular products such as axles, frames, transmissions, universal joints, clutches, engines, and other parts sold to manufacturers of on-highway motor vehicles and for use as service parts. Industrial products include those manufactured and marketed for off-highway vehicles.

> Employees: 35,200

Burgess-Norton
Geneva, Illinois

Manufacturers of piston pins, cold extruded parts, hardened and ground screw-machine products, powdered metal products and foundry products.

> Employees: 1,100

Onan Corporation (subsidiary of McGraw-Edison Company)
Minneapolis, Minnesota

Manufacturers of stationary power machinery including electric generator sets, generators, engines, and load transfer switches.
> Their goal is to penetrate the auto and truck diesel markets.

> Employees: 2,688

Sealed Power Corporation
Muskegon, Michigan

Manufacturer of precision metal products by casing, stamping, and extruding such as pistons rings, cylinder sleeves, valve tappets, filter products, and auto compressors. They also distribute internationally and domestically a complete line of gas and diesel engine parts produced by themselves and others.

> Employees: 5,000

OEM Profiles

Chrysler Corporation
Highland Park, Michigan

Manufacturer of automobiles, trucks, related parts and accessories, engines, powder metal products, chemical products, inboard marine engines, outboard motors, and vinyl fabrics. Chrysler is working on a truck diesel engine with ceramic wear parts. They have worked mostly with SiC but are good potential targets for using zirconia.

   SIC Codes: 3711, 2295, 2899, 3399, 3519, 3714
   Employees: 133,811

Cummins Engine
Columbus, Indiana

Cummins is the over-the-road engine manufacturer with 52 percent of the market. They are also the leader in adiabatic engine development and are already working with PPC and testing PPC zirconia parts. PPC should carefully cultivate and encourage this relationship because of the industry position of Cummins.

   Employees: 22,788

Caterpillar Tractor Co.
Mossville, Illinois

Manufactures earth-moving, construction, and materials handling machinery and equipment and diesel, turbine, and natural gas engines. Its engines are used in its own and other manufacturers of tractors and trucks. Fifty-six percent of its sales were to markets outside the United States in 1986. They are already evaluating ceramic components for diesel and gas turbine engines, but are not willing to talk at this time. They will need to be pursued eagerly but delicately.

Detroit Diesel Allison **(Division of General Motors)**
Detroit, Michigan

Manufacturer of heavy-, medium-, and light-duty diesel engines, heavy-duty transmissions and aircraft and industrial gas turbines.
   DDA is developing its own adiabatic engine, but they are not as far along as Cummins. They are still evaluating silicon carbide and zirconia as potential component materials. This relationship will also take time and work to cultivate.

   SIC Codes: 3519, 3511, 3714
   Employees: 25,000

Ford Motor Company
Detroit, Michigan

Manufacturer of passenger cars and trucks. Ford is testing materials but is not very open about its work. Relationship will need to be cultivated.

OEM Profiles—cont'd

Navistar International Corporation
Chicago, Illinois

Manufactures diesel and gas-powered trucks from 19,501 to 128,000 lb gross vehicle weight. They also manufacture equipment for agricultural and construction applications. They do not appear to be actively involved in the ceramic component research.

Employees: 39,020 in United States

Eaton Corporation
Southfield, Michigan

Product lines include electronic and electrical parts, and vehicle components, including truck components, mechanical transmissions, drive and trailer axles, brakes, locking differentials, engine valves, hydraulic valve lifters, tire valves, leaf springs, viscous fan drives, power steering pumps, thermostats, air conditioning equipment, couplings, hose and tubing for over-the-road trucks. Also supply passenger car and off-highway vehicle components.

They are actively investigating ceramic materials for engine components and are interested in zirconia. They have been receptive to PPC's overtures and are a good prospect to cultivate.

Employees: 48,933

Mack Trucks
Allentown, Pennsylvania

Their business includes manufacture of heavy-duty trucks and truck tractors. They are very interested in zirconia wear parts from PPC.

Employees: 13,011

---

over-the-road trucks, farm equipment, and construction machinery. These segments offered the greatest potential for the eventual adiabatic diesel applications. If the company could get started with zirconia by selling parts as a market entry, then by the time the adiabatic engine was ready, PPC could have its market reputation in the zirconia market. Exhibit C17-1 lists those companies that supply engines and engine parts. In addition to selling OEM, Phoenix Porcelain Company must placate the aftermarket, namely, the parts suppliers and distributors. Encouraging the OEM people to specify Phoenix's TTZ high-wear parts forces the aftermarket to stock these replacement parts. Hence, the company can drive or push the product through the replacement market. A list of OEMs appears in Exhibit C17-2.

SALES FORECASTING

The trend for many segments in the industrial market is toward greater durability and increased efficiency. TTZ is exactly the material needed to attain these objectives. The market for ceramic parts has existed since the middle 1980s for diesel-powered trucks, equipment, ships, and generators.

Jim Stone, working with the marketing research department, generated a sales forecast for the next 3 years that was based on two assumptions:

1. The United States will enjoy a stable economy during the forecast years of 1992, 1993, and 1994.

2. The sales forecasts are very conservative, using very conservative estimates and assumptions.

Stone concluded that the best potential market for Phoenix Porcelain Company would be the

TABLE C17-1	Sales Forecast, 1992-1994 (in units)		
Category	*1992*	*1993*	*1994*
Truck	30,436	97,258	173,364
Farm equipment	29,960	94,374	166,727
Construction	17,600	55,664	97,872
Mining	216	708	1,248
Oil field equipment	1,296	4,548	8,868
Pumps	132	432	756
Compressors	1,032	3,312	5,844
Boats	752	2,432	4,336
Ships	624	2,016	3,585

TABLE C17-2	Projected Sales, First Year, 1992, for Over-the-Road Trucks, Farm Machinery, and Construction (in units)					
Growth Rate Percentage of Total	*Units Sold*	*Percentage Using Ceramics*	*PPC Share*	*PPC Units*	*Numbers of Parts*	*PPC Total*
6.0% Over-the-road	289,910	.05	.15	2,174	14	30,436
5.0% Farm machinery	285,325	.05	.15	2,140	14	29,960
5.5% Construction	146,559	.05	.15	1,099	16	17,584
TOTAL PPC PARTS (1992)						77,980

medium and heavy diesel engines used in the following applications:

- Over-the-road trucks
- Farm machinery
- Construction equipment
- Mining
- Oil field equipment
- Pumps
- Compressors
- Ships and boats

The first three categories will account for more than 95 percent of the diesel engines sold, and PPC should identify these areas as their target markets. Since medium- and heavy-duty diesel manufacturers produce multipurpose engines, Stone expected to be able to cover virtually the entire diesel market by successfully marketing the value of the high-wear parts to the four key domestic engine manufacturers, namely, Caterpillar, Cummins, Navistar International, and Detroit Diesel Allison, to name a few. Table C17-1 shows Stone's sales forecasts.

Table C17-2 provides a finer breakdown in how Stone analyzed the first year, 1992, sales forecast for over-the-road trucks, farm machinery, and construction.

Questions for Discussion

1. Should PPC undertake the zirconia diesel engine market challenge projected in 1992 with the assumption that costs would be subordinate to revenues?

2. Should they tackle the gasoline market first and concentrate their efforts by consolidating their market position?

3. Evaluate the sales forecasting method used by Stone and suggest any improvements worth noting.

4. Define the major problems in the case and devise a forecasting solution.

CASE 18
Starnes-Brenner Machine Tool Company

The Starnes-Brenner Machine Tool Company of Iowa City, Iowa, has a small one-man sales office headed by Frank Rothe in Latino, a major Latin American country. Frank has been in Latino for about 10 years and is retiring this year; his replacement is Bill Hunsaker, one of Starnes-Brenner's top salesmen. Both will be in Latino for about eight months, during which time Frank will show Bill the ropes, introduce him to their principal customers and, in general, prepare him to take over.

Frank has been very successful as a foreign representative in spite of his unique style and, at times, complete refusal to follow company policy when it doesn't suit him. The company hasn't really done much about his method of operation although from time to time he has angered some top company men. As President McCaughey, who retired a couple of years ago, once remarked to a vice president who was complaining about Frank, "If he's making money—and he is (more than any of the other foreign offices)—then leave the guy alone." When McCaughey retired, the new chief immediately instituted organizational changes that gave more emphasis to the overseas operations, moving the company toward a truly worldwide operation into which a loner like Frank would probably not fit. In fact, one of the key reasons for selecting Bill as Frank's replacement, besides Bill's record as a top salesman, is Bill's capacity as an organization man. He understands the need for coordination among operations and will cooperate with the home office so the Latino office can be expanded and brought into the mainstream.

The company knows there is much to be learned from Frank, and Bill's job is to learn everything possible. The company certainly doesn't want to continue some of Frank's practices, but much of his knowledge is vital for continued, smooth operation. Today Starnes-Brenners' foreign sales account for about 25 percent of the company's total profits, compared with about 5 percent only 10 years ago.

This case was written by Philip R. Cateora, *International Marketing,* 7th ed. (Homewood, Ill.: Richard D. Irwin, Inc.,1990).

The company is actually changing character from being principally an exporter without any real concern for continuous foreign market representation to worldwide operations where the foreign divisions are part of the total effort rather than a stepchild operation. In fact, Latino is one of the last operational divisions to be assimilated into the new organization. Rather than try to change Frank, the company has been waiting for him to retire before making any significant adjustments in their Latino operations.

Bill Hunsaker is 36 years old with a wife and three children; he is a very good salesman and administrator, although he has had no foreign experience. He has the reputation of being fair, honest, and a straight shooter. Some back at the home office see his assignment as part of a grooming job for a top position, perhaps eventually the presidency. The Hunsakers are now settled in their new home after having been in Latino for about 2 weeks. Today is Bill's first day on the job.

When Bill arrived at the office, Frank was on his way to a local factory to inspect some Starnes-Brenner machines that had to have some adjustments made before being acceptable to the Latino government agency buying them. Bill joined Frank for the plant visit. Later, after the visit, we join the two at lunch.

Bill, tasting some chili, remarks, "Boy! This certainly isn't like the chili we have in America."

"No, it isn't, and there's another difference, too.... Latinos *are* Americans, and nothing angers a Latino more than to have a 'Gringo' refer to the United States as America as if to say that Latino isn't part of America also. The Latinos rightly consider their country as part of America (take a look at the map) and people from the United States are North Americans at best. So, for future reference, refer to home either as the United States, the States, or North America, but, for gosh sakes, not just America. Not to change the subject, Bill, but could you see that any change had been made in those S-27s from the standard model?"

"No, they looked like the standard. Was there something out of whack when they arrived?"

"No, I couldn't see any problem—I suspect this is the best piece of sophisticated bribe-taking I've come across yet. Most of the time the Latinos are more 'honest' about their *mordidas* than this."

"What's a *mordida*?" Bill asks.

"You know, *kumshaw, dash, bustarella, mordida;* they are all the same: a little grease to expedite the action. *Mordida* is the local word for a slight offering or, if you prefer, bribe," says Frank.

Bill quizzically responds, "Do we pay bribes to get sales?"

"Oh, it depends on the situation but it's certainly something you have to be prepared to deal with." Boy, what a greenhorn, Frank thinks to himself, as he continues, "Here's the story. When the S-27s arrived last January, we began uncrating them and right away the *Jefe* engineer (a government official)—*Jefe,* that's the head man in charge—began extra careful examination and declared there was a vital defect in the machines; he claimed the machinery would be dangerous and thus unacceptable if it wasn't corrected. I looked it over but couldn't see anything wrong, so I agreed to have our staff engineer check all the machines and correct any flaws that might exist. Well, the *Jefe* said there wasn't enough time to wait for an engineer to come from the States, that the machines could be adjusted locally, and we could pay him and he would make all the necessary arrangements. So, what do you do? No adjustment his way and there would be an order canceled; and maybe there was something out of line, those things have been known to happen. But for the life of me, I can't see that anything had been done since the machines were supposedly fixed. So, let's face it, we just paid a bribe and a pretty darn big bribe at that—about $1,200 per machine—what makes it so aggravating is that that's the second one I've had to pay on this shipment."

"The second?" asks Bill.

"Yeah, at the border when we were transferring the machines to Latino trucks, it was hot and they were moving slow as molasses. It took them over an hour to transfer one machine to a Latino truck and we had ten others to go. It seems that every time I spoke to the dock boss about speeding things up, they just got slower. Finally, out of desperation, I slipped him a fistful of pesos and, sure enough, in the next 3 hours they had the whole thing loaded. Just one of the local customs of doing business. Generally though, it comes at the lower level where wages don't cover living expenses too well."

There is a pause and Bill asks, "What does that do to our profits?"

"Runs them down, of course, but I look at it as just one of the many costs of doing business—I do my best not to pay but when I have to, I do."

Hesitantly Bill replies, "I don't like it, Frank, we've got good products, they're priced right, we give good service and keep plenty of spare parts in the country, so why should we have to pay bribes to the buyer? It's just no way to do business. You've already had to pay two bribes on one shipment; if you keep it up, the word's going to get around and you'll be paying at every level. Then all the profit goes out the window—you know, once you start, where do you stop? Besides that, where do we stand legally? Perhaps you've missed all the news back in the States about the Wedtech scandal, the Housing and Urban Development (HUD) billion dollar rip-off, procurement scandals at the Pentagon, and so on. Congress is mad, countries are mad; in fact, the Foreign Bribery Act makes paying bribes like you've just paid illegal. I'd say the best policy is to never start; you might lose a few sales but let it be known that there are no bribes; we sell the best, service the best at fair prices, and that's all."

"You mean the Foreign Corrupt Practices Act, don't you?" Frank asks and continues in an "I'm not really so out of touch" tone of voice, "Haven't some of the provisions of the Foreign Corrupt Practices Act been softened somewhat?"

"Yes, you're right, the provisions on paying a *mordida* or grease have been softened, but paying the government official is still illegal, softening or no," replies Bill.

Oh boy! Frank thinks to himself as he replies, "First of all, I've heard about all the difficulty with bribing governments, but what I did was just peanuts compared to Japan and Lockheed. The people we pay off are small and, granted we give good service, but we've only been doing it for the last year or so. Before that I never knew when I was going to have equipment to sell. In fact, we only had products when there were surpluses stateside. I had to pay the right people to get sales and besides, you're not back in the States any longer. Things are just done different here. You follow that policy and I guarantee that you'll have fewer sales because our competitors from Germany, Italy, and Japan will pay. Look, Bill, everybody does it here; it's a way of life and the costs are generally reflected in the markup and overhead. There is even a code of behavior involved.

We're not actually encouraging it to spread, just perpetuating an accepted way of doing business.

Patiently and slightly condescendingly, Bill replies, "I know, Frank, but wrong is wrong and we want to operate differently now. We hope to set up an operation here on a continuous basis; we plan to operate in Latino just like we do in the United States—really expand our operation and make a long-range market commitment, grow with the country. And, one of the first things we must avoid are unethical . . . . "

Frank interrupts, "but really, is it unethical? Everybody does it, the Latinos even pay *mordidas* to other Latinos; it's a fact of life—is it really unethical? I think that the circumstances that exist in a country justify and dictate the behavior. Remember man, 'When in Rome, do as the Romans do.'"

Almost shouting, Bill blurts out, "I can't buy that. We know that our management practices and techniques are our strongest point. Really, all we have to differentiate us from the rest of our competition, Latino and others, is that we are better managed, and as far as I'm concerned, graft and other unethical behavior have got to be cut out to create a healthy industry. In the long run, it should strengthen our position. We can't build our futures on illegal and unethical practices."

Frank angrily replies, "Look, it's done in the States all the time. What about the big dinners, drinks, and all the other hanky-panky that goes on? Not to mention House Speaker Wright, PAC (political action committee) payments to congressmen, and all those high speaking fees certain congressmen get from special interests. How many congressmen have gone to jail or lost reelection because of those kinds of things? What is that, if it isn't *mordida,* the North American way? The only difference is that instead of cash only, in the United States we pay in merchandise and cash."

"That's really not the same and you know it. Besides, we certainly get a lot of business transacted during those dinners, even if we are paying the bill."

"Bull—the only difference is that here bribes go on in the open; they don't hide it or dress it in foolish ritual that fools no one. It goes on in the United States and everyone denies the existence of it. That's all the difference—in the United States we're just more hypocritical about it all."

"Look," Frank continues, almost shouting, "we are getting off on the wrong foot and we've got 8 months to work together. Just keep your eyes and mind open and let's talk about it again in a couple of months when you've seen how the whole country operates; perhaps then you won't be so quick to judge it absolutely wrong."

Frank, lowering his voice, says thoughtfully, "I know it's hard to take; probably the most disturbing aspect of dealing with business problems in underdeveloped countries is the matter of graft. And frankly, we don't do much advance preparation so we can deal firmly with it. It bothered me at first; but, then I figured it makes its economic contribution, too, since the payoff is as much a part of the economic process as a payroll. What's our real economic role anyway, besides making a profit, of course? Are we developers of wealth, helping to push the country to greater economic growth, or are we missionaries? Or should we be both? I really don't know, but I don't think we can be both simultaneously, and my feeling is that as the company prospers, as higher salaries are paid, and better standards of living are reached, we'll see better ethics. Until then, we've got to operate or leave, and if you are going to win the opposition over, you'd better join them and change them from within, not fight them."

Before Bill could reply, a Latino friend of Frank's joined them and they changed the topic of conversation.

Questions for Discussion

1. If you were Bill, how would you respond?
2. What course of action would you take when you assumed full responsibility for sales in Latino?

The Top Plastics Company

Before the energy crisis and the myriad raw material shortages that occurred in late 1973, the Top Plastic Company (TPC) expected 1974 to be its best year ever. Preliminary forecasts for 1974 indicated that production would have to be increased 6 to 8 percent over the 1973 volume of 8 million pounds in order to meet sales expectations. Initial projections called for rising demands in all five product categories and in all four sales regions. Only in TPC's Mid Region territory was the outlook perceived as somewhat uncertain and this derived mainly from a projected weakening in the market for automotive-related plastics products.

However, a sudden shortage of liquid resin (a critical ingredient for plastics production), coupled with sharp increases in resin prices, caught Top Plastics' management unprepared. Within the span of just a few months, it became painfully apparent that the company's entire marketing strategy might have to be reappraised and perhaps drastically revamped to meet the realities of liquid resin availability. Moreover, the company's once-successful policies in dealing with liquid resin suppliers seemed to be in need of revision.

COMPANY HISTORY AND BACKGROUND

Top Plastics Company is a wholly owned subsidiary of Alpen Paper Corporation and was formed in 1960 as a result of Alpen management's decision to diversity its product line out of industrial paper products. In the late 1950s when plans for forming Top Plastics first were conceived, Alpen Paper operated three pulp mills, two paper mills, and ten paper products plants; Alpen's corporate headquarters was located in Meridian, Mississippi, the site of its biggest pulp mill. In addition to its Meridian facilities, Alpen had mills and plants scattered in several locations in Alabama, Georgia, Mississippi, and Tennessee.

Based on a case prepared by Gary P. Shows of the University of Alabama under the supervision of Professors Morris Mayer, Arthur A. Thompson, and A. J. Strickland, all of the University of Alabama. Permission to use granted by the authors.

As of the late 1950s, the parent corporation's principal products were linerboard, corrugating medium, and cylinderboard, which were used in assembling corrugated cases and paperboard cartons. Alpen's annual sales totaled $50 million and had grown at a moderate pace during the firm's 80-year history.

In 1958, several developments prompted the management of Alpen Paper Corporation to consider diversifying its product line beyond the confines of the paper industry. Both company and industry profit rates were low, partly because the industry produced a "commodity" type product. Demand conditions and technology offered little or no opportunity for Alpen to manufacture a distinctively different product and thereby gain a profitable competitive edge over rival firms. Furthermore, market demand for Alpen's products had weakened over the past 2 years, leaving Alpen with excess production capacity and shrinking profit margins.

A number of alternative diversification strategies were considered and after much analysis and deliberation, Alpen opted for a cautious move into the plastics industry. Alpen executives, being leery of jumping too fast into what was for them a new industry, stipulated that Alpen's initial investments in plastics be kept small. Diversification into plastics was deemed attractive to Alpen for a number of reasons. First, Alpen had an opportunity to sign a contract with German Plastics Company for the American patent rights to a new plastics manufacturing process. This newly developed process was thought by Alpen officials to be superior to existing plastic processes, and at the same time, met Alpen's requirement for a small capital investment. Second, market research studies indicated that the plastics industry had an excellent growth potential in both volume and profit. Third, it appeared that many of Alpen's industrial paper products customers would also be potential users of plastics, thereby allowing the company to use its present distribution channels to serve both lines of products, Finally, a good possibility existed that technological interfaces between paper and plastic products might permit the development of several entirely new products.

Thus, in early 1960 the Alpen Paper Corporation established Top Plastics Company, and $750,000 was allocated for the construction of a small multiproduct plant in Ellisville, Mississippi. The new management team at Top Plastics intended for the Ellisville plant to steer the company on a course that would (1) pinpoint the types of plastic products with the highest profit contribution, (2) test the effectiveness of the German process, and (3) build a base of technical and marketing expertise for further entry into profitable segments of the plastics industry. TPC's Ellisville plant began production in December 1961 and had as its initial products egg cartons, bakery trays, inner-carton partitions (such as were used in packaging cookies), and packaging containers for in-store use by supermarket chains.

The essential raw material required in the production of these products was a petroleum-based liquid resin produced by combining the petroleum substance with other polymeric materials in a series of petrochemical processes. Top Plastics selected Monsanto Company and Koppers, Inc., as its chief suppliers of liquid resin because of their ability to work closely with product development and assist where possible with technical expertise. Although other resin suppliers were available, TPC chose not to do business initially with them because they also marketed finished plastic products that competed with TPC's product line.

During the early months of operation, the products manufactured at the Ellisville Plant were sold in Mississippi, Alabama, southern Tennessee, and western Georgia. TPC's marketing force comprised four salesmen, each assigned to a specific product classification. One salesman called on egg producers, another on wholesale bakeries, a third on supermarket chains, and one salesman sold to both wholesale paper jobbers and wholesale grocers. By early 1961 the demand for TPC's plastic products was sufficient to warrant the limited use of Alpen Paper's sales force who were also selling the four-state area. Alpen's salesmen were mainly used whenever an Alpen customer was a potential user of TPC's products but was not being visited by one of the plastics salesmen. In mid-1961, TPC further expanded its sales coverage by contracting with two independent distributors in Memphis and Birmingham for the handling of TPC's plastic products. Sales during the first year of operation alone were $1.5 million, and expansion possibilities quickly became a prime consideration.

GROWTH AND EXPANSION AT TPC

During the next 10 years, TPC continued to grow and expand at a healthy rate. In 1965 TPC built a plant in Tawanda, Pennsylvania, the company's first plant outside of the Southeast. The Tawanda plant was designed to produce heavier plastic products than the Ellisville plant, but it still incorporated the patented and highly efficient German process. Another plan was built in Houston in 1967 and still another in 1970 in Charlotte, North Carolina. These latter two plants were engineered to manufacture heavy-weight plastic products while remaining versatile enough to produce lighter-weight items if and when demand conditions warranted. The Houston and Charlotte plants required significant capital investments, but the risks were deemed acceptable by TPC because of the projected long-term strength in demand. Throughout this phase of major expansion, TPC's management relied exclusively on internal growth rather than acquisition because TPC's patented German process was still felt to be superior to processes used by other companies in TPC's market area.

Between 1962 and 1972 TPC's annual sales rose from $1.5 million to $13.5 million. The initial four-item product line was expanded to 25 different product groups and more than 250 separate items. As of 1973, TPC's produce assortment consisted of the following five major classes:

> Group A—Heavy-weight plastics (children's toys, cabinets, shelves)
>
> Group B—Lightweight plastics (door and wall moldings, plastic notebooks, auto plastics)
>
> Group C—Packaging materials (egg cartons, inner-carton partitions)
>
> Group D—Disposable products (cups, eating utensils)
>
> Group E—Miscellaneous (pocket calculators, plastic screws)

REORGANIZATION OF THE MARKETING FORCE

Within a few years of TPC's formation as a division of Alpen, Top Plastics' management realized the company's marketing effort was gradually becoming less effective. The parent firm had cut back its sales force to try to reduce costs. Alpen salesmen were consequently spending less time servicing the accounts of the TPC subsidiary. Additionally, disagreements between paper salesmen and plastics salesmen were arising over the servicing of a number of plastics accounts. In 1967 Alpen and TPC agreed to assign responsibility for the entire plastics marketing effort to an expanded TPC marketing department, timing the move to coincide with the start-up of TPC's Houston plant. The Houston plant doubled TPC's production capacity and of necessity prompted adjustments in the marketing of TPC's expanded product line.

As of 1973, TPC's marketing department consisted of a direct sales force plus affiliations with eight independent distributors. The distributors, located in Atlanta, Memphis, New Orleans, Dallas, Chicago, Detroit, Louisville, and Richmond, gave TPC a greatly expanded sales coverage as well as providing feedback on changing market conditions. Some of the distributors even suggested what prices and advertising allowances should be offered to various customers. Each of TPC's distributors seemed to have a well-trained sales force and TPC was generally well pleased with the sales performance of its eight distributor outlets.

TPC's marketing department was headed by a vice president, who reported to the senior vice president of Alpen Paper Corporation responsible for the marketing of both Alpen Paper and Top Plastics products. Reporting to TPC's marketing vice president were the four regional sales managers. Sales regions were divided into five districts with one salesman assigned to each district. The geographical makeup of the four regions by district was as follows:

> South Region—Mississippi, Alabama, Georgia, Florida, and Tennessee
>
> West Region—North Texas, South Texas, Arkansas, Oklahoma, Louisiana
>
> East Region—South Carolina, North Carolina, Kentucky, Virginia, and Maryland, Delaware, West Virginia, Washington, D.C.
>
> Mid Region—Western Pennsylvania, Ohio, Indiana, Illinois, and Michigan

Regional sales offices were located in the same cities as TPC's production facilities.

RELATIONSHIPS WITH SUPPLIERS

From the outset of its plastics operations, TPC had encountered only minor problems concerning the availability and acquisition of raw material suppliers for its plants. The main raw material was still liquid resin and supplies were plentiful. As many as eight resin suppliers continued to solicit TPC's business. Resin prices were generally stable and both delivery time and service were considered good.

TPC's chief resin suppliers included Monsanto, Koppers, Eastman Kodak, Union Carbide, Foster Grant, Dow Chemical, and Diamond Alkali. It was company policy for each TPC plant to purchase its own supplies of raw materials based on economic order quantity calculations. Since most of the suppliers used were dependable, price was normally the determining factor in deciding which firm to purchase from. Typically, TPC "played" resin producers against each other to obtain the best possible prices. No long-term contracts were made with any supplier since the resin market was essentially a buyer's market. The average price TPC paid for liquid resin in the first quarter of 1973 at its Houston plant was 25 cents per pound, with a range of 15 to 35 cents per pound.

THE FORECAST FOR 1974

As late as the third quarter of 1973, it still appeared that 1974 would be a record year for TPC. Sales were expected to top $15 million and production volume was projected to reach 8 million pounds. Table C19-1 shows the anticipated 1974 demand in pounds, scheduled production in pounds, per pound production costs, expected market sales price, and

	TABLE C19-1	1974 Operations Forecast			
Product Class	Expected Demand (in pounds)	Production (in pounds)	Cost per Pound	Selling Price (per pound)	Profit (per pound)
A	2,500,000	2,500,000	$1.40	$1.90	$.50
B	1,200,000	1,200,000	1.50	2.20	.70
C	1,500,000	1,500,000	1.80	2.10	.30
D	1,500,000	1,500,000	1.60	2.00	.40
E	1,300,000	1,300,000	1.00	1.10	.10

TABLE C19-2   Regional Sales Forecast for 1974 (in pounds)

Sales Regions	Product Categories				
	A	*B*	*C*	*D*	*E*
South	500,000	150,000	300,000	400,000	200,000
West	500,000	300,000	300,000	500,000	400,000
East	600,000	150,000	500,000	400,000	300,000
Mid	900,000	600,000	400,000	200,000	400,000

TABLE C19-3   Forecast of Distributor Sales During 1974

Sales Regions	Product Categories (%)				
	A	*B*	*C*	*D*	*E*
South	30	40	60	70	20
West	25	30	50	60	25
East	35	30	50	65	15
Mid	20	25	70	60	20

expected profit per pound for each of the company's five product classes. TPC presently has the plant capacity to produce 8,075,000 pounds of plastics without having to schedule overtime production.

Table C19-2 depicts the expected 1974 sales by region; the figures are in pounds and include both sales by the direct sales force and the eight independent distributors. In drawing up its 1974 sales forecast in pounds, TPC assumed that per pound costs and selling price in each region would be constant within each product category and also across all four regions.

Table C19-3 shows the estimated percentages of total 1974 sales for TPC's eight independent distributors.

Top Plastics' 1974 budget allocation for advertising and sales promotion was $450,000—an amount 15 percent greater than 1973. The 1974 promotional effort was patterned after the 1973 campaign and called for $100,000 to be spent on trade journal advertising, $50,000 to be spent at trade shows, and $300,000 to be spent for direct mail advertising.

MOUNTING PROBLEMS AND UNCERTAINTIES

Although TPC management anticipated a record year in 1974, events ran counter to expectations. In the summer and fall of 1973, the rumors of a petroleum shortage became a fact. In November the shortage grew sharply worse when the Arabs imposed an oil boycott. Almost immediately, the cutbacks in crude oil supplies affected TPC's supply of petroleum-based liquid resin. TPC's suppliers, primarily Eastman Kodak and Monsanto, began allocating their reduced resin supplies, first to their own plastics plants and then to their contract customers. Buyers such as TPC who spread their purchases unevenly and irregularly among several resin producers according to who offered the best price found themselves last on their suppliers' priority lists. Resin prices climbed rapidly, and by late November 1973, TPC was paying from 45 to 75 cents per pound of resin whenever and wherever it could be obtained.

As shortage conditions worsened, TPC's purchasing agents in December estimated that during 1974 the company could expect to obtain only 65 to 75 percent as much resin as was bought in 1973; this was enough to permit production of just 5.2 to 6 million pounds of plastic products—a production level far below the once-anticipated capacity output of 8,075 million pounds. When this estimate was received, TPC's manufacturing executives called a meeting to consider whether and how to revise the 1974 production plan. TPC's marketing vice president also scheduled a meeting with his four regional sales managers to discuss whether adjustments should be made in the company's market strategy and 1974 sales plan; the marketing vice president was also wondering how the manufacturing people would react to whatever marketing change might be called for and the extent to which it might be necessary to compromise the marketing effort to meet the constraints of the manufacturing division.

Questions for Discussion

1. If you were the marketing vice president of TPC, what alternatives could you consider in allocating the liquid resin across the five product classes? Which alternative do you prefer?

2. What action will you take regarding prices for the five product classes?

3. Is there any way that Alpen Paper could help out during the resin shortage?

4. How would you handle distributor participation during the shortage?

5. Do you have any recommendations regarding TPC's purchasing policies?

C A S E   2 0
Trans-Europa Business Credit

Trans-Europa Business Credit (TEBC), a commercial finance company, was acquired as a wholly owned subsidiary by a large conglomerate holding company. It is headquartered in New York and has 30 branches, most of them located in North America and Europe, and a few in the Middle East. The branches have always operated separately and autonomously.

TEBC's primary business is accounts receivable financing, but it also books loans secured by inventory or other collateral when a borrower needs more money than can be secured by accounts receivable alone. The minimum loan is $100,000 and the average is $250,000. The district manager, who usually has four or five branch managers reporting to him, has authority to approve all loans.

When TEBC was acquired, the management of Trans-Europa Corporation decided it wanted more control over the subsidiary. There was an overall concentration of loans in a few business areas that could become dangerous should the world economy change and undermine one of those business areas. To reduce the risk, Paul Bergonzi, the president of the finance company, hired George Praeger, an experienced loan executive, as vice president of commercial finance lending. Praeger was to reorganize the branch system and diversify the loan portfolio. Bergonzi assigned Tom Baldwin to be Praeger's assistant. Over the years, Baldwin had worked in several areas of TEBC and knew most of the branch managers personally.

One of Praeger's first decisions was to centralize the loan approval process by requiring that the head office be notified of all loans more than $250,000 and that the head office made final approval on all loans more than $350,000. This would include any increases in existing accommodations that would bring the loan line above $350,000.

Praeger discussed this idea with Bergonzi who presented it to the conglomerate management. They approved the plan.

Praeger then drafted the letter in Exhibit 20-1, page 659, to the branch managers.

Praeger showed the letter to Tom Baldwin and asked for his opinion. Baldwin said he liked the letter but suggested that since Praeger was new to TEBC, he might visit the branches and meet the managers to talk to them in person about the new procedure. Praeger decided that there was so much to do at the head office that he could not take the time to go to each branch. He sent the letter instead.

In the next 2 weeks, most of the branches responded. Although some managers wrote more, the letter in Exhibit 20-2, page 659, is a characteristic reply.

For the next 10 weeks, the head office received no information about negotiations of loan agreements from any of the branch offices.

Executives who made frequent trips to the field reported that the offices were busy making somewhat more loans than usual.

This case first appeared in David A. Nadler, Michael L. Tushman, and Nina G. Hatvany, *Managing Organizations: Readings and Cases.* Copyright ©1982 by David A. Nadler, Michael L. Tushman, and Nina G. Hatvany. Reprinted by permission of Little, Brown & Company.

EXHIBIT 20-1

Dear _____.

    Paul Bergonzi and the directors of the Trans-Europa Corporation have authorized a change in our loan approval procedures. Hereafter, all Branch Managers will notify the Vice President of Commercial Finance Lending of any loans in excess of $250,000 before the preliminary approval and before TEBC's auditors conduct the survey. In addition, final approval of all loans for more than $350,000 will come from the New York office. This includes new accommodations and increases in the loan line, which brings the limit up to $350,000 or more.

    By centralizing loan approval, we can ensure that our monies are not concentrated in only a few areas and we can broaden our base of operation. I am sure you will understand that this step is necessary in such times of increasing economic uncertainty. By effecting this change, the interest of each branch and the company as a whole will best be served.

Yours very truly,

George Praeger

George Praeger
Vice President of Commercial Finance Lending

EXHIBIT 20-2

Dear Mr. Praeger:

    We have received your recent letter about notifying the head office about negotiations of loans of $250,000 and the change in the approval process for loans in excess of $350,000. This suggestions seems a most practical one, and we want to assure you that you can depend on our cooperation.

Sincerely yours,

Jack Foster

Jack Foster
Branch Manager

Questions for Discussion

1. What do you think is happening in the TEBC branches?

2. Should Praeger have initiated the changes differently? How?

3. How can he rectify the current situation without making matters worse?

Zactec Electronics, Inc.

INDUSTRIAL MARKETING MANAGEMENT STRATEGY

Zactec Electronics, Inc.,[1] has been a successful electronics firm in the optoelectronics or light sensitive industry since its founding in 1959. The company has thrived on the growth of integrated circuitry in the industry. The dominant method of integrated circuits fabrication involves silicon materials rather than the cadmium sulfide or cadmium selenium the firm is now using. As a result of a shift from cadmium to silicon in this technology, the firm wishes to add to the capability of producing light sensitive components using the newer methods.

Zactec has been successful in the manufacture and design of photoconductive and photovoltaic cells. It has continued to grow until the industrial trends showed a slow growth rate or stagnation in its industry. Zactec currently sells its products to the following types of manufacturers:

Class	Percent of Sales
Cameras	20
Musical instruments and audio equipment	10
Analytical instruments	10
Industrial equipment manufacturers	60
	100%

[1]Fictitious name. We would like to thank Dalip Miglani, Charles E. Olson, and Michael K. Riess for their help in constructing this case.

Optoelectronic devices (OED) find applications in a wide variety of products ranging from musical instruments and medical diagnostic equipment to cameras and industrial quality controls. Table C21-1 illustrates some of the market areas that use OEDs.

CHANGES IN THE OPTOELECTRONIC INDUSTRY

Industry trends indicate there is a developing change in the demand for OEDs, dictating the use of new technologies that offer the following advantages:

Smaller size

Greater total dependability

Greater resistance to environment

Low battery drain

Lower total circuitry cost

Easier circuitry replacement and repair

PRODUCTION CONCERNS AND BUSINESS ANALYSIS

Silicon Technology

Solid state electronics is totally dominated by silicon technology, with the exception of light-emitting diodes and a few microwave applications. Zactec intends to produce devices of moderate complexity by proven "mainstream" methods. This will entail hiring an engineer in this area and making capital investments in silicon wafer processing, integrated circuit packaging, and testing facilities.

Silicon wafer processing plus basic assembly and test equipment will require a $350,000 initial

TABLE C21-1 Electronics Sales in Various Market Areas (in millions of dollars)				
Area	1985	1986	1987	1988
Musical instruments	141.0	162.0	175.0	210.0
Test and measuring instruments	722.0	715.1	758.6	914.0
Medical diagnostic equipment	399.6	431.5	470.6	577.0
AM and FM station equipment	17.5	18.0	19.2	21.0
Industrial operations equipment	651.0	589.8	673.7	960.0

TABLE C21-2   Silicon Semiconductor Facility Project Schedule

	Planning, Marketing, and Finance	Production
Preparatory phase	Conduct market analysis and market survey, forecast equipment, financial, and personnel requirements Hire silicon technology specialists	
Installation phase (6 to 9 months)	Maintain market contact, monitor costs	Install wafer production equipment, begin phototransistor and photodiode design, integrated circuit R&D
First operational phase (2 years)	Maintain market contact, monitor costs	Begin Monsanto production of phototransistors, establish packaging and testing assembly line, continue research and development
	Begin advertising and promotion of silicon products	Begin Zactec production of phototransistors and photodiodes
	Repeat market survey	Begin installation of automatic packaging and testing equipment
	Make product decisions on integrated circuits	
Second operational phase	Maintain market contact, monitor costs	Begin production of integrated circuits

investment. The photodiode devices will be produced first, and the production of the integrated circuits deferred by 2 to 3 years. Efficient IC assembly and testing is estimated to cost an additional $150,000. Table C21-2 is an overview of the entire project.

Costs

Up to 7,500 devices can be "built" on a single 3-inch diameter silicon wafer, but the major production problem is quality control. By their very nature, not all devices will work and the good ones have to be sorted from the bad ones. If yields of good wafers exceed 20 to 25 percent of the total produced, then the cost of the silicon wafer per good device is trivial compared with the costs associated with testing and packaging the devices. Table C21-3 is a fixed and variable cost breakdown with resulting break-even points for different variable costs. The average variable labor cost of $270 per 1,000 devices implies a production mix with fewer ICs,

and it illustrates how automation and the experience curve can substantially reduce packaging and testing labor costs.

Prices

For the purposes of this plan, the market price of $0.75 per device was assumed. Current prices for phototransistors of the quality Zactec will produce range from $1.22 to $2.25, in large quantities. Since demand is relatively inelastic, this price range would avoid mutual throat cutting.

Pricing for integrated circuits will depend on the market and application. Cameras and some remote sensing applications will see high-volume, low-margin markets with prices perhaps as low as $0.80. Control, audio, and musical applications will have prices in the range of $1.00 to $5.00, and some instrument makers will be willing to pay up to $15.00 per device. The above price statements are based on current price trends, Zactec's expert opinion, and a market survey.

TABLE C21-3   Cost Analysis

Average Fixed Production Costs per Year
Salaries for engineer, technician, supervisor $ 55,000
General overhead: utilities, some equipment rentals,
   outside lab work, masking, filters, interest on debt, etc. 71,000
Recovery of fixed assets, $500,000 over 10 years 50,000
$176,000

Wafer Production Variable Costs[1]
Labor: 1.28 hours/wafer @$4/hour $5.12
Materials 4.00
$9.12/wafer

Wafer Production Variable Costs per Thousand Devices for Different Yields
Phototransistor—photodiode
   30% yield (worst case) $ 4.06
   60% yield (best case) $ 2.03
Integrated Circuit
   4% yield (worst case) $30.40
   20% yield (best case) $ 6.08

Packaging and Testing Variable Costs Per Thousand Devices[2]
Phototransistor—photodiode
   Labor: 30 man-hours/1,000 devices @$4/man-hour $120.00
   Materials 100.00
$220.00

Integrated circuit
   Labor: 35 man-hours/1,000 devices @$4/man-hour $140.00
   Materials 200.00
$340.00

Total Variable Production Costs per Thousand Devices
Phototransistor—photodiode
   30% yield $224.06
   60% yield $222.03
Integrated circuit
   4% yield $370.40
   20% yield $346.08

Break-Even Analysis
Assume average market price of $.75/device with 17% of sales going to advertising, selling, and administration.
With a variable production cost of $270/1000 devices, break-even volume is 486,000 units/year average for 10 years.
With a variable production cost of $320/1000 devices, break-even volume is 582,000 units/year average for 10 years.

---

[1]Zactec has the option of buying fully processed wafers from Monsanto at $14/wafer, but yields, continuity of long-term price and availability, and assurance of a particular technology are not guaranteed.

[2]Labor costs are based on the assumption that operations are primarily manual with little automation.

MARKET SURVEY RESULTS

Of the 187 survey forms mailed, 75 were returned (40 percent). The following results were provided from the survey.

1. The trend to silicon technology was verified.

2. IC characteristics valued the most by respondents were higher reliability, reduced product assembly cost, and reduced net component cost.

3. Few respondents desired unusual power, voltage, or temperature that would rule out an inexpensive IC.

4. Of the devices proposed, the optical Schmitt trigger and the operational amplifier integrated with a light were the most popular.

5. The most common applications were industrial controls, computer peripherals, photometry, laboratory instrumentation, and photon coupling.

6. The mean price was $3.07 per unit. Low-value items (controls, burglar alarms, remote sensors) wanted a low price.

7. Packaging preferences expressed leaned heavily toward the Dual-Inline Package and the metal can with a transparent window.

SALES FORECASTS

The marketing department will estimate future sales using two assumptions. Table C21-4 shows the estimated sales volume and net cash flow for Zactec's light sensitive devices if the company achieves 10 percent of the current market within 8 years. Table C21-5 shows the results if Zactec achieves 25 percent of the current market within 10 years.

BUSINESS MARKETING STRATEGY

Historically, large firms have not been sufficiently adaptive, or had low enough overhead, to find optoelectronics markets profitable. Zactec's principal competitor, Flairex Electronics, is also a small firm that has a substantial share of the silicon optoelectronics market (current total $11 million) and almost as large a share as Zactec (20 to 25 percent) of the photoconductor market, which totals $5 to $6 million.

Zactec proposes a two-prong offensive and defensive marketing effort. Zactec cannot afford to leave the burgeoning silicon market to its competitors, although it could survive by making CdS and CdSe

TABLE C21-4   Cash Flow (in thousands of dollars)

Assumption: Zactec achieves sales volume for its silicon light-sensitive devices equal to 10 percent of the current market within 8 years

Year	Fixed Production Costs	Variable Production Costs	Selling, Advertising, and Administrative Costs	Total Costs	Sales Revenue	Net Cash Flow
0	350	0	0	350	0	(350)
1	141	0	20[1]	161	0	(161)
2	141	72	34	247	200	(47)
3	281	99	47	427	276	(151)
4	121	173	82	376	481	105
5	121	252	119	492	700	208
6	121	279	132	532	776	244
7	121	317	150	588	881	293
8	121	360	170	651	1000	349
9	121	360	170	651	1000	349
10	121	360	170	651	1000	349

[1]Seed money to initiate advertising for silicon photo devices.

Internal rate of return=16.6%.

			Selling,			
	Fixed	Variable	Advertising, and			
	Production	Production	Administrative	Total	Sales	Net Cash
Year	Costs	Costs	Costs	Costs	Revenue	Flow
0	350	0	0	350	0	(350)
1	141	0	20*	161	0	(161)
2	141	72	34	247	200	(47)
3	281	107	50	438	296	(142)
4	121	209	99	429	581	152
5	121	288	136	535	800	265
6	121	342	162	625	950	325
7	121	396	187	704	1100	396
8	121	504	238	863	1400	537
9	121	666	315	1102	1850	748
10	121	900	425	1446	2500	1054

TABLE C21-5   Cash Flow (in thousands of dollars)

Assumption: Zactec achieves sales volume for its silicon light-sensitive devices equal to 25 percent of the current market within 10 years.

*Seed money to initiate advertising for Silicon photo devices
Internal Rate of Return=26.3%

photoconductors in applications requiring wide spectral response, low noise, or high temperatures. The long-term growth potential for this market is rather bleak. Silicon technology will assume increasing importance. Therefore, Zactec will continue in the cadmium device market but will also enter the silicon market to gain future sales and to sustain its future market share. The company proposes to develop a total capability for the design and manufacture of silicon devices.

Research and Development

Zactec's past success has been its ability to provide consistent product quality and maintain high levels of customer service. The company decided to develop a light-controlled oscillator (LCO), which produces a sine wave signal and has a frequency that depends on the intensity of the light incident on the device. An integrated circuit (IC) with this capacity has the desirable characteristics of serving a critical need in several markets, including cameras, instrumentation, remote sensing, and direct applications in electronic organs and musical instruments.

Promotion

Technical brochures, publicity, industrial advertising in trade journals, and personal selling will be con-

tinued. Promotion of Zactec's new line will incorporate promotion at the manufacturers' rep level and at the OEM and end-user levels. Direct mail will be sent to selected firms that can use the new product line. News releases will be sent, followed by advertising space in trade journals, such as *Electo-optical Systems Design, Electro-optical Master Catalog, Electronics, Electronics Buyers' Guide,* and *Electronics Design.*

Distribution Channels

Zactec currently uses manufacturers' reps but sells directly to very large customers, such as Kodak. There are twenty reps, who operate on a 5 percent commission basis. When the rep does routine clerical work on high-volume accounts, he or she receives an additional 2 percent. The present system offers many advantages:

1. The new product line can be offered quickly to the market.
2. The firm has experienced reps with ongoing accounts.
3. Lower initial expense will be incurred and the channel will be more adaptive to changes in sales volume.
4. This is a traditional channel, more acceptable for marketing business and industrial products.

Strategic Plan's Marketing Reach

Sales of OEDs are confined to industrial and research organizations. Although many applications exist for these devices, the realistic, potential market size numbers less than 200 organizations. Only domestic sales will be considered at this time; however, the vast foreign market cannot be overlooked, despite the numerous trade barriers that protect each country's domestic producers. It is not anticipated that the potential market will expand very much in the near future because most current and projected applications require a high degree of experience and sophistication. If new applications open up, the total number of OED sales could expand rapidly.

Questions for Discussion

1. Evaluate the entire strategic plan's feasibility and its potential profitability.

2. Is it unwise to be so conservative as to keep producing the cadmium line while shifting to the silicon line? Why or why not?

3. Should Zactec enter foreign markets, regardless of their inexperience with trade barriers?

4. Will the existing channel and promotion plans suffice to produce an eventual profit? If not, why not?

Glossary

accelerator principle As demand for a product at the retail level changes up or down, the impact at the wholesale and manufacturing levels is disproportionately greater.

accessories Short-lived tools or auxiliary equipment used in the administrative or manufacturing process.

advertising Any paid form of nonpersonal persuasive communication by an identified sponsor. In the business market, print media are used more frequently than radio or TV.

annual plan Detailed, short-term segment of the firm's long-term strategy; usually for a 12-month period. See *tactical planning.*

artificial intelligence The ability of a manmade mechanism to exhibit intelligent behavior; for example, computer programs that perform medical diagnoses or legal reasoning, understand human speech, or visually recognize written or typed characters. Most of these systems, though far from perfect, have been valuable in solving specific practical problems. See *expert system.*

benefit segmentation Market segmentation based on the benefits or desired results that a customer will gain from using a particular product or service.

brand manager See *product manager.*

break-even analysis Determination of what quantity must be sold at some given price for the firm to recover all of its costs.

break-even point The sales quantity at which a firm's revenue will equal its total costs.

brochure Any printed sales-promotion material that can be inserted into a direct-mail piece, left by a salesperson, or given to a prospect at a trade show.

business cycle Fluctuations in the level of business activity that do not occur at regular intervals but that follow a typical cyclical pattern.

business market All commercial, industrial, institutional, or government organizations that consume products or services for their own use or purchase these to resell to other organizations.

business services All nonproduct activities offered to the business market on a commercial basis; for example, accounting, engineering, legal counsel, advertising, and market research.

buyer-seller interface system Normally refers to a partnership between buyers and sellers who strive for mutually beneficial goals. The success of one partially depends on the other's performance. See *partnering* and *concurrent engineering.*

buygrid model A matrix that depicts the three types of purchases—new task, modified rebuy, and straight rebuy—across the eight phases of an industrial buying process.

buying center An organizational decision-making unit (DMU) that usually includes members from various functional departments (e.g., purchasing, production, engineering, quality control).

catalog A reference book containing a firm's complete product line and is given to buyers to aid and influence their purchase decisions.

channel intermediary An independent firm operating between a producer and the end user. In the business market, this can be a distributor, sales agent, or value-added reseller. In the consumer market, retailers would be included.

closed bid A sealed bid in answer to a specific request that listed item description and quantity. All bids are opened at a prescribed time and place. The purchase award often goes to the lowest bidder, particularly in the case of government purchases.

comparative advertising Advertising that promotes one firm's products by portraying the products of one or more competitors in a negative light. Most societies outside the U.S. do not condone such advertising, some even deem it illegal.

components Also called component parts, these products are purchased by OEMs for assembly into end products.

concurrent engineering (CE) Involvement of all concerned functional departments (e.g., engineering, production, purchasing, marketing, customer service) in the initial phase of new product development. This ensures that all aspects of the product's description or performance relative to customer satisfaction are considered. Suppliers and/or channel members may also be included. See *platform teams.*

consultative sales approach The salesperson concentrates on becoming thoroughly familiar with a customer's problem or need so that the most appropriate solution can be recommended.

contract manufacturing In international marketing, a firm contracts to have its product manufactured in the host country to avoid the problems of entering that market with a product manufactured elsewhere.

contraction defense When overextended and unable to withstand the rigors of an attack, a firm will sell off weak product lines or merge with another company to solidify its position in a given product area.

contribution-margin pricing Setting a price based only on those variable costs directly associated with the production and sale of that product. Overhead and fixed costs are omitted.

cooperative (co-op) advertising An advertising program in which producers and channel members share the cost and effort.

cost-driven pricing Setting a price with the primary emphasis on the cost of production rather than market conditions or the pricing strategy of competition.

counteroffensive attack Attack an aggressive competitor's target market or niche in retaliation for their attempt to increase market share.

County Business Patterns Periodic government reports containing market research data by counties; useful for sales forecasting and market potential analysis.

cross-docking Any system that provides direct flow from product to retailer, avoiding intermediate storage.

cross-elasticity of demand The degree to which the price change of one product affects the demand for another product; often occurs between products that can substitute for each other.

customer attitude tracking A longitudinal analysis of potential changes in customer acceptance of a company or its products; part of the control process.

customer service Refers to all the various activities undertaken to ensure a customer's satisfaction.

decision support system (DSS) A computerized database containing market information necessary for informed marketing decisions.

Delphi method Executives make individual sales predictions that are combined, smoothed, and reiterated until a group consensus is reached.

derived demand The demand for goods and services in the business market is derived from consumers' demand for the end products that are produced. For example, Ford will buy as many tires and air conditioners as are needed to produce the automobiles that they expect to sell.

desktop publishing A combination of computer software and hardware that allows a firm to produce its catalogs, brochures, newsletters, and direct mail program in-house.

direct exporting The producer makes the necessary contacts and arrangements to handle exporting without the aid of intermediaries.

direct marketing solicitation of orders via direct mail, catalogs, telephone, electronic mail, or computer.

directory A reference book published by a third party that lists suppliers by product category; a widely used and effective vehicle to bring buyer and seller together.

distribution channel The composite of firms that participate in the flow of products or services from the producer to the final customer.

distribution resource planning (DRP) A spinoff from materials requirement planning (MRP), DRP plans the distribution channel assets required to meet a customer's JIT programmed dates.

distributor A full-function channel member who takes possession of and title to a manufacturer's product and resells it to other business firms. Significant duties include local stocking, sales contacts, promotion, and customer service. Also referred to as wholesaler, merchant wholesaler, or industrial distributor.

dual distribution system A producer uses multiple channels to reach a broader spectrum of customers in a target market; for example, a company sales force to call on major accounts plus a network of distributors to service smaller accounts.

economic order quantity (EOQ) The purchase quantity at which procurement and inventory-carrying costs are optimized given a known level of demand.

economy of scale A reduction in total unit cost as the rate of production increases; at some point, the downward slope bottoms out and begins to rise again.

elastic demand When a price is reduced by some percent, total quantity demanded increases by a greater percent so that total revenue increases.

end user The final buyer of a business product who will use and not resell it.

exchange control A government control wherein a company holding foreign currency in the United States can only exchange it through the U.S. government to obtain payment in dollars.

experience curve A phenomenon wherein the quantity-related (variable) costs of production, administration, and marketing decline as the *cumulative* quantity of a product increases. Not to be confused with an economy-of-scale curve, which depends on the *rate* of production. Optimum results accrue when an innovative management actively seeks out cost-saving opportunities.

experience-curve pricing Basing the current selling price of a product on the average cost expected over some finite time period; that is, utilizing the predicted downward slope of the experience curve.

expert system A computer program that acts like an expert consultant in predicting the outcomes of events or diagnosing problems. It does this by referring to a large database of specific knowledge in a given area, and by using preset rules of inference to draw conclusions. See Artificial intelligence.

export management company (EMC) A domestic firm that acts as an international distributor or agent for a domestic seller.

export trading company (ETC) More complex than an EMC, an ETC acts as a consultant in researching, developing, and establishing a foreign market for a domestic producer. The Japanese successfully developed this business form, and many governments and businesses have emulated them.

fixed-order-quantity model Also called min-max inventory model. Orders are placed at a time that comprehends a supplier's current delivery cycle and in a quantity necessary to raise inventory to a level that will satisfy current market demand.

flanking attack A military strategy wherein an opponent is attacked from the side. In marketing terms, a firm attacks a competitor in its most vulnerable market segment.

freight forwarder Transportation firms with sufficient volume, flexibility, and warehousing to combine the small quantity shipments (LCL) of many shippers into a single (CL) shipment at a more economical rate.

full costing Pricing a product or service so that all costs associated with its production and sale are covered.

General Agreement on Tariffs and Trade (GATT) A treaty established in 1948 and signed by 96 nations, GATT provides a code of conduct for international trade, based on the principles that trade should be conducted without discrimination, that tariffs should be reduced through multilateral negotiations, and that member countries should consult together to overcome trade problems.

gross domestic product (GDP) the total market value of all goods and services produced *within* a country during a given period, usually one year. GDP is now used more regularly than GNP. See *gross national product (GNP)*.

gross national product (GNP) The total market value of all goods and services produced during a given period, usually one year. Its components include capital investment for new factories, machinery, or houses; personal consumption of goods and services; government expenditures for goods and services; and net exports (exports less imports). As computed yearly by the Department of Commerce, the U.S. GNP has included part of the value of goods and services produced abroad by United States-based companies. See *gross domestic product (GDP)*.

indirect exporting A firm sells into a foreign market through a domestic international distributor or importer-exporter.

industrial distributor See *distributor*.

inelastic demand When a price is reduced by some percent, total quantity demanded increases by a lesser percent so that total revenue decreases. This phenomenon is common in the business market.

innovation Introduction of something new (a new product) or an improvement in the way of doing something (an improved production process).

international distributor A channel intermediary that specializes in selling into international markets.

joint demand A product's demand is linked to the demand for another product, for example, computers and software.

joint venture Exportation by forming a partnership with a firm in the host country. In some countries, laws to protect domestic industries force joint ventures.

just-in-time (JIT) Delivery schedules that minimize the amount of inventory carried by the customer. This system places additional burdens on the seller.

learning curve See *experience curve*.

leasing A method of obtaining goods without the initial investment cost. Lease arrangements can be expensed rather than capitalized.

list price A published price used as the basis for any discounting.

maintenance, repair, and operating (MRO) The broadest range of industrial products and services; these are purchased to support the administrative and production processes.

manufacturers' representative (rep) An independent selling firm that contracts to sell the products of several manufacturers; does not handle competing goods and does not take title. Frequently called a manufacturers' agent or sales agent.

marginal pricing See *contribution-margin pricing*.

market challenger An aggressive firm that wishes to replace the market leader and is willing to withstand the leader's strength and pressures.

market-driven pricing Setting a price with the primary emphasis on customer demand and the pricing of competition rather than the cost of production.

market follower A company that maintains the status quo, shuns the spotlight, and follows the market leader.

market intelligence Information regarding customer and competitors that can provide the basis for a market strategy.

market leader The company with the largest share in a given market; it can have a strong influence on customer preferences and competitors' strategies.

market manager A marketing specialist who develops a detailed knowledge of the buyers, competitors, and conditions in a given market. Usually acts in concert with product managers.

market opportunity analysis Determining which market segments represent the firm's best chance to succeed; a classic product-market match analysis. See *S.W.O.T. analysis* and *success requirements*.

market potential The total sales possible within a specific market, given the firm's product line. See *served available market*.

market segmentation Division of a broad, heterogeneous product market into homogeneous segments based on applications, benefits sought, geographic location, volume potentials, etc.

market skimming price See *skimming price policy*.

marketing audit The systematic, exhaustive, and scheduled analysis of all marketing activities to determine where changes or improvements may be required.

marketing concept The idea that a firm should concentrate all efforts on satisfying the needs of customers rather than concentrating on making a profit; profits will flow from satisfied customers.

marketing expense-to-sales analysis Determining whether the cost of achieving a sales volume is justified by the volume and falls within a target range.

marketing intelligence system (MkIS) A total information system containing competitive data, internal costs, market potentials, and management science subsystems.

marketing research The systematic and logical process of determining answers to questions and finding solutions to problems; the marketing version of who, what, where, why, and when.

materials management The management of materials in all phases of procurement, use and processing; combines the functions of purchasing, production planning, inventory control, and even transport.

materials requirement planning (MRP) A computer planning process to determine what types of components, supplies, installations, etc. are needed, their quantities, and the control necessary to manufacture a given product. MRP is a subset of materials management.

merchant wholesaler See *distributor.*

min-max inventory model See *fixed-order-quantity model.*

modified rebuy One class in the *buygrid model;* a previous purchase is repeated but with alterations. For example, product specifications, pricing, or even the chosen vendor may be changed.

negotiated price Buyer and seller agree to a price for a specific purchase; differs from buying at a list price.

new task buy Another class in the Buygrid model; the buying firm has no past experience and relies heavily on the seller for guidance and information.

niche marketer A firm that concentrates in a narrow market segment, striving for optimal customer satisfaction and a dominant market share.

nontariff barriers Actions taken by countries to limit the amount of imports and protect local industries; may take the form of quotas, inspections, or the addition of quality specifications.

oligopoly A market in which only a few firms control the majority of the business volume. Most industries are oligopolies.

open bid A bid that is made and discussed between buyer and seller before a final purchase decision; the initial bid may be altered one or more times.

opportunity analysis See *market opportunity analysis.*

original equipment manufacturer (OEM) A company that produces an end product by assembling a broad array of materials, component parts, and subassemblies purchased from a variety of suppliers. The end product may be intended for the business market or the consumer market or both (for example, automobiles, computers).

partnering A joint effort between customer and supplier; likely to occur in the design and production of a new end product. Both firms seek to optimize product performance versus cost.

penetration price policy Entering a market with an aggressive price to gain market position, discourage competitors, and accelerate market growth.

physical distribution The actual movement and handling of a product from one point to another; transportation modes, warehousing, and materials handling systems are essential elements.

platform teams A term originated by the automotive industry to describe the multi-functional team assembled to design a new product. See *concurrent engineering.*

position defense Penetrating a well-chosen niche and warding off competitors from a position of strength.

product differentiation A means of product positioning; provides a product with distinctiveness. Without differentiation, a product becomes a commodity and is sold primarily on price.

product manager An individual responsible for the progress of a product from its inception as an idea, during its physical development and market introduction, and throughout its life cycle. Usually referred to as brand managers in the consumer market.

product positioning An attempt to differentiate a product by creating an image consistent with a customer's needs and priorities. Positioning may be based on the product or on services that enhance it, for example, technical support, warranty, and consigned inventory.

product quality Customers, not suppliers, determine quality based on the product's ability to perform an assigned task. The perceived level of quality depends on the level of performance weighed against price. In the business market, quality and consistency are regularly judged more important than price.

product service factors Those activities or attributes offered by manufacturers to enhance physical products, such as product quality, timely delivery, proper installation, and personal follow-up.

pull promotion Promoting a product by advertising its capabilities to end-users. Intel's "Intel Inside" program is an excellent example.

push promotion The opposite of pull; distributors are encouraged to resell the product through sales incentives, friendships, discounts, special training, prompt delivery, etc.

sales agent See *manufacturers' representative.*

sales forecast The actual volume a company expects to sell, given its sales potential (SAM), market conditions, and the allocated budget.

sales potential The total sales a given product could achieve if the firm monopolized the market; not to be confused with a sales forecast.

sales promotion Those elements that do not fall within advertising, personal selling, or public relations. Includes trade shows, incentives, special events, product and company literature, premiums, plant tours, calendars, and more.

served available market (SAM) That portion of a product market that a firm can serve with its current product line. For example, a producer of PC computers cannot serve the mainframe segment without converting customer demand. See *sales potential.*

skimming price policy Establishing a high price on a new product, given the absence of competition and a desire to recover sunk costs before the market becomes competitive.

Standard Industrial Classification Codes (SIC) A system for identifying all goods and services produced in the U.S. and the firms that produce them. Subdivisions separate manufacturers, wholesalers, retailers, and service providers.

straight rebuy One class in the buygrid model; a previous purchase is repeated without alterations.

strategic business unit (SBU) A relatively autonomous entity within a larger company; its business is planned separately, it has its own set of

competitors, and its management develops an individual strategic plan.

strategic marketing planning The systematic analysis of market opportunities and threats to determine a future course of action; followed by the SBU planning level, which includes the allocation and utilization of scarce resources.

success requirements Capabilities that a firm must have and the actions it must take to meet the demands of a given market.

S.W.O.T. analysis An essential analysis before forming any marketing strategy; compares the firm's strengths and weaknesses against market opportunities and threats. See *market opportunity analysis.*

tactical planning After strategic planning or the broad perspective, tactical planning deals with the who, what, where, when, and how details of implementation. See *annual plan.*

target markets The choice of one or more market segments that the firm chooses to penetrate. In business marketing, the targets are usually company types (e.g., end-products, size, technology), individual firms, or specific industries.

tariffs Governmental action that places a duty (charge) on imported goods to prohibit or slow the flow and protect the threatened domestic industry.

telemarketing Using a telephone to solicit sales, develop sales leads, determine the level of customer satisfaction, and keep the firm's name in front of the customer. Very helpful in reducing personal selling expenses.

total available market (TAM) The total demand within the several segments of a generic product market. For example, the automotive market includes sedans, minivans, convertibles, and pickups.

trade show A popular and effective way of developing sales leads. Many shows have 50,000 to 100,000 square feet devoted to exhibits, attract thousands of interested prospects, and feature a wide variety of products from huge earth-moving vehicles to industrial name tags.

transfer pricing The price charged by one corporate division selling its products to another division. The negotiated price may be lower than that charged to outside customers. affected by another business unit trying to maintain profits, transfer prices reflect the cost transfers that may set a price lower than the actual cost plus price model would dictate. The dictates of Robinson-Patman must be taken into consideration.

value-added resellers (remarketers) Wholesalers that deal with end users and help these customers design and choose multiproduct systems to suit their specific needs. These firms are very popular in the desktop computer market.

value analysis A systematic weighing of a purchased product's worth by the customer. Business firms consider the product's contribution to their net profit, its enhancement of the end-product's market acceptance, and any improvement in productivity.

wholesaler See *distributor.*

World Trade Organization (WTO) Oversees international trade agreements and has power to mediate trade disputes between nations. WTO members cannot veto the findings of the WTO's three-person panel as was true in the old GATT agreements.

Name Index

A

Abell, Derek F., 240, 241, 247
Abratt, Russell, 35
Acer 287
Achabal, Dale D., 551
Acker, David A., 531
Ackerman, Laurence D., 247
Adams, Arthur J., 187
Advanced Network Design, 397
Advertising Age, 441, 161
Airborne, 314
Airbus, 524, 572
Alberts, William W., 476, 487, 550
Alcatel Alsthom, 572
Alderson, Wroe, 247
Alexander, Ralph S., 97
Aley, James, 28
Alguire, Mary S., 216
Allegeny-Ludlum, 514, 525
Allen, Louis A., 49
Allred, James K., 95
Alter, Steven, 153, 157
America Online, 575, 577
American Can Company, 523
American Chamber of Commerce, 570
American Cyanamid, 547
American Premier Underwriters, 45
American Supply and Machinery Manu-
     facturing Association, 169, 347
American Telephone & Telegraph, 171,
     249, 455, 512, 565
Ames, B. Charles, 124, 247, 259, 273
AMF, 557
AMP, 288
Anderson, B.B., 435
Anderson, Eric, 96
Anderson, James C., 217
Anderson, M.J. Jr., 531
Anderson, Richard, 221, 246
Andreasen, Alan R., 156
Ansoff, A. Igor, 247
Apple Computer, 130, 148, 160, 165, 205,
     266, 300, 384, 512, 514, 536, 565
Aquila, August J., 317, 331

Arm & Hammer, 260
Armstrong, J. Scott, 187
Arnott, Nancy, 412, 461, 464
Arthur Anderson, 318, 543
Asahi Glass, 30
Asea Brown Boveri, Ltd., 71, 564
Atari, 266
Atmel, 524
Attanasio, Dominick B., 42, 64
Audit Bureau of Circulation, 455
Austin, Michael S., 273
Austin, Nancy, 407, 413
Avery, Susan, 361
Avlonitis, George J., 265, 268, 273, 274
Avnet, 359
Avon, 391

B

Bachrach, Samuel B., 124
Baker, Steven M., 157
Balachandran, Bala, 532
Baldwin, Steven R., 325, 332
Ballow, Ronald H., 365, 372
Banca Commerciale Italiano, 558
Banting, Peter M., 97, 404, 412, 435, 436
Barasch, Kenneth L., 242
Barclay, Donald W., 124
Barich, Howard, 217
Baris, Howard, 218
Barius, Bengt, 188
Barks, Joseph V., 361
Barksdale, Hiram C. Jr., 332
Barlas, Stephen, 576
Barnevik, Percy, 576
Barnhouse, Scott H., 112, 123
Barone, Joseph F., 208, 217, 218
Barrager, Dave, 217
Barrier, Michael, 216, 218
Barrowcliff, Stuart, 576
Barry, Thomas, 412
Bates, Donald L., 246, 247
Bateson, John E., 331
Bauer, Raymond A., 123
Bean, Alden S., 96

Beckman Instruments, 47
Beijing Jeep, 559
Beik, Leland, 549, 550
Bell Atlantic, 277
Bell Laboratories, 283
Bellenger, Danny N., 435
Bellizzi, Joseph A., 95, 96, 97, 462
Bello, Daniel C., 461
Benjamin, Gerald A., 332
Bennion, Mark L., 217
Beracs, Jozsef, 97
Bernhart, Kenneth L., 97
Berry, Leonard L., 313, 319, 320, 331, 333
Berry, Thomas E., 396
Bertrand, Kate, 193, 218, 331, 413, 461, 576
Bethlehem Steel, 88, 514
Biddle, Reginald, 332
Biggs, Joseph R., 123
Bird, Monroe M., 97, 122, 123
Black & Decker, 239, 526
Black, George, 461
Blasko, Vincent J., 462
Bleeke, Joel A., 217
Blenkhorn, David L., 435, 436
Bloom, Paul N., 274, 314, 331
Blue Cross-Blue Shield, 25
Boag, David A., 306
Bobrow, Edwin E., 362
Boeing, 12, 26, 160, 163, 179, 224, 239, 523,
     524, 565, 572
Boise-Cascade, 514
Bonoma, Thomas V., 64, 84, 96, 97, 110,
     124, 201, 202, 204, 216, 218, 435,
     436, 461
Boone, Louis E., 412
Boothroyd Dewhurst, Inc., 288
Booz, Allen & Hamilton, 276, 305
Bopp, Donald C. Jr., 123
Borg-Warner, 195, 450, 452, 453, 454, 567
Borrus, Amy, 576
Boston Consulting Group, 475, 476, 487,
     546
Bostrom, Gert-Olof, 332
Bouchard, Micheline, 332

Subject Index

683